Saint-Simon and the Court of Louis XIV

Duke de Saint-Simon, engraving by Louis-François Mariage after a portrait by Van Loo
By courtesy of the Bibliotheque Nationale, Paris

Saint-Simon,
AND THE COURT OF LOUIS XIV

Emmanuel Le Roy Ladurie

WITH THE COLLABORATION OF JEAN-FRANÇOIS FITOU
TRANSLATED BY ARTHUR GOLDHAMMER

THE UNIVERSITY OF CHICAGO PRESS • *Chicago and London*

Emmanuel Le Roy Ladurie is a professor at the Collège de France and a member of the Académie des Sciences Morales et Politiques. He is the author of numerous books, including *The Beggar and the Professor*, published by the University of Chicago Press. **Jean-François Fitou** is the deputy prefect of Langon, France. **Arthur Goldhammer** is an award-winning translator who has translated books by Georges Duby, Jacques Le Goff, and Jean Starobinski.

The University of Chicago Press, Chicago 60637
The University of Chicago Press, Ltd., London
© 2001 by The University of Chicago
All rights reserved. Published 2001
Printed in the United States of America
10 09 08 07 06 05 04 03 02 01   5 4 3 2 1

ISBN (cloth) 0-226-47320-1

Originally published as *Saint-Simon, ou le système de la Cour*, © Librairie Arthème Fayard, 1997.

The University of Chicago Press gratefully acknowledges a subvention from the government of France, through the French Ministry of Culture, in support of the costs of translating this volume.

Library of Congress Cataloging-in-Publication Data

Le Roy Ladurie, Emmanuel.
    [Saint-Simon, ou, Le système de la cour. English]
    Saint-Simon and the court of Louis XIV / Emmanuel Le Roy Ladurie, with the collaboration of Jean François Fitou ; translated by Arthur Goldhammer.
        p.   cm.
    Includes bibliographical references and index.
    ISBN 0-226-47320-1
    1. France—History—Louis XIV, 1643-1715.   2. France—History—Regency, 1715-1723.   3. France—Court and courtiers—History.   4. Saint-Simon, Louis de Rouvroy, duc de, 1675-1755. Mémoires.   I. Fitou, Jean François.   II. Title.
DC126.L4613   2001
944'.033—dc21

00-013227

To Professors Orest Ranum and Robert Forster

Contents

Preface

This book is the latest in a series of similar studies by Le Roy Ladurie focusing on the existential experience of one or more individuals or of a community. Among these are *Montaillou, Pierre Prion scribe* (in collaboration with Orest Ranum), essays on Gouberville and Rétif de la Bretonne, a book on the Platter family, and the memoirs of Jacques Le Roy Ladurie (edited by his son in collaboration with Anthony Rowley). Yet this book is even less of a chronological account than were these other works. Our "Saint-Simonian" text is by design analytical, which is why we have chosen "The Court System" for the title of part 1, and why in part 2 we study the "Regency System."

Since not all of our readers will be familiar with the life of Saint-Simon, however, we thought it might not be a bad idea to begin with a broadly sketched biography. Our opening pages are devoted to this task, in which we of course rely heavily on two admirable biographies of our subject, one by Jacques Roujon, the other by Georges Poisson. The analytical portion of our essay follows this introduction.

We also want to indicate what part each of us played in the writing of this book. Le Roy Ladurie prepared a draft of almost the entire text based on personal notes and other materials. Jean-François Fitou then reviewed this draft, filled in the footnotes, and revised the text itself. Finally, chapter 5, "Saint-Simonian Demography," is the fruit of joint research conducted intermittently over a period of several years. In contrast to the other chapters, chapter 5 was largely drafted by Fitou and revised by Le Roy Ladurie.

Emmanuel Le Roy Ladurie
Jean-François Fitou

Introduction

SAINT-SIMON IN THE AURA OF LE ROI
SOLEIL AND LE BIEN-AIMÉ

Born in 1675 to a father almost seventy and a mother not yet forty, Louis de Rou-
vroy succeeded to the title of duc de Saint-Simon in 1693. It has sometimes been alleged that Saint-Simon's obsession with the status of "duke
and peer" stemmed from insecurity about the ancientness of his title. In
fact, he was a scion of "good" family, but one whose roots can be traced
back to the lesser nobility. His father, Claude, the first duc de Saint-
Simon, had risen high enough to leave his son not only the title of duke
but also a substantial fortune, even if it was "in considerable disarray" and
beset by creditors. Louis was also blessed in youth by the good opinion of
Louis XIV. His father, who had served Louis XIII as "stable page," was
adept at sounding the hunting horn without spitting into the mouth-
piece—a talent much prized by Louis the Just. What is more, the younger
Saint-Simon enjoyed a personal friendship with Philippe d'Orléans, his
almost exact contemporary, who grew up to head the government of
France and even to rule for a time as regent.

Louis de Rouvroy received a more thorough education than most
other young men of his class and generation. Though not fluent in Latin,
he handled the language with considerable skill. His mother, the duchess,
loved her only son, coddled him, and kept a close eye on his activities.
With his family he moved in a world of aristocratic splendor and bourgeois solidity. At La Ferté–Vidame, the Saint-Simons possessed an estate
of more than twenty-five hundred acres, making it one of the largest in
the region even without its seigneurial appurtenances. To have put together such a large estate, Claude must have been a canny buyer—and
perhaps, in the early stages, not always a scrupulous one. As a child, Louis

1

spent part of every summer in the country, in the vicinity of a Trappist monastery as well as of an estate owned by an influential official in Colbert's ministry, the financier Desmarets. Although the Saint-Simons belonged to the nobility of the sword, in Paris they rubbed shoulders with wealthy families connected with the nobility of the robe, including the Pontchartrain-Phélypeaux clan, which supplied France with several ministers. And when legal papers had to be drafted or signed, it was the notary Arouet, Voltaire's father, who laid the necessary dossiers before the parents of the future memoirist.

A gifted child like Saint-Simon, living in a family with finely honed political sensibilities, would have begun to learn about the political milieu in which he moved at the age of nine or ten. His father, as a newcomer to ducal rank, had at times been slighted by those who considered themselves his betters. These incidents caused him pain, which he no doubt internalized and passed on to his son, thereby contributing to Saint-Simon's permanent anxiety about his status.

The years between 1684 and 1690 proved crucial in shaping young Saint-Simon's future. The Peace of Regensburg (1684) marked the height of the French monarchy's influence, especially abroad. Even more significant was the Revocation of the Edict of Nantes in 1685, a decision that Saint-Simon would later come in all sincerity to detest. Last but not least, the Glorious Revolution in England (1688) led to persecution of Catholics on the English side of the Channel, exacerbating Saint-Simon's existing anti-British sentiments. Though by no means fanatical, this nascent hostility would ripen in later years.

In 1683, the Saint-Simon family had moved into a new and unpretentious *hôtel particulier* in Versailles. The advantage of this move was that it allowed for brief stays at the royal court nearby. At least until 1723, however, obtaining an apartment inside the château would remain one of Saint-Simon's constant preoccupations. His Versailles residence was little more than a "downtown" pied-à-terre, a long way from the coveted place within the sovereign's lair.

In 1691, Louis de Rouvroy began preparing for a military career, which might well have shortened his life had he pursued it. But within a few years of his father's death, his superego fell silent, and he quickly abandoned this line of work.

As the only child of an elderly father, Louis was alone in the world. He had no close cousins or brothers-in-law to help him along. And by the end of the seventeenth century, France, too, was alone in the world, threatened by the very aggressive League of Augsburg, a coalition of maritime as well as continental Protestant powers that opposed not only the Revocation of the Edict of Nantes and the Bourbon annexation of Strasbourg but also efforts to extend French hegemony into the Palatinate and toward Cologne by military and diplomatic means. What is more, France's enemies included not only Lutheran and Anglican states but also Catholic powers displeased with the king of France. For the time being, these included the Habsburgs of Vienna and Madrid, who were outraged by the Regensburg treaty's sanctioning of French conquests of Iberian territory. Within a few years, it would take all the king's men to hold off the coalition that formed along the several borders of what we now think of as France.[1]

But let us back up a bit. In 1691, with the lukewarm blessing of Louis XIV, elderly Duc Claude had enrolled his small, frail sixteen-year-old son in the Gray Musketeers. The youth endured "democratic" training in military maneuvers, in which he took only mild interest at best. He took orders from a Sergeant Flick as well as a captain named Maupertuis, a decent but persnickety commander who rode his men hard.

It was in 1691 or 1692 that Saint-Simon first began to hone the pen that would make him famous. The *Memoirs* themselves were written during the reign of Louis XV, but the drama they recount began in the last decade of the seventeenth century. Among the events dealt with in his early writings was the capture of Namur (now in Belgium) in 1692, in which Saint-Simon took part as a musketeer. This success on land was overshadowed, however, by a naval defeat at La Hougue, which plunged Saint-Simon into despair despite his distance from the maritime theater. The forces of Louis XIV fared far less well at sea than in the cow pastures of the Low Countries.

Saint-Simon also wrote about certain "mixed marriages" involving the most illustrious personages of the realm. For example, the son of "Monsieur," the king's brother—in other words, young Philippe d'Orléans, Saint-Simon's friend who was ultimately destined to become regent of France—married an illegitimate daughter of the king. And another of Louis XIV's bastards, the duc du Maine, wed a blue-blooded Condé. It is easy to imagine the howls that these nuptials elicited from our memoirist, whose antipathy to royal bastards knew no bounds. These early texts also featured portraits of two other characters whom Saint-Simon would make it his business to hate, Abbé Dubois and the future maréchal-duc de Villars, whose father he praised as if in compensation for the nasty things he would later say about the son.

With the death of the octogenarian Claude de Saint-Simon in April 1693, Louis became a duke at the age of eighteen. In writing about his youth, however, he neglected to mention a few important episodes. One of these oversights was unavoidable: there was no way that Saint-Simon could have known about the death in 1690 of the talented Tallemant des Réaux, "the Saint-Simon of the poor." On the other hand, his omission of the famine of 1693, which reduced the population of France by more than a million, was inexcusable.

This devastating disaster began in the summer and fall of 1693. By July or August, grain prices on the Paris market had shot sky high. The poor could not afford to eat. Meanwhile, however, France scored a series of striking military successes. At Neerwinden the future author of the *Memoirs* courageously took part in a number of cavalry charges with his tutor at his side. This victory was followed by another at Charleroi and still others in Spain and Italy. In the same year the Order of Saint-Louis was established. It was a military honor, and its red ribbon is still used today to distinguish members of the Legion of Honor. France's victories no doubt justified the creation of the new order, but in alluding to it Saint-Simon was discreetly ironic.

The new duke also inherited his father's extensive estates and as a royal favor was granted the power to govern localities such as Blaye where his father had enjoyed the same privilege. He was made a colonel and gave some thought to marrying. Indeed, he courted the duc de Beauvillier, Colbert's son-in-law and a minister of quietly reformist bent, with an eye to asking for the hand of one of his daughters, but his suit went unrewarded. Saint-Simon also displayed precocious signs of litigiousness: when the maréchal de Luxembourg, noted for his brilliant battlefield exploits, had the temerity to ask that his place in the pecking order be raised from eighteenth among the dukes of France to second, thereby pushing his way ahead of Saint-Simon, who ranked twelfth, the young duke filed a formal protest.

After famine and war came new taxes to defray the costs of battle. The *capitation*, a tax on every family head, was introduced in 1694–95. Even the privileged had to pay an amount that depended on the family's social rank (experts had established 569 degrees of social status for the purpose). With this novel form of taxation, Louis XIV was playing an old game, but this time he went further than ever before. Forcing everyone to make a direct monetary contribution to the royal coffers was a way of leveling all distinctions and privileges before the majesty of the state. Yet at the same time, the new tax also respected and even gave official blessing to the existing social hierarchy.[2] The king thus played a paradoxical role: he was at once the highest-ranking noble in France and the great equalizer of French society. This strategy, though still hesitant and experimental, was a harbinger of things to come. Saint-Simon, who viewed fiscal exemptions as one of the privileges of the aristocratic order to which he belonged, took a dim view of these royal initiatives.

In any event, he spent the year 1694 in legal skirmishes stemming from the Luxembourg affair and in negotiations connected with his marriage to Mlle de Lorges. The duke's intended was a woman of quality in almost every sense, despite the fact that her maternal grandfather was a financier (which ensured that she would bring a large dowry). Yet her marriage to a duke could easily be construed as a glaring mismatch. Her father had been Saint-Simon's superior during the Rhineland campaign, however. It was therefore not a duke but a young colonel who was proposing to marry his general's daughter. Looked at in this light, the match was acceptable. The marriage proved to be a happy one, though it produced few children and even fewer grandchildren. By all appearances things went well right from the start. The honeymoon lasted from the wedding in April 1695 until the spring of 1696, when Saint-Simon was once again obliged to join the army in the east.

Another marriage close in time to his own made a great impression on Saint-Simon. His wife's sister, who was still hardly more than a child, wedded the duc de Lauzun, a man well into his sixties. Meanwhile, the Luxembourg affair continued to preoccupy our duke, though success still eluded him, to put it mildly. Posterity remembers this period, however, not so much for Saint-Simon's legal troubles as for several important literary and cultural milestones: among the illustrious figures of the seventeenth century who passed away around the time of Saint-Simon's marriage were the poet La Fontaine, the painter Mignard, the epistolary Mme de Sévigné, the moralist La Bruyère, and Louis XIV's former physician-in-chief Aquin, who, remarkably enough, counted Jews among his close relatives, a fact that elicited little negative comment. The first signs of the Quietist storm began to appear on the horizon: Fénelon was "kicked upstairs" to become archbishop of Cambrai, a sublime promotion that soon turned into a form of exile. That staunch *fénelonienne* Mme Guyon was subsequently dispatched to the Bastille. And finally, the gods of war, having bestowed their blessings on Louis XIV in the early stages of the last great conflict of the seventeenth century, suddenly withdrew their favor. In 1695, the French were obliged to surrender the city of Namur on terms that bordered on the humiliating.

Saint-Simon took part in the final phase of the War of the League of Augsburg, which was ended by a treaty signed at Ryswick in 1697. This ended his military career. To be sure, it may well be misleading to speak of Saint-Simon as having had a military career at all, because of the vast number of men who served in the French army of the period he was surely one of the less distinguished. In any case, his century ended not on the battlefield but in sumptuous debauch, these being the terms that Saint-Simon uses to describe the glittering wedding of Louis XIV's grandson, the duc de Bourgogne.

In war as in peace, Saint-Simon kept largely to the same unvarying routine. He might quarrel in the morning with his brother-in-law Lauzun and then take a moment to pray quietly or study the texts of the Jansenists, about whom he was just beginning to become curious. He also took an interest in the Trappists, in whose monastery Rigaud was painting his portrait of the abbé de Rancé (whose successor is remembered for the scandal he caused). Saint-Simon would later construct a complicated fable about this period involving the death of Racine, who had supposedly fallen out of favor with the king before he died.

The period around the turn of the eighteenth century, specifically the years 1699–1702, proved important to both Saint-Simon and the king. Saint-Simon's friend Pontchartrain became chancellor of France. In a game of musical chairs, Chamillart was then made comptroller general of finance and secretary of state for war. In other words, he was Colbert and Louvois rolled into one, albeit without their talent—though to be fair, Chamillart, who later became Saint-Simon's friend, was much less of a fool than some historians later made him out to be. The death of Monsieur, the king's brother, conferred the important title of duc d'Orléans on his son Philippe, the writer's friend. From that moment on, Saint-Simon could boast of powerful friends at court, including two additional ministers, Chevreuse and Beauvillier. Saint-Simon thus held a powerful hand, but only as long as young Louis did not deliberately snatch away his best cards. Unfortunately, Louis could be counted on to do just that, at times with ample justification.

By 1701, the conflict over the succession to the Spanish throne had become a central issue. Saint-Simon took the opportunity to retire from the army. The king favored the War of the Spanish Succession, and he was backed by his wife, Mme de Maintenon, and his son, known as Monseigneur, as well as by the Pontchartrain clan. The Colbert clan (including Beauvillier and perhaps Torcy) discreetly opposed the conflict, however; it was more interested in peaceful economic expansion than in a shooting war.

During the spring and summer of 1702, the "Anglo-Saxon and Germanic powers" (England, the Netherlands, and the Empire) one by one declared war on France, which they suspected of imperialist designs on the Iberian Peninsula. In this war France was less isolated than before, because Spain fought alongside her. Still, it was a very bitter conflict, complicated by the "little Ice Age," which affected France's allies and enemies alike. Conditions were particularly harsh during the terrible winter of 1709, but things had begun to go badly for France long before that, when royal forces lost the Battle of Blenheim in 1704. In the meantime, Saint-Simon's bête-noire Villars proved himself to be an excellent strategic advisor to Louis XIV. His friend the duc de Bourgogne joined the King's Council. A war with Huguenot partisans broke out in the Cévennes in 1703. Portugal, at odds with Spain, rallied to the English side, which thus benefited from an infusion of recently discovered Brazilian gold. Meanwhile, the death of Bishop Bossuet in 1704 spelled the end for a certain vision of the Gallican church, and the Jansenist opposition quickly rushed to fill the void. Also, the painter Boucher, whose erotic rococo touch would leave its mark on eighteenth-century French painting, was born in 1703.

Where was Saint-Simon in all this? Through a complicated arrangement with his relatives the Lorges and his friends the Chamillarts, he was able to move into a tiny apartment, a veritable rat hole, in the château de Versailles, where he spent a considerable portion of his time. For him this was a great boon, for it put him in a position to observe the never-ending spectacle of local and world history as it unfolded. Saint-Simon was at last at the center of things, sticking his nose everywhere and keeping his eyes open.

Seen from Versailles, things in France seemed to go from bad to worse. This pessimistic view, which at times coincided with reality, has exerted undue influence on many historians. To be sure, France suffered failure after failure through the end of 1708, and her successes were modest indeed. With his talents as a peacemaker Villars achieved a minor victory in the Cévennes, but the inept Villeroy blundered into disaster at Ramillies in May 1706. Philip V, the new Bourbon king of Spain and grandson of Louis XIV, lost Madrid. And even the capable Vendôme went down to defeat at Oudenarde in July 1708. Yet through all of this, French territory remained intact and safe from invasion, but for the enemy's brief seizure of Toulon in 1707.

In recounting this period, Saint-Simon mingles the anecdotal with the essential without clearly differentiating the two. For instance, when the dowager queen of Spain offers Philippe d'Orléans an armchair in Bayonne, our duke is offended because to his way of thinking, no one, no matter how highly placed, may sit in an armchair in the presence of a queen, even a dowager queen. During this period, there was talk of sending Saint-Simon to Rome as ambassador. The proposal, however, came to naught: this was not the first time, nor would it be the last, that his dreams of useful office would be frustrated. Meanwhile, the Jansenist controversy, which had been more or less dormant since the 1668 treaty with Rome, was rekindled by the 1705 papal bull *Vineam Domini*. Saint-Simon took a keen interest in the Jansenist revival.

The weather also had a major impact. The *grand hyver*, or great winter, of January-February 1709, killed seed already in the ground. Famine and epidemic followed, resulting in perhaps six hundred thousand deaths in excess of normal mortality. But the men and women who died had little to do with court intrigue, so Saint-Simon scarcely notices them. He does, however, mention and describe the famine and its lethal consequences. Strangely, the country's military situation improved at almost the same time. Villars and Vendôme thwarted allied offensives at Malplaquet and Villaviciosa in 1709 and 1710.

If Saint-Simon paid only scant attention to the famine of 1709, he did leave a splendid account of court cabals in that year. For him, the most important issue of the day was the question of his lodging at Versailles. He lost the pied-à-terre in the château that he had borrowed from the Lorges, but later in the year he obtained another from the Pontchartrains, a large room with a wardrobe. Finally, in 1710, culminating a hard-fought battle, he was rewarded with the ultimate in luxury, a five-room apartment with kitchen (actually more like a ten-room apartment) in the palace's northern wing. Now the writer was free to host guests for dinner as often as he liked. The view from his Versailles observatory grew considerably wider, and the quality of his observations improved accordingly, if it is possible to imagine such a thing, for they were already excellent (even allowing for errors both inadvertent and deliberate). Saint-Simon owed his good fortune to his wife's appointment as lady-in-waiting to the new duchesse de Berry, whose marriage the writer apparently played an important role in arranging.

For the memoirist, the central event of the postfamine period (late 1710 into 1711) was the death of Monseigneur, the son of Louis XIV. Saint-Simon's description is a magnificent set piece. The prince's demise raised his hopes for the future considerably, because now the duc de Bourgogne, his personal friend and eldest son of the late "Grand Dauphin," stood next in line to the throne. Misfortune intervened, however: the untimely death of the new dauphin in 1712 put an end to the optimism occasioned by his father's death the year before. Meanwhile, French classicism had also quietly exited the scene with the death of Boileau in 1711. And a year earlier, the duchesse de Bourgogne, not long for this world herself, had given birth to the future Louis XV. The Parlement of Paris also approved a new tax, the *dixième*, which would nibble away at the wealth of the privileged, much to the dismay of Saint-Simon, who was incensed at the shrinking of his aristocratic exemptions. His protests show him to have been a man unwilling to make a personal sacrifice even though his country was surrounded by enemies and threatened with invasion.

The ten months from April 1711 to February 1712 were thus framed by two important deaths. Monseigneur was gone. His ashes had been laid to rest. But the duc de Bourgogne, the embodiment of so many hopes, was still alive. Consequently, these few months mark one of the happiest periods of Saint-Simon's life. He had a charming and pretty wife, three children (who would not bring him all the satisfaction he hoped), a château in the country, and residences in Paris and Versailles, to say nothing of a fine apartment in the holy of holies, the palace itself, at the heart of the monarchical system. To be sure, he also had large debts, but he was not the only high-ranking nobleman in that situation. What determined how residents of the palace lived was not their income but the fact that men of rank were expected to spend extravagantly as befit their station.

The health of France would soon improve. True, the military situation was still less than ideal, with persistent tensions and difficulties along the northern border. But England's aggressiveness waned. She no longer heeded Marlborough's belligerent counsel. In 1710, the Tories, vaguely pro-French, came to power. They took cognizance of the death of Emperor Joseph I of Austria in 1711 and above all of the fact that the British people had tired of war. For Louis XIV, the rise of pacifist sentiment in England held out hope of salvation, much as the death of Czarina Elizabeth Petrovna in 1762 would raise the hopes of her enemy Frederick II of Prussia. By early 1712, the power shift in London had made it possible to convene peace talks in Utrecht. Meanwhile, Saint-Simon whiled away his hours of leisure by concocting reform proposals similar to those being formulated by other aristocratic liberals, such as Chevreuse, Beauvillier, Fénelon ("but nonchalantly . . . over billiards"), and above all the duc de Bourgogne, who in Saint-Simon's mind would have remained his friend and collaborator even after his ascent to the throne. In Saint-Simon's reform proposals one finds good ideas along with less good ones. One of his goals was to create a regime that more accurately represented the nation, a change that he hoped would cut the ground out from under the absolutist monarchy. But another was to give complete hegemony in government to a nobility more hierarchical and stratified than ever. In this respect, Saint-Simon's thinking was radically at odds with the much more egalitarian ideas that would gradually come to dominate French thinking toward the end of his life and afterward (c. 1750–55).

For Saint-Simon, the beginning of the War of the Spanish Succession marked the waning of Louis XIV's fortunes. But can one also make a counterclaim that the end of that war in 1713 marked the end, or at least the moderation, of the monarchy's misfortunes? In view of the monarch's advanced age (he was well into his seventies), such a claim might seem excessive. In our view, however, there is no good reason to take an unduly pessimistic view of the final years of the Sun King's reign (1713–15). What Louis lacked was a panegyrist like Carlyle, who sang the praises of another monarch who served his country no less gloriously than Louis served France, the stoic Frederick II. Poverty was certainly widespread in France in 1713, but it was by no means universal, and already the stage was set for the thirty, fifty, or even sixty glorious years that would follow the Sun King's death. Moreover, as François Bluche has pointed out, the Treaty of Utrecht (1713) was in no sense a total fiasco for France, which came away from the table with Santo Domingo, French America (especially Canada and Mississippi), territories in the north and east conquered in the last third of the seventeenth century (including Lille and Strasbourg), and a Bourbon on the throne of Spain. France would retain some of these prizes until 1763, others until 1789, and still others to the present day.

For Saint-Simon, who was always apt to feel sorry for himself, things were on the whole rather good. He was saddened, to be sure, by the deaths of both the duc and duchesse de Bourgogne in 1712, but through his wife he maintained close ties to the duc de Berry, one of the likely heirs to the throne. What is more, he had become a personage of sorts at court. He submitted elaborate documents, some signed, others anonymous, proposing an unofficial House of Lords, which he envisioned, in typical French fashion, as an informal body whose members would be recruited from among the dukes and peers and magistrates of Parlement. In an unsigned essay he took up the defense of the third estate and peasantry, the unfortunate victims of crises induced by war, thereby contradicting his not entirely unwarranted reputation as a selfish aristocrat. With respect to the fiscal privileges of the nobility, his thinking evolved in the direction of increased solidarity between the second order and taxpaying commoners. Proud of his ducal heritage, he vigorously defended his rank, challenging the pretensions of, for instance, the duc du Maine (on grounds of illegitimacy) and his wife (despite her role as a hostess who, at Sceaux, lavished her guests with the joys of Enlightenment). He also disputed the claims to higher rank of La Rochefoucauld, the grandson of the author noted for his famous *Maxims.* And he became enmeshed in bureaucratic struggles with his nemesis, the younger Pontchartrain, a most able secretary of state in the Department of the Navy. On occasion our author caught wind of impending disgrace or exile, ostensibly because he had fallen into royal disfavor. But invariably within a few weeks it had all blown over, and Mme de Saint-Simon, who found country life boring, was soon prodding her husband to return to the court without delay.

In Saint-Simon's eyes, Louis XIV's final year in power was marred by the "disastrous" royal edict on bastards, which Parlement was obliged to register in August 1714. This text declared the king's legitimized offspring and their descendants eligible to accede to the throne in the absence of any living prince of the blood. In 1714, however, there were at least half a dozen princes of the blood still alive and in reasonably good health. Saint-Simon's indignant response to this pro-bastard edict reflects a certain purist ideology prevalent at the time in court circles, an ideology about which we shall have more to say later on. In fact, however, there was little likelihood that the duc du Maine would ever ascend to the throne and even less that the comte de Toulouse would ever wear the crown, though with his stout common sense he might well have made a decent king.

Furthermore, one should not take literally Saint-Simon's jeremiads concerning his isolation and indeed ostracism by the court during the final two years of Louis XIV's reign. The writer was merely embroidering on the theme of solitude, which his mother had harped on when he was young. She had made him feel that he had been abandoned as a child by a decrepit old father who had died while Louis was still a young man. True, the royal ministers who were friends of Saint-Simon—men such as Chevreuse, Beauvillier, and Pontchartrain—had either died or resigned. And the woman friends who had kept him abreast of palace rumors had also been sidelined: indeed, his great friend Mme Chamaillart, *la grande biche*, had recently passed away. But to his great credit, the writer enjoyed, even if he did not reciprocate, the friendship and esteem of Fénelon, as well as of the duc d'Orléans. On two occasions, moreover, Louis XIV made a show of his esteem and friendship for Saint-Simon. Once, when the future regent was ill, the king had some very kind words to say about our duke. And later, when Sieur Courtenvaux was banished, the king immediately gave the disgraced courtier's apartment at Marly to Saint-Simon. One comes away with the impression that Saint-Simon was trying to gain the sympathy of his future readers and that he sought to cast himself as a martyr and opponent of the regime on the eve of what he saw as its possible collapse. In any case, he believed that the impending death of Louis XIV would be a moment of liberation, after which he would be in an excellent position to take part in any new government. In fact, however, when the Sun King died in September 1715, he left his heir a kingdom that was peaceful and well disciplined. But he also left a ticking time bomb, primed to go off at any moment: the papal bull *Unigenitus*, which the pope had imprudently issued at Louis's behest in 1713. It was as if the aging king had wanted to play a nasty trick on his successors. If so, he succeeded only too well.

For Saint-Simon, the great question was whether he would be called to serve after the king's death. The regency of Philippe d'Orléans, which began in September 1715, was for him the chance of a lifetime. But it was a chance that he did not know how to exploit to the full, and in many ways apparently did not wish to exploit, given that he categorically rejected important posts he might have been offered, such as chairman of the Finance Council and perhaps captain of the guards, which were by no means to be sneered at. He did, however, become a member of the Regency Council, a quasi-ministerial position in which he helped to organize a government by council—an effective way of allowing social elites to participate in the decision-making process. In theory, this was not an insignificant role. It allowed him to exert some influence over government appointments and dismissals. He followed the regent from Versailles to Vincennes and later waited on young Louis XV at the Tuileries. He was also an assiduous visitor to the Palais-Royal, the residence of Philippe d'Orléans, who for several years wielded supreme authority as regent. There he was able to observe the remarkable career and activities of Abbé Dubois, who advocated alliances with the Protestant powers England and Holland—a policy that proved quite beneficial to France but that Saint-Simon, obsessed as he was with France's dynastic ties to Philip V's Spain, utterly failed to grasp. By contrast, the Scottish economist John Law's rise to power and wealth after 1716 scarcely troubled him at all. If at times he was somewhat hostile to Law's ventures, at other times he was fairly receptive or even openly sympathetic.

Sops to Saint-Simon's vanity also came his way: the Croix de Saint-Louis was followed in 1728 by the Croix du Saint-Esprit. And the Regency generously bestowed another distinction: he was authorized to wear a special jerkin decked out with gold stripes and braid. The origins of this getup lay in Louis XIV's desire to foment jealousy among his courtiers: those not authorized by the king to wear such fancy dress envied those who were. Last but not least, the regent bestowed upon his friend Saint-Simon the signal honor of *grandes entrées* with the monarch. To be sure, since the monarch in this case was a child, there was little real advantage to be gained from frequent audiences. And the always urbane Philippe bestowed this particular honor quite freely. What is more, Dubois, shortly before his death, revoked the privilege from many to whom it had been granted, including Saint-Simon, who did not deign to complain. In the interim, the duke, like anyone who gains even the slightest notoriety in any political microcosm, became the butt of criticism and satire and was mocked in song as an insect, a "blighter" (*boudrillon*, a word not to be found in any dictionary but probably related to *boudrine*, a rural term for a wheat blight), a louse, and—rather puzzlingly—a cowardly bourgeois. Even today, to be the butt of satire in a newspaper like *Le Canard enchaîné* is a sign that one has arrived on the political scene. It was not entirely fanciful on Saint-Simon's part, therefore, to think that he did indeed have it made.

In August and September 1718, Saint-Simon had a hand in actions that transformed the Regency from a liberal to an authoritarian regime. Despite the formal changes in government procedure, however, basic policy retained its quasi-liberal orientation. The cornerstones of that policy remained alliance with England and Holland, tentative overtures to religious minorities, and stimulation of the economy by means of Law's issuance of paper currency.[3] For a time people felt wealthier, and the feeling was not entirely illusory. It would take a good economic historian to explain how Law's system worked. Saint-Simon simply admired it, or at any rate expressed confidence in it, without fully understanding its mechanisms.

In the fall of 1719, Saint-Simon moved into the castle of Meudon, where he would remain for several years. This was another sign of the extraordinary favor he enjoyed with the regent. Mme de Saint-Simon had fallen ill and required several rooms in a palace that had belonged to Monseigneur until his death in 1711. The duc d'Orléans gave the Saint-Simons not just a few rooms but the entire castle, where they were able to entertain in a lavish style that badly strained their budget. For several years they lived in a princely manner, holding court on the model of Versailles. But later on, when Saint-Simon was reduced to living in his own castle in the Perche, he felt no nostalgia for the grand manner, though he was glad to have sampled it once in his life.

Ensconced in his sumptuous redoubt at Meudon, Saint-Simon once again resisted all attempts to recruit him into government service. To hear him tell it, he was offered and refused the positions of guardian (*gouverneur*) of young Louis XV, almost an adolescent at the time, and keeper of the seals. The first of these posts was occupied by Villeroy, who was fundamentally at odds with the regent, and the second by d'Argenson, who was involved in a temporary dispute with the government. But for one reason or another Saint-Simon rejected both offers, which would have tempted many a man in his position. Is he therefore to be put down, as one of his biographers suggests, as a "Cornelian" character, a sort of El Cid who preferred honor to more substantial rewards, at times to an almost comical degree? Perhaps. What is certain, however, is that, El Cid or not, his sympathy for Spain never wavered.

From Meudon, Saint-Simon looked on with dismay as Dubois plotted his inexorable rise to power. A superb strategist, the abbé maneuvered behind the scenes, and his intrigues reached as far as Rome, with a cardinal's red biretta his ultimate goal. Dubois was well aware, moreover, that Saint-Simon privately held him in low esteem. Once the biretta was safely his, however, this *créature rougie*, as Saint-Simon contemptuously described him (alluding to the color of his holy headgear), had neither the wish nor the power to prevent Saint-Simon from being named ambassador extraordinary to Castile for the purpose of negotiating the marriage of the regent's young daughter to the son of Philip V, who for two decades had been making his mark as the first of the "Spanish Bourbons." Saint-Simon was by nature a great traveler, a sort of amateur ethnographer interested in the essential inequality of humankind. He loved to make scholarly observations about the kinds of hierarchies that developed under African kings and Asian potentates and eagerly savored details of the czar's visit to Paris. At Lauzun's he delighted in the refined conversation of the Ottoman envoy Mehemet Effendi. He was glad of any opportunity to travel, whether it was to the Atlantic coast of France, to Germany in his youth, or across the Pyrenees in the final years of the Regency. To write about hierarchical society, he needed to learn and gather information.

Favored by the regent, then, Saint-Simon went to Spain as ambassador extraordinary in the fall of 1721. Spain's economy had been growing for several decades. Its bureaucracy was being modernized along French lines. And its military and naval power were being restored, though not sufficiently to avoid several defeats on land and sea. Broadly speaking, the restoration begun by the last of the Habsburgs was continuing under the first of the Spanish Bourbons. Some excellent historians have questioned Philip V's intelligence. Be that as it may, he had the excellent idea of bringing with him to his new country the fruits of all that France had learned about organizing the administrative apparatus of government. He applied these lessons directly in Madrid and indirectly in Spain's bustling and independent-minded provincial capitals.

Saint-Simon's embassy to the Iberian Peninsula began with several not very glorious attempts to flatter Dubois, whose influence was then at its height. By way of atonement, the duke would later spit on Dubois's grave every bit as excessively as he had licked his boots in 1722. On his way to Madrid, Saint-Simon did not neglect to tour Segovia and Toledo or to sample Spanish cuisine. Despite several gaffes typical of amateur efforts at diplomacy, his mission met with almost total success. He negotiated two marriages between the French and Castilian branches of the house of Bourbon. One of these—that of the regent's daughter to the prince of Asturias, for which Saint-Simon was directly responsible—actually took place. Supposedly he also hoped to obtain a high position and various honors for himself in Spain, as another northerner, Ripperda from the Netherlands, had succeeded in doing. But this was not to be.

By April 1722, Saint-Simon was thus able to return to France with his head held high, despite the fact that his lavish expenditure in Spain had seriously depleted his fortunes. Dubois refused to compensate him sufficiently to defray the heavy costs he had incurred (more than 800,000 livres, or nearly a third of his capital). All in all, his embassy had lasted more than six months, during which two notable events had occurred in France. The first was the arrest of Cartouche, a bandit whose exploits coincided with the liberal phase of the Regency, which was also a period of heightened criminal activity. The other was the resignation of Antin, Noailles, and Villars from the Regency Council. These elderly holdovers from the Sun King's court did not wish to sully themselves by rubbing shoulders with the commoner Dubois.

After his mission to Madrid, Saint-Simon returned to his father's house and estates. A narrative of the period from 1722 to 1723 might well be entitled "Chronicle of a Disgrace Foretold," a chronicle that would end with the regent's death. Pressed by his domineering mother, the unhappy duke was obliged to give the hand of his seriously handicapped daughter to the ridiculous prince de Chimay, who in truth aimed to marry not the girl but her father, Saint-Simon himself, whom Chimay believed to be in tight with Philippe d'Orléans and capable of obtaining any favor he wished. Unfortunately, Chimay was the only one who believed this, although it is true that the friendship between the regent and the writer remained unshakable.

In August 1722, Dubois was named prime minister, much to the dismay of Saint-Simon, who was consequently squeezed out of the inner circles of government. Although his relations with the new head of government were not as bad as he would later make out, they were not good, either. Because Louis XV had now attained the age of majority, the Regency Council was replaced in February 1723 by the usual Upper Council (Conseil d'en Haut), of which Saint-Simon was not a member. In June 1723, he was evicted from the handsome castle of Meudon, where he had lived in spacious quarters with his wife since 1719. When Dubois died in the summer of 1723, however, he got his semiofficial residence back, only to lose it along with all of his other official and semiofficial positions in December, when the regent also passed away. Worst of all, he lost his standing at Versailles, to which the court had returned in the summer of 1722.

For Saint-Simon, it was hardly a matter of being cast out into poverty but only a more prosaic return to the routine of private life. For the next several decades, he would live happily as a *bourgeois de Paris* in the winter and in the summer as a country squire in some nearby province. After 1723, he slipped easily into the useful and fruitful role of a gentleman farmer with a penchant for modernizing his estates and improving the lot of "his" peasants. For the duc de Saint-Simon was in fact a man of thoroughly modern inclinations, who late in life even set up a forge to produce useful metal objects. Yet in a fascinatingly contradictory way, he was also a man of the past, as his aristocratic ideology and commitment to inequality make clear. Such ideas are hardly surprising, however, in a man who saw himself as a professional duke and peer.

From 1723 to 1740, Saint-Simon was happy and productive in what Georges Poisson has shown was a very active "retirement."[4] To be sure, he sought to elicit the pity of his readers by describing himself as "socially dead." But in fact, once freed from the cares of the court, which no longer aroused in him anything more than a vague bitterness, he "worked simultaneously on a variety of texts" pertaining to history and the aristocracy. He also devoted himself "to managing his lands and seeing a select group of friends." And he took steps to promote the fortunes of his offspring, especially his sons, whose military careers, though relatively brief, were considerably more distinguished than their father's. Whatever the aging nobleman may have lacked in military panache, however, he made up for with civic courage. In 1734, when he was almost sixty, he spoke out publicly in memory of Abbé Duguet, who had died the year before. As we shall see later on, the duke had embraced many of the abbé's ideas, which stemmed from his "renunciationist" and Jansenist beliefs.

Retirement from the court liberated Saint-Simon's creative energies, and he was quick to produce a number of substantial historical and polemical texts: these include the *Notes sur tous les duchés-pairies* [Notes on all the duchy-peerages], *Des Légères Notions sur les Chevaliers du Saint-Esprit* [Brief thoughts concerning the Knights of the Holy Spirit], *Grandes Charges de la Couronne* [High Crown posts], *Les Cardinaux français à la nomination de Louis XIV* [French cardinals appointed by Louis XIV], and *Etat des maréchaux de France depuis Louis XIV* [List of marshals of France since Louis XIV]. Then, in the 1730s, Saint-Simon immersed himself in Dangeau's journal, which he read pen in hand. To this bare carcass washed up on history's shore, he would soon give flesh and blood. In 1739, when he was already well into his sixties, he began work on the most important of his books, the *Memoirs*. By then he already knew that his sons would not give him the grandson he had hoped for, hence there would be no one to inherit his title. Was his hope in writing therefore to secure for himself a literary posterity, even if by his own wish his reputation was to remain confined within a narrow circle for many years to come? In any case, his writing gave meaning to his existence and helped him to endure (as it helps so many elderly men who turn to writing memoirs in their later years). To be sure, in composing his great memorial he used numerous texts written earlier, the earliest of which, he tells us, dated from 1694, when he received his baptism of fire during the War of the League of Augsburg. In this respect, Saint-Simon resembles Felix Platter, who in his seventies wrote his memoirs with the help of texts written when he was still a beardless adolescent traveling about Europe or later while studying medicine in Montpellier. Saint-Simon was not the only writer of his kind.

In doing what he did, Saint-Simon had no desire to be impudent or indiscreet. What he wrote was not destined for publication during his lifetime. Nevertheless, from 1739 on, he wrote constantly, except for a few months in the late winter and early spring of 1743 following his wife's death. From then until 1749 he wrote without letup. The *Memoirs* end, of course, with the death of the regent in December 1723. It remains uncertain whether Saint-Simon's plan to continue his text through 1743 and the death of Cardinal Fleury came to naught or whether he actually produced some number of pages that have been lost. In the present state of our knowledge, it would be idle to speculate. But we cannot end this brief introductory discussion of the *Memoirs* without mentioning Saint-Simon's stunning prediction of "the impending end and dissolution of the French monarchy" some fifty years before the fact.[5] This, he believed, would be the inevitable result of the debasement of the aristocracy that began with Mazarin and continued under both Louis XIV and Louis XV. On this point we disagree with the eminent Saint-Simon specialist Yves Coirault, who tends in our view to underplay the duke's astonishing prescience.[6]

Saint-Simon's final years coincided with the high point of Louis XV's reign. The Treaty of Aix-la-Chapelle (1748) marked the end of the War of the Austrian Succession, in which France for once proved to be the equal of Great Britain. Under the terms of the treaty, France held on to its empire in the New World, from the Saint Lawrence River to the Mississippi. Of course, it would not hold on for long, but the victory was still not without significance. The Treaty of Aix also established a certain balance of power in Europe. As a good disciple of the pacifist Fénelon, Louis XV refused to annex the territory that is now Belgium. Yet the government of Versailles was still enmeshed in chronic though not fatal financial difficulties. It therefore attempted with some success to impose on the hitherto privileged a new tax known as the *vingtième*. In some ways this was based on ideas proposed long ago by Vauban.

After he finished the *Memoirs*, Saint-Simon did not just fade away. He moved from one Paris residence to another, polishing his already almost perfect text, "lining up" *(graticulant)* his sentences, as he put it. Oddly enough, the word he used, *graticulant*, is rather unusual, and General de Gaulle, another memoir writer of note, would use the same word in a similar context some two centuries later. He also grudgingly served as a consultant on rank, a subject on which he became a recognized expert in his old age. He noted that one form or another of "rank" could be observed in Asia as well as among the savages of Africa and America. His ethnographic theory was based on the ideas that "gradations of social estate," as he excellently phrased it, are a universal phenomenon—a by no means unintelligent observation, even if it flies in the face of Rousseau's *Discourse on Inequality* (1754), which as it happens was written during Saint-Simon's lifetime. In the will he wrote shortly before his death in 1755, the duke asked to be spared the pomp of a baroque burial. This was consistent with everything he stood for as the rear guard of an ancien régime that took on almost mythical proportions in his writing, where he reduced prerevolutionary society to its hierarchical and "thearchical" essence.[7] But he was also in the avant-garde in his opposition to baroque Christianity and embrace of a purer, more Jansenist religion. After his death, these same religious ideas would give rise to a new and already revolutionary ideology among restless Augustinians, "Augustinoids," and post-Augustinians who were not dukes, much less peers, but angry commoners.

S aint-Simonism takes on a life of its own after Saint-Simon. In fact the author's literary and historical reputation developed almost entirely after his death, as he himself sincerely hoped it would. The vast manuscript of the *Memoirs* wound up first in the hands of a notary despite the existence of heirs, because the duke's estate was tied up in a tangle of debts. Later, around 1760, with help from Choiseul, the still unpublished text was transferred to the archives of the Ministry of Foreign

Affairs. A copy was made, and portions of this, often faulty, found their way into print even before the Revolution. Under Louis XVIII and after, thanks initially to the efforts of the writer's nephew, the valiant general de Saint-Simon, a more serious effort was made to publish the text. Three editions appeared, one during the general's lifetime and two more after his death. Chéruel published the complete text starting in 1858. Boislisle and his successors followed suit between 1879 and 1927. And finally, a new edition edited by Yves Coirault began to appear in 1983 and is happily now complete. In our work, we have used different texts depending on the quality of each for our purposes. The vast majority of our notes refer to the Boislisle and Coirault editions, both of which are admirable, superbly indexed, and in any case complementary. The interested reader can easily refer back and forth between the two.

It may be worth saying an additional word or two about these editions. The scholars have done an excellent job of reconstructing what remains of the original, which is a great deal. The Boislisle, at more than forty volumes, is an irreplaceable instrument. Its footnotes and monumental two-volume index are indispensable when it comes to drawing out the wealth of material contained in the *Memoirs*, which some have compared to a tapestry and others to a film.[8] The Coirault, printed on thin paper, is more like a portable computer. With its massive index and dense type it is possible to find a specific passage of the text very quickly, if need be after consulting Boislisle.

The various biographies tell us what we need to know about a life that was one of observation and action but not activism, except for a few short years of at times reluctant political engagement during the Regency.[9] We also learn about the enlightened if not terribly profitable way in which Saint-Simon, like other great landowners of his day, managed his estates. One author has even attempted a pyschobiography of the *petit duc* with a lack of success characteristic of the genre. Yves Coirault has done as much as can be done to penetrate the secrets of Saint-Simon's prodigious writing.[10] Finally, Mme Hélène Himmelfarb, together with her learned and intrepid collaborators at the *Cahiers Saint-Simon*, have year after year provided solutions to many of the riddles surrounding the achievements, ideas, and social milieu of a nobleman who ranked among France's highest.

One would like to be able to say that the Annales school and what was later dubbed, somewhat demagogically, the "new history" have not lagged behind. Nevertheless, despite a very rich article by Jacques Revel,[11] almost everything remains to be done in this area. The problem is that the Annales school's approach—call it anthropological, sociological, or historical-ethnographic as you will—was for too long dominated, not to say suffocated, by Norbert Elias's way of looking at the problem. Until recently, Elias's views have all but monopolized the attention of the *annalistes* whenever they turn their attention to the *Memoirs* or the court system, to say nothing of the Regency.[12] Unorthodox opinions, even when put forward by credentialed *annalistes* such as ourselves, have been stifled.[13] Since 1973, we have published some of our findings, but now the time has come to lay our cards on the table. What we propose in the present work is, we hope, a systematic and comprehensive interpretation of Saint-Simon's thought and work (but not of his writing or style). We look not at the form but at the substance of the text, and our approach owes little or nothing to the work of Elias. It is divided into two parts, like the work of the *petit duc* himself: "The Court System" and "The Regency System."

If we were to cite the main influences on the research that we have quietly been pursuing for the past twenty years, two names come to mind: Alain Besançon and Karl Popper (especially his *Open Society and Its Enemies*). These thinkers influenced our thinking in part 2, the "Regency System." As for part 1, the "Court System," which is the longer and we think more substantial of the two, our inspiration came mainly from Saint-Simon himself, as well as from the work of innumerable historians. But at many points in our work, two luminaries showed us the way and eased our task. The first was Pseudo–Dionysius the Areopagite, a writer, or perhaps one should say theologian, of the first millennium, who concerned himself with *hierarchy*, whether human, ecclesiastic, or angelic. His meditations on rank, the sacred, purity, and renunciation were of the utmost importance to us. What is more, as Yves Coirault has shown in his *Dans la forêt saint-simonienne* (183), the pseudo-Areopagite's ideas about hierarchy may well have been known to Saint-Simon himself through a series of medieval and modern intermediaries. And finally, it goes without saying that we have been deeply influenced by the similar or analogous approach taken by Louis Dumont in his immortal *Homo hierarchicus*. For us, Dumont's title alone defined a whole program of research. And of course there was much to learn from the text.

Sanctus Simo hierarchicus: much of our text, especially in part 1, is summed up by these seemingly simple words whose implications become profound once one has steeped oneself in the thought of Pseudo-Dionysius the Areopagite and in the universal "hierarchology" of Louis Dumont. And also, of course, in the thousands of pages of Saint-Simon, whose writings we know well, though we are not so presumptuous as to take ourselves for an Yves Coirault or a Hélène Himmelfarb or a Georges Poisson, all far more expert in this regard than we are. As for ideas about court networks and family systems, especially within the king's patrimonial household, the work of British historians in the Namierite mold as well as of countless European historians of the family, such as André Burguière, Antoinette Fauve-Chamoux, Peter Laslett, and many others, were of the greatest importance in our research.

part one

The Court System

Hierarchy and Rank

1 *This chapter will take up the problem of rank and hierarchy at the* royal court of Versailles in the period 1690–1715. It will also deal with what might be called the "post-court" of the Regency period (1715–23). Our basic source will be the *Memoirs* of Saint-Simon, at times supplemented by other, independent sources, such as the letters of Liselotte, also known variously as the Princess Palatine and Madame (wife of Monsieur, brother of Louis XIV). Liselotte and the *petit duc* never saw each other's texts, which remained unpublished until after their deaths.[1] Hence, we are dealing here with two truly independent sources, all that any historian concerned with objectivity could hope for. From the writings of these two authors, one has at least some access to the ideology of a relatively limited circle, a subset of the royal court. By ideology we mean a "set of ideas and values defined to a certain extent socially," or more simply, a "system of ideas and values."[2]

Our goal is different from that of Louis Marin in his book *Le Portrait du roi*, which was inspired by the work of Ernst Kantorowicz.[3] Marin's analysis focused on the king's body. This is a relevant object of study, but of limited value for the questions we wish to raise. Despite the fact that the monarch was fundamental to the system of aristocratic centralism, one cannot understand the ideology of the residents of Versailles in terms of the king's body alone. It was at most a focal point, but no more than the head of a needle compared with the rest.

Another work that we encountered in the course of our research was Christian Ehalt's book on "forms of expression under absolutist rule" at the Habsburg court in Vienna.[4] Ehalt deals mainly with problems associated with the theatricalization of power at the Habsburg imperial court. He is interested in the processes of "curialization," modernization, and rationalization whereby erstwhile warriors were turned into aristocrats. His ideas are interesting and rich but need to be fleshed out. Indeed, any court, whether imperial or royal, involves not only questions of power but also questions of status largely independent of power. What is more, Ehalt, following Norbert Elias, tends to exaggerate the degree to which the high nobility was demilitarized, a process he sees as civilizing and rationalizing. In fact, courtiers from the leading families in Louis XIV's entourage were still to some extent warriors, and the monarch expressly desired that courtiers retain a military role.[5] Some participated in duels. More significantly, many served when young as musketeers and later as officers in the bloody wars that ravaged Europe from 1688 to 1713. Their curialization was thus not purely and simply a modernizing transition toward nonviolence (as Elias would have it). Curialization was a unique phenomenon, which deserves to be studied in and of itself.

On the matter of court ranks and hierarchy—that "ceremonial and festival of abstractions," as Yves Coirault has put it—one may wish to consult J.-P. Labatut's recent thesis.[6] For more concrete images, one can turn to the engravings of Abraham Bosse, who was already acutely attuned to these matters during the reign of Louis XIII. See in particular his *Noblesse française à l'église* and *Cérémonies de l'Ordre du Saint-Esprit.*[7]

But let us return to our two authors, Saint-Simon and Liselotte. Although the letters of the Princess Palatine, or Madame, are not nearly as well written as Saint-Simon's text, they have the advantage of being more concise, of saying more in fewer words. Take, for example, a letter written at Versailles on 27 December 1713.[8] In this very dense text, which we reproduce in full in the notes and analyze below, Madame lists the various degrees of rank within the royal family as well as outside or "below" it.

At the head of the royal family was of course the king. Then came the "sons" or "children of France," including "le Grand Dauphin," also known as "Monseigneur,"[9] son of Louis XIV, and the king's brother, "Monsieur," son of Louis XIII. Next came the "grandsons of France": the sons of Monseigneur, such as the duc de Bourgogne and the duc de Berry, as well as the sons of Monsieur, such as Philippe d'Orléans, whose grandfather was Louis XIII. Immediately below the grandsons of France came the "princes of the blood," Condé and Conti. They were the king's cousins several times removed, because both they and Louis descended from a common ancestor, Charles de Bourbon, the grandfather of Henri IV. Finally, rounding out the royal family, came Louis XIV's bastards: the duc du Maine and the comte de Toulouse were the Sun King's illegitimate sons by Mme de Montespan. This little group, with its own hierarchy, was of course situated above plebeian dukes and peers, and it vexed Saint-Simon no end to see himself and others of his rank preceded by royal bastards. Madame's letter also alludes to various material and symbolic indicators of rank: whether or not one was allowed to eat with the king; how much time one was allowed to spend with him; whether or not one was permitted to be served by certain of one's officers in the monarch's presence; whether or not one was allowed to ride in the king's carriage; and so on.[10] We also learn of certain intrigues that altered this basic hierarchy without overturning it. For example, the status of royal bastards improved slightly, much to Saint-Simon's dismay. In her 1713 letter, however, Madame was not particularly worried about the promotion of the king's illegitimate offspring. They still ranked far below the princes of the blood, whom she and her children still outranked both legally and in terms of privilege. What Madame could not stomach, however, was the idea that her granddaughter should rank below the married princesses of the blood. This meant that not only her own blood but even more the blood of her husband—of Monsieur as well as Madame— was being devalued or "debased" as a direct result of intrigues initiated by Madame la Duchesse, an illegitimate daughter of Louis XIV who had married a Condé, that is, a prince of the blood, and who formed part of a cabal around the king's son. This duchess now and then wielded enough influence to slap the granddaughter of the Princess Palatine in the face and get away with it. Here, then, we have an example of the way in which cabals interfered with rank.[11]

Other texts detail the postures associated with each rank (that is, whether or not one was allowed to sit in any given situation).[12] As a sidelight, bear in mind that in the Catholic mass people used to sit, kneel, or stand depending on what stage, or "rank," the ceremony had reached. From Madame we learn that at the court of Louis XIV, her son, the duc de Chartres and future duc d'Orléans, a "grandson of France," enjoyed the right to be seated in the presence of a queen of France and to ride in her carriage.[13] These seemingly anodyne actions were forbidden, however, to "mere" princes of the blood, a Condé or Conti. As distant cousins of the king, they were already at some remove from the royal line and were therefore denied the privileges granted to a grandson of France such as the duc de Chartres. Once, however, Louis XIV invited a Condé to sit on the rear seat of the royal barouche, a privilege normally reserved for his dogs. This miraculous event was never to be repeated, however.[14]

Madame also addressed the burning issue of what types of seats could be used in what circumstances. The same question preoccupied Saint-Simon, who was not always as clear or as calm as Madame in his discussions of armchairs versus chairs with backs versus just plain stools, which served as physical symbols of the court hierarchy.[15] Here is Madame on the subject (1 October 1699):

> The king was unwilling to accept any compromise in the matter of the ceremonial. The duc de Lorraine insisted that he was entitled to be seated in an armchair in the presence of Monsieur and myself, because the emperor had allowed him one. The king replied that the emperor had one ceremonial and he had another. For example, the emperor permits cardinals to sit in armchairs, whereas cardinals may not be seated in the presence of the king. . . . Monsieur is willing to allow a chair with a back, and the king agrees, but the duke insists on being treated like an elector, and this the king will not allow. Monsieur proposed doing as the king of England does. That monarch insists that we not be given chairs, while we insist on having them. Therefore, when we are present he sits only on a stool. . . . But the king would not hear of this, and so as not to be compelled to insult the duke, we have put aside our plans to travel to Bar.

In this case the marks of distinction are clearly ordered: electors (whose votes selected the emperor and who therefore shared in his glory) were entitled to an armchair; the duc de Lorraine, who was not an elector, was entitled only to a chair with a back but wanted more; and for other high dignitaries, especially female dignitaries, there was the plain stool. Table 1.1 conveniently summarizes the answer to the question, Who was allowed to sit in the presence of whom, and on what?[16]

Under certain circumstances in the presence of Louis XIV, only the queen of France *in partibus*—that is, Mme de Maintenon—was entitled to an armchair. This was considered an outrage, but the king's abuse of his authority was covered up by invoking reasons of health. The *vulgum pecus*, including the dauphin, were denied this honor. Away from Versailles, however, anarchy reigned, especially at Marly and the Trianon, where courtiers and mere hangers-on sat anywhere and any way they pleased.[17]

The use of such material symbols of rank extended much lower in the hierarchy, all the way down to the level of the dukes and peers. We see this in an affair that greatly agitated the dukes, even if it seems ridiculous to us: the Affaire du Bonnet, which pitted the dukes and peers against the *premier président* of Parlement.[18] Saint-Simon was obsessed with questions of rank and their symbolic expression, and indeed, more generally, with questions of social architecture and its symmetries. For him, failure to respect symbols could have dire consequences. In 1718, when the Provincial Estates were convoked at Dinan, the maréchal de Montesquiou, commander-in-chief of Brittany, remained seated in his sedan chair when it was expected that he would first ride and then march at the head of

TABLE 1.1 SYSTEM OF SEATING

	Dauphin, dauphine, sons and daughters of France	Grandsons and granddaughters of France	Princesses of the blood	Princes of the blood	Cardinals	Duchesses, foreign princesses, Spanish grandees (female)	Dukes, foreign princes, Spanish grandees (male)	Women of Quality	Men of Quality
King, queen	stool	stool	stool	standing	stand before king, stool before queen	stool	standing	standing	standing
Dauphin, dauphine, sons and daughters of France	armchair	stool	stool	standing, then armchair	stool	stool	standing	standing	standing
Grandsons and granddaughters of France		armchair	chair with back	chair with back	chair with back	chair with back	stool	stool	standing
Princes and princesses of the blood			armchair	armchair	armchair	armchair	armchair	seated	seated

Note: This table is taken from Henri Brocher, *Le Rang et l'étiquette sous l'Ancien Régime* (Paris: Alcan, 1934), 28. Rows are labeled with the ranks of the royal family in descending order; columns with ranks including dukes and men of quality. Table entries indicate how persons of the rank indicated by the column heading were expected to behave in the presence of persons of the rank indicated by the row heading (at Versailles).

the Breton nobility.[19] To Saint-Simon's way of thinking, this open disrespect for the second order may well have contributed to the discontent that culminated in 1720 in a conspiracy of Breton aristocrats whose rebellion the government was then compelled to put down.[20] The duke also recounts another incident whose alleged consequences were far more serious (although his allegation is inaccurate). In 1688, the king ("who was now without a mistress and much given to building") noticed that one of the windows in the newly reconstructed Trianon seemed narrower than the others. He pointed this out to Louvois, who at first denied that it was so. In the end, Louis XIV had his way, but Louvois, according to Saint-Simon, was so furious at his master that he dragged him into the War of the League of Augsburg.[21]

Symbols that once attached only to higher ranks sometimes devolved to lower ranks as well, but such mutability only underscored the immutable principle of hierarchy itself. It was like the inflation of currency, which affected the value of a particular coin without diminishing the economic importance of monetary instruments generally. For example, the Princess Palatine was, by virtue of her marriage, a daughter of France. In a special dispensation, Louis XIV authorized her to keep four ladies-in-waiting as opposed to the two previously allowed. The right to a foursome of companions then passed to one granddaughter of France, the duchesse de Berry (the wife of one of the grandsons of France), and then to another (the duchesse d'Orléans), and ultimately to the princesses of the blood.

Or take another case of symbolic "trickle-down": when Monsieur (a son of France) died, his son, the duc de Chartres and future duc d'Orléans, who was only a grandson of France, was permitted to keep the same officers, guards, and Swiss guards that his father had had. This transfer of signs of honor from one generation to the next was more than a symbolic gesture, however. In this case, the monarch also granted his young nephew Philippe enormous material and financial advantages by way of compensation for his having married a royal bastard.[22]

The trickle-down phenomenon extended well below the summit of the social hierarchy constituted by the extended family of the monarch. Until the end of the seventeenth century, for example, velvet was found only in the jerkins and cloaks of the high aristocracy, not in the costumes worn by the nobility of the robe. Little by little, however, this custom "contaminated" the lower ranks as well. Caumartin, a state councilor and intendant of finance, was "the first man of the robe to venture to appear in a velvet jerkin and cloak." This happened toward the end of Louis XIV's reign. "There was at first a hullabaloo at Versailles. [Caumartin] endured it. People got used to it. For a long time no one dared to imitate him, but eventually nothing but velvet was good enough for the magistrates, and gradually it passed from them to lawyers, doctors, notaries, merchants, apothecaries, and even the more important *procureurs*."[23] This of course made it necessary for people of higher rank to find other status symbols to distinguish themselves from people of lesser "estate."

In sum, what was involved in these hierarchies was not a notion of mere social difference but a complex, comprehensive, "holistic" conception of relations between individuals and groups. From her vantage point at the summit of society, Madame could take in the whole panorama of rank, from the children of France to the grandsons of France, the princes of the blood, the legitimized bastards, the dukes and peers, and so on, all the way down to the bottom of the social ladder. The men who organized processions in Toulouse did the same. They distinguished six categories: magistrates, liberal professions, members of commercial guilds, bourgeois and rentiers, artisans and craftsmen (grouped in eighty-one different guilds, all hierarchically ordered), and finally "unincorporated" residents.[24] These Toulousains may have occupied a less exalted place in society than Madame, but they shared her zeal for classification. The hierarchy of estates was not the only pertinent parameter, however. Money and power upset the neat order of the social hierarchy. Béchameil, a man of considerable means, might well be lampooned by one count and kicked in the pants by another. He was nevertheless the lover of a duchess, the father-in-law of a minister and a duke, and an enlightened collector. The king consulted him, and he rubbed shoulders with the "best" society.[25]

Rank was not simply a consequence of a person's genealogical position in an all-encompassing hierarchy of families. It was rather like the vast blue cloak of the Virgin of Mercy, whose folds were ample enough to accommodate a range of qualities of the most diverse sort.[26] The ancientness of a noble lineage was certainly a consideration, but so were the number of impressive *alliances*, or illustrious marriages, and the number of important state posts held by family members, and the number of fiefs and great estates held by the family, and so on. As Saint-Simon put it, "antiquity, retinue, fiefs, marriages, positions held for some time—all these bestow true grandeur on a family from as far back in time as can be known."[27] Clearly, Saint-Simon held no brief for the idea that the nobles of France were all descended from the ancient inhabitants of Germania or from the warriors who invaded Roman Gaul between the third and fifth centuries. This was wise of him, even if he claimed that his own family was descended from Charlemagne, "at least on the distaff side."[28]

That said, it remains true that rank was largely a matter of birth. This was especially true in the case of the second order, or nobility. With the first order, or clergy, things were not so simple. A man could be of common birth, like Dubois, and still become an archbishop or even a cardinal, a prince of the church, without being in any sense a prince. Yet even here, the policy of episcopal appointments adopted by Louis XIV and his ecclesiastical advisors tended to make rank coincide with birth in the first order as well as the second. Higher posts such as bishoprics were awarded to "distinguished" ecclesiastics of noble birth. This was also true of court positions and high administrative posts, of magistracies in the sovereign courts and parlements, of military commands, and of provincial governorships.[29] Very few bishops were commoners. To be sure, Saint-Simon accused the Sulpiciens—"the filthy beards of Saint-Sulpice," as he calls them—of having encouraged Madame de Maintenon and the king to select as bishops "nothings" and "nobodies." By this he meant that the candidates to whom he was hostile were men who sprang from the obscure nobility of the robe or pen, but only rarely did they come from outside the second order.[30]

Besides rank and birth, Saint-Simon also esteemed merit. Meritocratic judgments were not a discovery of the late eighteenth century.[31] Seneca had already pondered the matter. In the seventeenth century, it was the subject of countless Latin essays and classroom exercises. Saint-Simon even alluded to it in a subtitle: "Hervault, archbishop of Tours: His Birth, His Merit, His Death."[32] He points to this prelate's virtue, Gallicanism, wit, learning, crypto-Jansenist leanings, and diligence. He also mentions that he is a true nobleman in property and honor, born to an ancient house tied by marriage to other such houses. Taken together, all of these qualities made him "an excellent and courageous bishop." Elsewhere Saint-Simon observes that birth into an illustrious family friendly to his own is in itself a merit worth more than merit as such. In 1715, at a time when he enjoyed a certain influence with the regent, Saint-Simon saw to it that Puységur was appointed to the War Council on account of his rare merit as a military man. He also had the duc de Lévis similarly appointed on the grounds that his relationship to the duc de Beauvillier (Lévis' uncle) was in itself a "transcendent merit."[33] In the case of Lévis, birth and merit were equivalent.

A t the turn of the eighteenth century, hierarchy as Saint-Simon understood it was recognized throughout Europe as a fundamental principle. In each country, however, it was embodied in a distinct series of ranks. An English duke had no aristocratic rank in France, and vice versa. If an English duchess wished to be seated in the presence of Louis XIV, she was obliged to wait until the French monarch granted her a "stool of favor." But such a gesture was simply a personal favor, with no implications for the status of dukes as a group on either side of the Channel.[34] A similar remark applies to the grandees of Spain. As late as 1696, they had no rank in France. When their wives appeared at the court of Versailles, they sat (on stools) only if Louis XIV granted them that favor.[35] But after a Bourbon acceded to the throne of Spain, all that changed.

This "nationalization" of hierarchy is perhaps one of the distinctive features of Saint-Simon's *Memoirs*, which occupy a position at the intersection of the hierarchical with the national. Culturally, Saint-Simon was a contemporary of Louis XV (he wrote his *Memoirs* during that monarch's personal reign). Politically, he coexisted with Louis XIV and Philippe d'Orléans. Existentially, he saw himself as a loyal subject of Louis XIII, the king who had made his father a duke and peer and to whom Saint-Simon gave his unstinting admiration.[36] Now, it was during the reigns of Louis XIII and Louis XIV, whose histories Saint-Simon passionately relived and deeply internalized, that great strides were made in the nationalization of hierarchy. Consider, for example, the nomination of bishops. Traditionally, these *grands seigneurs* had been drawn from the families of local or regional potentates. But, as Michel Péronnet notes, "Louis XIII sought to destroy geographic solidarities, and to that end he turned the episcopate into a national corps, whose members were recruited from across France."[37] What was true for the first order also had implications for the second: from 1600 on, the nobilities of France were in a sense unified nationally without damage to the hierarchical pyramid. Strict general rules were applied to nobles of all regions, especially in regard to the exclusion of bastards. Lax southern attitudes in this regard gave way to the more rigid standards of the north, which became the law of the kingdom.[38]

Wherever a national hierarchy existed, friction was inevitable when foreign ranks had to be integrated for one reason or another into the national court. Cardinals, for example, posed numerous problems, because they were princes of the Roman curia. They were nevertheless admitted with honors to the courts of France and Spain, particularly if they were French or Spanish nationals. Until 1696, for instance, they were entitled to use a folding chair at ceremonies of the Ordre du Saint-Esprit, whereas other knights of the order had to sit on a plain bench.[39] For a time, cardinals also shared with the king the right to mourn in purple, while the rest of the court wore black.[40] In Spain, Philip III allowed cardinals to sit in armchairs, but this pained him so greatly that he contrived never to sit with a cardinal except on stone benches placed on either side of a window.[41] Saint-Simon found these extra national privileges particularly annoying because he was a Gallican and therefore hostile to the popes and their *créatures rougies*.

Secular princes from other countries also caused trouble. Although they had no place in the national hierarchy, they tended to insinuate themselves between the princes of the blood, representing the lowest level of the royal house, and the dukes and peers, representing the highest level of the remainder of the aristocracy.[42] Saint-Simon's distaste for this solution is easy to explain: as a proponent of hierarchical nationalism, he had no way of accommodating non-French dignitaries in his system. As a duke and peer, he felt humiliated by them twice over. What is more, he was critical of them for having usurped a rank they did not deserve in the time of the League of Augsburg. On the one hand this was helpful to the Guises and the house of Lorraine, and on the other hand it encouraged a hyper-papist, ultra-bigoted Iberian mentality that filled Saint-Simon with horror.[43] Even the great Turenne, with his *princerie de Bouillon*, failed to find favor in our duke's eyes, despite the fact that Saint-Simon was related to him through the Lorges.[44] After tossing the marshal a few bouquets, Saint-Simon plunged a dagger into his heart: "Turenne, great captain, greater seditionist. His art, his *feigned* modesty, his *cloak* of probity *amongst his acts of disloyalty and criminality.*"[45]

A proper conception of hierarchy implies infinitely fine vertical subdivisions. The three orders—clergy, nobility, and third estate—failed to provide an adequate embodiment. Ranks tended to proliferate within these crude categories. Saint-Simon, for example, claims that the rank "granddaughter of France" was established by Louis XIII for his niece Mlle de Montpensier, the granddaughter of Henri IV, at the behest of Claude de Saint-Simon, the author's father and an enthusiastic proponent of hierarchy.[46] Allegedly this new rank was carried over into the age of Louis XIV for the benefit of the grandchildren of both sexes of both Louis XIII and Louis XIV. As a granddaughter of France, Mlle de Montpensier was entitled to a funeral ceremony in which a vigil over her body was held by three ladies of quality, including a princess and a duchess. A daughter of France would have been entitled to six, but a princess of the blood was allowed only her own domestic servants. (Hierarchy was most apparent in rituals of mourning, which included a religious component.)

To hear his son tell it, Claude de Saint-Simon was also responsible, as an expert on hierarchy, for obtaining a half stool for the wife of the chancellor of France, *la chancelière*. Supposedly she had wanted a full stool as if she were a duchess, but she had to settle for a half stool on which she was allowed to sit only during the queen's toilette. As a result, she was placed somewhere between the ordinary women of quality, who had to remain standing at all times, and the duchesses, who in many situations were allowed to sit when the royal couple was present.[47] Still, *la chancelière* never obtained the right to use scarlet seat covers in her carriages and sedan chairs; these were reserved for duchesses.

Was there no end to such distinctions? The duchesse d'Orléans, wife of the future regent, evidently thought not. In principle she was right, even if in the case in point she turned out to be wrong: "The duchesse d'Orléans had a head filled with fantasies that she could never realize. . . . Not content with the modern rank of granddaughter of France, which she enjoyed through her husband, she could not bear the idea that her children were only princes of the blood and dreamed up a rank for them that was betwixt and between: they were to be known as 'great-grandchildren of France.'"[48] In 1710 the subject came up again: "She could not bear the thought that her children were only princes of the blood, and from wishing that there were a distinct rank above the princes of the blood it was but a hair's breadth to contriving to obtain one. She therefore dreamed up a third estate *between the Crown and the princes of the blood* and set out to create one and have it approved."[49] Louis XIV sabotaged the project, which nevertheless had the merit of clarifying the distinction between "the crown" or "royal house" (king, sons, and grandsons of France) and the princes of the blood (who were also of royal blood, but more distantly related).[50] Together these two groups constituted the "reigning house," broader than "the crown" as such.[51] The rank of "great-grandchildren of France," which was never approved, would have further refined distinctions within "the crown."

A passage in the *Memoirs* goes into greater detail about all this.[52] Within the "reigning house," it was customary to distinguish the "houses" of the sons of France and of the first prince of the blood. However, the dauphin, or eldest son of the king, had no house of his own (and hence no military contingent), because he was totally identified with the king. Hence one had the following "houses": the king's house in the strict sense, comprising the king and dauphin (ruling family with primogeniture); the subsidiary houses of sons of France other than the dauphin; the crown, or royal house, comprising the king, sons, and grandsons of France; and the reigning house, comprising all Bourbon males and their families, including the princes of the blood.[53]

The texts and dossiers that Saint-Simon assembled in connection with the abortive effort to create the new rank of great-grandson of France number among the few surviving documents from his research archives.[54] They clearly indicate that not just one or two noblemen but everyone in the upper reaches of the court took a keen interest in the problems of hierarchy and the infinite subtleties of rank.

As an adept of ever more subtle "subdivisions," Saint-Simon opposed the actions of certain nobles in 1717. In that year, an ill-defined group challenged the "natural" superiority of the dukes and peers and sought to have questions involving succession to the throne submitted to the judgment of the Estates General.[55] In response, Saint-Simon insisted on the distinctive qualities of the peerage within the second order. Dukes and peers, he argued, constituted "by birth a distinctive rank separate from the reigning house . . . which has tacitly and consistently but clearly and palpably told the men of quality that [dukes and peers] are and have what the men of quality can never be owing to the disproportion of birth that separates them."[56] If the nobility ever forgot that it was made up of disparate ranks, it would be reduced to a "putative nobility" and cease to be itself.[57]

Naturally, the support that this minor *fronde* of the nobility received in 1717 from more or less occult sources only irritated Saint-Simon all the more. Among the upstart group's allies was Philippe de Vendôme, grand prior of the Order of Malta in France and allegedly a pox-ridden drunkard, who was joined by the brothers Mesmes, one of whom served as the Maltese order's ambassador to France and the other, a *créature* of the duc du Maine, as *premier président* of the Parlement of Paris.[58] Vendôme and Maine: a descendant of one of Henri IV's bastards and a bastard of Louis XIV. Saint-Simon's animus against bastards here converged with his interest in hierarchy and rank and led him to condemn the militancy of the broader nobility. In this respect, he differed somewhat from Boulainvilliers, another progressive theorist of the second order in the age of Enlightenment.[59] Boulainvilliers saw the nobility as a single group sharing the same blue blood and within that group advocated equality.[60] In a sense, Boulainvilliers treated nobility as a "substance." Or perhaps more tellingly, as a monolithic bloc capable of becoming involved in disastrous conflicts with other, more sizable "substances" (such as the third estate). By contrast, Saint-Simon saw the second order, and indeed French society as a whole, as "a fluid and structuring medium," with an emphasis on subtle internal distinctions between different interdependent levels.[61]

Hierarchy, in other words, implied separation and subdivision within an overall context of interdependence. It established distinctions not only between groups but also between individuals, or at any rate families. Individual qualities were not distinguished from family characteristics. It was not the individual nobleman who mattered but the scion of this or that distinguished family. In writing about Spanish festivals, for example, Saint-Simon noted that there were "distinct places in all ceremonies not only for the grandees but also for their wives, *their eldest sons, and the wives of their eldest sons.*"[62]

Hierarchy influenced not only the molecules but also the atoms of society. The categories discussed in Liselotte's letters (sons of France, grandsons of France, and so on) might at any point be empty or contain only one member. After the death of Monsieur in 1701, only one "son of France" remained, for example, and after the death of Monseigneur in 1711, there were none. Yet the category as such continued to outrank the princes of the blood and dukes and peers, despite their greater numbers.

Dukes and peers were ranked by head of household or, what comes to the same thing, family. In effect they were ordered by the ancientness of the peerage. "The maréchal de Luxembourg, proud of his successes and of the world's applause for his victories, believed that his position was strong enough to allow him to raise his rank from eighteenth by seniority among the peers to second, immediately behind M. d'Uzès."[63] To be sure, what enraged Saint-Simon about this high-handed maneuver was that he stood to be one of its victims if Luxembourg succeeded: his rank would be reduced from twelfth among the peers to thirteenth. The Luxembourg family would join the eleven others that already outranked the Saint-Simons. What is more, one of Luxembourg's supporters was none other than Achille III de Harlay, *premier président* of the Parlement of Paris, whom Saint-Simon detested. Harlay had hit upon the legal subterfuge that had made it possible to legitimate the "adulterine copies," or bastards, of the king and Mme de Montespan. Later he would conceive a stratagem for assigning the bastards a rank intermediate between the princes of the blood and the peers.[64] Saint-Simon, who disapproved of both bastards and preferential treatment of any kind, thus had more than one reason to dislike Harlay. In his own terms, it was perfectly rational for him to oppose a marshal's attempt to improve his standing in the peerage, even if that marshal had covered himself with glory in battle and bore the name Luxembourg.

The Luxembourg affair, which posed the problem of rank as a matter of both individual and family standing, is in every way exemplary. Saint-Simon's discussion of this affair was by his own admission "the bitterest and most acrimonious part of the *Memoirs*."[65] It shows what enormous importance he attached to even the subtlest of distinctions. His interpretation of Luxembourg's claims is typical of his interpretation of court customs and the court spirit in general. We have already discussed part of that interpretation in connection with Harlay. But there is more. Luxembourg had sought to violate the sacrosanct principle of hierarchical rank. Hence it came as no surprise to Saint-Simon when the marshal tried to arrange a marriage between his daughter and the obscure, elderly bastard of a prince of the blood, a dissolute drunkard who spent the better part of his time in taverns.[66] In Saint-Simon's mind, bastardy and bibulousness were of a piece: both came under the head of impurity, whose central importance in his thinking we shall see in what follows. Furthermore, among those who supported Saint-Simon and the dukes in their suit against Luxembourg was Henri-François d'Aguesseau, an *avocat général* who went on to become a *procureur général* and ultimately chancellor. As it happens, the estimable d'Aguesseau was also an "enemy of the Jesuits."[67] Luxembourg, who was linked to bastardy, bibulousness, and Jesuitism, therefore stood for everything that Saint-Simon hated about the assault on hierarchy. What is more, all of this carried over from one generation to the next: Jean de Maisons, a *président* in the Parlement who openly lived with a woman to whom he was not married, favored Luxembourg, who shamelessly greased the palm of the magistrate's mistress.[68] And the magistrate's son, Claude de Maisons, also a *président* in the Parlement, was an impious man as well as a warm, if secret, partisan of the duc du Maine, Louis XIV's notorious bastard. Once again, adultery, bastardy, and impiety attached to the hated Luxembourg by way of his agents.[69]

Saint-Simon became involved in other affairs that were similar in character although perhaps with fewer aggravating circumstances than the one involving Luxembourg. In 1714, for example, he won a suit against François VII, duc de La Rochefoucauld, who chafed at being only the thirteenth peer of France when Saint-Simon, though clearly inferior by birth, ranked twelfth.[70] Our duke owed his victory to his friend Chancellor Pontchartrain. In a show of gratitude, he kissed the chancellor "as one might kiss a mistress."[71] Note that this dispute was really a family affair, because Saint-Simon's father was already on bad terms with La Rochefoucauld's father, the author of the famous *Maxims.*[72]

Dukes were not the only nobles to be ranked more or less individually. So were princesses, even illegitimate ones: two of the king's natural daughters were obliged to address a third as "Madame" when she became a granddaughter of France through her marriage to the duc de Chartres. But the new Madame had only to address each of them as "my sister." Displeased by this unequal treatment, the two sisters tried to address the duchesse de Chartres as "Mignonne," only to be scolded by Louis XIV.[73]

Even monarchs were "indexed" in relation to one another. According to Saint-Simon, the French king addressed the Danish king as "Your Serene Highness" but insisted on being addressed in return as "Your Majesty," which was much more exalted.[74] The ranking principle also covered royal councils and the like. In 1721 the maréchal de Montesquiou joined the Regency Council, also known as the "old seraglio," where he ranked thirtieth in terms of seniority and dignity.[75] Members of chivalrous orders were likewise ranked by seniority. This was true of the French Ordre du Saint-Esprit and the Spanish Golden Fleece. When Philip V arrived in Madrid to assume the throne, he received the Golden Fleece from the most senior knight of the order, the duke of Monteleone Pignatelli.[76] The orderly ranking of the Golden Fleece made a pleasant contrast with the informal anarchy that otherwise reigned among the grandees of Spain: "They respect no ranking by seniority or class (except for granting priority to the archbishop of Toledo as primate of Spain). They fall into line one after the other as chance may dictate."[77] For Saint-Simon, this informality was one reason why the court of Madrid was inferior to the court of Versailles, where a more rigorously hierarchical spirit prevailed. Spain was but a pale imitation of France, just as France was an imperfect version of Germany. It took the degrees of the Golden Fleece, originally imported from late medieval Burgundy, to bring a little order to the ranks of the Iberian aristocracy, which still suffered in Saint-Simon's eyes from the backwardness that the Moors had brought to peninsular affairs.

The numerical ranking system was not essential, however. It was subordinate to the more general principle of hierarchy and could in some cases come into conflict with it. Take the so-called *ordre du tableau* that Louvois introduced in the army: "Promotions were now made only on the basis of seniority, which was called the *ordre du tableau*. Hence all the [great] nobles [were mingled] with the mass of officers of every sort. This led to confusion . . . and to general neglect . . . of all differences of person and background in what had become the people's military service."[78] Historians have shown that on this point Saint-Simon was exaggerating. Individual merit and talents were taken into account in promotions.[79] Birth also mattered to the group as a whole (the officer corps remained almost entirely of noble origin). Yet although the historians are right about the facts, this does not contradict the deeper logic of Saint-Simon's position. To his severe and judicious way of thinking, ranking by seniority was valid in principle only so long as it reinforced and did not contradict the essential hierarchy of families based on dignity of origin or birth, in absolute contrast to "the vile populace in which all are equal."[80]

When it came to socializing among officers, Saint-Simon had nothing but sarcastic things to say about noble army officers who invited only men of equivalent rank to dine in their homes, excluding officers of lower rank, when according to the duke they should have invited guests to their dinner table solely on the basis of birth.[81]

Saint-Simonian sociology was bound up with biology. A man did not become a duke or prince; he was *born* one. The child was already what it would become upon leaving its mother's womb, or even while still inside it. A son born to a princess was a duke; a son born to a queen was a prince. "On 6 June we heard the news that the queen of Spain had given birth to a prince in Madrid, who was to be called Don Felipe. . . . On 8 January Madame la duchesse de Bourgogne gave birth to a duc de Bretagne."[82]

Retrospectively speaking, a woman could even give birth to a prelate. Take the case of "Florence Pélerin, an actress and dancer at the Opéra, who was long the kept woman of M. le duc d'Orléans and by whom he had the archbishop of Cambrai (as he is today)."[83] Birth was a time to reaffirm certain hierarchies. Prior to Louis XIV, duchesses assisted at the queen's deliveries. On occasion the queen and daughters of France would visit duchesses in labor.[84] But these customs had more or less disappeared.

The taxonomy, though quasi-biological, was nevertheless vertically hierarchical as well. The higher one stood on the ladder of rank, the more recognition one expected from those on lower levels, and the less recognition one gave. This was especially true in the case of kings, and most of all in Madrid. Kings received visits but did not make them. Saint-Simon was not aware of *any* royal visit to a lesser personage in Spain from the time of Philip II to that of Philip V. That is why he was so beside himself when the incredible occurred in 1710: "During the three days he spent in Madrid, King Philip V did something that is almost unheard of in Spain. . . . He called upon the marquis de Mancera in his home, and the recipient of this visit was nearly overcome with joy."[85] True, Mancera fully deserved such a visit because of his patriotic attitude during a recent war. Having lived to the ripe old age of 102 thanks to a macrobiotic diet of ice water and preserved roses, he could boast of having been paid an honor not seen in Spain since the duke of Alba's death in 1582.[86] As Saint-Simon remarked, "I am not sure that any king of Spain has ever visited anyone since Philip II went to see the dying duke of Alba, who, when he saw the king walk into his bedroom, told him that it was too late and without another word turned his face to the wall."[87]

To be sure, Louis XIV paid more visits than did his Spanish counterparts. But these were considered to be events of such magnitude that the host felt obliged to put on a lavish display even when the king was only represented by a page.[88]

When young Louis XV decided to visit the former chancellor Pontchartrain, who had retired to a life of piety, Pontchartrain contrived to prevent such a violation of protocol from actually taking place. In the politest way imaginable, he virtually barred the door to his house to prevent the young king from entering.[89]

As Montesquieu shrewdly noted, distinction of ranks implied corresponding distinctions in land tenure: common, freehold, noble.[90] In their mobile essence, these degrees of ownership reflected the possible ascent of noble masters and landlords up the ladder of status: "The king [Louis XV] has just designated the estate of Marigny-en-Brie, near Coulommiers, a marquisate, in favor of M. de Vandières [a relative of the marquise de Pompadour], who inherited the Marigny estate from his father."[91]

Yet even though Saint-Simon was deeply interested in social relations and the social pyramid, he was not interested in the property relations that made some men the owners of property and others workers.[92] Unlike the economist Quesnay, he would never have defined the nobility as "the landowning class." (As we shall see later, however, he did come fairly close to this on occasion, when he spoke of his blue-blooded colleagues as "landed" gentlemen.) He was not well versed in political economy despite his enlightened admiration for Vauban and Boisguilbert.[93] He tended to invoke human stupidity or wickedness to account for what economists would one day blame on the whims of nature and insufficient productivity. To his way of thinking, governments were often more responsible for human woes than were events themselves. He slyly blamed the disastrous Loire floods of 1707 on the fact that the inept maréchal de La Feuillade, whom he detested, had eliminated certain natural stone barriers that had previously served as a sort of providential dam.[94] Since La Feuillade was also a thief, a homosexual, and an incompetent, to say nothing of an enemy of Saint-Simon's friend the duc d'Orléans, everything fit together.[95] Human failings adequately explained why the river had overflowed its banks. There was no need to indict nature, though she had presumably lent a hand.

Saint-Simon's attitude toward famine may serve as a test case. For us, the famines of this period were an inevitable byproduct of a certain phase in the development of man's relationship to his environment. In premodern agricultural societies, a year or two of bad weather could mean an insufficient supply of seed for subsequent plantings, leading to rising food prices, depressed marriage and birth rates, increased death rates, and food riots. To be sure, real grain shortages due to bad weather could be compounded by nefarious speculators and black marketeers, but these were secondary effects. Yet Saint-Simon either ignored the weather, as he did in describing the famine of 1693, or incorporated it into his all-encompassing theory of society, in which seasonal factors counted for far less than social intrigue.

Take, for example, the famine of 1693–94. In the summer of 1692, Saint-Simon was a young musketeer taking part in preparations for the siege of Namur. "The fine weather turned to rain more plentiful and unrelenting than anyone in the army had ever seen, and people thought of Saint Médard, whose festival was celebrated on 8 June. On that day it rained buckets, and people pretended that the bad weather would last for forty days and forty nights. And so it did. Soldiers made desperate by this deluge swore oaths against the saint and sought out icons, which they smashed or burned. The rain became a plague upon the siege."[96] Obviously Saint-Simon is here discreetly distancing himself from the almost medieval religious beliefs of the common soldiers, who blamed the overabundant rain on the saint. His own Christianity was of the purer sort that would never think of blaming a meteorological phenomenon on a holy man when it was obviously the work of Providence (God) and lesser causes (chance). Saint-Simon, whose thinking about nature was on the whole quite similar to that of Malebranche, took it no farther than this. But what he had actually witnessed in that rainy June of 1692 was the "beginning" of the great famine of 1693–94. Indeed, that summer, fall, and winter were all quite wet, and the excess moisture proved disastrous for the harvest of 1693. The upshot of all this was that in 1693–94 France suffered a "human deficit" of more than a million people, if we take account of both the higher-than-normal death rate and the lower-than-normal birth rate—a 5 percent loss of population. But Saint-Simon says not a word about this famine, even though he was perfectly well aware of its meteorological "prodrome." We thus have every right to find him guilty of a crime of omission for writing only about court trifles and military matters while a cataclysmic event was taking place before his very eyes.

By contrast, Saint-Simon had a great deal more to say about the famine of 1709–10. This was only natural, since he had in the meantime become a personage at court, if only of the second tier. He was a secret advisor not only to the duc d'Orléans but even more to the ducs de Bourgogne, de Beauvillier, and de Chevreuse, who together constituted a reformist party much concerned with the impoverishment of the population. Saint-Simon mentions the scholarly works of Vauban and Boisguilbert for the first time in his discussion of the year 1707. Both writers were concerned with reducing misery and improving state finances.[97] In this connection, Saint-Simon also discusses the great chill of 1709. And he goes into great detail about the famine that resulted from this chill in 1709 and 1710.

These passages should be read with care, however. Saint-Simon's account of the chill and subsequent famine is tendentious. He blames much of went wrong in 1709 on individuals and on the authorities, when in fact the thermometer was probably the primary culprit. He even goes so far as to suggest that d'Argenson, the *lieutenant de police* whose pro-Jesuit views Saint-Simon disliked, had joined the provincial intendants in a nebulous plot whose most visible result was to plunge the populace into famine.[98] He was in fact projecting back onto 1709 charges that were current in the 1740s, while he was hard at work on the definitive version of his *Memoirs*. He shared the traditional mind-set: rather than face up to the realities of low agricultural productivity and meteorological unpredictability, he preferred to believe that a secret plot had been deliberately fomented to starve the people. He was obsessed with thoughts of bread, not for himself (he had plenty) but for the poor (toward whom he felt a sincere generosity). Little by little this concern of his developed into an obsession with a conspiracy later dubbed the "famine pact." Because the government in 1709–10 disposed of rotted grain and tried to store unspoiled grain, the duke charged officials with both waste and hoarding. The idea of a "famine pact" or conspiracy "thus gained credence not only among the people but also among magistrates and merchants," to say nothing of Saint-Simon himself. With varying degrees of good faith all alleged that the famine was "artificial, deliberate, and orchestrated." The perpetrators and beneficiaries were the people in power and the "gentlemen of finance" detested by the peerage.[99] The monarch himself (Louis XIV in 1709, Louis XV in 1740 and later) was seen as the more or less witting accomplice of spineless bureaucrats and shady monopolists. The mystical image of a paternal, providential monarchy suffered from the vagaries of an ever more complex market for grains, coupled with a traditional view of price fluctuations: people blamed evil operators rather than bad weather and inadequate infrastructure.[100] Thus Saint-Simon's ideology was rooted in the hierarchical structure of the society of his time as well as in the images that most people formed of the way society worked. From the top to the bottom of the great chain of being, people believed that the enigma of famine and the "cruel manipulation of wheat" could be better explained by sociological factors than by natural, economic, and ecological ones.

Within this narrow and limited framework, Saint-Simon's hierarchical conception tended to create finely differentiated hierarchical structures composed of a large number of distinct ranks. Ideally, each family stood in a hierarchical relationship to every other family. Ultimately this resulted in a hierarchy with dozens, if not hundreds, of subdivisions. All of this, including the very upper reaches of the hierarchy, was encompassed within the simpler, broader structure of the three estates: clergy, nobility, and third estate.

Although Saint-Simon had little taste for anything not purely hierarchical and little understanding of economics, he did at times see the three orders as exercising a certain influence of a purely material order. As he saw it, the second order (nobility) consisted of landed gentry: "land and swords—this is the nobility's only property."[101] By contrast, the third order was associated with *rentes* (interest on bonds) paid by the royal treasury to magistrates, merchants, and ordinary bourgeois. The upper reaches of the third estate thus consisted of rentiers.

Note that in relegating the magistrates of the *parlements* to the third estate, Saint-Simon the sociologist erred from a legal point of view. In law as well as in theory, *parlementaires* were ennobled.[102] In Paris they were nobles of relatively recent date, in the provinces in some cases more ancient. But if Saint-Simon was wrong about the parlement of Brittany, he was "right" insofar as the snobbery of the high court aristocracy was concerned. What is more, this snobbery was shared by the *robins anoblis* who were victims of aristocratic condescension.[103] They internalized the same hierarchical disdain to such a degree that they felt "contempt for bourgeoisie [*sic*] of every kind, even when clad in purple, authentically ennobled, and seated on *fleurs-de-lys*." As Roland Mousnier notes, the high nobility of the robe was nothing more than a "bourgeoisie" in the eyes of a true *gentilhomme*. Mousnier quotes the *Mémoires* of the abbé de Choisy, written under Louis XIV: "My mother, who was an Hurault de L'Hôpital, often said to me, 'Listen, my son, curb your pride and remember that you are merely a bourgeois. I know that your fathers and grandfathers were *maîtres des requêtes* and *conseillers d'Etat*, but I am telling you that in France the only recognized nobility is that of the sword. The glory of the entire nation rests in arms.' "[104]

To repeat, then, correcting Saint-Simon the snob but recognizing the spirit of the group of which he was a member: for him, the *noblesse d'épée* was a landed aristocracy, whereas the *noblesse de robe* and the upper strata of the third estate were by and large rentiers.[105]

Saint-Simon saw the difference between the top of the hierarchy and the very bottom (which in ill-humored moments he referred to as the "dregs of the populace") in two very different lights. At court there were individuals who were not "men of quality" and whose only title was *valet de chambre* or *premier valet de chambre* to the king. Yet these people could in fact wield considerable, not to say awesome, power, since they actually served as the king's trusted agents. Such men dined easily with great lords. A man like Louis Blouin, *premier valet de chambre* to Louis XIV and lover of the painter Mignard's splendid daughter, was on intimate terms with the ducs de Villeroy and de La Rocheguyon (alias La Rochefoucauld), "who supped with him almost every night."[106] And Beringhen, who was *premier valet de chambre* to Louis XIII as well as having distinguished himself by daring deeds on the battlefield, obtained the considerable post of *premier ecuyer* (first equerry) of the court under Mazarin.[107]

Saint-Simon took a different and not always consistent view of the vast distance separating the highest ranks of the court nobility from the mass of commoners. At times he adopts a protective, almost friendly tone toward the lower orders or estates. In discussing the technically remarkable accomplishments of farmers in Alleu, for example, he notes that the region "is rich but populated only by prosperous yeoman, clever men of stout common sense."[108] He also mentions Captain Le Fèvre, an erstwhile swineherd and illiterate who nevertheless won the Croix de Saint-Louis and promotion to the rank of officer by dint of valiant exploits. Aristocrats in the army admired and liked him.[109] He also tells us about the wife of the postmaster of Nonancourt, a "most respectable woman of spirit, good sense, brains, and courage." Supposedly she saved the Stuart pretender to the English throne from assassins hired to do him in.[110] And Saint-Simon describes the humble priest of La Ferté, a village of which he was lord, as a "man of spirit and a scholar."[111] Finally, a man named Ducasse, said to be the "son of a humble hog butcher who used to sell ham in Bayonne," is described as a valiant seaman who earns a well-deserved promotion to squadron commander.[112]

Saint-Simon also sincerely deplored the poverty of much of the population. In several places, however, he can scarcely conceal his contempt for individuals sprung from the lower orders or even the middle class, as well as for dynasties of similarly humble origins, so that we are left in little doubt as to his private sentiments, at least as regards people whom he detested. We are told, for example, that Cardinal Dubois started out "as nothing more than a penniless knave." (Saint-Simon was exaggerating: in fact, Dubois was the younger son of a physician and pharmacist from Brive. As an adolescent he attended the Collège Saint-Michel in Paris on a scholarship.)[113] Cardinal Fleury was the son "of a collector of tithes in the diocese of Lodève." This was in fact a bourgeois background, perhaps even a noble one, and not nearly as insignificant as Saint-Simon makes out, but this did not prevent him from expressing his contempt: "As a young man Fleury wormed his way in among Cardinal Bonsy's valets."[114] Fleury had indeed been a protégé of Bonsy, but there was nothing discreditable about that. Another of Saint-Simon's bêtes noires, the Jesuit Tellier, was described as the "son of a poor peasant from the wilds of Normandy," hence obviously good for nothing.[115] The Lantis were illustrious members of the Roman and even French aristocracy, but for Saint-Simon "those Lantis are nothing at all. They took the name della Rovere because they had a mother who belonged to that family, but in any case the Roveres themselves belonged to the dregs of the populace before their pontificate," that is, before Francesco della Rovere became Pope Sixtus IV in 1471.[116] The phrase "dregs of the populace (lie du peuple)," which Saint-Simon used fairly frequently, suggested that the lower orders were somehow impure. When he wrote, for example, that a certain duke had married "a creature from the dregs of the populace," he meant a "bar girl." He also used the term gueux, or tramp, to suggest poverty and, by association, ancestors of low birth: "Abbé Tencin was a priest and a tramp, the great-grandson of a goldsmith. . . . Guérin was his name, and Tencin was the name of a small property that supplied the whole family's needs."[117] No reader of this disdainful passage would be likely to guess that the Tencins (whose nobility, though modern, was by no means as recent as Saint-Simon suggests) were one of the most distinguished, as well as wealthiest, families of the Dauphiné.

Like father, like son. A commoner, even one of notarial or parlementaire ancestry, was likely to be a crook or a scoundrel. "My father's steward, a man by the name of Tessé who was with him for several years, suddenly vanished with fifty thousand livres . . . for which he had produced false invoices."[118] To be sure, the elder Saint-Simon should never have trusted this slick clerk: "He was a small, affable, soft-spoken, clever man, who had demonstrated some talent and who had friends, including an *avocat* in the Parlement of Paris." So much for the crook. The scoundrel was even worse, for he was not just useless but downright harmful to his country: "I won't say that Arouet would have been put in the Bastille [in 1717] for writing impudent verses if he hadn't made a name for himself through his poetry and adventures and hadn't enjoyed society's indulgence. He was the son of my father's notary, and I saw him many times when he brought documents to be signed. [The boy's father] had never been able to make anything of his libertine son, who ultimately made his fortune under the name Voltaire, which he took in order to conceal his true name."[119]

Families were ranked in decreasing order of dignity. Under the law, rank was transmitted from generation to generation as governed by the rules of primogeniture. Beyond this de jure transmission of rank, *grands seigneurs* wished to add de facto heritability of offices. But the nature of office holding did not always lend itself to this idea. An office could become vacant not only when its incumbent died but also when the king died. For example, the office of first physician was automatically vacated on the king's death, because the royal physician was a part of the king's personal and even domestic entourage.[120] But this was a special case. Such dynasties of bureaucratic mandarins as the Colberts and Phélypeaux-Pontchartrains did everything they could to pass offices from father to son: "Maurepas became secretary of state while almost still a child, replacing his father Pontchartrain, who was dismissed."[121] This desire to perpetuate the lineage extended to offices and dignities that brought more honor or status than genuine power. Take orders of chivalry, for example: the marquis de Listenois obtained the Golden Fleece thanks to the support of his mother-in-law, the comtesse de Mailly, née Saint-Hermine. She managed this with help from Mme de Maintenon, partly as compensation for her failure to provide her daughter with a suitable dowry.[122] The honoree in question "seemed rather savage," for a short while earlier Listenois had swindled his mother-in-law out of 1,200 pistoles allegedly needed as ransom to free him from (a nonexistent) captivity.[123] Mme de Mailly nevertheless decided to shut her eyes to the truth. Somewhat later, Listenois was killed at the siege of Aire-sur-la-Lys.[124] In the following year (1711), Bauffremont, Listenois's brother, obtained the position in the order left vacant by the original recipient's glorious death.[125] Although the initial acquisition was dubious, this honorific symbol ended up a family heirloom.

Provincial governorships were treated in a similar way. The development of the intendant system had made the position of governor somewhat honorific,[126] although governors retained certain military powers.

Take the case of Anjou: the comte d'Armagnac passed the governorship to his son, the comte de Brionne, but later prevailed upon Brionne to pass it on to his grandson, the prince de Lambesc.[127] Sometimes there was a price to be paid. Ségur (who belonged to the entourage of the duc d'Orléans) stood "in line" to succeed his father as governor of Foix. But to make sure he would get the post, he married the unacknowledged bastard daughter that the duc d'Orléans had had with the actress Desmares.[128] The new father-in-law, who also happened to be the regent, expressed his gratitude by giving Ségur 200,000 livres tournois and the governorship of Foix, which Ségur's father had originally bought from the maréchal de Tallard with Louis XIV's permission.[129] The same pattern—purchase followed by appointment followed by de facto inheritance—was followed in Douai: upon the death of the elderly Pomereu (a former captain of guards and brother of a state councilor), the regent gave the gubernatorial post to Comte François d'Estaing, a lieutenant general who had served under him in the Spanish wars.[130] D'Estaing, who knew his way around high society, had previously arranged a marriage between his son Charles and a wealthy heiress, the only daughter of a Fontaine-Martel. This proved to be an inspired move. Unbeknownst to d'Estaing, the girl's mother was a protégée of the regent. With his connection to the regent and the support of the mother, d'Estaing had no difficulty in making sure that the lucrative governorship would pass to his son. The regent raised no objection.[131]

In periods of inflation, transfers of this sort were often accompanied by an increase in the emoluments of office. In 1710, the maréchal de Matignon, a tightfisted Norman, arranged the marriage of his son Gacé to the daughter of the maréchal de Châteaurenault, who brought with her a dowry of 100,000 écus (the marriage, incidentally, would prove to be an unhappy one). To further enhance his son's fortune, Matignon resigned the governorship of La Rochelle and Aunis in the son's favor.[132] The office was valued at 230,000 livres and yielded an income of 16,000 livres. In 1719, when times were better and the cost of living was higher, Matignon arranged with the regent to increase the governor's compensation by 6,000 livres.[133] To be sure, the Matignon family was well versed in state finances. During the Chamillart ministry, it had drawn on his treasury.[134] Louis XIV was quite willing to approve these de facto hereditary transfers of provincial governorships so long as the beneficiary did not come from the province in question, for this would have encouraged subversive intrigues through collusion with the local nobility, a prospect that the Sun King wisely wished to avoid.[135]

Court offices and related positions (paramilitary and other) could also be passed on easily under the lax conditions that prevailed during the Regency. In 1717, Philippe d'Orléans attached the right of survivorship to the positions of captain of gendarmes, grand falconer, grand chamberlain, captain of light horse, first gentleman of the chamber, and grand master of the wolfhunt.[136] Henceforth these positions could be passed from father to son, even if the child was as young as twelve. The regent's favors thus "opened the door to all children who survived their fathers." The Rohans, La Trémoille, Chaulnes, and others less illustrious all benefited from these favors of the regent. The same period also saw an increase in the lucrative *brevets de retenue*, which in some cases profited the same families. These attached important financial rewards to what had been honorific offices and in some cases allowed the benefits to be passed on to one's children even if the associated title was not heritable.[137] In a similar vein, Philippe granted the Maulévriers the right to pass the office of royal chaplain, not from father to son, obviously, but from uncle to nephew.

Favors were handed out in a steady stream. In 1721 the Beringhens were allowed to transfer the office of first equerry from father to eldest son (and eventually to his younger brother). This was valued at 400,000 livres, and the man who held it was allowed to wear an embroidered blue jerkin. The d'Antins were no less fortunate: they were permitted to pass the lucrative office of superintendent of buildings directly from grandfather to grandson.[138] In 1722, the Courtenvaux, who were in fact Le Tellier–Louvois, received a similar boon: a baby still in the cradle was allowed to inherit his father's post as captain of the Hundred Swiss, which the father had already inherited from the grandfather.[139] The Mortemart family could boast of three generations of first gentlemen of the king's chamber.[140] The La Trémoilles could make the same claim until Cardinal Fleury took the position away from them in order to give it to his nephew.[141] The Tessé family already enjoyed the good fortune of a marshalship and an ambassadorship. In 1723 they obtained the right to pass on from grandfather to grandson the post of first equerry to the future queen.[142] And the duc de Tresmes scored when he was allowed to transfer his prized positions as governor of Paris and first gentlemen to his son (not without complications, however).[143] All of these posts brought emoluments and pensions.[144] In 1718, the Charosts, Luxembourgs, Berwicks, and Ségurs were granted the right to pass on to their children their lucrative provincial governorships and lieutenant generalships (in Picardy, Normandy, the Limousin, and Foix).[145]

Louis XIV was more reluctant than his nephew the regent would be when it came to allowing offices to be (provisionally) inherited. By taking a relaxed view in this regard, Philippe d'Orléans won for his government the support of the high aristocracy. He consolidated the society of ranks, adding a second classification to the "eternal" ordering of families. This second classification was based on length of service in high office. Of course, such tenure could hardly compare with the centuries across which noble titles were transmitted through the male line. The secondary ranking pertained to offices that were honorific yet lucrative. Among the most persistent dynasties in this regard were the Beringhens, whose name we encountered earlier. They started rather low on the ladder, with an immigrant from the duchy of Clèves whose son, grandson, and two great-grandsons would succeed one another in the post of first equerry from 1645 to the time of Louis XV.[146]

Even more remarkable was the case of the guardians and governesses of the kings and children of France. The maréchal de Souvré was the guardian of Louis XIII. His daughter, Mme de Lansac, was the governess of Louis XIV, and her granddaughter, the maréchale de La Motte, was the governess of the children, grandchildren, and great-grandchildren of Louis XIV. Her daughter, the duchesse de Ventadour, inherited the office of governess, and she was succeeded by her grandson's wife, the princesse de Soubise, and her granddaughter, the duchesse de Tallard. In all, then, there were seven generations, five of them active, of guardians and governesses of the children of France, including three kings and several dauphins.[147] The maréchale de La Motte and the duchesse de Tallard alone brought up twenty-three children of France. Here we see the importance of succession through the female line, whose remarkable efficiency is sometimes obscured by the prestige of the male line, which often failed to endure.

The noble qualities that determined rank did not depend solely on the male or female pedigree. Military valor also counted. Blood transmitted recalled blood spilled. Norbert Elias liked to describe the "civilization" or acculturation of warriors, who thereby became more "civil." By this he meant that courtiers were descendants of the warriors of the Middle Ages made gentler by the new "civilization of manners." What was lost in soldierly coarseness was gained in modernity. But Elias's work is not entirely immune from challenge. Indeed, under Louis XIV the court nobility and its kin sacrificed itself abundantly on France's frontiers. It was far *more* military and bellicose than were many uncourtly nobles of the Renaissance. In fact, the rise of the court from the late fifteenth century on coincided with the development of modern forms of warfare.[148] It was not uncommon for the down-at-heels nobles of the boondocks to hole up in their manors in order to avoid serving the king: the case of the sire de Gouberville is instructive in this regard.

A quick perusal of Saint-Simon's pages is enough to erase any doubt about the military risks run by courtiers. The marquis de Beaumanoir, Noailles's son-in-law and lieutenant general of Brittany, became the last of his line when he died childless in the battle of Spire in 1703.[149] Killed along with him were a Choiseul-Pracomtal—a protégé of Boufflers and

Mme de Maintenon as well as the son-in-law of another courtier, Mont-chevreuil—and also a prince of Hesse serving in the enemy ranks. The son of the maréchale de Clérambault died at Hoechstaedt, admittedly with his back turned to the enemy. Blainville also perished there (the third Colbert to die in the service of the king), as did Zurlauben, a nephew by marriage of the duc de Montausier, and La Baume, the son of the rather hapless maréchal de Tallard.[150] At the battle of Luzzara in 1702, two Lorraine princes, Commercy and Vaudémont, met their deaths in the imperial ranks.[151] On the French side, a La Rochefoucauld died, as did the marquis de Créquy, son of the marshal of the same name as well as son-in-law of the duc d'Aumont and nephew by marriage of Louvois. The duc de Lesdiguières was merely wounded, while Louis XIV's grand-son, the king of Spain, conducted himself courageously. At Cassan (1705), five officers known at court or members of it were killed, including a Choiseul-Praslin: "Noted lords thus died in common tasks."[152] At the battle of Turin in 1706 four officers close to the court were among the fifteen hundred French dead, including the "clumsy, stupid, and inept" Mursay, a relative and protégé of Mme de Maintenon, whose relationship to the dead man was no doubt an aggravating circumstance in the eyes of the merciless Saint-Simon.[153] In 1705, the prince of Hesse-Darmstadt, who was rumored, probably inaccurately, to have been the lover of the former queen of Spain, died at Barcelona while fighting in the ranks of the enemy.[154] A Nangis, who was more plausibly reported to have been the lover of the duchesse de Bourgogne (hence of a woman in line to become the queen of France), served heroically in his youth, though he would live to become a lackluster marshal of France.[155] In his prime, how-ever, his amorous exploits were rivaled only by his exploits on the field of battle. Mention should also be made of the names Rupelmunde, Lau-trec, and the prince d'Elbeuf, who left their bones on the *champ d'honneur* alongside many others.[156] The duc de Chevreuse lost his son Montfort and his son-in-law, Morstein junior, while the duc de Beauvillier lost his brother-in-law Marillac.[157] At Chivas on the Po in 1705, Marcillac, the former aide-de-camp to the maréchal de Villeroy, received ten wounds, one of them in the stomach, and his hands were mangled.[158]

When all is said and done, much of Saint-Simon's work is summed up in the dictum that "war is nothing to trifle with."[159] In this he was merely following Castiglione, who insisted in *The Courtier* on the impor-tance of military training for men at court. But Castiglione was writing at a time when jousting was still practiced, whereas Saint-Simon was a contemporary of the first "bureaucratic" armies. Their views of warfare differ accordingly.

Saint-Simon took a passionate interest not only in warfare but also in dueling. Recent research has shown that dueling was still important under

Louis XIV and even more important during the Regency, despite efforts by pious meddlers to put an end to it.[160] The death of the Sun King in 1715 "revived the duel."[161] The young duc de Richelieu was imprisoned in the Bastille for engaging in a duel, and the dukes who visited him there insisted on wearing their swords into the prison, this being a privilege granted to dukes but not to other nobles. In this respect, the typical duke and peer was simply "a nobleman better-armed than the rest" and permitted to retain his weapon while his inferiors were obliged to hang theirs in the vestibule.[162] According to Saint-Simon, aristocrats were much given to spilling each other's blood in duels. The prince de Lixin (from Lorraine) killed his mother-in-law's brother in a dispute over some minor historical point.[163] The young duc de Richelieu in turned killed Lixin for casting aspersions on his birth and for daring to marry a daughter of the house of Lorraine, the sister-in-law of a Bouillon. Their duel took place in 1734, at the beginning of the siege of Philipsbourg, during which Berwick, another great lord, also died, but not in a duel. Much earlier, 1716, Coigny and Mortemart met in yet another duel. Saint-Simon showed his friendship for Coigny in the matter of young Richelieu's last battle.[164] In his view, duelists were culpable only when they were of "low estate," by which he meant members of the nobility of the robe.[165] By contrast, dueling was a perfectly suitable pastime for great lords. In 1716, when Jonzac met Villette in a duel, Saint-Simon displayed sympathy for the families of both young men.[166] A point of honor obliged them to fight when neither had any interest in killing the other.

Heroic feats of arms were not Saint-Simon's style. He does honor his father's memory, however, by recounting the story of his duel with Vardes. The elder Saint-Simon was on the point of cutting his opponent's face.[167] But the two "gallant men civilly parted company" after failing to eviscerate each other. For Saint-Simon, dueling was unjustified only if one of the two participants was a recognized coward, in which case it was wrong of his adversary to take advantage of him. Such was the case in the abortive duel between the prince de Conti and Philippe de Vendôme, the grand prior of France and a notorious coward.[168]

The question of cowardice calls for a brief digression. For Saint-Simon, it was personified by men he disliked. The grand prior had all the marks of a true coward: a drunkard (allegedly) born into a bastard line though himself legitimate. Furthermore, his successor as head of the Order of Malta was "also" a bastard, in this case, of the regent.[169] D'Antin was afraid of battle.[170] He was also the friend and half-brother of bastards, as well as of the illegitimate Madame la Duchesse. As always for Saint-Simon, the absence of a noble virtue (in this case bravery) is associated with the impurity of illegitimacy or even with excremental filth: a Bullion-Fervacques, who was cowardly in battle and therefore doomed to revert to the inferior ranks of the robe, was descended from the great financier Bullion, who always carried a small box filled with "the freshest shit." To be sure, this anecdote, however accurate it may have been, had been embellished by tradition and perhaps "improved" as well by Saint-Simon, but this only makes the equation of cowardice with impurity of origin all the more significant.[171] In any case, cowardice, like courage, was a fact of nature, consubstantial with a person's genetic heritage, just as nobility was supposed to be "genetic."[172] The parallel is no accident: a man was born brave or cowardly just as he was born with or without blue blood. No one could alter these basic facts of nature.

"At the other extreme," Saint-Simon's aversion to cowardice went hand in hand with his profound contempt for men who imitated the outward marks of courage. He detested boastfulness and bluster, which were mere "verbiage" compared with action. This, he felt, was the bad side of the duc d'Orléans, a "braggart in crime," whom he nevertheless portrays on the whole in a positive and sympathetic light.[173] It also accounted for his hatred of Villars, a consummate braggart whose "Gascon" munificence scarcely concealed his extreme avarice.[174] Once again the critic is not innocent: in his heart of hearts, Saint-Simon disliked Villars the braggart for being the protégé of Mme de Maintenon and, later, an ally of the duc du Maine.[175] In this respect, the older Villars was "worth little more" than his son the marshal: although admittedly a man of piety and courage, he was of "low" birth and a friend of Maintenon and did not deserve his promotion to the Ordre du Saint-Esprit.[176]

To return for a moment to d'Antin, it is worth noting that Saint-Simon also referred to him as a "Gascon" (his family did indeed spring from the southwestern part of France).[177] D'Antin fell short of being a true aristocrat in two respects: he was both a coward and a braggart (boastfulness was supposed to be a Gascon quality). In Saint-Simon's mind, "Gascony" was thus a highly pejorative term encompassing a boundless region stretching from Villars's Dauphiné to the southwest from which d'Antin's ancestors sprang.

The subjects of war and dueling bring us to the question of honor. A sense or code of honor was indeed a characteristic of the second order. It was also characteristic, according to Montesquieu, of the society of ranks in general.[178] The wellborn official disdained bribes because of his sense of honor—at least when the bribes in question were too visible.[179] A person might refuse an honorific post if accepting it for some reason did not accord with his or her notion of honor.[180] In 1710, for example, the duchesse de Saint-Simon tried (ultimately in vain) to avoid accepting the position of lady-in-waiting to the duchesse de Berry, a position she saw as suitable for a "standing" lady but not for a "seated" lady such as

Marie-Gabrielle de Saint-Simon, who enjoyed the right to sit on a stool at court.

The passion for honor was also evident in another court pastime: gambling. Like dueling, it ran afoul of Christian principles whenever a pious courtier wished to make an issue of it. Two value systems thus came into conflict. The duc de Mortemart lost 100,000 livres at the gaming tables at a time when he was already heavily in debt to any number of merchants.[181] The *dévots*, or religious zealots, including Chevreuse and Mortemart's father-in-law, Beauvillier, insisted that the duke's debts "to the suffering merchants and workers" be paid "as a matter of conscience." For his part, Saint-Simon tries to impress on Beauvillier "how much honor is at stake in the prompt payment of gambling debts and how inflexible society is in such matters." Here, the aristocratic concern with honor was in conflict with the promptings of the Christian conscience. Saint-Simon's unflattering portrayal of Mortemart, not only in this affair but in the *Memoirs* generally, also stems from the fact that it was Mortemart who revealed to the dominant party at court Saint-Simon's hostility to the princesses of Lorraine (protégées of Mme de Maintenon), the Soubises (abject flatterers of Louis XIV), and d'Antin, who coveted the duchy of Epernon, to which his rank did not entitle him. What is more, Mortemart was a threat to the continuity of his noble line: when his gambling debt was made public, his wife suffered a miscarriage. It took every bit of Saint-Simon's diplomatic skills to keep for Mortemart's son the office of first gentleman of the king's chamber, which the father's folly had nearly forfeited.[182]

For Saint-Simon, gambling implied strict segregation, another characteristic of the society of ranks. One day, without warning, he and the duc de Chevreuse entered the rooms of the duc de La Rochefoucauld and found him playing chess with one of his lackeys. All three dukes blushed at this unseemly discovery.[183] Only a La Rochefoucauld "preyed upon by his valets" could have stooped so low.

The high noble who in a sense owed his place to fortune was nevertheless expected to participate in games that were not purely games of chance but required some degree of skill or intelligence. Dangeau won an honest fortune by gambling—legally and with great skill—for money.[184] Chamillart owed his ministry to many things, among them the important contacts he made through his skill at billiards.[185] By contrast, pure games of chance such as *biribi*, *pharaon* (faro), and *bassette*, where everything turned on the luck of the draw, were disapproved and often banned (at least in theory). The marshals of France, who stood as the ultimate guardians of the tribunal of honor, even laid down that a man was not obliged to pay debts stemming from amusements of this sort.[186] In the case of a true nobleman, debts acquired in more honorable games could lead, however, to suicide, if they could not be paid, or at the very least to exile.[187]

Gambling could therefore be fatal.[188] Conversely, it was only right that gambling should come to a halt when a death occurred. Saint-Simon was scandalized when gambling resumed at Marly too soon after the deaths of Monsieur, Monseigneur, the duc de Berry, and the duc and duchesse de Bourgogne.[189]

A prince who did not gamble lost face, even if he had the excuse of saving in order to build. Monseigneur "used to be a big gambler, but since he started building he has taken to sitting in a corner of the salon at Marly and drumming on his snuffbox. He opens his eyes wide but hardly sees anyone and sits without conversation, without mirth, and I would almost say without feeling or thought."[190]

L et us turn now from questions of honor and gambling to the vast realm of linguistic and physical symbols of rank. When it came to titles, even punctuation could be important. For example, the daughters of France were addressed either as "Madame" or "Madame *comma* something": Madame, duchesse d'Orléans, for instance, was a daughter of France by marriage, whereas Madame *la* duchesse d'Orléans (with the comma replaced by the definite article) would have indicated a "mere" granddaughter of France.[191] When the king or regent engaged in dialogue, he used terms of kinship (such as "my uncle," "my brother," "my nephew") only with close blood relatives. This convention distinguished between those in whose veins flowed the most precious dynastic blood ("the Crown")[192] and more distant relatives, such as the princes of the blood, whom the king addressed by title; the latter of course belonged not to the Crown but to the "reigning house." Thus the ultimate title was to have no title and to be addressed by the king simply as "my uncle" or "my cousin."

Indeed, all titles were subject to a certain slippage or inflation, which diminished their value without rendering them altogether worthless. Over Saint-Simon's objections, the regent reluctantly agreed to address the king of Denmark as "Your Majesty" and the Estates General of the United Provinces as "High Powers."[193] In an odd assault on the majesty of the French crown, the duc de Lorraine prevailed upon the regent in a moment of weakness to address him as "Your Royal Highness," a salutation denied to Danish, Swedish, and Florentine princes.[194] Conversely, certain princelings promoted themselves by eliminating part of their title rather than adding to it. The elector of Bavaria, for instance, contrived to have himself addressed as "Electeur" rather than "Monsieur l'Electeur," an abbreviation that he deemed immensely gratifying because it made him more like a king (one never said Monsieur le Roi or Monsieur l'Empereur or Monsieur le Pape).[195] At a slightly lower level, the custom of bestowing on princes of the blood, especially the Condés, titles such as Monsieur le Prince, Monsieur le Duc, and Monsieur le Comte is said to have originated during the Wars of Religion.[196] The title Monseigneur had always been widely used, but only in writing. In spoken forms of address, its use in the secular realm had been limited originally to le Grand Dauphin, son of Louis XIV, but was later usurped by princes of the blood, royal bastards, and even provincial army commanders.[197] Even bishops were not addressed as "Monseigneur" until the middle or late seventeenth century, but the new title stuck. Yet Saint-Simon, to hear him tell it, preserved his archaic purity by addressing only sons of kings as Monseigneur.[198] A similar inflation was evident in Madrid: at first "Excellency" was used only in addressing Spanish grandees and foreign ambassadors, but later it was "prostituted" and applied to any number of lesser lords.[199]

These examples can be seen, as Saint-Simon saw them, as an indication of a general devaluation of signs. In a more pedestrian sense, however, they suggest simply that titles have a history. Nevertheless, that history illustrates the transcendent importance of the hierarchical principle. Even the elimination of a title can be interesting in this regard. Take Louis XIV's revocation of the title of Monsieur le Prince from the prince de Condé. The king acted as he did, not to humiliate his most noble cousins, but to exalt the position of first prince of the blood. Owing to the continual "branching" of the royal bloodline, however, that honor now belonged to the Orléans clan and not to the Condés.[200]

As for material symbols of rank, some were quite mundane. In Spain, Saint-Simon tells us, one could find excellent wine and olive oil on noble tables, while other people used mediocre substitutes because they were lazy. The best Spanish ham was served by only a few grandees: it was made from hogs fed on snake meat (the ultimate in impurity and wickedness thus went to feed the noblest Spanish lords).[201] A more telling material distinction was instituted in 1709, when the king of France ordered *les Grands* to give their silver tableware to the Mint; he contributed his own gold tableware. From then on the king and royal family ate from dishes of vermeil and silver, while the princes of the blood ate from china, despite "the uncleanness of the earth" (the idea of impurity figures here in a context of material hierarchy).[202] The reader may object that this measure was the result of an unusual situation stemming from the financial crisis of 1709. But there were other material correlates of rank: at court balls in Spain, the wives of grandees sat on velvet, while the wives of their eldest sons (not yet "grandees") sat on ordinary satin or damask.[203]

The foregoing example pertains to the very high Spanish nobility. At this level, the type of seating and the right to eat with individuals of higher rank were also important symbols, as in France. At the court of Madrid, *infantes* were entitled to an armchair (even in ceremonies involving the king and queen). The covering was always of a less sumptuous fabric than the monarch's chair, however. "It is true that in public the *infantes* do not eat with Their Majesties."[204] The rules of hierarchy took precedence over what would be a normal expression of family togetherness in a household of lower rank.

Signs of honor might also be classified in terms of the parts of the body to which they pertained.[205]

The head. Under certain conditions grandees could wear their hats in the presence of the king.[206] In Genoa, Philip V followed the example of Emperor Charles V in addressing the doge as "Your Highness"; certain senators were obliged to cover their heads.[207]

The hand. "Consider two lords of unequal rank, C and D. Say that D receives C, and suppose that D is of inferior rank. He must give his guest the place of honor and seat him at his right hand. This is called 'giving the hand.'"[208] For example, an ambassador "'has the hand' at the table of a prince of the blood. In other words, the prince seats the visitor to his right, because he is the representative of a sovereign or a friendly power."[209]

The seat. The gradation of armchairs, regular chairs, and stools has already been mentioned. Hierarchical seating was not limited to royalty or even to the vicinity of royalty. Individuals of quality "conceded" an armchair or some other type of chair to the king and the more prestigious members of his entourage, but in the presence of inferiors they insisted on their right to occupy the same chair: "Saint-Pierre was no more than a petty Norman noble who never sat in the presence of the old duchesse de Ventadour, mother of the maréchale de Duras, when he went to Sainte-Marie nearby to pay her court."[210]

The foot. The foot of the queen of Spain was sacred. No one was supposed to touch it. The duke del Arco, who served snake-fed pork at his table and was a favorite of Philip V, had the good fortune to free the queen's foot when a horse partially threw her and left her dangling dangerously from a stirrup. The great lord was also a shrewd rescuer: after saving the queen's life, he was clever enough to take refuge in a monastery until "pardoned" by the king for violating the taboo against touching the queen's foot. Philip V quickly obliged. The same taboo also explains why the queen was left virtually alone during the few seconds it took her each day to put on her shoes. Such moments of solitude had their uses, for they allowed the indispensable *azafata* (chambermaid) to pass secret messages to the queen.[211] The feet also had honorific uses: in France the king's guards clicked their heels to salute a passing duke-peer, whereas they "presented arms" to salute princes of the blood and captains of the guard.[212]

Moving up from the foot to the mouth, let us pause a moment to consider the formal kissing practices of the queens and prospective queens of France. Take, for example, Louis XIV's granddaughter-in-law and sister-in-law, the duchesse de Bourgogne and Madame Palatine. To give or receive a kiss was a mark of distinction separating *les Grands* and their spouses from everyone else, including their daughters. *Les Grands* who were entitled to "kiss Madame" included the princes of the blood, the dukes, the grandees of Spain (after 1701), the officers of the Crown, the marshals of France upon their return from a campaign, and ambassadors. When the king was present, however, the queen (present or future) kissed no one.[213] This taboo was significant. In the king's absence, the dauphine could be kissed because she was then merely an "emanation" of the monarch, who was temporarily unavailable. This symbolism was itself a consequence of the rule that husband and wife were of one flesh. Hence the wife or eldest daughter-in-law could represent the majesty of the absent royal husband. This is not the place to delve into the rules governing the priority of kisses in bourgeois circles, far below the court and aristocracy. Readers of Molière will remember the famous line, "Baiserai-je, Papa?" (Shall I kiss, papa?).

The mouth is used not only for kissing but also for eating. The act of feeding involved certain rituals of distinction whose meaning was ambiguous. Dining joined people together as much as it set them apart.[214] In theory, the king dined alone, or at least apart. "Except when with the army, the king never ate with anyone under any circumstances whatsoever [apart from wedding feasts]."[215] In 1700, when the young duc d'Anjou became Philip V of Spain, he immediately began to eat alone and even to hear mass virtually alone, apart from his brothers.[216] After all, the mass was in essence a meal (the Eucharist). It would be more accurate, however, to say that the king sat alone at the center of several concentric circles of conviviality. The situation was similar to that involving the formal kisses, for kissing was like eating: to kiss was metaphorically to eat. When Louis XIV dined *au grand couvert*, members of his immediate family were present and ate with him, although at some distance. Included in this group were royal children and grandchildren, both male and female.[217] They constituted the first circle. At royal family weddings, princes and princesses of the blood were invited to dine as well. They constituted a second circle. Finally, when the king was with the army and dined in the field, his table was open to a wider circle of guests.[218] Yet even here admission was limited to the privileged upper echelons of the military aristocracy and *les Grands* (in this instance the two expressions were synonymous). This third group included the royal family, both immediate and not so immediate, dukes, marshals of France, captains of the king's bodyguard (who were themselves great lords), and perhaps a few heroes of the current battle. "As luck would have it," however, these heroic warriors always came from very good families or enjoyed both a high military rank and noble birth. Birth, moreover, counted for more than rank. The clergy was excluded from this martial table, except for cardinals and bishop-peers (because they counted as princes or dukes). Finally, even the most august nobles of the robe, whether of Parlement or the Council, would never have presumed to dine with the king. At best the wife of a high *robin* might be honored by being allowed to serve the *grande* or *petite dauphine.*[219]

These dinner circles did more than many a learned treatise to define the reciprocal relations between the king and the upper ranks of the laity. To begin with, they made it clear that the royal entity stood on the fringes of the sacred. It besieged and colonized the sacred, as it were, but was by no means a central element of it. The fact that ecclesiastics were excluded from the royal table unless they were of rank equivalent to the lay guests (princes or peers) is significant in this regard. This exclusion did not diminish men of the cloth; it exalted them. In no way did the king feel superior to the sacred. On many occasions, Louis XIV acknowledged his inferiority to the church and reaffirmed his spiritual allegiance. As one who could heal scrofula with his touch, the monarch could claim to have a foothold in sacred territory, but no more. He stood camped outside the temple, or at the foot of the altar. The downgrading of the anointment ritual following the end of the Middle Ages had diminished the king's "priestly" role. The king was indeed an image of God, but only one of several, and only on earth: a "bishop outside the church," as he was called.

The royal dinner table also served as a concrete representation of the royal bloodline, both immediate (descendants of Louis XIV) and remote (princes of the blood). It focused a spotlight as well on the high court and military aristocracy (the dukes and the marshals of France, paragons of blue blood and military valor). The king thus presided over the second order, or to put it another way, over the second (noble and military) function of the well-known trifunctional schema.

Nobles of the robe and officeholders, whether servants of the state or *parlementaires*, were excluded from these dinner circles. Their rejection had far-reaching consequences. To be sure, the king was in one sense the first officer of the realm and the head of a more or less centralized bureaucracy. But when it came to signs of honor, the paper-pushers were out of the picture. The king was above all the first nobleman and, in theory at least, the first soldier, and in his veins ran the most precious blood of the aristocracy of the sword. Blood (inherited or spilled) was thus preeminent; only the sacred was more important, and there too the king had a role, albeit a marginal one. He was first and foremost what Joël Cronette has called a *roi de guerre*, a king of war.

T he highest dignitaries of the realm bore titles that were inscribed in the very geography of France. But they also enjoyed a more direct form of territorial privilege: they were permitted to drive their carriages into the courtyard of the Louvre, whereas others were not. This privilege was relatively new: not only were hierarchies not fixed *ad aeternum*, but carriages were a fairly recent invention.[220] The custom in question dated back no further than the middle of the sixteenth century.[221] This privilege too was reserved for the enchanted circle of men and women entitled (on rare occasion) to eat with the king and kiss the queen or her stand-ins. Included were the princes of the blood, dukes, marshals of France, officers of the Crown, and their wives.[222] In Spain the palace of the Buen Retiro also had a special courtyard reserved for the carriages of cardinals, ambassadors, and grandees.[223] Cardinals, to reiterate, were princes, hence treated the same as lay princes. As a general rule, however, the highest dignitaries of the clergy, or first order—bishops and even archbishops—were not entitled to the honors of the Louvre, which were reserved for the supreme representatives of the second order.[224] This was only natural: could one imagine a bishop "kissing the duchesse de Bourgogne?" Still, Chancellor Pontchartrain (who was less strict in this respect than his predecessor Boucherat had been) opened his court "parking lot" to the aristocracy and high clergy but closed it to nobles of the robe, no matter how rich. In this instance, we have a personage far less important than the king setting the bar of exclusion very high indeed.[225]

If we look at *entrées*, or access to the king, we find that the rules were very similar. The principal *entrées*, *de devant* and *de derrière*, the front way and the back way, were available to the highest officers of the court and the king's immediate family, both legitimate and illegitimate. These privileges "intersected" with the more informal comings and goings associated with the actual business of government. Officials designated as having *entrées par les derrières* could enter the monarch's cabinets at any time except when the Council was meeting or the king was with a minister.[226] The less prestigious *entrées de la chambre* and *entrées du cabinet* were extended to princes of the blood and cardinals.[227]

Let us take a closer look at the discreet *entrée de derrière*, which made the fortune of one d'O, guardian of the comte de Toulouse, one of Louis XIV's bastards. This *gouvernement*, or guardianship, and its associated responsibilities gave d'O "a presence, a handsome income, a continuous relationship with the king, private audiences, [and] *entrées* at all hours," and all this for a man "who had no such privilege *par devant*, like the first gentlemen of the chamber, but who was far more important and enjoyed freer access since he could enter the king's *cabinets par les derrières* at almost any hour."[228]

To say that a minister had power and that a prince of the blood or duke had none is to simplify the reality of the situation. Illustrious aristocrats could approach the king (through the *entrées* just discussed). They could solicit from him and his collaborators favors, pensions, and lucrative financial opportunities.[229] The ducs de Chevreuse and Beauvilliers, who were by no means *robins*, nevertheless acted as ministers, officially in Beauvillier's case and unofficially in Chevreuse's.[230] True, both were sons-in-law of a very formidable *robin* of the Council, namely, Colbert. Descendants of other dukes, intermarried with leading mandarin families, would serve as full-fledged ministers under Louis XV. One example was Choiseul (who married a Bouthillier-Brûlart, a clan typical of the ministerial *noblesse de robe*). Maurepas, who served as minister of the navy under Louis XVI, became a *grand seigneur* like any other even though he descended from the Phélypeaux-Pontchartrains, the prototypical Bourbon ministerial clan. In the time of Louis XIV, dukes may have lacked the power to decide, but they still had the power to prevent, which was no mere token. For instance, Harcourt and La Rochefoucauld prevented Chevreuse, another duke whom they disliked, from playing an open role in the Conseil d'en Haut, which Chevreuse never publicly joined.[231]

Furthermore, while *les Grands* may not have wielded direct influence over the bureaucracy, they still enjoyed considerable influence over the military. When seven new marshals of France were appointed in 1693, five were *grands seigneurs:* Choiseul, Villeroy (despite his ineptness as a soldier), Joyeuse, Noailles, and Boufflers.[232] Similarly, when ten new marshals were appointed in 1713, only two, Rosen and Vauban, were drawn from the lower ranks of the nobility.[233] The other eight were men, as one said at the time, "of the highest honor," whether by birth (Harcourt) or marriage (Châteaurenault). Many of them served admirably in war. The military power of the high nobility is therefore beyond doubt, even if when all is said and done the *grands seigneurs* were dominated by civilians only recently promoted to the *noblesse de robe*, men in the Louvois-Barbezieux mold, who ran the ministry of war with an iron hand.[234]

Ultimately, of course, an important distinction has to be made between *status* and *power*, the one as different from the other as the left hand is from the right.[235] In the minds of contemporaries obsessed with matters of hierarchy pure and simple, status was clearly more important than power, especially when that power was purely military. No wellborn individual was in any doubt about the relative position of a duke (a hereditary status of substantial dignity) and a marshal of France (who wielded armed force but only for life). Harcourt, who traced his roots to the most ancient Norman nobility, said "out loud that his only goal was to be a duke, and if he knew for sure that he would become a marshal of France but not a duke, he would quit the service at once and return home."[236] The difference between being a marshal and being a duke was a bit like the difference today between being a professor at the Collège de France and being a member of the Académie Française, except that the status of academician is not hereditary. Functional status or mark of honor: the debate is perennial.

Like many of his contemporaries, Saint-Simon was struck by the disparity between the status hierarchy, whose material and symbolic signs he so diligently enumerated, and the real hierarchy of power. While allowing for a distinction between status and power, the spirit of hierarchy nevertheless implied a hope that eventually he who had status would also become powerful. For the *petit duc* the continuing disparity was therefore a source of unending complaint.

To begin with, he complained about the power of the king's ministers. Louis XIV, unlike his predecessors and Mazarin, chose his ministers almost exclusively from the upper ranks of the administrative *noblesse de robe*. His Upper Council did not include any princes of the blood, dukes and peers (except for Beauvillier), *nobles d'épée*, or court aristocrats. Ministers, of course, stood far below *grands seigneurs* so far as the symbolism of rank was concerned. They therefore sought to enhance their status, deviously at first but later legitimately, so as to rival lords over whom they already "reigned in authority," oppressing even princes of the blood.[237] Ministers began to dress like men of quality and to wear swords.[238] Under certain circumstances, the wives of ministers, like the wives of great lords, were permitted to eat in proximity to the king. Like duchesses, they were allowed to ride in His Majesty's carriage. Ministers also sought and obtained for their children honorific court posts, such as master of the wardrobe, grand quartermaster, captain of the king's door guards. A guard captain enjoyed the not insignificant benefit of being close enough to the monarch to converse with him and beg his favors, which could yield financial rewards.[239] This privilege profited such ministerial clans as the Chamillarts, Colberts, Desmarets, and Louvois–Le Telliers.

The four secretaries of state enjoyed similar advantages. Each one headed a department of the royal administration, but unlike the ministers they were not automatically included in meetings of the Conseil d'en Haut. The king, Saint-Simon tells us, "was in the habit of filling these positions with men of no account [in fact they were often highly distinguished *robins*] so that he might, if the fancy took him, dismiss them as he would a valet, and also to prevent them from profiting unduly from their authority. . . . He would never have made a *seigneur* a secretary of state."[240]

Saint-Simon's assessment in this instance is partially corroborated by a text that comes straight from Louis XIV himself. The Sun King did indeed pride himself on being able to dismiss his ministers and secretaries at will because they were men of relatively low rank. Yet this was not the only reason why they were chosen. Indeed, it had become customary in France to fill government posts with *robins,* who were reputed to be more competent administrators than *nobles d'épée* or *de cour,* often thought of, rightly or wrongly, as inept.

These "insignificant" secretaries of state nevertheless wielded considerable power and as viceroys lording it over the rest of humanity usurped the outward trappings of quality and rank. Following an example set by Louvois and certain foreign princes, they refused to address dukes as "Monseigneur" and insisted that in correspondence they themselves be addressed by that title by anyone who was not a duke or prince.[241] Although they were in essence royal notaries, they wiped away the stain of low status by ceasing to sign marriage contracts for *les Grands.* They came to occupy a sort of hybrid status, aping the court nobility.[242] Even worse, they began to think of themselves as de facto equals of the dukes and peers and had the temerity to attempt to marry into the most distinguished noble families.[243] They wore swords, which *robins* were not allowed to do.[244] They gave up their cloaks and bands and black garb and began to dress like other courtiers, though less colorfully and with a smaller amount of gold braid.[245]

Much the same thing can be said about state councilors, men who took part in the work of the various councils. In the system of government adopted by Louis XIV, they were the equivalent of what might today be called "political insiders" or "decision makers." They were far below the princes of blood in terms of rank, prestige, and probably wealth but above them in terms of collective power. In other words, state councilors were little gods set above the rest of humanity but below the ministers, who were viewed, in a sort of hierarchical polytheistic system, as gods of the earth.[246] This was the *robe du Conseil:* some of its members had enjoyed nobility for some time, but most were nobles of relatively recent date. A very few were descended from families that had belonged to the *noblesse d'épée* since the late Middle Ages.

On the whole their status was low but not negligible. They gave way only to princes of the blood, cardinals, officers of the Crown, dukes and peers, and marshals. In the councils, at any rate, they vied for priority with any noble of less than ducal rank, with lieutenants general, and even with bishops and archbishops, who of course refused to hear of such pretensions.[247] In the Conseil des Parties, councilors even sat in armchairs, but these were prudently referred to as *chaises à bras* in order to distinguish them from the *fauteuil* reserved for the king, if he deigned to attend.[248]

The state councilors' insistence on priority over "untitled persons of quality" (meaning nobles of less than ducal rank) was probably a recent innovation, dating back perhaps no earlier than 1714. If this assumption is correct, it suggests that the councilors saw themselves as moving up in the world and that they intended to bring their symbolic status into line with the actual power they wielded. In this they found defenders among the most august aristocrats, such as Noailles, who thought it grotesque of Saint-Simon to maintain that state councilors were in fact members of the third estate who ought therefore to stand aside for *any* noble, no matter how humble in rank.[249]

Despite the efforts by the *robe du Conseil* to climb the cascade of contempt, the disparity between the symbolic status of *les Grands* and the enormous actual power of the *hauts robins* remained great under Louis XIV.[250] From the beginning of his personal reign, the Sun King, unlike Mazarin, sought to maintain and even to widen the gap by excluding from his councils nearly all important aristocrats, including princes of the blood, nobles of the sword, and ecclesiastics. The chasm was narrowed somewhat under Louis XV, notwithstanding the contrary view of the ever-frustrated Saint-Simon. To a certain extent, we can say that Saint-Simon's ideas were implemented by Louis le Bien-Aimé, even though Saint-Simon himself was excluded from power. The aristocracy of court and church did invade the councils and ministries, including the prime ministry, and filled the secretary of state positions. To be sure, the *robe du Conseil* held on to many important posts, most notably the *contrôle général des finances*. But if the gap between power and status was reduced, it was never abolished. Paradoxically, the distinction between the two, so characteristic of societies based on hierarchy, would reemerge in all its force after the Revolution, which deprived the aristocracy of much of its power but left its prestige and de facto superiority of status intact.

The Sacred and the Profane

2   *Monseigneur, the son of Louis XIV and next in line for the throne,* while "on his way to Meudon on the day after Easter, encountered in Chaville a priest who was taking Our Lord [that is, the Host] to the bedside of a person who was ill. [Monseigneur] climbed down [from his carriage] and knelt to pray. . . . He was told that the patient was suffering from smallpox. Greatly afraid of this disease, he was struck by this, and that night told his doctor that he would not be surprised if he had it."[1] And sure enough, he very soon took to his bed and died a few days later.

The king, too, once prostrated himself before the Host in transit and accompanied it to the deathbed of the patient for whom it was intended.[2] These examples show that the men at the very top of the "worldly" or political hierarchy, kings and would-be kings, did not hesitate to kneel before the symbols of the sacred, incarnated here below by the Eucharist.

The sacred permeated every aspect of the profane hierarchy. Take, for example, the celebration held at the Hôtel de Ville of Paris on 24 January 1705, to mark the appointment of the duc de Tresmes as governor of that city. The duke was received in great pomp.[3] The *prévôt des marchands*, or provost of merchants, addressed him as Monseigneur. At the banquet, "the gentlemen [that is, aristocrats] of both the court and Paris, and of sword and gown, were seated on the *right* side of a long table in thirty *armchairs*. Opposite them, seated on *chairs with backs*, were the aldermen [and other municipal personages]. The *prévôt des marchands* and the duc de Tresmes sat alone *at the high end of the table, in two armchairs, the provost to the duke's left*. . . . *The meal was of fish because it was*

Saturday. The duc de Tresmes tossed coins to the people upon entering and leaving the Hôtel de Ville."[4] In this remarkable text, the elements of protocol are clearly spelled out: aristocrats and aldermen, duke-governor and provost of merchants, "high end" and "low end" of the table, right and left, armchair and chair with back, *grands* and *peuple*. The fish menu adds a "sacred" touch: it signifies religious abstinence on Saturday, a day when the impurity of meat was not tolerated.

More generally, the sacred played a dominant role as an invisible structuring and harmonizing influence. Here, in Saint-Simon's mind, theology joined anthropology to undermine any and all theories of equality, whose day was nevertheless soon to come. "Nothing could be more misleading than the assertion that everyone is equal before the king . . . [because] kings are images of God on earth. They are charged with imitating him insofar as it is given to any of his creatures to do so." From there Saint-Simon went on to invoke both thearchy and hierarchy, "Scripture and the Fathers." And who could prove him wrong? There was, he argued, "a hierarchy in heaven, nine choirs or *orders* of angels, one above the other," along with "seven angels above all the rest," whose eyes, according to the Book of Tobias (not to mention Pseudo-Dionysus the Areopagite), feasted always on God. Was the society of ranks like the society of angels? Saint-Simon also tells us that John the Baptist "was the greatest among the children of men." The church prayed to the Virgin Mary "as Queen of heaven and of the angels and saints: here is a hierarchy which is well founded because it rests on faith." The saints thus occupied their rightful place below God and Mary, and for Saint-Simon the ancientness of their cult was proof of the truth of Catholicism, a proof inscribed, he notes, on countless cathedral portals.

Descending from heaven to earth, Saint-Simon also cited the existence of hierarchy in two republics he took to be aristocratic: Switzerland and the United Provinces. He leaned even more heavily on the example of certain savage tribes: "Everywhere in the states of Asia and Africa we find hierarchies of rank, even in the minor African monarchies of Cape Verde, the Gold Coast, and Senegal . . . whose palaces are huts scarcely larger than those of the king's subjects. If one turns to nations without kings or *police* (order), one finds the same gradation among the Hurons, the Iroquois, and indeed all the savage nations. Even though these people live in movable, impermanent dwellings, each one has a chief, who has councilors and elders whom the other savages respect and to whom they defer in council as well as in their activities and dances and banquets, in what little they have of ceremony, and indeed in everything." Even wild boar have hierarchies, according to Saint-Simon.

But getting back to humans, Europeans, and the problems of priority among duchesses that were uppermost in his mind, Saint-Simon once again denies "that everyone is equal before the king. The king's grandeur and majesty derive from the fact that in his presence his subjects are unequal. His throne, to which one must ascend by degrees, symbolizes this inequality. Without gradation, inequality, and difference, order is impossible." The despot Cromwell failed, according to the *petit duc*, because he wanted to make everyone and everything equal. Degrees of hierarchy are found not only in the aristocracy, Saint-Simon tells us, but also in the army, the magistracy, and corporations of merchants, as well as in villages, where the church warden leads processions, and, last but not least, in the clergy. Equality earns his contempt wherever it can be found: in princes of the blood, bastards, armchairs,[5] formulas of style, visits, the trains worn by women in mourning and at other times, funerals, and coats of arms.

I cite these texts and a few others because they give an anthropological and theological dimension to hierarchy, or *gradation*, as Saint-Simon often calls it.[6] Archangels and angels, devils, and even savages are included within this conception of hierarchy which encompasses heaven and hell along with a "sublunary" world in which distinctions even finer than those of nature predominate.[7]

In Saint-Simon's view, humankind was hierarchical even before it was civilized, and it remained so after acquiring culture. In this he was ahead of anthropologists and even ethologists, who have discovered pecking orders and dominance among animals. Thomas Hobbes, of course, began with the opposite premise: initially there was equality. In a state of nature, order and hierarchy do not exist. Under these conditions uncivilized men wage the war of all against all. Hence their lives are solitary, sordid, nasty, brutish, and short. For Hobbes, the savages of the New World exemplified this violent, chaotic existence, for which the only remedy was the creation of a Leviathan, a monster-state with total control, whose mission was to establish "holism" wherever the reign of the individual had led to disaster.

Thus where Saint-Simon saw sacred hierarchy, Hobbes saw brutal, individualistic, egalitarian atomism. The contrast was absolute. French culture, or at any rate the portion of French culture that Saint-Simon represented, had long emphasized gradation. After Rousseau this would no longer be the case. By contrast, British thinkers such as Hobbes, John Locke, and Adam Smith laid the foundations of egalitarianism and economic individualism.[8] If we want to find a hierarchical thinker to compare with Saint-Simon on the other side of the English Channel, we have to go back more than a century to the Shakespeare of *Troilus and Cressida* (act 1, scene 3). Perhaps this is yet another sign of the relatively advanced state of England, where mercantile values held sway as early as the seventeenth century, whereas it took the French much longer to free themselves from the aristocratic model.

On the matter of hierarchy and its relation to the sacred, Saint-Simon's thinking was very similar to the Princess Palatine's. To reiterate, each was unaware of the writings of the other, so their texts tend to corroborate one another. For Liselotte, as for the author of the *Memoirs*, to hierarchize was to sanctify. What is all the more remarkable in the case of Monsieur's wife is that the princess's religion was enlightened, tolerant, beset by doubts, and already prey to what Paul Hazard would call the "crisis of European consciousness." Late in life, Madame, who had what she called a private religion of her own, developed a more emotional attachment to her faith. There was nothing stiff or formal about her beliefs. But when it came to society's hierarchies, or to the court's, Madame's piety became as ritualized and ceremonial as could be:

> You must remember that here *distinctions of rank* are observed in the mass. For example, only *granddaughters of France* are allowed to have a chaplain give the responses during mass and hold a candle from the *Sanctus* of the *Preface* to the *Domine non sum dignus*. *Princesses of the blood* are not allowed a candle or chaplain of their own, and their pages must give the responses. At the end of the mass the priest brings the *corporal* to be kissed: this goes only as far as the *children of France*. As for the chalice in which wine and water are served, *only we* [that is, the *children of France*, a group to which Madame belongs by virtue of being married to a younger son of Louis XIII] are entitled to drink from it, and it is not passed to the *princes of the blood*. Here, as you see, there is ceremony in everything, even religion. In all things spiritual in this country, one always has regard for the temporal. If this is not as pleasing to God as might be desirable, there is nevertheless a temporal side that is good. So all is not lost, as you see.[9]

Despite the writer's irony, the scene is clearly described. The children of France were allowed to kiss the corporal. This cloth, upon which the Host was laid, was the supreme symbol of *purity* (and we shall have more to say later on about the problem of the pure and the impure in relation to hierarchy). The children of France were also allowed to taste the water and wine in the holy chalice. The granddaughters of France were entitled to have a chaplain read the responses during mass. In this way they participated directly in the work of the "clergy," though to a minimal degree, since the chaplains in question were probably very junior priests. Finally, the princesses of the blood had their "pages give the responses." The pages were thus like altar boys, closer to the laity than to the priesthood. Hence the princesses of the blood were a little more remote from the sacred than were the women who ranked above them in the hierarchy, yet they still had some contact with it. Note in passing that great ladies partook of the mysteries of religion through their servants, chaplains or pages who were members of their families or personal servants. One is reminded of two sisters of the highest nobility who wished to do penance for their sins. One turned to the other and said: "Ma soeur, faisons jeûner nos gens" [Sister, let us order our people to fast].

As soon as Madame turned her thoughts to the question of rank, then, she envisaged a religion different from that of her customary devotions, at times sincere and at times skeptical. The social perception of the sacred tapped into a more archaic form of religiosity. Here, the spiritual informed the temporal and vice versa, whereas more "modern" or *renonçant* worshipers wished to sever the fervor of faith from the social. One of these more modern worshipers was the abbess of Maubuisson. Although born a German princess, she refused to observe or respect the "priorities of the [right and left] hand" because she no longer distinguished, she said, between one hand and the other except to make the sign of the cross.[10]

A passage of Saint-Simon's further elucidates the hierarchy of rank with respect to the Eucharist:

It was [at the hot springs of Forges-les-Eaux in 1707] that I learned of a new foray by the princes of the blood [against the dukes]. . . . Kept powerless by the king, they shamelessly took advantage of his desire to improve the position of his bastards, whom the king had placed among them, in such a way as to acquire new advantages for themselves. The superiority and marked preference of rank accorded to the grandsons of France was unbearable to them. . . . One of the distinctions [among high-ranking nobles] involved the king's communions. After the elevation of the mass, a folding table was placed below the altar and covered with fabric and a broad cloth. At the Pater, the chaplain of the day stood and whispered in the king's ear the names of all the dukes present in the chapel. The king then named two, who were always the most senior, and the same chaplain then went and bowed to each. After the priest's communion, the king rose and walked to this folding table, where he knelt without a carpet or *carreau* [a square cushion used for sitting and kneeling during the service], and took hold of the cloth. . . . The two dukes, who along with the captain of guards on duty were the only ones to rise from their cushions to follow him, the senior duke on the king's right, the other on his left, then each took a corner of the cloth, which they held close to the king, while the two chaplains of the day held the other two corners of the cloth on the altar side. All four knelt, leaving the captain of guards standing alone behind the king. Then, within a few moments, communion received and ablution taken, the king . . . returned to his place, as did the captain and the two dukes. If a son of France happened to be [in the chapel], he alone would hold the right corner of the cloth, and no one would hold the other corner. If a grandson of France [the duc d'Orléans] happened to be present without a son of France, it was the same thing: no prince of the blood in attendance would serve along with him. If there was only a prince of the blood, one duke was tapped instead of the usual two, and he served on the left, with the prince of the blood on the right. The king named the dukes in order to show that he had the power to choose among them without regard to seniority [of their peerage]. In no case, however, did he ever choose a less senior duke over a more senior one.[11]

Ultimately, however, the princes of the blood succeeded in eliminating the dukes from the royal communion ceremony.

The text just quoted is of the utmost importance. It tells us that the sacred took precedence over the semi- or nonsacred. In the presence of the Host, the king knelt on the bare floor. The side of the cloth facing the altar was raised above the side facing the nave, and the right enjoyed priority over the left. Before the Body of Christ, then, the hierarchy went from the king to the sons of France, then to the grandsons, then to the princes of the blood (who sought to improve their position still further), and finally to the dukes and peers in order of seniority. Again, seniority brought the classification down to the level of individuals, or at any rate, of their respective families.

It is interesting to consider these rites and gestures in the light of a remark by Tocqueville: "Catholicism," he wrote, "likes to bring all classes of society together at the foot of the same altar, for in the eyes of God all are one. . . . Hence it does not prepare the faithful for inequality."[12] Clearly, the sage of Cotentin was on occasion misguided. At Versailles, in any case, no horde of equal individuals gathered under God and behind the king. There was instead a sophisticated hierarchy. The monarch stood at the head of a chain with many links. Distinctions were made manifest by priorities of rank and seniority that determined who would hold the royal communion cloth. Before the obscure sanctuary of Christianity's central mystery, the Eucharist, knelt the monarchy, the central mystery of the state. The king, God's image on earth, stood at the head of the second order (aristocracy and nobility), just as God and his mitered representatives here below stood at the head of the first order (clergy). It is worth noting, moreover, that in two essential activities, eating (see above) and partaking of the Lord's Body in the ceremony of communion (another form of eating), the king placed himself at the head of a purely aristocratic hierarchy (royal blood plus dukes plus persons of lesser quality), excluding altogether the *noblesse de robe* (whose nobility was of a lesser degree) and the *vulgum pecus*.

If we look now at rites of mourning, we can round out this picture of the subeucharistic, subroyal hierarchy. Mourning rituals involved a sacred element, because they grew out of and extended the religious burial ceremony. Nobles of the robe and commoners were excluded from the most central elements of a set of rituals that confirmed and even quantified the essential hierarchy of *les Grands*, the most illustrious nobles in the land. Indeed, a *queue de deuil*, or mourning train, of a specified length was prescribed for each great lady. "Duchesses were the last [after the daughters of France, princes of the blood, etc.] entitled to wear these mourning trains." The honorific *queue de deuil* was denied to ladies below this rank. Lengths were prescribed according to each lady's position in the hierarchy: "The queen's mourning train was eleven *aunes*. Daughters of France were entitled to nine *aunes*, granddaughters of France to seven, princesses of the blood to five, duchesses to three. The invention of the rank of 'granddaughter of France' made it necessary to lengthen the trains of the queen and daughters of France by two *aunes* each."[13]

During rites of passage and mourning, time, ordinarily a secularized quantity, briefly took on qualities of the sacred. These rites therefore afforded an opportunity to reaffirm the hierarchical order and thus led to unbelievable disputes over priority. In this regard, it is worth noting that the earliest surviving text of Saint-Simon's, written in 1689 when he was fifteen, deals with the funeral ceremony that followed the death of the dauphine and features details about the hierarchical placement of various individuals and about the disputes that not unexpectedly arose between monks and chaplains.[14]

The king was the image of God—a pale, faded image. He was *like* a god. But he certainly was not God, much less "a" god, whatever the words of Bossuet may have implied to certain readers. Standing at the head of his aristocratic, hierarchical cohort, the king functioned more like a kind of saint, a role consistent with his status as the Lord's anointed, even though this quality had been deemphasized since the time of the last Valois and further deemphasized under the first Bourbons. The king's body produced not only persons of royal blood but also relics. "The Jesuits asked Henri IV for permission to remove his heart after his death so as to display it in a reliquary."[15] Under Louis XIV, too, various organs (including the heart and intestines) were removed from the bodies of members of the royal house, including the king, for display in the various churches of the capital.[16]

The king, in addition to being a source of relics, was also a wellspring of the sacred in a more institutional sense. Under the terms of the Concordat of 1516, the sovereign enjoyed the power to appoint 10 archbishops, 80 bishops, and 527 abbots. The pope retained only the right to instate bishops, but he could not reject the king's nominees.[17] Furthermore, new bishops swore an oath of loyalty to the monarch. Thus to use today's terminology, the Gallican church was indeed an established church, a state religion, even though in many respects it transcended the state.[18] Benefices were handed out, for example, on the king's communion days, in consultation with his confessor Tellier, a Jesuit of common and perhaps rural birth. In other words, the only advice that the king received came from a man who was in effect his servant, so that in theory nothing prevented His Majesty from doing as he pleased, although in practice the Jesuit naturally exerted an important influence.[19] Once a bishop was appointed, moreover, all communication between him and Rome was expected to pass through the king. Mailly, the archbishop of Arles, earned himself a severe reprimand for breaking this rule.[20]

By contrast, cardinals were appointed by the pope, but the king of France retained control over a certain number of nominations, as did certain other European rulers. Coislin, the bishop of Orléans, benefited from this royal prerogative in 1695, as did Noailles (Paris) in 1700, and Rohan (Strasbourg) in 1712.[21] Note that all three of these king-appointed cardinals were great lords. Furthermore, regardless of whether a new cardinal owed his nomination to the pope or to the king, when the courier arrived from Rome with the red skullcap, the king insisted on placing it personally on the prelate's head. This was to remind the new cardinal of his temporal and even spiritual dependency on the monarch. When Cardinal Le Camus placed the red cap on his own head, he came close to forfeiting it permanently and for the rest of his life remained cloistered in his Grenoble diocese.[22] True, Le Camus, who was by all accounts an excellent bishop, also offended the king in other, less trivial ways: He criticized the Revocation of the Edict of Nantes and the Jesuits. He also supported Quietism and Jansenism. These offenses contributed to his disgrace as well.[23] When it came to the skullcap, a new cardinal was well advised to receive it from the papal courier, stick it in his pocket, and later present it to the king to be placed on his head.[24]

The king (as well as others of royal blood) was of course less sacred than the church. There was more mystery in the little finger of any priest consecrating the Eucharist than in the king's entire body. But at the moment of communion and indeed throughout the mass, the king (or dauphin or any son or daughter of France) occupied a strategic position at the foot of the altar. This spot was physically marked by a *drap de pied*, or foot cloth, on which the monarch and his "descendants" by blood or marriage were allowed to stand. Princes of the blood and dukes were excluded; as in the case of the royal communion cloth, their relation to the foot cloth was determined by hierarchical rank. The royal foot cloth thus marked the transition from the divine to the human, or more concretely, between the priests (who officiated at the altar) and the high aristocracy, arrayed in proper order (princes, dukes, and so on) behind the king and his closest relatives. The monarch therefore served as a link between the sacred and the profane, or to put it another way, between two major orders, the clergy and the nobility.

Once again we can turn to Madame Palatine, "daughter of France," for yet another revealing description of the relation between hierarchy and the sacred. The occasion was the taking of the habit by one of her granddaughters, the regent's daughter, who upon entering the convent immediately became its abbess. Although Madame, at heart still a Protestant, detested the monastic life in general and nuns in particular, she described this event with scrupulous attention to the question of hierarchy because it involved the sanctification of rank:

> We arrived at Chelles at nine-thirty. My grandson the duc de Chartres was already there. Shortly after ten, we went to the church. The abbess's prie-dieu was already in the nuns' choir. It was covered with purple velvet embroidered with gold fleurs-de-lys. My prie-dieu had been placed against the balustrade of the altar. My son [Philippe d'Orléans, grandson of France] was at my side. His daughter, my granddaughter, was behind my chair, *because princesses of the blood are not allowed to kneel on my foot cloth. This right belongs only to grandchildren of France such as my son and daughter.* . . . Cardinal de Noailles officiated. . . . After the cardinal read the epistle, the master of ceremonies went to the nuns' choir and beckoned to the abbess [that is, to Madame's granddaughter]. She came. She curtseyed to the altar, and again to me, and then climbed the steps and knelt before the cardinal, who sat in front of the altar in a large armchair. The confession of faith was ceremoniously brought before the abbess, who read it and then prostrated herself on the top step of the altar.[25]

The same rank order as before applied even to kneeling on Madame's foot cloth: first children of France and then grandchildren of France were permitted to do so, but princes of the blood were not. The hierarchies of the sacred dominated all others, however: the new abbess, born a princess of the blood, prostrates herself before God, who is worthily represented by a cardinal.

All of the various factors at work in the foregoing ceremony (hierarchical order interacting with sacred and subsacred order, space reserved for the royal blood as a transition between the first, or religious, order and the second, or aristocratic, order) are illustrated to perfection in the plan of the Spanish royal chapel. In this sanctuary all the customary observances common to the French and Spanish courts were scrupulously codified. (The strong bond between the two monarchies—a bond forged first by intermarriage and later by dynastic fusion—tended to bring customs north and south of the Pyrenees into harmony if not identity.)[26]

The king of Spain knelt at the foot of the altar on his own prie-dieu and "royal carpet" or "foot cloth." During the mass, the representatives of the royal blood (the king and, in a less prominent position, the prince of Asturias, or heir apparent) stood on this rug. The cardinal and patriarch of the Indies offered the king incense and presented the Bible to him to be kissed. Before Philip V, this double ceremony was conducted within a small tabernacle or tent, which isolated the sovereign. Although the king was a sacred personage, he was less so than the cardinal, before whom His Majesty knelt to receive the Candlemas candle. By way of compensation, however, the cardinal's armchair was made of wood, whereas the king sat in an armchair upholstered with splendid fabrics. But this was a minor point. Behind the royal carpet, toward the nave, stood the bench of the grandees, who were the only lay persons authorized to sit during the royal mass. Facing this, on the other side of the nave, was the bench of the high clergy. Ordinary ecclesiastics remained standing. The secular nobility of the robe and commoners might be allowed into the royal chapel but had to remain standing as spectators. They had no official role in the ceremony and were not even mentioned in accounts that listed persons in attendance. The sacred position of the "Catholic King" was that of first gentleman of the kingdom. Kneeling on his carpet, he became once again the bridge between God and the clergy on the one hand and the lay high aristocracy on the other. As the most sacred representative of the nobility, the monarch was in direct contact with the first order, which considered itself the repository of the divine.

Inspired by a similar ideology, Louis XIV organized his chapel in much the same way. In provincial and parish churches, moreover, great lords sought to occupy a position analogous to that of the king (in his absence). They each had their own prie-dieu, their foot rugs at the foot of the altar, and priests facing them as the cardinal faced the king, in Spain on the Gospel side: Dangeau enjoyed such privileged treatment and "strutted amid such pomp" at Saint-Germain-des-Prés,[27] as did Noailles in Languedoc and Saint-Simon himself when he served as ambassador to Spain. All this was obviously a far cry from the egalitarianism that Tocqueville imputed to Catholicism on theoretical grounds: all Christians, he assumed, are equal in God's eyes. But the truth is that when mass was said at Versailles, "the crowd of courtiers appeared to worship the prince, and the prince to worship God."[28] Nowadays one can think of any number of secular versions of this system. In 1992, for example, I had the honor of attending a gala concert at which France's head of state was present. While the president watched the orchestra, the television cameras remained focused on the president.

Not only was royal ceremonial steeped in the sacred, but so too was the monarch's daily life. Again, this was especially true in Spain, whose king was known as the "Catholic King," whereas the king of France was *only* "Most Christian." A glance at the daily schedule of King Philip V and his second wife, Elizabeth Farnese, will serve to illustrate this. The day began with breakfast, followed by prayer, then by the official rising ceremony, toilette, mass, confession, communion, and dinner (at midday). After that came hunting (the aristocratic occupation par excellence), followed by the king's daily work with Grimaldo, his secretary of state. While the king was thus engaged in bureaucratic labors, the queen went to confession. The day concluded with supper, followed by prayers and spiritual readings before bed.[29]

The sacred often interfered with the ordinary protocol of hierarchy. Courtiers, both secular and ecclesiastic, vied for a strategic place near where the king knelt. Could a mere *maître de chapelle* don a black cape and station himself on a stool close to the monarch's prie-dieu—a status symbol ordinarily reserved for bishops?[30] Who would present the Bible for the king to kiss during the grand mass of the Ordre du Saint-Esprit? Would it be the chaplain on duty that day or the cardinal de Polignac, who was not a member of the order but who happened to be stationed next to the king's prie-dieu?[31] And who would occupy the fourth place behind the august prie-dieu? The duc de La Rochefoucauld, grandmaster of the king's wardrobe, or the bishop of Orléans, first chaplain?[32]

Hierarchy and religion occasioned disputes not only at court but even in small towns: "Something that has never been seen and in all probability never will be seen in this world is a small town that is not divided into factions . . . where a marriage does not lead to civil war, where disputes over rank are not rekindled by every offertory, by incense and blessed bread, by processions and funerals . . . where the deacon gets on with his canons and the canons do not look down on the chaplains and the chaplains do not find the cantors impossible to bear."[33] Here, the rites of the church are depicted as perpetually reawakening the demons, or rather the angels and archangels, of an easily offended hierarchy. Boileau's *Lutrin*, an astonishing poem about nothing, or almost nothing, is a remarkable illustration of this.

The king's coronation was another occasion when the sacred impinged on the summit of the social hierarchy, and at the precise moment when the enduring essence of that hierarchy was reaffirmed. To be sure, the coronation ceremony had lost some or even much of its importance since the fifteenth century, when Joan of Arc had looked to it as the primary goal of her efforts to restore the monarchy. In the sixteenth century, the coronation still existed, but the strategic moment in the transfer of power came earlier, when the late king was buried and his banners were lifted from the grave to shouts of "The king is dead! Long live the king!"[34] Until this burial, an effigy of the dead king continued to serve as the symbolic seat of power. The new practice did not diminish the sacred aspect of the transfer; one could even argue that it was enhanced. The end-of-mourning ceremony, which was in no sense profane or secular but steeped in the most profound religiosity, thus complemented or perhaps prefigured the coronation.

Things changed with the accession of Louis XIII, the first Bourbon king to be more or less assured of his place. Now the transfer of power was marked by an initial *lit de justice*, at which the new king was presented to Parlement—a ceremony almost purely secular in essence. In the case of little Louis XV, who acceded to the throne when his great-grandfather Louis XIV died on 1 September 1715, a first *lit de justice* was scheduled for 7 September, but the young king was ill and the ceremony was postponed until 12 September. Do Saint-Simon's complaints about various abuses connected with the coronation suggest that the importance of the sacred had diminished and that people were less conscious of hierarchical matters? He was of course disappointed by the edict of 1711 granting priority in the coronation ceremony to the princes of the blood and the king's legitimized bastards, who filled the six roles assigned to lay peers and all but eliminated the dukes and peers from the ceremony.[35] This edict confirmed the fact that "a broad segment of society felt all but excluded from a coronation now conducted essentially by the male kin of a hereditary monarch," and of course under the auspices of Salic law, which was peculiar to France. There was no longer a role for the dukes and peers, who stood as representatives not of the nation but of hierarchy itself and hence of society as a whole, the very pillar on which the royal family rested. Saint-Simon's criticisms of the coronation ceremony proper may seem relatively trivial: the *robe du Conseil* and ministries were overrepresented at the expense of the high nobility, and an important element of the ceremony—the acclamation of the new king by the "people" in the nave—was omitted. Yet these details might appear to suggest that already under Louis XV less value was being attached to the sacred character of the monarchy.

Did the legists seize control of the anointment ceremony from the priests? Even if they did—which is highly debatable—the whole ritual obviously retained a sacred aspect. What is more, whatever "desacralization" may have occurred had no effect on the monarch's daily routine, which was still replete with religious moments: mass, vespers, benediction of the Holy Sacrament, and above all communion. This religious routine survived even though Louis XV went on strike, as it were, when it come to the Eucharist: he was too inveterate a fornicator to permit himself to ingest the consecrated Host.

The court hierarchy basked in this sacred climate not only at its summit but also at less exalted levels. This was apparent to everyone.

For example, the Ordre du Saint-Esprit, which only nobles could join, maintained an acute sensitivity to rank even as it paid its respects to the third person of the Trinity. Each member of the order was assigned a specific place in processions according to seniority. Saint-Simon spilled a great deal of ink over the order and its *cordon bleu*, and he was not the only one to complain of abuses. Much of what he wrote will seem incomprehensible to our egalitarian and disenchanted eyes. Yet there can be no doubt that the order did in fact respect both rank and religion. It observed three annual holidays. Of these, one was devoted to purification (Candlemas) and another to the infusion of the Holy Spirit (Pentecost). On these occasions, at least until 1661, the knights of the Saint-Esprit received communion in full knightly regalia.[36] When the necklace of the order was fastened around the neck of a new knight, he uttered the very words once addressed to Christ by a man about to be miraculously cured: "Domine non sum dignus" ("Lord, I am not worthy [but say the word and my body will be healed]").[37]

To an aristocrat, the Ordre du Saint-Esprit was perhaps a less coveted honor than the title of duke and peer, but it could mark the culmination of an international career that had already garnered a Golden Fleece and a title of Spanish grandee. Scotti, an "extremely thick and heavyset" fellow born into one of Parma's most distinguished families, was the favorite of the queen of Spain (Philip V's second wife). Through the lady's kindness, Scotti was named guardian of the king's youngest son, obtained the Golden Fleece, and was ultimately made a grandee. "To top it all off," the queen, "having made him who had been very poor extremely rich, obtained for him the Ordre du Saint-Esprit."[38] By the same token, a career that began in Spain but continued on the French side of the Pyrenees could lead first to the Ordre du Saint-Esprit and then to the Golden Fleece. The two orders were all but equivalent in the eyes of those honored to receive both. When the duke of Uceda, who held the title and exercised the functions of Spanish ambassador, abandoned Philip V for the Habsburgs, he immediately returned his Saint-Esprit necklace to Louis XIV. In return, the archduke of Austria, whom the emperor and the English both recognized at that point as "king" of Spain, awarded Uceda the Golden Fleece. Indeed, he not only traded a Saint-Esprit for a Golden Fleece but also exchanged a Golden Fleece awarded by Philip V for another awarded by the archduke.[39]

Further possible permutations of the Saint-Esprit and Golden Fleece can be seen in the peregrinations of Maulévrier-Langeron, a client of both the Condés and the duc du Maine. In 1720 this nobleman went to Madrid to deliver the *cordon bleu* of the Saint-Esprit to Don Felipe, the newborn prince. As a reward, he returned home, not without incident, with a promise from the king of Spain of a Golden Fleece for himself.[40]

In theory, the major orders of religious origin or significance were intended to honor men who had enjoyed meritorious careers, but only those whose high birth made them suitable to receive such distinctions. Kings were nevertheless accused of debasing the marks of honor: the marquis de Bay, a courageous soldier, had the misfortune (as Saint-Simon saw it) of being the son of a man who kept a tavern in Franche-Comté. Hence it was "seriously wrong" of Philip V to have awarded him the Golden Fleece.[41] But His Catholic Majesty may have been exactly right, regardless of Bay's merits as a soldier, if the stories that he was actually the son of a lord and not a saloonkeeper were in fact true.[42] On the other hand, the Golden Fleece awarded to d'Asfeld was even more dubious in Saint-Simon's eyes. D'Asfeld was the son of a merchant who sold gold- and silver-embroidered silk and velvet on the rue aux Fers in Paris.[43] The queen of Sweden had bestowed on this tradesman the noble title of Asfeld, which sounded vaguely German, as a reward for acting as the queen's agent. The son, an honorable and talented fellow with a knack for building fortifications and managing logistics, joined the entourage of the duc d'Orléans. Philip V awarded him the Golden Fleece in recognition of his military skills, which were indeed impressive and made up for his otherwise unimpressive background. Purists were nonetheless appalled.

The same purists also objected when a Golden Fleece was awarded to Morville. True, Morville was wellborn, but his family belonged to the *noblesse de robe*. His father was d'Armenonville, a member of the Fleuriau clan of "technocrats," who were related to the Le Peletiers, clients of the Le Tellier–Louvois. D'Armenonville had been gently pushed aside by Desmarets but regained favor under the Regency, which he served as secretary of state for foreign affairs and later Keeper of the Seals. Morville enjoyed a similarly brilliant career, which took him from the Châtelet to Parlement and the Great Council (Grand Conseil), after which he served as ambassador to Holland, received the Ordre de Saint-Louis, joined the Council of State (Conseil d'Etat), and became minister of foreign affairs from 1723 to 1727. He fell into disgrace under Fleury, however, at roughly the same time as the fall of Monsieur le Duc. Morville was a protégé first of Dubois, then of the duc d'Orléans, and later of the Bourbon-Condés. He was also an anglophile and a collector of titles, with a weakness for honors that flattered his vanity. In 1723 he was elected to the Académie Française and shortly thereafter received the Golden Fleece from Philip V, who hoped to buy himself a friend in the French government, despite the fact that Morville had hitherto shown himself to be more of an anglophile than a friend of Spain. In wooing him for the Spanish cause, Philip V broke no new ground: he had often bestowed the Golden Fleece on influential members of the French elite who enjoyed good relations with the king and Mme de Maintenon (Villars and Caylus, for example) and later with the duc d'Orléans (such as Ruffec, the son of Saint-Simon, who was himself a friend of the regent). But Saint-Simon was not entirely wrong to complain that Philip V, in thus rewarding Morville, broke with what had hitherto been his standard practice when bestowing the Golden Fleece on Frenchmen, namely, limiting his choice to men of distinguished, albeit in some cases illegitimate, birth (such as Toulouse and Berwick), court aristocrats (Béthune-Sully), and soldiers who, though undistinguished by birth, had nevertheless distinguished themselves in battle (Villars and d'Asfeld). In awarding the Fleece to Morville, who was nothing more than a *robin* who had been made a minister, a garden-variety technocrat, Philip V had thus stooped as low as Monsieur le Duc, who in making his 1724 appointments to the Ordre du Saint-Esprit had, in Saint-Simon's somewhat exaggerated opinion, "tossed in a lot of nondescript riffraff."[44]

The Duke of Ossone's Hispano-French career was less arduous and his rise more spectacular. Ossone's elder brother ruined himself with lavish gifts to dancers from the Opéra. When the childless spendthrift opportunely died, the title of duke passed to the younger man, who was dispatched in splendor as ambassador to Paris to negotiate the marriage of the duc d'Orléans's daughter to Philip V's heir apparent. The regent could do no less than reward the ambassador with the *cordon bleu* of the Saint-Esprit, capping a dazzling rise.

In some cases, the *cordon bleu* was obtained by unusual or even disreputable means. Blackmail was not unknown: D'Estampes had stumbled onto the homosexual affair between Monsieur, the king's brother, and Châtillon. Sword in hand, he accosted Monsieur somewhere near his commode and threatened to expose him unless his victim agreed to make him a member of the Ordre du Saint-Esprit in 1688. In the event, his name was placed in nomination by none other than Monsieur's son, the duc de Chartres.[45]

Without resorting to such nefarious means, a man could be named to the order as a favor (provided, of course, he was sufficiently wellborn and had the requisite titles, however insignificant). This is what happened to Saint-Simon's father. Louis XIII, a (presumably) platonic admirer of young men, was pleased to name the elder Saint-Simon a knight of the order at the age of twenty-five and less than two years later made him a duke and peer. And Louis XIV appointed his friend Puyseulx to the order when he was past sixty. Puyseulx was a man of many talents, but his *cordon bleu* was in part the result of a promise the king had made when the two played blindman's buff together as children half a century earlier.[46]

Not all favors came from the king. As minister, Louvois favored La

Trousse with nomination to the Ordre du Saint-Esprit in 1688. In that same year, Mme de Maintenon honored Villarceaux, a courtier for whom she had long felt affection of the most honorable sort, by seeing to it that his son, in his forties at the time, was awarded a *cordon bleu*. The younger Villarceaux had been a lieutenant-captain since 1677. In 1690, two years after joining the order, he was promoted to brigadier general. In effect, the *cordon bleu* was a harbinger of future promotions, as in the case of Saint-Simon's father. It was also a mark of favor to those who knew how to read it. In the case of Villarceaux, however, it had tragic consequences: at the battle of Fleurus he fought heroically but was captured by the enemy. At the sight of his *cordon bleu*, they murdered him in cold blood.[47] The times were cruel.

Nominations to the order illustrate the way in which religion and rank intersected.[48] The same hierarchical pecking order we have seen at work elsewhere exerted an influence here as well. Each time nominations were opened, the sons of France claimed the right to propose two or even three candidates, whereas the grandsons of France and the first prince of the blood were entitled to only one apiece. Other princes of the blood were entitled to propose one candidate each, but only if the total number of candidates exceeded eight. Saint-Simon of course believed that these rules were new, dating back no earlier than 1688, or perhaps no farther than 1724, when, as we have seen, Monsieur le Duc threw in the names of all sorts of people whom Saint-Simon dismissed as riffraff.[49] But even if the specifics of such privileges changed, they still underscored the traditional distinctions among the highest-ranking nobles in the land.

In any case, the Ordre du Saint-Esprit represented the "top drawer" of the sacralized hierarchy, as is clear from certain sixteenth-century documents on which Saint-Simon drew while studying processions in which knights of the order participated. These documents described the order of march in religious processions as a sort of Jacob's ladder extending down from the dominant peak, which was the church, to the lower peaks of the royal house, and so on: religious authorities first, followed by the king and queen, followed by princes and high barons such as the Montmorency, knights of the order, *gentilshommes* (that is, qualified lords holding high offices), and finally *robins* of the Parlement and other sovereign courts, who were expected to bring up the rear.

The two orders, Saint-Esprit and Golden Fleece, were part of the national hierarchies of their respective countries, France and Spain, as were the dukes and peers of France and the Spanish grandees. When circumstances required, Louis XIV was capable of making a point of the difference between the two nations. For daring exploits at Girone, two Frenchmen, Montmorency-Estaires and Noailles, received the Golden

Fleece from Philip V, who also made them grandees of Spain in 1711. This greatly displeased the Sun King, who at the time was contemplating a divorce between France and Spain in order to entice his enemies into signing a peace agreement. The maréchale de Noailles was even forced to "cough up" the compliments she had received for the honors bestowed on her son. Shortly thereafter, however, the differences were smoothed over, fortunately for Montmorency-Estaires, who, as the prince of Robecq, went on to enjoy a brilliant career in Spain. For him, the Golden Fleece had been but a stepping stone to even more illustrious rewards.[50]

Orders of knighthood thus marked out a man's career progress and indicated whether or not he was on his way to better things.[51] The marquis d'Harcourt was a shrewd, cunning, and ambitious Norman of very ancient nobility who held a number of important commands along France's northern and eastern borders during the wars of Louis XIV. In 1693, when he was thirty-nine, he was promoted to lieutenant general; in 1697 he became ambassador to Spain; in 1700 he became a duke; and in 1703, he was named marshal of France and captain of the king's bodyguard. In 1705 he became a knight of the Ordre du Saint-Esprit.[52] He obtained a peerage in 1710 after a lucrative reappraisal of his post as lieutenant general for Normandy in 1709. To cap his career, he was invited to join the Regency Council. He was hampered by a stroke, however, and suffered financially from the economic depression of 1690 to 1715. Much of his enormous income went to feed his troops. He therefore profited less from all his advantages than would his descendants, who were destined to govern Normandy until 1789 and who in one capacity or another remain with us even today.[53] Cleverly chosen alliances with the Villeroys and the Louvois-Barbezieux further contributed to the family fortune, which passed in 1718 to the marshal's son, François d'Harcourt.[54]

When it came to knightly orders, the Saint-Esprit was the one that Henri d'Harcourt truly coveted. The Golden Fleece was secondary in his mind. When he received it for services rendered to Spain, he voluntarily passed it on to his brother Sézanne, and when the brother died childless, Henri passed it on to his second son and then, after that son's death, to his third son.[55] "After the third son's premature death," Saint-Simon acidly comments, "this *much-inherited* Golden Fleece left the hands of the Harcourts."

For Saint-Simon himself, the Golden Fleece was mainly an amusement, a young man's decoration that he passed on to his older son as a stopgap until the boy could inherit the more substantial position of duke and peer.[56] As for his younger son, Saint-Simon chose the more direct route of having him made a grandee of Spain. This was supposed to console the younger boy for not being a duke and peer of France, an honor of course destined for his older brother, who in the meantime had been sowing his wild oats and enjoying his Golden Fleece.

Villars, that grasping and courageous "Gascon," went even farther than Saint-Simon and Harcourt, simultaneously holding for himself the Saint-Esprit, the Golden Fleece, a duchy peerage, and a title of grandee. Like Harcourt, Villars was a protégé of Mme de Maintenon as well as a self-made man who owed everything to his valor. He started lower on the social ladder than Harcourt: his nobility was relatively recent, even if Saint-Simon was exaggerating when he portrayed him as the son of a "bailiff from Condrieu" in Dauphiné (which may be in the south of France but is not, as Saint-Simon would have it, part of Gascony). Born in 1653, Villars served as lieutenant general in the War of the League of Augsburg. In 1702 he married a rich and beautiful woman from Normandy, and in that same year he was made marshal of France following the battle of Friedlingen. In 1705 he became a duke and a knight of the Ordre du Saint-Esprit. Then he was dispatched to restore peace to the Cévennes. In 1709, after being wounded at Malplaquet, he became peer of France, and in 1712 he won the battle of Denain, which led to the Treaty of Utrecht in 1713, with the happy result (for France) that a Bourbon ascended to the Spanish throne. At about this time, Villars began to covet Spanish titles, even though he had barely ever set foot on Spanish soil. In 1714 he obtained the Golden Fleece, along with a (French) pension of 3,000 livres for his sister's husband Choiseul.[57] In 1723 he was made a Spanish grandee. Was this perhaps a reward for the discreet support he had offered Cellamare and the duc du Maine in their conspiracy against the regent? In any case, it made for a dazzling conclusion to Villars's career and excited the bitter and surely unjustified jealousy of Saint-Simon. Under Fleury, Villars, by now in his seventies, joined the Upper Council. His son married a Noailles, a family of the highest nobility and of course of "Maintenonist" sympathies. Villars had been clever enough to live a long life, demonstrate his valor, win the favor of Mme de Maintenon, the old court, and Cardinal Fleury, and to parlay a Saint-Esprit into a French peerage and a Golden Fleece into a grandee's title in Madrid. Harcourt's French and Castilian titles were scattered among his children and other relatives. By contrast, Villars held onto everything for himself in the hope of passing it all on to a single heir. He kept his feet on the ground and put all his eggs in one basket—his own. He plundered the Germans on whom he successfully waged war and with the booty bought the splendid castle of Vaux-le-Vicomte, which cost him a fortune.

But let us return to the subject at hand, hierarchy in relation to religion. In this respect, the ceremony in which the Golden Fleece was conferred was fairly typical. Even though the name of the order was of course an allusion to ancient mythology, the ceremony was steeped in Christian religiosity.[58] Before being dubbed with Gonzalo de Cordoba's heavy sword, the knight aspirant knelt before a table upon which were placed a vermeil crucifix, a missal opened to the Canon, and the Book of John. This says it all. The sacred table occupied a privileged location even in relation to the king's armchair, which was itself privileged in relation to the position of all others present. These included the other knights of the order, who, with their hats still on their heads, sat in order of seniority on an upholstered bench. Also present were the (bureaucratic) officers of the order, who sat on a bare bench with hats off. Finally came the ladies, who remained standing as simple onlookers, or *voyeuses*. (Saint-Simon often uses the word *voyeur* to imply a position outside the ranks of the hierarchy, which was the position of Saint-Simon himself in writing his memoirs. This may be compared, as we shall see later, with the position of "renouncers," men and women who turned their backs on the world and yet remained in it.)

Saint-Simon carefully notes that in the Golden Fleece ceremony, the king's armchair occupies a privileged position with respect to the lay participants but a subordinate position with respect to sacred objects such as the crucifix and missal.[59] Indeed, the royal seat was displaced slightly to the left in order to make room for the august central table "and out of respect for what is on it."

For Saint-Simon, the sacred was transmitted to the hierarchy at three distinct levels. For the clergy, or first order, ecclesiastical institutions proper filled this role. For the king, there was the coronation at the beginning of his reign, together with specific ceremonies such as royal communion throughout. The king also served as a bridge, or point of transition, between the first and second orders. And finally, there was the knightly dubbing ceremony for the second order proper, or at any rate for those members of the second order deemed worthy by dint of birth or valor to join a knightly order such as the Saint-Esprit or Golden Fleece. Dubbing, which Saint-Simon described in such detail when his son became a knight of the Golden Fleece, "speaks in mystical religious terms or in a language of initiation that bears the impress of Christianity. It is almost a sacrament according to Augustine's definition of the sacred sign." When first formulated in the Middle Ages, the dubbing ceremony was intimately associated with the theory and practice of the priest-king on the model of David and Melchizedek.[60]

The question of the sacred thus brings us face-to-face once again with the problem of rank. Note that a man's age on entering the Ordre du Saint-Esprit tended to be inversely proportional to his rank in the hierarchy. Sons of France and Spanish *infantes* received the *cordon bleu* at birth, immediately after baptism.[61] Princes of the blood automatically became knights of the order when they turned twenty-five. In the waning years of Louis XIV's reign, the age was reduced to fourteen in order to prevent royal bastards from getting in ahead of them.[62] Less highly placed personages had to wait until later in life. In such cases, military exploits often made up for birth that fell somewhat short of the mark.

These genealogical rules were eventually internalized by everyone the king might consider eligible to receive the Saint-Esprit. Saint-Simon admiringly cites several examples of individuals who refused the *cordon* when it was offered. These were people who deemed their own pedigrees too common for such an honor. Among them were two military commanders, Fabert and Catinat, distinguished by their battlefield exploits, and an archbishop of Sens by the name of Fortin de La Hoguette, whose parents were by his own estimate "nothing at all."[63] As for Catinat, who was on good terms with le Grand Dauphin but was disliked by Mme de Maintenon, his refusal did not distress the king unduly.

When everything was as it should be, however, the religious honor was the reward for martial valor. Aristocratic values easily accommodated sacred rituals of knighthood and dubbing. On occasion the reward was a long time coming: Charles de Revel, an impecunious younger son of the rising de Broglie family, climbed the ranks of the military hierarchy one step at a time, showing much courage if little flair, until he became a lieutenant general. In 1702, when he was well into his fifties, his heroic defense of Cremona plucked him from an obscurity that would have been total but for his brief affair with the actress Champmeslé. For his battlefield exploit, he was awarded not only the Saint-Esprit but also the governorship of the city of Condé with its lucrative emoluments of 22,000 livres per year. The latter stages of his career were honorable if not particularly remunerative, though he did marry the sister of the duc de Tresmes, a woman well past her prime and without a large dowry who may have married only to avoid the convent. Revel, grown fat and gouty, did not live long after his wedding, not even long enough to become a marshal. Without a marshal's baton, he had to make do with his Saint-Esprit.[64]

The Saint-Esprit could thus cap a career, but most people preferred to use it as a stepping stone to higher position and greater monetary reward than Revel managed to obtain. For example, Louis-Vincent, marquis de Goesbriand, whose birth was honorable but no more, made a rich marriage with the daughter of the minister and financier Desmarets.[65] Then, for putting up a courageous fight in Aire in 1710, he was awarded the Saint-Esprit, together with an annual pension of 20,000 livres and the government of Verdun, which was worth another 20,000 livres a year.[66] In 1712 his father-in-law, Desmarets, obtained for him another pension of 12,000 livres.[67] Having become rich, Goesbriand was able to arrange a wedding between his son and the daughter of the marquis de Châtillon. This marriage, which brought honor to the Goesbriands, was also advantageous for the Châtillons, whose daughter was accepted without dowry.[68] The Saint-Esprit, essential and lucrative as it was, was only one of the ingredients that went into the making of Goesbriand's brilliant career, whose crowning touch came at the coronation of Louis XV.[69] As a knight of the Saint-Esprit, he was one of four nobles chosen to carry the offerings for the coronation ceremony (a pitcher of wine, a golden loaf, a silver loaf, and a red velvet purse containing thirteen gold pieces). He sat in the front row of choir seats in the Reims cathedral. In an earlier phase of his career, between 1700 and 1725, Goesbriand had enjoyed the backing of Desmarets, the maréchal de Villeroy, and Mme de Maintenon. He managed to put together a solid chain of material advantages around which he wove a decorative braid of honors. His brother-in-law Maillebois, marshal of France and son of Desmarets, also received the *cordon bleu*. The order was a very posh club in which family connections were a definite advantage.[70]

The Ordre du Saint-Esprit also figured in yet another career strategy: that of Navailles, a valiant but dull Gascon noble who gave his allegiance to Mazarin, as his wife did to Mme de Maintenon (indeed, the woman to whom the king was secretly married had as a young girl tended turkeys for the mother of Navailles's wife). Navailles was awarded the *cordon bleu* in 1661, along with the government of Le Havre, which was worth an estimated 300,000 livres and yielded an annual income of 18,000. After a brief period of disgrace, Navailles was made a marshal of France in the 1670s as well as guardian of the future regent. The *cordon bleu* did not save him from poverty, however (his servants starved), and he bungled the opportunity to become a duke. Still, the honor was a good omen for the Navailles family, which was firmly though not comfortably ensconced at both Versailles and the Palais-Royal. One of the marshal's daughters made a brilliant marriage with Prince Charles III of Lorraine, duke of Elbeuf and member of a ruling dynasty, who is famous for having struck a colonel with a shoulder of lamb, leaving an indelible scar on the unfortunate soldier's cheek.[71] The duchess of Elbeuf was thus put on notice that she had best behave herself.

Appointment to the order theoretically indicated a combination of good birth, courage in battle, honorable situation, and political backing. A Breton noble by the name of Coëtanfao had all the requisite qualities: his brother was a bishop, he was bold in battle, and he held the distinguished post of knight of honor to the duchesse de Berry (which Saint-Simon's influence during the Regency had helped him to obtain), the chief advantage of which was that whoever held it could expect to receive a nomination to the Ordre du Saint-Esprit. Unfortunately Coëtanfao died too young and never received the *cordon bleu*.[72]

The sacred emanated from the clergy to the nobility and on from there to the entire society of *corps*, or corporations. As recently as the turn of the eighteenth century, much of the French population still belonged to one corporation or another. The court basked in emanations of the sacred: masses, vespers, and benedictions of the Holy Sacrament followed one upon the other in the chapel of Versailles, which stood one story higher than the rest of the palace. Was the court itself a corporation, or was it more a hodgepodge of sometimes warring corporations? Lower down the social scale, among artisans and villagers, guilds and corporations supplanted the confraternities that had been organized around the cult of a patron saint (such as Saint Crispin for the shoemakers and Saint Eligius for blacksmiths) or the Holy Spirit (as was often the case with urban and village confraternities in southeastern France). Even today's trade unions, distant heirs of the corporations of old, would be unthinkable without some form of ideology, a substitute for the religious underpinnings of an earlier time. And union members often stage "processions" in city streets, tying up traffic endlessly.

Religion thus linked the court hierarchy to the heavenly hierarchy not only at the highest level, but all the way down the line. Even though sanctity was the supreme value and the sacred was contrasted with the profane, religious intolerance was not intrinsic to the system. The fact that the sacred stood at the top of the hierarchy indicated that legitimate exemptions from its prescriptions could be claimed lower down. Saint-Simon and the Princess Palatine were both perceptive observers of court hierarchies to which they subscribed with every fiber of their being, yet both were receptive to religious pluralism. Neither was prejudiced against Jansenism, even though it was persecuted by the authorities. Their hostility manifested itself only when the Jansenists formed a party within the church. Saint-Simon even wrote several paragraphs about the Solitaries of Port-Royal, for whom he displayed a deep sympathy. He admired their ascetic, scholarly style, in part because of his own persistent interest in Augustinian theology and morality.[73]

Saint-Simon and Madame also categorically opposed outright acts of religious intolerance such as the Revocation of the Edict of Nantes. The expulsion of the Huguenots (1680) coincided with the formation in France of a modern national state characterized by the union of throne and altar. In England, too, aggressive antipapism served as the mortar of national unity in the seventeenth century. The French state already had egalitarian tendencies. But equality applied to those who were regarded as full-fledged members of the state or nation, as distinct from the scapegoats whose exclusion confirmed and promoted national unity. The period from 1680 to 1700 thus witnessed a wave of persecution in both France and Britain. South of the Channel, the Huguenots were the ones persecuted, whereas to the north and northwest it was the Catholics and the Irish.

A theorist of hierarchy, Saint-Simon never wavered in his hostility to these manifestations of intolerance. He severely condemned the Revocation as barbarous.[74] What about charges that French Protestants had been responsible for the civil wars of the sixteenth and seventeenth centuries? Saint-Simon hinted that the real fomenters of the Wars of Religion had been the Guises and other *ligueurs*, not the Protestants.[75] He wisely deplored the fact that French Calvinist workers had been lured to Prussia after being persecuted in France under Louis XIV, and he admired the king of Prussia for having been shrewd enough to take advantage of France's blunder.[76] Yet although Saint-Simon was inclined to be tolerant, he was less so than the duc d'Orléans, who toyed with the idea of rescinding the Revocation and bringing Protestant émigrés back to France.[77] On the whole, Saint-Simon took a wait-and-see attitude with respect to the Huguenots. He regretted the repressive actions of 1685 but did not press for a reinstatement of the policy of peaceful coexistence. Accordingly, it is not difficult to understand why he did not always sympathize with Dubois's pro-English diplomacy.

His general cast of mind made him extremely hostile, moreover, to the revolt of the Camisards, whom he regarded as fanatics.[78] In some respects this hostility was justified: the unnecessary cruelty of the Camisards horrified him, not without reason. In any case the crucial point remains: Saint-Simon, *homo hierarchicus*, and Madame, *domina hierarchica*, refused to support the waves of expulsions of religious dissidents and outbursts of religious intolerance that followed the Revocation. Because the society of ranks to which both of them subscribed was a strict hierarchy, it could easily accommodate Protestants of every station, high or low.

Saint-Simon knew or had known Huguenots at various levels of the cascade of contempt—and not always at the bottom. His father-in-law, Lorges, was a close ally of Louis de Durfort, count of Feversham, who had fled to England on account of his religion and capped his career with a brilliant coup when he secretly married Charles II's widow, England's dowager queen.[79] Lorges's sister, the comtesse de Roye, was another Protestant émigré who lived in England, and Saint-Simon remained on the best of terms with her children.[80]

The *petit duc* also displayed considerable respect for Lutheran ideas. To him it seemed only logical that Germany, an extremely hierarchical country, could afford the luxury of being partially Protestant. Admiringly he related the story of the count of Nassau-Saarbrück, a foreigner who served as a lieutenant general in the French army: "He was the best-built man in the world, with the most grand and imposing manner, highly polite, extremely brave, and altogether honest, and though he lacked wit, he was well respected. He was also quite rich, but Lutheran, and not old. The king himself launched several gentle attacks against his religion and let him know that he would go very far indeed if he became a Catholic, but this failed to shake him."[81]

If Saint-Simon respected Lutheranism in Germany, he also respected Gallicanism in France and Anglicanism in Great Britain. So long as a church was both Christian and national—in other words, not ultramontane—it earned our author's approval, though not without certain caveats. Writing of the duke of Ormond, a Jacobite and Anglican who for political reasons had sought refuge in Madrid, Saint-Simon had this to say: "The duke of Ormond was short, fat, hunched up, yet graceful in every way, with the air of a very great lord who conducted himself in a polite and noble manner. He was deeply attached to his Anglican religion and in Spain consistently refused the substantial inducements he was offered to give it up."[82] Saint-Simon liked Anglicans, provided that they had been Jacobites.

As for the Huguenots, Saint-Simon, who had no use for ideological monopoly, was naturally a proponent of Realpolitik toward the Protestant powers, great and small, with the exception of Hanoverian England. He never forgave Du Luc, the French ambassador to Switzerland, for renewing France's alliance with the Catholic cantons but not the Protestant ones, who took their grievance to the court of Versailles.[83] The French alliance with the Helvetic Confederation as a whole was not renewed until much later.[84]

Can we therefore say that Louis XIV's rigorous persecution of Protestants reflected a certain modern ideology of the state as "equalizer" and agent of political and religious unification: *une loi, une foi, un roi* (one law, one faith, one king, as the saying went)? By contrast, Saint-Simon's religious pluralism, however limited, accords well with the various ways in which hierarchical thinking allowed for flexibility: "In the house of my Father there are many mansions." There were many niches, of many kinds, even "multiconfessional" ones, along the vertical axis that led from the lowest to the highest rank of the social hierarchy. Conversely, racism was born in more modern societies that were egalitarian in tendency. There, the fine discriminations of the past gave way to brutal exclusion of vast religious or "genetic" minorities first identified as such and then declared undesirable.[85]

At bottom, Saint-Simon was rather close to Edmund Burke, another aristocratic thinker. It is worth noting that the two authors shared the

same theory about the Glorious Revolution of 1688 and its aftermath—
a theory that incidentally makes good sense. Although the British coun-
terrevolutionary was unaware that the French duke had preceded him,
both saw the events of that time as a simple maneuver designed to place
the English crown securely in the Protestant line.[86]

In other respects, however, the two writers differed. One finds little
trace of Burke's vehement anti-Semitism in Saint-Simon. (Or, for that
matter, in the Princess Palatine, who was a great reader of the Old Testament. But one would have to read her correspondence in its entirety to
be sure.) The worst one can say about Saint-Simon in this regard is that
he harbored a vague anti-Semitic prejudice with respect to certain Spanish grandees, whose ancestry he thought could be traced to bastard,
Moorish, or Jewish roots.[87]

Had the duke been an anti-Semite, his feelings might have manifested
themselves when d'Aquin, Louis XIV's first physician, was banished in
disgrace in 1693 at the behest of Madame de Maintenon.[88] D'Aquin was
in fact the grandson of an Avignon rabbi, who had "converted at Aquino
[in the kingdom of Naples] and taken the name of that city." To be sure,
Saint-Simon might appear to have shared the stereotypical image of the
Jew when he described d'Aquin as greedy and grasping. Elsewhere, however, he expressed sympathy for the man, and at no point did he allude
again to his Jewish ancestry, which seems not to have concerned him.

Saint-Simon does, however, state clearly that the maréchal d'Estrades
had a father whose mother was "of the Spanish Jewish race." The attack
he launched against this lady shows that he regarded her as lower than
a bastard, on a par with her husband, a "bourgeois from Bordeaux recast
as a councilor in Parlement." Clearly in Saint-Simon's mind, Judaism
blurred together with the impurity of the bastard and the filth adhering
to a bourgeois barely disguised by a thin coat of professional whitewash.[89]
These are mere fleeting references, however. Indeed, there were almost
no Jews in Louis XIV's France, where the Protestant problem was far
more important than the Jewish question and far more likely to result in
diatribes and acts of discrimination. It was not until the persecution of
the Huguenots was ended that France, in ceasing to be anti-Calvinist,
discovered that part of itself was anti-Semitic.

When all is said and done, it is hardly surprising that the sacred took
on such importance in a hierarchical society. Saint-Simon's memoirs are
set in a sacralized society in which outright atheism was almost unheard
of. In discussing the duc d'Orléans's impious attitude, Saint-Simon remarked that the prince "was too intelligent to be an atheist, atheists being
a species of madmen far rarer than people generally believe."[90]

Thus there were many ways in which religion affected the secular hierarchy, especially that of the high nobility. But one can equally well turn

the question around and consider the impact of hierarchy on the sacred, or at any rate on the first order. Of course, even today one still speaks of the "ecclesiastical hierarchy." The expression was even more pregnant with meaning in Saint-Simon's day: religious ranks were graded and numbered just like the ranks of aristocrats. For example, the abbot general of Cîteaux was declared to be entitled to an armchair in the Estates of Burgundy. This decision was made by the king himself, who dismissed a claim by the bishop of Autun that he alone was entitled to an armchair in the Burgundian assembly.[91] Similarly, Villeroy, the archbishop of Lyons and "primate of the Gauls," insisted on his "primacy" over the archbishop of Rouen, who happened to be the younger son of the great minister Colbert ("primacy" implied such privileges as standing closer to the royal prie-dieu along with certain rights of appeal, officiality, and devolution of benefices). Louis XIV served as arbiter in this hierarchical dispute as well (aided in this instance by a *maître des requêtes*). On a single day, he convened two council meetings to deal with this matter alone and in the end found in favor of young Colbert.[92] But the Villeroys, who held high positions in Lyons and at Versailles, found a way to take their revenge: availing themselves of various favors, they "saw to it that two Villeroy archbishops of Lyons would take precedence over more senior archbishops when admitted to the Ordre du Saint-Esprit."[93]

The ultimate snobbery of the sacred was exemplified by the requirements for admission to the Strasbourg chapter of canons, whose members—counts as well as canons—were required to provide proof of their noble birth.[94] Rank was a sensitive issue in Strasbourg because Alsace had once been a part of Germany, whose aristocracy was famous for its haughtiness. No one could be admitted to the chapter without proof "based on duly notarized documents indicating sixteen quarters of high paternal nobility and an equal amount of maternal nobility": in other words, candidates were expected to provide proof of the existence of thirty-two male and female forebears belonging, in the case of Germans, to a family of princes or counts of the Empire or, in the case of the French, to a family of dukes and peers or marshals of France.[95] "Owing to these strict standards, the chapter became the patrimony of a few families." Contrast this with the chapters of Languedoc, which in this period were largely open to commoners. Nevertheless, Louis XIV, who sought to Gallicize the ultra-selective Strasbourg chapter and find places in it for his protégés, managed to gain admission for Armand de Rohan, the son of Mme de Soubise, an old friend who may or may not have been his mistress.[96]

Hierarchy also intersected with religion in the universities, which were of course deeply involved in training a competent clergy. When a high noble destined for the priesthood (and ultimately a bishop's miter) defended his thesis—be he the son or bastard of a prince, duke, or minister, a Bouillon, Orléans, Colbert, or Chamillart—the entire court would turn out to view the spectacle, except for the younger La Rochefoucauld, who never left the king's vicinity. This provided yet another opportunity for disputes, as dukes vied with *parlementaires* for priority. Despite what Saint-Simon says, the latter seem to have come out on top in many instances. But when it came time for a bastard grandson of the Princess Palatine to defend his thesis, she claimed the right (unheard of for a woman) to listen to the proceedings—and not only that, to listen while seated in an armchair. Nothing of the kind had ever been seen at the Sorbonne.[97] But this would not be the last such episode.

Holidays were another excellent occasion for displaying ranks and subranks, estates and corporations, in their requisite order. Processions were especially suitable for this purpose because they were built around the spatial representation of rank. In the annual Assumption procession commemorating Louis XIII's dedication of his kingdom to the Virgin, the Parlement of Paris claimed the right to march ahead of the regent. Saint-Simon's commentaries on the ensuing ruckus are a useful source of information.[98] Among the precedents he cites, based on ancient records, was a procession in 1557 marking the capture of Calais, in which prelates were followed by the king, princes of the blood, duchesses, countesses, and so on, with Parlement and the Chambre des Comptes bringing up the rear.[99]

Were processions always rank-ordered? No. For penitential purposes, the usual hierarchies were sometimes tampered with. In the time of the Ligue or perhaps even earlier, Henri III ignored his exalted rank and joined parades of pious penitents, flagellants, and mortifiers of the flesh. Traces of this penchant for self-humiliation can be found in the *Memoirs.* Saint-Simon makes fun of the behavior of Adrien, duc de Noailles, who in 1722 was exiled by the regent to his estate (located between Tulle and Aurillac).[100] "There the duke played at being pious, wore a cope in processions and at parish lecterns, and provoked laughter both at home and in Paris, where people knew him and where, the better to please the regent, he had kept an actress from the very first days of the Regency." Saint-Simon had similarly derisive words, no doubt mixed with rage, for Henri de Lorraine, duc de Guise, who was assassinated in 1588. In order to curry favor with priests and townspeople, the duke had conceived the odd idea of having himself named honorary churchwarden of his parish as well as councilor in Parlement, a ridiculous title when applied to a *grand seigneur.*[101] Saint-Simon was scornful of the self-abasing behavior of men like Noailles and Guise because he believed that it was motivated by false piety. For our purposes, however, such behavior, whatever its motivation, serves to underscore the fact that religious processions and other pious activities could either reinforce the hierarchy or undermine it for evangelical reasons that people more or less clearly understood. Although Catholicism sometimes had egalitarian implications, Tocqueville was obviously wrong to think that this was always the case.

Finally, one finds in Saint-Simon a whole realm of the sacred, or rather the supernatural, which, though not Christian, nevertheless involved quasi-religious or sacrilegious rites. Fortune-telling comes under this head. Mme Du Perchois told the comte de Coëtquen that he would be die by drowning, for example.[102] Saint-Simon scolded the youth for his "mad and dangerous curiosity" and denounced the ignorance of fortune-tellers. But another soothsayer in Amiens made the same prediction, and in fact the young aristocrat did drown in the Scheldt in June 1693 while his entire regiment looked on. Similarly, the younger son of the maréchal d'Humières was killed in Luxembourg in 1684, and his death "had been so clearly and accurately foretold that he mentioned it to friends as something about which he had not the slightest doubt."[103] Saint-Simon's attitude toward such things was ambivalent. As a Christian, he warned against mysterious and supernatural powers of divination, yet they made an undeniable impression on him. He did not like to believe in such things, yet they caused him to tremble in spite of himself.[104] Catholic theology sought to circumscribe the supernatural, but to Saint-Simon it was of far wider import than the theologians imagined. In 1706, for instance, a little girl looked into a glass of water and interpreted what she saw as a sign that the king's sons and grandsons would die and the duc d'Orléans would one day become regent.[105] And so it came to pass. Saint-Simon disapproved of such things as machinations of the devil, but he did not discount their claims to veracity.

Saint-Simon was more skeptical about a woman in the Sarre said to be possessed by the devil and upon whom an exorcism was performed. Even without firsthand knowledge of the case, he concluded that the victim was either mad or a poor wretch looking for a way to get food.[106] It had been a long time since anyone—even a man as attached as Saint-Simon to the age of Louis XIII—believed that it was possible for a whole town to be possessed, as at Loudun.

Or consider another case, this one involving a blacksmith from Salon-de-Provence, a character out of Nostradamus, who in 1699 had a vision in which he saw the late queen, Louis XIV's erstwhile wife, many years after her death, in the shape of a blonde woman standing next to a tree in Provence. Later, the same visionary told the king of a ghost he had seen in the forests of Saint-Germain, where the specter had supposedly manifested itself in the hope of inducing Louis XIV to make official his secret marriage to Mme de Maintenon.[107] To believe Saint-Simon and his colleagues, this story was as true as the king was noble. Here, too, sacrality and hierarchy were linked, even if the sacred element in this case had a strong odor of the heretical about it. The writer of the *Memoirs* also reported on another ghost in whose existence he believed, Marshal Fabert's "familiar spirit," with which the soldier had argued about religion late into the night while a friend lay sleeping in his bed. What is more, the spirit in question had lent Fabert a helping hand that had enabled this grandson of a peasant and son of a bookseller to become a marshal of France.[108]

And then there was a man by the name of d'Effiat, an alleged murderer who, in his eighties, shortly before his death, conversed nightly between the hours of seven and nine with mysterious visitors said to be the devil's minions.[109] Saint-Simon's credulity in this instance will come as less of a surprise if we remember that his library contained works by De Lancre published under Louis XIII and possibly inherited from his father, along with various speculative works about deviltry. In this respect, too, Saint-Simon demonstrated his nostalgia for the age of Louis XIII, the king he loved so well. This interest in deviltry lends a certain piquancy to his comparison of Maine and Noailles, two men he thoroughly disliked, to Satan himself.

The Pure and the Impure

Hierarchy has an affinity for the sacred as iron filings have an affinity for magnets. But it is repelled by the impure. The opposition of sacred to profane, with which we dealt in the previous chapter, is therefore reinforced by the opposition of pure to impure, to which we turn next.

Louis Dumont discussed this problem at length in connection with the castes of India. The purest castes, such as the Brahmins, are expected to avoid physical contact with members of lower castes and to perform rituals of purification after certain types of bodily secretion (defecation, menstruation, and so forth). Frequent bathing ensures cleanliness, and purity is hedged about by various taboos. For instance, pipes cannot be shared by members of different castes lest the pure lips of a high-caste individual come into indirect contact with the impure lips of a person of lower caste.[1]

In a hierarchical society such as the court of France (which epitomized European cascades of contempt in their most refined form), things were different. To begin with, there were no castes in Louis XIV's entourage but only ranks. Moreover, while high-ranking contemporaries of the Sun King could be just as demanding in regard to physical cleanliness as any Brahmin, they were concerned with different parts of the body.

Brahmins cleanse the body's exterior: the skin. By contrast, in the highest circles of French society at the turn of the eighteenth century, people were primarily concerned with purifying the body's insides: men and women of quality used emetics to induce vomiting, clysters to administer enemas, and lancets to let blood.[2] Taboos concerning excrement did exist, but they were weak, much weaker than they are today. Saint-Simon devoted page after page of the *Memoirs* to purgatives and commodes, including the commodes used by the king of France, the Spanish royal couple, and Mme de Maintenon. Many distinguished gentlemen took a keen interest in purging their systems, among them the stalwart Richelieu. The old duke was in the habit of taking cassia every night and often an enema in the morning, after which he would "walk around for three or four hours and then, wherever he happened to be, unburden himself" in a commode "so copiously that the bowl could scarcely hold it all."[3] Every month Louis XIV submitted to what were called *jours de médecine*, or medicine days, which in fact meant purges. These became even more important after Dr. Fagon, a proponent of the clyster, replaced Dr. d'Aquin, who favored bleeding. After the king was purged, a mass was said and the royal family visited the sovereign in his bed. On these occasions le Grand Dauphin remained on his feet, but the duc du Maine was allowed to sit on a stool because of his lameness.[4] This was also the only day on which Mme de Maintenon would visit her husband as she might visit a sick friend. Since their marriage was secret, the king normally went to see her, rather than vice versa.[5]

Bleeding was also seen as essential for maintaining a vital equilibrium. Saint-Simon was not the first to insist on its importance. The higher a person's rank in society, the more frequently he or she was bled and purged. Indeed, Louis XIII died as a result of such treatment. Never once does Saint-Simon express the slightest doubt about the reasonableness of drawing blood or cleansing the intestines. Even when he developed a phlegmon as a result of repeated bleedings, he never questioned the corporation of surgeons or their methods. He held Mareschal, the king's first surgeon as well as a pious man of Jansenist bent, in the highest esteem. Madame was more dubious, but like it or not, she submitted to purgation and bloodletting as did everyone else of august rank. Gloomily she came to believe that these procedures for cleansing the body's internal plumbing were indeed a good and necessary thing. Beneath an engraving by Abraham Bosse entitled "The Doctor and the Bloodletting," one can read this caption: "Bleeding with the lancet cleanses the mind and purifies the blood of all that is rotten."[6]

Piero Camporesi has shown that these cathartic techniques were among a range of procedures used to purify the body and rid it of pollution, to say nothing of demons.[7] Sometimes combinations of purgatives and emetics were used, along with lotions, plasters, and vesicants, to treat tapeworms, black and melancholic humors, pituitary engorgement, and phlegmatic excess, even though these treatments sometimes induced nervous exhaustion in the patient. The recourse to such hypercathartic techniques was intimately related to an obsession with filth and a medical-religious ideology that Camporesi relates to baroque witch-hunting. This purgative conception of medicine can be traced all the way back to Hippocrates and Galen. It was perpetuated by an academic hierarchy within the social hierarchy. Apothecaries provided an arsenal of medications, including hellebore and various emetics (which "exorcised, obsessed, and made martyrs" of their clients), while physicians and surgeons wielded the clyster and lancet. Meanwhile, as Camporesi also shows, women discreetly relied on a gentler regime of herbal medicine, which tended to be nonhierarchical in its administration as well as soothing in its results.

The focal point of the French obsession with purity was therefore different from that of Brahmin India. French "hierarchs" were not much concerned with prohibiting contact with excrement or menstrual blood but insisted on the need for deep internal cleansing. Saint-Simon was, of course, also concerned with symbolic and hereditary taints in the blood, with congenital "blemishes" and sexual vice, as was the Princess Palatine.[8]

Tainted blood. Execution by decapitation did not impugn the honor of the executed man's family, but putting a man to the wheel deprived his kin of their good name. This was especially true in Germany and the Netherlands, according to Saint-Simon, "because in those countries there is a large and important difference among the penalties imposed upon persons of quality who commit crimes. So ignominious is the wheel that no noble chapter will accept a victim's uncles, aunts, brothers, sisters, or any of their progeny for three generations. Such a death is thus not only a source of shame but a material disadvantage, for it precludes pardon, prevents marriages, and dashes any hopes the family might have had of obtaining places in abbeys and sovereign bishoprics." Take the Horn family, which had been known in the Netherlands since the eleventh century. Among its forebears were two men whose heads had been honorably severed in the sixteenth century. When the count van Horn murdered a speculator in 1720, the family therefore pleaded to have him decapitated rather than broken on the wheel.[9] Their pleas went unheeded.

Congenital blemishes and sexual deviance. For Saint-Simon, the chief issue here was the question of royal bastards, who introduced the greatest possible impurity (illegitimate birth) into the heart of what was supposed to be the sanctuary of ultimate purity (the royal person and family). In his eyes, illegitimacy was therefore an absolute scandal. Young Louis XIII felt the same way, according to Madeleine Foisil, and it was therefore perfectly understandable that bastardy should have so enraged Saint-Simon (and to a lesser extent Madame). To us the scandal is hard to fathom only because we no longer grasp the logic and rules of a system based on hierarchy. To be born a child of adultery or fornication was to be stamped with a mark of impurity antithetical to all sacred values. A statute of the Ordre du Saint-Esprit adopted in 1597 stated that "no bastard shall be admitted to the order unless he be a recognized and legitimized bastard of a king."[10] (Naturally this exception displeased Saint-Simon.) Partially excluded from the order, bastards were prohibited from holding the royal communion cloth.

Saint-Simon used violent language in speaking of the royal bastards of both sexes whom Louis XIV "shamelessly" married off to princes and princesses of the blood and even in one case to a grandson of France. The *petit duc*'s vehement words make it clear that illegitimacy constituted a threat to the very idea of purity. On this point, one could easily cite dozens of passages from the *Memoirs*. I will limit myself to summarizing one of several places in which Saint-Simon sets forth the principles that underlie his thinking on the matter.[11] He begins by roundly condemning the marriage of the duc de Chartres (son of Monsieur, the king's brother) to the king's daughter by Mme de Montespan (Chartres, of course, later became the duc d'Orléans and regent of France). He also has harsh words for the marriage of Monsieur le Duc (a prince of the blood and a Condé) to a sister of the new duchesse de Chartres, also a bastard. He then goes on to note that the (legitimate) daughters of these two half-bastard marriages subsequently entered into still other unions, which corrupted the progeny of a Berry and a Conti, the king's grandson and nephew respectively. Another bastard, whose mother was Mme La Vallière, had married a Conti of the previous generation but "thank God" had had no children. Saint-Simon even went so far as to allege that William of Orange became an enemy of France when he refused to marry a royal bastard, leading to wars that proved disastrous for the French state and gave rise to the many miseries that afflicted the country after 1700. And he forcefully linked the theme of impurity to the mixing of blood and the violation of boundaries: "This *mixing* of *the purest blood* of our kings, and one boldly dares to say, of the entire universe, with the *foul muck* of double adultery has thus been the steady work of the king's entire life. He has done his utmost to achieve a *mixing never seen* in any previous century."

The marriage, life, and death of the duc de Chartres, the future regent, were of paramount importance in shaping Saint-Simon's thinking about impurity. The *Memoirs* open with the wedding of young Philippe, thus under the sign of bastardy. And they end with the death of the same Philippe, by then duc d'Orléans and regent, in the arms of a courtesan, hence in the shadow of adultery and ultimate damnation. That the marriage of "Chartres-Orléans"[12] represented the ultimate in impurity for Saint-Simon is clear from his choice of chapter title: "Marriage of the duc d'Orléans, . . . *intrigues* associated with this marriage, *shame* of Monsieur, very public *despair* of Madame, *embarrassment* of Monsieur le duc de Chartres, *stupor* of the Court, *rage* of Madame la Duchesse, elder sister of the bride."[13]

This marriage soiled everything it touched and everyone who touched it. The original sin of Dubois, the future cardinal and epitome of all vice, was to have persuaded Chartres to consent to such a bastard union.[14] The taint spread from Dubois to Noailles, whose crime was to have been an "old associate" of Dubois's long before he became a cardinal.[15] It comes as no surprise, then, when Saint-Simon forcefully sums up the situation in yet another chapter title alluding to the "abyssal horrors" of the duc de Noailles.[16] Indeed, the bastard Maine, the "pro-bastard" Dubois, and the "pro-Dubois" Noailles are among the arch-villains of the *Memoirs*.[17]

In Saint-Simon's admittedly biased view, the remainder of the duc d'Orléans's life and career was dominated by his relations with bastards and their kin, who repeatedly figure in the chapter titles of the *Memoirs*.[18] To begin with, there were Orléans's relations with his own bastards, whom he shamelessly indulged after he came to power: "The chevalier d'Orléans, a legitimized bastard of M. le duc d'Orléans, [scandalously] obtains the grand priory of France, the abbey of Auvillé, the generalship of the galleys, and the title of grandee of Spain."[19] Then there were the duke's conflicts with Vendôme, who was the descendant of one of Henri IV's bastards and stigmatized as such by Saint-Simon. And finally there were the duke's relations with the bastards of Louis XIV, who insulted him endlessly but whom he nevertheless treated with "surprising sympathy."[20] His wife, the duchesse d'Orléans, also demonstrated "extreme folly in regard to her royal bastardy."[21]

Orléans's reprehensible indulgence of bastards extended to other European dynasties as well. He treated a bastard son of the Elector of Bavaria as though the man were the product of one of his own adulterous relationships, having him named a grandee of Spain, the same honor he bestowed on his own illegitimate son. He also prevented the young man from fighting a duel and promoted his military career.[22] When Saint-Simon was not railing against the "foul muck of double adultery," he was describing Paris as the "sewer which gathered in the spawn of all Europe's sensuality," an allusion to the Parisianized offspring of any number of the continent's princes, not just Louis XIV. "Foul muck" and "sewer" are related notes in the key of the impure:

> The taste, example, and favor of the late king [as adulterous lover and father] had made of Paris a sewer which gathered in the spawn of all Europe's sensuality, and this state of affairs continued long after him. In addition to the late king's mistresses, there were his bastards and those of Charles

IX (including the widow of one and her daughter), the bastards of Henri IV, [who made] a vast fortune, the two [bastard] branches of the Bourbon brothers Malauze and Busset, the Vertus, bastards of the last duc de Bretagne, the bastard daughters of the last three Condés, and even the Rothelins, bastards of a bastard, to wit, a younger brother of Longueville . . . [the very] Rothelins who have lately presumed to pass themselves off as somebodies and, by having the gall to crown themselves princes of the blood, have almost persuaded other people that they truly are. Besides this mob of French bastards, Paris has also welcomed the mistresses of the kings of England and Sardinia, two mistresses of the Elector of Bavaria, and countless bastards from England, Bavaria, Savoy, Denmark, Saxony, and even Lorraine, all of whom have made huge fortunes there and amassed heaps of orders and commissions and an endless variety of favors and distinctions, including some of the highest honors and ranks, though none of them would have drawn so much as a second look in any other country in Europe. And last but not least, there was even that most vile fruit of a thoroughly monstrous and notorious case of incest involving the young duc de Montbéliard, the scion of a family that has had the audacity to put itself forward as a maker of princes. . . . It should be added, however, that in the midst of all this scum, which no other nation but France would have dreamed of taking in, there were two men, one a bastard from England and the other from Saxony, who rendered glorious service to the state as military commanders.[23]

This passage is as intriguing as it is impassioned. The wife and daughter-in-law of a bastard of Charles IX are summarily branded with the illegitimacy of a man who was husband to one and father-in-law to the other, even though both women were perfectly legitimate under the rules governing birth and marriage. In this general indictment of bastards, however, Saint-Simon grants exceptions to two, both of whom happen to have been marshals of France and military heroes: Saxe and Berwick. It was as if the warrior virtues, traditionally the monopoly of blue blood, somehow compensated for or redeemed the foul corruption of their ignoble birth.

This "sewer" passage is crucial. It proves that Saint-Simon's hatred was not limited solely to *royal* bastards because of the political danger they represented owing to their potential claim on the throne. His passion was far more comprehensive than that: it was of an existential order, directed at bastards in general, or in any case, at bastards of the high nobility, whose exalted rank was impugned by the mark of the impure. Saint-Simon's aversion to bastards knows no bounds: he even goes so far as to associate the taint of illegitimacy with the ultimate impurity, incest. In discussing the Montbéliard bastards, he mentions their "audacity," "their intrigues, their impudence," and last but not least, "their hypocrisy" and "egregious incest."[24] Had not Léopold-Eberhard, prince de Montbéliard, arranged marriages between pairs of his illegitimate offspring (by different mistresses to be sure)?[25] It comes as no surprise to learn that the prince's attempt to legitimize his dubious progeny was "denounced by the Aulic Council" in Germany, while much to Saint-Simon's relief a royal edict in Paris "relegated this vile rabble" to the pit from which they had crawled.[26] Nor is it surprising to learn that these incestuous bastards were also devoted followers of the Jesuits, the Sulpiciens, and the Rohans—three additional marks of infamy in Saint-Simon's eyes.[27]

It may be worth pointing out, moreover, that the English word "bastard" can be translated into French as *salaud*. Attested in French since at least the sixteenth century (according to Littré), *salaud* is of course etymologically linked to *saleté*, or filth.

In a sense, quantitative history bears Saint-Simon out. In earlier periods there were substantial numbers of bastards in France, especially noble bastards, although illegitimate births never outnumbered legitimate ones. But in his own time, the late seventeenth and early eighteenth century, illegitimate children were extremely rare. This suggests that most French men and women had calmly and resolutely embraced and internalized the antibastard values that Saint-Simon exemplified with an energy bordering on the fanatic. In the Beauvaisis in the time of Louis XIV, just half of 1 percent of all births were illegitimate. In Crulai in Normandy between 1604 and 1799, the figure was six-tenths of 1 percent. In more indulgent areas such as the Auge region, the illegitimacy rate stood somewhere between 2 and 5 percent, no higher. And in the middle of the eighteenth century, it was just 1.2 percent for all of France, including cities as well as rural areas. Compare that to the 12 percent illegitimacy rate of the 1970s. In the age of Louis XIV and Louis XV, it was only in such exceptional social groups as the children of the monarch and the proletariat of a large city such as Paris that one finds significantly higher rates of illegitimacy, which was all the more "condemnable" as a result.[28]

Owing to his phobic hatred of bastards, Saint-Simon developed views that may have been extravagant but were nonetheless vigorously and logically argued. He established in his own mind a connection between his preoccupation with hierarchical purity and the injunctions of Christian morality. In this synthesis, one finds elements of a certain traditional distrust of the sexual instincts and amorous passion unconstrained by social preference and ecclesiastical sacrament: "We were dealing with a man who was not only deaf but, worse than that, in love," Saint-Simon wrote of his relative Sandricourt, whom he tried in vain to talk out of a foolish mismarriage to Mlle de Gourgue.[29]

Let us pause for a moment to consider the terms in which Saint-Simon discusses the impure. In speaking of bastards, his images are excremental: "foul muck" (boue infecte) and "sewer of sensuality" (égout des voluptés). When describing less egregious forms of impurity having more to do with base origins than with illegitimacy, he uses words like "dregs" (lie) and "mire" (bourbe). Here the allusion is not to excrement but to the residue at the bottom of the wine barrel or the filth of the swamp. For instance, speaking of the Lantis, descendants of the Della Roveres from whose midst came Pope Sixtus IV in 1471, Saint-Simon writes: "Before their pontificate these Roveres belonged to the dregs of the populace: Francesco Della Rovere was the son of a fisherman from somewhere near Savona."[30] Never mind that for two centuries already, from 1471 to the time at which Saint-Simon wrote, the Della Roveres had enjoyed any number of impressive papal distinctions: nothing could hide the fact that they sprang from the "dregs of the populace" and once hauled fishnets to the sea. Cardinal Sala stood even closer to the "dregs" and was therefore even more repulsive.[31] "This monk sprang from the dregs of the populace, was a coachman in his youth, and then became a Benedictine in order to have bread to eat and to make something of himself.[32] He had a peculiar cast of mind and an odd notion of enterprise, which led him to stir the people of Barcelona to revolt against the king of Spain and to play a leading role in the Catalonian rebellion, [so much so that] he was seen as the heart and soul of the archduke's party."[33] (The Spanish king, Philip V, Cardinal Sala's nemesis, was in many respects one of Saint-Simon's "cherished few," a symbolic substitute for the defunct duc de Bourgogne, his brother, as we shall see in greater detail later on when we discuss Saint-Simon's embassy to Madrid during the Regency.)

"This Sala was a wild man capable of anything." Note that wildness is here adduced as characteristic of the dregs of the populace, notorious for their hot temper, which could boil over just as grape mash will froth at certain stages of the fermentation process. Pope Julius II, nephew of Sixtus IV, also sprang from the dregs, and to Saint-Simon he, too, was a wild man. In the Cévennes, moreover, the dregs among the Camisard rebels were wild men as well, yet they succeeded in inflicting the ultimate humiliation on an army led by the comte de Broglie, a mediocre military commander whom Saint-Simon vilifies on account of his connections with Basville and the Jesuits: "A few [Camisard] leaders were hanged after being captured in small skirmishes.[34] They all came from the dregs of the populace, and the hangings neither daunted their party nor slowed it down."

Obviously, the "dregs of the populace" were at the opposite extreme from the high aristocracy, so Saint-Simon believed that marriages between these two groups were by their very nature mismatches: "The duc de Saint-Aignan [a widower who had been married to a Servien, a woman whose family included dukes and ministers] had committed the folly of choosing for his next wife a creature from the dregs of the populace, who began by taking care of his wife's dogs and later rose to become her chambermaid."[35] In this instance, the phrase "dregs of the populace" is a purely sociological concept, not a value judgment. Despite her low origin, the woman in question (who actually sprang from a family of the lesser nobility) was witty and virtuous. Indeed, she "was so modest . . . [and] lived such a withdrawn and virtuous life that she commanded respect throughout her lifetime, which was long."[36] To say that she came from the "dregs," then, meant not so much that her birth was ignoble but that she had performed a degrading service (taking care of the first duchess's dogs). It was in this sense that Mme de Maintenon could be said to have sprung from the "dregs of the populace," because she had performed degrading services for Mme de Neuillan when she was an adolescent.[37] Indeed, upon "returning young and poor from America," the future Mme de Maintenon "ended up living with Mme de Neuillan in Poitou. That lady could not bring herself to give the young woman bread without requiring her to perform some service. She therefore bestowed upon the girl the keys to her loft so that she might supervise the feeding of hay and oats to the horses." The young woman was also assigned the job of tending turkeys.

Also less pejorative than "foul muck" and "sewer of sensuality" (with their excretory associations) was *bourbe*, meaning "mire" or "mud" and thus hinting at plebeian and indeed rural peasant origins: "No gown was shorter than that of the Chauvelins, who had been barefoot peasants without judicial pretensions when the fortune of Chancellor Le Tellier plucked them from the mire *(les débourba)*."[38] In fact, the Chauvelins were descended from a *procureur* who had served in Nivernais under François I.[39] Such—metaphorically speaking—was the mud in which the Chauvelins had once waded without shoes, according to Saint-Simon, who immediately linked this metaphor with other themes associated in his mind with impurity: monstrosity, forbidden mixing, homosexuality (purely figurative in this instance), and even Jesuitism. When Louis Chauvelin, the *avocat général* whom Saint-Simon saw as having sprung from the mire, became treasurer of the Ordre du Saint-Esprit and thus eligible to wear the *cordon bleu*, Saint-Simon was quick to plunge the dagger in: "An *avocat général* [that is, a magistrate of relatively low rank, much inferior to a *premier président*] wearing a *cordon bleu* seemed such a *monstrous* thing that even Parlement was revolted, but this *avocat général* was the darling of the Jesuits and therefore the king's favorite."[40] For Saint-Simon as for all theorists of the impure, the ideal of purity was intimately associated with a repugnance for the mixed and therefore the monstrous.[41] When the bastard Maine was unfairly elevated to the rank of royal heir, he became a "monster of grandeur," a master of "infernal deceit" who for his own purposes manipulated *premier président* de Mesmes in the depths of the "swamp" *(bourbier)* in which that magistrate habitually wallowed.[42]

A swamp compounded in this instance of personal immorality and base (peasant) origins: if the Chauvelins waded barefoot in the muck, the Mesmes had long plodded through it in *sabots*, or wooden shoes, symbols of their rustic roots. "These Mesmes are *peasants* from Mont-de-Marsan. The first to leave his *sabots* behind was a professor of law in Toulouse, whom the sister of François I hired to tend to her affairs."[43] With his usual flair for exaggeration, Saint-Simon lists the various clerical and judicial employments that enabled the Mesmes to "wipe" the mud off themselves, ascend to the nobility (of the robe), obtain exemption from taxes, and even, as "base" as they were, to marry their sons to daughters of the high nobility.

Two other words that Saint-Simon was fond of using to denote sociological impurity were *crasse*, or filth, and *vilain*, which can mean villein as well as "sordid." *Vilain* evoked medieval serfdom, which was a thing of the past in the seventeenth century except in a few provinces of eastern France. Saint-Simon applied the word to ennobled descendants of bourgeois or peasants who agreed to let their sons marry daughters of the nobility "for nothing," that is, without dowry. If the daughter-in-law's illustrious lineage expired for want of a male heir, these usurpers were then in a position to lay hands on the entire fortune.[44] In speaking of such *vilains*, Mme de Sévigné kept a rather cooler head than Saint-Simon: she referred to them as turkeys in peacock feathers.[45]

"Filth" was a word that Saint-Simon applied on occasion to the king's secretaries of state, who had succeeded in "cleansing" themselves of their modest condition as royal scribes to become personages of almost ministerial rank.[46] They resorted to a variety of procedures to "to scrape the mud off their lives" *(décrasser leur existence)*. "When they were mere royal notaries, they used to be caked with it." By these means "the secretaries of state became first half-breeds, then apes, then phantoms, courtiers of a sort and men of quality. . . . Gradually, they rid themselves of the filth of their origins. . . . These pygmies turned into giants and at last shed the mud of their notarial offices." Here we encounter a mild form of the concept of impurity or filth, which as usual is associated with the concepts of mixture (half-breed, ape), disproportion (pygmies becoming giants), and insubstantiality (the secretaries' phantomlike state is the result of an incomplete transition from social insignificance to full-fledged existence).

The bastard is a more extreme instance of the same type: all exemplify a general form of sociological impurity, which afflicts individuals who lack self-respect and attempt to escape from the sordid condition Providence presumably intended them to occupy.

The passion to promote the fortunes of bastards was therefore an affront to common decency. It was this passion that unhinged Louis XIV, a monarch normally courteous and "proportionate" in his behavior toward men and women of all conditions. When his son Maine was accused (perhaps wrongly) of incompetence and cowardice in battle, the vexed monarch broke a reed cane over the back of the valet who happened to be serving him dinner.[47]

A legitimate child issued from the sacrament of marriage, whereas a bastard was the issue of a crime.[48] Nevertheless, there were men of the cloth prepared to rise to the defense of the illegitimate. Naturally Saint-Simon was not one to let pass an opportunity to criticize the Jesuits on this score. It was indeed true that Father Daniel of the Society of Jesus alluded in his *Histoire de France* to the existence of Merovingian kings who were also bastards, although he was more discreet about it than Saint-Simon lets on.[49] The *petit duc* roundly condemned the Jesuit for implying that "such bastardy was capable of ascending to the throne" and expressed regret that the book had been so successful with the king, who was of course delighted by it, not to mention the general public. "Everyone snapped it up, including the women."

Another case in which the implications of bastardy were far-reaching was that of the Soubises, whom Saint-Simon detested. François de Rohan-Montbazon, prince de Soubise (1631–1712), counted among his ancestors of the previous century the bastard son of the last duke of Brittany. In the eyes of Saint-Simon, this was no claim to glory, and ordinarily it should have been enough to bar the prince's son from admission to Strasbourg's canonical chapter, which suffered from the Germanic allergy to bastards no matter how remote. But that was not all: even worse was the allegation that Soubise had acted as pimp for his wife, whom he had supposedly prostituted to Louis XIV in exchange for substantial rewards. On top of that, the prince's great-grandfather on his mother's side, La Varenne, had supposedly held the degrading position of chef to Henri IV, and he, too, had allegedly acted as pimp in service of that monarch's pleasures. To add insult to injury, moreover, he became, at the end of his life, an ally of the Jesuits.[50]

Bastardy, procuration, Jesuitry, and violation of a canonical chapter's hierarchical scruples: by Saint-Simon's scheme of values, the Soubises deserved to be condemned four times over. And for good measure, the charges were largely false and slanderous. Soubise and his wife were honorable people, not the Sun King's pimp and whore. Indeed, the lady had never even been the king's mistress. La Varenne had been in youth not a kitchen boy but an equerry of the royal kitchens—not nearly as base an office as Saint-Simon pretends. As historians of the court system, however, what matters to us is not the actual facts—these would interest the positivist historian—but rather the ideological models that guided Saint-Simon's pen.

The prince de Soubise was not the only person who raised the snobbish writer's hackles. Saint-Simon also alludes to the "*soubisquesque* infamy" of the marquis de Prye, who allowed his wife to become the mistress of Monsieur le Duc, the man who became prime minister after the regent's death.[51]

Just as an anti-Semite may say, "Some of my best friends are Jews," Saint-Simon might have said that some of his best friends were bastards. Despite his hatred for the fruit of adulterous relationships, the *petit duc* felt a certain sympathy for the comte de Toulouse, the bastard son of Louis XIV and Mme de Montespan who became an admiral. Or at any rate, if what he felt was not exactly sympathy, it might be characterized as "benign neglect."[52] To be sure, Toulouse was neither abominable nor monstrous, whereas the duc du Maine was allegedly both. Toulouse was a cold, not to say glacial, individual, curt and abrupt in manner, upright and honest in character, and blunt and candid in his dealings, not quick-witted but valiant and enterprising. As can be seen from this description, Saint-Simon was not hostile to him and on balance perhaps even rather well disposed.[53]

The writer exhibited a similar tolerance for the maréchal de Saxe, the bastard son of the king of Poland and Maria Aurora von Königsmark.[54] The source of his sympathy was Saxe's victory at Fontenoy in 1745. Saxe had a notable ancestry: his adulterous mother's brother was Philip Christoph, count von Königsmark (1640–94), who became the lover of the duchess of Hanover. The jealous duke had him burned alive in a lime oven or, in a more plausible version of the story, had him killed and then buried in lime.[55]

Berwick, another illegitimate offshoot of a royal line and illustrious soldier, also found grace in Saint-Simon's eyes. His military virtues earned him an esteem comparable to that reserved for Saxe and Toulouse. Berwick was "gentle, reliable, loyal, vigilant, and energetic."[56] For Saint-Simon, Berwick was the exceptional bastard who proved the rule. He held him up in contrast to his enemy Vendôme, who was that dreadful abomination, the legitimate descendant of a royal bastard.[57] The maréchal de Puységur, Berwick's friend and Vendôme's enemy, who did his best to bury Vendôme completely after his disgrace, serves Saint-Simon as a convenient touchstone for highlighting the difference between the "good but illegitimate" Berwick and the "evil bastard" Vendôme.[58] The eagle-eyed writer was thus willing to forgive the bastard who proved competent and courageous in battle, whether on land (Saxe and Berwick) or sea (Toulouse), but Vendôme, who was not even a genuine bastard, was not entitled to such indulgence. Was this perhaps because he was (allegedly) a sodomite?

To sum up, then, the bastard, notwithstanding the few exceptions just mentioned, was the antithesis of the aristocrat. An aristocrat was courageous, generous, and valiant in battle, whereas a bastard was cowardly and greedy. The duc du Maine "trembles in his wife's presence. He is always deathly afraid that she might lose her head."[59] With his infernal spirit, the timid and clumsy Maine was "an utter poltroon in heart and mind."[60] By contrast, his wife, a legitimate daughter of the Condés, hence of the most precious royal blood, was characterized as "courageous to excess, enterprising, audacious. She treated her husband like a Negro and made him bow and scrape before her. . . . She drove him with a stick."[61] The contrast between the cowardice of impure blood and the bravery of pure blood could hardly be better drawn. D'Antin, too, was pusillanimous in war, according to Saint-Simon.[62] (One is tempted to say, Let him who has never been afraid in combat cast the first stone.) True, d'Antin may have been born legitimate, but through his mother, Mme de Montespan, he was the half-brother of Louis XIV's bastards. In any event, Saint-Simon tends to lump him together with the latter, his brothers in infamy.

A bastard was not only fearful but also greedy, in contrast to the munificence of the great lord born of lawful wedlock. For example, the princesse de Carignan ("bastard daughter of the duc de Savoie and the comtesse de Verue") and her husband exhibited "unparalleled greediness." The couple "raked it in by the handful on all sides, a hundred-franc profit here, a gain of a million there, including several million from Mississippi."[63] Yet Saint-Simon himself had made half a million in Mississippi, so that one might have thought that he was hardly in a position to cast stones at the Carignans.[64]

Besides being greedy and pusillanimous, the bastard race was also by nature treacherous. Betrayal dogged its steps and afflicted even its marriages through a kind of contagion. The marquis de Lassay married a somewhat crazy bastard daughter of Monsieur le Prince (Condé), so of course it was only fitting that Lassay later betrayed Condé for the sake of his bastards.[65] Betrayal became hereditary: Elisabeth, princesse d'Espinoy, was the daughter of a bastard daughter of Charles IV de Lorraine and Béatrix de Cuzance.[66] The reader will not be surprised to learn that treachery was in Elisabeth's blood: she passed the secrets of the French court to the Habsburgs in Vienna and spied on the duchesse de Bourgogne on behalf of Mme de Maintenon.[67]

Given Saint-Simon's views on the matter, he naturally believed that bastards should not reproduce: like the mule, born of the coupling of a horse with an ass, the bastard should have been condemned to sterility by nature. Even Louis XIV said of his own illegitimate sons that "no issue should come of such species," but he never made his practice coincide with his theory and ultimately arranged proper marriages for his bastard offspring. When a possible bastard line was nipped in the bud, Saint-Simon rejoiced: "Though married, the unacknowledged bastard daughter of the late Monseigneur died without children," he noted twice, thereby doubling his pleasure at this minuscule triumph.[68] Similarly, in 1713, he carefully concealed his private satisfaction at the death without children and in impoverished circumstances of Charles IX's "bastard daughter-in-law," by which he meant the belated (and legitimately born) bride of Charles's elderly illegitimate son, who, as Saint-Simon himself readily concedes, was a perfectly pious and virtuous gentleman.[69]

It was better for a bastard line to die out lest the indelible stain reappear in subsequent generations. All the water in the sea would never suffice to wash it away. Take, for instance, the case of Victor-Amédée, duc de Savoie.[70] He had the scandalous idea of following Louis XIV's lead by legitimizing his bastard sons and marrying his illegitimate daughter off to a prince of his own ducal blood. But his behavior was hardly surprising, since Victor-Amédée himself was none other than the great-grandson (on his mother's side) of César de Vendôme, the bastard son of Henri IV and the beautiful Gabrielle.[71] Breeding always will out. The bastard is like a mongrel dog, with the head of a spaniel, the body of a collie, and the paws of a German shepherd. No amount of grooming can hide the truth.

In the end, bastardy and its retinue are like gangrene, corrupting everything in the entourage of the prince who tolerates it. Take the case of Monseigneur, the son of Louis XIV, about whose legitimacy there could be no question. With his mistress, Mlle Choin, he spent time at Meudon in the company of the "Lorraine sisters" Espinoy and Lillebonne, both children of an illegitimate daughter of Charles IV de Lorraine. One of them acted as a spy on behalf of Mme de Maintenon. Also close to Monseigneur were Vaudémont, an illegitimate son of Charles IV and the uncle of these two sisters; Madame la Duchesse, Louis XIV's illegitimate daughter; d'Antin, her legitimate half-brother; and Vendôme, descended from one of Henri IV's bastards. There was probably no other court that Saint-Simon hated as much as he hated the court of Monseigneur at Meudon, which he characterized, not without exaggeration, as adulterated and bastardized to the core.

Although bastards were intrinsically impure, purification was not impossible. If the bastard himself could not be cleansed of pollution, his mother could, on condition that she make a pious retreat from the life of society. Mme de La Vallière lived a life of strict renunciation in a Carmelite convent, enduring "harsh penitence of body and spirit . . . [and even] going so far as to abstain entirely from drink for a full year, during which she fell ill and lay on the point of death."[72] Mme de Montespan also took up residence in a convent in her old age: "She arrived at a point where she gave everything to the poor. She worked for them several hours each day at low and vulgar chores such as mending shirts. . . . Her dining became as frugal as could be, and her fasts more frequent. . . . She dressed in crude fabrics. . . . She wore a belt studded with iron spikes, which cut into her flesh."[73] The theme of renunciation, which would occupy such an important place in Saint-Simon's work, was here broached for the first time, in connection with his phobia of the impure.

If bastardy resulted from a perversion of procreation, sodomy was seen at the time as a deviation of sexuality. In the domain of the impure, it was often associated with illegitimacy, not only in the *Memoirs* but also in other contemporary documents. It was as if homosexuality were an aggravating circumstance, magnifying impurity to the utmost degree. The chevalier de Lorraine, a homosexual and lover of Monsieur, the king's brother, represented Mme de Maintenon in the negotiations with Monsieur's son Philippe d'Orléans concerning his impending marriage to Mlle de Blois, the illegitimate daughter of Louis XIV. In this instance, the connection between sodomy and adultery was explicitly and vehemently condemned by both the Princess Palatine and the *petit duc*. The "criminal" associations compounded the impurity of bastardy and its attendant dangers. Bear in mind, moreover, that both Madame and Saint-Simon believed, probably wrongly, that the chevalier de Lorraine was guilty of poisoning Henriette d'Angleterre. Sodomy, poison, and the defense of bastardy thus came together in one person to yield the highest imaginable degree of impurity.

Another homosexual of note was Cardinal de Bouillon, who may well be depicted as a pedophile in a fine painting that now hangs in the museum of Perpignan. His colleague Maidalchini was in the habit of referring to him as *il cardinale coglione* (Cardinal Balls). Saint-Simon's hatred of him was a foregone conclusion: Bouillon was a foreign prince, sovereign in Sedan. It was therefore difficult to fit him into the French system of ranks that was so important to Saint-Simon, as it was also to the great genealogist d'Hozier.[74] Indeed, Bouillon was a foreign prince twice over, since as a cardinal he held rank in the Roman curia. He was also a relative of Turenne, whom Saint-Simon secretly detested.[75] And he was allied with those masters of deceit, the Jesuits, and with their friend Fénelon, whose cause he championed to the pope (but in vain): for these "errors," too, Saint-Simon disliked him. Last but not least, Bouillon deliberately perverted the system of ranks: he provoked the ire of his fellow cardinals when he flouted custom and wore his red skullcap in the presence of the pope. The reader will not be surprised to learn that a sodomite whose sin was compounded by so many other character flaws not only betrayed the king but became a forger, with the all too obliging assistance of Etienne Baluze, a great scholar who wittingly or unwittingly offered the cardinal the benefit of his somewhat murky learning.[76]

Other sodomites in the *Memoirs* fare no better. The inept general La Feuillade is said to have a "soul of filth." Saint-Simon accuses him of having relieved his uncle of his gold and jewels and of coming close to being excommunicated by Cardinal Le Camus on account of a presumably scandalous masquerade. In addition, he was an enemy of the party of the duc d'Orléans, with which Saint-Simon was associated.[77] Another homosexual, Huxelles, was false, deceitful, immoral, lazy, feckless, jealous, base, and if that were not enough, a prostitute (metaphorically speaking).[78] He made himself the accomplice of the king's bastards and joined the duc du Maine's conspiracies.[79] His huge head, vast wig, and "loud" hat served him instead of intelligence, if not wit.

Yet another homosexual, not to mention bibliophile and accomplished Hellenist, was Longepierre, whom Saint-Simon, simplifying the facts, links to his three arch-villains, Maine, Dubois, and Noailles. In fact, Longepierre was associated with the comte de Toulouse and through him with the duc de Maine. After Maine sent him away, he was "picked up" by Noailles—a complicated history for one man.[80] Bouillon's nephew, the abbé d'Auvergne, shared his uncle's vice as well as his underhandedness. He tried by unscrupulous means to wrest the archbishopric of Cambrai from the hands of Cardinal de La Trémoille.[81] Although the Bouillons were sworn enemies of the Noailles, whom Saint-Simon also detested, this fact did nothing to diminish our author's animosity toward the abbé d'Auvergne.[82] The enemy of my enemy is not necessarily my friend. The abbé Servien, who counted many illustrious ministers among his forebears, was a man of wit and a courageous satirist whose only flaw was that he was also a sodomite. He met with a scandalous but very "modern" end, in the home of a dancer, thereby bringing to an end one line of ministers whose rising fortunes had posed a continuous challenge to the aristocratic hierarchy.[83]

And then there were Rémond and Canillac, whose names are linked by their shared predilection for "Greek" debauchery.[84] One was Dubois's spy, the other—in addition to being in the pay of Parlement and reconciling the sodomite La Feuillade with Orléans—was his croupier.[85] As for the only transvestite in the *Memoirs*, the abbé d'Entragues, his sins included a weakness not only for the duc du Maine but, even worse, for Protestantism.[86] And to round out this list of sodomites, there was Brissac, afflicted with gout, a man with the plain appearance of an apothecary and the feet of an elephant, who had been expelled from the Ordre du Saint-Esprit and had no one to dine with, no war to fight, no one to pay him homage or wait on him, and who lived off the property of his wives.[87]

In general, there can be no doubt that for Saint-Simon sodomy was a negative trait associated with other negative traits: complicity with bastards, involvement in conspiracies hostile to Saint-Simon's friends, affronts to hierarchy, unscrupulous dealings, treachery, espionage, expulsion from the precincts of the sacred, and behavior unbecoming an aristocrat. There are, however, two exceptions that confirm the basic rules of Saint-Simon's purist view of the world. Conti was a homosexual, yet Saint-Simon portrays him as a sympathetic and courageous figure, the "French Germanicus," who is entitled to a good deal of indulgence because of the "purity of his blood, the only royal blood not adulterated by bastardy."[88] Saint-Simon is also quick to pardon Monsieur, the king's brother: though effeminate and homosexual, this prince was brave in battle and respectful of hierarchy. This was hardly surprising, since the blood that flowed in his veins was that of Saint Louis and Louis XIII, the purest in all the world. In the end, not even the most extreme impurity (sodomy) could overpower the supreme purity of a monarchical race unblemished by the taint of illegitimacy.

In a more direct way, sexuality was also the source of another major form of impurity: syphilis. For Saint-Simon, Vendôme's character was blackened by the combination of bastardy, sodomy, and pox, yet history remembers him mainly as a capable military commander who saved Louis XIV from defeat in the War of the Spanish Succession. But Vendôme was the grandson of one of Henri IV's bastards, and Saint-Simon was uncompromising when it came to the purity of the blood, particularly in people he detested. He could not forgive the stain on Vendôme's escutcheon. Furthermore, Vendôme made no secret of the fact that he was a sodomite. And pox had destroyed his nose. To top it all off, he married a princess of the blood, Mlle d'Enghien, with the support of that archbastard, the duc du Maine.[89] The royal blood that flowed in the veins of this daughter of the Condés was tainted three or four times over by her husband's multiple flaws.[90]

Vendôme was impure, moreover, not only by dint of his ancestry, his morals, and his diseases, but also for another reason: "On Vendôme everything looked good: his notable and exaggerated filth, his heavy use of tobacco, which the king could not tolerate in anyone else, . . . his morals . . . in their most depraved aspect [homosexuality], etc."[91] The presence of tobacco in this litany of "filth" is interesting. Saint-Simon took a dim view of this plant. He believed that the duc de Noailles's tobacco might have been used to poison the dauphine.[92] Boudin, one of the henchmen of the duc du Maine, "is dying of tobacco, and his face is always smeared with it," as was Vendôme's.[93] Huxelles, another sodomite, was filthy in his use of tobacco, and his "clothing and tie are always covered with it."[94] And so on. The duchesse de Bourgogne could not stand it when young Pontchartrain, the one-eyed, Jesuit-loving upstart, spit gobs of tobacco at the very feet of the monarch. The duke of Ossone, who died in a fit of sneezing, was allegedly poisoned with tobacco, as was the duchesse de Bourgogne, who had to contend not only with tobacco but also with the Jesuits—too much for any woman to bear.[95] Was there anything in the world *filthier* than Nicot's weed, regardless of whether it was smoked, snuffed, or chewed?

When it came to impurity, however, tobacco was less important to our authors than sex and matters related to reproduction (bastardy, sodomy, and syphilis). In India, impurity involved improper or unhealthy contact of many kinds: with excrement, pipes (tobacco again), what have you. It could also be hereditary, as in the case of the untouchables. We have no intention of examining the Indian case here. Suffice it to say that our French authors believed very strongly in the inheritance of acquired characters, which could be transmitted by various kinds of contact, including the merest glance. Here "contact" is to be construed in the broadest possible sense.

After a pregnant princess was poked in the eye, her baby was born with eyes as black as ink.[96] When a husband lost his temper with his pregnant wife and threatened to throw her out the window, the baby was born "quaking" and all its life would carry the nickname "Trembleur," forfeiting its rights as firstborn as a result.[97] Madness was also in the blood, at least in the maternal line.[98] A facial tic could be transmitted to a baby in the womb if the mother spent too much time looking at the person with the tic, which itself had been acquired by imitating a similar tic in a nun.[99]

In general, pregnancy was a dangerous, vulnerable condition. In the *Memoirs* we often hear of miscarriages, and women who miscarried were said to have suffered an "injury." Even the most intelligent minds of the seventeenth century regarded the reproductive process as fraught with all sorts of perils that modern science has shown to be illusory. Hence it is not surprising that homosexuality, venereal disease, and illegitimacy, seen as forms of impurity, were believed to threaten the purity of families of exalted rank. However plausible the logic, Saint-Simon as usual pushed it to extremes—hence his usefulness as a paradigm.

In the writings of Saint-Simon (and to a lesser extent of Madame), we find a geography of the pure and the impure. Sodomy was definitely southern, the Greek or Italian vice. Whether we read Madame's *Letters*,

Saint-Simon's *Memoirs*, or Tallemant des Réaux, these two peninsular countries recur again and again. Saint-Simon often applied Mediterranean adjectives to homosexuality: "Greek" referred to classical or Hellenic times, whereas "Italian" alluded to habits commonly attributed to seventeenth-century Romans and other inhabitants of "the Boot," who as "ultramontanes" were prima facie suspect.[100] The Iberian Peninsula was "impure" in another way, congenitally one might say, owing to a deeply ingrained toleration of illegitimacy. "Nearly all the most distinguished and respected houses in Spain are bastard, and often repeatedly so, and almost all the grandees and noblest lords of Spain are steeped in bastardy."[101]

What statistical evidence we have appears to bear Saint-Simon out. Demographers who have studied Spanish cities in the Golden Age have found rates of illegitimacy and premarital conception higher than in France, even among the nobility.[102] Seventeenth- and eighteenth-century Castilian and French writers expressed alarm at the Iberian propensity to tolerate bastards, which they explained in terms similar to Saint-Simon: the adulteration of the kingdom's population under Philip V was said to be a consequence of Moorish influence and the Moors' "commerce in mixing" with Spaniards "almost until the time" of the Catholic Kings. Whether or not this assertion had any basis in fact is not important. Implicit in it was the notion that impurity was indicative of insufficient fidelity to sacred values. Impurity increased as Christianity, long held in check or diluted by Islam, declined.

In Saint-Simon's writings, statements of this kind were closely related to a more general view of the world "beyond the Pyrenees." For now I will simply sketch a broad outline of that view, which Saint-Simon probably formed well before his embassy to Madrid in 1721–22, although he certainly refined his thinking during his diplomatic mission. Although he was pro-Spain and anti-England when it came to foreign policy, he nevertheless deplored the bar sinister that in his eyes marred the Castilian escutcheon.[103] His anthropological convictions were thus radically at odds with his diplomatic commitments, which were entirely devoted to the Spanish cause. He believed, for example, that Spain's royal bastards held too many high state posts and claimed too many honors.[104] Castilians also shunned what Saint-Simon considered the "healthy" French practice of staging a ceremony in which members of the court escorted the king and queen to the marriage bed on their wedding night.[105] The virtue of this practice was that it offered a symbolic guarantee that the children of the marriage would be legitimate. Here was an example of the ridiculous prudishness of the Spaniards, yet another unfortunate consequence of the Muslim conquest. For it was of course widely believed that Muslims could not be trusted around Iberian women, who were therefore kept out of sight, especially in their bedrooms.[106]

According to Saint-Simon, Spain not only failed to take adequate measures against bastardy but also lacked sufficient respect for hierarchy. To be sure, Castilians had a highly developed sense of courtesy and honor.[107] This was a truism that nobody could deny. Indeed, their rituals of politeness were sometimes exaggerated, overscrupulous, and even downright ridiculous, as when they saw guests into and out of their homes.[108] But true hierarchical authenticity in its most august forms was not their strong suit. For example, Castilians had no royal coronation ritual. The Iberian kingdoms were small and had been subject to constant harassment by the Moors, so that it had been impossible for their courts to perform all the requisite rituals when crowning a new monarch.

Spanish monarchs and grandees wore no ceremonial costumes, nor did they place insignia of rank on their carriages, coats of arms, or houses.[109] It was only when French influence began to make itself felt after 1700 that the first ducal mantles appeared on a few carriages in Madrid.[110] Spanish grandees did not outrank other knights of the Golden Fleece, nor were they ranked by seniority relative to each other.[111] They were willing to accept assignments so modest that a French duke and peer would have been ashamed to be associated with them.[112] And there were far too many of them, because Spain's kings had awarded the title of grandee far too liberally, primarily for financial reasons.[113] Castilian fecklessness when it came to hierarchy so irritated Saint-Simon that he cited innumerable examples in addition to those already mentioned. He was scandalized, for instance, by the sight of a Spanish grandee eating his *puchero* alone, as if he were a Dutch burgher munching on a sandwich of bread and cheese.[114]

Even worse, visiting was not part of any genuine social ritual in Spain. Visits were nothing more than occasions for interminable displays of annoying good manners. Spanish grandees deserved praise for drinking small amounts of wine and avoiding drunkenness, but they lacked the beautiful teeth and blond hair of their German counterparts.

Meat was supposed to be impure, and a notable feature of the Catholic religion was the ban on eating meat during Lent. This necessitated a brisk trade in ocean as well as freshwater fish, and in France, a civilized country, it was easy for wealthy people to buy as much as they needed for the Lenten period. But Castile was underdeveloped in this respect, owing chiefly to the "laziness" of the Castilians. During Lent there was but a single species of fish for sale at the market: *vesugo*. One was therefore reduced to fasting in the Spanish manner, on eggs and even chocolate.[115] This was lamentable, for wasn't chocolate the favorite food of the Jesuits?[116] It would of course be possible to point out that in a hot climate, like Spain's, fish are difficult to transport and preserve, but Saint-Simon was so wrapped up in his own reasoning that he would have brushed the objection aside.

Here one glimpses an assumption that lies everywhere just beneath the surface of the *Memoirs*: that France is hierarchically, "purely," more *developed* or accomplished than Spain, though perhaps less so than Germany (especially in regard to disapproval of illegitimacy). In France the society of ranks was more fully realized than was the case south of the Pyrenees, even though the process of decay had begun in France as well.

Of course, the opposition development/underdevelopment applied to more than just questions of rank or purity/impurity. In comparing France and Spain, Saint-Simon frequently sounds quite modern. For example, he suggests that the women of Philip V's court did not allow sufficient time to pass between pregnancies. This may have been unintentional, or it may have been to please the king's second wife, a devout Italian.[117] By contrast, the dukes and peers of France, including Saint-Simon, knew how to limit the number of their offspring. It was rare for a duchess to have more than two children.[118] The younger Pontchartrain may have wearied his spouse with repeated pregnancies, but at the court of Louis XIV he was the exception that proved the rule, and for his trouble he earned some highly abusive rebukes from Saint-Simon.[119] We have become accustomed to regarding birth control as a criterion of development, but Saint-Simon already saw it in that light in the seventeenth century. Despite his rigid advocacy of hierarchy, he had in some ways an authentically modern cast of mind, as this example shows. His "split personality" is evident in his criticism of Castile, which is at times old-fashioned and at other times up to the minute: he complained that the Spanish aristocracy was neither pure enough nor hierarchical enough, yet he also protested that its women were too prolific and its monks too crude and superstitious.

More marked even than Saint-Simon's disdain for Spain was his contempt for Italy. Beyond his aversion to "Italian ways" (read homosexuality), he railed against the pope's Roman associates, the perpetually rebellious Neapolitans, and the Sicilians with their penchant for treachery.[120]

If one hoped to find a proper respect for purity and hierarchy, one had to look to the north, to Germany and, to a lesser extent, Britain. The German nobility not only abhorred bastards but detested mésalliances. Madame was a living, breathing example of this Germanic attitude, as is clear from any number of passages in her letters and Saint-Simon's *Memoirs*. When informed of Louis XIV's decision that her son was to marry one of the king's illegitimate daughters, she slapped the poor boy, and when the king, in announcing the news to her himself, bowed deeply, her response was so icy that the king, "unbending himself, saw only her back, as she had already taken a step toward the door."

Saint-Simon, who was not only a germanophile but also a germanophone, even in his style, deeply admired the Teutonic cult of hierarchy.[121] He appreciated the daughters of the German nobility, whose purses may have been empty but whose blue blood was as refined as any.[122] In the Rhineland, sensitivity to hierarchy was acute: to become a canon of the noble chapter of Strasbourg, for instance, one had to be descended from noble ancestors on both sides, whereas in equivalent French institutions it was enough to be descended from nobility in the paternal line only. In Germany the womb was just as important as the phallus in the transmission of nobility. Yet even if blue blood flowed in women's veins, the wives and daughters of the German aristocracy received virtually no inheritance in order that the bulk of the family estate might pass to the eldest son.[123] In noting this disparity, Saint-Simon once again underscored the distinction between noble *status* (which was carried, as it were, in the chromosomes of males in France, but in Germany in the chromosomes of females as well) and *wealth*. Primogeniture enabled illustrious families to maintain their rank more easily. Of course, the Germany that Saint-Simon described was in part a Germany that existed only in his imagination. Still, his text tells a great deal about its writer's obsessions.

This fascination with France's neighbor stemmed from the "Germanist" predilections of the French aristocracy. After 1550, a number of writers and historians (including Hotman, Vignier, and Belleforest) encouraged French nobles to think of themselves as descendants of the forest tribes that had crossed the Rhine to invade Gaul in the third, fourth, and fifth centuries C.E. In the seventeenth century, monarchist propagandists tended to play down this idea, but the Germanic theme came back into vogue in the writings of Saint-Simon and others.[124] Our duke had in his library the works of Pasquier and Boulainvilliers on the subject. Indeed, Boulainvilliers was a more subtle student of the matter than is generally believed.[125] As Saint-Simon saw it, the bellicose Franks of Germania had invaded Gaul and been civilized by Christianity under Clovis, and from this stock came France's lords, suzerains, and vassals, as well as her fiefs and her knights. The conquered Gauls became serfs of these Germanic lords, and when they were emancipated, they formed the third estate. The Frankish lords had shared power with the king through the institution of assemblies in the fields in March and May. The great Merovingian and Carolingian vassals were thus the ancestors or predecessors of the peers of France, or so Saint-Simon believed (in fact, the peerage was not introduced until much later, in the thirteenth century).[126] The "Germanism" of the French aristocracy (which one hesitates to characterize as a "pan-Germanism" of nobles everywhere) was therefore fundamentally inegalitarian. Not only did the Franks dominate the third estate, they were also stratified internally and divided into a number of hierarchical castes. In the top rank were the great vassals, who ultimately became dukes and peers.[127] The seventeenth-century French nobility saw itself in the mirror of the German nobility, with its respect for tradition and hierarchy—reflected, as it were, in the blue eyes of the Junkers. In this regard, Saint-Simon was deeply indebted to Boulain-villiers's studies of Germany, which he read and to a considerable extent simplified. But Boulainvilliers had the very modern idea of instituting equality within the noble order, in accordance with what he claimed had been the laws of the ancient Germans, and this of course dismayed Saint-Simon.[128] That is why he mildly attacked a man whom he recognized as a learned scholar and great genealogist but nevertheless accused of being an astrologer, a friend of the dreadful, not to say diabolical, Noailles, and a dilettante.[129]

Moving from hierarchical Germany to the Low Countries, Saint-Simon was under no illusion about the purity of the blood or the antiquity of the noble houses of Flanders, despite the fact that it was linked to Germany linguistically. Speaking of Bergeyck, a Brabantine mercenary in the pay of Spain whom he held in high esteem, he observed that while the man was neither a count nor a baron he was "nevertheless from the best of such families as one is likely to find in the Low Countries."[130] For all its wealth, Flanders was but a poor man's Germany when it came to nobility. Saint-Simon was also critical of Dutch "avarice," which he found even among high officials and deemed to be utterly incompatible with aristocratic values. As we saw earlier, moreover, he believed that Flemish nobles liked to dine on sandwiches of bread and cheese that they carried about in their pockets, a predilection that rendered them unfit for aristo-cratic society.[131] Even ambassadors shunned their company.

With Germany's neighbor to the east, things were even worse. Poland had long been a thorn in the side of France's princes, who had tried in vain to have themselves crowned kings there (most notably the prince de Conti). And it was best not even to speak of Henri III. According to Saint-Simon, Poles were grotesque drunkards.[132] And the former queen of Poland was a Frenchwoman who had betrayed the country of her birth.[133] Only one "Polish" prince found grace in Saint-Simon's eyes: the son of the Polish king. But physically he resembled a German or perhaps a French dignitary: "He was a tall, strapping lad of eighteen, a very healthy-looking blond [youth] with good color, who resembled M. le duc de Berry."[134] Apparently it troubled Saint-Simon very little that this charming young man's father, Augustus II of Saxony, king of Poland, was also the father of 354 bastards. And his legitimate son was no better behaved.[135] For Saint-Simon, the Russians were like the Poles, only worse—alcoholics "not quite rid of their barbarous customs, given to tantrums, and full of strange ways." One of them, Prince Kyrakin, had traveled widely but "still smelled of Russia, and extreme greed spoiled his talents."[136]

Thus Germany, surrounded by the unsavory Low Countries, Russia, and Poland, stood out like a diamond of hierarchical purity. It reminded Saint-Simon of another of his fascinations, extremely clear gems such as the "peregrine," a "pearl of the very first water . . . unique in all Europe and perhaps in all the world for its perfection, weight, and size," or the "Regent diamond" the "size of a greengage plum, almost round in shape, . . . perfectly clear, free of any blemish, cloud, or flaw, of admirable water, and weighing more than five hundred grains."[137] Seeking to extol this gem of purity as the antithesis of all that was impure, Saint-Simon even claimed that the Regent diamond had been secretly exported, "concealed in the buttocks of a factotum of the Great Mogul whom the authorities had neglected to purge."[138] This was of course a tall tale, yet it is instructive in its own way for what it reveals of Saint-Simon's ideas of the pure and the impure, the limpid and the crude, the anal and the astral. Similarly, the celebrated "kick in the behind" administered to Madame la duchesse de Berry by her husband at Rambouillet in 1714—a kick that was generally approved at Versailles as a just punishment of a woman by her spouse—tells us everything we need to know about the difference between the crystalline Berry, in whose veins flowed the purest blood in the world (that of the French royal family), and his mysterious, incestuous, dissolute wife, the daughter of a bastard.[139]

Saint-Simon would have liked to include Great Britain in his list of countries scrupulous in matters of hierarchy. He notes, for example, that Berwick, who is "extremely English, cannot tolerate any inversion of rank."[140] The issue was a topical one, because Berwick was at the time an opponent of d'Antin's efforts to usurp the title of duke and peer of Epernon. D'Antin, who was a legitimate son of Mme de Montespan, hoped to make use of his mother's influence with the king, an influence that according to Saint-Simon derived from the lady's "culpable fertility."[141] Berwick, the bastard son of a king of England, thus became a champion of hierarchy out of hostility to d'Antin, the legitimate son of a woman who had given birth to bastards while a mistress of the king of France. A bastard, in other words, advocated legitimacy in opposition to a legitimate son who advocated bastardy.

Indeed, Saint-Simon was not entirely wrong about England. Unlike in France, royal bastards there were held to be "nameless, no-account nullities unless rescued from nothingness by the award of some title defining their precise social rank."[142] Although by the end of the eighteenth century England would become quite tolerant of bastards, it appears to have been much less so at the end of the seventeenth century (hostility to bastards apparently having peaked between 1650 and 1660).[143] In general, however, the English case was a considerable embarrassment to Saint-Simon, because British mothers carried nobility in their wombs and did not simply reproduce it.[144] Social mobility on the English side of the Channel was much greater than in France, and the rules of derogation from nobility were less strict.[145] Furthermore, Saint-Simon hated the British and the "Anglomaniacs."[146] He therefore simply omitted Britain from his bipolar geography of the pure and the impure. Basically, he stuck to the Continent and proposed a fantastic cosmology. Bastardized Spain, flanked by sodomite Italy and Greece, were set against "decent Germany," a conservative country that respected the hierarchies of birth. France, caught between north and south, was pulled in both directions, torn between two competing models: the Mediterranean, or impure, and the Germanic, or pure.

Saint-Simon's attitude toward bastardy in particular, as well as impurity in general, was not typical of ranking members of hierarchies, aristocrats, or the broader category of nobles. In fact, the noble order, especially in southern Europe, was fertile in illegitimate offspring. Provincial customs in southern France, modeled on those of Spain, were tolerant of bastards when it came to inheritance, legitimization, and ennoblement. By contrast, Saint-Simon, with his rigorous logic, represented a tendency, a geographical and cultural region, and a moment in the history of blue blood and its attitudes toward illegitimacy. A principal reason for this split was religion. Calvinism and Jansenism, with their Augustinian mistrust of carnal passion, demonstrated increasing severity toward extramarital sexuality and any fruit that might come of it. The *petit duc* was influenced by the theologies of exigent grace, or at least by the Catholic version of those theologies, which is to say, Jansenism. He was therefore all the less tolerant of adultery and children of adultery.

Regional attitudes were also important. As a member of the northern nobility, Saint-Simon shared the anti-bastard sensibility of northern Europe. "The *échiquier* of Normandy, the *coutume* of Paris (art. 158), the *coutume* of Calais (art. 169), the *coutume* of Etampes (art. 182), and many other texts of the same type exclude bastards from successions."[147] The customs of Anjou, Maine, Melun, Poitou, and Brittany prohibited, or at any rate limited, the generosity of fathers toward bastard sons. In Lorraine, as late as the fifteenth century, the property of a bastard reverted upon his death to the lord exercising powers of high justice over his place of residence. By contrast, in southern regions influenced by Roman law and Occitanian culture (Toulousain, Dauphiné, Auvergne, and even the Marche), there was a general unwillingness to dispossess bastards entirely. Saint-Simon liked to contrast Spanish laxity with German rigor. The same north-south opposition existed in France, however. The portrait needs to be touched up a bit, however: in Flanders (and the Low Countries in general) there was greater tolerance of bastard heirs than in northern France. Must we conclude that the Flemish were half-baked Germans?

In France it was the *langue d'oïl*, the language of northern France, that set the tone. It was of course the language spoken in key centers of power and influence. In Auvergne, whose nobility spoke the *langue d'oc* of southern France, the typical blue-blooded family included at least two bastards during the reign of the Valois and early Bourbons. By contrast, the nobility of the Beauce (a region in which the *langue d'oïl* was spoken) produced far fewer "impure" offspring. What is more, a royal edict of March 1600 concerning the tax known as the *taille* came down squarely in favor of the more rigorous custom of the north. Article 26 of this text stipulated that bastards of nobles were ipso facto commoners unless granted explicit letters of ennoblement in recognition of their personal merit or the merit of their family. Colbert's reforms of the nobility reduced many illegitimate sons of noblemen to common status in order to limit the number of nobles entitled to tax exemptions. Henceforth, any bastard claiming a noble exemption would be liable to prosecution for fraud. Even Louis XIV, who in his later years took pride in his bastard offspring, was at first ashamed of them. He kept them out of sight as much as he could, unlike his grandfather Henri IV, who was something of an exhibitionist in this regard. What this shows is that between the last third of the sixteenth century and at least the third quarter of the seventeenth century, the attitude of the royal family had subtly changed, even as royal males went right on fathering illegitimate children. Saint-Simon exemplified the more stringent attitude of pious northern aristocrats. During the reign of Louis XIV, this attitude gradually gained ascendancy over the laxer view that had prevailed earlier. The noble order attempted to purge itself of some of the more glaring examples of impurity in its ranks. Indeed, demographic statistics showing that illegitimacy reached its lowest level in the period between 1660 and 1730 suggest that Saint-Simon's way of thinking influenced the entire society and not just the nobility.

In Saint-Simon, this widespread obsession with illegitimacy was coupled with a generally hierarchical cast of mind notable for its rigor and intellectual consistency. The puritanical, or at any rate Jansenist, attitudes of the late seventeenth and early eighteenth century did not abate with time. Public opinion condemned Louis XV's sexual adventures far more harshly than it had criticized Louis XIV's *gambades* or the amours of Henri IV. In retrospect, it is easy to understand Saint-Simon's deep (and posthumous) affection for Louis XIII, that most chaste of kings. And weren't his attacks on bastards also directed at the love affairs of Louis XV, which, though almost never mentioned in the *Memoirs* (which end in 1723), were nevertheless ever-present in the mind of a writer who was an attentive and critical observer of the behavior of all heads of state, including the one under whom he lived while writing his magnum opus? After moving to Paris in 1723, moreover, Saint-Simon would hardly have turned a deaf ear to the buzz in that city concerning the young monarch's notorious adventures with the Nesle sisters and, later, Mme de Pompadour.

Cabals, Lineages, and Power

4

Having discussed the pure and the impure, let us return now to the central concept of hierarchy, which of course shaped Saint-Simon's thinking about the court in general and court conflicts in particular. We have thus far encountered at least three different ways of describing the court hierarchy. At the very summit, the royal couple ranked above the children of France, who in turn outranked the grandchildren. A second scheme set the royal family in the strict sense apart from the princes of the blood. And finally, the distinction between legitimate and illegitimate children, between lawful wedlock and royal adultery, established a third axis (with the pure and the impure at opposite poles, establishing the system's upper and lower limits).

The first of these three schemes is by far the most useful when it comes to analyzing court conflicts and cabals. Madame and Saint-Simon never discussed such matters. They saw little of each other. The *petit duc* was socially beneath the great lady's notice. To her, Saint-Simon and the other peers ranked far below the Counts Palatine. As we have seen, moreover, neither knew of the other's writing. Hence we may once again assume that since both analyzed the situation in the same way, their information was accurate and tells us something about how the court (in the person of its most sociologically perceptive members) saw itself.

Let us begin by quoting from a letter that Madame wrote to the duchess of Hanover on 28 September 1709:

The whole court is filled with intrigue. Some hope to obtain the favor of the powerful lady [Mme de Maintenon], others that of Monsieur le Dauphin

[Monseigneur, son of Louis XIV], and still others that of the duc de Bour-gogne [son of Monseigneur], for he and his father do not like each other. The son is contemptuous of the father; he is ambitious and wants to govern. The dauphin is under the absolute domination of his bastard sister Madame la Duchesse. The princesse de Conti [another bastard] has become her ally so as not to forfeit all power over him. All are opposed to my son [the duc d'Orléans]. They are afraid that the king might favor him and may be plan-ning to arrange a marriage between his [that is, the duc d'Orléans's] eldest daughter and the duc de Berry. But the duchesse de Bourgogne, who would also love to control the dauphin as well as the king, is jealous of Madame la Duchesse. She has therefore entered into a pact of friendship with our Mme d'Orléans in order to thwart the other alliance. The result is an amus-ing comedy of intertwined intrigues, and as the song says, "If we weren't dying of hunger [the famine of 1709–10 had just begun], we'd die of laugh-ter." The old lady [Maintenon] has set all these people against one another so that she might govern all the more freely.[1]

And here is another sketch of court cabals by Madame, this one from 1710:

Now for some news about how things currently stand at court. The king is more charmed than ever by his aging beauty. Everything passes through her hands, and everything is out of kilter, like the old lady's waist. She is bent on feathering her nest, sucks money out of everything, and teaches the duchesse de Bourgogne how to do the same. She knows all the state's secrets and keeps the duchess so well apprised that none remain secret for long. Monsieur le Dauphin is still smitten with the Choin woman, whom he may have married. The lady is a cunning one. She refuses to appear at court, because if she did she would be obliged to bow down to the dauphin's mother-in-law [Mme de Maintenon], and this she has no intention of doing. She sees only the duchesse de Bourgogne and her favorites, and Madame la Duchesse, who happens to be the favorite of Monsieur le Dauphin. She [Choin] does them a great favor by allowing them to eat with her. Here they call this privilege the *parvulo*. More secret and more private than this does not exist. Choin has her creatures everywhere. The maréchal d'Hux-elles, Albergotti, and state councilor Bignon are also her advisors. Mon-sieur le duc de Bourgogne [le Grand Dauphin's son] is the leader of the *dévots*, who are: M. le duc de Beauvillier, the duc de Chevreuse, M. d'O.[2] This cabal does not always take a favorable view of the other two and often opposes them in council [Beauvillier, in particular, opposed Pontchartrain and Maintenon]. The entire court is divided among these three cabals.[3]

In the two letters just quoted, Madame refers to three cabals, each associated with a different generation of the royal family: king (Louis

XIV and Mme de Maintenon), son of France (Monseigneur, or le Grand Dauphin, and his mistress, possibly his secret wife, Mme Choin), and grandson of France (the duc de Bourgogne). Although historians credit Bourgogne with having been the leader of a group of enlightened liberals (including Fénelon, Beauvillier, and Chevreuse), Madame sees him primarily as the head of a *camarilla* of *dévots* (and her judgment was not totally wrong).

In a superb passage dealing with the same year, 1709, Saint-Simon describes the same three cabals: the father's, the son's, and the grandson's.[4] The king's cabal—or, rather, Mme de Maintenon's—was conservative, seigneurial, and military. That of his son, Monseigneur, went in for base intrigue. And his grandson, the duc de Bourgogne, headed a cabal that was intelligently reformist and ministerial, despite a tinge of Jesuitical bigotry. In a moment we will explore Saint-Simon's important account in greater detail.[5]

For now, however, let us go back in time a quarter of a century. On 11 August 1686, Madame wrote a letter in which she described a Louis XIV who was not yet old; hence the question of succession was of little immediate concern. The three-way split between the king, his son (born in 1661), and his grandson (born in 1682) had yet to emerge, if only because the son and the grandson were still so young. In attempting to describe the court, therefore, Madame had to cast about for another model. She settled on one that pitted the royal family proper against the granddaughters of France and the princes and princesses of the blood. In this instance "royal family" meant the king and his secret wife, Mme de Maintenon. The granddaughters of France were the two daughters of Gaston d'Orléans, brother of Louis XIII (otherwise known as la Grande Mademoiselle and Mlle de Guise). The princes and princesses of the blood included members of the Conti and Condé-Bourbon families (Monsieur le Duc, Madame la Duchesse, the princesse de Conti, and "Mme de Bourbon"). Madame gives the following account of the situation:

> In truth, anyone not obliged to sort things out here would laugh until he cried at the sight of how things are done at court. The king imagines himself to be devout because he no longer sleeps with young women. He flatters his brother's favorites and torments everybody without exception. The old lady, Maintenon, takes pleasure in making all the members of the royal family odious in the king's eyes and in lording it over all but Monsieur [Louis XIV's brother], whose praises she sings in the king's presence.
>
> Think of what I tell you here as describing the lay of the land at court as it now stands. No one speaks well or ill of Mlle la Grande Duchesse and Mme de Guise. They are seen as nullities, which seems an enviable

condition to me, and I would gladly change places with them. M. le Duc [son of le Grand Condé] will crawl on his belly before anything that looks like favor, and his abject behavior is the butt of universal mockery. Mme de Maintenon toys with the princesse de Conti and Mme de Bourbon [wife of M. le Duc] as if she held them in a pair of scales. She raises one and lowers the other, or she maneuvers one into favor and sends the other packing. Right now Mme de Bourbon is in favor and the princesse de Conti in disgrace. But that will soon change. The reason why the princesse de Conti is in disgrace is that spies have told the king that she made fun of Maintenon to her cousin Choiseul. Mme la Duchesse [de Bourbon] is no happier than the rest of us, because her husband treats her as if he were a real tyrant.[6]

The scene described here is far less comprehensive that that set forth in the trigenerational model discussed earlier. In that model, three generations of the royal family (along with their supporters) contended with one another based on their estimates of when and how the monarchical succession would take place. The whole apparatus of government became caught up in their veiled disputes: ministers, high-ranking bureaucrats, military commanders, prelates, Jesuits, aristocrats. In 1686, on the other hand, real power, insofar as it was not wielded personally by Louis XIV, was in the hands of dynasties of mandarins: the Le Tellier–Louvois family, the family of the late Colbert, and the Phélypeaux clan (see below). Quarrels involving the Condés or Contis were far less important than disputes between the Le Telliers and the Colberts. What is interesting, however, is that Madame, in keeping with her hierarchical vision of society, was already trying in 1686 to decipher the court system in terms of a model involving the upper echelons of the social hierarchy, namely, the various components of the royal family. Although her analysis is flawed, its shortcomings do not invalidate the basic principles of a worldview shaped entirely by the court.

Between 1711 and 1715, le Grand Dauphin, the duc de Bourgogne, and Louis XIV passed from the scene one after another. Hence the trigenerational model of 1709 no longer made sense. Madame therefore developed yet another model of the court during the Regency (even as the court system was falling apart because of the move to Paris). In decoding the power struggles of this later period, she moved to a model based on the opposition of pure to impure, or legitimate to illegitimate. In one camp, we find young Louis XV, the frail son of the duc de Bourgogne, and the regent, Philippe d'Orléans, the legitimate offspring of the "blood" of Louis XIII. As regent, the duc d'Orléans supported the young king and for cash turned to the financier John Law (or Las, as contemporaries called him). In the other camp, out of the depths of the impure came the bastard duc du Maine, who had previously been encouraged by that old witch Maintenon (the royal bastards' erstwhile governess) and backed by Parlement. What made the clash even more dramatic was the fact that Maine was the brother-in-law of Philippe d'Orléans through his wife, the duchesse d'Orléans, also a royal bastard and Maine's sister. But let Madame speak for herself:

> It is only too true that Parlement [that is, the Parlement of Paris] is causing embarrassment to my son [the regent, Philippe d'Orléans]. He has told me that those Messieurs are sticking their noses into things that are none of their business and that as long as royal authority remains in his hands, he will keep it intact so that when the king reaches the age of majority he may pass it on just as he received it. He will not permit anyone to tamper with it. Thus far there is nothing to fear. The people have not budged, nor have the other parlements in the provinces. My son's wife's brother [that is, the duc du Maine] and his wife are his worst enemies. They are the ones who have stirred everyone up against him. If my son had listened to me, he would not be a brother-in-law to these people and would be able to act without fear. My son needs to find new ways to pay the late king's debts. This Las, who is the object of such hatred, is a highly intelligent Englishman.[7]

In fact, the legitimate/bastard opposition fails to capture the complex realities of 1718. Saint-Simon, who at this point was directly involved in government, paints a far more sophisticated portrait of this period. But for the years 1712–15, when the court was still in Versailles but le Grand Dauphin and the duc de Bourgogne had already been removed from the scene by premature death, Saint-Simon, too, relied on the same legitimate/bastard model: Orléans versus Maine. He relied on it extensively for his descriptions of the court and government during those three years, just as Madame would do a short while later.

A variant of the legitimate/bastard opposition—another way to say pure/impure—was legitimate/adulterous. Mme de La Fayette used this hierarchical key to elucidate the court structure and cabals with brio in *La Princesse de Clèves* (1678). Ostensibly the novel dealt with an earlier period coinciding with the reign of Henri II (1547–59):

> Mary Stuart, queen of Scots, who had just married M. le Dauphin and to whom people referred as *la reine dauphine*, was perfection itself. Her mother-in-law the queen and the king's sister Madame also loved verse, comedy, and music. . . . And since the king [Henri II] loved physical exercise, all the pleasures were represented at court.

After this passage of ludicrously admiring prose comes a description of the Guises: the duc de Guise, the cardinal de Lorraine, and the chevalier de Guise. Then the text switches back to the dauphine (Mary Stuart) by way of the duc de Nemours:

The duke often called on *la reine dauphine*. Because of this princess's beauty and her particular esteem for this prince, many people believed that he lifted his eyes to gaze upon her. Through her marriage her uncles Messieurs de Guise had gained considerable credit and respect, and now their ambition was equality with the princes of the blood, and power, the kind wielded by the constable, Montmorency. The king, who relied on Montmorency to handle most government affairs, made favorites of the duc de Guise and the maréchal de Saint-André. But those drawn to his side by favor or affairs could not remain there unless they submitted to the duchesse de Valentinois [that is, Diane de Poitiers, Henri II's mistress]. Although she was no longer either young or beautiful, she ruled with a power so absolute that she could fairly be called the mistress of both the king and the state.

The king had always loved the constable, and no sooner had his reign begun than he recalled him from exile, where he had been sent by François I. The court was divided between Messieurs de Guise and the constable, who was backed by the princes of the blood. Both parties had long dreamed of winning the duchesse de Valentinois to their side. The duc d'Aumale, brother of the duc de Guise, had married one of her daughters; the constable aspired to a similar marriage. He was not content simply to have married his elder son to Mme Diane [not to be confused with Diane de Poitiers, duchessse de Valentinois], the daughter of the king and a lady from the Piedmont. This marriage had faced many obstacles owing to promises that M. de Montmorency had made to Mlle de Piennes, one of the queen's ladies-in-waiting. Patiently the king had conquered these obstacles one by one, but still the constable had lacked sufficient support: he needed to win the backing of Mme de Valentinois and drive a wedge between her and Messieurs de Guise, whose great influence had begun to worry the duchess. She had done all she could to delay the dauphin's marriage to the queen of Scots. To [Mme de Valentinois], the young queen's beauty, her able and accomplished mind, and the advantage that her marriage would have given to Messieurs de Guise [Mary Stuart's uncles] were all unbearable. She particularly hated the cardinal de Lorraine [one of the Guises], who had spoken to her in a sharp and even contemptuous tone. At some point she learned that the cardinal had been meeting with the queen. The constable therefore found her ready to form an alliance with him through the marriage of Mlle de La Marck, her granddaughter, to M. d'Anville [Montmorency's second son], who has since succeeded him as constable under Charles IX. The constable did not believe that M. d'Anville would object to this marriage, but even though the reasons for it were kept from him, the difficulties were scarcely diminished. M. d'Anville was madly in love with *la reine dauphine*, and however hopeless this passion may have been, he could not bring himself to make an engagement that would have obliged him to divide his attentions. The maréchal de Saint-André was the only courtier who did not take sides. He was one of the favored, and his favor depended on himself alone.

Leaving aside such diversionary matters as the (conjugal) alliance between a Guise (Aumale) and one of Diane de Poitiers's daughters and the younger Montmorency's unrequited love for the dauphine, we see from this passage that what divided the court in Mme de La Fayette's reading was the opposition between legitimate and adulterous. (Whether or not this account corresponds to the realities of the 1550s need not concern us here.) On the side of legitimacy we find the queen, Catherine de' Medici, the dauphine, Mary Stuart, and her allies, and with them the Guise, who were princes of Lorraine, hence foreigners, along with the duc de Nemours. On the other side we find adultery, together with those who abetted or made use of it: Diane de Poitiers (de Valentinois), the royal mistress, figures here alongside Montmorency and the princes of the blood. And finally, within the court, a molecule comprising two atoms, moved a single free electron: the maréchal de Saint-André.

The sly novelist pretends not to take sides in this conflict, in which the role of Diane de Poitiers prefigures that of Mme de Montespan. In the 1670s, when *La Princesse de Clèves* was being written, it was Montespan's favor that determined who was up and who was down. But the unfolding of the tale shows clearly which side Mme de La Fayette was on. At the beginning of part 4 of her novel, Henri II is accidentally killed. Diane and the Montmorencys lose their influence. The queen, the dauphine, and the Guises—on the side of legitimacy—take command under the auspices of the youthful new king, François II. It is in their entourage that Nemours and the princesse de Clèves will be able to love each other platonically—*purely*.

To sum up, then, the hierarchical principle shaped not only the system of court ranks but also contemporary analyses of that system. That principle manifested itself in a variety of forms: through the generations of the royal family, proximity to the royal blood, purity versus impurity, legitimate versus bastard, legitimate versus adulterous.

L et us turn now to what Saint-Simon wrote about the year 1709.

I lack words for what I want to say. Because of the great changes affecting the conditions and fortunes of Vendôme and Chamillart [both of whom had fallen into disgrace], the court was more divided than ever. To speak of cabals might be too much, and the proper word for what went on eludes me. So I will say "cabal" even though it is too strong, with the warning that it exceeds what I mean to imply. . . . The court was divided among three parties, which included all the leading personages.

This introduction is followed by a digression in which Saint-Simon evaluates the relative degrees of selfishness and disinterest motivating each of these three parties. In order to clarify the situation for the reader, we have compiled a table listing certain salient characteristics of each "cabal" (see table 4.1). Note that the center column of this table is headed by Louis XIV and his wife, Mme de Maintenon, whose marriage, though clandestine, was known to everyone. Below them is Monseigneur, the king's legitimate son and heir apparent (he would die, however, a few years before his father). Situated at the very center of the table, Monseigneur can be regarded as the central point of the entire system. Below him is the duc de Bourgogne, who married Marie-Adélaïde de Savoie, thereby making her the duchesse de Bourgogne. As the son of Monseigneur, the duc de Bourgogne was second in line for the throne. And

TABLE 4.1

First Generation (Two brothers, one wife, one mistress)	(Monsieur, brother of Louis XIV)	Louis XIV, husband (in second marriage) of Madame de Maintenon	Madame de Montespan, former mistress of the king
	↓	↓	↓
Second Generation The dauphin, known as Monseigneur, along with his brother-in-law and half-brothers	The duc d'Orléans, future regent, son of Monsieur; and his wife, the duchesse d'Orléans (a bastard), sister-in-law and half-sister of Monseigneur and sister of the duc du Maine	Monseigneur, son of Louis XIV; and his mistress, Mlle Choin (Meudon cabal)	The duc du Maine, bastard of Louis XIV and Montespan, half-brother of Monseigneur, and brother-in-law (through his sister) of the duc d'Orléans
		↓	
Third Generation Unlikely heir to throne: the duc de Bourgogne		The duc and duchesse de Bourgogne and their party (Fénelon, etc.)	
		↓	
Fourth Generation The actual heir to the throne		The future Louis XV	

finally, below him, the central column ends with the future Louis XV, who would not be born until the following year, 1710.

Saint-Simon's text now continues with three crucial points about the personages in the central column of our table (the couple Louis XIV–Maintenon, followed by Monseigneur, followed by the duc and duchesse de Bourgogne):

> Under the wings of Mme de Maintenon gathered the first [cabal], whose principals, pouncing on the spoils of [disgraced minister] Chamillart's fall made still more piquant by the fall of [the maréchal de] Vendôme, whom they had also done their utmost to push out, were spared and in return spared Mme la duchesse de Bourgogne; and they were also on good terms with Monseigneur.

Next comes a description of this first cabal, that of Maintenon, including a list of the various personages and personalities it included. Indeed, a "cloud of questions" surrounded the oldest surviving generation of the royal line, symbolized to perfection by the monarch (whose supreme functions raised him above any cabal) but above all by his wife Maintenon, the "old lady," as Madame called her, or "the omnipotent Maintenon," as she was described more recently by a leading historian of French finances, Daniel Dessert. Without granting the lady greater importance than she deserves (historians disagree about her actual power), let us state simply that she was at least a symbolic figure around whom various forces, pressure groups, and conspiracies could come together. Today we might refer to these as "lobbies."

The members of the "Maintenon cabal," Saint-Simon writes,

> enjoyed the esteem of public opinion and the benefit of Boufflers's renown. Others came to bask in his glory or to make use of it. Harcourt, even from the distant banks of the Rhine, kept a hand on the tiller. Voysin and his wife were the instruments [of Maintenon and Harcourt] and relied in turn on their support. In the second rank were the chancellor [the elder Pontchartrain], who was dismayed by Mme de Maintenon's aversion to him and his consequent estrangement form the king; [the younger] Pontchartrain [the chancellor's son], who made things happen at a distance by bouncing one ball off another, as in billiards; the first equerry [Beringhen], grown old in intrigue, who had brought Harcourt together with the chancellor and worked everyone into a frenzy; his cousin Huxelles, apparently a philosopher, cynical, epicurean, false in every way, gnawed by the darkest ambition, of whom Monseigneur had formed the best possible opinion thanks to Choin [Monseigneur's mistress], who was infatuated with Huxelles owing to the efforts of Beringhen, his wife, and Bignon; the maréchal de Villeroy, who even in the depths of disgrace had never lost his hold on

Mme de Maintenon, and whom the rest went easy on because of this and because the king's old love [for Villeroy] might, with [Maintenon's] help, be rekindled at any time; the duc de Villeroy [the marshal's son], egged on by him but with his own way of doing things; La Rocheguyon [François VIII de La Rochefoucauld], who laid traps while sneering in silence; and [through] Blouin [first valet of the king's chamber] and other secret agents, [Maintenon and Harcourt] knew everything and enjoyed all the credit of youth with Monseigneur, and had a hand, however remote, in the fall of Vendôme and Chamillart; and they were abetted by the duchesse de Villeroy, whose limited intelligence was compensated by common sense, much prudence, impenetrable secrecy, and the confidence in many things of Mme la duchesse de Bourgogne, whom she kept on a tight and firm leash.

In brief, this was the Maintenon cabal, which we may now examine more closely. Because the king was bound by marriage to the lady who headed this group, we may assume that it exerted considerable influence on him. In the diagram in figure 4.1, we have placed the Maintenon group in the upper left for convenience. Here we find, of course, Mme de Maintenon; Blouin, the king's first valet de chambre; the maréchal de Boufflers; the duc de Villeroy, Louvois's son-in-law; and the duc de La Rocheguyon (La Rochefoucauld), also a son-in-law of Louvois. In other words, we find here remnants of the Louvois clan. Although Mme de Maintenon had been on bad terms with Louvois personally, she was nevertheless a skillful enough politician to bring the late minister's sons-in-law into her cabal.

Other names also appear in the upper left corner of the diagram: Chancellor Pontchartrain and his son, whose relations with the king's wife were unbelievably complicated; along with Beringhen, Bignon, the "maréchal" d'Huxelles, and Voysin. A whole close-knit group, tied together by varying degrees of friendship (and in some instances, paradoxically, by antipathy), as well as kinship and patronage (as indicated in the legend below the diagram).

Précieuse and *dévote*, married to a king who saw himself as an apostle, universal abbess and mother of the church, Madame de Maintenon maintained a variety of extremely close relationships with the members of her group. There was an inner circle, her own general staff, which in fact if not in law constituted *the* general staff of France, or at any rate part of it. Its most important member was Harcourt, commander of the Army of the Rhine, whose vast patronage network extended throughout Normandy. Apoplectic and calculating, he was a man with many secret connections and countless stratagems. He also had ties to the Louvois clan, or what was left of it, through an old friendship with Louvois senior

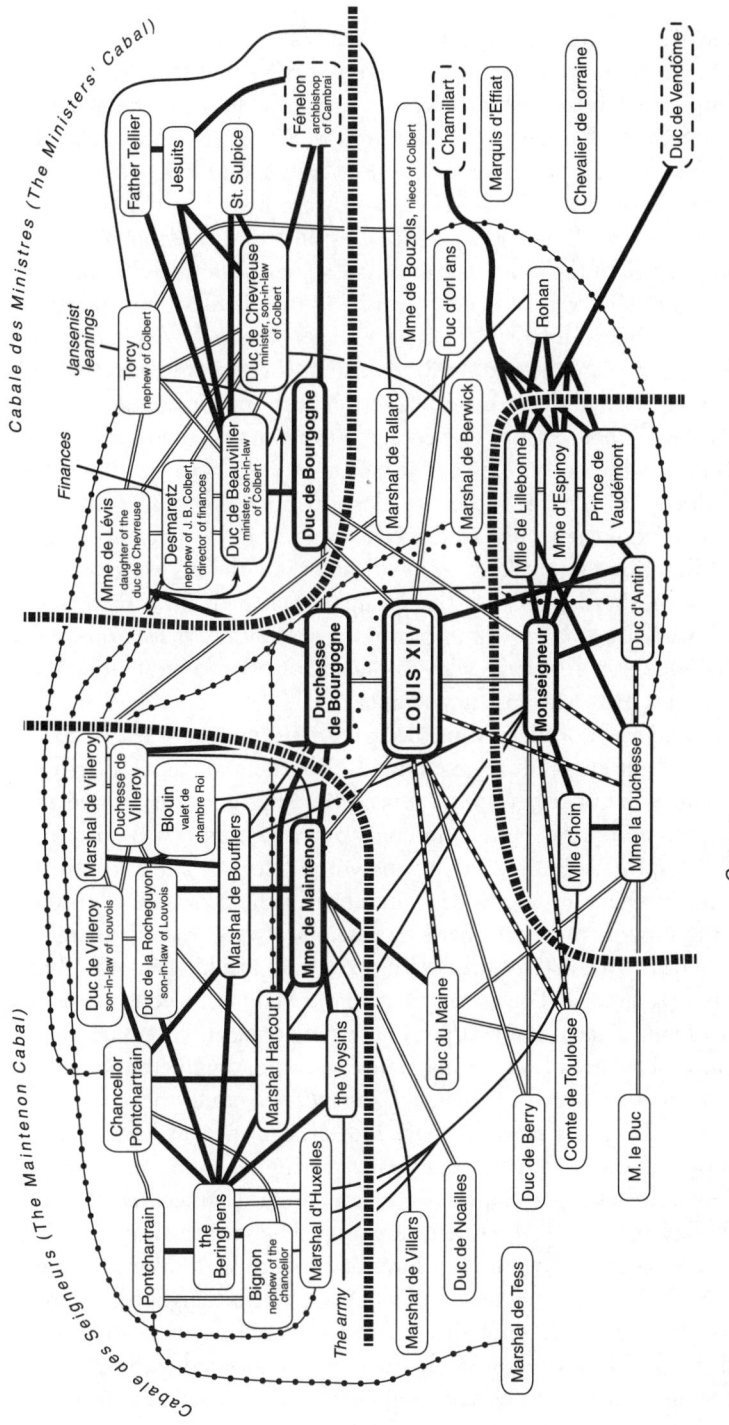

Figure 4.1. The Cabals

and his son Barbezieux. (Later, Harcourt's eldest son would marry first a Villeroy and then, after her death, Barbezieux's daughter.) Harcourt had a complicated relationship, friendly but difficult, with the King's Council, on which Maintenon, his patron as well as his follower, sought in vain to win him a seat. He more or less systematically opposed the ducs de Chevreuse and de Beauvillier, who were linked to the Colbert clan and the duc de Bourgogne, hence hostile to Maintenon. An old friend and protégé of the king's second wife, an ally of powerful ministerial families, the son of a Le Tellier, husband of a Brûlart, and father-in-law of a "Louvois," Henri d'Harcourt was a wise old Norman who had been born into an ancient family. Nothing short of apoplexy could halt his rise. He earned the most prestigious honors: major military commands, a marshal's baton, a duchy-peerage, a captaincy of guards, a Saint-Esprit, a Golden Fleece, an embassy in Spain, and the favor of Philip V and the princess of Ursins. He came close to obtaining a seat on the Upper Council (aborted only at the last minute) and was lavishly rewarded for his efforts by the king. As the head of the Maintenon group— or as one of the heads, because the group in fact had more than one center and was also known, significantly, as the *cabale des seigneurs*, or lords' cabal—he met regularly with the heads of other aristocratic and military families of the utmost importance.

Among them was Boufflers, who, along with his military allies, constituted a sort of "supreme military command." Boufflers was also a marshal and duke and a national hero who adored the king and was adored in Paris. Public opinion, or what counted as public opinion, was putty in his hands—despite his limited intelligence. Boufflers was a man of great courage and Spartan simplicity. His presence in the Maintenon group earned it the support of certain Parisian patriots, always ripe for the taking. Certain other marshals of the comic-opera variety added color to this highly militarized mafia. They strengthened the Maintenon constellation with their immense fortunes, vast patronage networks, and regional governorships, which were of some importance in contending with the powerful intendants in charge of provincial *généralités*. Among this group of marshals were Huxelles and Villeroy. Huxelles, dishonest "beneath a husk of probity," was an ally of Phélypeaux, Beringhen, and the Louvois clan.[8] Villeroy, a stage general, was an incompetent disgraced by defeat, yet he still had the ear of Mme de Maintenon. His son, the duc de Villeroy, Louvois's son-in-law, did not have to contend with disgrace. And his daughter-in-law, the duchesse de Villeroy ("not intelligent but sensible"), constituted a link—not the only one—between the Maintenon cabal and the duchesse de Bourgogne, who was associated (through her husband, at any rate) with the opposing faction, the so-called ministers' cabal of the duc de Bourgogne.

Harcourt stood for Normandy. Villeroy stood for Lyons. Huxelles to some extent stood for Alsace. The importance of regional roots and patronage networks (operating through provincial governorships) is not to be overlooked.

Other marshals of France were either allied with the cabal of Monseigneur (Vendôme, for example) or else not linked to any cabal (Vauban). The *other* cabal, that of the duc de Bourgogne, counted virtually no high-ranking military officers among its members. Bear in mind that Chevreuse and to an even greater extent Beauvilliers were quasi-pacifists. If peace could be had, they were more than ready to abandon the Spanish Bourbon to his sad fate.

But to get back to the Maintenon cabal, recall that "Voysin and his wife were the instruments [of Maintenon and Harcourt] and relied in turn on their support." Voysin belonged to a family of *maîtres des requêtes*, one of those families of "mandarins" that served as a breeding ground for future state councilors and intendants and played such an important role in the government and the court. His adroit wife had advanced her own fortune, according to Saint-Simon, by ingeniously arranging hospitality for Mme de Maintenon during the campaign of 1692 in Hainault when her husband was intendant there. Voysin replaced Chamillart as secretary of state for war and later became a minister of state, and in these positions he played an important role in Mme de Maintenon's maneuvers. The king did not automatically embrace the opinions that la Fée ("the Fairy") whispered in his ear—quite the contrary—so that it was one of the lady's constant objectives to make sure that there was always a minister beholden to her on the King's Council, someone who could present her views to the king as he sat among his ministers. She had hoped that her favorite, Harcourt, might fill this role, but in the end she entrusted it to Voysin. This mission of trust turned out to be of the utmost importance at the end of Louis's reign, when it came time to force the council to swallow two bitter pills: the king's testament and the codicils bestowing certain privileges on the royal bastards. After becoming chancellor, Voysin retained his position as secretary of state as well. By currying favor with the king's wife, Voysin's spouse had done him an enormous service.

We come next to the second rank, at the head of which Saint-Simon placed Chancellor Pontchartrain, "who was dismayed by Mme de Maintenon's aversion to him and his consequent estrangement from the king." Here we encounter one of the basic rules of cabals as Saint-Simon understood them: it was possible for someone not in the good graces of a cabal's leader—in this case Mme de Maintenon—still to be a key player in the cabal owing to his position, allies, and enemies. Mme de Maintenon may have had an aversion to the elder Pontchartrain, but this meant only that he was demoted to the "second rank," not expelled from the group. The case of the Phélypeaux-Pontchartrains is interesting in several respects. This was one of the great "bureaucratic" families of the seventeenth century and destined ultimately to join the high aristocracy in the eighteenth century. Furthermore, the department of government headed by the younger Pontchartrain was responsible for overseeing the city of Paris. He was therefore aware of all the information that the police turned up about the city's residents, information he reported to the king. This was an undeniable source of power, even though young Pontchartrain's relations with the police, headed and indeed incarnated by d'Argenson, were complicated.

Through "Blouin and other secret agents, [Maintenon and Harcourt] knew everything." With the Pontchartrains we encountered the question of the police, which was one key to the Maintenon group's power. With Louis Blouin, first valet of the king's chamber and a close friend of two of the group's mainstays, the duc de Villeroy and the duc de La Rocheguyon, we come to the question of espionage, but now in the court rather than the city.

As governor of Versailles, Blouin supervised the Swiss guards and other clandestine observers and palace factotums. Reports on the behavior of any number of courtiers passed through him on their way to the king.

Beringhen, the first equerry, known as "Monsieur le Premier," was in charge of the *petite écurie*, or small stable, and thus head of a department that might seem far less important than the guards or police. But at Versailles, the *petite écurie* was in a state of permanent rivalry with the *grande écurie*, presided over by Louis de Lorraine, the grand equerry, known as "Monsieur le Grand," and an intimate friend of Louis XIV. Notwithstanding the somewhat pointless competition between these two equestrian organizations, Beringhen occupied a key node in the Maintenon network. He was on good terms with Huxelles and also served Harcourt and Chancellor Pontchartrain as go-between: he had "grown old in intrigue . . . brought Harcourt together with the chancellor, and worked everyone into a frenzy."

Rocheguyon, "who laid traps while sneering in silence," offers another interesting example of the importance of position. He was the son of François de La Rochefoucauld, who, like Monsieur le Grand, was a close friend of the king but on bad terms with Mme de Maintenon.[9] But La Rocheguyon was Louvois's son-in-law and the brother-in-law of the duc de Villeroy. He was a friend of Blouin but cool toward Beauvillier and Torcy, that is, toward the Colbert clan, which figured prominently in the Bourgogne cabal. Through a process of attraction and repulsion, a system of what one might call "natural valences," he thus wound up in the Maintenon cabal.[10]

The duc du Maine was the illegitimate son of the "double adultery" of Louis XIV and Mme de Montespan. He was loved by both the king and Mme de Maintenon, who raised him, and he, too, joined the *cabale des seigneurs:* "M. du Maine, who reigned in the hearts of the king and Mme de Maintenon, arranged everything, obeyed no one but himself, was full of mockery, did as much harm as he could to everyone, and was feared and known by all." Maine was not alone: whether by chance or by design, he was the leader of a clique within the larger Maintenon cabal.

In addition to such important allies as Albergotti, d'Effiat, d'Antin, Voysin, and of course Maintenon, the Maine group, whose members often appeared at the glittering court over which the duchesse du Maine presided at Sceaux, could also count on various satellites, such as the duc d'Aumont and the duke of Albemarle (bastard of James II), the marquis de Pompadour, the marquis de Montmorency-Laval, the marquis d'Ancezune, the comte de Langeron, the baronne de Staal, and the demoiselle de Montauban.[11] There were also ecclesiastical satellites such as the cardinal de Polignac, Bishop Chambonas, and Abbé Brigault, and judicial satellites such as Bargeton and above all Mesmes, the *premier président* of the Parlement of Paris. And there was also a poet, La Grange–Chancel. Maréchal de Villars even seems to have compromised himself for Maine in the Cellamare conspiracy.

In the course of Saint-Simon's analysis, the family ties of each of the cabals emerge with remarkable clarity. As noted earlier, each cabal was tied to the royal family tree at a different point. The Maintenon cabal was linked to the father, Louis XIV. We turn next to the cabal of Monseigneur, the son. "D'Antin, Madame la Duchesse, Mlle de Lillebonne and her sister, their uncle, from whom they were inseparable, and the intrinsic court of Meudon formed this [second] party," writes Saint-Simon. In this brief passage we see the two poles of the cabal whose center was the château de Meudon. Blood ties constituted the first pole: Madame la Duchesse was the (natural) half-sister of Monseigneur, the legitimate son of Louis XIV, since she was the king's bastard daughter, the product of what Saint-Simon calls Louis's *tendres amours* for Mme de Montespan. She was also the half-sister of d'Antin, another influential member of the group, the legitimate son of Mme de Montespan and her husband Louis-Henri de Pardaillan, marquis de Montespan. The second pole of the cabal involved Lorraine: Mlle de Lillebonne and her sister (the "two Lorraines," as Saint-Simon calls them), erstwhile protégées of Louvois, were both princesses of Lorraine, and their uncle Vaudémont was a prince of Lorraine. All three counted bastards among their ancestors. As in the time of the Guises, but with less bloody panache and flamboyance, the (semi-bastardized) house of Lorraine intervened in the cabals of the French court. And in generational terms, it intervened at the level of the "son," Monseigneur.

Linked to both of these poles was what Saint-Simon calls "the court of Meudon proper," in other words, the court of Monseigneur.[12] For the "perfect courtier" anxious about his career, this posed a problem. It was all a question of "timing," of the impossibility of being in two places at once. One naturally followed the king to Marly, but in anticipation of the coming reign, one was also obliged to go to Meudon to pay court to Monseigneur (since of course no one knew that he was going to die before his elderly father). So one made arrangements to "mix visits to Marly with visits to Meudon." This was one of the great ideas of the reign, or at any rate, one of the ideas of the noble population of Versailles.

At this point let us turn back to our basic reference text:

> Neither of the two other [parties, that is, the Maintenon and Bourgogne cabals] wanted anything to do with [the members of Monseigneur's cabal], and both feared and distrusted them. But everyone was polite to them on account of Monseigneur [who of course stood in line to become king], and even Mme la duchesse de Bourgogne was polite to them. [In the Monseigneur group] d'Antin and Madame la Duchesse [half-brother and half-sister] were as one. They were equally condemned. Yet they headed this party. In d'Antin's case this was because of his private meetings with the king, which increased with each passing day, and which he better than anyone else knew how to flaunt and even, together with Madame la Duchesse, parlay into a solid advantage for their own [private meetings] with Monseigneur. Not that the two Lorraines did not enjoy even more of the confidence [of Monseigneur] and Mlle Choin [his mistress], more at any rate than the other two. They [the two Lorraines] also had another advantage, but one that was unknown at the time and long afterward, of which I spoke earlier . . . which was the connection with Mme de Maintenon, whose basis was shameful but substantial and for that very reason well concealed [one of the two Lorraine princesses was Mme de Maintenon's spy and regularly wrote her about what went on at court]. But they were still stunned by the thunderbolts that had just fallen on Vendôme and Chamillart [both disgraced]. Boufflers, Harcourt, and their chief lieutenants detested [Vendôme's] pride and the high rank and position of command he had achieved. . . . This second party [that is, Monseigneur's cabal] was strictly speaking Vendôme's.

Or at any rate, it had been until the marshal's recent disgrace. We can now add a further level of complexity to our description. Monseigneur's cabal included foreign princes (of Lorraine), two bastard females and the half-brother of a bastard female (the princesse de Conti, Madame la Duchesse, and d'Antin), soldiers (Luxembourg and for a short time Vendôme), and finally, more remotely connected, the families of the princes of the blood, Conti and Condé, themselves married to bastard daughters of Louis XIV, who were close to Monseigneur. The king—endogamous and initially polygamous before settling into monogamy with Mme de Maintenon—arranged marriages during his lifetime between four of his natural children, both male and female, and princes or princesses of the royal blood belonging to families whose male members had some possibility of acceding to the throne. Both the Condés and Contis were descended from Charles de Bourbon, the grandfather of Henri IV. Arranging marriages between cousins was a clever way of keeping the peace at home. If there were genetic dangers in such marriages, the benefit was worth the cost: there would be no *frondes* or wars of religion.

Under these conditions, the ties between Monseigneur and his group on the one hand and the bastards and Condé-Contis on the other were of far-reaching significance. The alliance thus created reached into the inner sanctum of the heir apparent. Monseigneur was paired with his mistress, Mlle Choin: "a large, short, ugly, witty brunette, who became extremely fat and stank as she grew old, but was modest, honest," and disinterested (according to Saint-Simon's various portraits of her). Before taking up her position as Mme de Maintenon to le Grand Dauphin and his cabal, she had been lady in waiting to the first princesse de Conti (the "dowager" princess), who was herself a bastard daughter of Louis XIV and Louise de La Vallière. This princesse de Conti was thus also the half-sister of Monseigneur and for a long time acted as his private advisor, until she was supplanted in that role by another woman who was half-sister to both her and Monseigneur, namely, Madame la Duchesse, also a bastard of Louis XIV but by Mme de Montespan rather than La Vallière. (Monseigneur definitely could not do without the advice of one or the other of his bastard half-sisters.) Indeed, it was the dowager princess who arranged the affair between Choin and the dauphin.

Monseigneur's cabal was highly ingrown. The dowager princess had been married to a Conti, who soon left her a widow. Her rival was the dauphin's other half-sister, Madame la Duchesse, who married not a Conti but a Condé known as Monsieur le Duc. Conti, Condé: the difference was unimportant. What mattered was that it was "all in the family," indeed, in the lineage of the Condés, *bourbonnique* par excellence.

The Conti-Condé-Bourbon ties in Monseigneur's immediate and extended entourage were further reinforced by other marriages, as well as by illegitimate amours. Indeed, the younger prince de Condé, the younger brother of the dead prince, married another Condé, the sister of Monsieur le Duc. And to top it all off, this prince was the lover of Madame la Duchesse. Monsieur le Duc was thus cuckolded by his sister's husband, who was also his cousin, as well as the kissing cousin of his wife. It is all too easy to lose track. Suffice it to say that in Monseigneur's entourage, everyone knew everyone else quite well.

There had been similar intrigues in the dauphin's entourage fifteen years earlier, in the period 1692–94. Hoping to influence the king's son and heir apparent, the maréchal de Luxembourg had, as it were, extended a pseudopod in his direction in the person of his relative and aide-de-camp Clermont-Chaste. Luxembourg had initially tried to push his aide into the arms of the dowager princesse de Conti as a way of manipulating that lady, who exerted a powerful influence on Monseigneur. Then, in a more subtle maneuver, he had installed the versatile aide as lover of none other than Mlle Choin, this being the most direct way to gain a hold over Monseigneur. Louis XIV thwarted this intrigue, however, by reading his bastard daughter (the princesse de Conti) love letters seized by the *cabinet noir*. As the princess listened in tears, political strategy turned to vaudeville.

It would take too long to explain how Vendôme, one of the great military leaders of the day and the grandson of a bastard of Henri IV, came for a time to embody the "Meudon cabal," which, thanks to his participation, became part of what might be called the military lobby. Within this Meudon cabal, or Monseigneur cabal or Vendôme cabal as it was also known, there were two subgroups, however, whose ambitions, hinged to the fate of Monseigneur, the heir apparent, did not always coincide. One faction centered on Mme de Montespan's two children, d'Antin and his half-sister Madame la Duchesse, who was herself the half-sister of Monseigneur (by the left hand). The other was led by the two Lorraine princesses, Espinoy and Lillebonne, and their uncle Vaudémont: "D'Antin and Madame la Duchesse, entirely united as to their views, mutual needs, vices, and motives, were highly suspicious of the two Lorraines, despite confidential and outwardly most cordial relations between the two groups sustained during the king's lifetime by their common aims, awaiting the moment when they would slit one another's throats for sole possession of Monseigneur after he became king."

Seen from outside, the Meudon cabal, with its intricate interpersonal relations and tangled intrigues, might be likened to an octopus with its tentacles all twisted and entwined. Seen from inside, however, it was more like a jellyfish. Monseigneur was the soft underbelly, the central point not only of his group but, as we said earlier, of the entire system. Monseigneur, Saint-Simon wrote in substance, was as unintelligent as could be, stout but not squat, sensible but not witty, petty in a thousand ways, easygoing because of his dullness, yet tightfisted with his mistresses. What little enlightenment he possessed was snuffed out by too much education, and all he ever read was the society pages and obituaries in the *Gazette de France*. The historian François Bluche has tried to revise this portrait of Monseigneur by putting intelligence back into the picture—a difficult task but perhaps not impossible.

Was Monseigneur's cabal truly independent of the dominant faction symbolized by the name if not the person of Mme de Maintenon? To answer this question in the affirmative would be to give much credit to le Grand Dauphin, who, however voluminous, and undeniably legitimate, nevertheless lacked substance. His vast presence was not surrounded by the effervescence of talent and ideas that one finds around the duc de Bourgogne, whose entourage included such first-class men as Fénelon, Saint-Simon, Chevreuse, Beauvillier, what was left of the Colbert clan, and even some Quietists. More important, the Monseigneur cabal was in fact linked to the Maintenon group, if only through the princesse d'Espinoy, who, as was mentioned earlier, was both a "Maintenonist" and a fixture among the *parvulos* of Meudon.[13]

One last point: important courtiers and ministers who belonged to the Maintenon group took care to remain on the best of terms with Monseigneur in anticipation of his coming reign (which of course never came). Among them were Huxelles, Beringhen, Harcourt, Boufflers, Villeroy, and La Rocheguyon (La Rochefoucauld). Even more important, because they were or stood to become ministers, were the members of the Phélypeaux faction, most notably Pontchartrain senior and La Vrillière. In addition, the Monseigneur cabal had substantial ties to the financial world. And last but not least, the Lorraine princes had not put all their eggs in one basket. Among the members of this important family from the border region to the east were Monsieur le Grand, whom Louis XIV valued highly and even adored; the princesse d'Harcourt, wife of Alphonse de Lorraine, who was on intimate terms with Mme de Maitnenon; the two Lorraine princesses Espinoy and Lillebonne, who spent every evening with Monseigneur; and the chevalier de Lorraine, who was Monsieur's lover. In another sign of the distinctiveness of the Bourgogne cabal, it alone among the three had no room for the invaders from Lorraine, who liked to think of themselves as dynamic figures on the model of the Guises.

The two "senior" cabals (of Monseigneur and Maintenon), together with the bastard subgroup (Maine in association with Maintenon), formed a "cluster" within the court that allows us to define what might be called the dominant party at Versailles. This "party" dominated not just the court but also the few hundred, or at most a thousand or so, principal "technocrats" who ran the apparatus of government and formed the "political class": *maîtres des requêtes, conseillers d'Etat*, intendants, financiers, military leaders, bishops, and *premiers présidents*. These three intertwined cliques—Maintenon, Monseigneur, and Maine—occupied the heights of power and influence. Many key decision makers belonged to one or the other of these groups.

What we are dealing with, then, was a flexible, decentralized, yet supreme power structure, a sort of protean "holding company" under the aegis, real or mythical, of "la Patronne," Mme de Maintenon. It included the following alliances.

1. *A camarilla of leading noblemen.* Well-placed in society and close to (or at any rate, within a respectful distance of) the king's wife, this group included the Richelieus, Monaco, Noailles, Estrées, Brissac, La Roche-foucauld, Clermont-Tonnerre, Huxelles, and Beringhen, to name a few.

2. *Military leaders.* If one includes Vendôme, who would later be disgraced, one can even say *the* military leadership, important generals who were also great nobles, namely, Luxembourg, Boufflers, Villars, Guiche (through his wife), Harcourt, Albergotti, and (until his fall) Vendôme— the group to which Saint-Simon referred as "the fresh air of the court and the armies"—in short, all those gentlemen who strapped on swords, whether real or ersatz, and cultivated good, in some cases deferential, relations with Mme de Maintenon and, of course, her royal spouse. What this shows is that the high aristocracy, though stripped of its civil power by the nobility of the robe that filled the councils and parlements, retained extremely important advantages when it came to war, which was the monarchy's great and constant preoccupation. A woman of soaring ambition such as Mme de Maintenon naturally took this situation into account when she formed her crucial relationships.

3. *Key ministers.* These were the men who controlled important segments of the bureaucracy and financial machinery as well as the armed forces, which were vast for the period. Specifically, key departments included the Office of the Comptroller General for Finance, the Chancellery, and the Secretariats of State for War and the Navy. The chancellor and above all the comptroller general supervised (through a variety of councils) the work of the *maîtres des requêtes* and *conseillers d'Etat*, the provincial intendants, and the many tax farmers who dealt with indirect taxes, military supplies, and the like. The royal couple, Louis XIV and Mme de Maintenon (who discreetly influenced each other without appearing to lift a finger), intervened in this machinery in various ways with the help of one or another of the great ministerial families, relying initially on the group constituted by the Phélypeaux clan, Bignons, and Caumartins. In particular, Phélypeaux–La Vrillière held one of the four secretary of state positions. Even more important were the Phélypeaux-Pontchartrains, father and son, who simultaneously or successively headed the Contrôle Général, the Chancellery, and the Navy (which had been set afloat again after Colbert). At first both father and son enjoyed a good reputation at court, but at some point relations between the elder

Pontchartrain and Mme de Maintenon (but not the king) turned sour enough to result in his estrangement, though never total disgrace. Mme de Maintenon also relied on other families headed by notable individuals: first the Chamillarts and then the Voysins for Finance, War, and the Chancellery (and here again a subtle game of favor and disfavor resulted in a transfer of influence from Chamillart to Voysin).

The mechanics of personal and family influence do not change much from century to century. Things were much the same three hundred years ago as they are today. Accordingly, it is interesting to note that early in his career Chamillart served as superintendent of Saint-Cyr, an institution founded by Mme de Maintenon and dear to her heart. (One thinks of Georges Pompidou, who as a young man directed the Fondation Anne-de-Gaulle under the supervision of General de Gaulle's wife.) Voysin also made the journey from obscurity to power by taking up the post of superintendent of Saint-Cyr. Contemporary witnesses, beginning with the highly reliable d'Aguesseau, confirm the influence of Mme de Maintenon's desires on the decisions that the king would later make to the detriment of the elder Pontchartrain and in favor of Chamillart and, subsequently, Voysin.[14]

Whether octopus or ectoplasm, la Patronne also clasped to her ecumenical bosom what was left of the Le Tellier–Louvois clan, despite the fact that she had previously felt an aversion to Louvois. When it came to mending fences, however, she was a past master, and she established a very businesslike relationship with Louvois's son Barbezieux, whom she liked better than she had liked his father, just as she preferred the younger Pontchartrain to the elder and saw to it that he eventually became secretary of the navy. In addition, most of the illustrious aristocratic families that had opportunistically allied themselves with the Le Tellier–Louvois faction through marriage were on the best of terms with the king's wife at the turn of the eighteenth century. Finally, such ancient ministerial families as the Le Peletiers, Villeroys, and Brûlarts still maintained footholds in the high administration (Le Peletier) or were powerfully if unimaginatively represented at court (Villeroy). All came under the aegis of "the group," that vast and durable collection of smaller cliques whose later stodginess earned it the appellation of "old court" under the Regency. Mme de Maintenon was notable for her adaptability. During the early years of her marriage, she relied on the orphans of the great minister Colbert to the detriment of the Le Tellier–Louvois clan. Later the subtle lady dropped the Colberts in order to facilitate her alliance with Louvois's son Barbezieux. This turn of events coincided more or less with a withdrawal of favor from the sons- and daughters-in-law of Colbert, who were suspected of Quietism.

4. *The "super-group."* The "super-group" took charge of the relics,

emotional and biological, of Louis XIV's love affairs and friendships with women, including both former mistresses (such as La Vallière and Montespan) and intimate friends (such as Mme de Soubise). The king managed his love life rather well.[15] His emotional odyssey took him from a Nausicaa (La Vallière) to a Circe (Montespan) and finally to a Penelope (Maintenon). All of these women came from excellent, or at any rate respectable, families. They were therefore "presentable," as were their offspring, even those of the left hand. At most the Sun King allowed himself a few blunders, such as his affair with one of the women who tended the royal gardens, whose child, the product of his royal amours, he married off to La Queue, an obscure gentleman from Brie, to whom Bontemps every now and then gave a few écus.[16] In this respect Louis XV would be much less well behaved, or more negligent at managing his majestic "image." Some of his affairs were with women well down the social scale, and he even contracted a venereal disease, something that the Sun King had always been careful to avoid: this sun had no spots.

As Louis XIV grew old, "the group" maintained excellent relations with some of these women (such as Soubise) as well as with their families. If they were disgraced and cloistered (as La Vallière and Montespan were), and later after they died, the group watched over their offspring, with Madame de Maintenon as governess. Among the children of royal mistresses cared for in this way was the duchesse d'Orléans, whom la Patronne had once dandled on her knees and who eventually saw to it that Mme de Maintenon was admitted to the residence of the future regent at the Palais-Royal.[17] Another was Madame la Duchesse, married to the elder Condé and deeply involved in Monseigneur's cabal. And last but not least was the duc du Maine, whose subgroup we have already briefly examined. In this vast network of bastards, the cardinal de Rohan, a legitimate son of Mme de Soubise and her husband, enjoyed a special status as "honorary bastard" because the royal couple lavished upon him a portion of the affection that the king quite properly reserved for his lawfully wedded parents.

5. *The royal bastards.* From the standpoint of the state, the question of the royal bastards largely hinged on the rulings of the Parlement of Paris, which issued a series of ad hoc judgments in favor of "legitimized" bastards. Because of Parlement's role, the royal couple, Louis and Françoise, were convinced that they had no choice but to continue down a road they had started on long before. They continually pressured, not to say corrupted, two *premiers présidents* of Parlement, Achille III de Harlay and Jean-Antoine III de Mesmes, who in turn adopted a high-handed approach to the magistrates under them, magistrates who were, potentially at any rate, far less docile to royal authority than were their hierarchical

superiors, caught between a rock and a hard place.[18] Mesmes's nomination to be *premier président* in 1712 confirms the complex anatomy of the dominant group and its bastard subgroup: indeed, Mesmes basically obtained this key post thanks to the support of the duc du Maine, who wrote a letter of recommendation to Mme de Maintenon.[19] Thus the "super-group" kept a close watch on the *robe du Conseil* (that is, the *conseillers d'Etat and maîtres des requêtes*), but it also maintained monarchical control over the *robe du Parlement* (the high officials of the sovereign courts), far better control, in fact, than in other periods, such as the Fronde or the Regency of Philippe d'Orléans. Not only the courts but also the police were kept under firm control in Paris as well as Versailles, thanks to La Reynie and later d'Argenson, Pontchartrain junior, and the first gentlemen of the king's bedchamber (Bontemps and Blouin).

The group also wielded a certain international influence, especially in Spain through Mme des Ursins and the first wife of Philip V, who was none other than the sister of the duchesse de Bourgogne and hence a descendant of the dukes of Savoy. Both of these princesses were on good terms with Mme de Maintenon and with each other. The king's wife also had ties to the family of the Elector of Bavaria as well as cordial relations with the Jacobites and especially with the royal Stuart family, which had sought refuge in France, but only after losing power at home.

In religious matters, the dominant group, symbolized by la Patronne, had been clever enough to adopt a "centrist" or, rather, "center-right" position, which proved advantageous, since in many power structures the center coincides with the summit.[20] The group was generally anti-Jansenist. How could it have been otherwise under the reign of Louis and Françoise? (Some of its members, such as the elder Pontchartrain, made no secret of their Gallican leanings, however, which may explain the cooling of relations between him and Mme de Maintenon.) In any case, the group refused to align itself totally with the Jesuits. Owing to the influence of la Patronne, it tended to follow the more moderate lead of the Séminaire des Missions Etrangères (which differed in some small ways from the Jesuits, whose tolerance of Chinese ceremonies met with disapproval).[21] To an even greater extent, it also followed the lead of the Sulpicians. (Saint-Simon always made a point of disparaging the "filthy beards" of Saint Sulpice, who wielded such great influence in the seminaries.[22] The Sulpicians in a sense oversaw the training of the lower clergy.)

A figure such as Godet des Marais, bishop of Chartres, is a good symbol for Mme de Maintenon's "centrism" or "Sulpicianism." As confessor to the lady and honorary Sulpician, Godet apparently prevailed upon his penitent to influence the king with respect to the distribution of benefices and nomination of bishops. (We know, moreover, that Mme de Maintenon's modest power over the sovereign was exerted not so much in the realm of great decisions, such as the Revocation, over which she had little sway, as in the selection and appointment of officials, both clerical and lay. In this area her tactics of insinuation worked wonders.) Is not the power to appoint the ne plus ultra of real power? After Godet's death in 1709, the torch of clerical influence was taken up by Cardinal de Bissy and the curé La Chétardie, who jointly assumed Godet's role with respect to Mme de Maintenon. But Bissy's talents as a negotiator were not the equal of Godet's, and he made himself ridiculous by trying to reconcile the regent's cabal, represented by Abbé Dubois, with the old court, represented by the maréchal de Villeroy.

"Let us sink the prelates." Like military leaders, bishops wielded *some* power, chiefly regional, even if they lacked the extensive powers of ministers. Through the prelates, not only the court aristocracy and nobles of the sword but also nobles of the robe and even the aristocracy of finance were able to find hugely profitable places for any number of younger sons, for their own greater glory as well as that of God. This constituted a network of considerable influence, as la Patronne was well aware, just as she was aware of the value of her cherished marshals.

Finally, the Maintenon group also contrived to shape the future, beyond the innovative interlude of the Regency and the successful initiatives of its three godfathers, Orléans, Dubois, and Law. After the death of Dubois and the disgrace of Monsieur le Duc, Cardinal de Fleury became in effect young Louis XV's permanent prime minister. Fleury was well versed in the arcana of the old court and knew the shadowy ins and outs of the Maintenon clan long before the death of Louis XIV. He made a point of befriending la Patronne (and the friends of la Patronne) through the Dangeaus, the Lévis, Maine, and Villeroy—the very heart of the dominant "super-clan." He shared their discreet doubts about the Jesuits, in all friendship to be sure, yet he knew how to bargain with them once he had the tiller in hand. Knowing all this, Louis XIV set it down in his will that Fleury was to be the tutor of little Louis XV, thus ensuring that this son of a Languedocian financier would enjoy a most astonishing career, from which the old court, or what was left of it after 1723, would to some extent benefit. It was not entirely an accident that one of Fleury's first steps as prime minister was to evict from Versailles an enemy of that same old court: the duc de Saint-Simon.[23]

Having reviewed the cabals of Mme de Maintenon and Monseigneur, who were not so much enemies as hostile allies, let us turn now to the cabal of the third generation, that of the duc de Bourgogne, also known as the "ministers' cabal."

Drawn to the hopes nourished by the birth, virtue, and talents of Mgr le duc de Bourgogne and utterly devoted to the cause by undeniable affection was the duc de Beauvillier, who was more visible than any of the others; the duc de Chevreuse [by virtue of his *esprit géométrique*] was the soul and strategist [both dukes were sons-in-law of Colbert]; the archbishop of Cambrai [Fénelon], from the depths of his disgrace and exile, [was] the pilot. Of lesser prominence were Torcy and Desmarets [both with family ties to the Colbert clan]; Father Tellier [the king's confessor]; and the Jesuits. Desmarets was friendly with the maréchal de Villeroy and the maréchal d'Huxelles. And Torcy, close to the chancellor [Pontchartrain], joined with him on matters concerning Rome [both were Gallicans] and consequently opposed the Jesuits and Saint-Sulpice. In this particular area Torcy was thus at odds with his cousins Chevreuse and above all Beauvillier [who were both pro-Jesuit], so that relations between them were awkward and often embarrassing. The latter tightened their alliance when necessary, always concerting their views, as they had occasion to see each other constantly without seeming to go out of their way to do so [because they were brothers-in-law, Colbertians, and unofficial or official ministers]. [They were] immune to darts because of their positions and quick to take everything in; in a position to divert others with illusions and, with a wave of the hand, to turn realities into fantasies . . . because throughout this reign the ministry totally controlled affairs, however much confidence Mme de Maintenon may have usurped. . . . They had only to parry [here the actions of the two brothers-in-law are described]. . . . Their devoutness . . . was easy to ridicule [this was a cabal with religious overtones]. Frippery, fashion, and envy were on the other side, with la Choin and Mme de Maintenon. The two cabals [that of the duc de Bourgogne and that of Mme de Maintenon, the grandson and the "grandmother," so to speak] eyed each other warily. [The Bourgogne cabal] proceeded in silence, the other noisily, and seized upon all available means to injure its rival. All the elegant people at court and in the army were on the side [of the Maintenon cabal], whose ranks were further swelled by disgust and impatience with the government, and many sage people were drawn in by the probity of Boufflers and the talent of Harcourt.

Despite the snobs' disdain, the Bourgogne or ministers' cabal did count several notable figures among its members, first and foremost the duc de Bourgogne himself, the son of Monseigneur and grandson of Louis XIV. The childish duke was given to daydreaming while engaged in such favorite pursuits as killing wasps and mashing grapes, but toward the end of his youth (and life) he apparently matured. He might have made a great king had he not succumbed to an early death in 1712, at age thirty. He was also a devout boy, even something of a religious bigot.

The duc de Beauvillier, Colbert's son-in-law, was disciplined in every sense of the word: early to rise, pious, humble, precise, and immune from extravagant fancies (to paraphrase Saint-Simon's various descriptions). As a minister of state, Beauvillier was one of the few nobles of high rank but not of the gown who attended meetings of the King's Council. It was his ministerial presence, along with that of Desmarets, Torcy, and even Chevreuse (minister *in partibus*), that earned the duc de Bourgogne's group the sobriquet "ministers' cabal." In a sense it was the rump of Colbert's group.[24] By contrast, the Maintenon group (which had less access to the ministry despite the powerful influence of la Patronne, the chancellor, Chamillart, and Voysin) was known as the "lords' cabal," presumably because it counted so many illustrious aristocrats among its members.

The duc de Chevreuse, Beauvillier's brother-in-law, served as unofficial advisor to the king, to whom he had access at all hours "through the back door." He whispered advice in the king's ear. This close relationship with the monarch ultimately gained him an appointment as minister of state, although he did not participate in meetings of the King's Council.[25] According to D. H. J. Van Elden, Chevreuse (despite his penchant for illogical argument) was Pascal's prototype of the *esprit de géométrie*, as opposed to the *esprit de finesse* so common among the descendants of Mortemart (most notably Mme de Montespan and her children, almost all of whom were blessed with the much-vaunted *esprit Mortemart* that so fascinated Marcel Proust).[26]

Next comes Fénelon: despite his exile to Cambrai, where he was archbishop, the author of *Télémaque* was still a key figure in the Bourgogne cabal, indeed the quintessential figure of the liberal and more or less aristocratic opposition. Saint-Simon was lukewarm toward Fénelon, of whose pro-Jesuit leanings he was critical and whom he regarded (not altogether fairly) as an intellectual charmer, pleasant enough but capable of turning it on and off "like a faucet" and of giving each person just the right amount of syrup along with his intellectual, moral, and social gruel. In fact, Fénelon was a man of very high intelligence and a precursor of modern pacifism, educational methods, and perhaps even socialism. Of all the cabals, the Bourgogne was the one with ideas, which it owed largely to Fénelon, the brilliant ideologue in this theoretical and speculative company.

Two other members of this "sodality" are worth a brief glance.[27] Both were ministers belonging to the Colbert clan: Torcy, secretary of state for foreign affairs, wrote well and had a good memory, and Desmarets, comptroller general of finance, also served in a sense as a bridge between the government and the world of high finance (especially through his contacts with such important men of affairs as Samuel Bernard, contacts that proved to be highly beneficial to the state).[28] But Desmarets, who had close family ties to Voysin, was actually somewhat aloof from the Colbert clan and in the latter stages of his ministerial career enjoyed the favor of Mme de Maintenon, as well as the friendship of Villeroy and Huxelles, both members of the lords' cabal, or dominant party.[29] When it came to the decisive issue of calling French troops home from Spain, the Colbert-Bourgogne (or Beauvillier-Bourgogne) clan was naturally pacifist or "dovish" and therefore in favor of withdrawing French troops, whereas the "dominant" group, with Voysin, Monseigneur, Boufflers, Villeroy, La Rocheguyon, and, characteristically, Desmarets (who split with his Colbert cousins over this issue) remained "hawkish" and therefore in favor of keeping some of Louis XIV's soldiers in the Iberian Peninsula.[30] To complete the switching of partners, the elder Pontchartrain, a member of the dominant group, became a pacifist, which drew him closer to his old adversary Beauvillier. As for Madame de Maintenon, peace was all she hoped for, because as usual she was far more interested in what she could get out of men she had backed for high office than in what they thought about issues of war and peace, over which she had relatively little influence.

The Bourgogne group occupied important positions in the apparatus of government. For instance, Torcy's de facto and later de jure control of the postal system and secret censorship proved to be crucial.[31] The group was also powerful within the networks of tax farmers and other contractors who had done business with the government under Colbert and remained loyal to the Colbertians. These contractors had ties to Beauvillier but above all to Desmarets. Nevertheless, the Bourgogne group had its weaknesses. In contrast to the Maintenon cabal, which was an entire Gotha unto itself, in the Bourgogne cabal aristocratic families were relatively rare, although there were some: among them, thanks to Quietism, were the Béthune-Sullys, who oddly enough embraced what was left of the Fouquet clan, whom Colbert had oppressed (Béthune-Sully was linked to Fénelon, Beauvillier, and Chevreuse, and Béthune-Orval was Desmarets's son-in-law). Mention should also be made of a Mortemart, a foul-mouthed fellow, who married a Beauvillier daughter, and of course there was Saint-Simon himself, who was not as lowborn as his detractors and other ill-informed commentators claimed at the time and afterward. The group had little influence with the army, even though some of its members, such as Morstein and Montfort, fought in the ranks and died heroically (but in positions of relatively low rank). The former was the son-in-law and the latter the son of Chevreuse (and Montfort's death was all the more unfortunate in that as the son of Chevreuse and son-in-law of Dangeau he seemed destined to serve as a bridge, however tenuous, between the Bourgogne and Maintenon clans). The weak influence with the military will come as no surprise since this was a group with pacifist leanings, apart from the bellicose Desmarets, who was a Colbert to be sure but also had ties through a series of marriages to those inveterate warmongers Voysin and Lamoignon-Basville.[32]

In the religious, or rather ecclesiastical, realm, the Bourgogne-Colbert group's investments were overly diversified, some on the "right" (via the Jesuits and their friends the Quietists) and others—but these were in the minority—on the "left" (Jansenists and Gallicans). On religious issues, in other words, the group was not united in either action or philosophy, and this was a serious disadvantage. In this respect, it differed sharply from the Maintenon group, which shrewdly occupied the decisive center position (with the Sulpicians and Missions Étrangères), attacking vigorously to the left (aiming at the Jansenists) yet without totally surrendering to the right (the Jesuits and a fortiori the Quietists). Among the "Burgundians," by contrast, Beauvillier, Fénelon, Béthune-Sully, and Cardinal de Bouillon (a Fénelonist) were pro-Jesuit. This accounts for a phenomenon that would otherwise be astonishing, namely, the discreet presence, in an outer orbit of the Bourgogne cabal, of Father Tellier, the king's confessor. This Jesuit, whom Saint-Simon describes as the son of "poor Norman farmers," had therefore, by the *petit duc*'s (probably erroneous) reckoning, risen from "the dregs of the populace."[33] In any case, he was a hard man, stubborn, cruel, fierce, false in every way, a dreadful person, beyond the reach even of [fellow] Jesuits (all but four or five of them anyway), and born to do evil, at least to hear Saint-Simon tell it. We are not obliged to take him at his word.[34]

But the Bourgogne cabal, or rather its Colbertian subgroup, also included anti-Jesuits. Chevreuse, despite his Quietist leanings, was somewhat recalcitrant when it came to the followers of Loyola. And Torcy especially, following in the great tradition of his parents-in-law the Arnauld-Pomponnes, saw himself as discreetly Gallican and even pro-Jansenist. As Saint-Simon put it, "Chevreuse and Beauvillier, who kept no secrets from each other, were reserved with their supporters, and though cousins of Torcy, their suspicions of his Jansenism put substantial distance between him and them." While the Maintenonians held the center and the summit, the Burgundians fought on the flanks on opposing sides: with them, as we have seen, were both Tellier, the redoubtable Jesuit and royal confessor, and Torcy, the closet Port-Royalist [that is, Jansenist—trans.]. This was an undeniable weakness: a house divided against itself cannot stand.

N one of these three cabals existed in isolation. There were links between them. These were formed, if the reader will permit us to abuse scientific terminology, by atoms with "multiple valences." One

such atom was the astute, shrewd, and appealing duchesse de Bourgogne. Her husband was, of course, the central figure in his own cabal,
but she was also a dear friend of Mme de Maintenon: "Mme la duchesse
de Bourgogne . . . swam between the two cabals," as Saint-Simon
puts it. The duchesse de Bourgogne was thus a siren with a double loyalty. The same role of go-between, but this time between the Monseigneur and Bourgogne cabals, was played by Marie-Françoise Colbert
de Croissy, marquise de Bouzols, who, though ugly and malicious, was
also charming:

> For the ministers' [i.e., Bourgogne] cabal, there was no enemy greater than
> [the Monseigneur cabal], although Torcy [of the Bourgogne cabal] and
> Madame la Duchesse [of the Monseigneur cabal] and consequently d'Antin
> [also of the Monseigneur cabal] were on good terms with Mme de Bouzols,
> Torcy's sister and long an intimate friend in every way of Madame la Du-
> chesse and who, though her face was hideous, was nevertheless charming
> and had the devil's own wit.

Saint-Simon ends his magnificent "Sketch of the Court" with this sentence: "Such was the inner face of the court in those tempestuous times,
marked by two spectacular falls [of Vendôme and Chamillart], which
seemed to clear the way for others."

C an Saint-Simon's texts be used to develop an analysis of the political
leadership of the ancien régime as a modern political scientist
might go about it? To tell the truth, the discipline of political science is
not exactly in favor with historians, except for those who study the very
recent past. Perhaps this is because its conclusions do not take us very
far, or perhaps it is for some other reason. In the study of very old political
systems, political science has played almost no part. When it comes to
the seventeenth century, for example, everyone agrees on the existence
of coteries, factions, camarillas, and "sodalities," perhaps even of real political parties, though parties very different in nature from those whose
influence André Siegfried, studying the twentieth century, would map in
Ardèche and Brittany. The environment in which these older structures
took shape was so different from today's, however, that the lessons of
political science—whether that of Siegfried or that practiced in the
United States—are of little use.

Leaving contemporary methodological issues aside, one can nevertheless approach these texts of Saint-Simon's with certain broad questions
in mind. The *petit duc* here relies on a notion that was central not only
to his thinking but also to the reality of the court: the idea of a cabal. A
cabal was a temporary construct, though it might last for up to two decades or even longer. Its purpose was to obtain various advantages in

court and government circles such as power, prestige, money, appointments to high clerical or military positions, and promotions within the ranks of dukes, princes, and so on. For Saint-Simon, the study of cabals, which in his mind was inseparable from the task of portraying the individuals who belonged to them, was one of the chief purposes of history. Indeed, he criticized Father Daniel, who sometime around 1714 wrote a history of France, for having sacrificed everything to "battle history" while neglecting what one might call "cabal history" or "portrait history."[35]

In the case of the court of Louis XIV, the cabal system revolved around the system of royal filiation. Independent of that, however, each cabal can be seen as a "network" of relationships based on kinship, patronage, friendship, and the like. Furthermore, different cabals could be separated by hostility and quarrels between individuals or families. A cabal might be supported in part by a substructure associated with some social, sociopolitical, institutional, or religious force: the army, the church, the world of finance, the bureaucracy, the nobility, the princes of the blood, or the dukes and peers, for example.

Still, Saint-Simon's fundamentally individual, atomistic (and consequently molecular) vision of the three cabals and of the cabal system makes our rather sociological analysis seem somewhat forced. In a system in which there was no official opposition, however, or in which that opposition could not accede to power, the study of cabals is of some comparative interest. Such methods have been applied to the study of contemporary systems very different from one another and from the French ancien régime, systems in which power is obtained by jockeying for position among those already in place rather than by an alternation of roles between people in power and some sort of opposition. Examples of such continuity-based contemporary systems (which are by no means examples of "preestablished harmony") include various communist regimes, whose bureaucratic workings used to be studied by "Kremlinologists." Think, too, of France, where in a very different climate, of course, the Gaullist system merged into the post-Gaullist or "Giscardian" system. Here, the mechanics of succession were complex, but they worked without a hitch to achieve a certain measure of continuity, without opposition, until May 1981. Like the genealogical axes invoked by Saint-Simon, the channels of Gaullist succession involved the formation of "cabals" within a larger group whose members were, broadly speaking, in agreement as to essential matters but who assessed the future in different ways. They disagreed only in regard to the advantages they might hope to obtain from a possible change at the top. As different members of the group chose different individual strategies, factions developed.

Political sociology has often tried to emulate one of the natural sciences. The concepts of social class and class struggle (such as those of Guizot, Thierry, and Marx) were of course linked to various facts about the ancient and/or modern world: think of Servius Tullius's Roman census by "class" or the "classes" of maritime inscription prior to the French Revolution. Think, too, of the tax schemes proposed by Vauban and others: "taxpayers of the first class," second class, and so on. And then there were the classifications of animals and plants proposed by Linnaeus, Buffon, and Tournefort. Whether in zoology or sociology, such notions of "class" often imply rigid divisions (between mammals and birds, bourgeois and proletarians, and so on), which leads to problems about boundaries and overlaps, problems that can be difficult to solve even for the most subtle Marxist or the most illustrious entomologist.

Some American sociologists have worked with more flexible concepts borrowed from geology. For example, Pitirim Sorokin (who was actually European, or to be more precise, East European, though he taught in the United States) introduced the concept of social "stratification." In some ways the idea of "stratum" is richer than that of "class," because strata can be turned upside down, riven by faults, folded over on themselves, squeezed together, or pushed about and mixed by landslides. With the geological metaphor comes a certain variety, therefore. But geology is a science of the inanimate and inert. There is no real fusion, no synthesis, no active exchange between geological layers. That is why the stratifications of Sorokin and his many American followers are nearly as unsatisfactory as the botanical-zoological theories of Thierry, Guizot, Marx, and Tournefort.

Lucien Febvre was well aware of the problem and irritated by "stratigraphic" thinking based essentially on the opposition of high and low (even if the high and the low were eventually mixed together). He suggested an analogy between social structure and the complex structures and infrastructures of a large city: water mains, gas mains, and electrical cables snaking every which way to link the high and the low in unforeseeable ways, thus abolishing the hierarchies of sociological stratification and the rigid divisions of botany and zoology.

Saint-Simon followed a course quite similar to that advocated by Febvre. One of the duke's admirers, the twentieth-century German novelist Ernst Jünger, once remarked that the memoirist's methods were not all that different from those of organic chemistry and molecular biology, sciences which of course did not yet exist when Saint-Simon wrote. "Saint-Simon studies the court as if it were a huge organic molecule. His was a very modern spirit," Jünger wrote. Indeed, as is clear from our reference texts, Saint-Simon did not confine himself to identifying cabals and factions. He also recorded the valences of many types that linked this or that member of one cabal to this or that member of another.

He also noted the negative valences within each cabal: the elder Pont-chartrain was not on good terms with Mme de Maintenon, for example, or at any rate he had fallen out of favor, yet he remained part of the Maintenon cabal. Beyond his delineation of the three cabals, Saint-Simon was thus able to describe a concrete situation: the broad outlines of his account do not hide the less important and sometimes contradictory details. The court was of course a relatively closed and circumscribed unit, with only a few hundred important participants and perhaps a few thousand people involved all told. This hermetic character helps when it comes to writing a monograph.

At this point, we must abandon the realm of natural or physical science for that of social science and consider the rigorous methods that anthropologists have developed for the study of small communities: think, for example, of Evans-Pritchard's work on the Nuers or, at a simpler level, Lawrence Wylie's work on French villages. Obviously Saint-Simon had no notion of modern anthropology, even if he did have certain intuitions about the subject (he had apparently read some accounts of travels in Africa and America). His terms of reference were clock-making and the fabrication of automata: these were the advanced technologies of his day. He also uses metaphors based on gambling, which would have been constantly before his eyes at court.

Clock-making: We have a rather interesting text concerning Saint-Simon's efforts to put together a cabal of his own, although the truth is that he was more skilled at analysis than at machination. His plan was to use the networks and connections provided by the three existing cabals described above. Pursuing what he took to be his own best interests, he hoped to arrange a marriage between "Mademoiselle," the daughter of the duc d'Orléans (and grandniece of Louis XIV), and her second cousin, the duc de Berry, son of Monseigneur and grandson of Louis XIV. Yet another instance of serpentine endogamy: the monarchy was like a snake eating its own tail. In order to bring about this marriage, through which he hoped to improve his position, he employed various women and even the odd Jesuit. Saint-Simon had this to say about his efforts:

> Such were the machines and combinations of machines that my friendship for those to whom I was attached, my hatred for Madame la Duchesse, and my alertness to my present and future situation were able to assemble, arrange, and set to work in a precise and disciplined manner with proper adjustment and appropriate tugs on various levers, and which I inaugurated and perfected during the season of Lent. I was kept apprised of the workings of all of these machines, of the various obstacles they faced, and of the progress they made, and each day I regulated their clockworks accordingly.

From this perspective, the court was like a huge clock or timepiece, which Saint-Simon took apart and reassembled for our edification as well as for purposes of his own. He was of course aware that the comparison was not perfect. Clockworks made of metal last forever, or nearly so. By contrast, the mechanisms of the court were vulnerable to unpredictable reactions. They were like "cubes of ice" that melted in the sun. Within a few days of her wedding, the duchesse de Berry would get drunk, embark upon a dissolute life, and consequently disappoint the hopes that Saint-Simon had placed in her. In later years, a cabal assembled for the purpose of arranging the marriage of the duc de Berry would turn out to be one of the great regrets of Saint-Simon's life.[36]

Saint-Simon's analyses also draw our attention to games and gambling. He was concerned, first of all, with the idea of the *wager*. To put together or join a cabal was to wager on the future, to bet that the central figure in the cabal (whether Maintenon, Monseigneur, or Bourgogne) would retain power for a certain period of time (in the case of Mme de Maintenon) or acquire power (in the case of Monseigneur or the duc and duchesse de Bourgogne). Betting, moreover, was an activity with which Saint-Simon was familiar. When he bet that the city of Lille would be captured, he nearly ruined his reputation with the king for the sake of a few pistoles. And given his Jansenist sympathies, he was no doubt aware of Pascal's wager.

One game that interested him was *billiards*, which of course involves the indirect action of one ball on another ball by way of yet a third ball. The game was popular at court. Chamillart, who excelled at it, launched his brilliant ministerial career at the billiard table (even before he became acquainted with Mme de Maintenon through his post as intendant of Saint-Cyr).[37] And then there was Bishop Langres, "good Langres," who after humiliating himself at court because of his ineptness at billiards, began practicing back in his diocese and ultimately returned to Versailles, where he surprised many courtiers by beating them hands down.[38]

In some ways the cabals worked like a game of billiards. Take, for example, the case of Clermont-Chaste, whom the maréchal de Luxembourg used as an instrument, establishing him as the lover first of the princesse de Conti and later of Mlle Choin in order to influence the lackadaisical Monseigneur. Through these intermediaries, Luxembourg thus manipulated the man he regarded as the future king: Clermont-Chaste, the princesse de Conti, and Mlle Choin were his "balls" in a game of billiards.

Saint-Simon himself played billiards in connection with the duc de Berry's marriage. Through Father Tellier, the Jesuits, and a whole series of women, he tried to influence the key actors, namely, the king and

Mme de Maintenon. Neither Monseigneur nor the duc and duchesse d'Orléans had much power to make decisions in such matters, since the king more or less monopolized the field.

S aint-Simon's text, coupled with general knowledge of his work, allows us to form a picture of what might be called the "political class" of his time, or at any rate its upper echelons. This is not to say that the court exercised power. It did not, or at any rate not as such. But it was through the court that one could most effectively grasp the levers of power, especially since the ministers of government, the members of the leading bureaucratic families such as the Phélypeaux family, the Chamillarts, the Colberts, and the Louvois clan, were at court and married their children there. Marriages were constantly being arranged.[39] People met one another at social gatherings and elsewhere. The bureaucracy and the aristocracy mingled. In the eighteenth century, moreover, part of the high aristocracy (including Maurepas and others) consisted of none other than the descendants of men who had been "bourgeois" ministers in the seventeenth century. The "fusion of elites" was well under way, much to the benefit of the mandarin dynasties.

Saint-Simon's text is also interesting for the extensive use it makes of genealogical analysis. Once again we find three generations of the royal family: father, son, grandson, and their wives. And once again we discover the influence of kinship within the royal family and other important families: bastards, princes of the blood, and so on. Finally, let us say a word about ranks: the bastards sided mostly with Maintenon; the princes of the blood and certain female bastards were tied directly or indirectly to the Monseigneur cabal; and the dukes were associated with the Bourgogne and Maintenon cabals (among others).

Sociological factors also came into play. Various forces, such as the church, the very high nobility, the world of finance, and the army, aligned themselves with one or another cabal or else divided their support among several. The principle of hierarchy, which was at the heart of Saint-Simon's thinking, enabled him to impose order on all this by linking the cabals to the three top levels of the system: the king, together with his wife; the son of France (Monseigneur, le Grand Dauphin); and the grandsons of France and new dauphin (the duc d'Orléans and especially the duc de Bourgogne).

It would be interesting to look at how major groups aligned themselves. The most important were these:

- the marshals of France, who formed a sort of military lobby (primarily associated with the Maintenon cabal and, through Vendôme and Luxembourg, with the Monseigneur cabal)

- the princes of the blood and female bastards (mainly linked through the ladies to Monseigneur)
- the court's "internal valets," who were charged with police functions
- the dukes and peers and the nobility more generally
- the ministers
- the high-ranking clergy, some of whom had "invested" in the Maintenon cabal, others in the Bourgogne cabal

Clearly, the categories set forth above have little in common with those of Marxist analysis, or at any rate its more simplistic versions, which is hardly astonishing. The bourgeoisie is scarcely in evidence. One thinks of the intuitions of historians like Daniel Dessert, who argued that power was exercised within a very narrow circle of people, almost all of them noble (whether nobles of recent date and of the robe or of long standing and of the court). Most merchants and industrialists were excluded, but financiers were allowed in (most of them recently ennobled and involved with the state sector). One found them in the Maintenon cabal (associated with the princesse d'Harcourt), as well as in the "dominant party" in the broad sense, especially in the entourage of the Pontchartrains.[40] The receiver general Claude-François de La Croix, a friend of Mlle Choin, was part of Monseigneur's cabal. And there were also financiers with the duc de Bourgogne, Beauvillier, and Desmarets (from the powerful group of government contractors who were formerly clients of Colbert), as well as with the Orléans clan (Béchameil was Monsieur's intendant) and in the bastards' entourage (the comte d'Evreux, an associate of the comte de Toulouse, a royal bastard, was the son-in-law of the immensely rich financier Crozat). But to describe matters thus is to look at things through the wrong end of the telescope. In reality, finance was everywhere. Financiers were one of the four pillars of the regime's *nomenklatura;* the others were the high nobility of the sword *(grands seigneurs)*, the lesser nobility *(hommes de qualité)*, and the bureaucrats (including both the *robe du Conseil* and *haute robe du Parlement*). Financiers managed the property of the princes and dukes, offered the hands of their richly dowried daughters in marriage, and insinuated themselves into high administrative offices. By so doing they solidified the unity of the broad ruling group, to the exclusion of those doing business in the nonstate sector (commerce and industry). This group would divide into no more than three or four cabals and two main factions, the party of *resistance* (Maintenon) and the party of *change* (Bourgogne/Orléans), but division itself only confirmed the everyday reality of unity in administrative practice, social relations, and even the broad outlines of policy.

Before wrapping up this description of the cabals, we would do well to say a few words about the duc d'Orléans, for whom the period 1700–

1715 was one of wandering in the desert. "In 1709 Monsieur le duc d'Orléans was in no position to exert his will or participate in government in any way." In total disgrace with Louis XIV, Orléans had some connections with the "Bourguignons" but was alienated from them by his radical impiety. He remained "on standby," as it were, awaiting political changes to come. In the mean time, he enjoyed relatively cordial relations with the duc de Bourgogne and especially Fénelon, but genealogically he stood a notch higher, at the same generational level as the duc du Maine and Monseigneur, his half-brothers-in-law by the left hand and first cousins by the right. Orléans therefore allowed things to take their course. Having nothing to lose by biding his time, he was prepared to wait.

Let us return now to our basic pattern, based on the three generations of the royal family at the very summit of the hierarchy. A more "violent" version of the same pattern existed under Louis XIII with Marie de' Medici, Gaston d'Orléans, and Anne d'Autriche. One might extend this analysis by looking at the sociopolitical and religious forces that each of these strong personalities represented. For the period of the Fronde, a matrimonial or genealogical analysis in the style of Saint-Simon would be less pertinent, because the power of revolutionary forces after 1648 somewhat swamped the influence of family structure per se. Still, one does find Condé, a prince of the blood, opposing the duc de Beaufort, the son of a bastard of Henri IV. At the center of the system was Anne d'Autriche and her friend Mazarin, the minister, along with la Grande Mademoiselle. These players pursued "family strategies" with the backing of various "outside" forces (the nobility, Parlement, "the populace") whose allegiances shifted over time.

Even before the Fronde, cabals forged by various clan or factional interests tended to rally around an official or unofficial member of the royal family. Writing in his *Memoirs* of the period 1643–44, La Rochefoucauld observed that "a cabal was organized that included most of the people who had been loyal to the queen [Anne d'Autriche] while the late king [Louis XIII] was alive; it was known as the Cabale des Importants. Although the people in it had different interests, ranks, and professions, all agreed to be enemies of Mazarin, to publicize the imaginary virtues of the duc de Beaufort, and to pretend to a false honor, which Saint-Ibal, Montrésor, the duc de Béthune, and a few others took it upon themselves to bestow."[41] Anne, the late king's wife and soon to become the very dear friend of Mazarin, hence a disappointment to *les Importants*, and Beaufort, Henri IV's grandson by the left hand, briefly occupied strategic points in the system (as other princes and princesses would do in the 1700s). For a time this or that provisional group or coalition found their support useful in pressing specific demands.

What makes Saint-Simon's work interesting beyond the period it covers is that general considerations of this sort are spelled out with precision. With the aid of his texts, one can combine a modern "socioeconomic" analysis with a "genealogical" analysis that is not only traditional and "hierarchical" but also anthropologically illuminating.

One caveat, however: between the Fronde and the end of the seventeenth century, France witnessed the development of another, somewhat different system of cabals not amenable to this type of analysis. It was in the 1690s, owing to divisions stemming from the advent of Quietism, that the system of three cabals associated with three generations of the royal family emerged. It was this system that Saint-Simon described and that we have analyzed at length in this chapter. Earlier, however, in the 1650s, Mazarin, the queen mother's intimate friend, had gathered all power into his own hands. Little Louis XIV was still too young and too dependent on the cardinal to have much of a say in how things were done.

No bi- or tri-generational system was available for the cabals to attach themselves to. It would take forty years, the time necessary for Louis's children and grandchildren to be born and come of age, for such a network to form. The princes and princesses of the blood might have imparted a collateral rather than a multigenerational structure to the cabals of 1650–90.[42] But Mazarin, having been burned by the Fronde, took great care to prevent this: "The cardinal's lessons to the young king turned on general maxims, which came down to this: keep the princes of the blood down as much as possible."[43]

Since Cardinal Mazarin was the only person in authority to enjoy the affectionate confidence of Queen Anne, he became the center around which formed the various cabals and factions that would occupy center stage until 1690 (well after Mazarin's death). The abbé de Choisy, a highly intelligent man who may have dressed as a woman but described what he saw without embellishment, gave a clear analysis of the way things stood in 1661, from the eve of Mazarin's death until shortly thereafter:

> Fouquet, Le Tellier, and Lionne were the three ministers the cardinal used. Fouquet was superintendent of finance. Le Tellier, as secretary of state for war, had extensive knowledge of the government. Lionne had been a minister of state since attending the Frankfurt conferences and though he held no official appointment had for several years served unofficially as secretary of state for foreign affairs. The cardinal frequently complained about him and said unpleasant things but could not do without his services. All foreign matters were settled with him before being brought to old Brienne or his son, who were obliged to sign without examination. Colbert lurked in the

shadows. The cardinal had recommended him to the king as a private secretary, a good valet whose only thought would be of service and who would never try to influence him. [After Mazarin's death,] the king therefore held a first council meeting with his three ministers. Colbert [who would become the king's fourth minister] was not publicly admitted until long afterward. The queen mother was offended not to be included. She spoke of this rather openly.[44]

This remarkably clear text offers an elegant conceptualization of the situation. One man (an unmarried cardinal) was able to parlay his own genius and the queen mother's almost conjugal love/friendship into a position of unchallenged supremacy at the summit of the monarchy. He played the role of father or tutor to the young king, who was kept on a short leash, and governed through his "servants" (Fouquet, Lionne, and Le Tellier) and his "valet" (Colbert). After his death, he bequeathed this quartet of men, or rather, families, to Louis, who because he had no descendants old enough or relatives powerful enough, was similarly able to reign for a quarter of a century as sole sovereign.[45] His Majesty thus retained the cardinal's servants. Eventually he got rid of one (Fouquet) with the help of two others (Le Tellier and Colbert). From that point on, he had to deal only with a triumvirate (Le Tellier, Colbert, and Lionne), but Lionne soon ceased to take part in the struggle for real power: "Father Lionne," Choisy writes, "did not aspire to influence the king. He was content to discharge his duties honorably, to wangle substantial remuneration out of the court—remuneration that he often squandered on useless expenditures—and to abandon himself unreservedly to all sorts of pleasures."[46] This left two main contenders for power, or rather, two rival clans, each of which had its own network of clients and sub-cabals. Indeed, the Colberts and Le Tellier–Louvois faction sought to assign various parts of France to each of their loyal clients. The patrimonial and domestic system thus bequeathed to Louis XIV by Mazarin survived until after 1683, as Colbert, Le Tellier, Louvois, and Seignelay-Colbert passed away one by one between that year and 1691.

There followed a period of transition, which lasted from 1691 until 1697, during which the monogenerational system of the early reign (supported by the major clients of the head of the royal family) was replaced by the trigenerational system of the later reign, which lasted from 1697 until the deaths of Monseigneur and the duc de Bourgogne. At first Mme de Maintenon relied on what remained of the Colbert clan to thwart Louvois. Then, after Louvois's death, she distanced herself from the Colberts and entered into a brief rapprochement with what was left of the Le Tellier–Louvois clan. Meanwhile, the Colberts regrouped around the third generation of the royal family (the duc de Bourgogne). At that point, Mme de Maintenon turned to mandarin families that had not been among the most prominent of the previous period (in particular the Phélypeaux family, who were much in favor with la Patronne after 1690, and, later, the Chamillarts and Voysins).[47] In addition, an intermediate group centered on Monseigneur formed between the dominant clan (Maintenon) and the semi-oppositional clan (Bourgogne-Colbert). This third cabal was actually much closer to the dominant group than to the "opposition."

In this way a logical transition from a monogenerational to a trigenerational system was accomplished. But the network of cabals, or if you will, of clans and parties, continued to depend not on a partisan popular "base"—which was at once nonexistent and mute—but on that supreme patrimonialist summit, the royal house, the keystone of the entire edifice. Nevertheless, the cabals did eventually expand to include several thousand people: ministers, powerful bureaucrats, great lords, men of quality, high magistrates, financiers, generals, and prelates, who were like the ribs holding up the upper reaches of the regime.

Saint-Simonian Demography

and Female Hypergamy

5 *Saint-Simon mentions by name roughly ten thousand individuals,*
nearly all of whom belonged to the elite of France, along with
a smaller number from the elites of Spain, England, or Ger-
many.[1] A few came into the world in the sixteenth century,
but most were born in either the seventeenth century or the
first three decades of the eighteenth. As the age of Louis XIV gave way
to the Enlightenment, their numbers naturally dwindled.

Here we shall focus on the French, for this was the group that Saint-
Simon knew best, although he did become fairly well acquainted with a
few Castilian nobles while serving as an emissary to Spain. (Under the
heading "French" in this context, we include Savoyards, Lorrains, and
Walloons even though they were not subjects of France per se.) We know
the dates of birth and death of 2,616 of the "French" individuals (1,834
men and 782 women) whom Saint-Simon mentions. This information
can be gleaned from his text itself, the notes and index to the Boislisle
edition, the index to the first Pléiade edition (which has to be checked
constantly against Saint-Simon's text and Boislisle's footnotes), and the
new and noteworthy Pléiade edition edited by Coirault.

Table 5.1 breaks this "French" population down by sex and date of
birth, grouped by decade except for those born in the sixteenth century,
all of whom are listed in the first column, and those born in the 1720s
and 1730s, who are grouped together in the last column. (The samples
from these two periods, which mark the starting point and end point of
our survey respectively, were too small for analytical purposes.) Glancing
at table 5.1, we find 43 women born "in the sixteenth century," that is,

TABLE 5.1

	Sixteenth Century	1600	1610	1620	1630	1640	1650	1660	1670	1680	1690	1700	1710	1720–30	
Number of Women	43	32	30	45	61	80	79	99	81	86	88	35	16	7	A
Total Years Lived by These Women	3,179	2,238	2,092	3,093	4,133	5,403	5,310	6,160	4,850	4,883	4,929	1,957	596	370	B
Average Life Expectancy (in years)	73.9	69.9	69.7	68.7	67.8	67.5	67.2	62.2	59.9	56.8	56.0	55.9	37.2	52.9	C
Number of Men	194	68	86	135	151	215	221	207	190	164	105	49	32	17	D
Total Years Lived by These Men	13,180	4,527	5,788	9,476	10,630	15,068	15,000	13,331	12,046	9,971	5,755	2,704	1,806	1,012	E
Average Life Expectancy (in years)	67.9	66.6	67.3	70.2	70.4	70.1	68.3	64.4	63.4	60.8	54.8	55.2	56.4	59.5	F
															G
Boys and Girls Dead before Age 20	1	0	1	0	1	2	1	4	6	2	9	10	4	1	H

before 1600; 32 between 1600 and 1609; 30 between 1610 and 1619; and so on through the 1720s and 1730s, the last decades discussed by Saint-Simon and covered by the Boislisle and Pléiade indexes.

The second section of the table gives a similar breakdown for males. In addition to the figures on births, the table also records the average life expectancy of men and women decade by decade. Take men born in the 1690s, for instance: 105 are mentioned in the text and included in Boislisle's scholarly biographical notes. We find that they lived a total of 5,755 years, for an average life expectancy of 54.8 years.

Special attention should be paid to the last section of the table. It records the number of boys and girls mentioned in the *Memoirs* (and previously cited indexes) who died before reaching the age of twenty. These early deaths have been excluded from the totals in lines B and E. Saint-Simon took such little interest in infant and child mortality (defined as death before the age of twenty) that the numbers are too small (and no doubt inaccurate) to be useful. Indeed, the question did not interest him at all until he dealt with the 1660s, and even then his interest was feeble. Given this bias, we have decided to ignore the 42 deaths of "very young people" from the bottom line of the table. The remaining 2,616 individuals in our sample all lived at least twenty years and often much longer.

With this decade-by-decade breakdown, we are able to explore the workings of Saint-Simon's memory in a new way (see figure 5.1). Look first at the men. The numbers tell an interesting story. The males in whom the duke was most intensely interested intellectually belonged to the "cohorts" born between 1630 and 1690. When Saint-Simon, who was born in 1675 and began to write in the 1690s, turned twenty-five, these men ranged in age from twenty to seventy. The generations most amply represented in the *Memoirs* (and most fascinating to their author) were those born between 1640 and 1670, a period that includes the Fronde and the beginning of Louis XIV's personal reign. Whether motivated by hatred or friendship, praise or blame, the *petit duc* lavished the lion's share of his attention on men who were between forty and sixty when he turned twenty-five. A man of the past, Saint-Simon preferred his elders to his immediate contemporaries.

When it came to women, however, Saint-Simon, chaste and monogamous though he may have been, was primarily interested in females of roughly his own age, hence younger than the males mentioned in the previous paragraph. This was the group on which he performed his feats of memory. Figure 5.1 shows clearly that when it came to the "fair sex," Saint-Simon discriminated in favor of youth. His sample of men gives preference to age, but the women he paid attention to were scarcely older than he, and a fair number were still of tender age.

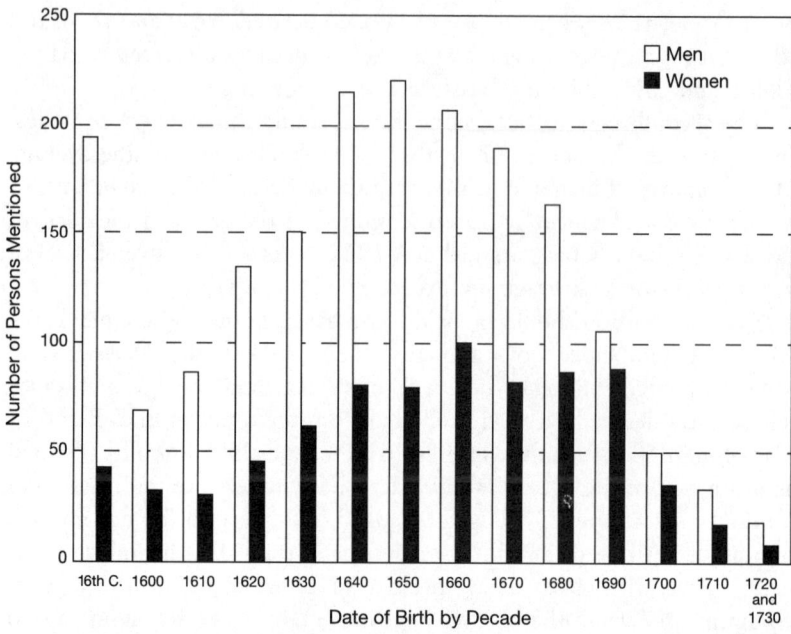

Figure 5.1. Distribution of "Saint-Simonians" by Decade and Gender

Figure 5.2 suggests another interesting finding. The life expectancy of men and women born in the writer's youth and early adulthood appears to be shorter than that of individuals born at other times. Take those born in the 1620s, for example. Survivors from that group would have been in their eighties when Saint-Simon was still young. Saint-Simon was primarily interested in these survivors, or at any rate, in others of this group who had only recently died. This accounts for the longevity of those born between 1620 and 1629 among his heroes and heroines: roughly sixty-nine and seventy years for females and males respectively. But as we move farther into the seventeenth century, Saint-Simon remembered more and more people whose birth dates were later than those in the first group. This meant that even if they died relatively young, the writer still might have known them directly or through someone he knew. Thus the samples grow progressively "younger" as we move from the beginning of our period toward the end. In these later samples, the higher proportion of people who died in youth or adulthood brings the average life expectancy down to 56.7 for the 232 women and 367 men born between 1680 and 1740 (a total of 599 individuals who lived collectively 33,983 years). Of course the average life expectancy in France did not really decline between the Revocation and the Regency. Indeed,

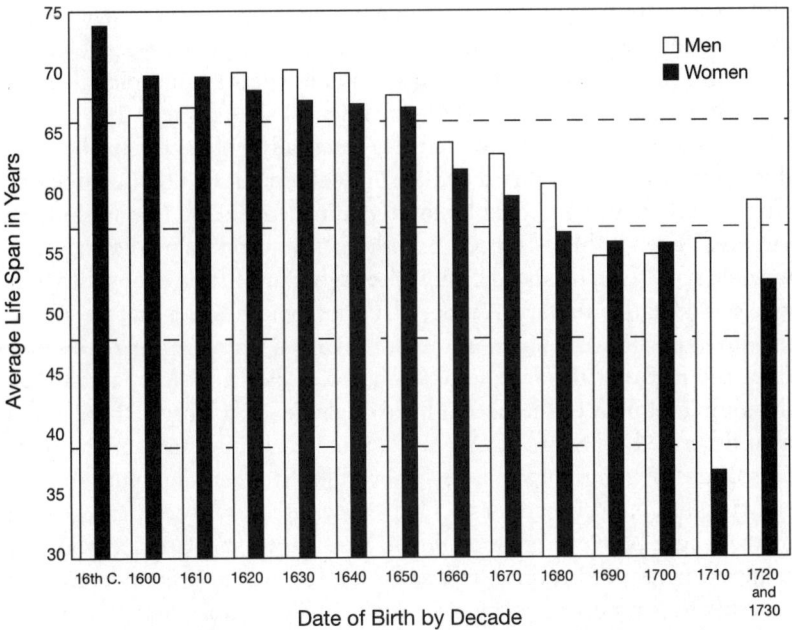

Figure 5.2. Average Life Span of "Saint-Simonians" by Gender

the final half century of our sample may fairly accurately represent the life expectancy of socially prominent people of the time. Those who rounded the "Cape of Good Hope" in their twentieth year could expect on the average to live another thirty or forty years.

The fine points of this discussion can be left to specialists in prosopography. Our goal is simply to compare social groups: men and women in high society, for instance, or *robins*, aristocrats, and soldiers.

When it comes to men and women, the sample reveals a striking fact. Look at table 5.1. Going back from the 1720s and 30s to the 1620s, we see that the life expectancy of Saint-Simon's women is sometimes equal to, or in the 1690s and 1700s just barely greater than, that of men, but more often than not it is lower, markedly so in the 1710s.

On the whole, women born between 1620 and 1739 appear to have lived noticeably less long than men. For the 677 women born in that period, the average life expectancy was 61.6 years, whereas for the 1,486 men it was 65.2 years (ignoring the fact that life expectancies are artificially inflated for those born in the earlier decades because of the effect of perspective or mirage described earlier).

The contrast between the figures for men and women in ten out of twelve of our sample periods is attenuated only slightly by the two aberrant decades, the 1690s and 1700s. That men could expect to live longer than women may have been true only subjectively, not objectively, but to Saint-Simon's contemporaries it was nonetheless an unavoidable reality. We would therefore do well to ponder its significance.

Was the mortality rate for females unusually high, perhaps because they gave birth too frequently under difficult conditions that contemporary obstetricians, hampered by limited knowledge, could do nothing to improve? Even if this was true—and there is no proof of it whatsoever—it would have to be balanced against the high mortality rate for aristocrats who served in the military. A more plausible hypothesis, therefore, is that the observed difference in mortality for men and women after 1620 stems from the fact that the sample of women was markedly less biased than the sample of men in the period from Richelieu to Fleury. Of the 1,486 men described by Saint-Simon and annotated by Boislisle, many were personages of some importance. They enjoyed a certain status and social visibility, however modest. Their notoriety was also a consequence of their age. Not everyone could be like the Grand Condé, who had achieved fame by the time he was twenty-two. The preponderance of noteworthy or notorious figures in the male sample makes it much "older" than the female sample. And while we can also detect the effect of notoriety, hence age, on the female side, it is less frequent than on the male side. Hence the apparent life expectancy of males is longer. Indeed, Saint-Simon (and therefore Boislisle) frequently mentions a man because he is important, which usually means that he is also old. It makes no difference that the memorialist's bias was involuntary and in any case inevitable. On the other hand, he might mention the same man's wife simply because she was the wife of a notable personage. For wives there was no "celebrity effect" as such and consequently no "age effect." This tends to reduce the average life expectancy of the women in our sample, even though celebrated women are of course discussed in the *Memoirs*.

For women born before 1620, however, the female notoriety effect, however minuscule, is much greater than for women born after that date. Saint-Simon mentions a number of women born in the sixteenth century or the first two decades of the seventeenth century. They are present in the text only because they were singled out by their contemporaries and by posterity, whose judgment Saint-Simon merely echoed. They were noteworthy because they were involved in activities that brought them some measure of glory—and because they lived long lives, which was in itself a source of distinction. Statistically speaking, the women who fit this description turn out to be as old as the men in the male sample for the same period (up to and including the third decade of the seventeenth century). Before 1620 the "longevity gap" ranges from two to five years, but now in favor of women. What accounts for these differences? The pre-1620 samples reflect very special circumstances: here, the notoriety or longevity effect applied equally to men and women. Indeed, the life expectancy of women in the samples is even longer than it is for men, while the reverse is true after 1620. It seems entirely plausible that this apparent advantage for women had more to do with the nature and quality of the information available to the writer than with anything else. Concerning the period before 1620, he could have learned from his elders or from his reading about any number of men not deemed worthy of the very first rank yet still worthy of recognition. But posterity remembered only women who had enjoyed the limelight. For the period after 1620, however, the situation was almost always the exact opposite: the notoriety/longevity effect worked in favor of men. Hence the masculine sample is biased, and that is why it appears to show that men enjoyed a longer life expectancy.

If our goal is to explore Saint-Simon's memory as such, it therefore makes sense to concentrate primarily on the male and female samples from the period after 1620. This is especially appropriate, moreover, since we are then dealing with a group of people who were either rough contemporaries of Saint-Simon or slightly older. For the historian, Saint-Simon really gets to the heart of his subject when he takes up the period beginning in about 1620. For earlier years, the information he provides is of the mundane sort often found in biographical dictionaries.

For the purpose of comparing the life expectancies of different social groups (*robins*, aristocrats, and soldiers), we now want to break down Saint-Simon's sample, not by date of birth, as we did previously, but by social or hierarchical position, vertically rather than horizontally, as it were. To that end, we have computed the average life expectancy of the various people mentioned in the *Memoirs*, grouped by rank and occupation (as well as gender, as before).[2]

When we do this, one group immediately stands out: the *robins*, both secular and ecclesiastic. Under this designation we include not only magistrates of the parlements and other sovereign courts but also the *robe du Conseil (maîtres des requêtes* and *conseillers d'Etat)*. We also include writers, artists, and men of science, many of whom sprang from backgrounds not unlike those of *robins* and who held some sinecure at court or in the tribunals or bureaucracy as a way of keeping the pot boiling until they were able to live on the income from their books or paintings (which few ever managed). All told we count 583 such individuals in Saint-Simon's text, including 246 ecclesiastics.

Our second group consists of military officers (the vast majority of whom were nobles), of whom we count 656. Later we will break this

Robe (583)

I. Ecclesiastics (246)

Cardinaux 19
Archevêques 30
Évêques 78
Aumôniers du roi 3
Doyen de la faculté de théologie 1
Abbés 65
Doyen de chapitre 1
Chanoine 1
Archidiacre 1
Jésuites 26
Oratoriens 8

Capucin 1
Carme 1
Génovéfain 1
Sulpicien 1
Bénédictin 1
Dominicain 1
Trappiste 1
Moine 1
Curés 2
Pasteurs 3

II. Intellectuals, Artists, and Principal Royal Servants (80)

Secrétaire perpétuel de l'Académie fra-
    ņaise 10
Membres de l'Académie française 10
Poètes 5
Écrivains 10
Directeur de Saint-Cyr 1
Membres du Collège de France (profes-
    seurs au Collège royal) 2
Professeurs 2
Docteurs en Sorbonne 2
Historien 1
Historiographe 1

Surintendants des Bâtiments 2
Peintres 3
Architecte 1
Musiciens 3
Comédien 1
Maître de musique 1

Économiste 1
Directeur de l'Observatorie 1
Généalogiste 1

Directeur général de la Maison du roi 1
Surintendants de Monsieur 2
Maître des cérémonies 1
Gouverneurs du duc de Chartres 2
Maréchal des logis 1
Premier valet de chambre du roi 1
Valets de chambre du roi 5
Premiers valets de chambre 3
Valet de chambre 1

Premier chirurgien 1
Chirurgiens 2
Médecins 10
Apothicaire du roi 1

III. Officials, Funtionaries, and Court Officers (257)

Chanceliers 5
Ministres d'État 22
Contrôleur général 1
Secrétaires d'État 8
Gardes des Sceaux 2

Premiers présidents du Grand Conseil 2
Président du Grand Conseil 1
Conseillers d'État 52
Maîtres des requêtes 14
Membre du Conseil de commerce 1

Lieutenant général de police 1

Lieutenant de police 1
Lieutenant civil 1

Directeur des Monnaies 1
Trésorier de France 1
Trésorier général 1
Trésoriers de l'Extraordinaire des guerres 2
Gardes triennaux du Trésor 2
Trésorier général de la Navigation 1
Receveurs généraux 2
Fermier général 1
Financiers 3

TABLE 5.2 *(continued)*

Directeur des Ponts et Chaussées 1
Ambassadeurs 2
Introducteurs des ambassadeurs 2
Sous-introducteur des ambassadeurs 1

Intendants 21
Intendant général du clergé 1
Intendants des finances 4
Intendant des postes 1
Intendant de la marine 1
Intendant des armées 1

Premiers présidents du Parlement 16
Présidents à mortier 21
Présidents de parlement de province 4
Conseillers au Parlement 16
Conseiller à la Grande Chambre 1
Procureurs généraux au Parlement 5
Avocats généraux 4
Présidents de la Chambre des comptes 5

Military Personnel (656)
Maréchal général 1
Maréchaux de France 68
Lieutenants généraux 282
Brigadiers 71
Maréchaux de camp 66
Inspecteur des armées 1
Généraux 6
Généraux des galères 3
Général d'artillerie 1
Généralissimes 2
Gouverneur des Invalides 1
Capitaine général (en Estrémadure) 1

Divers (Grande Condé, Prince Eugène) 2

Grand amiral 1
Chefs d'escadre 6
Vice-amiral 1

Colonels 25
Majors généraux 2
Mestres de camp 18
Commandants 4
Aides de camp 4
Majors 2
Commandant des gardes suisses 1
Caitaines 6
Capitaine de la garde personnelle du roi 1

Maître des comptes 1
Auditeur à la Chambre des comptes 1
Bâtonnier des avocats 1
Avocat au Parlement 1
Avocats 4

Secrétaires du roi 4
Notaire 1
Greffier 1
Robe 1

Maître des Eaux et Forêts 1
Grand maître des Eaux et Forêts 1
Conseiller général de la Chancellerie 1
Envoyé au Maroc 1
Premier commis à la Guerre 1
Commis du secrétaire d'État à la Guerre 1
Compagnie des Indes 1
Prévôts des marchands 3

Capitaines-lieutenants 3
Enseignes 4
Enseigne de chavau-légers 1
Lieutenants 6
Officier des gardes françaises 1
Officier de cavalerie 1
Sous-lieutenants 3
Cornettes 4
Guidon 1
Mousquetaire noir 1

Mousquetaire 1
Officier de marine 1
Lieutenant de vaisseau 1
Capitaines de vaisseau 9
"Achète un régiment de cavalerie" 2
"A un régiment" 8
"A une compagnie" 3
Ordre de Malte 1
Ingénieur militaire 1
Gouverneur de Jersey à fonction essentiel-
    lement navale et militaire 1
"A fait la guerre" 1
Tués au combat 8
Blessés 4
Militaires 14

contingent down further into three subgroups so as to analyze more carefully internal differences within the ranks of the military. (Table 5.2 provides a detailed breakdown of these two groups.)

Our third and final group is based on rank rather than occupation: it consists of princes and dukes. More specifically, we have included princes of the blood, foreign princes, and dukes (both *ducs et pairs* and *ducs à brevet*). All told we have compiled some 258 "profiles" of individuals fitting this description.

Let us state our most significant findings at the outset in the form of a table (table 5.3). Notice the significant gap here between the *robins* (regardless of the nature of the robes they wore, as ecclesiastics enjoyed only a slight advantage over their secular colleagues) and the rest: sixty-nine to seventy years for the former versus sixty to sixty-three years for the latter.

Although it is true that people like the Brid'oisons and Trissotins may have lived quiet, comfortable lives, their apparent longevity is in the first instance an artifact of the way in which the sample was constructed. It was common for a man to become a duke when he was still young, in some cases very young. By contrast, the prelates, ministers of state, provincial intendants, and to a certain extent even the *conseillers d'Etat* and *maîtres des requêtes* who make up the sample of *robins* achieved these enviable positions only toward the ends of lengthy careers, hence at a relatively advanced age compared with the dukes and, a fortiori, the lesser nobles who formed the bulk of the officer corps.

What is more, death in combat decimated the ancient nobles "of the court" or "sword," whose vocation was to go to war when called upon (even Saint-Simon, not much of a soldier, had his day in battle).[3] By contrast, only a minuscule number of *robins* lost their lives in combat.

With the aid of figure 5.3 we hope to clarify these observations. For each of our three "socioprofessional" categories, we have graphed longevity by decade. Thus for each group we can read off the proportion of the total number who died between the ages of twenty and twenty-nine, thirty and thirty-nine, forty and forty-nine, etc.

Consider the first three sets of bars in the graph, representing those who died in their twenties, thirties, and forties respectively. In all three sets, *robins* are underrepresented. Dukes were more likely than members

TABLE 5.3

	Average Life Expectancy	Number of Individuals
Robins, including	69.4 years	583
ecclesiastics	70.4 years	246
Dukes and princes	59.6 years	258
Military	63.0 years	656

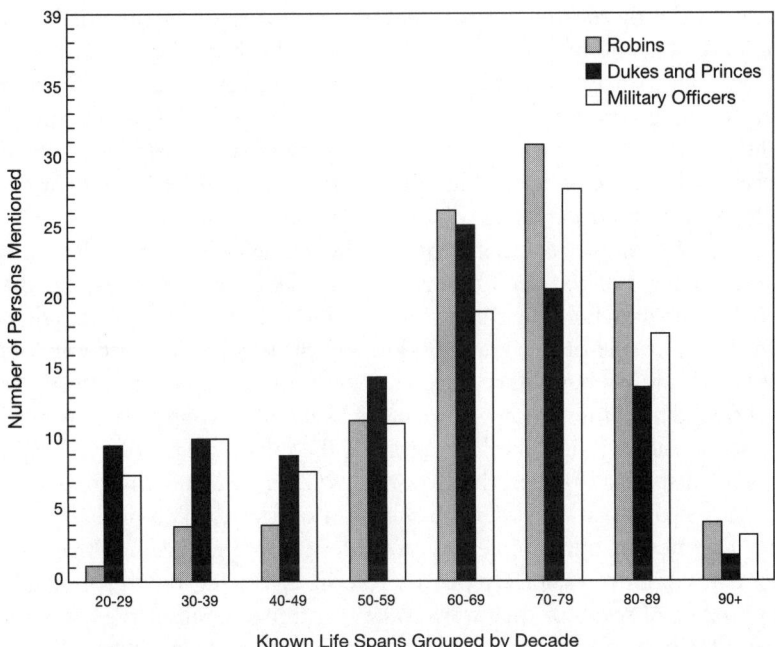

Figure 5.3. Life Spans of Robins, Dukes, and Princes, and Military Officers

of the other two groups to die young, followed closely by professional soldiers. Many young lawyers who died before they could rise to higher *robin* positions simply do not appear in the *Memoirs*. Had they lived, they might have come in for some of Saint-Simon's ample disdain for their profession. Their absence from the text makes it seem that dukes and military officers were more likely to die young, but this impression is misleading: during the Age of Louis XIV, dukes and princes were in fact no more likely to die before the age of forty than were *robins*. It is just that Saint-Simon was much more aware of premature death when the deceased happened to bear one of the most illustrious names in France. That alone was enough to earn the unfortunate personage a mention in the *Memoirs*, even if he died before having a chance to make his mark, whereas Saint-Simon would have been all but blind to the premature death of a young *robin* because such people were beneath contempt. Only those who had risen to the highest posts merited any kind of mention, scornful though it was likely to be.

The high proportion of military officers who died between the ages of twenty and forty-nine needs no explanation: the Sun King's wars took a heavy toll.

When we come to the fourth set of bars in the graph, representing deaths between the ages of fifty and fifty-nine, we find that the differences between the three groups have diminished. For the first time, it is not the *robins* but the military men who are least likely to die.

Another glance at the graph suffices to show that the last four sets of bars are an inverted image of the first three. Here the *robins* are consistently in the lead, proving that the hierarchs of the courts and council occupied far more of Saint-Simon's attention than did magistrates at the beginning of their careers.

Thus the *gens de robe* mentioned in the *Memoirs* tend to die late, between the ages of sixty and ninety, with a peak in the seventies, but the number of surviving dukes and princes falls by comparison after eighty. On the right side of the graph, dukes and princes are far outnumbered by *robins* and even military officers. Aristocrats—or at any rate those mentioned by Saint-Simon—were more likely to die young, and few lived as long as *robins*. The dukes' histogram is the mirror image of the *robins'*.

This disparity between the two groups leads us to modify somewhat our earlier observation about the effect of notoriety, which made it seem that the men in our sample enjoyed a longer life expectancy than the women. Certainly notoriety plays a role in increasing the apparent life expectancy of *robins*: if they were to be mentioned at all in the *Memoirs*, they first had to live long enough to gain high state positions. It was different with dukes: their birth alone was sufficiently "notorious" in Saint-Simon's eyes. The "notoriety effect" thus breaks down into a "career effect," which makes it seem that *robins* lived *longer* on average than they actually did, and a "birth effect," which makes the life expectancy of dukes and princes seem *shorter* than it actually was.[4]

Outcomes, however, matter to us more than causes. Saint-Simon's work is, of course, one long brief on behalf of dukes (or more precisely, dukes and peers) and, to a lesser extent, on behalf of the aristocracy generally. This brief was largely directed *against* the *robins*, whose distinctive quality Saint-Simon considered to be an absence of quality. For him, the *robins* were a "vile bourgeoisie" composed of "men without qualities." This judgment was inaccurate, to be sure, but it was not Saint-Simon's alone. It reflected the thinking of many other members of the elite.

This is where our statistical data become interesting, because they show that the conflict between aristocrats and *robins* was also a conflict of generations. Young dukes confronted elderly *robins*: Saint-Simon versus Chancellor Pontchartrain, Desmarets, Chamillart, and Dubois, for example. This was not simply a matter of relations between individuals; it was also a matter of dukes, who were often young (and certainly aggressive), taking on the "burgraves" of the robe. There was some logic to all this. In the course of his various ventures, our memorialist often clashed with powerful *robins* (and generally came off the worse for his trouble). In his

anger, he saw government ministers in particular and the "technostruc-
ture" in general as the primary threat to what he saw as France's traditional (or aristocratic) constitution. Now, the ministers and technocrats
whom he feared were in fact *robins* who had reached the pinnacle of their
careers after years of impeccable service. By the time Saint-Simon had
to contend with them, these detested burgraves (as well as ministers with
whom he carried on a love-hate relationship such as Pontchartrain and
Chamillart) were already a bit gone to seed. What is more, these elderly
veterans of the parlements and councils spent much of their time managing the matrimonial strategies of their families, hoping to improve their
status by marrying their handsomely dowried daughters to scions of old
noble dynasties. In so doing they posed a threat to the purity of ducal
bloodlines, which only left the "blighter" *(boudrillon)* Saint-Simon all the
more outraged and aghast.

As for the 656 military men in our sample (whose average age at
death was sixty-three), it makes sense to break them down by rank:
group A includes admirals, marshals, and lieutenant generals, group B
officers of middle rank, and group C officers of lower rank.

The average life expectancy of the military burgraves in group A was
69.8. Although not all of these superior officers died in their beds (think
of Turenne and Berwick, for example), as a group they did almost as well
as the churchmen (which shows, incidentally, that celibacy was by no
means the primary reason for the remarkable longevity of the clergy).
The officers in group B lived an average of 61.2 years, barely more than
the dukes and princes. And those in group C faced the alarming prospect
of living just 50.9 years.

Further analysis shows that the military contingent split along two
lines. The lower an officer's rank, the more likely he was to die young.
This is hardly surprising: officers of lower rank stood a greater chance
of dying in battle. Furthermore, many of the men in group C would have
risen to higher rank if they had lived and thus would have ended up in
group B or even A.

The resulting disparity was what one might call a "manifest" inequality
rooted in the organization of the military. But there was also a "latent"
inequality, which also shows up in our sample though not in quite so
obvious a fashion. In the army of the ancien régime, a man was more
likely to achieve higher rank (or even to start out in an important position
of command)[5] if he held a position of high rank in the aristocracy. The
military hierarchy was largely shaped by the civilian hierarchy, a phenomenon that was noticed long ago by Tocqueville.[6]

Since most military officers were nobles, it follows that most lesser
nobles held relatively low ranks in the military and that most of the offi-

cers killed in combat belonged to this group. By contrast, the scions of the high aristocracy were relatively well protected, not because they were innately courageous warriors but because their duties tended to be at a fairly high level.

Hence the functional inequality of the three groups of officers was compounded by an "injustice" in the distribution of rank, which became an injustice in the face of death. In other words, the injustice of civil society was in a sense injected into the military, since the ranks of the social pyramid were fairly faithfully reflected in the order of battle. For example, officer group A consisted largely of dukes and princes and other nobles of ancient lineage (although there were notable exceptions, such as Vauban and Catinat). Group C consisted essentially of nobles who were not dukes (and a fortiori not princes). Group B was more mixed: distinguished aristocrats, who often started out at high rank, rubbed shoulders with lesser gentlemen who owed whatever fame they achieved to their martial exploits.

Turning now to women, we find that differences among females from the various groups were less pronounced than the differences among males (see figure 5.4). The 173 *robines* (that is, female *robins*) in our sample lived an average of 63.4 years. The difference between those

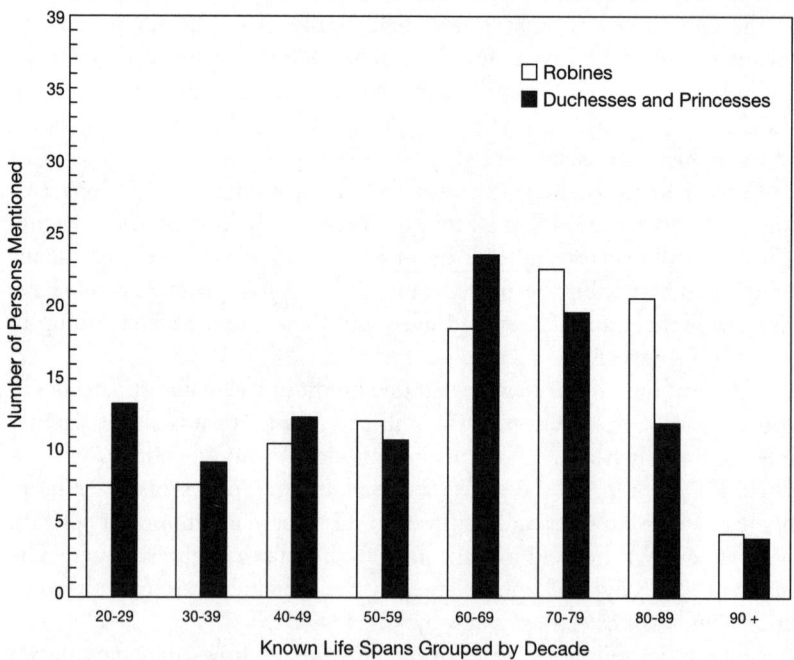

Figure 5.4. Life Spans of Robines and Duchesses and Princesses

who married a *robin* and those who were born *robines* but married nobles is insignificant: 63.7 years for the 85 "wives of *robins*" versus 63.1 years for the 88 women "born to the *robe*." The 253 duchesses and princesses constituted a somewhat "younger" group: their average life expectancy was 57.8, similar to that of their husbands (dukes and princes).

Differences in life expectancy between these two groups of women were somewhat less than the differences between the corresponding male groups (a six-year difference for the women and a ten-year difference for the men). *Robines* tended to live longer, at least to judge by appearances. To judge by these statistics, generational conflict was much more of a problem for men more than for women.

It is safe to assume that we have in Saint-Simon's text a fairly complete roster of the duchesses and princesses of the day, as well as of their male companions. Hence the figures given represent the "normal" life expectancy of court nobles during the reign of Louis XIV. The "career effect" that makes the (male) *robin* group seem older than it actually was is not in evidence for the *robines*.

One stubborn fact remains, however: *robines* do appear to have lived longer than duchesses and princesses, even if the difference was not as great as that between *robins* and dukes. Even though the *robines* mentioned in the *Memoirs* were probably more representative of their group than the *robins* were of theirs, it still seems likely that the resulting picture of life expectancy is somewhat distorted. What we suspect is this: although there is no career effect to make the *robine* life span appear longer than it actually was (as in the case of *robins*), there was also no celebrity effect for *robines*, who lacked that early visibility and prominence that came of birth or marriage and that earned princes, dukes, and their wives and daughters mention in the *Memoirs* at a tender age, regardless of what they might or might not do in later life or how long they survived on this earth.

This situation arises for the following reason: Saint-Simon does not mention *robines* because they are famous in their own right but only because they are married to or perhaps daughters of famous *robins*. Thus he pays relatively little attention to young women who died before their as yet unknown husbands and fathers played the role that earned them the writer's scorn. Only spouses and daughters of magistrates and "technocrats" who had held the highest government offices were likely to float to the surface of his memory. Hence the wives and heiresses mentioned in the *Memoirs* were women who had themselves survived long years during which their husbands and fathers still toiled in relative obscurity.

Still, these women, unlike their *robin* counterparts, were not obliged to traverse the various stages of a long career in order to appear in the *petit duc*'s pages. Some died relatively young. But like sherpas on a long climb, they accompanied their husbands and fathers part of the way up the ladder, hence they appear on average to have lived longer than the representatives of the aristocracy. If we are right in thinking that the aristocrats in the *Memoirs* suffered from the birth effect and the male *robins* benefited from the career effect, the women of the robe stand in a sort of intermediate position. They seem a little older because they were pulled along by their husbands as a locomotive pulls the cars behind it. But they are no more able to pass their husbands than the cars in a train can pass the engine, because our memorialist was interested primarily in the careers of men. Hence for statistical purposes if nothing else, he failed to pay sufficient attention to the fair sex.

I f we look now at women who took the habit (figures 5.5 and 5.6), we are in for still more surprises. For the women in the text who became nuns (of whom, admittedly, our sample is quite small—only forty), the average life expectancy was 62.3 years, significantly less than the remarkable longevity achieved by male ecclesiastics. When we look at the sample more closely, however, the reason for this becomes apparent. It includes only abbesses, prioresses, and superiors of the plushest convents in the realm. These institutions admitted only girls and women of the highest

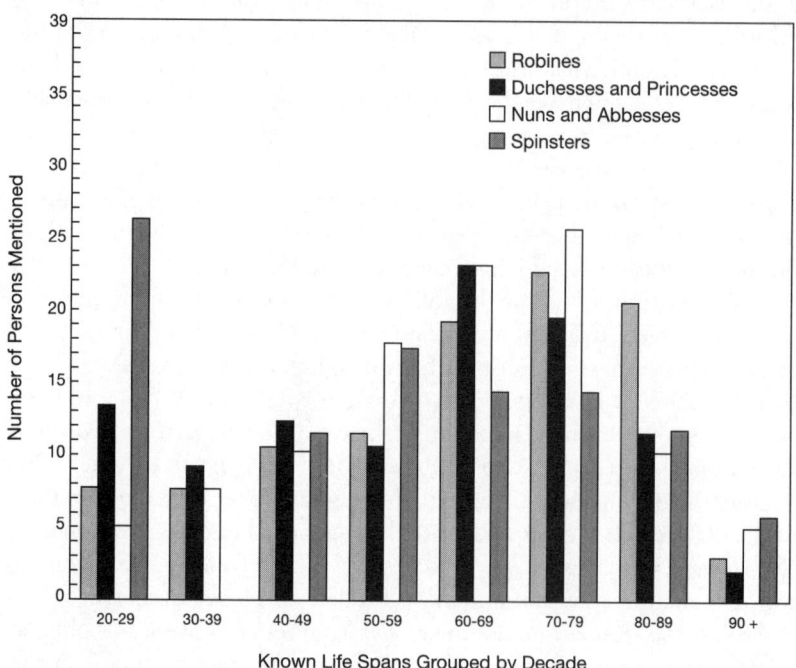

Figure 5.5. Life Spans of Robines, Duchesses and Princesses, Nuns and Abbesses, and Spinsters

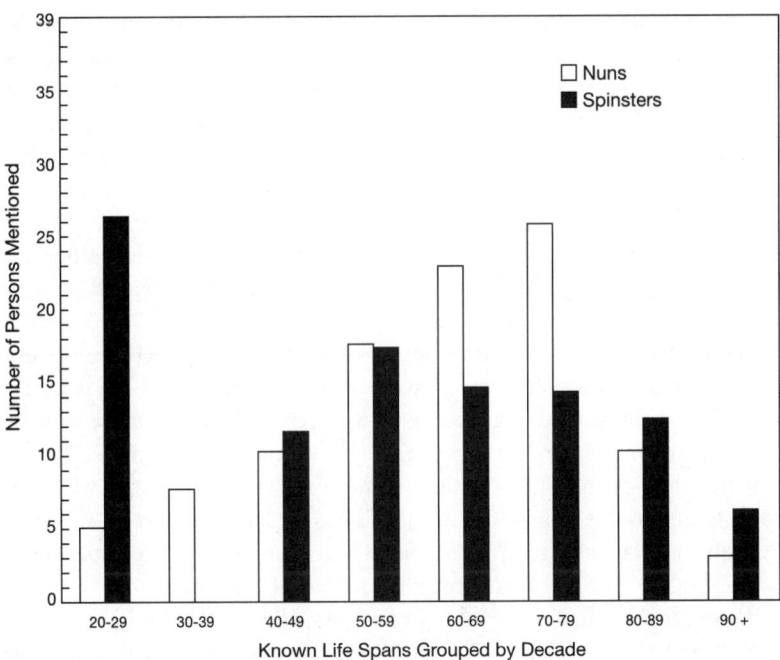

Figure 5.6. Life Spans of Nuns and Spinsters

nobility, especially as their heads. Among our abbesses and nuns, for example, we find a Torcy, a Lorraine, a Guise, a Lillebonne, a Gramont, a Fiesque, a Caumont, three La Rochefoucaulds, a Condé, a Rohan-Guéméné, two Rohan-Soubises, two Villeroys, a Villars, a Rochechouart, a Mesmes, the sister and five daughters of the devout Beauvillier, the regent's daughter, abbess of Chelles, and two more or less penitent mistresses of the great king (de Ludres and La Vallière).[7]

This enumeration alone is enough to reveal the similarity between this "religious" group and the group of duchesses and princesses. Although nuns lived longer on average than duchesses and princesses, the lives of "spinsters" tended to be relatively short. The spinster group is small (just thirty-five women), but its "performance" was deplorable: the lowest life expectancy of any of the groups in the survey, male or female, at just 55.1 years. Along with their unimpressive longevity, spinsters exhibit a markedly atypical pattern of mortality by decade. For spinsters to die between the ages of 30 and 89 was relatively unusual compared with other women, but at either extreme of the graph we find them beating all records. A very high proportion died young (25 percent of these unmarried women died before the age of 30). This is odd even linguistically in French, because the phrase for spinster is *vieille fille*, literally "old maid," but many of these "old maids" were in fact young but prevented from marrying either by fate or by the deficiencies of contemporary medicine. Here a "reverse notoriety effect" may have come into play, because Saint-Simon liked to note the deaths of young women when their families experienced those deaths as tragic, thereby making them worthy of his pen. That such an effect did in fact operate despite the memorialist's usual predilection for the old over the young seems clear from the fact that all of these women who died young came from families belonging to the court nobility. In this sad cortege we find a Condé, a Bouillon, and a Lorraine, all of whom died at 25; Mlle de Beaujolais, the regent's daughter, who died at 20; and Fontanges, who was Louis XIV's mistress for a short time (it could hardly have been otherwise). Three La Rochefoucauld daughters died at 21, 24, and 28 respectively. All of these women unfortunate enough to die before the age of thirty thus belonged to the "duchess and princess" group and some were even connected with the royal family to one degree or another. Thus we have an extreme instance of the way in which the *Memoirs* make it appear that the life expectancy of the highest nobility was shorter than that of the *robins*.

If we wish to understand this phenomenon, we must look at women who died young in relation to aristocratic women generally. Take the slightly greater longevity of nuns and correct for the propensity of young unmarried women to die prematurely and you come up with a figure for life expectancy fairly close to that of duchesses and princesses as a group. Taken together, these three categories (nuns, duchesses and princesses, women who died before 30) form a relatively homogeneous "intergroup" of 328 women whose average age at death was 58.

The group of thirty-five spinsters also includes another noteworthy subgroup: those who lived to be 85 or 90. It may well be that Saint-Simon was inclined to mention these women relatively frequently merely because to live so long was in itself such a remarkable feat (a "normal" phenomenon of notoriety). There is no point in wondering about the supposed benefits of a chaste way of life presumably exempt from the often lethal consequences of pregnancy and committed to the shelter of quasi-seclusion. The simple fact that among these vaunted octogenarians was Ninon de Lenclos (age 85) should suffice, we hope, to explain why we avoid going into tortuous detail about the multiple meanings of the word "spinster" that we have applied to this group.

In any case, the life expectancy of women seems firmly established at around 63 (63 for nuns and 63.4 for *robines*). No subgroup of the "second sex" came close to the life expectancy of nearly 70 achieved by male *robins*.[8]

The thoroughly biased way in which the scrupulously "discriminatory" labors of the duke's vindictive memory constructed his samples can also be seen in his matrimonial preoccupations. The various types of marriage mentioned in the forty-two volumes of the Boislisle edition give an interesting view of the social structure.

Boislisle's indispensable critical apparatus enables us to check (and on occasion correct) the memorialist's lapidary and at times downright unjust judgments. We are bound to point out, however, that the quantity and in some cases quality of the critical and biographical notes in Boislisle's alphabetical index diminishes somewhat after the letter "P": no doubt the great scholar (or more likely his successor) wished to hasten the completion of the index by limiting the amount of information to a useful if reduced level. Because of the resulting deficiencies, relatively insignificant when compared with the scholarly monument of the Boislisle edition as a whole, we have made use whenever necessary of the recent and admirable Pléiade edition edited by Yves Coirault.

By restricting our attention mainly to France, we assembled a sample of 1,366 marriages.[9] In order to make this a representative and homogeneous sample of Saint-Simon's world, we included only marriages celebrated after 1600, omitting examples from the sixteenth century (or even earlier) about which Saint-Simon would have possessed only indirect knowledge (generally gleaned from books).[10]

In order to establish a typology of aristocratic marriages, we had to adopt Saint-Simon's view of society, which was based on what Louis Dumont calls a "holistic" ideology.[11] The duke did not catalog hundreds of marriages simply for the pleasure of remembering them. A *homo hierarchicus* if ever there was one, Saint-Simon was passionate about ordering social relations in terms of rank, of status granted by birth. In his mind, the most important thing about any marriage was whether or not it tended to preserve or destroy the differences of degree that he believed were necessary to the stability of aristocratic society, indeed of society generally. For Saint-Simon, to think was to classify.

Without going so far as to characterize as "racist" the duke's frequent (but not universal) indifference to or contempt for people of lower rank,[12] we cannot ignore the fact that his attitude was one of disdain, hauteur, and *esprit de caste.*[13] Note, however, that his ideological conception of society had nothing to do with his judgment of individuals. He was not an essentialist. His expressions of contempt for a person's base *origins* sometimes coincided with genuine *personal* sympathy for the individual in question. Take, for example, his brief comment on the death of the maréchale de Chamilly:

The maréchale de Chamilly died in Paris on 18 November at the age of sixty-seven. *She was a woman of wit, enormous good sense, great piety, and constant virtue who was also extremely amiable and well-suited to high society and public display.* The bulk of her husband's fortune came from her; the couple had no children. *She was one of our closest friends, and we missed her greatly.* She had many friends and always enjoyed the greatest esteem and respect. *Du Bouchet by name, she was a wealthy heiress of utterly common birth.*[14]

Despite her "utterly common birth," then, this rich heiress was one of Saint-Simon's and his wife's few true friends, and he makes no bones about crediting her with the loftiest of moral as well as social virtues. The *Memoirs* abound with similar examples, which seem somewhat odd to our democratic way of thinking because of the radical disjunction between the writer's (unstated) ideology and his affection or esteem. Nevertheless, Saint-Simon believed that men and women inherited a certain quality that established immutable hierarchical relations among them— or at any rate he believed that those hierarchical relations ought in principle to remain immutable, even if he recognized that in fact they did not.

How closely did such hierarchical notions match the social realities of Louis XIV's long reign? To answer this question, we ordered our sample of marriages according to the husband's status either at birth or (in the case of *robins* who acquired their rank) in early youth. We did not wish to be swayed by the literary flair of Saint-Simon's judgments, however. We therefore quantified, counted, and weighed various categories of marriage using a system of classification as close as possible to the writer's traditionalist vision.

Specifically, we characterize marriages between a man and a woman of the same rank as endogamous, or intrinsically egalitarian. Thus, if a prince of the royal blood married the daughter of a prince of monarchical blood, that marriage was endogamous. Or if a "foreign" prince (Bouillon, Rohan, or Lorraine) married the daughter of a foreign prince, that marriage was endogamous. Or if a duke married the daughter of a duke. Or if a *gentilhomme* born into the *noblesse d'épée* (or *noblesse native*, as Loyseau calls it in his definition of "gentility") married the daughter of a *noble d'épée*. Or if a *robin* (blessed with "dative" nobility, the nobility of office) married the daughter of a *robin*. Or if an ordinary commoner (not even a *robin*) married a woman of similar extraction. All these examples of endogamous marriage preserved the "social order" and therefore earned Saint-Simon's highest seal of approval.

When a man and a woman belonging to different groups married, however, we refer to that marriage as "hypergamous" if the man is of higher rank and "hypogamous" if the man is of lower rank than the women, regardless of the magnitude of the difference in rank. For instance, if a duke married the daughter of a noble who was not a duke, we classified that marriage as hypergamous. And we did the same if a duke or indeed any noble of the sword married the daughter of a *robin*.

Let us attach labels to ranks as follows: (A) princes of royal blood; (B) foreign princes;[15] (C) dukes and peers, dukes, brevet dukes; (D) *gentils-hommes;* (E) *robins;* (F) commoners who were not *robins* in the strict sense (including financiers, intellectuals, and so on). Using this notation, we see that any marriage in which the bride and groom come from the same group (A-A, B-B, C-C, etc.) is classified as endogamous. Any marriage in which the male belongs to a higher group than the female (such as A-B, A-C, B-C, etc.) is an instance of female hypergamy, regardless of the absolute magnitude of the gap. Finally, any marriage in which the wife's rank is higher than the rank of her husband (B-A, C-B, etc.) is classified as an instance of female hypogamy.

Figure 5.7 illustrates each theoretically possible case of each type of marriage. Using this scheme, we obtain the following results for our sample of 1,366 marriages: 740 involved husbands and wives of equal rank, hence are classified as endogamous; 378 involved female hypergamy of

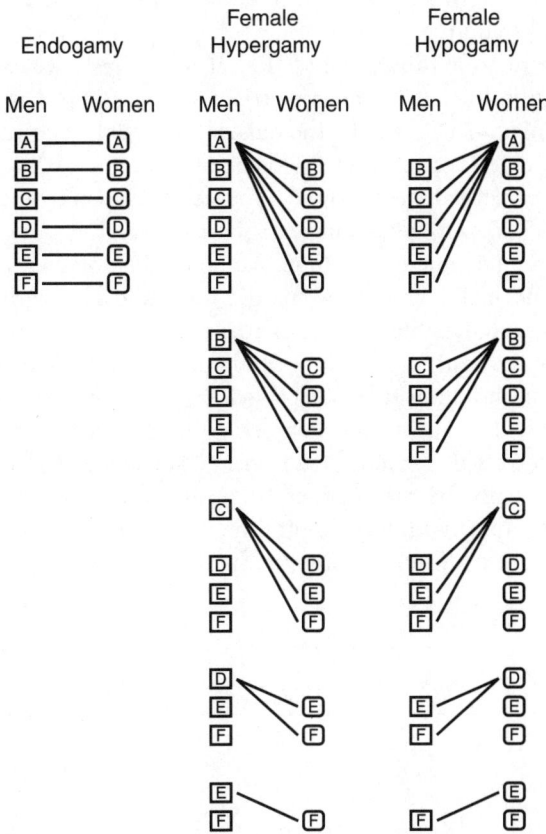

Figure 5.7. Types of Marriages

one degree or another (that is, the bride's rank was lower than that of her husband); 133 involved female hypogamy (a woman married a man whose social standing was below her own); 115 marriages could not be accommodated in this scheme and call for more specific commentary.

We summarize these results in table 5.4. One fact jumps out right away: the majority of marriages (54.2 percent) were endogamous. At all levels of the society of ranks, people married their own kind. Each rank "recruited internally," to borrow an expression from Louis Dumont.[16] Each group was able to reproduce itself without drawing new members from other groups, even as "replacements" or mere "breeders." Sons, as the inheritors of rank (whether in the form of a father's title or function), married the daughters of men who belonged to the same category as their own progenitors.

The fact that endogamous unions constitute a majority of our sample shows that hierarchical thinking remained influential well into the reign of Louis XIV if not beyond. All groups were apparently keen to maintain the stability of court society.[17] There is less evidence of social mobility than of social stability.

Using information drawn from J.-P. Labatut's thesis, we can flesh out this predilection for endogamous marriage in the group that was Saint-Simon's primary focus, namely, the dukes.[18] Although relatively small in number and therefore more likely than other groups to "recruit" from without, dukes nevertheless showed a marked preference for endogamy. According to Labatut, dukes and peers married daughters of other dukes and peers 35.7 percent of the time. Younger sons of dukes and peers (who in the normal course of events did not stand to inherit the ducal title) also married daughters of dukes 20.4 percent of the time. And fully 47 percent of the daughters of dukes and peers married dukes and peers.

To be sure, the ducal title was passed on only to the eldest son, and the daughters of dukes had to compete with dangerous outside rivals (about whom we will say more later on). Nevertheless, Labatut's statistics, together with the more general figures given above, suggest that curial groups preferred internal recruitment whenever possible.

To believe Saint-Simon, moreover, he himself narrowly escaped the

TABLE 5.4

Marriage Type	Number	Percentage of Total
Endogamous	740	54.2
Hypergamous	378	27.7
Hypogamous	133	9.7
Special cases	115	8.4
Total	1,366	100.0

consequences of this group pressure to marry within. In a passage devoted to the memory of his uncle, the marquis de Saint-Simon, the memorialist mentions that this uncle's "passion was to marry me off to Mlle d'Uzès."[19] The lady in question was Catherine Louis-Marie de Crussol, two of whose brothers bore the title of duc d'Uzès. After avoiding marriage to Saint-Simon, she was nearly chosen by the king to marry the duc du Maine. Ultimately she married Louvois's son Barbezieux. Here—at least in the first part of the story—we glimpse part of the reason why the question of endogamous marriage so preoccupied Saint-Simon.

Although the pattern of endogamous marriage developed largely as an effect of convention, it was also a product of necessity. In a rigid society of ranks, a person was far more likely to encounter a kindred spirit in the group to which he or she belonged, particularly where the families were involved in bringing the couple together. Protocol was so strict that people were unlikely to mingle outside a narrow group united by many common characteristics, birth foremost among them.

Even when people married "for love" (and there are examples of this in the *Memoirs*), they were frequently of the same rank.[20] Saint-Simon did not see society as a sort of dough in which people remained stuck wherever they happened to be and were not free to move around. Even though he preferred marriage according to the proper forms (hence endogamous), he was not blind to the fact that many people preferred freedom of choice, and he was perfectly capable of applauding a good love match as long as no mismarriage or other catastrophe was involved. But disaster always lurked in the wings, as is evident from this passage devoted to the marquis de Villequier's two daughters, to whose charms our memorialist was clearly not indifferent (Boislisle notes, moreover, that the mother of these two girls had made a great impression on Colbert):

> Châtillon had married Mlle de Piennes for love. This pair was by general agreement the handsomest couple at court, the best and noblest looking of all. They quarreled and separated, never to see each other again. She [the wife] was lady-in-waiting to Madame and sister of the marquise de Villequier, who also married for love.[21]

Sometimes the desire to end a life of celibacy was enough to push a man (or woman) into the arms of a "convenient" partner. But "convenient" generally meant someone of similar rank (for instance, a superior officer of noble extraction, but perhaps of the lesser nobility, might marry a girl of good noble family). Consider this:

> Des Alleurs was a Norman of negligible background but fine-looking, a fit subject for a painter, and this served him well in his youth. He had long served as captain of the guards and spent the entire war as a major general

in the Army of the Rhine, in which capacity he excelled. Eventually he became a lieutenant general and obtained the Grande Croix de Saint Louis. He was a clever fellow, gentle, respectful, and affable with everyone, and everybody knew him well. He had courage and great wit, skill, and finesse yet always seemed unaffected and at ease. In Strasbourg, where he spent the winter, he fell for Mlle de Lutzelbourg, a statuesque beauty from a superb family who had had more than one lover, and though all he had going for him was his wit and cleverness, he aspired to make a good match for himself. And at this he was so successful that she married him.[22]

M atrimonial egalitarianism was obviously a desirable goal, but it did not preclude other types of marriage, of which female hypergamy was undeniably the most significant. By female hypergamy we mean marriage under the following conditions: "A family belongs to an inferior group and is wealthy in terms of money but not prestige. This family offers a daughter, together with a dowry, to a man belonging to a superior group in exchange for a measure of prestige. Prior to the marriage, the family that gives the daughter is of relatively low status."[23] Of the 1,366 marriages in our sample, 378 (or 27.7 percent) fit this description.

Hypergamy as Saint-Simon understood it occurred mainly when the daughter of a *robin* married a *gentilhomme*. This was the classic hypergamous marriage. But there was also the case of marriage between a duke and the daughter of a *noble d'épée* who was not a duke (which might be called "lesser hypergamy" in contrast to the former situation, which we may call "greater hypergamy"). Numerous passages in the *Memoirs* describe both cases.

Take the marriage of Lanjamet, a Breton nobleman (of dubious ancestry, according to Saint-Simon) and court insect "whose insignificance was the most significant thing about him": "At almost the same time people learned of Lanjamet's marriage to the daughter of a Paris *procureur*, a woman whom he had kept for a long time before secretly marrying her three or four years before the news became known. She had beauty, but along with it intelligence and cunning enough for four demons and was as wicked and perfidious as fourteen devils."[24] A few sentences later, Saint-Simon, who shuddered at the mere thought of a "democratic" wedding, plunges the dagger in: "Insignificant though he was, his fickle wife, who was already the widow of a *procureur*, was a shameful match for him."[25] Daughter of one *procureur* and wife of another, and a flirt besides: in Saint-Simon's eyes such a wife could only tarnish the escutcheon of a nobleman, no matter how recently he, too, had wallowed in the mire of "insignificance."

Other young women, who to be sure sprang from the loftier echelons of "the robe," apparently had no difficulty marrying noblemen from old families despite Saint-Simon's pleas. Take, for example, Marie-Antoinette de Mesmes, born into a powerful family of jurists:

> The *premier président*, a widower, had only two daughters. They were rich and would have made apt subjects for a weird tale: one was dark, unctuous, terrifyingly ugly, stupid, and of course a perfect prude as well as marvelously devout; the other had hair as red as a cow, a pale complexion, wit, and friends and wanted to be free and first in all things. Although the latter was the younger of the two girls, she was the first to be married, to Lautrec, Ambres's son, who did her the favor of falling in love with her. He was ill paid for his ardor. He never managed to tame his beauty, who divined what manner of man he was and knew how to make the most of it. The poor husband left her service and Paris—to tell the truth this was no great loss—and shut himself up in the provinces. They had no children. It was Lautrec's elder brother, today a lieutenant general and chevalier of the Order, who married one of the duc de Rohan's sisters.[26]

The Lautrecs were the cream of the *noblesse d'épée*, as can be seen from the fact that a brother of the "poor husband" managed to find a Rohan for a wife (true, the Rohans seemed to breed eligible young women who came equipped with fabulous dowries). From Saint-Simon's description of the wife (and her sister) and satisfied rehearsal of the calamities that befell the couple, we know what moral we are supposed to draw: in the writer's view such an unequal marriage could only end badly.

Another instance in which a woman enjoys a lightning-quick rise, which in this case benefits her husband as well, can be found in volume 11 of the *Memoirs*:

> Pontchartrain arranged a marriage between one of his stepbrothers, a ship's captain then at sea, and the only daughter of Ducasse, a man thought to possess a fortune of 1,200 thousand livres. Ducasse hailed from Bayonne, where his brother and father sold ham. He made a fortune as a freebooter and got to know a lot of people, which gained him a commission as an officer on one of the king's ships, and soon thereafter he was promoted to captain. He was a man of great courage, with a cool head and big ideas and much loved in the navy because of the generosity with which he shared everything and the modesty with which he kept to his place. He got into a furious quarrel with Pontis when the latter captured Cartagena and pillaged the city. Ducasse would go much farther still, as we shall see. Apart from the lure of gain, which on the one hand resulted in this marriage and on the other secured the protection of the Ministry of the Navy, [Pontchartrain] found it entirely proper to use Ducasse's money to buy his stepbrother the post of lieutenant general of the galleys, the only one of its kind, which carried with the rank of lieutenant and marked a major step

forward for this ship captain. The post was vacant because of the death of Noailles's bailiff, and no buyer had come forward since.[27]

In this bargain, the son of a man who "sold ham" traded his daughter for the protection of a powerful family of ministers especially influential in his domain of maritime commerce. And the Pontchartrains, for their part, were only too glad to divert some of the "1,200 thousand livres" amassed by the former pirate into their own coffers.

Others were no more scrupulous than the Pontchartrains. Witness the La Rochefoucaulds, one of whom, the duc de La Rocheguyon, married a woman who, though the daughter of a mere marquis, was nevertheless a wealthy heiress: "At the same time the duc de La Rochefoucauld arranged for his son, the duc de La Rocheguyon, today duc de La Rochefoucauld, to marry Mlle de Toiras, a wealthy heiress born and raised in Languedoc in her mother's home, which she had never left."[28]

Another common hypergamous scenario in the *Memoirs* was for a daughter of the *noblesse d'épée* to marry into ducal ranks. Obviously the young woman's charms were a plus not to be neglected. If a duke condescended to marry a woman of lower (but still respectable) rank, it was not merely because he was after her dowry (about which we shall have more to say in a moment). Many a graybeard responded to a midlife (or post-midlife) crisis by seeking a young female companion. In social jockeying at court, beauty apparently sufficed to overcome differences of birth, but only if those differences were not too glaring. Many families of the old nobility could claim that their lineages were as old as those of any duke and equal in quality, lacking only the ducal title. Feminine allure was yet another way of reducing social distance. Even Saint-Simon recognized this, for all his harping on principle.[29] As an example of the strategy of seduction, consider the misfortunes of the duc de Gesvres, which we beg the reader's indulgence for recounting here:

> The elderly duc de Gesvres remarried at the age of eighty-one . . . [The bride was] Mlle de La Chesnelaye, a Rommilley. She was a beautiful woman of striking figure, and very rich, who agreed to the marriage because she coveted a [ducal] *tabouret* [stool]. The king tried to talk [Gesvres] out of [marrying], but the old man could think of no better way to hurt his son, whom this marriage greatly wronged, and would not be dissuaded, looking forward as he was to carrying on like a young buck at the supper before the wedding. He was punished for it, and his young bride was punished even more: he fouled the bed so badly that both of them had to be scrubbed down and all the linen changed. The reader can judge for himself what such a marriage led to.[30]

Another example from the very highest levels of the aristocracy is even more enlightening:

The duc de Saint-Aignan, left a widower by Servien, mother of the duc de Beauvillier, committed the folly of marrying eighteen months later a creature from the dregs of the populace, who after taking care of his wife's dogs for many years had risen to the position of chambermaid. He died six years later, totally ruined, leaving two sons and a daughter from this fine marriage. The mother had wit as well as virtue. The king himself, who liked M. de Saint-Aignan, urged him more than once to offer the lady his *tabouret*. She would not hear of it, however, and sought only to please and take care of M. de Saint-Aignan in his own home. Although she had no wish to appear in public, she did wear the ducal cloak and mantle. Her conduct earned her the good will of M. and Mme de Beauvillier, who took care of her after M. de Saint-Aignan died and raised her children as though they were their own, lavishing equal affection on all.[31]

There is much to be learned from this passage. To begin with, the Beauvilliers (and no doubt other ducal families) did not share Saint-Simon's aristocratic prejudice, or at any rate did not carry prejudice so far as to refuse to take care of the elderly "creature from the dregs of the populace" who had married the duke's father. Aristocratic pride did not stifle their feelings for a fellow human being. (According to Boislisle, moreover, the "creature" in question actually sprang from the lesser nobility.) Furthermore, even though the king felt kindly toward her, the duke's bride confined herself to playing duchess *in partibus* and *intra muros*. She refused to accept the *tabouret* that the king was willing to allow her because to do so would have called unwelcome attention to her astonishing social ascent.

Louis XIV evidently did not view this marriage as a hangable offense. As Boislisle remarks in a note, "Although M. de Saint-Aignan had already transferred the duchy to his son, the king invited the new bride to accept the honors of the Louvre, which, incidentally, she declined out of modesty. By contrast, according to Luynes's *Memoirs*, he absolutely refused to grant this distinction to the duchesse de Gramont because she was of low extraction and had indeed served as a chambermaid."[32]

Thus we see that Saint-Simon's rigid conception of noble (and specifically ducal) quality may well have led him to exaggerate the significance of certain cases of female hypergamy, which some contemporaries preferred to deal with in a relatively low-key manner. Nevertheless, the case of the duchesse de Gramont to which Boislisle alludes shows that the writer's prejudices were widely shared (albeit with less scrupulous vigilance and annoyance) by people of his rank and above in the hierarchy, including the king.

In any case, it would be a mistake to treat the 378 hypergamous marriages in Saint-Simon's text as aberrations. Because of their number and variety, as well as the importance that the writer ascribed to them and the reactions of the people involved, they deserve to be set in historical context. To that end, we propose the following (modest) theory of female hypergamy.

The 378 hypergamous marriages mentioned in the *Memoirs* represent 27.7 percent of the total number of marriages that we have cataloged. The figure is almost exactly half the number of endogamous marriages (of which we count 740, or 54.2 percent). Clearly, then, under the hierarchical conception of society of which Saint-Simon was only the most vocal exponent, it was perfectly acceptable if some marriages (a minority to be sure) permitted upward mobility for women rather than exactly reproducing the same social landscape generation after generation. Under what conditions was such upward mobility possible?

A. In Louis XIV's France, "it was considered normal for the status of the wife's family to be slightly inferior to the status of the husband's family, and this had no bearing on the status of their children."[33]

It was an accepted tenet of matrimonial strategy that daughters should marry as high as possible above the station to which they were born, regardless of the father's position in the hierarchy. No one, not even Saint-Simon, was shocked if a duke married the daughter of a wellborn nobleman. By contrast, "prejudice" came into play whenever a *noble d'épée* tried to marry a commoner of any sort. Such unions were regularly deplored as "depreciative." If a young woman of noble extraction married a duke, this was seen as a social promotion (as in the case of Mlle de La Chesnelaye discussed earlier)—a normal, expected case of advancement. The jump from one rank to another immediately or "mediately" above it was seen as problematic only if it involved leaving the world of the *robe* for that of the *épée*, for such a leap meant crossing the imaginary gulf that, in the mind of Saint-Simon and certain of his contemporaries, divided humanity in two.

Consider the diagram in figure 5.8, which represents Saint-Simon's, and, more generally, the aristocracy's, view of women's trajectories. The horizontal line represents the major social cleavage, the sole source of resistance to upward mobility for women. Indeed, some people found crossing this barrier easier to accept than Saint-Simon did. If this barrier was not crossed, there was no reason to get excited even if a woman skipped one or more intermediate rungs in clambering up the social ladder.

B. The compensation or, rather, the impetus for hypergamy (or "the gift of marriage") was the dowry, which helped many a girl along the tortuous path to higher status. The family of the bride gained new luster

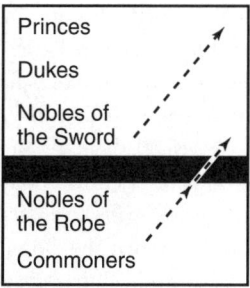

Figure 5.8. Women's Trajectories

through the marriage and obtained a status that only the husband could provide. It was a glorious and in a sense meritorious act to bestow a "damsel" upon a man of superior rank. In most cases, however, the gift of the girl was not enough. She had to come with a dowry or the prospect of "great expectations."

Saint-Simon, for example, tells the story of the marriage of the comte de Tessé to the daughter of a "mere" *robin:* "Toward the end of the year, Tessé gave his eldest son in marriage to the daughter of Bouchu, a state councilor of whom I spoke not long ago. She was the opposite of Mme de Roquelaure: without wit, talent, birth, or beauty but blessed with an unlimited number of écus, which was exactly what Tessé needed."[34] Because this marriage allowed a *robine* (even if she enjoyed the august status of daughter of a state councilor) to worm her way into the *noblesse d'épée,* Saint-Simon regarded it as a mismatch: it flew in the face of his chief prejudice.

One can cite even more clear-cut examples in which a man's wealth enabled his daughter to make a rapid run up the cascade of contempt, like a trout or salmon swimming upstream to spawn. In this respect, the most eloquent passage in the *Memoirs* to our way of thinking is the one devoted to the marriage of a princely Bouillon, the comte d'Evreux, to the daughter of Antoine Crozat, known as "the Rich Man":

Shortly thereafter this pride [of the Bouillons] succumbed to the desire for riches. The comte d'Evreux, M. de Bouillon's third son, had found in the king's good graces, procured for him by M. le comte de Toulouse, and in the pocketbooks of his friends, all he needed to acquire the post of colonel general of cavalry that had belonged to his uncle. But he had nothing to repay them with and nothing to live on, and neither M. de Bouillon nor the cardinal [de Bouillon] could or would give him what he needed. He therefore resolved to swallow the pill of mésalliance and, with the king's permission, make a princess of the daughter of Crozat, who, having risen from common clerk to petty financier to money man to the clergy, had plunged into adventures on the high seas and in banking and was justly regarded as one of the wealthiest men in Paris. Mme de Bouillon, who brought us the news, urged us to visit all the *many relatives made grotesque by their attempt to pass themselves off as descendants* of the dukes of Guyenne. She gave us the list, and we visited them all and found them puffed up with joy. The only one who kept her wits about her was the mother of Mme Crozat. She received visitors with a respectful yet tranquil air, said that it was *an honor so far above her* that she did not know how to thank us for the trouble we had taken, and added that she thought it better to show her respect by not returning our visit and disturbing people so different from herself who had already been kind enough to do her such an honor; and then she did as she had promised and stayed home. She never approved of the marriage, whose prompt consequences she foresaw and predicted. Crozat made a splendid wedding at his home and provided the newlyweds with room and board. Mme de Bouillon referred to her daughter-in-law as her "little gold ingot."[35]

We have emphasized some of the more pungent phrases in this eloquent passage. We learn that the shock of the mismatch (Crozat was erroneously believed to have been a coachman)[36] was considerably attenuated by the size of the financier's fortune. We are also told that the Crozats made themselves ridiculous by claiming illustrious ancestors in Guyenne in order to reduce the distance between themselves and the Bouillons (a desperate measure, to be sure, which they knew perfectly well was unlikely to reduce the disparity one iota). And we discover that the bride's grandmother was dismayed by the presumptuousness of the match (Saint-Simon, who shared her view but from the other side of the divide, clearly appreciated the good sense of this mature and sober traditionalist). Finally, we witness the unflappable cynicism of the Bouillons, which augurs ill for this marriage made for money. (Evreux would treat his wife with contempt, and eventually she returned to her father's home. There was even an attempt to annul the marriage, which the duc de Bouillon, the groom's father, had unsuccessfully opposed.)

C. The main consequence of points A and B above was that upward mobility in the social circles associated with the French court in the seventeenth century was achieved primarily by women. Men remained at the ranks they inherited from their fathers.

The holistic conception of men like Saint-Simon and many of his peers depended on a prejudice and a convention: the prejudice was that noble blood possessed an indelible quality of superiority; the convention, modeled on Salic law, was that only the male line was taken into account in determining the presence or absence of that precious quality. Although Saint-Simon protested glaring mismatches more loudly than many others, he paradoxically ignored the consequences of such marriages in that he looked upon their offspring as full-fledged members of the father's group. The mother's background did not disqualify the children in any way.[37]

Madame's letters reveal a more specifically Germanic form of aristocratic prejudice, which differed in various subtle ways from Saint-Simon's attitude.[38] Although the Princess Palatine was at least as scrupulous as the *petit duc* about people's backgrounds, she paid attention to *both* the paternal *and* the maternal branches of the family tree. When a bad match was made, Saint-Simon tended to complain vociferously and then forget about it (at least as far as the next generation was concerned), but Madame, that tireless letter writer, permanently and categorically condemned the guilty.

D. Another consequence of the system was that the possibility of upward mobility for young women eventually led to a glut of women in the higher ranks of society.[39]

Many women born into the upper ranks were unable to find worthy mates owing to competition from lower-ranking outsiders. Noble families refused, moreover, to allow their daughters to marry men a notch or two below them on the social ladder.

Because of this, as well as the fact that the Sun King's wars at times killed off excessive numbers of wellborn males, some women belonging to high-ranking groups (princes, dukes, *noblesse d'épée*) were condemned to a celibacy that was often sublimated as a religious vocation, whether sincere or not. In a sample of 369 daughters of dukes and peers from the seventeenth century, for instance, we count 105 nuns.[40] This reinforces our earlier remark that the forty abbesses we looked at in the section on demography all came from the highest nobility. Some were even related to the royal family, although admittedly in unorthodox ways (there were royal bastards and former royal mistresses such as La Vallière). Recall, too, that the thirty-five "spinsters" we looked at earlier were mostly young aristocrats of high rank.

On the whole, female hypergamy does not appear to have been incompatible with the dominant endogamy. It was not totally excluded by the system, nor was it merely tolerated. Hypergamy made it possible to replenish the ranks of the court aristocracy and bring new blood into highly placed families.[41] Although Saint-Simon emphasizes the common, or at any rate less distinguished, background of wives as compared with their husbands, the fact is that hypergamy and endogamy together defined the pattern of permissible aristocratic marriages, which we summarize in the table 5.5. Attentive observers of aristocratic morality preferred case A but accepted case B as normal, even if the fussiest arbiters like Saint-Simon complained when the woman crossed the "red line" between robe (or

TABLE 5.5

Case	Husband	Wife	Denomination
A	Rank x	Rank x	Endogamy
B	Rank x	Rank inferior to x + dowry or wealth	Female hypergamy

common herd) and sword. Taken together, the 740 endogamous and 378 hypergamous marriages account for 1,118 of the nuptials in Saint-Simon's sample, or 81.8 percent of the total.

Even though Saint-Simon distinguished between the two types of marriage in theory, in practice he and his kind behaved in such a way as to confirm their deep unity: together they constituted a system that defined the acceptable ways in which superior groups might perpetuate themselves and replenish their ranks.

The 133 cases of female *hypogamy* cry out for analysis. Most of these marriages took place within the *noblesse d'épée*. It seems that certain ducal and princely families were willing to allow "surplus" daughters to marry noblemen of good family but lesser rank. Such marriages were not regarded as mésalliances. To be sure, the husband was required to possess certain notable qualities. Indeed, he was expected to belong to an illustrious family in good standing at court. Thus the groom's family would have been just a cut below the bride's in terms of court protocol.

Of the 133 hypogamous marriages in our sample, 77, or 58 percent, involved marriages between daughters of dukes and nobles of somewhat lesser rank. A smaller number involved daughters of princes who married dukes. To Saint-Simon's discerning eye, such marriages marked a "step down" in society, but apparently such a strict interpretation did not prevent such prestigious dynasties as the Rohans, Luynes, and Noailles from allowing several of their daughters to marry men who did not possess titles as prestigious as their own.

Note, however, that none of these families *ever* allowed one of their daughters to marry a *robin* or, a fortiori, a commoner. Although it is true that women who married did not always maintain their station or rise to a higher one, an "invisible hand" seems to have prevented the daughters of the highest aristocracy from descending below the line separating sword from gown.

The foregoing observations do not contradict but in fact corroborate our earlier remarks about endogamy and hypergamy. As "tokens of exchange" in the economy of power, women were supposed to move in one direction only: up. They replenished the ranks of the aristocracy by swimming upstream, against the powerful currents of the cascade of contempt.

At worst, a young woman might think herself condemned to a rather mediocre fate if she failed to marry a man as titled, honored, and distinguished as her father or eldest brother. But such a minor individual loss of status rarely spelled disgrace for the girl's entire family.

Widowhood sometimes led to female hypogamy. For a second marriage, a woman might give up a position of high rank (generally shared by her late husband and father) for a somewhat more modest place. It was as if a woman's exchange value decreased as age diminished her allure (or perhaps simply as a result of having been married before).

Such cases are described in the *Memoirs*. Already somewhat "the worse for wear," the celebrated duchesse de Chevreuse, wife of the duc de Luynes and daughter of a duc de Rohan-Montbazon, took as her second husband a "mere" marquis by the name of de Laigue. Similarly, the daughter of the prince de Beauvau first married the prince de Lixin but after being left a widow settled in her second marriage for the duc de Mirepoix. To be sure, this was only a small step down, but a step down nonetheless given our ineffable Saint-Simon's strict criteria in matrimony.

There is anecdotal evidence, moreover, that some young women chose hypogamous marriage over not marrying at all. This seems to have been the reason for the marriage of "Mlle d'Estrées, the spinster sister of the last duc d'Estrées, [who] announced her wedding to d'Ampus, an obscure gentleman from Provence whose [family] name is Lurens."[42] Her sister then married a brother of this country gentleman, and eventually the mismatches precipitated a falling out between the two couples and the entire Estrées clan.

Sometimes, as in the best (or worst) melodramas, hypogamy was the price to be paid because the prospective bride was somehow disabled, disgraced, or dishonored. *Faute de mieux*, a great family might consent to a marriage between a disgraced daughter and a man of lesser quality, who might find it advantageous to ally himself with a powerful family. Saint-Simon discusses this case explicitly:

Pezé was from the Maine region, a gentleman through and through, but quite simple, a distant relative of the maréchal de Tessé according to the genealogists but closer according to the ways of love: he had a mother of whom the marshal was quite fond. Pezé was a younger son. Tessé looked out for him and early on saw to it that he became a page of Mme la duchesse de Bourgogne, whom he served as first equerry. Courtarvel, Pezé's elder brother, had some property but for himself alone and lived with Pezé in the country. Their grandfather had married the eldest daughter of Artus de Saint-Gelais, lord of Lansac, and a daughter of the maréchal de Souvré, whose family had thought themselves fortunate to get her decently off their hands in this way because of her physical disgrace. The man who took her deemed himself quite honored to make such a match, whatever the price.[43]

Female hypogamy, we note in passing, was also an "intra-*robin*" phenomenon. Indeed, the daughters of the greatest *parlementaire* dynasties sometimes married men whose careers had not taken them as far as their future fathers-in-law—at least not as of the time of marriage. For our purposes, the important point is that where female hypogamy did occur, it took place within the major groups (sword and gown, and to a lesser extent among commoners) without crossing the divide that separated them.

It is therefore fair to say that hypogamy was often in the eye of the beholder, and in Saint-Simon's case that eye was very severe. The families involved often did not share the writer's all-consuming prejudice. Still, our investigation of hypogamous marriages reinforces our earlier statement about the persistence of the sword/gown cleavage.[44] At the same time, the existence of hypergamous marriages establishes a model of upward mobility for women, upward mobility that was especially significant when a woman moved across the boundary that divided the two main groups into which Saint-Simon divided the only society that mattered to him.

Attitudes toward hypogamous marriage show that while both major groups tended to view intragroup marriages as more or less alike (unlike Saint-Simon, who was keenly sensitive to even the slightest differences of rank), neither normally permitted its daughters to marry men from the group below. In the ideology of court groups, then, there was a sharp distinction between sword and gown that resulted in an asymmetry between the choices available to men and women. Men could marry women of inferior rank, even those who fell below the "bar of mésalliance," or beyond the line between sword and gown. Women could marry men less titled than their brothers but only if the husbands came from the same curial group.

Saint-Simon was simply an exponent of this ideology, which he helped to refine, complicate, and in some ways confuse by applying it to subgroups, ranks, and even individuals, whereas many of his contemporaries applied it only to the fundamental distinction between sword and robe. In this and many other respects, Saint-Simon was a fundamentalist of hierarchy, a zealous proponent of the cascade of contempt.

Let us turn now to the 115 "special cases" that we did not include under the heads of endogamy, hypergamy, or hypogamy. These can be broken down fairly readily into two groups of unequal size. Included in the first group are just twenty-five marriages that quite simply do not fall within our criteria. Many of these were marriages within the extended royal family, some of them secret, such as the probable marriage of Monseigneur, le Grand Dauphin, to Mlle Choin, his mistress, "a short, fat, ugly brunette with a snub nose, a good mind, and a flair for intrigue and maneuver."[45]

In this small group, we have also included the marriages of a few bastards born to a father of royal blood and a commoner mother, such as the future regent's illegitimate daughter and the daughter that Louis XIV had with a gardener. At once "subaltern" and grandiose, these bastards generally found mates among the *noblesse d'épée.*

In addition to various other special cases (in particular, marriages between French nobles and foreigners of comparable birth), this miscellaneous category also includes the marriages of the illegitimate children that Louis XIV had with the duchesse de La Vallière and the marquise de Montespan. We hardly need call attention to the scandals that erupted (only to be quickly snuffed out) when one of these royal bastards married a prince or princess of the house of Bourbon (a Condé or Conti), or even a grandson of France such as the duc de Chartres (the future regent). In a brief passage of the *Memoirs,* Saint-Simon discusses the maneuvers leading up to the marriage of Philippe d'Orléans and succinctly states his numerous objections:

> The king, concerned with establishing his bastards, whom he raised higher day after day, had married off two of his daughters to princes of the blood. Mme la princesse de Conti, the only daughter of the king and Mme de La Vallière, was a childless widow; the other, the eldest daughter of the king and Mme de Montespan, had married Monsieur le Duc. For a long time Mme de Maintenon even more than the king thought of nothing else but how to raise the status of these children higher and higher, and both hoped that Mlle de Blois, the second daughter of the king and Mme de Montespan, would marry M. le duc de Chartres. He was the king's only nephew and far outranked the princes of the blood because he was a grandson of France and because Monsieur [his father] kept his own court. The marriages of the two princes of the blood to which I just alluded had scandalized everyone. The king was not unaware of this, and he was therefore able to gauge the likely effect of an even more glaringly disproportionate marriage. For four years he had turned this over in his mind and had even taken some steps toward achieving his goal. Those steps were made all the more difficult by the fact that Monsieur was minutely scrupulous about anything to do with his standing and Madame came from a country that abhorred bastards and mésalliances and was of a character such that one dared not count on persuading her to accept such a match. In the hope of

overcoming these many obstacles, the king turned to Monsieur le Grand, to whom he had always been close, in order to win over his brother the chevalier de Lorraine, who had always controlled Monsieur.[46]

To deal properly with the problem of the royal bastards and their establishment, we would need to write another book. Let us therefore say simply that the twenty-five marriages in this special category were so unusual that it is best to leave them out of our analysis.

There is, however, a second set of special cases that is particularly interesting for the present discussion. The ninety marriages in this group all involved a government minister (or the son or daughter of a government minister), hence a person associated with the highest echelons of the *robe du Conseil*, and either a *noble d'épée* or the daughter of a *noble d'épée*.

Sixty-six of these ninety marriages elevated a minister's daughter to the "native" *gentilhommerie*, or nobility of the sword, and a few even achieved ducal status. All these count as female hypergamy in the strict sense. The remaining twenty-four marriages involved a minister or minister's son wedding a daughter of the native gentry. Hence these count as cases of female hypogamy.

This presents a problem, however. The ministerial families involved in these unions belonged in theory to the nobility of the robe. Saint-Simon complains frequently and emphatically about this throughout the *Memoirs*, in which he harps on the low ancestry of *robin* dynasties whose origins lay in the "vile bourgeoisie."

We stated earlier, however, that while great families, and in particular ducal families, were perfectly prepared to tolerate female hypergamy for the benefit of their males, they did not allow their daughters to descend beneath the social barrier between sword and gown. They accepted hypogamy only if it did not take their daughters outside the native noble order, the nobility of the sword. What, then, allowed these twenty-four ministers or sons of ministers to benefit from a de facto dispensation of some sort?

The answer is simple: these ministers or sons of ministers were no longer considered to be men of the gown. Because of the role that ministers played on the King's Council, ministerial families were comparable to aristocratic lineages of ducal rank. Apart from a few fossils (such as Saint-Simon and the Princess Palatine) who held firmly to the distinction between gown and sword, dukes and their sons did not disdain to marry the daughters of ministers or to allow their daughters to marry ministers or sons of ministers.

Ministerial families thus constituted a quite special subgroup of the aristocracy: plucked from the cream of the nobility of the robe, they formed a distinct echelon between the high robe and the sword, not to say the dukes. Ministers and their male offspring, future ministers in embryo, apparently had no difficulty marrying women of ostensibly higher station, in some cases so high as to appear beyond the reach of ordinary *robins*. To cite one extraordinary example, Barbezieux, Louvois's son, married the daughter of the duc d'Uzès, who had previously been "promised" to none other than Saint-Simon. The daughters of ministers had no difficulty marrying into the most distinguished ducal ranks. Some ministerial families were even unwilling to accept marriages for their daughters with anyone less than a duke. Each of the three daughters of the great Colbert married a duke: Chevreuse, Beauvillier, and Mortemart, respectively. Hence it would be misleading to think of such marriages as hypergamy in the usual sense. For want of a better term, we will refer to them as cases of female pseudo-hypergamy. Similarly, when a minister or the son of a minister married the daughter of a noble of the sword, the marriage did not really "lower" the woman socially. We therefore classify such marriages under the head of female pseudo-hypogamy.

In order to clarify the special situation of ministerial lineages, we therefore adopt a special terminology. We call the marriage of a minister's daughter to a noble (often a duke) a "female ministerial marriage" (pseudo-hypergamous). And we call the marriage of a minister or minister's son to the daughter of a *noble d'épée* a "male ministerial marriage" (pseudo-hypogamous).

If we adopt the idea that, socially speaking, a minister was the equal of a duke, certain complexities simply vanish. The special situations described above complete, and to some degree complicate, our analysis of aristocratic marriage. Ministerial marriages blurred the traditional hierarchy by allowing ministerial families, despite their roots in the nobility of the robe, to leap the abyss of mésalliance not only by giving away a daughter but also by accepting the gift of a son. Ministerial families belonged more to the aristocracy than to the world of the gown. Much to Saint-Simon's dismay, they accomplished a "fusion of elites" by breaking the standard model of curial reproduction outlined above.[47] That model linked endogamy (in the majority of cases) to female hypergamy (in a relatively small number of cases, to be sure, but frequent enough and on the whole well tolerated). Thus the ministerial families, to their own benefit, laid the groundwork for a new type of society, a society that differed from the old, and in some ways utopian, society of ranks. By 1750 that old society had ceased to exist: France had become post-baroque, or post-rococo or neoclassical, under the aging Louis XV, and so it would remain under Louis XVI.

Renouncers and Jesuits

The worldly spirit praises the great of this world in proportion to their treasures; the divine spirit assigns to the children of the Lord deserts in proportion to their scorn for riches.

—Father Pasquier Quesnel,
Réflexions morales sur le Nouveau Testament
(Amsterdam edition, 1736), 5:59.

Does an oppressive system of ranks allow for any form of escape? Louis Dumont refers to individuals who seek to escape social constraints as "renouncers" and to groups that do the same as "sects." Both assert the rights of the individual against the oppressive holistic society. Or perhaps it would be more accurate to say that the assertion of individual rights complements and in a sense reinforces the constraints imposed by the universal, hierarchical values of the rank-stratified temporal realm.

Madame has little light to shed on this matter, though there are clues in her wish to rediscover what she called "Nature" as well as in her nostalgic (or was it Germanic?) longing for "eating cherries on a mountaintop at five in the morning" and constant references to the Abbey of Maubuisson. She repeatedly wonders whether she ought to retire to this convent, whose abbess was a relative of hers. By doing so she might escape the unpleasantness of the court. At other times, however, she asks if she ought not rather to resign herself to the difficulties, complications, and dangers of Versailles and Marly. When Monsieur dies, she finally makes up her mind. Before burning her late husband's correspondence with his male lovers, she loudly proclaims to anyone who will listen that she wants "no convent! Let no one speak to me of convents!"

Saint-Simon has more to tell us than Madame has. In the very first volume of the *Memoirs* (covering the year 1692), he describes the "solitaries" of Marlagne, south of Namur. Having withdrawn from the world, they live alone in cloistered poverty. Within the walls of their monastery they drink only pure water, eat only food from their own gardens, and dedicate themselves to work, silence, and prayer:

Marlagne is a monastery situated on a pleasant low plateau surrounded by a park and a forest of tall trees. It was founded by Archduke Albert and Isabelle as an isolated retreat for Discalced Carmelites, an order that maintains similar establishments in each of its provinces so that its members may make retreats of a year or two. They live in perpetual silence in bare cells quite similar to those of the Carthusians but take their meals in a common refectory. Those meals are quite frugal, because the monks fast almost all the time and are diligent in prayer, dividing their days between manual labor and contemplation. They each have four small rooms, a tiny garden, and a small chapel, along with an abundance of the freshest water I have ever tasted. Some of it comes from wells in or near the houses or scattered about the grounds, but most comes from flowing springs. The park is a rolling expanse of land with plenty of tall trees and is surrounded by walls. It is vast. Eight to ten small houses are scattered here and there and equipped with gardens somewhat larger than that of the cloister along with a small kitchen. A monk of the order lives in each of these houses for a month at a time, rarely longer. Such a retreat requires the permission of the superior, who alone makes occasional visits. Life in the houses is more austere than in the cloister and entirely isolated. All the monks attend Sunday services, take their rations from the convent, and during the week prepare their own meals. They never leave their tiny houses. When the time comes to say mass, they ring a bell, and a neighbor comes to give the responses, after which he returns without uttering a word. The monks spend their time in prayer, contemplation, household chores, and basketweaving like the *laures* of old.

Later in this same passage, which deals with the military campaign of 1692, Saint-Simon contrasts the simple piety of these solitaries with the "underhandedness" of the Jesuits, who prefer politics to renunciation:

After Namur was captured, something happened that caused quite a stir and might have led to trouble had any prince but the king been involved [Saint-Simon believed Louis XIV to be pro-Jesuit]. Before [the king] entered the city, where it would hardly have been suitable for him to stay while the castle was under siege, everything was subjected to scrupulous inspection . . . the mines, the magazines—in a word, everything was laid out in plain view. In the final inspection conducted after the castle was taken, the Jesuits were included. They opened their gates, but not without a show of surprise, to put it mildly, that their word alone was not good enough. But the inspectors looked in places [that the Jesuits] had not anticipated and found their basements filled with powder, about which they had said nothing. What they were planning to do with this powder remains unclear. It was taken away, and because they were Jesuits, nothing came of the incident.

This contrast—between those who renounce the world, like the solitaries of Marlagne, and those who are in the thick of it, like the Jesuits of Namur—is marked, and it recurs throughout the *Memoirs*. Saint-Simon reserves a special place for those who withdraw from worldly life and the society of ranks. He himself periodically retreated to meditate in the company of individuals and groups that were, if not Jansenist, at least sympathizers of the Jansenists. He sought the advice of men who lived solitary lives, men for whom he professed wholehearted admiration. One such was Rancé, the abbot of a Trappist monastery. Another was the very pro-Jansenist comte du Charmel, who left the court for lengthy retreats with the Trappists.[1] Certain bishops and other ecclesiastics also chose to reside in their dioceses and provinces rather than seek proximity to the king and his entourage: as innocent as babes, they cared for the poor, fasted, and ate only vegetables ("Oh, my beloved vegetables!" one was heard to exclaim). Despite his sympathy for renouncers, Saint-Simon was deeply suspicious of pseudo-mystics and others of the zealously devout who did not truly turn their backs on the world and whose aims were more political than religious. Among them were some Jansenists: Saint-Simon's sympathy for the sect, though quite genuine, was not unalloyed. He also distrusted Quietists such as Fénelon, whom he thought hungry for power. And of course there were the Jesuits, up to their necks in worldly, not to say world, politics.

Which renouncers did Saint-Simon believe to be the most pure? Heading the list was Jean-François Le Haguais, an *avocat* in Parlement from Caen, a friend of Chancellor Pontchartrain, and at one time a great hunter as well as skirt-chaser. In his later years, however, Le Haguais lived as a penitent far from Paris and put a lock on a tongue that had gotten him into trouble as a youth much given to scathing witticisms. Saints, even latter-day saints, were renowned for their silence, and Le Haguais lived up to his reputation.

As did the duc de Rouannez, a mathematician born into a prestigious family and a friend of Pascal's, who, as a disciple of that Jansenist master, refused a rewarding offer of marriage and, though he never formally took orders, donned an ecclesiastical habit that he wore until death surprised him in 1696, while he was living in pious seclusion in a Home for Devout Gentlemen and Friars Minim.

Another man cut from the same cloth was François de Chandenier, a scion of the illustrious Rochechouart family and former captain of the guard. During the Fronde, he became involved in a murder plot that disgraced him in the king's eyes and landed him in a cell in the fortress of Loches, where he survived on meager rations. Eventually he was freed and soon thereafter entered the Abbaye Sainte-Geneviève (on the site of the present-day Panthéon in Paris). From then until his death, he occasionally went on remote retreats with the Jansenist Nicole.

Also worth mentioning in this connection was the Transylvanian prince Ragotzi, who at one time had been a Hungarian rebel leader. In a backhanded way, he was therefore Louis XIV's ally against the court of Vienna. After suffering military defeat at Austrian hands, he embarked on a series of adventures that eventually landed him in France, where he lived in seclusion among Grosbois's *camaldules* in an establishment modeled after the oldest European houses of retreat.[2] In this refuge, Ragotzi made do with few servants, saw almost no one, lived on bread and water, did good works, and was diligent in prayer both day and night. Later he made yet another retreat to the Ottoman Empire, but despite the folly of this plan, he lived happily among the Turks, content with whatever Providence provided.

Charmel, a nobleman from Champagne of superficial intelligence but deep spirituality, made enough of an impression on Saint-Simon to appear frequently in the *Memoirs*. At one time a great gambler and habitué of the court, Charmel later gave himself part and parcel to the Catholic faith of his childhood but only after reading *De la vérité de la religion chrétienne*, a book by the Protestant minister Jacques Abbadie that in its day was greatly admired by many among the Catholic elite. Such admiration was evidence of uncommon broadmindedness—a quality more often associated with Jansenists than with Catholics. Charmel then took to wearing hair shirts, spiked belts, and other instruments of penance, not to say torture (or "masochism," as people like to say nowadays). In the Trappist monastery on Good Friday he remained on his knees, "without support and without changing his position," from four in the morning until ten.[3] Yet he kept up both his good spirits and his ties to Jansenism. The latter led to his disgrace in 1706, but by then he had long since abandoned the court. He died in 1714 after an operation for gallstones, more penitent than ever, though one wonders why, since he had led an utterly pure life for more than a quarter of a century. Yet who would dare boast of being saved?

Another associate of the Trappists was much like Charmel: the chevalier de Saint-Louis, a gruff and not very intelligent old soldier who was touched by grace in the year 1684. A lull in the fighting became his pretext for leaving the army and heading for the marshes and bogs of Trappist country. There he led an ascetic existence for thirty years as a lay brother among the "predestined." He became famous later on when the worldly Cardinal de Bouillon answered his edifying sermon on death with the words, "No, Monsieur de Saint-Louis, not death, don't speak to me of death. I do not wish to die."[4]

Another "honorary Trappist" was Joseph de Forbin, the nephew of a cardinal and brother of an archbishop, a canon, and a soldier-monk. He himself had long served as a musketeer and was seriously wounded at Ramailles (a disastrous battle that was not among the finer moments of Louis XIV's reign). After his wife died, he withdrew to a monastery of Minims on the grounds of his castle in Provence. Although he remained a lay brother, he lived a life of rugged solitude wholly taken up with prayers and good works, and died a saintly death.[5] Yet another brother of his was an avid duelist until he, too, underwent a conversion experience and became a Trappist.

Clearly the central figure in all this was the abbé de Rancé, the superior of the Trappist monks. Born, like his close friend the pro-Jansenist bishop Barillon, into an illustrious family of the *robe du Conseil*, Armand-Jean Bouthillier de Rancé was Saint-Simon's model par excellence of a man who cultivated silence, found joy in austerity, and ardently embraced suffering. Like his father before him, Saint-Simon felt a tender affection for the abbé, so tender that he later developed a great affection for his younger brother, the chevalier Henri de Rancé, a galley captain and commander of the port of Marseilles, when the gallant captain, who was the spitting image of his elder brother, paid a brief visit to Paris. By then the abbé had been dead for eighteen years, having expired on a bed of straw and ashes in a state of high anxiety and distress despite a blameless career as a monk. He had plumbed the depths of mysticism and renunciation and eschewed as too worldly even the scholarly work on which the Benedictines of Saint-Maur prided themselves.[6] Yet he was no extremist but a man who kept to the middle of the road, and this, too, attracted Saint-Simon, even though Rancé had been a sympathizer of the Fronde and an intimate of Cardinal de Retz. A loyal friend of Bossuet's, Rancé had remained aloof, keeping an equal distance from the three vertices of the fatal "Bermuda Triangle:" the ultramontanism of the Jesuits, the charlatanism of the Fénelonian Quietist zealots, and—politically the most dangerous of all despite Saint-Simon's unspoken sympathy—Jansenism. Saint-Simon liked to visit his good master and neighbor at the Trappist monastery during preparations for Holy Week.

He was not the only one to make this pious journey. Mme de Guise, the daughter of Gaston d'Orléans (by his second wife), also known as Elisabeth d'Orléans, duchesse d'Alençon, was a misshapen hunchback who married the next-to-last duc de Guise, Louis-Joseph by name (the last duke was their son, who died young). Louis-Joseph de Guise had in his veins the blood of those princes of Lorraine despised by Saint-Simon because of their involvement in the League, which had been much too

Jesuitical for his liking. But our author deemed the duke's wife innocent of the past excesses of her in-laws, in whose dynasty she was a mere outsider. Indeed, the duchesse de Guise, widowed early on, served as patron of the Trappist monastery. She was a woman of extreme goodness, who spent all her time in prayer, fasting, and good works and made frequent and regular retreats to the Trappist monastery, where Rancé housed her in a building adjacent to the abbey walls.

Elisabeth, moreover, was quite insistent about her rank, which was very exalted indeed: she was a granddaughter of France, since her father was a son of King Henri IV. Although her husband was a Guise and therefore quite wellborn himself, there was no question of his being seated in an armchair in his wife's presence. He was entitled only to a folding chair: "Every day at dinner he would hand his wife her napkin, and after she had sat down in her armchair and unfolded her napkin while M. de Guise remained standing, she would give orders that a place should be set for him. The necessary items were always kept in readiness on the buffet, and now they could be set at the far end of the table. Everything was done, day after day, with the same scrupulous attention to detail, without diminishing the lady's rank one iota or raising that of M. de Guise despite his august marriage." Not that Saint-Simon felt the slightest pity for this descendant of *princes ligueurs*. In Alençon, "the duchesse de Guise lorded it over the intendant as though he were a mere apprentice and treated the bishop of her diocese in much the same way, keeping him standing for hours on end while she sat in an armchair, never deigning even for a moment to allow him to sit off in a corner somewhere out of her sight."[7]

This was the same Elisabeth who made retreats, was a generous patron to the Trappists, renounced the worldly life with all its vanities and responsibilities, and deliberately cut herself off from the pleasures of this world, for she had it on good authority that from dust she came and unto dust she would return. Yet at the same time, she behaved like a *domina hierarchica*, insisting on every privilege of her supreme position. It was as if she wished to place in the balance a proper dose of renunciation against the weight of such supremacy, while exhorting others to do the same. The court system, built as it was like a vertical espalier, needed this counterweight, this leaven of spiritualist egalitarianism. Otherwise it would have forfeited some of its divine justification and ceased to function properly or even to endure for very long. In the same spirit, Mme de Guise saw to it that her death would be in harmony with her penchant for austerity—dazzling austerity because it was hers, shrouded not by a dark cloud but by a bright one.[8] She asked to be buried not in Saint-Denis, as her illustrious birth would have entitled her, but at the convent of Carmelites in the faubourg Saint-Jacques, and as a simple nun. In life she had contrived to combine a courtly existence with the Carmelite spirit, to temper hierarchy with the solitude of the cloister.

We find the same ability to transcend contradictions in Maréchal Catinat, who in this respect was not so very different from Henri IV's granddaughter. Catinat was the poor man's Vauban: like Vauban he was an austere patriot, but he lacked the talent of his colleague from the Morvan for making himself famous by publishing, informally at first, a work destined to become a best-seller like Vauban's *Dîme royale*.[9] Catinat had nothing but scorn for death on the battlefield and, by the end of his life, for the world. In his unique way, he fused Christian renunciation with Roman stoicism. His Catholic piety was notorious, but his ultimate retreat to the tiny château of Saint-Gatien near Saint-Denis was not just a lonely zealot's flight into the desert but a statement comparable to Cincinnatus's turning his back on Rome and the blandishments of power in order to trudge behind his plow. Emulating Plutarch, Rousseau himself would later extol the virtuous marshal as the prototypical citizen of the Enlightenment. At once a hermit and an apostle of hierarchy, Catinat, if we believe Saint-Simon, combined a marked taste for Christian solitude, in which he took secret pleasure, with a fundamental distrust of commingling of the social orders, of that horrible confusion of *estats* that he believed ought to remain separate and carefully arrayed one above the other. Asceticism, yes, but even in asceticism there must always be hierarchy.

Except for Rancé, all the renouncers we have mentioned thus far were laymen, but one can easily cite any number of clerical examples as well. For instance, the abbé de Charost was the son and brother of a duke. He withdrew from the world and went to live in his father's home, where he later died. According to Saint-Simon, Charost was a very pious abbé and worthy of being elevated to the rank of bishop, but other writers skewered him for his allegedly unecclesiastical morals. A less dubious example was the abbé de Coetelez, who withdrew first to a Carthusian monastery and later to Brittany, where he lived a pious life of solitude. So did Père de Chevigny, a former soldier born into a Parisian bourgeois family that washed away its base origins by acquiring an ennobling office (the so-called *savonnette à vilain*, or commoner's cleanser). Upright and honest, Chevigny was a man of simple virtue who was also a friend of the La Rochefoucaulds, who had ties to the Jansenists, among whom Chevigny was a man of considerable importance. Indeed, his Jansenist leanings had seriously compromised his reputation with the "royals" long before he withdrew from the world. He died in 1698, after years devoted to study and care of the poor, years during which he rarely emerged from his retreat.

Two other abbés merit inclusion in this austere gallery. To Saint-

Simon, the abbé d'Estrades was a man of "mixed" background. His father's family had opposed the League, which for Saint-Simon was a big plus, but his mother "sadly" traced her descent to a family of Spanish Jews. Despite this, the memorialist commended d'Estrades highly, because he had ruined himself in the service of France, spending freely on any number of embassies before embarking on an exemplary life of solitude in Chaillot and Passy, where he lived cheaply in a rented house.

The portrait of Abbé Jean Vittement is more subtly drawn. Vittement sprang from humble Picard roots. An energetic teacher, he had moved up in society in the usual way. Eventually he became rector of the Sorbonne and tutor or assistant tutor to the grandsons of Louis XIV. Later, after the king's death, he made a name for himself as assistant tutor to the child king Louis XV. Quick and intuitive, he soon realized, however, that all power would ultimately pass to the young king's head tutor, the prelate Fleury. A wary Fleury pressed him to leave the court, and Vittement soon agreed, rejecting various consolation prizes, including a seat in the Académie Française (paltry compensation though it was). He then took vows and embarked upon a life of poverty and solitude with the Brothers of the Christian Doctrine, specialists in the catechism. This decision compelled the admiration of the court, whose power his retreat at once challenged and reinforced. In doing what he did, Vittement followed in the footsteps of Nicolas Le Fèvre, who returned to a life of solitude after completing his work as a tutor to princes. Vittement's story held particular significance for Saint-Simon, who, like the abbé before him, was expelled from the court by Fleury in 1723 and obliged to live in "solitude"—comfortable solitude, to be sure, in a Parisian *hôtel* most of the year and in his castle in the country the rest of the time.

Continuing our exploration of men who renounced the world late in life, let us turn now to the highest levels of the government and begin by considering two ministers charged with very high responsibilities indeed: Le Peletier, a comptroller general of finance, and Pontchartrain, a chancellor. Claude Le Peletier, who retired from his last government post in 1697, was a man of overscrupulous conscience who hoped to live out his final years in pious retreat: the very definition of "ultimate renunciation." He divided his time between piety and gardening and managed to complete a manuscript about each, the *Codex theologicus* and *Codex rusticus* respectively. His son and grandson, both *présidents* of Parlement, would both follow suit: when the time came, each would voluntarily abandon the high judicial office he held. But another son, Charles-Maurice Le Peletier, was different: a "dull and glorious animal" and seminary director, he never got over being the son of a former minister of state.

The elder Pontchartrain had been a friend of that minister as well as his successor as comptroller general of finance. Eventually, however, he surpassed Le Peletier in both his career and his retirement. Overcome by premature modesty, the latter had passed up the supreme post of chancellor, settling for lesser but still powerful positions in finance and the post office before plunging into retirement. But Pontchartrain went all the way to the top, so that his renunciation was even more spectacular. He had many reasons for resigning his post at the beginning of Louis XV's reign and living out his days in modest retirement, and not all of them had to do with Christianity. Age was a factor (he was already past seventy). He was also a widower (Mme de Pontchartrain had died a short while earlier). And finally, he was afraid of having to place his official stamp on measures favorable to the royal bastards, measures of which he profoundly disapproved but that he would have rubber-stamped out of instinctive respect for sovereign authority.

That said, it remains true that religion played a central role in his decision. Like Le Peletier, Pontchartrain wanted a pious interval between life and death, a time of refuge from a corrupt world during which he could give himself over fully to prayer but without any trace of baroque mummery, which would have been unbearable to a discreet disciple of Jansenius such as the chancellor. He sought to shun the court, where Tellier and other Jesuits exerted a magnetic influence. And he hoped to get away from Mme de Maintenon's favorites, the Sulpicians, and spend more time with his own favorites, the pro-Jansenist Oratoire, in whose headquarters he had sometimes slept while still chancellor, in a room specially set aside for him. Every retreat began with a definite plan: Pontchartrain's was to move into the bachelor quarters formerly occupied by that illustrious renouncer M. du Charmel (see above), who had lived for a time in a suite in Pontchartrain's home. The chancellor's unprecedented resignation had the further advantage of allowing him to avoid having anything to do with the implementation of the papal bull *Unigenitus*, whose hostility to Jansenism was patent. Last but not least, it would give him the opportunity in 1716 to give the court a fine lesson in virtue and humility: when Louis XV came to call on him, he hastened to the sidewalk to greet the young king rather than accept the immense honor of receiving the king inside his own home, as the boy monarch's then-guardian Maréchal de Villeroy wished. The extraordinary thing about Pontchartrain's resignation was that never in living memory had a chancellor ever left his post for any reason short of death. One had to go back to the sixteenth or perhaps even the fifteenth century to find a precedent: a full-fledged keeper of the seals who voluntarily gave up his post. Thus Pontchartrain's retreat, steeped as it was in spirituality, seemed a miracle to his contemporaries.

Nevertheless, the fact that Pontchartrain meditated upon his renunciation for a long time before acting was in fact typical. It was not uncommon for people at court or in power suddenly to turn their backs on both. Early in 1697, for example, Louis XIV reorganized the highly exclusive Upper Council, the tiny but powerful areopagus of his regime.[10] One of those included was Claude Le Peletier, who would resign within the year.[11] Another was Pontchartrain, who would do the same in 1714, as would Beauvillier a few years later. Only Pomponne, the fourth and final member of the council, would avoid the common fate of his colleagues: whatever ideas of retreat or renunciation he may have had remained mere whims until his death. But his father, Robert Arnauld d'Andilly, who led a saintly life of retirement at Port-Royal-des-Champs, in the eye of the Jansenist storm, had renounced more than his share of the world, enough for himself and all his offspring.

We have yet to discuss the fourth member of the council, Beauvillier. He had much in common with Le Peletier and Pontchartrain, except that he liked Jesuits. Late in life, following the death of his intimate friend and brother-in-law Charles, duc de Chevreuse, minister and duke Paul de Beauvillier would also make the standard decision to retire to a life of piety. As early as 1711, it was reported that the duc de Beauvillier had "an unshakable taste and penchant for retirement."[12] Alas, his retirement proved to be short-lived. In 1714, "he lay sick for nearly two months in Vaucresson, to which, *a short while earlier*, he had retired and shut himself away from the world, even from his most intimate companions, so as to think of nothing but his salvation and devote his every moment of solitude to nothing but this" [emphasis added]. He died there on the last Friday in August (the same day of the week as Christ's passion), "in the death of the Just, having kept his head to the end." He was sixty-five. After his death, his wife broke off all commerce with the world both at home and at the convent of Benedictine sisters in Montargis, where several of her daughters were nuns. The duchess would remain in pious retirement until her death, eschewing not only the pleasures of the "table but amusement of any kind."[13] Again there is not the slightest hint of Jansenism in any of this, not surprising in view of the pro-Jesuit sentiments of the Beauvilliers. Much the same description could be given of the duchesse de Mortemart, another leading light in a group with Quietist tendencies whose members included Fénelon, Mme Guyon, and Beauvillier. A young woman of striking good looks, Mme de Mortemart had been quite fond of both the court and the world, but suddenly she abandoned both and, "in Paris, plunged herself into a devout solitude that overwhelmed all resistance, and in spite of everything she would persevere in this course to the end."[14]

As for the elderly duc de Beauvillier, we saw earlier that his decision to renounce the world predated the mortal illness that ultimately claimed his life. Since Beauvillier was close to the Jesuits and therefore free of any taint of Jansenism, it is clear that the practice of making a pious retreat was not exclusively linked to any particular religious ideology, even if it was often associated with Jansenism. The entire Christian elite, whether pro-Jesuit or pro-Jansenist, was drawn to the practice: as life drew to a close, many people sought to deepen their faith and assure themselves of eternal salvation. An example was set at the highest levels of the state by a trio of pious ministers: Le Peletier, Pontchartrain, and Beauvillier. Indeed, with this "threesome" of pious Catholics at the head of the French government, any hapless Huguenots who remained in France found themselves in deep trouble.[15]

With such high-level renouncers, the edifying retreat could of course only be a culminating event. Others, however, were at liberty to renounce the world repeatedly, a little at a time. The marquise Marthe de Caylus was adept at this, as were the comtesse Françoise de Saint-Géran and the marquis Armand de Lassay. So was Troisville (pronounced Tréville), the grandson of a bourgeois from the Basque town of Oloron and son of the illustrious musketeer later made famous by Alexandre Dumas. Troisville was a highly cultivated man but, unlike his father, not much of a soldier. He cut a glittering figure in high society as well as among the cream of the demimonde gathered around Ninon de Lenclos. But later, in the grip of remorse, he sought refuge in pious solitude—only to find himself bored stiff. Eventually he returned to the high life, which he found difficult to do without. After shuttling back and forth several more times, he finally settled in among the Jansenists, whose ideology was widely shared by "educated and intelligent people of good taste," not unlike the "caviar left mentality" of the late twentieth century.[16] Louis XIV took offense at this and refused to see him anymore, and His Majesty's displeasure led to Troisville's failure to win a seat in the Académie Française.

The Sun King was more forgiving toward others than toward the "foreigner" Troisville, a genuine Basque. Louis demonstrated a certain indulgence, for example, in the case of pure-blooded Frenchmen such as the younger Gesvres and Fieubet. These gentlemen at least found it possible to interrupt their pious exercises once or twice a year to pay their respects to the monarch. Fieubet, incidentally, became so depressed in solitude that he eventually died of boredom (and jaundice). And then there was Lassay, who eventually married an illegitimate daughter of Monsieur le Prince.[17] He had been in love with the daughter of an apothecary, a beautiful, modest, sensible, witty young woman, who became his first wife. When she died, "he believed that he was losing his mind, began thinking of himself as devout, and went into retreat with the Incurables of Paris on the rue de Sèvres, where for several years he led a most edifying life.

Ultimately, however, he became bored, attempted to return to society, and soon found himself right in the thick of it, where Monsieur le Duc found him much to his liking."

U ntil now we have said little about female renouncers. Those who have been mentioned thus far, such as the duchesse de Guise and the duchesse de Beauvillier, became not nuns but lay sisters in Trappist or other convents. Among women, as among men, there was a double standard in renunciation: secular or cloistered (one is tempted to say civilian and military). Saint-Simon discusses at least a dozen women who renounced the world: not many compared with the hundreds and hundreds of women who appear in the *Memoirs* but still a substantial number, and significant in the sense that these women conformed to an "ideal type" that was very much present in the thinking not only of Saint-Simon but also of many of his contemporaries both at court and in Paris.

Perhaps the simplest approach is to begin with two of Louis XIV's former mistresses, one of whom chose the cloister while the other went the secular route. Louise de La Vallière became a nun, a Carmelite of the rue Saint-Jacques convent in Paris. She expiated her "sin" by doing "unremitting penance every day of her life," going well beyond the rule of her order: she abstained as much as possible from drinking, even water, and as a result became ill and eventually died.[18] By contrast, Mme de Montespan may have fallen into disgrace but she kept both feet firmly planted in society, albeit a backwater society of sorts. But God had touched her. A Jansenist Oratorian, Père de La Tour, supervised her closely. She gave almost everything she had to the poor. At dinner she cut back on the amount she ate even though eating had once been one of her greatest pleasures. She prayed virtually around the clock.[19] And she imposed upon herself myriad unbelievably tedious penitential chores.

Any number of women followed the example of Mme de La Vallière by withdrawing from the world to become authentic nuns. One of those mentioned by Saint-Simon is Louise Hollandine of Bavaria. She was the daughter of a Palatine elector who served for a time as king of Bohemia. She was also the aunt of three kings of England and the niece of a fourth, as well as the great-aunt of an empress of Austria. Though a princess to the bone, she had been brought up under the influence of Port-Royal. This helps to explain her subsequent choices. She became first a nun of the Abbey of Maubuisson and later its abbess. Such a promotion was no cause for wonder given the lady's extraordinary rank, yet for more than half a century she chose to live in conditions of utmost deprivation.

Was her fate so unlike that of Marie-Madeleine Gabrielle de Rochechouart, abbess of Fontevrault and sister of Mme de Montespan? Marie-Madeleine was placed in the convent by her father, "locked up quite young" and more or less against her will: the veil was not something to which she wished to subject herself. In time, however, she became a good nun. With some help from her sister, the king's mistress, she became the (highly competent) superior of Fontevrault, an abbey housing a very unusual order in which men were subordinate to women, that is, monks to nuns—modern feminists should be overjoyed. A theologian, polyglot, and prolific letter writer, Marie-Madeleine led an ascetic life in her convent in accordance with all the rules, "purifying her heart of any filth that might have found its way in." At regular intervals another sister would castigate all her flaws, and she would do the same in return. Occasionally she would visit the court, but she took no great pleasure in it. She was obliged to go, however, because it pleased the king, who adored her almost as much as he did his *maîtresse poulette*, Mme de Montespan (Saint-Simon's slangy expression for the royal mistress is rather audacious, roughly equivalent in contemporary English to referring to the lady as a "babe"). Yet the abbess of Fontevrault ruled her world and her order with an iron hand, when necessary cloaked in the usual velvet glove.

An even "better" example, closer to the standard of humility set by Mme de La Vallière, is that of Anne-Louise-Christine, duchesse d'Epernon, granddaughter of Henri IV by the left hand, who was to be betrothed to the Polish king Casimir but preferred a crown of thorns to the crown of Poland. She even eschewed the position of abbess, which, no matter how austerely the women who held it lived, always carried with it a certain taint of lust for power. Anne-Louise joined the Carmelites of the rue Saint-Jacques at the age of twenty-four. She would spend the next fifty years and more in the same convent in an odor of sanctity, humility, and spirituality by general agreement of all the sources.[20] Similarly, the marquise de Faudoas also became an ordinary nun after suffering a profound shock: her husband's brutal death in 1697, apparently in connection with certain obscure doings involving witchcraft. She took the habit in 1701 and spent the rest of her life with the Benedictines of Montargis.

Having looked at several nuns, let us turn now to the case of a "deminun." Mme de Miramion was a very wealthy Parisian woman who, after Bussy Rabutin abducted her, thwarted the designs of her would-be rapist by taking a vow of chastity on the spot.[21] Out of her own fortune, she later endowed a community of women known as *miramionnes* so that she might live in retreat among them and devote herself, among other good works, to teaching the daughters of the poor how to read.

As for non-nuns, consider the case of Anne de Châteautiers, a talented, unselfish woman of redoubtable virtue who for a long time waited on Madame, to whom she was a "favorite, and worthy of it." Anne turned down a superb offer of marriage from a prince and, when her patroness died, went into retirement, spending the next two decades in a rented or borrowed house in Paris, where she saw virtually no one and seldom went out except to go to church. And then there was the marquise Anne de Grignan, Mme de Sévigné's granddaughter-in-law and the daughter of a *fermier général*: her enormous dowry arrived just in time to fertilize the estates of the illustrious letter writer's grandson (who was sorely in need of cash). Anne had no children. Widowed early, she became a sad and lonely saint: "She shut herself up in her house, which for the remainder of her days she never left except to go to church; and she never saw anyone."[22] In other words, she was a second Mlle de Châteautiers, but without the model's charms. Also worth mentioning is Mme de Dangeau, a Bavarian princess by birth and one-time "star" of Versailles.[23] Her husband was very old, however, and stopped going out altogether, so she, too, fell into a life of very pious retirement. And then there was Louise de Cavoye, née Coëtlogon: she adored her husband even though he was unworthy of her. At court she lavished him with praise while he looked on with anxious gravity. After he died, she "never spent a night away from the house" in which she had lost her darling spouse. Indeed, her only excursions were to Saint-Sulpice, where she went twice daily to pray. She devoted herself entirely to charity and soon wore herself out with unflagging ardor, "perpetually overcome by religion."[24]

In a somewhat different vein, consider the case of the marquise Anne-Charlotte de Créquy, who was not only the niece of Archbishop Le Tellier of Reims but also his lover: "Until his death she loved him as more than an uncle." Later she became the mistress of the abbé d'Estrées, and when this second ecclesiastical lover died in 1718, the marquise was "widowed" for the third time, her lawfully wedded husband having died in 1702. At this point she "suddenly underwent an amazing and durable conversion" that brought her simplicity, humility, and peace. She exhibited "extraordinary joy amidst the most repulsive austerities and was extremely generous with the poor, constantly in prayer, and a regular visitor of prisons, dungeons, and hospitals, where she witnessed the most horrible workings of nature," and she kept all this up until she died—a very lengthy penance indeed.[25]

The princess of Pettorano was a daughter of the maréchal de Boufflers, who contracted syphilis from a husband unworthy of her, after which she went into pious retreat with the *Descalzas reales*, as the Discalced Carmelites were known in Spain. As for the maréchale de Villeroy, her husband's defeat at Ramillies shocked her to such an extent that "she withdrew from everything," cut herself off from the world, and spent her life in an armchair "in prayer and pious reading." Morality and penance were her only topics of conversation. Under the direction of her confessor, Père Polinier, a saintly man but crude and gruff in his ways, the maréchale de Villeroy embarked on a life so contrary to nature that it killed her within a year or two, though by way of compensation she "died the death of the Just."[26]

Then there was the maréchale d'Humières, who, shortly after the death of her husband (who was a duke as well as a marshal), retired to a home outside the walls of the Carmelite convent on the rue Saint-Jacques. Of course she kept her carriage with its ducal emblems, but she respected her vocation to the point of giving up the velvet or scarlet cover that duchesses normally draped over their carriages and sedan chairs.[27] Such humility in a great lady commands admiration.

Turning now to British exiles in France—of a "papist" and Jacobite stripe to be sure—first prize for renunciation must surely go to the former queen Marie-Béatrice d'Este, the widow of James II (who died in 1701) and the survivor of a long series of misfortunes that ended with her death in 1718. Among those misfortunes was the Glorious Revolution, to which she fell victim in 1688. She bore her fate with Christian fortitude to the very end, repeatedly humbling her natural haughtiness through gifts to God: "penance, prayers, good works, [and] all the virtues of the saints." Honorable mention goes to the French-born duchess of Portsmouth, the former mistress of Charles II. By 1718, however, she was quite elderly "and truly converted and repentant, though her affairs were in such a sorry state that she was reduced to living in the country."

All told, then, our sample consists of a dozen non-nuns and half a dozen nuns. Many other nuns receive brief mention in the *Memoirs*. Saint-Simon saw no reason to dwell on any but the few discussed above, whose motivations seemed to him sincere and widely acknowledged, in any case worthy of a few choice words. Taking both the nuns and the non-nuns together, we find that only two or three members of this small group were *robines* (noble or otherwise). To be sure, the majority of these "renouncing" ladies sprang from dynasties of the sword that had entered into profitable marriages with dynasties of the robe. By contrast, among the male renouncers, the proportion of *robins* is much higher. In other words, piety among women frequently ignored well-established social boundaries, but among men it was closely associated with certain forms of (Jansenist, Gallican) education and culture typical of the robe.

Bear in mind that we are here neglecting the many nuns who were "put away" by their own families, whether by force or emphatic persuasion, either because there was not enough property for a suitable dowry or for some other reason. If we confine our attention to women who sincerely and voluntarily renounced the world, whether nuns or lay sisters, we find that most did so in response to some kind of "shock": the end of an affair or death of a highly placed lover, syphilis, old age, a husband's misbehavior, the death of a spouse or high-ranking patroness, the terrifying prospect of a prodigious marriage, kidnapping with or without the threat of rape, military defeat (or other serious failure in time of war), political revolution, or the simple trauma of having been subjected in childhood and adolescence to a rigorous or even harsh Jansenist upbringing. The women we have looked at thus far, whom some might judge a trifle hastily to be religious fanatics or "church mice," were actually part of a mainstream broad enough to accommodate both renunciation of the world and worldliness. That stream runs through all forty volumes of Saint-Simon's *Memoirs*.

"T o the bottom with the prelates": when Saint-Simon wrote these words, he meant not that he wanted to hurl them into the sea but rather that he wanted to get to the bottom of certain questions he had about bishops. Fewer than a dozen bishops are linked to the theme of renunciation in the *Memoirs:* enough for our purposes but surely not an exhaustive sample. All but two are French, and both of the exceptions are Latins, whose careers therefore resemble those of their French counterparts.

One of these Latins was Cardinal Marescotti. After serving in various departments of the Vatican, he declined all further assignments, even in his capacity as cardinal, and withdrew to his residence in the Eternal City. He was very old, to be sure, but still had his wits about him, a circumstance that the Augustinian Saint-Simon took as the very mark of predestination. Thereafter Marescotti divided his time between prayer, alms, celebration of the mass, and spiritual readings by hand-picked priests. He died at the age of ninety-nine.

From the other "Latin" peninsula, the Iberian, came Cardinal Portocarrero, who at the very beginning of the Bourbon dynasty in Spain was still an extremely powerful statesman. Later, however, he fell into disgrace and retired to his bishopric, where his every thought was devoted "to his diocese and his salvation." He died a magnificent and edifying death.[28] On his tombstone, a simple slab, he ordered these words inscribed: "Here lie ashes, dust, and nothingness." To be sure, a vertical stele not far from the spot told visitors and tourists the name of this illustrious eminence and his exact titles. In Spain, where bishops were required to reside in their dioceses, there were no "court prelates."[29] Many therefore conscientiously attended to the welfare of their flock, but at the same time they turned their backs on the world and devoted themselves to spiritual pursuits in the manner of the aging Portocarrero. Perhaps this partly explains why the Catholic faith became so solidly entrenched on the Iberian peninsula, where resident bishops kept a close eye on things—closer than in France, in any case.

Turning now to French bishops, we come first to a bishop *in partibus:*

Artus de Lionne, the son of a minister of Louis XIV. When it came to renunciation, Artus took after his father, a stalwart Gallican who may have had Jansenist proclivities. His mother, a penniless widow who held the world in contempt, completed his education after retiring to a life of indigent piety. Artus's niece by marriage, the daughter of a well-to-do Alsatian innkeeper whom a Lionne had stooped to marry only to abandon shortly thereafter, had entered a convent as a lay sister, whereupon she was transformed into an estimable benefactress of the poor. Artus's brother, apparently after giving up wine, made do with twenty to twenty-two pints of water from the Seine every morning, in addition to which he quaffed still more gallons of the liquid at dinner.[30] Meanwhile, "Bishop" Artus served as a missionary in Asia, but after quarreling with the Jesuits, he made a pious retreat and lived until his death in a small room in the Missions Etrangères. To the end of his days, he continued to sport a full missionary beard. So here we have a whole family of renouncers of both sexes: the last generations of Lionnes, led by Bishop Artus.

Another renouncer was François Bouthillier de Chavigny, the son of one of Richelieu's ministers (originally a *robin*). Bouthillier, a relative of Rancé, began as a worldly court prelate. Although he was an effective administrator of his Troyes diocese, he spent little time there. He gambled large sums, was a favorite of the ladies (who called him *le Troyen* and *chien d'évêque* and *chien de Troyen*—"the Trojan," "doggy bishop," and "Trojan dog," canine appellations that refused to go away after sinking their teeth in, as it were). Before he reached the age of sixty, however, Bouthillier awoke to the unworthiness of his dissipated life and one fine day decided to drop everything and devote himself exclusively to his eternal salvation. He had previously consulted Père de La Chaise, a Jesuit and confessor of Louis XIV. Note in passing that Bouthillier, though a first cousin of the abbé de Rancé, was by no means a rigorist a priori nor a Jansenist a fortiori: not only did he consult with the highly Jesuitical Père de La Chaise, but he later became a staunch supporter of the ultramontane bull *Unigenitus*.[31] In any case, he left the administration of his diocese and the title of bishop of Troyes to his nephew, in whose house he took up residence toward the end of the seventeenth century. There he would remain for many years "in the most scrupulous and uninterrupted retreat," with occasional excursions to an even more remote Carthusian monastery in Champagne. Although Bouthillier became an authentically devout solitary, at no time did he seem "soft-headed or foolish or disoriented or doddering."[32]

Another bishop of note was François-Théodore de Nesmond, bishop of Bayeux during a period that coincided exactly with Louis XIV's personal reign (1661–1715). He, too, traced his origins to the robe, for he was the son of Guillaume de Nesmond, *premier président* of Parlement. François-

Théodore did not withdraw fully from the world, for he continued to administer his Norman diocese. But there are many reasons to classify him as a renouncer, or semi-renouncer: his frugality; his tremendous generosity to the poor, to the point of giving up most of his income for their benefit; his total and at times ridiculous naïveté in sexual matters; his utterly pure and virginal ecclesiastical existence; his permanent residence in his diocese, where he remained almost a recluse (but for occasional trips to Paris and Versailles to please the king); and last but not least, his simple way of life. He differed greatly from most of his episcopal colleagues, for even those who were pious and chaste lived in the manner of great lords.

Another former debauchee whose ancestors belonged to the world of the robe was Cardinal Le Camus, who later in life developed Jansenist proclivities. He thus resembled Bouthillier de Chavigny in some ways but not in others. Le Camus was still young when he repented of his libertine "errors." He went "into a deep retreat and suffered the austerities of the harshest penitence." Later he was named bishop of Grenoble over his own objections. Ultimately the pope made him a cardinal, despite the opposition of Louis XIV, who as usual shunned anything that smelled of Jansenism. In Dauphiné, where Le Camus continued to reside, he continued his life of penance: he sentenced himself to a vegetarian diet for the rest of his days. "He ate at home in the refectory with all his domestic servants and even his valets," who had quantities of meat while he limited himself to the vegetarian diet of an eremite in the wilderness. Despite this, he did an admirable job of reforming his diocese, through which he traveled constantly, visiting even remote areas like the rugged Breda valley. Wherever he went he brought with him the spirit of the Council of Trent leavened with a touch of Jansenism. A little Jansenist austerity may indeed have been welcome in Grenoble, a city notable at the time for the presence of one Nicolas Chorier, a talented forerunner of today's pornographers. Le Camus nevertheless came in for some venomous comments from Saint-Simon, perhaps because the duke disliked cardinals in general, whom he found too Roman for his taste even when, like Camus, they were closet disciples of Jansenius of Port-Royal.[33]

Another energetic bishop who nevertheless turned his back on any number of the pleasures of this world was Louis-Antoine de Noailles, bishop of Châlons-sur-Marne and later archbishop of Paris and cardinal. As a young "diocesan" with a beatific air, "a thick nasal accent," and a stupid face, he lived with his mother at the center of his Champenois see. The two of them lived in a state of perpetual communion, of almost incestuous hyperspirituality. In Châlons and later in Paris, the chaste Louis-Antoine ate nothing but "boiled meat along with two modest uncooked appetizers."[34] Whenever possible, he limited himself to such monklike fare. His mother's maiden name was Boyer, "which is to say, nothing," in Saint-Simon's unkind characterization. In fact, she was the daughter of a very wealthy tax farmer who had withdrawn from society and lived with her son for many years.[35] "There she entrusted herself to his guidance and confessed to him every evening," after which he owned up to whatever minor sins he might have committed during the day. Their isolation could not have been more complete. Despite the apparent naïveté and simplicity of this lonely existence, Noailles disliked the Jesuits intensely and was a discreet Jansenist. The obscene exhumation of bodies at Port-Royal and destruction of the Jansenist center there caused him great pain.[36] Because he made no great effort to hide his feelings, he incurred the enmity of his former protectress Mme de Maintenon and stirred up trouble in the diocese of Paris during the first three decades of the eighteenth century. When it came to Jansenism, Noailles was far more of a *robin* and a Boyer than a noble of the sword and a Noailles. In oedipal terms, he was far closer to the rigorist devotion of his "bourgeois" mother than to the aristocratic and religious conformism of the Noailles in general and his father Anne de Noailles in particular. Despite his renouncer tendencies, however, he retained a keen sense of hierarchy. He claimed precedence over dukes at meetings of the Regency Council[37] and was the very first to toast the marriage of his niece, the daughter of a duke, to Prince Charles of Lorraine. In this instance, a classic case of female hypergamy—the daughter of a duke becomes the wife of a prince—earned the blessing of this super-austere prelate.[38]

Yet another model of the bishop as resident reformer, solitary, and renouncer was Cardinal de Coislin. This prelate used instruments of penitence to pierce his skin and even dig into his flesh. He rose every night for an hour of prayer. He stayed put in his Orléans diocese but for inevitable trips to Versailles at the king's insistence. Coislin founded a number of extremely useful schools in the Orléans area. He lavished gifts on poor nobles (many of whom did not deserve them). He spent freely of his own money to protect the Huguenots of the region from the *dragonnades* of 1685 and after. More than that, he spread Jansenist ideas throughout his Loire Valley diocese. The Jansenist virus also afflicted his brother, the chevalier Charles-César de Coislin, who would ultimately be buried at Port-Royal, much to the fury of Louis XIV and of his nephew, Henri-Charles de Coislin, bishop of Metz, who was highly Augustinian in matters of doctrine, despite his entanglement in a sordid affair involving a choirboy who was the son of a light horseman of the guard. Allegedly he had ordered the boy whipped—and that may not have been his only sin with respect to the unfortunate youth. But he ended his days in a saintly manner. In any case, Cardinal de Coislin died a virgin, and his tomb became a focal point of popular veneration, not unlike the tomb of Deacon Pâris in the next reign. The Jesuits had good reason, therefore, to arrange for the quiet removal of the marker at Coislin's gravesite. But the same prelate, ordinarily such a humble man, also set great store by hierarchy, and he provoked a scandal when the duc de La Rochefoucauld (the son of the author of the *Maximes*) usurped his place of honor in the royal chapel, just behind the king, next to the grand chamberlain, during a sermon.[39]

To conclude this list, let us mention a few other names that Saint-Simon could hardly leave out. The bishop of Avranches, Pierre-Daniel Huet, lived for many years in retreat in a Jesuit house in Paris, which he never left.[40] There he devoted himself to study and led a very frugal life.[41] Cardinal de Retz was, of course, closer to the Jansenists than Huet was. After many skirmishes in love and war, he retired to Commercy "to do penance in total solitude for his previous life."[42] Finally, moving outside the ranks of bishops, indeed outside the clergy altogether, we find a tragic couple, the Fouquets—a husband and wife separated against their will by order of the king. Before being sent to prison, Nicolas Fouquet had been *surintendant des finances*. Involuntarily incarcerated, he became a voluntary renouncer, isolated from the world not just because he was in prison but because he considered it his duty as well as a test of his mettle. He took to heart a situation that had been forced upon him and died in 1680 at the age of sixty-five in the fortress prison of Pignerol, where for many years salvation had been his sole concern. Mme Fouquet lived much longer, until 1716, "in great piety and great solitude and engaged in charitable works throughout her life."[43]

R eligious renunciation is but one form of a broader sociological phenomenon of "withdrawal from the world," or perhaps, to put it in more secular terms, "withdrawal from society" (a withdrawal that in many cases has nothing to do with spirituality). In Louis XIV's France, people often withdrew from society because they grew old, but sometimes they also had more personal reasons, such as scandal, illness, or poverty.

Take scandal. The abbesse de La Joye, whose destiny resembled that of the "Portuguese nun" of literature,[44] was in fact the daughter of the duc de Saint-Aignan. She was seduced and made pregnant by the marquis de Ségur, who in this true-life story plays the role of the "handsome musketeer." Actually, he was a cavalry officer from the Périgord who lost a leg in the battle of Marseille. He also played the lute. His grandson would serve as a minister under Louis XVI. After giving birth unexpectedly and almost publicly, the abbess, a passionate and fascinating woman, was obliged to leave the convent she had headed and spend the rest of her days in another. She was reduced to living once again as a simple nun but consoled herself in her cell by contemplating a portrait of Saint Cecilia playing a lute, which for the abbess represented her lost lover,

Ségur.[45] The marquis went on to enjoy a splendid career, his rich reward for the sordid misfortune he inflicted on his poor mistress.

Other, less spectacular scandals led, if not to the more austere forms of renunciation, at least to withdrawal from society. Take, for example, Marie-Thérèse Eustachie de Barbezieux, the daughter of the maréchal-marquis d'Alègre and wife of Louis-François de Barbezieux, himself the son of Louvois and secretary of state under Louis XIV. Marie-Thérèse's wedding to Louis-François was worthy of a prince of the blood, and shortly thereafter the young bride was welcomed into the entourage of the duc de Bourgogne. An alleged infidelity with the duc d'Elbeuf soon led to a separation, however, after which Barbezieux died. The handsome chevalier de Bouillon then fought a duel with the scheming marquis d'Entragues to decide which of the two would marry the young widow. After this unfortunate incident, Marie-Thérèse withdrew or was packed off to a convent, where she died at age twenty-nine. A portion of the vast Louvois-Barbezieux fortune passed through her to her daughter, the duchesse d'Harcourt, and thus to the Harcourt dynasty.

Like Mme de Barbezieux, the comtesse Jeanne-Baptiste de Verue withdrew to a convent, at least for a short period of time. Like Mme de Montespan, she had begun by refusing to submit to her sovereign, in her case, Victor Amadaeus of Savoy. And (again like Louis XIV's future mistress) she had warned her husband of the dangers of such an extramarital adventure. But when her husband refused to intervene, the countess became Victor Amadaeus's lover. She thereby added millions to her fortune but eventually tired of the Savoyard duke's obsessive surveillance and sought refuge in a Paris convent, but more for the sake of her private tranquillity than out of a sincere religious vocation.

Another case may or may not belong under the head of marital scandals leading to nonreligious withdrawal from society. Françoise-Adélaïde de Noailles was a scheming, religious woman who at the age of thirteen had married the prince and grand equerry Charles de Lorraine, comte d'Armagnac. When her husband banished her for obscure reasons, she took refuge in a convent of Filles de Sainte-Marie in the faubourg Saint-Germain. But she was completely innocent in whatever had taken place four years earlier; the only scandal, if there was any, was on her husband's side.

Romain Dalon served with the parlements of Pau and, later, Bordeaux. The son of a magistrate, he was noted mainly for his debts, mischief, and bribes of ministers. Because of this, he was removed from office, a rare punishment in an age when most men held their offices for life. For a while, he pounded on doors in the hope of finding a job or stipend of some sort. In the end, however, he withdrew from society and lived "until his death in 1738 forsaken and scorned by all."[46]

Like criminal behavior, madness could also lead to early retirement. Such was the case with Charles-Denis de Bullion, of whom it was said that "a touch of madness" ran in the family. His grandfather, Claude de Bullion, *surintendant des finances*, exhibited some rather unusual scatological tastes, which offended the regent, Anne of Austria (though nothing came of Anne's distaste).[47] Charles-Denis himself was provost of Paris and governor of Maine and Perche. But he fell victim to bizarre moods and episodes of dementia, which led to his removal from office, and he was obliged to retire to his country estate, much to the dismay of his wife, a Rouillé, who lived only for the court and was bored to death in her country castle.

It will come as no surprise that illness was a more common reason for withdrawing from social life. The chevalier de Grignan, comte d'Adhémar, a valiant youth, retired from the service and the court in 1689 because he was in constant pain from gout. He enjoyed a delightful retirement in Mazarques, near Marseilles, where he lived until 1713, dying childless even though a late marriage was arranged in the hope that his wife might bear him an heir.[48]

Poverty (in relative terms, to be sure) forced at least one distinguished princess to leave the court and retire to an estate a long way from both Paris and Versailles. Françoise de Nargonne, a kind, majestic lady, married the duc d'Angoulême (a bastard son of Charles IX) in 1644, when the duke was already a widower of seventy-two. In Louis XIV's eyes, Angoulême was not the right kind of bastard, for he was of Valois rather than Bourbon extraction. The Sun King therefore more or less shunned his distant cousin, who "ordinarily" should have become a princess of the blood. She wandered from refuge to refuge, in both Paris and the provinces, before finding a mediocre final asylum with her niece, Françoise Apoil de Romicourt, at the château de Montmort, in what is now the département of the Marne. There she died in 1713 at the age of ninety-two, 63 years after her husband's death and 139 years after the death of her royal father-in-law Charles IX.[49]

Finally, there was disgrace. From disgrace to retirement—not necessarily devout or voluntarily austere but endured in bitterness, indifference, or resignation—was but a short step. One who took that step was Marie-Casimire de La Grange d'Arquien, French by birth but married to the (elected) king of Poland, Jean Sobieski. After the death of her royal mate, she took to wandering about Europe, but she ended up as a pitiful refugee in Blois because Louis XIV would not have her at Versailles. He complained that although she had been born French she had always acted against the interests of the Kingdom of the Lilies when her influence over Sobieski was great.

The former queen of Poland was not the only woman for whom disgrace meant enforced withdrawal from society. The princesse des Ursins and a few others joined her in exile. But for the most part, this was something that happened to men. Louis, comte de Guiscard, governor of Dinant, Namur, and later, Sedan, chevalier du Saint-Esprit, and former ambassador to Sweden, was very much a man of the court, but it was his misfortune to have been one of the losers at Ramillies in 1706, a cruel and crucial defeat for Louis XIV. Even Villeroy, whom the king loved, lost favor for a time because of it. Guiscard was disgraced, and though he moved heaven and earth to regain his former position, he never managed it. In the end, he retired to his estate at Magny in Picardy. There he was afflicted with a mild case of gout and a more serious case of melancholy. Though he had no fever, he took to his bed and, virtually alone, died for no apparent reason. Actually, disgrace ran in his family: two of his brothers "tugged at his ears like heavy earrings."[50] One of them, Jean-Georges de Guiscard, after an honorable military career, made the mistake of ordering the torture of a servant he suspected of theft. For this and other misdeeds, he was banished from France. The other brother, Antoine de Guiscard, abbé de La Bourlie, enjoyed a number of excellent ecclesiastical benefices but was compromised by his involvement in the abduction of several young girls as well as by his more honorable implication in the opposition to Louis XIV. He fled to England, where he fared no better than he had in France and ended up in prison for assault. There he was seriously injured and more or less killed himself—a rather violent form of withdrawal from society.

Ministerial disgraces were legion. Chamillart's was not particularly terrifying: although the king liked him, he ordered Chamillart to resign from his various governmental posts in 1708 and 1709, whereupon the former minister retired to his Paris hôtel. There he remained until his death in 1711, seeing few people but of an agreeable sort. John Law, who was for all practical purposes a high minister of the regent, was obliged to leave France in 1720 after his financial manipulations "failed." He went to Venice, where until his death he lived quietly with his family in dignified solitude.

The "long century" from 1615 to 1730 was marked by three major disgraces: Concini, dismissed by young Louis XIII; Fouquet, dismissed by young Louis XIV; and Monsieur le Duc, dismissed by young Louis XV (at the instigation of Fleury). These three cases illustrate the talent of the young Bourbon kings for secrecy. Each announcement came as a bolt from the blue. As often happens, the dismissed statesman was in each case the last to learn of his unhappy fate.[51] The severity of the punishment diminished with time, however: Concini was summarily put to death; Fouquet spent his retirement in prison; and Monsieur le Duc was merely "exiled" to his superb castle at Chantilly. One factor remained constant:

with the beginning of each new reign, the man who had served as de facto prime minister in the reign before was almost immediately disgraced and, if not executed, at least forced into "retirement" (broadly interpreted). When Louis XVI came to the throne, the same thing happened to Maupeou. Under the current French system of "republican monarchy," it has become almost a constitutional obligation for each new president of the Republic to dismiss the former prime minister.[52] Edouard Balladur did not survive the election of François Mitterrand any more than Jacques Chaban-Delmas had survived that of Georges Pompidou or Raymond Barre that of Valéry Giscard d'Estaing.

Saint-Simon was not himself a minister. The most that can be said was that he served for a time as the "right-hand man" of the regent, Philippe, duc d'Orléans. After Philippe died, Saint-Simon learned from highly placed individuals that he had become persona non grata at court, where he had been living since the end of the seventeenth century. Fleury and La Vrillière took it upon themselves to deliver the hemlock. Through his wife, they let him know that they would rather see him in Paris than in Versailles. The warning from Fleury was sugarcoated; La Vrillière's was more blunt. Saint-Simon did not have to be told twice: he soon moved into his Paris *hôtel*. People in those days retired young, especially when they had no other choice, even if they were born dukes like Saint-Simon or princes like Monsieur le Duc. To be sure, Saint-Simon had been thinking about the need for retirement, indeed for a religious retreat, ever since the death of the duc de Bourgogne in 1712. Inwardly he was therefore prepared for what amounted to nothing less than banishment in disgrace.

Unlike Saint-Simon, who performed his ministerial duties from the sidelines, Marc-René de Voyer, marquis d'Argenson, was a full-fledged minister and *garde des Sceaux*, or keeper of the seals, but in 1720 he too was obliged to endure the (relative) torture of disgrace and subsequent retirement. D'Argenson became *garde des Sceaux* after a distinguished career as a policeman: prejudices to the contrary notwithstanding, law and order can thus lead to justice (is the reverse also true?). The regent liked d'Argenson but dismissed him after a few years in order to make d'Aguesseau, the acting chancellor, keeper, apparently at Law's behest. D'Argenson took his disgrace hard, but he found a way to enjoy retirement, moving into a comfortable apartment he maintained in a convent whose superior was allegedly his mistress.[53]

R eading Saint-Simon, one could easily forget that there were people at court and elsewhere who retired simply because they were old. The proportion of older individuals in the population was much smaller than it is today because people on the average died much younger. The typical aristocrat or *robin* therefore remained active until the end of his life unless he withdrew in his prime for one of the reasons examined above (piety, scandal, illness, poverty, disgrace, etc.).[54] "Retirees" in our modern sense did exist, although their numbers were small. They were "old," but like their far more numerous counterparts today, they might still be energetic and vigorous, or as Tallemant des Réaux put it, "fresh and clean."[55] Take, for example, Guillaume de Lort de Sérignan, who died in 1721 at the age of ninety-two, still as lucid as he had been at fifty. He had retired from the king's bodyguard twenty years earlier. Shortly thereafter he married, and his health remained good for the next two decades of well-deserved rest enlivened by marital bliss.

Another retirement that might seem at first glance to be of the "modern" type was that of Bergeyck, a native of Antwerp. Born in 1664, he was the stepson of Rubens's widow. He began his career as a treasurer general in the Spanish Netherlands. After being dismissed from that post in 1699, he managed to wangle an appointment as comptroller general for war in 1702. By 1711, he was working for Philip V in Madrid and was chosen as one of three Spanish plenipotentiaries for the negotiations leading to the Treaty of Utrecht (the others were the dukes of Osuna and Monteleone). In 1714, at the age of seventy, Bergeyck decided to give it all up. He left Castile and withdrew from government service "in order to live out his life quietly on one of his Flanders estates." For twelve years, he led a tranquil existence. One is therefore tempted to say that this was indeed a modern sort of retirement, worthy of any high civil servant today. In fact, however, things were not that simple. Bergeyck would have remained on the job in Madrid, even in his seventies, had it not been for the all-powerful princess of Ursins, who, along with her henchman Orry, was forever laying traps for him. Bergeyck made up his mind to retire before one of these traps could be sprung. He then had the consolation of seeing his nemesis, the princess herself, disgraced the following year.

The retirement of another "high civil servant" was a less complicated affair that conforms more closely to present-day norms. There were no ulterior motives or frustrations with power. The official in question was one Bouchu, intendant of Dauphiné, who had ably governed his north-alpine district and made a good deal of money, some of it possibly illicit. Tired of the burden of administering a province, he hoped to find a less taxing job, perhaps with the Council of State in Paris, or simply to retire, even though he was barely fifty. If possible, moreover, he hoped to find a place far from his wife, a courageous but pretentious (or perhaps ambitious) woman whom he could perfectly well live without. On the way from Grenoble to Paris, he passed through Tournus, where his brother had a house.[56] He decided to settle down there, did some gardening, and saw no one but local *robins* and insignificant *gentilshommes à lièvre*, gentry who killed time by sallying forth from their crumbling castles to hunt hares with rusty épées. There he died a happy man ten years later. A sage? His wife did not follow his example. Consumed by the desire to become a duchess, she married the legless duc de Châtillon only to die a short while later of pneumonia "because she insisted on going to Versailles in the bitter cold in order enjoy her ducal *tabouret*" during the harsh winter of 1740.

The age of retirement in France has always varied widely from individual to individual. This statement was no less true centuries ago than it is today. A sergeant quits the army at thirty-five to return home to Corsica; a railroad engineer or schoolteacher lives for retirement at fifty-five; a university professor stops teaching at sixty-five; a professor at the Collège de France might retire at seventy, a president of the Republic at seventy-seven. What is the common denominator? At the court of Louis XIV, the range of ages at retirement was similar, but the reasons for retirement were considerably more varied. Age was not the only consideration. In particular, spirituality played a far more important role than it does now—meaning, of course, Christian spirituality, which brings us back to the central subject of this chapter: ascetic renunciation (abetted in some cases by more mundane considerations). It therefore makes sense to pause for a moment to consider works of theology and ethics that influenced Saint-Simon. Among them were books by a Protestant, Jacques Abbadie, and two Jansenists, Quesnel and Duguet.

I n pondering the reasons for religious renunciation, Saint-Simon did not hesitate to delve into works by certain Protestant writers. Yet he was not much interested in Huguenots individually or collectively, except when it came to discussing the possible conversion (to Catholicism) of his father-in-law (Lorge), Mme Dacier, and a few others.[57] Occasionally, however, he alludes in his writing to the indomitable resistance of French Calvinists and to certain of their religious beliefs. Although he was in most respects a good Catholic, something deep in his conscience responded to particular aspects of the Protestant faith.

Charmel and certain other renouncers whom Saint-Simon admired chose as bedside reading matter a spiritual guidebook by the Protestant pastor Jacques Abbadie entitled *Vérité de la religion chrétienne* (1684). Born in Béarn, Abbadie was a distinguished Huguenot who, in the wake of the repression of his sect ordered by Louis XIV, was obliged to preach first in Sedan, later in Berlin, and ultimately in the British Isles. Despite the hostility to Huguenots in the period leading up to the Revocation, Abbadie's book was a best-seller not only among Protestants but also among Catholics, especially Jansenists and their sympathizers.

What did Abbadie, along with his assiduous readers of "the two faiths," want and hope for? Above all, he sought to castigate, if not castrate, two major sources of disorder: sensual pleasure, or the lower part of man's nature, and pride or conceit, which La Rochefoucauld had also attacked as the most dangerous and deep-rooted of all the passions and a hindrance in man's effort to persevere in his embrace of divine revelation. The pastor from Béarn consequently insisted that the passions must be curbed. Pride and conceit must be stripped of all glory and chimerical illusions, and the flesh must be denied its illicit pleasures. Indeed, what else could be the goal of those who renounced the world and embraced suffering in order to persuade their fellow man (tautologically) that they had indeed forsaken the here and now? To renounce was therefore to risk everything and lose everything, yet this "folly of the Cross" was the only way to guarantee the eternal salvation of mankind.[58] According to Abbadie, those who wished to be true disciples of Christ must "pluck out their eyes, cut off their hands, detest their own bodies, and renounce their own selves along with their greatest pleasures and fondest habits," all for the purpose of "hating their souls all the more through strain and pain."[59] Sad and mortifying duties indeed! But through them the splendid promises of the gospel could be made concrete.

Compensation would come, of course, in the other world: eternal life in heaven for some, an eternity of infernal misery for others. On this and other points, Abbadie was a fundamentalist: he rejected Spinoza's ideas (which were studied in the Huguenot circles in which he moved) as crypto-atheist or anti-Christian. The ex-Pyrenean pastor was an anti-Spinoza fundamentalist à la Jurieu, and unbeknownst to himself he persuaded Saint-Simon, who may have been unaware of the philosophical implications of his choice, because Spinoza's name is never mentioned in the *Memoirs*.

In any case, for Abbadie what guaranteed the renouncer that salvation would be his ultimate reward was the miraculous power of Jesus Christ, his Resurrection as demonstrated by his Ascension. How could a body that had not been resurrected ascend to heaven? As for the Ascension, even though there is but one eyewitness account in the New Testament (in Acts), it was supposedly confirmed by the testimony of the Apostles, who, being serious men, could not have lied about this or any other matter. The argument is tenuous: an ascent by helicopter proves nothing about the previous discovery of a buried treasure. It is also circular, since the proofs of the validity of renunciation are given by men who, Abbadie tells us, were willing to be hanged, whipped, broken, and burned. Thus they were themselves extreme renouncers, bound and determined to prove that their arguments in favor of renunciation were correct and to persuade others to follow the same course.[60] Whatever the defects of

Abbadie's argument, however, the Resurrection and Ascension clearly had high symbolic value, and not just in his writing.

One question obviously remains, the shocking question of the fundamental injustice of this whole system, a subject of endless discussion since the time of Saint Augustine. The man (or woman) who renounces the world does not succeed in doing so on his (or her) own initiative. He does what he does only because indispensable grace has been bestowed upon him by the invisible hand of a divine being. It is this grace that enables the individual to renounce the world, but it is at the same time a sign that the individual is one of the chosen—a renouncer a priori, as it were, predestined rather than "pre-damned." Thus, renunciation is not a freely chosen meritorious act; it is simply the sign of an election willed by God. In this there is a fundamental lack of equity, especially when judged by the light of egalitarian Christian doctrine according to which all souls are a priori equal in the eyes of the Lord; the commoner is just as good as the prince. There is a lack of equity in the fact that those destined for hell are denied the right of renunciation for all eternity, for if they were to renounce, it would be a sign that they were saved (a reductio ad absurdum). Max Weber, one of the last twentieth-century disciples of Saint Augustine, spilled a great deal of ink over this thorny issue, which became the crux of theological disputation during the ancien régime. These pages of Weber's are still read avidly, if not always with deep comprehension, on college campuses in Europe and above all in North America.

Abbadie takes the commonsensical approach of shrugging his shoulders. In sum he tells his readers this: "Do not try to understand. Do not try to understand why God wants to save some and not others. Leave that to the philosophers, who in any case merely reason. Predestination exists. It is quite simply one of the mysteries of the faith. There is no point arguing about it. It must be accepted blindly. In any case, you are admonished to pluck out your eyes. God is not really as spiteful as he might seem. It is wrong to say in the name of predestination that God hardens the heart of the sinner.[61] In reality, the Hebrew text of the Bible says only that God does nothing to soften the hardness that is already there." A double negative is "less bad" than an affirmative. Faith, moreover, is essentially as much a matter of submission as of knowledge.[62] Does the Almighty want to humble my reason? Very well, then. Let his will be done. Do I ponder the mysteries of digestion? Why, then, should I quibble endlessly about the enigma of grace—whether it is sufficient, efficacious, or who knows what? The mysteries of the Christian religion are like the pillars of fire that guided the Hebrews through the desert. They have a bright side and a dark side. About the darkness of the depths we can do nothing. It is simply a sign of the infirmity of the human condition, and we must be satisfied with such stars as glimmer here and there in the vastness of the dark. We must not insist on the impossible.

Saint-Simon, for his part, speaks quite rightly of "the ineffable and incomprehensible mystery of grace, as far beyond the reach of our intelligence and our reasoning as the mystery of the Trinity."[63] Like Abbadie, whose work Saint-Simon's renouncer friends all studied, the *petit duc* was in some respects a fundamentalist, and it is important to remember this when considering other aspects of his activity,[64] especially in politics, or more precisely, in the politics of religion.[65] Can we not say, moreover, that Saint-Simon was a fundamentalist of hierarchy?

The "Abbadian" style of renunciation was by no means incompatible with the principles of hierarchy. Indeed, it took those principles for granted and reinforced them. To the pastor from Béarn as to Saint-Simon himself, the practice of renunciation was the indispensable buttress that shored up the whole edifice of hierarchy, without which it could not stand. Social and familial distinctions—between husbands and wives, children and servants, princes and subjects, debtors and creditors, slaves and masters, peasants and monarchs—could not help but be reinforced by the rough discipline imposed by abstention from pleasure and acceptance of the need for penitential humiliations. Throughout the "long" seventeenth century, distinctions such as these were only strengthened by a "mutualist" system of interpersonal relations within which renunciation ensured that, even as hierarchy was to be respected, "what is in one man's interest will be in the interest of all, and there shall be neither hatred nor jealousy nor competition."[66] Each person was expected to thank God for the greater wealth and more exalted rank that others had received from the hands of the Almighty, so that even a highly inegalitarian society could be thought of as a single family: "The good fortune of one shall be the good fortune of all." The debits and credits accumulated on earth by Monsieur de X and Madame d'Y would be compensated by either infernal punishment or blessed immortality. In everyday politics, people would continue to be treated as slaves, as if a man's life were worth no more than an animal's. But in religion, under the aspect of eternity, everyone was equal before God, and nothing else counted.

S aint-Simon had Huguenot ancestors on his father's side, and his wife's family belonged to a line that had long been Protestant and maintained links to distinguished "heretical" dynasties (such as the Orange and Bouillon). Calvinist traditions flourished in several of the locales in which he either resided or enjoyed seigneurial powers (such as Blaye and La Ferté). He added to this store of old Huguenot chrism through his reading, including the works of Abbadie and others.[67] For all his ardent Catholicism, Saint-Simon thus felt the magnetic attraction of Jansenism, the Catholic version of Huguenot Augustinianism, which found numerous adherents in Catholic regions.

Indeed, it was from Jansenism that Louis de Saint-Simon took many of his ideas about "renunciation" and "detachment." The memorialist was a great admirer of "Saint Augustine's system" and felt close to the "illustrious solitaries of Port-Royal."[68] To be sure, he did not subscribe except in his more whimsical moments to the narrow doctrine upon which Bishop Jansenius had bestowed a name.[69] But Saint-Simon felt at ease with ideas that were in effect Augustinian, if broadly interpreted, ideas in which he had been preceded by Saint-Cyran and would soon be followed by the great Arnauld. Rather like Racine, Pomponne, and Fieubet, Saint-Simon placed himself in distant but loyal orbit around the star of Port-Royal. But he never drew too close to its burning heat, or at any rate did so only rarely, because of the danger of being consumed. Of the various dukes and peers, he was one of the few to flirt with Jansenism in this cautious way. Other dukes with whom he was friendly, such as Beauvillier, preferred to flirt with Quietism or even with the Jesuits, sworn enemies of the Jansenists.[70] Still other peers of France followed Vendôme's lead and amused themselves in a libertinism that seemed almost atheist or pagan.[71] A generation earlier, the Saint-Simons had been close to the deeply Augustinian *hôtel* de Liancourt, alias La Rochefoucauld—and in this connection there had been a whiff of heresy. At the turn of the eighteenth century, young Louis was himself a familiar of the ultra-Gallican Pontchartrain senior, a sympathizer of the anti-Jesuit Oratorians.

Despite the difference in age, moreover, Saint-Simon was a close friend of the Oratorian Malebranche. The philosopher was of course not a Jansenist but a staunch Augustinian. He advocated renunciation because he detested greed and lust: both horrified him.[72] Neither could be overcome without divine grace, in principle a gratuitous gift having nothing to do with a person's merits as an individual: grace was a gift from God. According to the Oratorian philosopher, it could not be transferred to human nature except by decree of the Almighty.

Saint-Simon consciously embraced many of Malebranche's views. Of the Jesuits, the implacable enemies of the Jansenists, he liked to say that "there is some good in them, but also some things that are less good and some that are even execrable." By contrast, Port-Royal, according to the author of the *Memoirs*, was "the saintliest, purest, most learned, most edifying, most practical and yet most elevated . . . most luminous and pellucid thing that the last few centuries have produced."[73] His approval is clear. He modeled his judgment after that of his mentor Rancé: Saint-Simon clearly tapped the well of Port-Royal but resisted moving too far in the direction of Jansenism. Perhaps out of prudence, perhaps out of conviction, he declined to join a faction within the church that he feared might give rise to a schism. He was a staunch sympathizer of the Augustinian cause. At most, he may have been a fellow traveler of a Jansenist-tinged group when to his regret such a group came into existence. But he was hardly a man to become an activist in some sort of clandestine Jansenist network, no matter how Augustinian its views. He lurked around the edges, flirting with Jansenism but never consummating the relationship. Hélène Himmelfarb is categorical about this, and her findings are confirmed by a chronological reading of the *Memoirs*.[74]

By 1698, it was enough for a person to be linked to the notorious Jansenists for Saint-Simon to consider him or her as "upright, honest, and true"—touched by the grace of God. Anyone who had formed "the most intimate" bonds with the Jansenists was ipso facto classified as one of the most perfect of human beings.[75] When the scholarly Benedictines of Saint-Maur published an edition of the works of Saint Augustine, the Jesuits branded it Jansenist. That was all it took for Saint-Simon to declare it *urbi et orbi* a "beautiful edition," which indeed it was.[76] When the authorities developed a "suspicion of Jansenism" in regard to the ultra-honest d'Aguesseau, Saint-Simon immediately correlated this with "a deep and true talent" and an ardent love of the good.[77] When an allegation was made that someone in the church was "taking over the Sorbonne," clearly it had to be some abject instrument of the government such as Bishop Péréfixe, a man who had abetted the court in all its undertakings against M. Arnauld and his academic and Jansenist friends.[78] Was it reported that a certain countess was apt to frequent Port-Royal even at the risk of arousing the king's ire? Saint-Simon dutifully notes that this lady was "blessed with more intelligence and grace" than any other woman at court.[79] Did a certain French statesman believe in clear rules for dealing with Rome, always in a scrupulous and tactful manner? Was he, in other words, a Gallican sympathizer, a good Frenchman? It turned out of course that he had a tinge of Jansenism about him. Were the Oratorians reputed to be crypto-Jansenists?[80] If so, it was because they were "regular, scrupulous, and rigorous in their conduct as well as studious and penitent"—no less.[81] When the nephew of a great Jansenist bishop died, Saint-Simon found him to be a man "of great intelligence, a very agreeable gentleman" who would of course be missed.[82] When a prelate took steps to foster morality and discipline, the authorities immediately developed a strong "suspicion of Jansenism" concerning him.[83] We also learn of a determined renouncer who spent his entire life doing good works and subjecting himself to "harsh penance" and humiliation, trusting only in Jesus: "[H]e is a very respectable and very trustworthy man with a gift for friendship, sweet and pleasant."[84] It comes as no surprise to discover that this same man had made of Jansenism a true and inexpugnable religion.[85]

Easy salvation and pride in the human spirit: these were dangerous Jesuitical doctrines, and Jansenism, Saint-Simon suggests, is the best way to combat them, because it teaches that divine grace is omnipotent and everything must bow down before it as before an all-powerful sovereign.[86] In 1709, the royal authorities embarked on the scandalous project of razing the abbey of Port-Royal-des-Champs and the no less scandalous project of exhuming the sainted persons buried in a nearby cemetery.[87] Saint-Simon seized the occasion to praise the "celebrated Pascal," a Jansenist if ever there was one, whose ingenious *Lettres provinciales* made palpable and ridiculous the doctrine, ethics, and practice of Molina and the Jesuit casuists.[88] Did a pious bishop conceive an implacable hatred of Jansenism? Making use of his powerful influence with Mme de Maintenon, this man, notwithstanding his many august virtues, filled the episcopacy with "nobodies, uneducated ignoramuses."[89] The archbishop of Reims was reputed, rightly or wrongly, to be a Jansenist. He was a staunch proponent of the idea of all-powerful divine grace and denied that individual merit played any part in salvation. That was enough for Saint-Simon to overlook his fornication and declare him an enemy of the Jesuits, "learned in matters spiritual as befits his estate," and an effective administrator of his diocese, "which is the best run in the kingdom and the most richly endowed with most excellent subjects of every variety."[90] The maréchal de Bezons was suspected of Jansenism because he had raised his children in his own home and refused to send them to a Jesuit school, a decision that the Jesuits resented. Naturally Bezons was "upright, forthright, and honest with virtue."[91] A duchesse de Lesdiguières was vaguely suspected of Jansenism, and Saint-Simon was therefore quick to judge her a woman of great piety, "gentleness, merit, virtue, and abundant wit."[92] Among the countless virtues of his beloved wife, Saint-Simon set great store by the fact that she regularly went to confession with M. de La Brüe, curé of Saint-Germain-l'Auxerrois, a protégé of Cardinal de Noailles. Saint-Simon tells us that this curé was suspected of Jansenism, but this was an understatement: in fact, he was nothing less than a Jansenist militant.[93] Amelot, an ambassador and state councilor, was above reproach "as to his abilities, integrity, and all aspects of his official performance." Hateful individuals therefore chose to attack him in the only way they could, by persuading the king that he was a Jansenist.

Saint-Simon, moreover, did not shrink from adding that Jansenist ideology was in his opinion essentially quite innocent and that the authorities used it simply to blacken the names of people whom they wished for one reason or another to destroy.[94] In his mind, Jansenism, despite its rigorous exterior, was almost a doctrine of mutual affection: the fact that Fénelon left the Jansenists in his diocese alone and did not persecute them was one reason why the Swan of Cambrai was so beloved by his people.[95]

Jansenius had been bishop of Ypres, and his ashes were believed by some to have antiseptic or prophylactic properties. In the 1700s, he was succeeded in the episcopal see of Ypres by one Ratabon, who, it seems, succumbed to fainting spells whenever he entered his cathedral, where Jansenius had once been buried. In this way the defunct bishop, who had passed away in 1638, seemed to indicate disapproval of his successor, who was overly friendly toward the Jesuits. The spells became so severe, in fact, that the unfortunate Ratabon had to be transferred to another diocese: in 1713, he was named bishop of the southern town of Viviers, where he was at last able to escape whatever Jansenist emanation was causing him to lose consciousness.[96] It was almost as if Jansen's lingering scent served as a useful insecticide, exterminating his enemies long after he was gone.

And what about Cardinal de Noailles, who had many affinities with Jansenism, or at any rate, with a certain variety of Jansenism? To hear Saint-Simon tell it, the reforms that the cardinal instituted around 1715 were "a masterstroke of religion, of gentleness certainly," but also of wisdom.[97] He was "the first prelate of France, the most firmly established, the most universally beloved and unanimously revered." What is more, he was backed on questions of dogma and many other matters "by the Sorbonne, the other schools, the curés of Paris, the majority of the second order, the regular monks, and the parlements," especially that of Paris, which unanimously supported an archbishop "who had all hearts on his side."[98] Noailles, prelate of all hearts! Who could have put it better?

Saint-Simon accepted Noailles's view that in 1717 to oppose the anti-Jansenist constitution *Unigenitus* was ipso facto to keep faith with the laws of the church and the "maxims and customs of the kingdom based upon the liberty of the Gallican church."[99] In this respect, Cardinal de Noailles was "the very soul of righteousness, piety, simplicity, and truth." By contrast, the pro-constitutional bishops were so deeply enmeshed in worldly things that they were paralyzed to the core.[100] The anti-*Unigenitus* party had to contend with "the ambitious, the mercenaries, and the ignoramuses." It was composed, according to Saint-Simon, of the most learned prelates, as well as the most virtuous, disinterested, pious, and decent.[101] As a Jansenist sympathizer, Saint-Simon continued to support the church pact of 1668, an irenic agreement that had taken a rather hard blow from the bull *Vineam Domini* in 1705 even before the "odious" *Unigenitus* was promulgated in 1713.

Saint-Simon took his ideas about renunciation and detachment from the best sources. He "drank deeply," for example, from that limpid font of Jansenist rigor, Father Pasquier Quesnel's *Réflexions morales* on the New Testament, a work widely read during the reigns of Louis XIV and Louis XV and unjustly forgotten today. It was one of Saint-Simon's favorite books.

As a diligent, or at any rate competent, reader of Quesnel, Saint-Simon was familiar with the facts of the theologian's life as well as with his ideas. Born in 1634, Quesnel was an Oratorian, a friend of Arnauld, and a Jansenist who long enjoyed the support of many prelates, including Noailles and Bossuet. A prolific and combative writer, he spent the last thirty years of his life in exile in Brussels and, later, Amsterdam. When he died in 1719, he enjoyed a reputation for heresy as great as the all but total oblivion into which he has since fallen. Today he is remembered only by historians of Jansenism inside or outside the Catholic Church.

From one end of his vast text to the other, Saint-Simon had only good things to say about Pasquier Quesnel. As early as 1698, he remarked on the very positive relationship between the persecuted theologian and Cardinal de Noailles, who was of course for Saint-Simon the very epitome of righteousness.[102] The duke also exonerated the author of the *Réflexions* of the charge of republicanism (a frequent and not altogether groundless accusation).[103] He saw an authentic miracle in Quesnel's escape to Brussels and Holland toward the end of Louis XIV's reign.[104] He noted that the king's confessor, Père de La Chaise, "a just, upright, sensible, wise, gentle, and moderate priest," always had Quesnel's *Réflexions* on his table even though he was a Jesuit. In Saint-Simon's estimation, the book was "excellent and abundantly instructive," as well as "a work approved of and respected by the entire Church, which it edified."[105] Quesnel was above all the butt of ridiculous, zealous, baroque persecutions instigated by the high clergy.[106] Saint-Simon's obituary for the fugitive priest was as eloquent as any eulogy: we learn that Quesnel was an obedient, orthodox priest, learned and enlightened, who had always worked "in solitude [?], prayer, and penitence."[107] Saint-Simon's affectionate indulgence toward Quesnel is astonishing in view of the fact that the man was a suspicious and somewhat overwrought agitator, "a first-class crackpot," as Céline might have called him. But he was an intelligent advocate of ideas that were important to Saint-Simon, a tireless proponent of renunciation, "detachment," abandonment, and self-denial, and a believer in the value of withdrawing from the world in order to seek salvation in the wilderness—salvation through penance, which could make even a heart of stone as tender as a child's.

Quesnel believed that we are "in the beginning," first and foremost, citizens of heaven, provided of course that we are saved, that is, chosen beneficiaries of divine grace—the Jansenist-Catholic equivalent of the

Jewish or Puritan covenant. As citizens of heaven, we are as strangers on earth, mere voyagers and vagabonds. We live here below only so long as our bodies endure, sampling the material world, which in reality is nothing but a cemetery for the already dead, whose apparent life is only an illusion. Saint-Simon's library contained numerous volumes of the works of Quesnel, volumes filled with allusions to renunciation on almost every page. Quesnel insists on the celestial and therefore essentially otherworldly vocation of the saved.[108] It is this vocation that nourishes the heart in this lifetime and points toward the ecstasy of the divine in the next. For Quesnel, ego, or love of self, was to be proscribed. So was pride, along with blind ambition for the grandeur of this world, the stumbling block that had tripped up so many unworthy bishops. He insisted even more, if such a thing is conceivable, on the prohibition of fornication, adultery, indecent behavior, sodomy, libertinage, criminal pleasures, worldly impurity, "unbridled exploitation of creatures," ardent and voluptuous passions, and physical pleasure outside the marriage bed (of which bastards were often the unfortunate byproduct).[109] In his disapproval of bastards, the views of the Amsterdam exile again coincided with Saint-Simon's unbending attitude, which Quesnel and other theologians had done so much to mold.

Mortify yourself, Quesnel preached, repent, and desire nothing but Christ's grace. So say the law and the prophets: It would be foolish in the extreme to give up our claim upon eternity for a moment of pleasure. Our mortification and suffering are the measure of our hope. We must learn to delight in them as in a refreshing beverage, a cool and salutary bath. We must therefore learn to behave sincerely as if we were innocence crucified. The cross "is the altar of sacrifice, the tribune of the truly learned man,"[110] the court of the sovereign Judge, and the marriage bed of the Husband, that is, of Christ, from whose wounds we are reborn. "Let us therefore fasten our lips to those wounds, which are for us the source of life, the source of the milk that will nourish us, which is grace." Penitence: by increasing our capacity for suffering, we can learn to renounce still more of what passes for life. Mortifying the flesh diminishes the effects of sin. If all the good people of the world renounced the world, the earth would be no more than a vast desert, no more than a dark figure of contrast to set against a heaven filled with the souls of the good and the just, émigrés from a diabolical planet free at last to enjoy the eternal bliss of paradise. Let us therefore resolve here and now to be good and to seek our glory in humility, in imitation of Christ, to the consternation of the worldly. We must therefore shun the court unless otherwise bound by professional obligation (as bishops were, for example). Even more, we must shun the favor of kings and princes and turn our backs on worldly honors. The true Christian thrives now and for all eternity not on material prosperity but on the spiritual prosperity of the heart. This spiritual wealth can reach all the way into the realm of darkness and death, which the Apostles humbly made their specialty. Avarice and luxury are of course to be rejected. The easiest way to do this is to divest ourselves of superfluous property and perishable wealth for the benefit of the poor: to endow a hospital bed, help a dying man, or feed a pauper is to nourish Christ. Too many rich men remain obdurate in the face of misery. Let us pray that they may show mercy. Let us abstain from eating meat in a spirit of penance and renunciation. Let us shun meat in favor of vegetables. Ah, vegetables, lovely vegetables! And last but not least, let us not hesitate to speak our minds to certain prelates: many a bishop is guilty of amassing wealth and abandoning his diocese for the court. Bishops who behave in this way dishonor themselves and become as wolves to their fellow man. Obviously Quesnel, who was often persecuted by certain bishops, knew how to pay them back in kind.

Nevertheless, for Quesnel, as for Saint-Simon and Abbadie, renunciation was in no way incompatible with the hierarchical spirit. The heavenly hierarchy of angels and archangels was Quesnel's model (as it was Pseudo-Dionysius's model) for the hierarchical structure of the earthly church:[111] at the top was the pope, directly under whom served the bishops, whose responsibility it was to educate and supervise ordinary curés and vicars.[112] By analogy, it was the same in civil society: "[T]he peace of families, of communities, of public societies, and of states is assured by order and *subordination*, just as the peace of the Church is so assured." Quesnel invokes the parable of the body and the members (1 Cor. 12: 12–21) to justify his view, for according to Saint Paul, "the eye cannot say unto the hand I have no need of thee, nor again the head to the feet, I have no need of you." And vice versa. Of course the eye guides the hand and the head the feet, as everyone knows. The metaphor applies to society and the church as well as to the body. The noble stands above the commoner, and the prelate above the rest of the flock.

Renounce and renounce again: something will always remain. Like Quesnel, his faithful pupil Saint-Simon tells many tales of renunciation with an abundance of detail. The persecuted Jansenist luminary was not the only influence on the *petit duc*, moreover. Among the apologists of "detachment" who had the greatest impact on the memorialist was Jacques-Joseph Duguet, born in 1649 and the son of an *avocat* in the *présidial* of Montbrison. An Oratorian like Quesnel but a moderate and perhaps naïve Jansenist, Duguet spent a great deal of time in retreat at the Trappist monastery with du Charmel and M. de Saint-Louis. There he became close to Saint-Simon, who appreciated his sincere humility and holiness coupled with wide learning and competence in practical as well as theoretical matters. Several of Duguet's works, including the celebrated *Institution d'un prince*, a "prodigy of erudition, breadth, and justice,"[113] figured in Saint-Simon's library, and not just as decoration: he really read them.

Duguet was an intellectual and spiritual follower of the Port-Royalist Pierre Nicole, who in 1678 wrote the *Traité de l'éducation d'un prince*. Duguet, who began writing as early as 1675, wrote his own *Institution d'un prince* around 1700, although it was not published until 1739 (Duguet died in 1733). Recent historians, including those of religious orientation, have focused mainly on the political and pre-Physiocratic aspects of the text. As Raymond Darricau rightly notes, Duguet insisted that the "tenant of the throne" incurred certain obligations toward his people, and he proposed plans by which government could promote agriculture, encourage commerce, "ban usury, strictly economize on state spending, and establish a prompt, honest, and economical system of justice." In a similar vein, Duguet advocated the creation of a fund on which the prince could draw in case of public calamity so as to encourage the creation of new manufacturing enterprises: "The abbé saw himself as a participant in the battle against unemployment." Such down-to-earth concerns met with the approval of the duke-and-peer Saint-Simon, an aristocrat who was an energetic proponent of "improving" his own estates.[114]

In the *Institution d'un prince*, Duguet also explored the question of renunciation, especially on the part of sovereign princes. Indeed, it was obligatory for any prince to rise above the mundane in order to consider the spiritual implications of every decision. This way of looking at the matter made Duguet a Physiocrat before the fact. His ideas applied explicitly to secular heads of state, beginning with Louis XIV, whom he had in mind as he secretly penned recommendations that would not see the light of day until after his death. But he also intended them for potentates of another kind: princes of the church, including bishops and above all cardinals. Saint-Simon, too, wrote of prelates at times with admiration, at other times with the whip of satire, depending on the degree to which they were willing to give up the pleasures of this world, though of course without abandoning their essential pastoral duties.

According to Duguet, every prince, whether lay or ecclesiastical, had a duty to immerse himself in the affairs of his state or diocese. Yet in so doing, he must preserve a certain essential inner distance: in short, he had to cultivate contempt for the very world that it was his duty to govern. He must base his hope of future riches—the bounty of eternal reward—on his disdain for riches here and now.[115] There were no two ways about it: for a prince, according to the abbé, contempt of the world meant disdain of pride, of praise, of the desire to stand out and dominate—a desire dangerous enough in princes but more perilous still in bishops.[116] In the privacy of his study, Duguet in the early years of the eighteenth century repeatedly attacked Louis XIV, but without mentioning him by name. By this time, to be sure, the king was less drunk with pride than he had been in earlier years. Indeed, his preoccupation with his own grandeur had been on the wane since 1680. The trials of a long life had matured him, and already he had had to cope with the first misfortunes of the *fin du règne*. But pride was not the only problem, nor was false humility, which was merely pride by another name. For Duguet, ambition was also the enemy—indefatigable, hateful ambition. One saw it in the "plague-ridden men *(hommes empestés)*[117] who infect church and state with their pernicious example to the detriment of true merit." If pride and ambition were vices, then what was virtue? Once again, the answer was humility—true humility, that of Saint Louis. Every prince had a duty "to humble himself profoundly before the hand of God," to humble himself through an arduous baptism of tears and penitential works. Of course, such humiliation in no way weakened the sovereign's authority or power.[118] For a king or prince, to be humble meant to exemplify simplicity: simplicity of dress, of furnishings, of servants, of living quarters, however palatial (was Duguet thinking of the château de Versailles, which in 1700 looked more splendid than ever?). Glory, too, came in for condemnation: here was yet another stone hurled at the Sun King, a monarch at one time obsessed with his own glorification, or as we would call it nowadays, his "image."

Duguet also played down the importance of birth. For most aristocrats in the 1700s, birth was a source of pride: how could it have been otherwise among those who considered themselves "wellborn"? Duguet took the opposite view: birth ought to be the grounds for humble meditation on human misery. Man was born helpless and naked, and he was not much better off when he died. Such negative, or at any rate depreciative, thinking stood as an indictment of that prestigious but contemptible place known as "the world." The worldly person walked on a bridge above an abyss, buffeted by the violent winds of his own passions.[119] Be he courtier or confessor to kings, he was moved by worldly things: jealousy, self-interest, prejudice, politics, hypocrisy, a culpable will to please, an ostentatious display of wit or wealth. By rights the world ought to be no more than a temporary bivouac for men and women whose true objective was eternity, but for many it became the be-all and end-all. In contrast to this world, with its idolatry of pomp and achievement worse than the idolatry of the pagans, the idea of poverty, of renunciation, took on its full value, or rather, revealed its full ambivalence: for the prince, great as he was in the eyes of men, was but a pauper before God, a pauper with neither possessions nor entitlements.[120] Yet God also imposed august duties upon the sovereign, "pauper" though he was. The Lord in his infinite goodness entrusted the prince with the duty to care for the poor (the "real" poor), as well as for orphans, widows, and foreigners—

in other words, all who were without protection or shelter.[121] Included under this injunction were not only renouncers but also the "renounced," those who for one reason or another were excluded or rejected by society. If the prince failed to take care of these people as a father would, there was a danger that the menacing revolutionary cries of the poor against the rich would become ever more insistent.[122]

Whether secular or religious, the prince had a duty to become a penitent, to thumb his nose at the pleasures of the senses. No more sumptuous feasts for bishops, who, like the prelate of Bayeux admired by Saint-Simon, were enjoined to limit their diet to vegetables and herbs. One prince of the church later identified three things that according to him could help young priests escape the flames of hell everlasting: terror, beans, and spaghetti. The vegetarian diet supposedly suppressed the sexual urge, thereby enabling young men to avoid sins of the flesh. Sexuality was not held in high esteem, even if it was never openly discussed for fear of arousing temptation in the reader. Suffice it to say that the prince was expected to remain pure and without blemish and to shun worldly corruption.[123] One good way to do this was to avoid the theater. That erstwhile Christian and secular saint Jean-Jacques Rousseau would later put the point in his own inimitable fashion. But in addition to the theater, Duguet also condemned large buildings (such as Versailles and the palaces of the bishops), as well as expensive ecclesiastical accoutrements (such as precious chasubles and sumptuous gold and silver vessels and calyxes). Such luxuries were of dubious value when it came to saving souls.

Duguet's puritanical political philosophy may seem austere. In fact, it was not hostile to personal happiness or the gratification of individual desire, provided that these were displaced from this world to the other. Moreover, the sovereign was supposed to be concerned not only with his own salvation but also with the salvation of all his subjects. Not that he was expected to make renouncers of all twenty million Frenchmen: many were called, but few were chosen. For monarchs as well as prelates, the ideal of renunciation had both collective and individual dimensions. On the collective plane, the prince had an obligation to preserve and protect a temporal "city" (that is, his state) even though its days were numbered: it would crumble when Providence so decreed.[124] In his heart, however, he was expected to look forward to another "city," the City of God, to borrow a phrase from Saint Augustine, a city designed by its omnipotent architect to rest on unshakable foundations. A king, an emperor, or a duke—a Charles, a Louis, or an Amédée—might have occupations in Vienna, Versailles, Madrid, or Chambéry, but his spiritual treasure was supposed to be stored elsewhere. At a purely individual level, princes were supposed to emulate a manner that Saint-Simon observed in certain

pious provincial bishops, whose repudiation of luxury, frugal ways, abstinence at the dinner table, simple manners, plain clothing, and patent
humility were pleasing in the eyes of the Lord. This ideal demanded not
only self-effacement and humility but also faith, for the "so-called wisdom of infidel princes" was limited to the goods of this world, whereas
the poor man, "if he is humble and faithful," could look forward to being
lifted up and placed upon a throne from which he would visit divine
justice upon proud kings.[125] *Deposuit potentes de sede et exaltavit humiles.*
These words of the Virgin Mary (in which the Jansenist-influenced Saint-
Simon took little interest)[126] were therefore of great topicalconcern. In
any case, those whom Saint-Simon deemed worthy of the name "Christian" adhered to an ethics of complete or at any rate partial detachment.

Earlier we pointed out that a philosophy, or rather a theology, of renunciation was by no means incompatible with the hierarchical social
structure that flourished in France under the Sun King. On the contrary,
the former reinforced the latter simply because it operated outside the
hierarchical framework. It negated hierarchy, but *from outside* the system,
hence in a sense respecting that system and making it de facto untouch-
able. Clearly, Abbé Duguet was no exception to this rule. His *Institution
d'un prince* was by no means a primer in antihierarchical egalitarianism
and the spirit of democracy. The prince, he wrote, must be "thoroughly
instructed in the proprieties" in order to carry out his governmental duties, but he must also "give the people common signs of affection and
kindness by wearing upon his face a friendly air, equal for all, which,
through a kind of mute eloquence, charms and wins the allegiance of
all."[127] So much for egalitarianism. Lest anyone mistake his meaning, the
abbé sought immediately to correct any hint of a "leveling" intent in
what he wrote. In terms that Saint-Simon would have found perfectly
acceptable, he observed that "in addition to the common language, the
prince has a peculiar language of his own, which he adjusts in a manner
appropriate to the birth, employment, service, and merit [of each individ-
ual]. He is careful not to allow his approving glances to fall indiscrimi-
nately. He does not give away freely what ought to be a reward and does
not debase what ought to be a distinction." In his enumeration Duguet
thus awarded pride of place to the advantages of birth (by definition aristocratic in the minds of contemporaries) and high noble *emplois* (that is,
provincial governors and marshals of France). As was inevitable for a man
of his time, he thus conceded a great deal to the hierarchical mentality.
To be sure, the allusion to service and merit reflected the spirit of the
early Enlightenment, but Duguet remained well aware of who he was—
and how insignificant. Nor did he forget that princes and their subjects,
no matter how much they renounced the world, remained obedient to

the stratifying imperatives of the time. The society still saw itself as aristocratic and monarchical in its very structure.

W e have said enough to situate Saint-Simon with respect to the question of renunciation, which we have discussed at length.[128] We now want to consider how he stood with respect to the related matter of Jansenism.

Like his teacher Rancé, Saint-Simon was entirely on the side of those whom he believed to have been wrongly accused of subscribing to Jansenist teachings, some of whom were persecuted for their beliefs. To believe Saint-Simon, these people were in fact quite "orthodox," by which he meant entirely in accord with the Catholic faith. One such person in his view was Bishop Pavillon d'Alet, even though all other commentators on this case believed that the bishop was Jansenist to the core. Perhaps Saint-Simon was being disingenuous, but how are we to plumb his heart and mind? In the *Memoirs*, he went so far as to state flatly that he even supported those who had in fact joined the Jansenist faction, wrongly perhaps, but who would nevertheless "be saved by their good faith in conjunction with their good works and genuine penitence."[129] To make such a statement was to invite the attention of the anti-Jansenist authorities, though to be sure there was little risk of a crackdown on the château de la Ferté-Vidame, since Saint-Simon's religious views did not become known until after his death. The allusion to "good works" is comical, given the sacred horror that Jansenists always professed with respect to the theology of works in any of its forms, but the gist of the duke's feelings is clear enough. This was as far as he ever conceived of going. When it came to true Jansenists in the strict and rigorous doctrinal sense—not mere sympathizers but hard-core party activists, resolute "doctrinologists" (to borrow a phrase)—the *petit duc* inevitably concluded that such people lacked both honesty and good faith. Hence they could expect no indulgence from him. In this seemingly harsh attitude, there was certainly an element of tactical prudence. In the end, his caution was such that even the most delicate prober cannot penetrate the veil. Saint-Simon was a wary writer, and less concerned with sincerity than is sometimes claimed.

In view of all this, it seems reasonable to classify Saint-Simon, despite his frequent self-corrections, deceptions, and pretenses, as belonging to the camp of "politicals," a "member" (loosely speaking) of what Emile Appolis has felicitously dubbed the "Catholic third party." Politicals spanned the entire breadth of the "middle way" (*voie mitoyenne*, as Saint-Simon called it)[130] between the Augustinian fanatics of grace and the Jesuit apologists of personal merit. To the Augustinian, Jesuit-hating,

Port-Royalist faction, the very concept of personal merit was all too redolent of the excessive claims being made for human freedom and against the Almighty. Saint-Simon's prudent prose staked out a position somewhere between Jansenius and Jesus—Jesus, that is, as revised and corrected by Molina, hence already somewhat suspect to Saint-Simon's way of thinking. In his own calculated way, the duke stood closer to the pro-Jansenist Augustinians than to their opponents, although his Augustinianism was prudently warmed over to make it palatable to as large an audience as possible.[131]

Here Saint-Simon found himself in good company. In the late seventeenth and early eighteenth century, the quasi-Jansenist third party counted any number of august personages among its members. To begin with, there was the eminent jurist and chancellor Henri-François d'Aguesseau. There were also men like Bossuet, a leading anticasuist who nevertheless always tried to bridge the gap between the two sides, the party of grace and the party of laboriously accumulated individual merit. Saint-Simon's position was also close to that of Mabillon, who held Quesnel in high esteem and who sought to purify or expurgate the cults of certain saints who in his estimation appealed rather too vividly to the popular imagination. And he had much in common with Abbé Claude Fleury, that great enemy of excessive credulity. He naturally shared the informally expressed opinions of the abbé de Rancé, a Quesnelist of sorts and an assiduous enemy of the Jesuit *zelanti*. Finally, his position was close to that of Père de La Tour, the Oratorian superior general as well as a Jansenist, and of the archbishop of Ephesus, Domenico Passionei, whose list of acquaintances was very impressive indeed: he often visited the great scholar Montfaucon, admired Mabillon, and worshiped Rancé and Cardinal Le Camus (himself a suspected Jansenist). In this list of men belonging to the *juste milieu* but leaning toward the center left, one also has to include Archbishop Le Tellier, a judiciously "middle-of-the-road" prelate despite certain regrettable lapses of personal behavior.[132]

Beyond the theological subtleties of Jansenism, the related question of renunciation crops up frequently in the *Memoirs*. Here Saint-Simon's ideas about hierarchy turn out to have a great deal in common with Louis Dumont's thinking in *Homo hierarchicus* about hierarchy in twentieth-century India: "In the society of castes itself, and alongside the caste system, [there exists] an institution which contradicts it."[133] Renunciation is the institution he has in mind. Seeking "detachment," a man becomes a *sannyasi*, meaning that he is "dead to the world." Accepting himself as an individual, he becomes the nucleus of a social group sui generis consisting of others like himself: a sect. In the case of the Jansenists, one thinks of the sectarian solitaries of Port-Royal and, later, in a more grotesque form, the sect of *convulsionnaires* of Saint-Médard.[134]

There are two ways, Dumont continues, to negate a very rigid hierarchical social structure. The first is by inversion of values, which in India is commonly associated with Tantrism, and in Europe with the dramatic or comic auspices of carnival, both well attested at Versailles in the late seventeenth and early eighteenth century.[135] Saint-Simon on the court carnival is a subject worthy of special treatment in its own right, but this is not the place. The second way of negating a hierarchical social structure is, of course, renunciation. This might seem in part symbolic or even, ultimately, cosmetic, a method of escaping or evading rather than negating hierarchy. Broadly speaking, renunciation was a technique by which individuals or sects sought actively or passively to achieve salvation in this world, a terrestrial preparation for the ineffable joys of the hereafter awaiting those who successfully navigated the "straits of death." In heaven, those ineffable celestial joys would become as divorced from renunciation as before death they had been wedded to it.

It is not enough, however, to look at Saint-Simon's idea of renunciation as simply an abstract ideal. And it is not enough to use the light from Dumont's luminous pages as a tool for exploring the comparative history of cultures and civilizations. Saint-Simon's treatment of spiritual detachment was linked to the concrete history of the court and to the behavior of powerful officials and aristocrats in Paris as well as Versailles. Doctrinally, it was related to the teachings of Augustinian theorists, both Huguenot and Jansenist, whether émigrés from Calvinist Ariège, residents of Brussels and Amsterdam, or members of the Huguenot and Jansenist diaspora, exiles of one sort or another whose attitudes toward renunciation exhibited certain common traits.

With the aid of certain bibliographic information, we have been able thus far to clarify our understanding but not to get to the bottom of the matter. Saint-Simon certainly would have read any number of well-known penitential works, to say nothing of numerous passages of the New Testament concerned with the mortification of the flesh. As we have seen, he was intimately familiar with the works of Quesnel (1672), Abbadie (1684), and the late Duguet (1739): *Réflexions sur le Nouveau Testament, De la vérité de la religion chrétienne, Institution d'un prince*. The *Institution*, written in about 1700 but not published until 1739, came too late to have shaped Saint-Simon's thinking, but it could not help but confirm views on renunciation that he had formed much earlier. A clear process of intellectual convergence was at work.

Of the three authors just mentioned, Quesnel's work was the first to appear, and for Saint-Simon as well as for any unbiased observer today, he was the most important person in the whole affair. Quesnel's *Réflexions* were undoubtedly one of Abbadie's major sources for *De la vérité de la religion chrétienne*, published twelve years later, and for Duguet's *Institu-*

tion d'un prince, composed in secret roughly two decades after that. The *Réflexions* were also a source for the great Bossuet's admittedly mediocre *Méditations sur l'Evangile* (1695). Although this work fell far short of Quesnel's in quality, it may have been intended as a discreet rival. Some passages of the *Réflexions* are not unworthy of the *Pensées* of Quesnel's teacher Pascal, at least for the purposes of teaching and more or less intimate private preaching. Père de La Chaise, who until his death in 1709 served as Louis XIV's confessor and who despite being a Jesuit was a man of quite moderate views, meditated deeply upon Quesnel for many years. He kept the *Réflexions* always at his side and read it before retiring at night. His successor, Père Tellier, was by contrast an outspoken "anti-Quesnelian." It was his baleful influence that ultimately drove Louis XIV to the extreme of promulgating *Unigenitus*, a bull "made to order" by a pliable pope in 1713 for the private use of the king of France. Saint-Simon was under no illusions regarding the unfortunate pro-Jesuit "swerve" *(flexure)* of 1709–13.[136]

Clearly, the intense hostility that Quesnel and his work aroused led directly to the disastrous *Unigenitus* of 1713, which explicitly and uncompromisingly attacked the Jansenist ideas of Quesnel and his disciples. The controversy surrounding this papal bull became the "mother of all battles," the *unigenitrix*, as it were, of the anti-*Unigenitus* reaction associated with the Jansenism of the Enlightenment. That reaction was by no means reactionary, moreover. Eventually it became one of several currents— Gallican, clerical, *parlementaire*, *avocassière*—that fed the vast revolutionary tide of 1789. Quesnel, unjustly neglected by most students of French history, was thus one of the fathers, or rather grandfathers, of a certain segment of the French left, whose ancestry can be traced back through the Revolution to the militant Jansenism of the Enlightenment.[137] Since that time, of course, that left has had its ups and downs, not to mention sectarian episodes of its own.

If the opposition to *Unigenitus* constituted a "left," what constituted the "right"? The terminology is of course anachronistic, and we do not want to insist on it. Without abusing the terminology unduly, however, one can say that the opposition to the party of renunciation (that is, to the Jansenists, many of whom were renouncers in theory if not in practice) was the worldly party, *les mondains* (no pejorative connotation intended). Paradoxically, however, even "men of the world" were tempted at times by the prospect of renunciation. Some who were immersed in the social world managed to persuade themselves that they thereby served a righteous cause. They sought to use the world of which they were a part. They even hoped to change it. The prototype of this sort of worldly individual, within the church at any rate, was the Jansenist's born enemy, the Jesuit, to whom Saint-Simon felt a deep aversion.

Not that he was unalterably prejudiced against each and every one of the Good Fathers. Some of his best friends were Jesuits, so to speak. Or to quote his own words: "Whatever is said about the Jesuits, one mustn't think that there are not a few among them who are very holy and enlightened men." One such "good" Jesuit was the remarkable guide and teacher Père Sanadon. Our memoirist, like Voltaire after him, was himself a "spiritual son" of the Jesuits, even if both subsequently bit the hand that had fed them.[138] Saint-Simon's friendship with Sanadon remained intact despite *Unigenitus*, and the duke continued to receive spiritual lessons and suggestions for pious reading from his former teacher.[139] He was even more strongly drawn to Père Gaillard, a superb preacher suspected, astonishingly enough, of having been a closet Jansenist within the Society of Jesus.[140] Allegedly Gaillard wore the habit of the order without sharing its doctrinal beliefs.

What about the reverse? It was one thing to be a Jansenist among Jesuits, but a Jesuit among Jansenists? The idea was far less pleasing to the author of the *Memoirs*. A case in point was Père Le Vassor, an Oratorian by outward appearance but in reality a Jesuit "spy" who had allegedly infiltrated that highly pro-Jansenist order. When caught red-handed, Le Vassor had no choice but to flee to England, where he became, of all things, a Protestant, was appointed to high posts, and wrote best-selling works on the history of France. Here, then, was a man who professed Jansenism, hid his Jesuit connections, and ended up a Protestant—an intriguing career trajectory. The only equivalent in the *Memoirs* is Ripperda, who served first as Holland's Protestant ambassador to Madrid and later as prime minister under Philip V of Spain, an appointment that required him to become a Catholic. Ultimately he was disgraced and sought refuge in Morocco, where he converted to Islam. One thinks also of the recantations of Palissot, that zealous enemy of the philosophes, who he charged had been led astray by Rousseau. But after 1789, he changed his mind and embraced the Revolution, a decision for which he was rewarded with an important appointment as a librarian.

For now, however, let us confine our attention to those Jesuits whom Saint-Simon considered "good." In view of his prejudice against the Fathers, he naturally thought of the "good Jesuits" as exceptions, at least in the present. When he contemplated an earlier period, however, "exceptional" members of the order seemed more plentiful. We see this "flashback effect" at work in an anecdote that he sets in Spain. During his visit to that country in 1721, Saint-Simon stopped in the town of Loyola where the adventures of Saint Ignatius began. From there, the

Jesuit empire had grown to unprecedented size, stretching from America to China by way of India and Europe. As a result, nearly everything in Loyola partook of the miraculous. Riding a mule at a slow and stately pace, Saint-Simon visited the fine baroque church built on the very spot where Ignatius's career began. There he was served delicious chocolate by the local Jesuits. But this only reminded him of the misdeeds of the Jesuits of his own time, the contemporaries of the elderly Louis XIV and the young Louis XV. In 1701, it seems, the Fathers had had heavy bars of chocolate shipped to them from America. Before long, however, customs inspectors discovered that the "chocolate" in these bars was but a thin layer of brown camouflaging gold that the Jesuits had contrived to smuggle from the New World to the Old. In Saint-Simon's mind, then, chocolate signified two entirely different things: the good old days of Saint Ignatius on the one hand, the deplorable present state of Loyola on the other.[141] This episode calls to mind the Jesuits of Namur, who, as we saw earlier, had allegedly amassed a cache of gunpowder for use against the French army. Although the camouflage in that case was more elaborate, it, too, proved ineffective.

What other charges did Saint-Simon level against the Jesuits? Were they perhaps murderers (if only indirectly)? On two occasions, it seems, children of illustrious families died while attending Jesuit preparatory schools in Paris, victims of alleged mistreatment by the Fathers. One of these victims was a nephew of Mazarin, who in 1658 died of a skull fracture after being tossed into the air by classmates who hated his very unpopular uncle. Young Antoine de Boufflers, the marshal's son, met with a similar fate after being whipped for a childish prank. The boy, fifteen at the time, supposedly died of shame, or perhaps it was rage. The king, Saint-Simon tells us, took a certain (unspecified) interest in both cases, but since the Jesuits were involved, "he let it rest there." The same words appear in the story about the gunpowder in Namur. If Saint-Simon is to be believed, the powers-that-be were always ready to pardon the Society of Jesus in advance, no matter what they did.[142]

Rightly or wrongly, Saint-Simon thus believed that the Jesuits enjoyed a certain immunity, and it horrified him: immunity not only from prosecution but also from taxation. He complained, not entirely without justification, that the Jesuits, by alleging financial difficulties, had gained exemption from certain taxes normally paid by the clergy, whether regular or secular.[143] The Jesuits, for their part, could argue that there were justifications for such an exemption. The Society of Jesus, however powerful it may have been, was a relatively new organization and lacked the vast resources in land that the Benedictine abbeys and other ecclesiastical institutions had amassed over the years through gifts. Consumed by his rage against the Jesuits, Saint-Simon does not mention the fact that they controlled little land, though he was well aware of it. In a similar vein, he also criticized the Fathers for having wangled special dispensations of benefit to former members who quit the Society after twenty years or more and returned home to claim their share of the family heritage. Brothers and sisters who had imagined themselves permanently quit of such claims were dumbfounded when a former Jesuit sibling returned home demanding a piece of the "pie."[144] To Saint-Simon, such mischief was intolerable.

With barely restrained anger, the duke enumerated the Society's every peccadillo. He fulminated, for instance, against the demolition (begun in 1605 and completed in 1689) of a pyramid marking the attempted assassination of Henri IV by Jean Chastel. The monument's inscription had accused the Jesuits of inspiring Chastel's attack, and Saint-Simon naturally had nothing but sarcasm for the Jesuit-loving official charged with overseeing the final phases of the pyramid's destruction. This was none other than Fourcy, the provost of Paris, supposedly a mere cat's-paw for his father-in-law, Chancellor Boucherat. By doing this favor for the Jesuits, Fourcy allegedly launched himself on a brilliant ecclesiastical career with the Society as his protector.[145]

Another exploit of Jesuitical imperialism aroused Saint-Simon's customary ire. It was a rather trivial incident, to be sure: a direct or indirect seizure of power in the parish of Brest, which at the time was still a small town. What Saint-Simon forgets to add is that one side effect of this little coup was to raise the level of mathematical teaching after the Jesuits took over the schools; ultimately this proved to be of great benefit to the city's nautical future.[146] Saint-Simon also alleges that the Jesuits were responsible for depriving the duc de Nevers of his right to appoint the bishop of the tiny "bishopric" of Bethléem in Clamecy, a mini-diocese on a par with the minikingdom of Yvetot or the grand duchy of Gerolstein, whose revenue was little more than a thousand livres tournois, if that. Obviously all this was quite petty, on top of which Saint-Simon's account of the Clamecy episode is somewhat biased.[147]

He is on rather firmer ground, however, when he lashes out at some of the Jesuits' intellectual ventures. In 1699, the Fathers savaged a Benedictine edition of Saint Augustine on the grounds that it exhibited Jansenist tendencies.[148] No doubt the charge was not entirely off the mark, since Fénelon himself was anxious enough about the dangers of publishing the text to have warned the authors against it. They were Benedictines of Saint-Maur, where Père Mabillon trained his minions in the most exacting techniques of scholarship. In any event, the pope, Louis XIV, the chancellor of France, and several secretaries of state offered the Jesuits no more than lukewarm support in their campaign against this Benedictine publishing venture, tinged with Augustinianism though it was. Indeed, it would not be too much to say that the royal government lent the anti-Benedictine offensive of 1699–1700 no support whatsoever. This hands-off attitude was in effect mildly pro-Jansenist, and it delighted Saint-Simon, who was overjoyed to see the sons of Saint Ignatius routed for once by the papal and monarchical authorities acting in concert.[149]

He was considerably less pleased, however, with what happened in 1713 in the case of Père de Jouvency.[150] Jouvency, a French-born Jesuit residing in Rome, was one of several contributors to a history of the order. The volume for which he was responsible covered the period of Henri IV, and Jouvency adopted a very indulgent attitude toward the Jesuits of the time even though they were *ligueurs*, troublemakers, enemies of the established order, and if not regicides then at least backers of regicides. The consistently Gallican, not to say pro-Jansenist, Parlement of Paris, reacted sharply to Jouvency's provocation and subjected his *Histoire de la Société de Jésus* to close scrutiny. But Louis XIV took a different view. Perhaps he had been manipulated by Père Tellier, whose influence had increased markedly. Or perhaps he was worried about his eternal salvation. Or perhaps in his anti-Jansenist zeal, the king had become an outright proponent of the Jesuits. The most he would agree to was a relatively mild sanction (to be sure the date was 1713, the year of *Unigenitus*). Jouvency's book was to be "banned" in France but "not shredded or burned." To Saint-Simon, the king's moderate if not downright pro-Jesuit attitude seemed nothing short of complicity or provocation.

For Saint-Simon, the straw that finally broke the camel's back was the *Histoire de France* published by Père Daniel, S.J. One of the duke's criticisms, shared by Voltaire, was that the Jesuit historian devoted too much space to military history. Saint-Simon also faulted Daniel for failing to take a critical view of Jesuit involvement in the agitations and disturbances that gripped France during the time of the League. It was a pleasure, he said, to watch Father Daniel skate over thin ice (in his treatment of these ultramontanist and possibly seditious episodes) with "Jesuit skates." Even worse, Daniel's condemnation of royal adultery and the ensuing bastards was to Saint-Simon's way of thinking insufficiently vigorous—a mortal sin at a time when the duc du Maine, himself a bastard, was engaged in every possible kind of intrigue in the hope of seizing the advantage after Louis XIV died. Clearly, Saint-Simon felt no great affection for Daniel, whose typically Jesuitical penchant for "skating on thin ice" annoyed him no end.[151]

What was the real reason for Saint-Simon's visceral hostility to the Jesuits? Was it that they conducted themselves like men of the world, or at any rate, men in the world? They poked their noses wherever they saw signs of vitality and activity. Their interests embraced life in all its

1. Hyacinthe Rigaud (1659–1743), *Louis XIV in Armor*, 1700. Here the king is portrayed as a warrior. Instead of the Roman tunics and other costumes in which the king had previously had himself painted, he is now shown in armor. The battle scene in the background was done by Parrocel, who specialized in the genre. Louis's face was painted by Rigaud himself, and he has given the monarch a disillusioned expression. Was this because he saw the difficulty and cost of the War of the Spanish Succession in which he would soon be enmeshed?

2. Antoine Benoist, portraits of Louis XIV in miniature, circa 1701. Benoist (1632–1717) was a court sculptor and medalist and in his way a Saint-Simon (or rather a Dangeau) of the graphic arts. Here we see a dozen profiles of Louis XIV, from early childhood to old age. What grew up around the king was not a "cult of personality" but a "cult of the royal person."

3. French school, circa 1715–1720, *Louis XIV and his Heirs*, circa 1706. The king is seated in an armchair. To his right is his son the Grand Dauphin, alias Monseigneur, a stout fellow but perhaps not as stupid as Saint-Simon made out. To the king's left we see the duc de Bourgogne, next in line for the throne. His son became Louis XV.

4. Antoine Benoist, portraits of the royal house in miniature, circa 1706. By row from top to bottom: Louis XIV; the Grand Dauphin and his wife, Marianne of Bavaria; the duc de Bourgogne and his wife, Marie Adélaïde of Savoy; the future Philip V and Charles de Berry; Louis XIII, Anne of Austria, and Marie-Thérèse.

5. Pierre Gobert (1662–1744), *Françoise-Marie de Bourbon, Mlle de Blois, Duchesse d'Orléans*. Saint-Simon's relations with Mlle de Blois, who became the wife of his friend the regent, were for a long time ambivalent and ended with a final "chill." She was a bastard, the child of the king's doubly adulterous affair with Mme de Montespan, and Saint-Simon despised bastards, but she was also the wife of his friend and protector, the duc d'Orléans.

6. François de Troy (1645–1730), *The Duc du Maine and Mlle de Nantes* [natural children of Louis XIV and Mme de Montespan] *as Paris and Venus*, 1691. The bastard Maine is one of the villains of the *Memoirs*. He was a principal in the relatively reactionary Maine-Maintenon cabal, but his wife, the duchesse du Maine, played a fairly significant role in the early Enlightenment. His sister, the duchesse de Bourbon, seen here as a young girl, belonged to the cabal of Louis XIV's legitimate son, Monseigneur, which was not very "progressive" either.

7. French school, seventeenth century, *The Comte de Toulouse* [another natural son of Louis XIV and Montespan] *Dressed as a Novice of the Ordre du Saint-Esprit.* Toulouse later became France's "naval bastard." He was an excellent naval officer, well liked not only by his crews but also by Saint-Simon, who in Toulouse's case made an exception to his general rule of detesting all bastards.

8. Pierre Bergaigne (1652–1708), *The Card Players*, 1699. Men and women playing cards in an "elite" setting. Saint-Simon reports that in 1712 "a number of men and women were banished from Paris for playing faro, a game that was rightly prohibited and that people stopped playing entirely after this expulsion" (B. 22:241). Faro, which originated in Italy, was an improvement on the French game of *bassette*. As late as 1717, the comic opera put on a production entitled *Le Pharaon* (Faro), and in the following year Dancourt composed *La Déroute du Pharaon*, which was never produced.

9. Etienne Allegrain, *Versailles, the Gardens and Court*, 1689. Louis XIV and his court "taking the air" at Versailles. The paths in the background radiate from a central point in much the same way as the avenues that radiate out from the Invalides chapel in Paris.

10. Charles Chatelain (1672–1755), *Louis XIV at Versailles before the Buffet d'Eau of the Grand Trianon*, oil, 1713. The "precious liquid" flowing over this monument was a major preoccupation of the period's innovators. Toward the end of his life, Vauban dreamed of nothing but water for irrigation, drainage, canals, and many other things.

11. Antoine Pezey (active until 1710), *Louis XIV Receiving the Oath of Dangeau, Grand Maître de Saint-Lazare*. At the end of the seventeenth century the king made Dangeau grand master of the Order of Saint-Lazare, a somewhat decadent knightly order. Among the knights of the order was the marquis de Rivarolles, an excellent soldier born in the Piedmont, who received the order's Grand Cross (C. 2:457). A courageous soldier, Rivarolles was hit by a cannonball during the battle of Neerwinden and lost his wooden leg.

12. Louis de Silvestre, *Louis XIV Receiving the Elector of Saxony at Fontainebleau*, 1714. Frederick Augustus, the elector of Saxony and later king of Poland, traveled incognito to the West in 1714 and called on Louis XIV at Fontainebleau. According to Saint-Simon, he was "a tall, plump youth of eighteen, very healthy looking, blond, with a nice color."

13. Hyacinthe Rigaud (1659–1743), *Philip V Wearing the Ribbon of the Saint-Esprit and the Necklace of the Golden Fleece*, 1700–1701. Because he was so laden with decorations, some contemporaries would have compared the prince unfairly to the ass laden with relics in La Fontaine.

14. François Marot (1666–1719), *Louis XIV Inaugurating the Ordre de Saint-Louis*, 1693. Louis XIV is standing and wearing his hat, while all the other courtiers and soldiers present are bareheaded. The Ordre du Saint-Esprit was the "religious" forerunner of today's secularized Legion of Honor. The order that Louis created in 1693 was supposed to reward martial courage, among other things, courage being a value that the royal army sorely needed in that difficult year of the War of the League of Augsburg.

15. Nicolas Lancret (1690–1743) *Award of the Ordre du Saint-Esprit by Louis XV,* 1724. In the chapel at Versailles, which looks more or less the same today, the young king, wearing his hat, awards the kingdom's highest decoration.

16. Laumosnier, *The Maréchal de Tessé, Ambassador to Madrid, Receiving the Golden Fleece*, 1725. Tessé received his Golden Fleece from Philip V of Spain, before whom he is shown kneeling. Philip as depicted in this portrait resembles some later pictures of Voltaire.

17. A. F. Van Der Meulen (1632–90), *Saint-Germain-en-Laye, New Castle.* Saint-Simon much preferred this royal residence to Versailles, which he disliked for many reasons. Louis XIII, whom Saint-Simon much admired, was raised here in the early seventeenth century along with several of Henri IV's bastards (a fact that Saint-Simon does not dwell on). After the Glorious Revolution of 1688 in England, Louis XIV ordered that Saint-Germain be given to James II, who played the role of a comic-opera king. The château was spacious enough to accommodate both James and the Assembly of the Clergy. Never short of ideas, Saint-Simon even proposed convoking the Estates General to meet here after the death of Louis XIV.

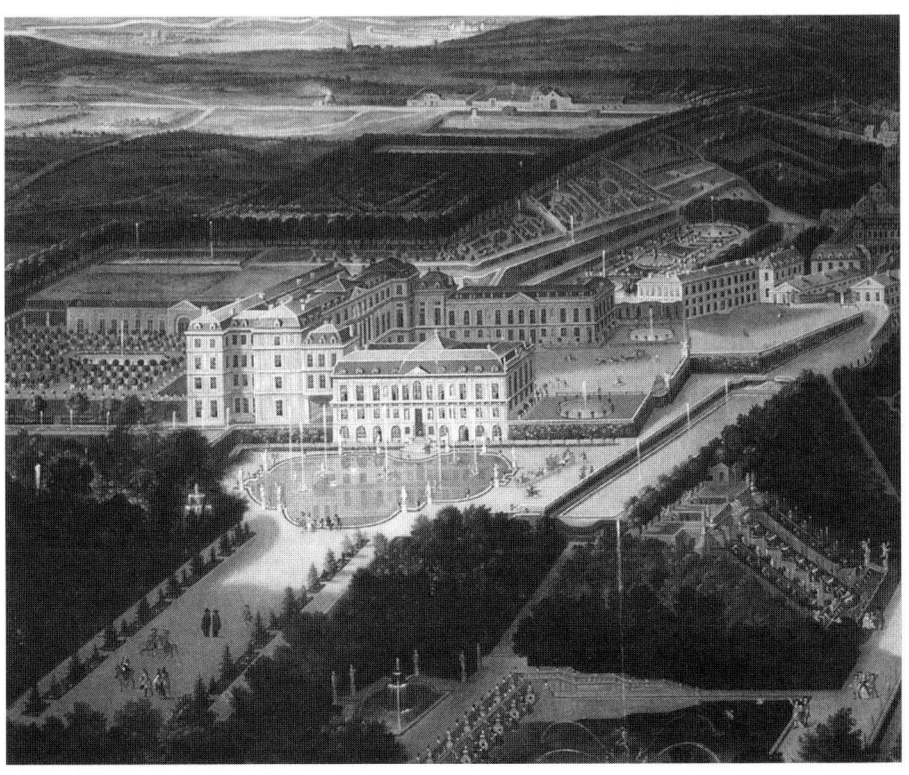

18. Etienne Allegrain, *Saint-Cloud, Seen in Perspective*, circa 1700. A residence of the Orléans, Saint-Cloud, like Versailles, resembled a vast barracks. Aesthetically it was rather ordinary, but it was quite serviceable for housing an important family's numerous guests and servants of many different ranks. Unlike the Palais-Royal, which was designed as an urban residence, Saint-Cloud served the Orléans as a country house. The regent's mother, Madame, spent every summer here. Like Versailles, the château boasted an *orangerie* and a menagerie.

19. Pierre-Denis Martin (1663–1742), *Marly, Perspective View of the Château and Gardens from the Basin Side*, 1724. Marly, Louis XIV's splendid residence, is today all but forgotten compared to Versailles, which survived, whereas Marly was totally destroyed. The atmosphere at Marly was more relaxed than at Versailles. The service was more intimate and less disciplined. On some occasions everyone kept their hats on, even in the presence of the king, and it was against the rules to be bored.

20. Jean-Baptiste Oudry (1686–1755), *Fable of La Fontaine, "The Sun and the Frogs."* In this graphical commentary on a fable of La Fontaine, Oudry gives an overview of the ancien régime hierarchy: the royal Sun dominates the city, residence of the elite, which in turn dominates the countryside, populated by frogs (peasants).

21. Nicolas de Largillière (1656–1746), *J.-B. Colbert de Torcy.* Torcy, nephew of the great Colbert, was one of the great "Colbertians" of Louis XIV's reign, though he lacked his uncle's panache. For a time he worked in the Ministry of Foreign Affairs under the orders of his father-in-law, Pomponne. In his maturity, he became head of French diplomacy until the death of Louis XIV.

22. Hyacinthe Rigaud (1659–1743), *Philippe de Courcillon, Marquis de Dangeau,* 1702. Not to be confused with his son, also named Courcillon, who was maimed in battle. Dangeau's colorless but detailed diary was one of the documents on which Saint-Simon based his memoirs.

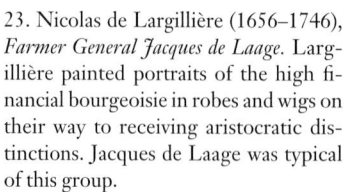

23. Nicolas de Largillière (1656–1746), *Farmer General Jacques de Laage.* Largillière painted portraits of the high financial bourgeoisie in robes and wigs on their way to receiving aristocratic distinctions. Jacques de Laage was typical of this group.

24. Joseph Vivien (1657–1734), *Fénelon.* The archbishop of Cambrai inspired the political thinking
of the discreet liberal opposition led by the duc de
Bourgogne. A teacher, pacifist, and utopian,
Fénelon was the most original thinker of the latter
part of Louis XIV's reign.

25. French school, eighteenth century, *Cardinal
Louis-Antoine de Noailles.* His father was a duke and
peer, and his mother came from a family of financiers. Despite his stupid expression in this portrait,
he was the leader of the capital's crypto-Jansenists.
He died a virgin.

26. F. Stiemart, after H. Rigaud, *Cardinal André Hercule de Fleury,* 1728. Fleury
was from Langeudoc. He came from a family of modest though by no means impecunious financiers. After serving as Louis XV's tutor, he became prime minister.

27. Jean-Baptiste Martin, known as des Batailles (1659–1735), *Siege of Namur,* 1692. The victorious siege of Namur was the scene of Saint-Simon's baptism by fire at the age of seventeen. The command of the besieging forces was a prestigious assignment, but the king did not always choose competent leaders. Instead he relied on his son Monseigneur, his brother Monsieur, the son of le Grand Condé, and maréchal d'Humières. Louis XIV's natural son Toulouse was slightly wounded in the arm not far from the elevated site from which His Majesty observed the battle.

28. Studio of H. Rigaud, *The Duke of Berwick before Nice*, 1706. The natural son of a king of England, Berwick was a "Jacobite" who became a Frenchman. To Saint-Simon, for once indulgent, he was the very type of the "good bastard." He was a competent soldier and well regarded despite his "unfortunate" birth.

29. Hyacinthe Rigaud (1659–1743), *The Duc de Villars*. Villars was another of Saint-Simon's nemeses. Through Maintenon's favors and his own talents he gained promotion and waged war in Germany and Flanders as well as in the Cévennes and Savoy, sometimes successfully.

30. Jean-Pierre Franque (1774–1860), *The Duc de Vendôme*. Vendôme was a man whom Saint-Simon could not forgive for his relations with Louis XIV's son Monseigneur and his "pseudo-bastardy" (he was born legitimate but was descended from a bastard of Henri IV). A homosexual, he saved Louis XIV from disaster as commander of the French army in Spain. He was quite popular as well.

31. Jean-Baptiste Santerre, *Philippe d'Orléans, the Regent, and Mme de Parabère as Minerva*. Wearing the blue ribbon of the Saint-Esprit and a soldier's armor, Philippe d'Orléans is here depicted with attributes usually associated with royalty but in this case indicating only that he is regent. These are symbols of the sacred and military functions of the monarchy. Minerva tenderly embraces France's provisional ruler. The goddess of wisdom is of course a symbol of Philippe's political sagacity, but she also bears a strong resemblance to his mistress, the comtesse de Parabère.

32. French school, eighteenth century, *Philippe d'Orléans in his Study*. The regent, seated, is with a young boy, standing. Is this perhaps Philippe's son, the duc de Chartres?

33. Pierre Subleyras (1699–1749), *Anointment of Louis XV*. This ceremony, in which the king kneels devoutly, signified the way in which hierarchical society and the monarchy itself were steeped in the sacred. To believe Saint-Simon, whose account does not accord with the image presented here, "the disorder of the anointment is impossible to convey in words."

34. Antoine Watteau (1684–1721), *L'Enseigne de Gersaint*. Watteau was another contemporary of Saint-Simon, who was born earlier and died later than the great painter of the Regency. This masterpiece of masterpieces of the post–Louis XIV "thaw" show the portrait of the late king being packed away unceremoniously. Was this intentional? When an authoritarian regime crumbles, it is not uncommon for effigies of the "egocrat" to be crated and hauled away to storage. But *comparaison n'est pas raison.*

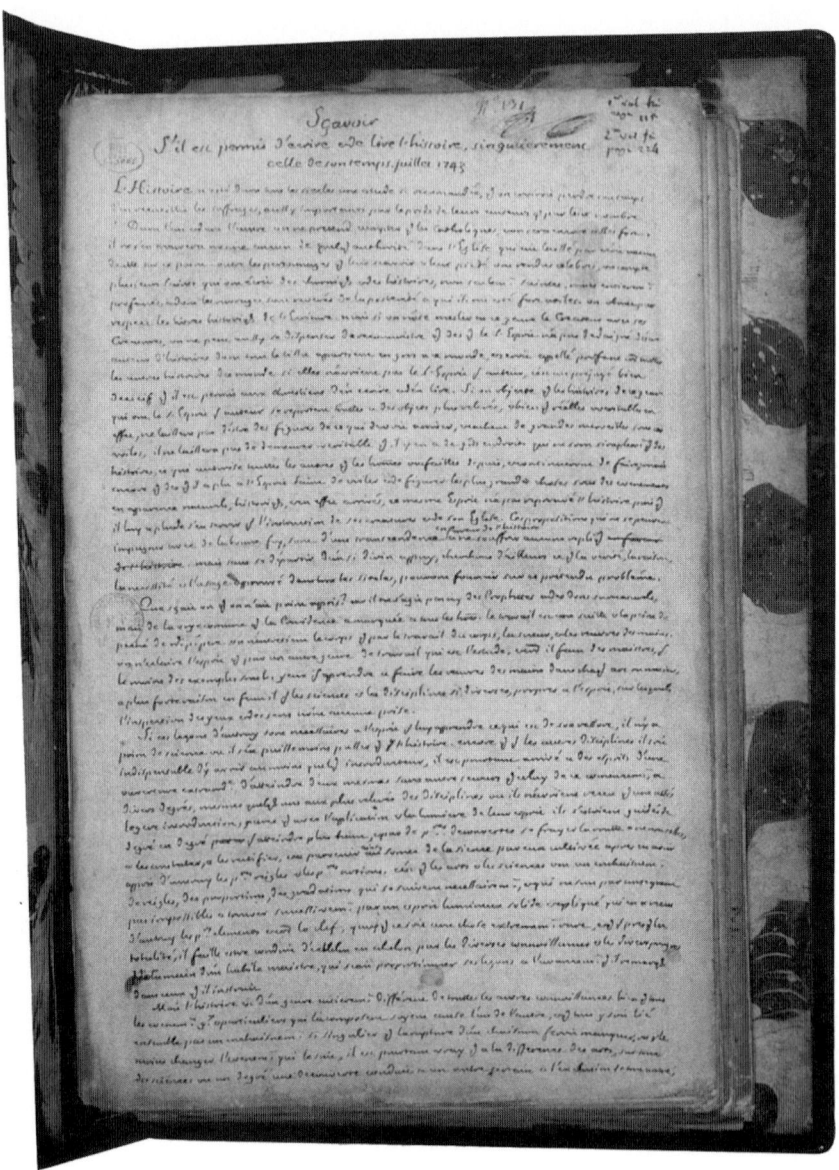

35. A manuscript page in Saint-Simon's hand. This extract contains a famous passage: "If reading and writing history are allowed. . ." Like the rest of the *Memoirs*, these few dozen lines are quite elaborate in style but show few signs of erasure, hence there must have been an earlier draft. "Is a Christian allowed to write history?" Yes, because the Holy Spirit expressed itself in part in historical style in sacred texts. And there were many other justifications for the "Christian historical" genre as well, at least if we believe Saint-Simon.

aspects, whereas the Jansenists were mainly concerned with death, or at any rate, with preparing for death through penance, austerity, and renunciation. Président Harlay captured the difference nicely in an insolent gibe: at a meeting with Jesuits he said, "How pleasant it is to live with you, my Fathers!" And then he turned to the Jansenist Oratorians who were also present and said, "How pleasant it is to die with you, my Fathers!"[152] Indeed, anyone who wished to die a good death was well advised to turn to the Oratorians after leading an agreeable life in obedience to the laxer standards of the Jesuits. Pro-Jesuit in life, pro-Jansenist in death: this rule was obeyed by Monsieur le Prince, Henri-Jules de Condé, son of the Grand Condé. On his deathbed, he dismissed his Jesuit confessor and turned to a Jansenist Oratorian, following the example of the prince de Conti and Mlle de Condé.[153] A few years later, the young duchesse de Bourgogne followed suit: sensing that death was near, she summoned a Recollect friar to replace the Jesuit who had previously filled the difficult role of confessor to a woman with numerous lovers. Her sister, the queen of Spain, did the same just before she died in 1714.[154] In this the two princesses were obedient to the custom of the house of Savoy from which they sprang: the dukes of Savoy were inveterate enemies of the Jesuits.[155]

To revert once more to Henri-Jules de Condé, Monsieur le Prince, it is true that he took his preparations for death farther than most. His grandfather before him had become convinced that he was a wild boar, but Henri-Jules, toward the end of his life, at about the same time that he changed confessors, was seized by the conviction that he was already dead. He therefore began taking his meals in an underground cell, which he believed to be the home of M. de Turenne.[156] Still convinced that he was dead, he took other meals in the company of guests who, playing along with the macabre fantasy, pretended to be dead themselves while heartily devouring the food that the prince placed before them. During these strange dinners, the conversation revolved around the hereafter. The prince's physician, Dr. Finot, who was also Saint-Simon's doctor, nearly split his sides with laughter when he recounted these bizarre banquets to the duke, who savored every detail. The important point here is that the Jansenist ideas that Monsieur le Prince embraced in the final months of his life were informed by a culture of death, a culture that he shared with others of sounder mind than he appears to have been. In contrast, the Jesuits proposed a culture of life, a culture of the Faustian world of the living—and not just those living in high society. Why not cite a line of Goethe in homage to the Good Fathers: "Green is life's golden bough" *(Und grün des Lebens goldner Baum)*.[157]

The Jesuits' appealing verdure left Saint-Simon rather cold, and it would be easy to conclude from the continual anti-Jesuit gibes in the

Memoirs that his hostility to the "Ignatians" was unadulterated. But that would be an exaggeration. In fact, his attitude was rather moderate, and oddly similar to his attitude toward the Huguenots. Was there a connection? Saint-Simon despised everything about the Revocation of the Edict of Nantes. But during the Regency, when an opportunity arose to annul it, to revoke the Revocation, as it were, and invite France's Protestant émigrés to return, he took a very cautious line. By contrast, the regent, Philippe d'Orléans, was inflamed: he wanted to act immediately to undo the blunder, or rather the crime, of Louis XIV by opening the door to the departed Calvinists. Saint-Simon kept his cool: "If you recall the Protestants," he said in substance to Philippe d'Orléans, "you run the risk of rekindling the Wars of Religion that so disfigured the sixteenth century. And if you do that, you will also revive the Catholic League." Thus the Huguenots were twice stigmatized: first for what they were in themselves and second for the ultra-Catholic forces—the Jesuits and the League—that they called into existence to destroy them. Saint-Simon could not abide what he regarded as fanaticism in reverse: he disliked both the "heresy" of the Protestants and the fiery antiheresy of the League and the Jesuits. He hated the "heretics" for provoking the viciousness of their persecutors. Yet the (left-wing) enemies of his (extreme right-wing) enemies did not thereby become his friends: in hindsight, and in a purely platonic way, he simply pitied them for what they had suffered in the time of Louis XIV, long before any thought of revoking the Revocation arose. When the opportunity came to do something about that injustice during the Regency, Saint-Simon waffled.

As for his attitude toward the Jesuits as such, independent of their relation to the Huguenots, his reasoning was similar but at the other end of the political-religious spectrum. Our author disliked the Jesuits; at times he even hated them. Yet one day the duc de Noailles came to see him and out of the blue proposed that the Society of Jesus be dissolved (eventually this did happen, but not until 1762). All Saint-Simon could do was throw up his hands. He pointed out that the Jesuits were doing important work in France—teaching in the secondary schools most notably—and that there was no one to replace them. Saint-Simon liked to carp, but from a distance. When he actually had a chance, or a possible chance, to do something for the Huguenots or against the Jesuits, he hesitated, though verbally his criticism remained as sharp as ever.

Who, according to Saint-Simon and other critics, were the enemies of the Jesuits? And who were their supporters? Here we must deal with factions and even cabals. Foremost among those unfriendly if not downright hostile to the Society of Jesus were the great bishops of the Gallican generation, that is, the generation that joined the Assembly of the Clergy in 1682 and supported the Revocation three years later. Among them were Bossuet, born in 1627; Cardinal de Coislin, born in 1630; Cardinal de Bonzi, archbishop of Narbonne, born in 1631, who for a long time reigned supreme in Languedoc and even at court; and Le Tellier, the archbishop of Reims and brother of Louvois, born in 1642. Cardinal d'Estrées (born in 1628) and Cardinal Janson (born in 1630) might also have played a role in the discreet battle against the Jesuits, but both were elderly courtiers and Janson was in bad health.[158] Bonzi and Le Tellier were handicapped, moreover, by illicit relationships with women, Bonzi with the comtesse de Ganges, who was married to the king's lieutenant in Languedoc, and Le Tellier with his niece, the marquise de Créquy. Among the younger adversaries of the Society were the virtuous Cardinal de Noailles, archbishop of Paris, born in 1651, who eventually became the Jesuits' favorite target. Oratorians regardless of age were of course pro-Jansenist and therefore strongly opposed to the Society, as were Jansenist theologians such as Quesnel, himself an Oratorian. As for laypersons associated with Port-Royal and therefore allergic to "Jesu-itry," there was the great jurist d'Aguesseau; Chancellor Pontchartrain (senior) of the Maintenon cabal; Madame la Duchesse and her half-sister Conti, royal bastards associated with the Monseigneur cabal and both highly "Jesuitophobic"; the maréchal de Bezons, an associate of the duc d'Orléans; and finally, in the Bourgogne cabal, Torcy (a Colbert) with his "aroma" of Jansenism and, later, Saint-Simon and his wife, as well as the duchesse de Bourgogne herself, a Savoyard by birth and therefore no fellow traveler of the Good Fathers.

Let us turn now to another "sodality," the one that backed the Jesuits. If we take a microscope to the *milieu parlementaire*, which in theory was Gallican, not to say Jansenist, in outlook, we nevertheless find a number of prominent lay backers of the Society. They include Harlay, the "old monkey" who ultimately bequeathed his library to the Jesuits; Lamoi-gnon, one of whose offspring, Basville, as an *intendant de généralité* and uncrowned monarch in Languedoc, was frequently a zealous enemy of Protestants as well as a tenacious adversary of Cardinal Bonzi, whom he managed after numerous intrigues to have disgraced; and the Chauvelins, who in a subsequent generation gave a minister to Louis XV.

Shifting our attention now from Parlement to the court cabals, we find that the most ardent pro-Jesuits at court belonged to the very Bour-gogne cabal of which the Jesuit-hater Saint-Simon was also an active member. As a result, he was never entirely at ease with other members of the group, whose dynamic pro-Jesuit wing included Père Tellier, the king's redoubtable confessor, along with Colbert's nephews, the duc de Chevreuse and the duc de Beauvillier. They were in clandestine contact with Fénelon, who, from exile in his archbishopric of Cambrai, remained as anti-Bossuet and antiabsolutist as ever. Fénelon, for his part, was delighted by the duc de Bourgogne's quiet but intense affection for him, and in Rome he could count on the support of Cardinal de Bouillon, another pro-Jesuit. (Note in passing that the Good Fathers produced few bishops. When a Jesuit became a bishop, as in the case of Lafitau, the brother of a celebrated ethnographer, the Society continued to rely on his services but no longer counted him as one of their own.) Other pro-Jesuits in the Bourgogne faction included the elderly duc de Lauzun, Saint-Simon's brother-in-law, whose nephew Belzunce, his uncle's pride and joy, was bishop of Marseille. Like Lauzun, Belzunce soon became a hero, although in a different way: when plague struck the city in 1720, he courageously cared for the sick. But he was also an outspoken proponent of the highly Jesuitical *Unigenitus*. There were also diplomatic connections: one of them developed toward the end of the Wars of the League of Augsburg between state councilor Crécy and a writer by the name of Callères, the former with ties to the Jesuits and the latter to the duc de Chevreuse.

We come now to the dominant cabal of Mme de Maintenon—dominant because the group's central figure was secretly married to the Sun King. Here Jesuit influence was perhaps not as strong, or at any rate not as direct, as it was in the milieu that included the Bourgogne cabal, Fénelon, Chevreuse, and Beauvillier—the Jesuit faction par excellence. Nevertheless, the Society enjoyed considerable support in the Maintenon camp, which wielded enormous power, not to say omnipotence. For one thing, their influence here gave them access to Louis XIV, a king who at times claimed to prefer atheists to Jansenists, whom he accused of constituting a "republican party within church and state." Louis had always been a strong Gallican, but at some point he changed. To be sure, he never became an ultramontane, but he was to some extent "boxed in" by his wife and, of course, Père Tellier. Over time, His Majesty made many concessions to the Good Fathers. There were even charges, ridiculous to be sure, that he belonged to a clandestine third order somehow linked to the Society of Jesus—in effect, the Sun King himself was accused of being a Jesuit. Although this slander was without foundation, it indicates that the king was perceived as an ideological sympathizer of the Good Fathers. This perception was not entirely wrong: the king's role in the inception of *Unigenitus* is evidence of a certain anti-Jansenist, hence pro-Jesuit, stance.[159]

Although the king's wife and "cabal leader," Mme de Maintenon, was somewhat suspicious of the Jesuits, she nevertheless entered into an "objective" alliance with them. Her beloved ward, the duc du Maine, was a devotee. Crucially, she joined the Jesuits in their anti-Jansenist crusade, working through common influential friends. Some of these held key "institutional" positions, such as the priests of the Missions Etrangères and the Sulpicians. Others were bishops devoted to both organizations and therefore allied with the Jesuits out of common interest if not genuine affection: Godet des Marais and Bissy, the latter aided by La Chétardie, the curé of the parish of Saint-Sulpice. Both of these bishops were younger than Bossuet and Le Tellier. They were also less cultivated, less erudite, less prestigious, and less talented than those two illustrious prelates so typical of the period of the Revocation (which preceded the years of Saint-Simon's maturity). But Godet and Bisset, assisted by the Jesuit royal confessor, Père Tellier, contributed mightily to the recruitment of a new generation of repressive, *constitutionnaire* bishops loyal to Mme de Maintenon. These outspoken younger men ruled the church of France after 1713, the year in which *Unigenitus* was promulgated, and for that matter after 1730, the year in which the Jansenist *convulsionnaires* of Saint-Médard caused trouble in Paris. *Constitutionnaires* versus *convulsionnaires*: it was hardly a fair contest, in view of the fact that the *convulsionnaires* drew repression as surely as a lightning rod draws lightning. Generational issues likewise arose among laymen in Mme de Maintenon's entourage. Chancellor Pontchartrain, an eminent member of the group, was a Gallican and Jansenist sympathizer. His relations with the unofficial queen gradually deteriorated. By contrast, his son Jérôme, secretary of state for the navy, turned with the prevailing wind: he presented himself as pro-Jesuit and *constitutionnaire*, and this, along with the generational transition, greatly facilitated his relations with the "old lady."

Did Saint-Simon think it possible to be on good terms simultaneously with both the Jesuits and their renunciation-prone Jansenist adversaries? Perhaps it is worth mentioning a bizarre example of this with an admittedly humorous twist. The person involved was the abbé de Soubise, the son not (as Saint-Simon slanderously alleges) of a royal mistress but of a woman whom the king liked well and held in high esteem. The young abbé de Soubise, ironically described by Saint-Simon as a "marvel of knowledge and a miracle of piety," was indeed on the best of terms "with the [pro-Jansenist] Oratorians as well as with the Jesuits, with the Sorbonne and Père de La Tour [both pro-Jansenist], with Père de La Chaise [a Jesuit], and with the [pro-Jansenist] archbishop of Paris." One would be hard put to be more ecumenical.[160] Soubise was no bastard, but he was certainly a well-loved child, the darling, it seems, of all the cabals. This did not please Saint-Simon, who had no respect for the universally liked. In any event, Soubise steered a shrewd course between the Gallicans and the Ignatians and as his reward enjoyed a brilliant career, much of it in Strasbourg, where he succeeded his uncle as bishop. The palace of the Rohans in the Alsatian capital remains an enduring symbol of his success.

To return to the Jesuits: Did they pull strings behind the scenes, manipulating officials who basked in the limelight? Was all the world really a stage? Pushed to extremes, the idea was mad, paranoid, and it was not what Saint-Simon believed. He didn't believe it about the Spain of Philip V, where the king's confessor, Father Daubenton, was only the tip of an "Ignatian" iceberg.[161] Nor did he truly believe it about the Empire, where the Society of Jesus was hardly devoid of influence. Nor did he believe it about France or any other Catholic country except Savoy. In all these places, the followers of Loyola acted as "gatekeepers," to borrow a term from modern political science. They did not exercise power alone, nor did they have a major or even minor share in the exercise of power. To believe otherwise would be absurd, on a par with the paranoid delusion that France is run by the Masons or Italy by the Opus Dei. The Jesuits did, however, exert *indirect* influence through their gatekeeping role. By 1700, as Saint-Simon was well aware, they were in a position to shape the minds of at least a portion of the younger generation through their work as teachers. In the royal confessional they practiced another kind of pedagogy. They also influenced the nomination of bishops through the Tribunal of Penance and the Council of Conscience. If the Jansenists' subject was grace, one might say that the Jesuits' subject was *grâces*, or favors, be they royal, episcopal, or what have you. They were also, to put it anachronistically, masters of the media by virtue of their skill in exploiting the holy pulpit. In this they were not without competition, however: there were non-Jesuit preachers of the first rank, such as Bishop Massillon, an Oratorian. But many Jesuits distinguished themselves at the pulpit, including Père Bourdaloue, one Ignatian whom Saint-Simon genuinely liked. The power of the Jesuits was thus indirect: they made suggestions, they educated people, they exerted influence, they obtained appointments (if possible to the highest offices) for friends and sympathizers (witness the nominations of bishops that followed the promulgation of *Unigenitus*). Last but not least, there was the threat of regicide, about which they theorized and which some people accused them of actually making. This may have had a dissuasive effect on the royal conscience even if it remained merely theoretical.[162] Normally, the Jesuits did not enjoy sovereign decision-making power in any area. At times criticism therefore shifted its ground, and they were attacked, wildly, as mere manipulators, as meticulous as they were professional. In this respect, the rabid and abusive anti-Jesuit sentiment that later developed among freethinkers, where attitudes similar to Saint-Simon's were common, is reminiscent of the paranoid anti-Semitism of more recent times.

Malesherbes made this comparison as early as the end of the eighteenth century, and Léon Poliakov echoed him in the twentieth.[163]

We are now in a position to situate Saint-Simon within the broad crypto-Jansenist, anti-Jesuit current that ran through the Age of Enlightenment. In this respect, at least, our author was a man of his times. For Norbert Elias, Saint-Simon and the society of the court were precursors of modern sociability. In our introduction, we pointed out some weaknesses of this theory. But Saint-Simon was indeed a precursor of modernity in a sense quite different from that which Elias had in mind, namely, as a Jansenist sympathizer who discreetly and privately identified with the strong anti-Jesuit feeling that flourished for four or five decades under Louis XV, culminating in the dissolution of the Society of Jesus in 1762. This dissolution was in a sense a "revocation of the Revocation," which sounded the death knell for a certain type of clerical militancy. It was a long prelude ending in the Civil Constitution of the Clergy of 1790, which led to many further exclusions. Indeed, the "long" nineteenth century would be a time of tireless activity for countless "priest snuffers" and "devourers of Jesuits."

Had Saint-Simon lived to witness the first phase of this process, which culminated in the dissolution of 1762, he probably would not have approved of it or wished to see it proceed even though he did earlier acquiesce in temporary local bans on Jesuit activity imposed by Cardinal de Noailles in Paris and Victor Amadeus in Sicily.[164] Nevertheless, what happened in 1762 was the logical outcome of the kind of hostility toward the Fathers that the *Memoirs* exemplifies throughout, even if the author never in his wildest imagination dared raise the issue of an outright ban. Saint-Simon's constant apologies for renunciation, which came close to expressing a contempt for the world that he preached powerfully without fully or truly practicing, enlist him on the side of Enlightenment Jansenists who said "no" to the world of political and religious authority. Michel Antoine refers to the attitude of certain pro-Gallican or pro-Jansenist *parlementaires* as embodying a "Catharist" tendency. For the structures of absolutism, they felt nothing but undiscriminating distaste. And indeed, those structures would survive the dissolution of the Jesuit order by only a few dozen years before themselves succumbing to the hammer blows of 1789–93. Saint-Simon certainly would not have wanted this, and he would have despised the guillotine. Yet because of his obsessive hatred of the Jesuits, he was in his own quiet way an unwitting, unwilling accomplice and precursor of the urge to destroy. His frequent and ardent expressions of sympathy for the most aggressive gestures of renunciation, whether Port-Royalist or Quesnelian, tended in the same direction, even though he was only a moderate fringe supporter of the world-denying Jansenist tendency. As such he belonged to that uncomfortably situated middle-of-the-road group of "Jansenist sympathizers," a veritable "third party."

Among hard-core sectarians less sophisticated than our author, hostility to the world sometimes degenerated into what one might call Augustinian cretinism. The Jesuits, for their part, saw no reason to repudiate the ancien régime. On the contrary, they found fertile ground in absolutism and, following the lead of the royal confessor, Père Michel Tellier, they knew how to exploit it, though at times they permitted themselves to cast a sympathetic eye on the liberal reform projects that their discreet friend, or quasi-friend, Archbishop Fénelon cultivated in his secret garden.

After the Revocation and even more after the promulgation of *Unigenitus*, the Jesuits found themselves deeply implicated in the structures of the ancien régime. Yet they were not hard-core proponents of hierarchy. Paradoxically, the hierarchical society that the antiabsolutist Saint-Simon idolized was one of the cornerstones upon which Louis-XIV-style absolutism was built. Despite this, the absolutist regime, propelled by its own momentum, often turned against its aristocratic base, which it undermined, eroded, and subjected to the destructive effects of egalitarianism and social leveling. All of this reflected the somewhat suicidal logic of absolutism itself, which had a tendency to saw off the branches on which it sat perched (seigneurialism, aristocracy, hereditary rank).

Indeed, the legitimacy of aristocracy and monarchy depends on attaching a certain value to birth, on granting hereditary privileges to certain families at both the sovereign level and the level immediately below. "Birth precedes existence," as Yves Coirault once put it. This glorification of genetic invariability was of course sustained by a mythology wittingly or unwittingly constructed for the purpose. One's pedigree, inscribed in the social "herd-book,"[165] became a matter of honor, and without a concept of honor the old society would have forfeited all reason to exist or look to the future.

Between this ancien régime based on birth (as much the low birth of commoners as the high birth of kings) and the principles of Jesuitism, there was if not a contradiction then at least a divergence. To be sure, the Jesuits did not deny or underestimate the importance of being born if possible a prince or a duke. But they also attached considerable weight to *merit*, in part for purely theological reasons. And merit, at least a priori, was a nonhereditary value. It depended, first of all, on the performance of meritorious good works, legitimate products of the creative freedom peculiar to man. The theology of the Jesuit fathers, Lessius and Molina foremost among them, was unalterably opposed on this score to Augustinianism in all its forms: Jansenist, Calvinist, or Lutheran.[166] For Augustinians there were no good works but only divine grace. Good works, individual merit, and so-called free will were in their view mere fleeting reflections of that grace. The Jesuits also cultivated merit in another sense: in their schools, where young people were ranked in order of merit by their Jesuit teachers. Their written work was graded and recorded, and these grades were (in theory) independent of the student's birth. A student from the "lower classes" might outperform an "aristocrat." Finally, merit in a sociopolitical sense was something to which Enlightenment society increasingly attached value, even, and perhaps especially, within the reformed nobility of the age of Louis XV and Louis XVI, as Guy Chaussinand-Nogaret has shown.

Can we say that Saint-Simon unwittingly aligned himself with the protesting Jansenists, who disliked or perhaps even detested the world within which they were forced to operate? Leaving Saint-Simon behind, we suggested earlier that those same Jansenists were subsequently supplanted by Jacobins and sansculottes driven by an aversion to the old order.[167] In other words, these revolutionaries were driven by their rage against the world as it is, or was.

By contrast, the Jesuits, whom our duke indefatigably assailed, were meritorious for their insistence on . . . merit (begging the reader's indulgence for the play on words). True, their project was ultimately doomed to failure, since in the long run the ancien régime was condemned by history. That death sentence was carried out in 1792, but the absolutism to which it was applied had by then become fragile indeed. Still, the efforts of the Good Fathers in the schools were *meritorious* (to use that word again) insofar as they led to some of the eighteenth century's finest achievements in culture, government, and administration—and the century was by no means an underachiever in these areas.

part two

THE REGENCY SYSTEM

The Liberal Regency:

AUTUMN 1715 TO SUMMER 1718

7 *To this point, we have been trying to describe the court system as we find it in Saint-Simon, cabals and all. What we propose to do now is to describe the practical ramifications of that system in a critical period: the eight years of the Regency that followed the death of Louis XIV.* It is something of a misnomer to refer to the "court system" in this period, however, because the court collapsed when the government moved from Versailles to Paris. As it happens, fully a quarter of Saint-Simon's vast memoir is devoted to these eight years, during which his attention was focused primarily on Paris and only secondarily on Versailles.[1]

During the years in question (1715–1723), the writer was no longer simply a spectator (with one of the best seats in the house, to be sure). He was a key political player, a member of the regent's inner circle who played an active role in the decision-making process. Yet he was disconcerted by everything that was happening, a courtier without a court and therefore a fish out of water. Indeed, he was at times so bewildered by events that he simply lifted whole passages from Torcy's memoirs and included them in his own with only minor changes. In lending these borrowed passages the prestige of his signature, he behaved in a manner not unlike that of Marcel Duchamp or Picasso, who, by bestowing their signatures on found objects, turned them into "works of art."

If we are to understand what took place during the Regency, we will of course need to examine the machinations of the cabals, or what was left of them. To do this, we shall be obliged to grapple closely with the day-to-day events of the transitional period during which Philippe d'Orléans and his associates attempted to introduce certain reforms. Hence we cannot simply confine ourselves to deciphering Saint-Simon's statements as we did in looking at the Versailles years (1692–1715), when our man was still only a "voyeur." Those statements must now be seen in relation to the actions of the government (and political faction) to which the *petit duc* belonged between his fortieth and forty-eighth years.[2] This will be our task in the remainder of this volume.

For a long time, the history of the Regency was distorted by a peculiar moralistic and anti-English bias. Saint-Simon himself more than once succumbed to both prejudices. He criticized Dubois behind his back for having sacrificed the fortifications at Mardyck (near Dunkirk) in order to remain on good terms with England.[3] This charge would subsequently be repeated ad nauseam by some of the finest historians of the Regency, including the eminent Dom Leclercq.[4] Today the issue seems pointless. We no longer believe in Maginot Lines, and anti-British sentiment is no longer in season despite the vagaries of the "Entente Cordiale," most recently in the negotiations over the European Union.[5]

Furthermore, Saint-Simon's homilies about the "turpitudes" of the regent's private life, echoed by historians such as Lémontey and Leclercq, now fill countless volumes (some of which corroborate Saint-Simon's reports with evidence of their own).[6] To be sure, times have changed since 1714, when it was proposed that the duc d'Orléans be subjected to "civil excommunication" for allegedly attempting to poison the royal family.[7] But the change failed to deter André Ranson from writing a "private life" of the regent that featured a chapter entitled "Seraglio." Nor did it discourage Albert Meyrac, the editor-in-chief of the *Petit Ardennais*, from publishing a book entitled *The Regent, His Girls, His Mistresses, and the Lovely Ladies of the Regency* in a series of "Indiscreet and Amorous Chronicles of the Past" put out by Albin Michel. Screeds of this ilk have bestowed legendary status on the women who had the good fortune to please Philippe d'Orléans, including Madame's erstwhile maid of honor Mlle Séry, who became Mme d'Argenton; Mme de Parabère,[8] the daughter of a member of the queen's honor guard; Mme de Falari, a duchess with a papal title; Mme de Sabran, a spirited lady descended from a cadet branch of the house of Foix; and various others. Some writers have gone so far as to create categories for classifying the regent's numerous amours:[9] thus we have the early mistresses (little Léonore, la Grandval), the *grandes maîtresses* (Charlotte Desmares, Mlle Florence, Mme d'Argenton,[10] Mme de Parabère, Mme de Sabran, Mme d'Averne), a transitional mistress (Mlle Houël), and a last mistress (Mme de Falari). Yet even the author who dreamed up this elaborate typology concedes that the ladies in question "dominated the man without dominating the prince."[11]

As recently as a generation or two ago, tales of such escapades could still arouse virtuous indignation, but today such a reaction would seem quaint. Our era has no license to give moral instruction to the past, nor do we like to think of ourselves as lesson givers.

Nevertheless, the Regency remains interesting as a case study in political science. Granted, the French ancien régime was radically different from any of the regimes that have presumed to exert their power over people in the century just past. Then as now, however, political systems have had to deal with the problem of transition.[12] The questions we wish to raise are these: How does a state exit from a rigid, tightly controlled, authoritarian system in conflict with both its neighbors and its own people?[13] Under such circumstances, what kind of transition can maintain continuity while lessening or eliminating the intolerable stress caused by the regime? (Such continuity may of course be deemed more desirable by the rulers than by the ruled.) If peaceful transition fails and the tensions associated with political change are not reduced, violent alternatives are possible: a costly, prolonged period of unrest, civil war, or revolution leading to the destruction of the regime and its replacement by another.

The Regency cleverly managed to avoid these pitfalls. At relatively low cost, it succeeded in reviving not just a political system but a social and economic system that had been worn down by Louis XIV's costly and aggressive policies.[14] The Regency also launched an extended period of economic expansion. The reign of Louis XV, which it inaugurated, was to be one of France's most illustrious periods of growth.[15] Hence there is ample reason for historians of the ancien régime to revisit the three thousand days of Philippe d'Orléans (September 1715–December 1723) in a dispassionate, nonmoralistic way, with an empathic, even sympathetic, eye. In this second part of our volume, we will of course be continuing our commentary on Saint-Simon's *Memoirs*, but we will also be looking at texts by Buvat, Barbier, and Dangeau;[16] at the impressive oeuvre of Dom Leclercq; and at more recent histories, among which the work of J. H. Shennan is worthy of special mention,[17] along with the excellent recent overview by Jean-Christian Petitfils.

But first, in the spirit of Saint-Simon's own critique, we need to say a few words about the state of the kingdom in the summer and autumn of 1715, in the months just before and just after the death of Louis XIV. To be sure, peace had been restored in 1713 and 1714 by the treaties of Utrecht, Rastatt, Baden, and so on. But relations with neighboring countries (Spain excepted) remained bitter. That bitterness was the consequence of eighty years of war, both hot and cold, during which the state's primary, indeed consuming, preoccupation was to maintain its troops in the field. France's relations with England and other Protestant countries were strained because of the unavowed but at times overt French support for the Jacobite restoration, support so obvious that, as Saint-Simon rightly observed, the death of Louis XIV was one of the greatest misfortunes to befall the Stuart pretender (the would-be James III).[18] Although the Low Countries were at peace with the Bourbon kingdom, they nevertheless undertook to fortify the frontier as permitted under the Treaty of Antwerp. Suspicions ran high.

Philip V's "neo-Bourbon" Spain remained France's only important ally, but Philip turned out to be a difficult friend. On the banks of the Seine he was popular among reactionaries and bigots, whose loyalty the regent was never able to secure.[19] Despite the renunciations of Utrecht, the king of Spain clung to the hope that he might accede to the throne of France if Louis XV died young, even though such an eventuality would very likely have provoked a new European conflict. France, all but ruined in 1712, could hardly have afforded such a catastrophe. Other destabilizing factors included Spain's claims on vast portions of the Italian peninsula and islands and the Empire's designs on the throne in Madrid, which might have led to a war between Spain and the Empire that could easily have engulfed France as well.

Domestically, the king's death had left the country's elites fragmented and frustrated. In the past fragmentation had meant weakness. In the future frustration might lead to rebellion. Parlement, held in check since the Fronde and Colbert, had been kept on a short leash until 1715 by its *premier président*, who took his orders from the court and the Maine-Maintenon faction. In 1714 and 1715, Parlement had registered without protest various edicts declaring royal bastards full-fledged princes of the blood eligible to succeed to the crown. On 11 August 1715, however, a first sign of disobedience manifested itself: speaking through *procureur général* d'Aguesseau, the *parlementaires* flatly refused to register the anti-Jansenist constitution *Unigenitus*.[20] And the old king was not yet even dead.

Would this incident of outright resistance drain the abscess? The Jansenists, an active and pious minority, were until 1715 virtual outlaws within the church of France, but their situation was not as dire as that of the Protestants, driven out by the Revocation. The Jansenist faction enjoyed many friends among the regular and secular clergy. Among its other potential allies were the parlements of Paris and the provinces, the Sorbonne, and at court, part of the powerful Noailles clan. Cardinal Louis-Antoine de Noailles, archbishop of Paris, took a rather indulgent view of Augustinian theology. As we have seen, he could claim the loyalty of educated people "of good faith" in the episcopacy, the university, the religious orders, the chapters, the Parisian and provincial clergy, the parlements, and, more generally, "all laymen who were not slaves of the Jesuits."[21] The cardinal's nephew, the young duke Adrien de Noailles,

who through his wife had ties to Mme de Maintenon, gradually transferred his loyalty from the waning *camarilla* of la Patronne to the waxing
cabal of Philippe d'Orléans. And the duke's brothers-in-law, Guiche and
Estrées, held important posts in the war and navy departments. Finally,
the duke's sister was the daughter-in-law of d'Antin, the legitimate half-
brother of Louis XIV's bastards and one of the subtlest courtiers of his day.

At court, the reformist, pacifist aristocratic party of the duc de Bourgogne (whose friends included Fénelon, Beauvillier, Chevreuse, and
Saint-Simon) more or less evaporated when most of its leading figures
passed away. The "cabal" was thus marginalized, but not entirely. Certain
of its members had served as ministers, either officially (as in the case of
Beauvillier) or unofficially (as in the case of Chevreuse). Beauvillier's
ideas lived on in his disciple Saint-Simon. A loyal and trusted friend of
the duc d'Orléans, the memoirist was enlisted as a political advisor even
before 1715. Orléans, for his part, revered the theories of Fénelon, which
had brought the two men together. Not without courage, Philippe had
never concealed his admiration for the Swan of Cambrai and let it be
known that if he became regent his first dispatch would recall Fénelon
to his side and involve him in all the government's business.[22] Unfortunately, Fénelon died too soon, in 1715.

The second cabal, that of Monseigneur, the Lorrains, and the Bourbon-
Condés, broke up when le Grand Dauphin died. But some of its former members or "offspring" (such as d'Antin and young Louis de Bourbon, known as Monsieur le Duc) waited until the moment was right to
join the ultimately victorious group of Philippe d'Orléans.

We come now to the dominant cabal of the end of the Great Reign,
that of Mme de Maintenon and the duc du Maine. This was the group
that stood to lose the most when Louis XIV died. Composed of *grands
seigneurs* who were often though not always inept (the Villeroys, Harcourt, Huxelles), this group depended on the Sun King's wife and principal bastard (Maintenon and Maine) as well on as certain ministers (Voysin
and at one time the Phélypeaux clan), not to mention Desmarets, an
errant atom that split off from the Colbert molecule to go its own way, or
to put it another way, a brutal rogue vizier, a surly animal who abandoned
Beauvillier and Chevreuse to further his own ambitions. Saint-Simon
would later find it difficult to forgive Desmarets for his ingratitude.[23]
Real power did not lie with the *grands seigneurs,* so the cabal needed the
support of ministers who held the crucial levers in their hands: Pontchartrain, La Vrillière, Voysin, Desmarets, and so on. Along with other officials such as *maîtres des requêtes, conseillers d'Etat,* intendants, and financiers,
it was the ministers to whom the substance of power belonged. Apart
from Voysin, those ministers belonged to the great families of mandarin-
bureaucrats (the elder and younger Ponchartrain and La Vrillière were

members of the Phélypeaux clan, and Desmarets and Torcy were Colberts, Torcy having been closer earlier to the Bourgogne cabal).

On the outermost fringes of the system, finally, was Philippe d'Orléans, who did not hesitate to reduce his isolation by surrounding himself with men of great talent such as Law and Dubois and even Saint-Simon, whose genius, it must be said, was more literary than political. As a friend of the regent, Saint-Simon found it easy to imagine himself in the role of advisor to the prince or unofficial prime minister, inventor of polysynody, and defender of the rights of the nobility. But Philippe never granted him the importance that Saint-Simon ascribed to himself.[24]

The Jesuits, for their part, were eager to insinuate themselves into the enchanted circles of power, to gain access to the centers where the key decisions were made. Yet even though they manipulated many important people, their influence remained peripheral, though not at all marginal. Mme de Maintenon, though ambivalent toward them, relied on them when necessary.[25] In her nostrils, the Sulpicians and priests of the Missions Etrangères had more of the odor of sanctity about them than did the disciples of Loyola.[26]

In the end, the national consensus, such as it was, seemed shaken but not shattered by the king's death. Contrary to legend, the crowd did not jeer as Louis XIV's coffin wended its way through the streets. In 1715, the kingdom of France numbered some twenty-one or twenty-two million subjects, if one left out the countless subjects of discontent—to borrow a famous quip.[27] To be sure, the horrors of 1709–1710 were just a memory. In those years, war, cold, famine, and epidemic had conspired to make it seem as if France were literally on her last legs.[28] But since then, the peace of Utrecht (1713) had bolstered an economic recovery whose origins dated back as far as 1711. Salt consumption rose to levels that were still low, to be sure, but significantly higher than they had been during the "great winter" crisis of 1709–10; notarial documents tell a similar tale. Yet vast tracts of farmland still went unused in 1715, land that had only recently been abandoned as a result of economic distress and depopulation. As comptroller general of finance and friend to bondholders, Desmarets had imposed a harsh anti-inflationary policy that triggered a round of deflation. In 1715, he increased the precious metal content of the livre tournois to the high level of 1666–89, thereby raising its value 43.2 percent compared with the low value to which it had sunk in the spring of 1709. While this "recovery program" was attractive to the state and to creditors, it was hard on many people in debt: deflation only added to their burden (whereas Law's plan, adopted later, would decrease it, as we shall see). In short, there were as usual plenty of serious reasons for frustration, and if a crisis of the elite had been joined to a rebellion of the masses, or a portion of the masses, the result might have been as catastrophic as earlier regencies or "vice-governances" had been (think of the 1560s, the 1640s, and even the 1610s).[29] But nothing of the sort happened between 1715 and 1723.

Of course in 1715, the factors that had led to the disorders of 1560–95, 1610–30, and 1643–53 had all but vanished. Thanks to Louis XIV, the *grands seigneurs* and Protestants had been brought to heel, and centralism had progressed. But just how smooth was the sailing for Philippe d'Orléans at the beginning of his regency? Success was by no means assured, as is evident from an anxious passage in Saint-Simon's *Memoirs* on the regent's "assumption of power."[30] The death of the Sun King had brought hordes of flatterers and self-promoters to Orléans's door. They packed his apartment so tightly that it was impossible to slip a dagger between bodies. The new regent's old friends did not loiter in the rear, either. Saint-Simon hastened to Philippe's side to remind him of his promise not to tolerate Parlement's callous treatment of the ducal party. These early consultations were decisive in sealing the fate of the late king's ministers (such as Pontchartrain and Desmarets).

Demands were made and purges proposed. Would the system hold up? Looking forward or backward in time would not necessarily incline one to optimism on this point. Indeed, at the next succession, when Louis XVI ascended to the throne in 1774, things began well enough (with the war in America), but before long the new king had to face the crises of the 1780s and the disasters of 1789–93. When all is said and done, the fact remains that the only fully successful royal succession in the whole period from 1559 to 1789, a full 230 years, was that led by Philippe d'Orléans, the nephew of Louis XIV, from 1715 to 1723. The regent and his associates must therefore have hit on some very clever strategies. What course did they follow? How did they seek to assure Louis XV a happy youth and a maturity that, if not devoid of disaster, at least skirted the irrevocable?

This is not the place for yet another portrait of the regent. Many have tried to paint the man, with varying degrees of success.[31] Saint-Simon, ordinarily so stingy with praise, ascribed numerous gifts to his eminent friend, among which we might mention good taste, a fine memory, eloquence, and deep insight. Saint-Simon particularly liked Philippe's description of Henri IV: even the good king's faults were appealing, to hear the regent tell it, and Henri was by nature so easygoing that he "made a vice of the supreme virtue of forgiving his enemies." As for the regent's government, if Orléans himself was highly gifted, Law and Dubois were even more so, Saint-Simon to the contrary notwithstanding. Indeed, for the *petit duc*, Dubois was the epitome of all the vices that noisily vied for supremacy within his puny frame.[32] But surely the abbé deserves better than this, even if Madame condemned him in no less vitriolic terms (he reminded the Princess Palatine of a fox about to pounce on its prey). The regent's assessment was more accurate: "The abbé has more intelligence, I have more courage." Such was Orléans's judgment of his former tutor, who eventually became his prime minister. It is worth noting that until recently most portraits of Dubois drew heavily on Saint-Simon's biased diatribes.[33] One sees this in the otherwise excellent work of Dom Leclercq, whose portrait of the abbé might have been lifted straight from the *Memoirs*, including even the famous characterization of the minister as a bird of prey. Yet Leclercq does not cite Saint-Simon as a source in this instance.[34] Here, in any case, we will try to judge the intelligence and virtues of statesmen according to their performance in government.

By force of habit, habituation to force, and the blessing of a long reign, Louis XIV governed with the implicit support of the country's elites, many elements of which he had in any case relegated to the sidelines. Content to share in the profits of the system, segments of the elite, most notably the *grands seigneurs*, allowed government ministers to do as they pleased.[35] Philippe d'Orléans, whose power was new and therefore fragile, was initially obliged to seek the support and assistance of elite groups. He needed, to some degree at least, to broaden the consensus. To that end, he had first to secure the backing of leaders of the more active and influential groups and second to obtain, at a minimum, the passive consent of the middle and even lower classes. By looking at the way he handled the Jansenist issue, we can gain a better understanding of how he went about this.

The regent and his advisors hoped to secure, if not the support of the Jansenists, then at least their benevolent neutrality. By so doing, they also hoped to obtain a measure of support from the parlements and their allies, the archbishop of Paris, the Sorbonne, and the many pro-Augustinian curés.[36] In contrast to Louis XIV, who, confident of his power, had persecuted, repressed, destroyed, and at times crushed his adversaries, Philippe intended to woo the latent opposition, win its support, and disarm any threat. He made up his mind early but felt no need to make his decision public immediately. It was essentially a political decision: the regent was a skeptic with little interest in dogmatic refinements and subtleties.

Broadly speaking, Orléans's view was that by opposing the (pro-Jesuit) Constitution, he could secure the support of the parlements. On the other hand, the Jansenist party was weaker than the Jesuit party and suffered from the serious drawback of harboring "republican" tendencies. This fear of "republicanism" accounts for certain later reversals of policy, but to Philippe the overwhelming fact was the power of the Jesuits (who were of course *constitutionnaires*, that is, supporters of *Unigenitus*).[37] He therefore listened closely to the advice of *parlementaires*, academics, Parisian curés, Sorbonne theologians, and even mendicant monks, many of whom looked favorably on Jansenism.[38] The Augustinian party (toward which Saint-Simon was well disposed, as we have seen) had other things going for it as well. In particular, it was hostile to the Huguenots—in which respect it paradoxically resembled its Jesuit adversaries. It thus represented heterodoxy within orthodoxy—no small advantage. It allowed its adepts, who remained within the Roman Catholic Church, to taste the joys of nonconformism without running the risk of either total exclusion or dogmatic bigotry ("No salvation outside the Church").[39]

We have already alluded to the fierce hostility provoked by promulgation of *Unigenitus* in September 1713. Backed by the Jesuit Tellier, Louis XIV's confessor,[40] the papal bull was challenged in Parlement by the *procureur général* d'Aguesseau. Among other consequences, the debate before the high court led to the disgrace of Cardinal de Noailles (1714).[41] Had the king's death not intervened, the Parisian prelate would have been "de-cardinalized."[42] But he remained, a pro-Jansenist cardinal in the capital, and his presence there served as an essential rallying point for reviving the opposition to the absolute monarchy when the king died. What a contrast with an earlier time, when one of Noailles's predecessors, Hardouin de Péréfixe (1605–71), had galvanized the anti-Jansenist crusade in Paris.[43] What is more, the Augustinian-led opposition extended beyond the limits of the capital. Of 123 French dioceses, 106 received *Unigenitus*, but six contrived not to publish it. Six or seven others hedged their bets and refused to pledge total support. Orléans was a shrewd politician, and in 1714 and 1715 he tried to gauge the strength of the Jansenist movement, which he saw as a possible ally, powerful to be sure but also potentially compromising. Even before the death of Louis XIV, he saw d'Aguesseau, Joly de Fleury, and Abbé Pucelle but kept these meetings quiet. Influential *parlementaires* as well as convinced Augustinians, these men might well prove invaluable to him. Philippe thought of enlisting them against the duc du Maine and his henchmen, and in this he was supported by Saint-Simon, who saw this policy as a way to promote the healthier, better-educated, more pious elements in both the clergy and the laity.[44]

Shortly after the king's death, early in September 1715, the regent summoned Cardinal de Noailles, embraced him, and talked with him privately for half an hour. Philippe then rushed off to Paris without even waiting for his guards. There he saw d'Aguesseau, the "eagle" of Parlement. These two men, representing the Augustinian and *parlementaire* opposition, were to serve as heavy artillery in the regent's strategy. What was on Philippe's mind, obviously, was a crucial meeting of Parlement scheduled for the next day. Further steps toward liberalization or "détente" were soon taken. Isoré, the archbishop of Tours, and

Noailles's brother, the bishop of Châlons, were granted authorization to visit Paris, authorization that had previously been withheld.[45] Four or five priests with similar views, along with Abbé Servien, an elderly priest with "Italian tastes" (that is, a homosexual), were released from the Bastille.[46] On 2 December 1715, a majority of the Faculty of Theology in Paris voted to retract the approval of *Unigenitus* it had granted while Louis XIV was still alive.[47] In August 1716, Noailles felt bold enough to forbid Jesuits to preach or hear confession in his Paris diocese.[48] This was a major setback for the Good Fathers, and cost them dearly in terms of revenue, all the more so when the ban was extended to other dioceses, mainly in the north (Châlons, Metz, Verdun) but also in the south (Montpellier, on orders of Bishop Colbert, a hard-core Augustinian).[49] In the west, the universities of Rouen and Nantes took positions against Archbishop de Mailly, an outspoken pro-Jesuit.

In February 1717, Chancellor Voysin, an erstwhile *créature* of Mme de Maintenon, died, and in retrospect this event may be seen as marking the apogee of the Jansenist or pro-Jansenist party.[50] D'Aguesseau, whose Augustinian and quasi-democratic passions were quite strong, immediately became chancellor.[51] Joly de Fleury, who shared d'Aguesseau's religious views and who in the last days of the old king had displayed real courage in the affairs surrounding the Constitution, replaced him as *procureur général*, to the dismay of the Jesuits.[52] As late as 1717, Saint-Simon seems to have been able to influence the regent to take action against the Jesuits.[53]

The Jesuits, meanwhile, did not remain on the sidelines. The "conformist," or at any rate episcopal, majority within the church of France did not like the ideas of Jansenius any more now than in the past. In October 1715, the Assembly of the Clergy, still in the grip of the hysteria that followed the death of Louis XIV, reaffirmed its opposition to the Augustinian theses of Quesnel. In Marseille, Bishop Belzunce, soon to distinguish himself in action against the black plague, took up cudgels on behalf of the Constitution. A pet pupil of Père Tellier, the saint from Marseille was—if we believe the malicious gossip of people like Saint-Simon—a blend of evangelical morals, personal heroism, and crass ignorance.[54] "Reactionary" polemics spattered mud everywhere, even on the regent: one Jesuit preacher delivered a sermon in which he characterized Philippe as a "small man puffed up with pride, as unworthy as he is uninformed, who nevertheless lords it over religion and the state."[55] On Toussaint 1716, Père de la Ferté, a Jesuit from a ducal family, preached in the presence of the child king.[56] He exhorted Louis XV to follow the lead of his great-grandfather Louis XIV in the fight against Jansenism. This stirred up the anti-Jesuits, including Saint-Simon. A few small pro-Jesuit confraternities had apparently been organized in the army's Soissonnais regiment.[57] Pope Clement XI, said to be a "prisoner of Cardinal Fabroni, who had a hold on him, and of a handful of Jesuits," was obliged to encourage these developments.[58] According to Saint-Simon, the regent, a skeptic indifferent to theological disputation, wanted nothing so much as to impose a "respectful silence" on both sides. As "the middle ground between absolute authority and total liberty," the Regency presumably should have preferred a middle-of-the-road solution, but the disciples of Saint Ignatius strongly opposed any sort of compromise.[59]

In any case, the pendulum of Orléanist policy soon began to swing to the "right." In January 1718, Chancellor d'Aguesseau, who had been keeper of the seals for little more than a year, was sacked.[60] He was replaced by the pro-Jesuit d'Argenson, a slithery creature with a keen sense of which way the wind was blowing.[61] To be sure, d'Aguesseau's fall had nothing to do with religious conflict. It came about because the former chancellor, along with the duc de Noailles and an obliging Parlement, had organized behind-the-scenes opposition to John Law's new financial system. The Jesuits nevertheless realized that they had scored an important victory: to celebrate the pro-Jansenist chancellor's disgrace, they gave their pupils a day off from school (thus setting an unfortunate precedent that has frequently been imitated in France ever since).[62] Even as d'Aguesseau was forced out as chancellor, the duc de Noailles was dismissed from the Ministry of Finance, and d'Argenson assumed the responsibilities of both men.[63] Law and Dubois also profited from the change. The Jansenist party, meanwhile, suffered a hard blow with the defeat of its natural leaders d'Aguesseau and Cardinal de Noailles (the sacked duke's uncle). To be sure, the fortunes of the Jansenists under Philippe never sank as low as they had under Louis XIV with the bull *Vineam Domini* of 1705, the constitution *Unigenitus* of 1713, and the destruction of Port-Royal-des-Champs in 1709.[64] Nevertheless, Augustinians would soon face difficult times once again, with the impending close of the liberal Regency and an end to the tolerant treatment that had been accorded to friends of the Jansenists for the previous two years or more. Philippe d'Orléans's brief honeymoon with Augustinianism thus came to an end. The relationship did not end in divorce, however. In this respect, the intransigent Sun King was indeed dead and buried, along with his extreme anti-Jansenist and anti-Protestant predilections. After 1718, it was no longer a bed of roses for the Jansenists, but neither was it the hell on earth of Louis XIV–era repression—not even purgatory by comparison.

The tenuous, instrumental character of the regent's temporary benevolence toward Jansenism (1715–17) is easier to understand if one recalls that the Regency, though far more liberal in its first few years than the Sun King ever was, was still quite cautious when it came to dealing with

Calvinism. True, several dozen Huguenot galley slaves were freed in 1715, but arrests of Protestants resumed in the Cévennes in 1717, even if the repression was less harsh than it had been in the time of the "Great Monarch." Philippe briefly considered inviting fugitive Protestants to return home, but Saint-Simon, despite his principled opposition to the Revocation, talked him out of electing so "dangerous" a course. The regent, though motivated by humanitarian concerns, was well aware of the economic losses that the persecution of the Huguenots had entailed for France and her government. Saint-Simon, more lucid perhaps than was his wont in such matters, also detected a desire on Philippe's part to make a conciliatory gesture toward the liberal, Protestant, capitalist maritime powers of the north: England and Holland. But the writer believed that the Protestants would form a state within a state and that they were "only partly" subjects of the Most Christian King. Their "republic," or self-government, constituted a society apart that could potentially threaten the monarchy from within. Saint-Simon's possibly paranoid view was that the Huguenots' return would make them "the arbiters of France's conduct and masters of her fate both at home and abroad."[65] The Regency manifested a certain discomfort with the policies of the previous regime, but it continued to pull the heavy anti-Protestant machine bequeathed it by Louis XIV. Philippe's policy was more flexible than Louis's, but there were certain obstacles it could not overcome: it could neither revoke the Revocation nor give Jansenism free rein. Some things are not negotiable, or to put it more accurately, cannot be gotten around. For several decades to come, the Revocation would remain the "unsurpassable horizon" of the ancien régime.

As for the Jansenist question, which we discussed earlier, for those who knew the world of politics it immediately raised the problem of the parlements. True to the traditions of the robe, the parlements of the provinces and especially the Parlement of Paris harbored Augustinian inclinations.[66] They were also bulwarks of power and wellsprings of legitimacy—again, this was especially true of the Parlement of Paris. For instance, when Louis XIII wished to set forth the conditions under which he hoped France would be governed by a regent after his death, he summoned the princes of the blood, the leading nobles, the officers of the crown, and delegates of Parlement to appear before him in his chamber and in the presence of the King's Council.[67] Acting through *procureurs du roi* and *substituts du procureur général* scattered throughout countless *bailliages*, the Parlement of Paris had a finger in the affairs of a third of France (the northern third). To a far greater extent than is the case today, the judicial power was one of the fundamental pillars of the state, all the more so in view of its authority to promulgate statutes and even to exercise a form of police power (through the aforementioned *substituts*).[68]

For a man like Philippe d'Orléans, who did not enjoy the benefit of either a preexisting consensus or a charismatic authority comparable to that which had become routinized or customary under Louis XIV, the parlements were thus a force to be contended with, flattered, and even for a time admitted into the highest councils of government.

Of course, Saint-Simon despised and at times reviled the high magistrates of Parlement who dared to pose as rivals to dukes like himself. Rather foolishly, he dismissed them as besmirched by their common origins. He rejected the vast judicial organism's claim to rank first among the *corps* that constituted French society. Indeed, he went so far as to relegate the *robins* of Parlement to the third estate, alongside those crass commoners whom the magistrates pretended to rise above. By contrast, the magistrates saw themselves as an authentically noble *corps* situated above all three orders. In particular, Saint-Simon challenged the notion of some *robins* that the French Parlement was somehow the equivalent of the English Parliament, a representative body or Estates General authorized to speak for the entire realm. The duke rightly insisted that Parlement was a court of justice, not a representative body. Whatever his reasons may have been, Saint-Simon was right to emphasize the crucial difference between the English Parliament, the ancestor of all of today's national assemblies and houses of representatives, and the French Parlement of the time, whose brief was in theory simply to decide à la Brid'oison who had the better case, Maître Pierre or Maître Jacques.[69]

In keeping with this analysis, Saint-Simon would have preferred that Philippe not ask Parlement, which was in effect a kind of supreme court, to proclaim his regency. To perform that office the *petit duc* would have turned instead to an assembly of peers and high crown officers.[70] But Orléans was more politic than his whimsical advisor. He knew full well that he could not do without the stamp of legitimacy that Parlement bestowed not only on his regency but also on the new king. During the celebrated September 1715 session of Parlement that immediately followed the death of the Sun King, Philippe obtained full recognition of his regency by a vote of the magistrates.[71] The dukes added a picturesque note to the session by initiating proceedings to secure recognition of their rights in the so-called Affaire du Bonnet (though the episode was probably less dramatic than Saint-Simon maintains). In any event, Orléans managed on this occasion to strip his archrival, the duc du Maine, of the formidable military powers he previously possessed. All his wishes were fulfilled, therefore, and he found himself in sole command of the ship of state.

The regent might well have congratulated himself, moreover, on not having taken some additional advice of Saint-Simon's, namely, that he convoke the Estates General.[72] In Saint-Simon's mind, the Estates were associated with what he believed to be the state's impending bankruptcy, and his plan was to convoke the Estates in order to blame them for the "burden of extremely cruel and despicable remedies" that would eventually have to be imposed. In his view, "most people" would rather see the state go bankrupt than accept a hefty tax increase and would pay no attention to the misery and protest caused by this brutal but necessary expedient.[73] Law, on the other hand, opposed allowing the state to declare bankruptcy. To do so, he argued, would plunge many of the king's subjects into ruin, undermine commerce and industry, and revive a subsistence economy in agriculture.[74] In fact, to have convoked the Estates General, or assembly of the three orders, would have been to tempt fate with a plunge into the unknown. This is clear, of course, from what happened in 1789, though it is true that the Estates General of that year marked a legitimate transition to a new liberal, and indeed democratic, order, whose difficult inception would be completed in the nineteenth and twentieth centuries. Philippe's goal, however, was to make the monarchical administration more efficient, not to destroy it. Saint-Simon, goaded by vexation with Parlement, was proposing a leap into the unknown and thus courting revolution, which Philippe, wedded to the art of the possible, "wisely" refused to consider.[75]

Another index of Orléans's concern with the parlements was the composition of the new councils. During the first three years of the Regency, the business of government was conducted by a series of councils under a regime that came to be known as "polysynody." Saint-Simon and other members of the Bourgogne cabal had proposed such a council-centered organization of government even before Louis XIV's death. This group of "intellectuals" (to use an anachronistic term) and others hoped to strengthen the hand of the great lords and other aristocrats by seeing to it that they occupied key positions on any new councils. At the same time they sought to undermine the authority and silence the pretensions of the secretaries of state, who, under the five previous reigns, had been the real repositories of power, which they had used to exercise a harsh tyranny over even the noblest aristocrats in the realm of public affairs.[76] Paradoxically, however, Philippe used the new councils as a way of wooing *parlementaires*, a tactical maneuver that had probably never occurred to Saint-Simon.

In September 1715, in fact, Orléans officially granted Parlement the right of remonstrance, that is, the right to challenge authority by protesting directly to the king.[77] This marked a sharp departure from the policy of Louis XIV, who had allowed that right to fall more or less into abeyance after 1667. In the long run, the regent's concession on this point may have been dangerous. In the short run, however, it proved advantageous to His Royal Highness, alias Philippe. In any case, the new councils were filled largely with *parlementaires* and other *robins*. D'Agues-seau joined the Council of Conscience, on which he was replaced in 1717 by Joly de Fleury, who shared his pro-Jansenist views; Pucelle joined later. Together they reinforced Cardinal de Noailles and the Grand Vicar Dorsanne, thus marking the revenge of the Augustinians.[78] To sweeten the victory, the Jesuit Tellier and the papal nuncio Bentivoglio, both strong proponents of *Unigenitus*, were expelled from Paris.[79] For good measure, Saint-Simon recommended locking up a few very active Jesuits in the hope that they might die quietly in prison, but he also took the precaution of depriving them of all writing materials. In a spirit of Christian charity, however, our duke, generous with small favors, indicated that the prisoners should be treated well and fed decently. Philippe meanwhile limited himself to less visible but no less coercive measures against the Good Fathers.[80]

Consider, by way of illustration, the new Inner Council (Conseil du Dedans) under polysynody. D'Antin, its chair, presided over a group that included, in addition to the inevitable courtiers, two *maîtres des requêtes* (representing the *robe du Conseil*) and three *conseillers* from Parlement (representing the *robe de la magistrature*). The Finance Council was chaired by Noailles; Villeroy, whose dullness was no secret, was "head of the council."[81] But in a further concession to the *robins*, the membership also included four state councilors, three *maîtres des requêtes*, and two *présidents* of Parlement. In practice, "difficulties of rank" poisoned the atmosphere of the councils even before they had met: it was state councilors versus *gens de qualité*, ecclesiastics versus laymen, dukes versus *gens de qualité*, and Saint-Simon versus everyone.

In fact, it soon became apparent that these favors to Parlement were mere eyewash, as the diminished role of the councils became obvious to all. Nevertheless, for a time both the regent and Parlement worked hard to maintain courteous relations. In May 1716, for example, Parlement opposed a plan to revive a number of quasi-ministerial *surintendances* to be filled by Torcy and d'Antin (the grounds for this opposition were partly financial, partly political). It was a complicated affair, but Parlement made a number of tactical retreats that paved the way for a resolution. Then, in August 1716, Parlement insisted that it had the right to precede the regent in the annual Assumption procession. Conflict was averted, however, when the regent decided at the last minute not to participate. Piety, after all, was not his cup of tea. It was not difficult to persuade him that there was little point in sacrificing a pleasant evening's diversion to this religious ceremony.[82]

The latent divisions that had been developing within the high nobility became manifest in 1716–17. Broadly speaking, there were three groups. The *parlementaires* and princes of the blood, temporarily allied, enjoyed

the favors of the regent, as we have seen. The legitimized bastards (demagogically) sought the support of the nonducal nobility, which was tired
of being snubbed by the dukes and peers. And finally, the dukes and
peers had long been embroiled with Parlement in the so-called Affaire
du Bonnet. Ever since the 1640s, but especially since 1680,[83] the peers
had been obliged to suffer the tortures of martyrdom whenever they attended a session of Parlement: when the *premier président* asked for their
opinion or called upon them to vote, he did not remove his *bonnet*. But
since 1694, it had become customary for him to lift his headpiece (without
quite removing it) when asking for the votes of Louis XIV's legitimized
bastards. Such "hidebound" concerns about priority may well elicit little
more than snickers today, but one has to admire the perverse craftiness
of the magistrates. It will come as no surprise that Saint-Simon and other
dukes seethed with impotent rage at the low blow the *premiers présidents*
managed to administer by the simple expedient of tipping their hats.[84]
In so doing, they asserted their superiority over the dukes and peers while
at the same time cleverly paying court to Louis XIV. Their gesture indicated that they ranked the royal bastards between the princes of the blood
and the dukes, which naturally gladdened the heart of the elderly king.
They redefined the cascade of contempt to suit themselves, so that it
ran now from king to princes of the blood to legitimized bastards to
parlementaires and finally to dukes and peers. The magistrates' willingness
to tip their hats to some and not to others carried with it a whole series
of exquisitely subtle implications. Paradoxically, however, this expression
of contempt for the dukes in a way undermined the whole elaborately
tiered *Stufenkosmos* of the ancien régime.

As early as September 1715 and again in January 1716, the dukes
clashed with Parlement over this practice. They were egged on by an
outraged Saint-Simon, who saw this as the battle of a lifetime—and who
may have used up some of the political credit he enjoyed in the early
months of the Regency by virtue of being an old friend of the duc d'Orléans.[85] In the end, the dukes were cut down to size. Raising a ruckus
about the *bonnet* earned them chiefly the sarcastic gibes of pro-Parlement
pamphleteers, who charged (rightly) that some of the dukes' ancestors
had been bailiffs, butchers, fishmongers, apothecaries, servants, adven-
turers, bastards, and pimps. Elderly Madame, never one to take matters
of hierarchy lightly, went them one better: most of the dukes, she
claimed, were just barely nobles.[86] Saint-Simon, whose military record
was undistinguished, got his—richly deserved—comeuppance. Despite
the fact that the pamphlets in question were inspired by the *parlementaire*
nobility, one senses in them a whiff of egalitarianism that would not have
been out of place in 1789. By then, the intestine battles among the four

or five different segments of the nobility—robe, sword, court, service, and recently ennobled—had done more to undermine the second order than any hostility from the common herd. (It has been the misfortune of the "right" in France always to be divided.) Let us not get ahead of ourselves, however. In May 1716, following a series of bitter episodes, the Regency Council decided to defer decision on the matter of the *bonnet* "until it shall please the king after attaining his majority."[87] This was a victory for Parlement, whose support Philippe still hoped to secure. For the dukes it was a debacle. The regent had indeed promised to support them after the death of Louis XIV, but that was before he recognized the political necessity of appeasing the *robins*, to which he applied himself with the pragmatism of the Orléans family. The earlier promises seemed binding only to those to whom they had been made, not to Philippe who made them. In another sign of antiaristocratic bourgeois solidarity, moreover, the dukes' own notaries refused to forward their protests against this decision (in June 1716).

So for the time being, that was the end of the matter. The dukes had lost. What about the bastards? The Edict of Marly (1714) had granted them and their male offspring the full prerogatives of princes of the blood in perpetuity.[88] In addition, if no other princes of the blood remained alive, the bastards were now entitled to accede to the throne. As one might imagine, this decision caused tears to be shed and teeth to be gnashed. Many people—princes of the blood, dukes and peers, *parlementaires*, ordinary *robins*, and the regent himself—had already accepted the idea that government was, if not democratic, then at least subject to a contract between the king and his people. These representatives of the elite believed, as an edict of July 1717 put it, "that the French nation has the incontestable right to *choose* for itself a king [from among the members of a particular family] if in time it should come to pass that the race of *legitimate* princes of the house of Bourbon has expired."[89] More prosaically, the house of Condé, represented by such legitimate princes of the blood as Monsieur le Duc (Bourbon-Condé), the comte de Charolais, and the prince de Conti, did not wish to allow any bastards, even legitimized ones, to usurp a status that rightfully belonged to others. If such a thing were to happen, Saint-Simon believed, it would undermine not only law and order in France but all laws, divine as well as human.[90] "Real" princes looked upon these "nouveau" or "pseudo" princes as usurpers and refused to concede that they had any right to succeed to the crown, no matter how hypothetical or remote the possibility. On top of all this was a not very savory dispute over an inheritance that saw Monsieur le Duc and his mother Madame la Duchesse pitted against the duchesse du Maine, who was married to a royal bastard. At stake was the legacy of the previous Monsieur le Duc (who died in 1710, leaving his son and wife to do battle with the wife of the duc du Maine over his inheritance).

In August 1716 and June 1717, the Condés and Contis submitted their brief against the legitimized bastards to the king and Parlement (which was delighted to have been chosen as arbiter in the matter). The substance of their case was that the royal bastards had no right to pose as princes of the blood or succeed to the crown. The bastards defended their position vigorously, but the moment was ill chosen. They were obliged to do battle on several fronts: the princes of the blood enjoyed the behind-the-scenes support of Parlement and the regent—a difficult trio to beat. They also had to contend with the dukes and peers, who were not only disappointed by the outcome of the Affaire du Bonnet but even more annoyed by the emergence of the bastards as an intermediate rank between themselves and the princes of the blood.[91] This development effectively downgraded the peers by a notch. Here, then, was a golden opportunity for Saint-Simon to indulge his mania for hierarchical distinctions:

> As for M. le duc d'Orléans, I spoke to him forcefully about the princes of the blood and the peers versus the bastards. I reminded him of everything he himself had said during the old king's lifetime about their various apotheoses, given that the late king had deified them by degrees, and I did not let him forget the horrors that the duc du Maine had invented about him and tirelessly spread.[92]

Worried by this formidable array of enemies, the duchesse du Maine, who was no fool, sought other allies for the bastards' cause. The dukes wanted a share of the royal power, but so did nobles of lower rank, and the duchess's idea was to enlist the latter against the former. The "rank-and-file" nobles chafed at the pretensions of the dukes and peers, who insisted that they should take precedence over all "non-dukes" in the second order (mere *gentilshommes*). Saint-Simon was under no illusion when it came to human stupidity (except his own), and he believed that fatuousness was no less frequent among dukes than among their untitled inferiors.[93] In 1716 and again in 1717, Maine goaded the lesser nobles into action. With superb and laudable audacity they uttered the dangerous phrase "Estates General," which they argued must be convoked so that the nation might freely air its views on the rules governing succession to the crown. In the opposing—and more powerful—camp, Philippe was backed by Parlement and the princes of the blood (Condé and Conti). He was thus able to drive a wedge between the two wings of the nobility (dukes and non-dukes) while availing himself of the backing of both a service elite (Parlement) and the princes of the blood. The divisions that existed within the nobility weakened the noble order generally, even those segments of it that wished to "de-absolutize" the monarchy. "Divide and conquer" might well have been the motto of the house of Orléans.

What is more, Philippe managed to keep the ship of state afloat with a remarkable economy of means. A royal edict of July 1717 did away with the rank that the bastards had obtained only a few years earlier (in 1714), denying them the right to accede to the throne. Parlement voted to register this edict by a healthy majority of 133 votes to 73. The summer of 1717 may thus be taken as the high-water mark of Parlement's power. Although the magistrates were flattered and courted on all sides, they never really seized control of either the situation or the nation. The three-way split in the top echelons of the elite was thus reaffirmed, but it was to prove short-lived.

For the time being, however, the dominant group, whose unity would soon begin to fray, still consisted primarily of magistrates of Parlement, princes of the blood (Condé and Conti), and the regent himself, banded together in fraternal solidarity. To his great advantage, Philippe remained in control of the administrative apparatus and of the provincial machinery of government, because the office of *intendant de généralité* had not been abolished at the end of 1715 when the councils were set up, despite Saint-Simon's express wish that it be eliminated.[94] To be sure, the provisional suppression of the post of secretary of state had to a degree curtailed the centralization of government in Paris (at Saint-Simon's behest, or so he says in the *Memoirs*),[95] but centralism flourished nonetheless in the provinces, where the intendants served as representatives of the king in each *généralité*. One way or another, centralism—that French perennial—survived.

So much for the dominant group. The other two groups—the dukes and peers on the one hand and the bastards backed by segments of the newly restive non-ducal nobility on the other—clashed with the *cabale philippienne* over such "fundamental" issues as the *bonnet* and the question of bastardy (fundamental, that is, in the eyes of Saint-Simon). As we have seen, however, these two groups were at odds with each other over the proper rank to be accorded to the royal bastards. This consumed most of their energy, and the regent took advantage of this to secure a degree of consensus in the highest echelons of the elite, whose representatives he enticed into his government through the councils. Everyone had seats: dukes and peers, bastards, and *parlementaires*.[96] The time was one of progress coupled with reaction: progress because power was no longer concentrated in the hands of the king and the "technocrats" as it had been before 1715, reaction because the bluest of blue bloods now shared in decision-making power through the councils (and with the advantage of hindsight, we can now say that this was not the group that most adequately embodied the future of French society). In any case, Philippe was able to weaken the aristocratic elite by capitalizing on its internal divisions. With considerable tactical skill, he was thus able to exercise a power that Louis XIV had managed to wield through force of habit, indeed at times through force *tout court*.

Another source of consensus was the "old court," where, moreover, we find many of the same people. There, from 1700 to 1715, those who would become Philippe d'Orléans's most implacable enemies gathered around the duc du Maine and Mme de Maintenon. For years, the old court had had two focal points: the two eldest generations of the royal family. At the center of one group were the king and his wife, along with the bastards Maine and Toulouse, a number of military leaders, and the old and not-so-old court aristocracy (Harcourt, Beringhen, Huxelles, Villars, the leading Lorrains, Villeroy, La Rochefoucauld, La Rocheguyon, and Noailles). Noailles, incidentally, anticipated the impending end of the reign of Louis XIV and quietly and rather adroitly moved closer to Philippe and his own uncle, Cardinal de Noailles. The second royal generation (Monseigneur, son of Louis XIV, and his mistress Mlle Choin) formed the nucleus of a group that gathered in Meudon, a group notable for the presence of the two Lorraine princesses and d'Antin, the legitimate son of Mme de Montespan and half-brother of the royal bastards. The group was also allied with the house of Bourbon through Madame la Duchesse, Monseigneur's great friend and half-sister and the mother of the younger Monsieur le Duc, who was to play a considerable role in the Regency and an even greater role later on. This second cabal had broken up in 1711, when Monseigneur died. Certain of its leading figures, including the Lorraine princesses and d'Antin, then joined the dominant party of Maine and Maintenon.

After 1715, this bedlam of cabals in disarray, this welter of bickering nobles, came to be known in both Saint-Simon's *Memoirs* and the common parlance of the time as "the old court." The fact of the matter is that the ideological differences between, say, a d'Antin and a Villeroy were not sufficient to justify a divorce for very long. As early as 1712, it became possible for some old differences to be patched up, and of course after 1715, a broader reconciliation became possible. It was this reconciliation that created what became "the old court," whose position vis-à-vis the Regency was in some ways one of discreet opposition and in other ways one of de facto complicity.

As the visible portion of what was left of the old Monseigneur cabal, the house of Condé benefited from the fact that the heir to the title of Monsieur le Duc was still a young man (born in 1692). The new head of the Condé line was a man free of prior commitments, and after 1715 he openly displayed his allegiance to the rising star of the Palais-Royal, Philippe d'Orléans. For several years, Monsieur le Duc thus became an eager (if at times impatient and occasionally imbecilic) epigone of the new regent.[97] He was a stubborn and brutal man without the least spark of wit, uneducated and unintelligent, and driven by ambition, as well as by his mistress, the redoubtable Mme de Prye. His primary goal was always to benefit himself, and he worked hard to achieve it.[98]

We come finally to what had been the third cabal, that of Beauvillier-Fénelon, which from 1700 to 1712 had been linked to the youngest generation of the royal family, that of the duc de Bourgogne. Fénelon, Chevreuse, Beauvillier, and other members of this group had at times been audacious reformers, but one by one they succumbed to old age and poor health. Because they departed the scene even before the Sun King, all that remained of their ideas and their intrigues was what they had been able to pass on to younger men such as Charost, Chaulnes, and Belle-Isle, who had yet to come into their own. Only one surviving member of the cabal, a man with a powerful but eccentric personality—none other than Saint-Simon himself—joined the group around the duc d'Orléans, to whom he confided his ideas and his frustrations. The regent took note of the latter while rejecting the former with smiles and polite thanks. Always prodigal with projects and advice, Saint-Simon spent himself for the sake of the Regency; ultimately his influence evaporated. People began to think of him as a tiresome bore.

More complex than the other cabals, the Bourgogne group had included reformers with a variety of different aspirations. Some wished to go back to some imaginary primitive constitution, a "liberal-feudal" regime. Others, more or less outspoken progressives, hoped to move forward. But all, from Saint-Simon to Saint-Pierre, criticized the power of the ministries and the encroachments of the bureaucracy.[99] From this group the diversity of the aristocratic reaction is evident: some (such as Fénelon and Saint-Simon) called for a vaguely representative system, while others (such as Boulainvilliers and, again, Saint-Simon) were nostalgic for the noble prerogatives of an earlier era.[100] Some of the Bourgignons were proud of the fact that certain of their views were echoed by critics from the lesser nobility such as Vauban,[101] whose central project was to rationalize the state apparatus by subjecting nobles to a general tax. Toward the end of the reign of Louis XIV, a variety of critical voices converged to question the monarch's "absolute" power and urge the involvement of "great" and perhaps "not so great" nobles in affairs of state.[102]

Had Philippe been true to the traditional logic of the court system whereby cabals organized around successive generations of the royal family, he would have organized a cabal of his own intimates. Had he done so, the regent's faction might have been known as the "Palais-Royal cabal" (after his princely residence, just as Monseigneur's cabal was also known as the cabal of Meudon and Maintenon's cabal as the cabal of Versailles). But to have followed such a course would have been pure folly, for Orléans was surrounded at best by dubious allies. His wife, the duchesse d'Orléans, was a woman of monstrous pride, even when seated on her commode. Although her marriage to the duke was somewhat, shall we say, theoretical, her husband's behavior annoyed her. She could not abide the thought that the rank of other royal bastards might be diminished, because, as a bastard herself, their rank, controversial though it might be, was also hers. Hence she sided with Maine.[103] Saint-Simon, who served his friend Orléans as a close and even confidential advisor during the first few weeks of the Regency, had ceased to be taken seriously as a source of counsel (a mistake, perhaps). More recent arrivals in the regent's camp, such as the duc de Noailles, could not be counted on. So shrewd an operator was not to be trusted. As Louis XIV lay dying, young Noailles had made contacts left and right, determined to be on the winning side no matter how things turned out.[104] Philippe's son Chartres was a lout who crudely emulated his father's debauchery.[105] Roués such as Canillac and Nocé, the regent's comrades in carousing and lechery, were of little use.[106] Orléans' mother, Madame, haughty and arrogant, rarely left her apartment, where she penned interminable letters, pored over genealogies of the Counts Palatine, and cultivated or wept for her august relations as their rank required (in much the same way as other aristocratic women tailored the length of their mourning veils to the rank of the deceased). She wrote several letters a week to her kin, some of whom she scarcely knew.[107] Effiat and the chevalier de Lorraine, old friends of the regent's father, Monsieur, were in disgrace on account of their supposed vices and crimes, hence they figured prominently among the enemies of Saint-Simon, who accused them of poisoning Monsieur's first wife, Henriette d'Angleterre.[108] Chirac, Philippe's physician, was an intelligent but insolent man who killed more than his share of patients, not always by accident.[109] To whom could the regent turn?

To be sure, Orléans was assisted by two men of remarkable talent, and possibly genius. Abbé Dubois had been Philippe's preceptor and in a way served as his father. The regent rode Dubois hard but admired his intelligence—and feared its authority.[110] John Law of Scotland met the duc d'Orléans in 1715. Law was a man with brilliant insight into financial matters. His ideas went beyond funding the budget and restoring public confidence in the exchequer. Indeed, he was far ahead of his time, for France in those days and for many years thereafter still made a fetish of metallic coin. Saint-Simon found Law to be an inspiring teacher even if the *grand seigneur*'s contempt for economic matters led him to decline the chairmanship of the Finance Council. Despite Law's incomprehensible French and irremediable anglicisms, the *petit duc* had to admit that he had learned or imbibed from the Scotsman a great deal about the conduct of financial affairs, a sometimes difficult and always abstract branch of knowledge.[111]

At first, however, Philippe's grasp of the reins of government was as tenuous as it was new, or perhaps tenuous because it was new. He needed to consolidate his grip, and neither Law nor Dubois was in a position to help. Only later would they acquire the means to govern. In the fall of 1715, the regent dismissed a small number of aides as a sort of homeopathic remedy. By sacrificing a few scapegoats he hoped to disarm the opposition that lurked within the old government. Desmarets, though quite capable, was ingloriously sacked from his post of comptroller general of finance.[112] Voysin, who played his hand more shrewdly, quit the Ministry of War but hung on as keeper of the seals.[113] The Phélypeaux clan (of the Pontchartrain, Maurepas, and La Vrillière branches) remained in their posts thanks to a bit of familial legerdemain proposed, apparently, by Saint-Simon and eagerly embraced by the beneficiaries.[114]

But the real flavor of the early Regency is to be sought elsewhere. A rather vague plan about governing through councils was put into practice. This marked the first time in the history of France that the idea of representative government was tried—even if it was only the aristocracy that was represented. One cannot but tip one's hat to these councils as precursors—rather farfetched, perhaps, but still precursors—of the liberal nobility's more serious experiments with representation in the 1780s. To be sure, the idea of "councils" had been discussed at the highest levels of government long before the eighteenth century. Saint-Simon tells us what was said about them in the later years of Louis XIV's reign. The elderly monarch brooked no dissent when it came to matters of scheduling, protocol, or speech.[115] But Fénelon, Chevreuse, Bourgogne, and Saint-Simon were the first to propose the use of councils as an instrument of reform, and thus a delegation of royal authority to the nobility if not to the nation. Orléans followed his friends' recommendation in this regard, but he studiously avoided taking the next step, namely, to decentralize government by shifting power to the provinces (in this his attitude was thoroughly French). The new councils, as Fénelon had conceived them long before, were intended to initiate certain fundamental changes. But under Philippe, who did not go in much for political theory, they became instruments of a short-term strategy. Subtle as this strategy was, it was also shortsighted and, in historical terms, small-bore.

For one thing, the men who created the councils generally avoided choosing aristocrats who were truly dedicated to reform, as Fénelon, Beauvillier, and Chevreuse had been. (The deaths of these three men within a few years of one another seemed to clear the way for a new generation of reformers, but the movement petered out.) On paper the new "polysynodic" councils wielded powers that had previously belonged to the secretaries of state and their staffs. As we saw earlier, some *parlementaires* gained appointment to the councils and as a result threw their weight behind the concept of polysynody. Paradoxically, however, other seats on the councils were awarded as sinecures to members of the old court, which was intrinsically hostile to the duc d'Orléans—old wine in new bladders, as it were. Those so honored warmed to the idea that they might wield more power than they had under Louis XIV. In the days of the Sun King, not even the most prominent courtiers could influence decisions except through the ministers (who, to be sure, often proved accommodating).

By the end of 1715, the composition of the councils revealed a great deal about the direction of the new government. In addition to the *parlementaires* and *robins* whom Orléans had appointed for their competence, their Jansenist connections, and their knowledge of the apparatus of justice and government, one also found the leading lights of the Maine-Maintenon and Monseigneur cabals, even though these same individuals had been so unpleasant to Philippe (and to Saint-Simon) during the "setting of the Sun." True, aristocrats of high rank had been appointed to the ministries (or their equivalents), much to Saint-Simon's delight. Magistrates and clerks had been obliged to make way for the bluest of blue bloods. Blue indeed: at the Ministry of Finance, for example, we find a duke, Adrien-Maurice de Noailles, whose support for Philippe was lukewarm at best, as would become apparent later on. Everyone knew of Noailles's old ties to the Maintenon clique. Pious under the old king and debauched under the new regent, he was clever at cloaking himself in the fashion of the hour—or the quarter-hour.[116] A more worthy appointment, to the Council of Conscience, was Cardinal de Noailles, the duke's friend and uncle.[117] The two men were drawn together not only by family ties but also perhaps by the cardinal's Jansenist inclinations. The war and foreign ministries maintained a special relationship with the Spanish ambassador, Cellamare. Portfolios went to several estimable old soldiers. Two of them, Huxelles and Villars, had been stars of the first magnitude in the old Maintenon group.[118] Toulouse, another of the Sun King's bastards, turned up at the Ministry of the Navy.[119] His illegitimate status in itself suggests that he had no great love for Orléans or, for that matter, Saint-Simon, even though the memoirist held him in such high esteem that at times he toned down his usual fulminations against bastardy for Toulouse's sake. The Inner Council included d'Antin, Beringhen, and Brancas,[120] which is to say, a trinity embodying the very essence of the old court, with the Monseigneur element represented by d'Antin and the Maintenon element by Beringhen, of course, and Brancas, who had served as Louis XIV's ambassador to Spain toward the end of his reign. The Regency Council itself quite simply embodied the *Almanach de Gotha* or *nomenklatura* of the old court and the old regime. There were the bastards Maine and Toulouse; the *grand seigneur* courtiers of old, such as Harcourt and Villeroy; Chancellor Voysin, who was an extreme hawk; those perennial ministers of the Phélypeaux clan (La Vrillière, Pontchartrain, and later, Maurepas); and finally the young duc de Bourbon-Condé, who was above all a "Bourbonist" and therefore, for the time being, an "Orléanist," but not to the manner born. The only Orléanists on this Upper Council (Bezons, a friend of the regent, Saint-Simon, Torcy, and Bishop Bouthillier) were either half-hearted in their support of the regent or lacked clout.[121] As for Law and Dubois, future stalwarts of "Philippism," neither yet held a seat on the Supreme Council.

The councils remained intact from 1715 to 1718, but as time went on, they were given less and less to do. From September 1715 to August 1716 the Regency Council met 165 times, but from October 1717 to September 1718 it met only 98 times.[122] In the fall of 1718, Orléans eliminated at least some of the councils and returned to a centralized system under Dubois.[123] Thus the liberal Regency came to an end and was replaced by the authoritarian Regency.

It would be a mistake, however, to think that Orléans had set up the councils only for show and to please the ideologues in his entourage (Saint-Simon among them) and that he had intended from the first to get rid of them when the moment was ripe. Philippe was always a pragmatist first and foremost, and in this instance he was no more Machiavellian than he was doctrinaire. When he took control of the state, he found the council proposal on his desk, where Saint-Simon had left it. He had nothing against the idea, but neither was he wildly in favor of it. He abolished the councils in 1718 as blithely as he had created them in 1715. They had been of some use, but eliminating them cost him nothing.

The last straw was perhaps the abbé de Saint-Pierre's clever attempt to use the councils for ideological purposes in 1718.[124] Long a fixture of the Palais-Royal, Saint-Pierre wanted to amend the recently established polysynodic system by introducing elections and bringing in bourgeois members. With remarkable prescience he dreamt of a semiconstitutional monarchy.[125] He would have abolished the sale of offices and primogeniture. *Horresco referens*, he would also have restricted the rank of duke to the marshals of France. Unlike his lukewarm admirer Saint-Simon, the abbé believed that dukes "without employment" could not point to any merit to justify their claims of rank and privilege.[126] Here, then, we see a shift from Philippe's pragmatic idea of polysynody to a fertile but "dangerous" set of new, almost democratic ideas systematically set forth by an ideologue of considerable talent. Saint-Pierre's book was condemned, and the author himself was expelled from the Académie. Soon thereafter, the councils were abolished. Their historical function had been accomplished: by restoring a semblance of power to the old court, they had disarmed the potential opposition to the regent and enabled Orléans to implement ambitious plans for the reform of French diplomacy and finance. Once these projects were under way and had obtained some measure of success and garnered the support of the elite and even the nation, Philippe was able to forgo the always dubious and now unnecessary backing of the old court. Or, to put it more precisely, he was now able to take the grudging support of the old court for granted and was no longer obliged to pay for it with anything more valuable than cash. There was no further need to share power with the polysynodic councils. Law's banknotes, judiciously distributed to nobles in need, such as Monsieur le Duc, his wife, and others, proved to be an adequate substitute for participation in the councils.[127]

Despite the innumerable ulterior motives of both sides, this temporary alliance between the regent and the old court personified by Villeroy occasioned few pangs of conscience in any of those involved.[128] Even before the old king died, Saint-Simon, despite his disinclination to compromise or to forgive the Maine-Maintenon and Monseigneur cabals for their sins, had proposed a coalition along just these lines, a papering over of the differences between Orléanist innovation and old court conservatism. The names that Saint-Simon proposed for appointment to the new councils (Villeroy, Toulouse, Villars, the two Noailles, Harcourt, Huxelles, and so on) were precisely those that Philippe eventually chose.[129] Orléans and Saint-Simon shared almost identical values, as did Harcourt and so many others. All believed in hierarchy and its rituals (which did not preclude religious skepticism in some or a cynical attitude toward government on the part of the regent). To one degree or another, all of these people were wary of the Jesuits and the bastards. They formed cabals and engaged in intrigues. They feathered their nests with fat dowries contributed by wives and daughters-in-law chosen if necessary from the worlds of the robe, the quill, or the bank—female hypergamy at work. On all these matters, there was such deep agreement that adversaries could afford to work together for a while before eventually going their separate ways; they never really came to blows. And so there was a certain blurring of the difference between the aristocratic liberalism of someone like Saint-Simon and the opportunistic groveling of someone like Villeroy.

By 1717 or 1718, then, the new regime had to contend with the kind of situation that is faced by any regency, any monarchical government in which the king is theoretically or practically speaking a minor (as had happened before under Catherine de Médicis, Marie de Médicis, and Anne of Austria) or (as would happen later with the accession of Louis XVI) a successor whose grip on the throne is tenuous. That situation was one of noble or aristocratic revolt. In some cases, this might take the form of armed combat (e.g., the early Wars of Religion, the disturbances that marked the early reign of Louis XIII, and of course the Fronde). Under more modern if not more clement conditions, however, noble revolt might instead take the no less dangerous form of political unrest, especially after the centralized monarchy of Louis XIV had crushed or at any rate diminished the power of the great feudal lords and militarist cliques. Louis XVI would experience the effects of such unrest in the 1780s. Philippe's regency fell midway between the two types of aristocratic protest: military revolt, which worked its terrible mischief for the last time during the Fronde, and political agitation, whose destabilizing consequences would be felt before and during the period known in France as the "pre-Revolution" and even during the early stages of the Revolution itself.

In confronting these twin dangers, that of the past and that of the future, Philippe moved first to quell the *political* challenge of the nobility. The ideological ammunition that the Enlightenment would supply to liberal nobles under Louis XVI was not yet available or still in short supply.[130] Under the Regency, enlightened thought still spoke with a stammering voice. In the *Memoirs*, Saint-Simon has only a condescending smile for Voltaire. What astonishes him is the idea that the son of his father's notary could have become "a sort of personage in the republic of letters."[131] The aristocratic political opposition to the regent's government was deeply divided, and the "Saint-Simonian" hierarchical pretensions of the dukes and peers earned the nobility nothing but ridicule.[132] Last but not least, the suspect patronage of the duc and duchesse du Maine left the aristocratic opposition sterile.

As for *military* opposition, efforts were made to establish an armed presence in Brittany in 1717 or 1718, where the local nobility was far more insistent and active than the Armorican clergy or third estate. Briefly abetted by the Parlement of Rennes, the Breton nobles attempted to challenge the legitimacy of certain taxes such as the *dixième* and the *capitation*, which in their eyes did away with the exemption from taxation to which the second order was entitled. What we have here, then, is a run-of-the-mill revolt of the privileged. The nobles sought to capitalize on the resentment that such taxes engendered even among impoverished commoners.[133]

To make matters worse, the Breton aristocracy set out to secure the assistance of foreign allies, namely, the Spanish. In addition, the governor of Brittany, Maréchal de Montesquiou, an old fogy for whom discipline was nothing to be trifled with, exhibited a haughtiness and contempt that alienated the population and helped fan the flames of rebellion.[134] Yet a national conflagration was somehow averted. A suspect alliance did spring up between the Parlements of Rennes and Paris, however, when relations between the regent and the Paris magistrates began to turn sour.

I n the first few years of his regency, then, Philippe d'Orléans managed to appease the Jansenists, gain the (temporary) support of the Parlement of Paris, and draw the sting of the high aristocracy. Hence there was little opposition when he began to put in place the elements of what would became one of his most successful initiatives in the area of foreign policy. Before long, he was able to act with a free hand at home. To be sure, the publication of Cardinal de Retz's memoirs in 1717 temporarily rekindled the spirit of the Fronde.[135] But Maine was not Gondi, much less Condé. Villeroy was not Beaufort, opinions to the contrary notwithstanding. And a best-seller, even one signed by Retz, was not enough to spark a revolution. The Brittany affair and the Cellamare conspiracy would repeat the Fronde only as farce mimics tragedy.[136]

In these favorable circumstances, Dubois pulled off a masterstroke: backed by Orléans, he first forged an alliance with England and Holland. Then he expanded this Triple Alliance into a Quadruple Alliance and with the accord of the Empire established peace in Europe for a quarter of a century. But it would be a serious mistake to view these developments from the narrow perspective of diplomatic history. Saint-Simon fell into this very trap because he saw the alliance as nothing more than a conspiracy, a cabal of roués ultimately manipulated by the English ambassador Stair.[137] Our duke was an intransigent Catholic but not an inquisitorial one. Though wary of Spain as the home of the Inquisition, he nevertheless remained steadfast in his support of a Franco-Spanish alliance.[138] In his view, if the Bourbon of France wished to rival the grandeur of the Habsburgs, he had no choice but to establish his policy on a firm foundation, the most important pillar of which was Spain. Dubois's audacious pro-English strategy was therefore totally at odds with Saint-Simon's thinking, which in this respect was rather backward. The duke believed that English and French interests were fundamentally irreconcilable,[139] and that the goal of all policy toward England should be to provide the British with a "lengthy domestic occupation" that might dissuade them from undertaking any significant adventure on the continent. (This could happen, for example, if France were to renew its support for the Jacobites and back pro-Stuart incursions into England—a desirable goal in Saint-Simon's view.)

Notwithstanding Saint-Simon's (stupidly reactionary) opinion, the alliance with the powers of the north marked a "conceptual breakthrough" in French policy, one of the most important of the Regency, which could boast of only two or three others to rival it (not a bad record, all in all).[140] The other major innovations were John Law's new financial system and the liberalization that took place (however briefly and incompletely) from 1715 to 1717 on several domestic fronts (judicial, religious, and aristocratic). The alliance with England and the Netherlands was not just a diplomatic maneuver; it also marked a "cultural shift," a new era of cultural exchange that ushered in a period of "Anglomania" in France (an Anglomania that had already influenced fashion and hairstyles in the last years of Louis XIV's reign).[141] The French turned their backs on the narrow, Jesuitical Catholicism of their Spanish allies, who despite a reinvigoration of the economy after 1713 remained terribly traditionalist and hyper-papist.[142] French statesmen and writers took a new interest in Protestant, capitalist Europe, symbolized by the bustling cities of Amsterdam and London. France opened itself up not only to the sea but also to continental Europe: Hanover and the Empire as well as the Low Countries. The Channel and the Rhine narrowed, while the Pyrenees grew taller.

Considerable credit for this positive evolution must go to Orléans (but not, unfortunately, to Saint-Simon). After many vicissitudes, Louis XIV, owing to the influence of his mother, his wife, and his teacher Mazarin, ultimately committed himself firmly to Spain, to ultramontane Catholicism, and even to papist Italy.[143] To this mix he added a political Catholicism of his own that was at once anti-Protestant and anti-Jansenist.[144] But the duc d'Orléans was different: he knew and appreciated the nonconformist ways of his father, Monsieur, who as it happens was a homosexual as well as a man not suffocated by piety until late in life.[145] Philippe was emotionally quite strongly attached to his mother, Madame, as well as to her beliefs, her kin, and probably her tolerant attitude in matters of religion.[146] He was fond of the Palatinate and of his Hanoverian cousins and therefore of Germany and of Protestantism, both on the Continent and in Britain. He came to religion, moreover, with a certain skepticism of his own. In this he differed from his uncle Louis XIV, who was Iberian-Italian by ancestry, education, and "family romance." As early as 1708, Orléans suggested to Philip V "a real *English-style* government" for Aragon, Valencia, and Catalonia.[147] Here again we see his pragmatism at work, but it was a remarkably open-minded and well-informed pragmatism: contrast Philippe's outlook with Saint-Simon's, as expressed in his unfortunate words to Philip V, congratulating the king of Spain on his good fortune in having a government without "formal structures or Tories or Whigs or Parliament."[148] In 1715, even before the Sun King's demise, Philippe made numerous contacts with the British ambassador, Stair, whom Louis XIV, Torcy, and Saint-Simon all detested, rightly or wrongly, for his arrogance.[149] In Philippe's view, Europe's two "marginal" dynasties, the Hanovers and the Orléans, shared certain common interests. If young Louis XV were to die prematurely, both would want to prevent the accession of Philip V to the French throne. Such an eventuality would have been fatal to Orléans, of course, but equally dangerous for England and for the peace of Europe. It would also have been perilous for France, which, as people at the time liked to say, was so badly in need of "rest."

Stair therefore hoped to sever the ties between the French monarchy (and for the time being the Regency) and the fallen house of Stuart, and he worked hard to drive both France and the regent into the arms of the Hanovers.[150] In so doing, he sought to kill two or three birds with one stone and to secure support in Hanover for the new English dynasty against the Russians. Thus nationalistic and dynastic considerations aided the cultural shift heralded by Voltaire's popularizing of Shakespeare and Newton on the French side of the Channel (but that is another story). Changes of this magnitude would take time. As late as December of 1715, Orléans was still allowing himself to be manipulated by the pro-Stuart party in France, which included a significant portion of the more or less devout and Jacobite old court along with Torcy, Huxelles, and Effiat.[151] But the cross-Channel escapade of the Stuart pretender, the would-be James III, who narrowly escaped an assassination attempt in Nonancourt that Saint-Simon blamed on the British ambassador, convinced the regent that it would be foolish to encourage further ventures on behalf of the Stuarts just because France was supposed to be the "hereditary enemy" of the Anglican Church.[152] Such anti-British thinking would have to be eliminated root and branch. Fortunately, as it turned out, the sympathy that Philippe showed for England in the summer and fall of 1715 was translated into a new foreign policy by the spring of 1716.[153] The implications of this change soon became clear.

As for Abbé Dubois, actions for which he was long criticized (not least in a film by a talented filmmaker)[154] may well be counted in his favor today. Born into a family of middling rank in Brive, he managed to clamber his way up the social ladder—no mean feat in an aristocratic milieu where social mobility, though not totally nonexistent, often ran up against the snobbery of les Grands and their emulators as well as the tendency of acquired or inherited positions in the hierarchy to become "frozen." Dubois's brilliant mind and vast store of historical and geographical knowledge earned him Saint-Simon's flattery while he was alive; his need to earn a living while young by accepting such menial chores as chanting obits and giving private lessons earned him the duke's sarcasm after his death. Yet Saint-Simon kept in his study a portrait of Dubois by Rigaud.[155] The abbé was also the butt of Madame's haughty mockery. What is harder to understand is why he has until recently been a target of criticism and derogatory comment by so many historians, who have uncritically jumped on the hobbyhorse previously ridden by the *petit duc* and the epistolary Princess Palatine. No one any longer accuses Dubois of having been in the pay of the English or having accepted bribes from any number of sources simultaneously.[156] He was a man who defied convention, as his relationship with Mme de Tencin indicates, but he was not "depraved," at any rate not in the sense attached to that adjective by puritanical positivists, especially those such as Lémontey who claimed to be making judgments from a more "enlightened liberal" standpoint.[157] To be sure, Dubois could at times be crude. When he was close to death and Mme de Feuquières came to see him, he complained loudly: "I'm buried in work and still I have to put up with whores bent on making my life difficult."[158] And he was no model of piety: indeed, Saint-Simon called him *l'impie parfait*.[159] On his deathbed, he refused the last sacraments and dismissed the priest who had been sent to his bedside on the pretext that he wanted to look into the proper ceremony for cardinals in such circumstances.[160]

In fact, Dubois was that rare and unloved bird in French (and indeed continental) politics, the Anglophile (even the British dislike them).[161] His Anglophilia declared itself as early as 1698 on a mission to London, where the authorities unfortunately denied him permission to visit Oxford and Cambridge. In January 1716, Dubois was appointed to the Council of State over Saint-Simon's objections.[162] He thus became a member of the handful of men who wielded real power. His influence was now sufficient to drive his master Orléans (who wanted nothing more) into the waiting arms of the British.

A self-interested but fertile alliance thus developed between the two families that we earlier referred to as marginal: the house of Orléans, viewed with suspicion by French traditionalists, and the Hanovers, still seen by some as foreigners in England. As Saint-Simon observed, there were solid national as well as dynastic grounds for the new alliance.[163] Michelet concurred: the alliance with England was "a mutual insurance contract, one that bolstered both George I and the regent. It was a boon both to the two nations involved and to the West as a whole. It led to the genuine, solid, and earnest peace for which everyone had been yearning ever since the notorious 'peace' of Utrecht had failed to settle anything."[164] The core of the new alliance lay in article 5 of the pact by which it was sealed: this upheld the provisions of the Utrecht treaty and set forth the rules of succession applicable to the reigning dynasties in France and Britain. The mutual security agreement also contained provisions pertaining to Dunkirk and Mardyck and spelled out what was to be done about subjects of either party who refused to accept the terms of the accord: this clause was aimed squarely at the Jacobites and the pro-Spanish party in France.[165]

Concerning this issue, we now know about the secret negotiations that Dubois held with England's Stanhope at the Hague and in Hanover during the summer of 1716. (Secret diplomacy existed long before Henry Kissinger went to China.) Dubois and Stanhope had been friendly for quite some time.[166] In October 1716, England and France signed a defensive pact in Hanover, concluding months of secret talks between the two men. France agreed to end construction work on naval facilities in Mardyck.[167] As we mentioned earlier, various historians have been harshly critical of Dubois for this concession even though it was of little consequence. The abbé correctly sensed that this agreement laid the groundwork for a European settlement. The Treaty of Utrecht was reaffirmed. The stage was set for Spain to eventually forswear any designs on the throne of France and, beyond that, for the Empire to renounce any designs on the Spanish crown.[168] Thus the great powers—England, France, the Empire, and the United Provinces (to some extent subservient to the British)—began to work out a system of peaceful coexistence and collective security.[169] The ultimate goal—peace—had yet to be fully achieved, but by August 1718 it seemed within reach.

These developments also shed light on certain aspects of the regent's cabal. Dubois was not alone when it came to showing his master the way. He, too, engaged in intrigue behind the scenes. He enlisted the support of members of Philippe's entourage, some of them roués, some not: among them were three aristocrats, Canillac, Nocé, and Nancré.[170] Canillac and Nocé were both in one way or another linked to groups in Parlement. Another individual by the name of Rémond, the son of a *fermier général* known as "the Devil," had connections in the worlds of finance, the robe, Parlement, and literature that enabled him to conduct intelligence missions on Dubois's behalf.[171] Rémond also had long-standing ties to both the duc d'Orléans and Ambassador Stair. Dubois employed other agents as well, including his brother Joseph, who derived a good deal of benefit from the abbé's rise,[172] and especially the Chevignard de Chavigny brothers. The latter two diplomats were of good bourgeois *robin* extraction, but because the Chevignards had only recently been ennobled, their aristocratic braggadocio seemed excessive to some, and they were criticized by purists, including of course the inevitable Saint-Simon.[173]

The pro-English policy advocated by Dubois and the Orléanist entourage faced one major obstacle, however: the opposition of the old court.[174] That opposition was led by Huxelles and Torcy, surreptitiously joined by Adrien de Noailles, who had only recently—and not wholeheart-edly—rallied to Philippe's side. The final signature of the Franco-British treaty in the fall of 1716, followed by the inclusion of Holland in what thus became the Triple Alliance (on 4 January 1717), marked the success of the Anglophiles in the Orléans-Dubois group. Much water had flowed over the dam since the Dutch War of 1672. It almost seemed as if the time of Henri IV had returned. As Ambassador Saint-Aignan put it in a thoughtful text, "Peace with the British has almost always been more profitable for us than war, in spite of our victories." The truth of this observation was proven by contradiction later in the century, when senti-ment on the Continent turned against the British (not always at the urg-ing of the French): Louis XV's victory at Fontenoy in 1745 (annus mira-bilis) did not prevent the next war from ending with the disastrous Treaty of Paris in 1763 (annus horribilis). In any case, on 22 January 1717, Dubois was invited aboard the royal yacht in Utrecht for seven or eight hours of talks with King George I. The son of an apothecary from Brive-la-Gaillarde had come a long way indeed. By this point, the expansion of the alliance to include the Empire was only a matter of time and patience. The goal was finally achieved in August 1718, when the emperor re-nounced all claims to the Spanish throne on the understanding that the king of Spain would similarly renounce all claims to the French throne.

In March 1717, Dubois joined the Council of Foreign Affairs.[175] Within this august assembly, the regent now had a man (not to say hench-man) he could count on. Dubois proved to be totally loyal and devoted to Orléans because he knew that his many talents guaranteed him a free hand in the conduct of foreign (and especially diplomatic) affairs (the relationship between the two men is reminiscent of Henry Kissinger's relationship with Richard Nixon). The regent was therefore able to rely less on the support of the old Hispanophile court (Villeroy, Torcy, Hux-elles, and other "persnickety pedants"). Up to a point, he could even do without the support of Parlement. This was new, and it explains the simultaneous disgrace of the duc de Noailles and d'Aguesseau in January 1718.[176] Dubois was so pleased by this new state of affairs that he emitted "wild shouts of joy."[177] It was at this point that Nancré decided to aban-don Dubois in favor of Huxelles.[178] Rats sometimes abandon a ship not when it is sinking but when it is in full sail.

To be sure, the triumph of Dubois and Orléans, which is obvious to us in retrospect, was not obvious to everybody at the time. Nancré may have thought that the pendulum would soon swing back in the old court's favor. Or maybe he was a man of genuine conviction (appearances to the contrary notwithstanding). Throughout history there have been journées des dupes: in 1630, in 1718 (for Nancré), in June 1997. In 1630, of course,

Marillac had seemed on the brink of victory, but it was Richelieu who emerged triumphant. At times French history has resembled a farce by Feydeau. Nancré should have borne this in mind.

Jansenists, parlements, Brittany, the old court, even foreign policy— none of this amounted to much compared to Law's experiment. True, nothing Law did fundamentally changed France's economic situation, which had begun to improve as early as 1713. The recovery that got its start in the last years of Louis XIV's reign ended a period of misery and constant crisis, although the crisis was never as bad as the many not altogether unfounded jeremiads against the misfortunes of the time might lead one to think.[179] In any case, Law's experiment served as a stimulus to an already recovering economy. In addition, it once again changed the rules of the political game. It put an end to the Regency's liberal period and in the summer of 1718 ushered in its authoritarian phase, which we mentioned earlier. But even then there was no return to the harsher aspects of the Sun King's rule or to the tensions associated with his tenure.

In relation to the various cabals that pursued their intrigues around the court and the ministries, Law, a financier of unique genius, was very much the regent's man. He served his master as Dubois did, but in a different area.[180] Unlike Dubois and Rémond, however, he was never part of the "seraglio." From 1713 to 1715, Law was in contact with Stair (who in his own way was also an Orléanist) and had ties to Desmarets and to Philippe himself. After December 1715, the relationship between Law and the regent blossomed, leading to the creation of "the Bank" in May 1716.[181] For several years thereafter, Philippe would have two irons in the fire at all times: Law and Dubois. Eventually this enabled him to dispense with the services of men who had been slow to declare their allegiance. One such, the duc de Noailles, was soon dismissed in disgrace. Other eleventh-hour adherents to the cause were similarly sent packing. The regent's ability to rid himself of such dubious allies was enhanced by the fact that by this point he had already placed men he could trust in key positions. Of these, Law and Dubois were the most important. Ultimately, when "Law's system" collapsed, it was the abbé who dismissed the financier. But even after the bankrupt Law was sacked in disgrace, Orléans would continue to feel a certain affection for his former protégé from the improbable wilds of Scotland.[182] Law might have gone bust, but the regent still admitted him "through the back door" for talks about the possibility of working together on future projects.

The so-called system of Law, which held sway in France from 1716 to 1720, did not create paper money out of nothing. Paper currency existed in France before the Scot arrived. In the first decade of the eighteenth century, Desmarets had printed money to help replenish a treasury depleted by years of war under Louis XIV. Indeed, a system of credit based on letters of exchange, *rentes* (interest-bearing notes), and interest on dowries existed long before the eighteenth century. As we have seen, moreover, Law was not single-handedly responsible for the new phase of prosperity and slow but steady economic growth that began in 1713 and continued until at least 1770, perhaps even as late as 1785. Because of this expansion of the economy, the entire reign of Louis XV would bask in a climate of accumulating wealth (which is not to say, however, that this new wealth was equally distributed). The new prosperity first manifested itself in the Atlantic coastal region around Saint-Malo as early as the end of the seventeenth century. Its presence became apparent elsewhere after the end of the War of the Spanish Succession in 1713. Law arrived just in time to lend a fillip of his own to this "postwar economic boom." All he had to do was emulate his colleagues in England by expanding the system of paper credit and banknotes. The Scot had already explained his views on the benefits of inflation to Desmarets. With a more abundant money supply and a constant quantity of land, the financier hypothesized, demand for land would inevitably increase, hence more money would be required to buy any given parcel. Law expected that this would lead to higher prices for agricultural products, which would then make it easier for farmers to pay ground rents and taxes to their landlords and king.[183] According to Jean Meyer, one French household in ten began using paper currency as a direct result of Law's program. The system led to inflation, as debts borrowed in gold were repaid in paper *monnaie de singe*, or "funny money," and interest rates fell sharply. Debtors found their burden alleviated by the plentiful supply of cash. This stimulated enterprise in the modern sense of the term and encouraged social mobility. Of course enterprise and mobility would have increased anyway, but it is plausible to assume that the increase was greater than it would have been had Law not intervened and had the postwar recovery been allowed to take its natural course.

The duc de Noailles detested Law.[184] Saint-Simon's attitude was more ambiguous. With aristocratic hauteur the writer professed complete ignorance of financial matters and claimed to have nothing at all to do with them. In actuality, however, he was well aware of the potential benefits of Law's system as early as 1716: without levying new taxes, at no cost or burden to anyone, the new banknotes would at one stroke "double" the amount of money available and make it more "portable" (*portatif*) to boot. He also noted two potential dangers: first, the inflation induced by paper currency might undermine confidence in the system, and second, the "popular capitalization" that Law's system promoted was in Saint-Simon's view more suitable to countries like Holland and England than to a more or less absolute monarchy like France. Indeed, the monarchy might be all too tempted to scorn economic necessities and deplete the treasury through foolish expenditures.[185] To the monarchist Saint-Simon, capitalism and "republicanism" were paradoxically related. Translated into modern terms, one might say that a market economy requires a certain minimum of individual liberty and social autonomy (with respect to politics).

Saint-Simon's meditations aside, inflation can always be expected to cause political and even social conflict. Law shrewdly took advantage of this to make it through the summer transitional phase. By 1718, inflation, coupled with various other factors touched on earlier, had ushered in the authoritarian phase of the Regency. The liberal phase was over. Earlier, in 1713 and 1714, just after the end of the War of the Spanish Succession, Desmarets, though as respectful of the value of the currency as a comptroller general could afford to be, had attempted to revalue the livre tournois. Shortly before Louis XIV's death, the silver value of the livre, which had suffered greatly during the war, the *grand hyver*, and the disasters of 1709–10, had already climbed back to a level just below the highest value it had achieved under Colbert. Creditors approved of Desmarets's policy of revaluation because it meant that the interest payments they received would have full value and that their principal, much of it lent when money was soft, would be repaid in hard cash. But "smallholders" and others suffered. Indeed, anyone who owed money suffered, from *grands seigneurs* to farmhands. Noailles, as the first chairman of the new Finance Council, loosened the screws slightly with a brief devaluation in December 1715 but after that held firm on the livre tournois (whose metal content remained fairly stable until Noailles fell from grace in January 1718).[186]

Marc d'Argenson succeeded Noailles as chair of the Finance Council, a position he held while also serving as keeper of the seals, in which capacity he had replaced d'Aguesseau.[187] D'Argenson barely touched his predecessor's policy. Before long, however, the influence of Law, the rising star in the financial firmament, began to make itself felt. By the spring of 1718, the vastly increased circulation of banknotes led to monetary depreciation. The currency was devalued twice, first in February and then again in May of 1718, and the drop in value was one of the steepest in the history of the ancien régime.[188]

Parlement soon became enraged. By contrast, the non-robe aristocracy remained calm and began preparing to derive maximum profit from the new system. Saint-Simon, who was on the whole a fairly good analyst of the economy, proposed an important distinction between *rentiers* (whose income derived from interest on loans) and *fonciers* (whose income derived from agriculture and ground rents).[189] The *petit duc* understood full well that country folk and city folk would inevitably come into conflict over the "pruning" (abolition or reduction) of the *rente sur l'Hôtel de Ville* (a state-issued note) because the interests of *rentiers* and *fonciers* were incompatible regardless of where they stood in the hierarchy. Although taxes were inordinately high, tax revenues were eaten up by interest payments on state debts that enriched bourgeois bankers, *parlementaires*, and other "pillars of justice" who lent money to His Majesty. But *fonciers*, or landowners, wanted lower taxes in order to reduce the operating costs of their farms and increase profits. Saint-Simon lauded the *fonciers*, whom he rather hastily identified with the second or noble order, whereas the *rentiers*, he claimed, were all *robins* and thus symbolic of— what else?—the third estate. In his eyes, the *rente* was a bourgeois, not to say common, institution, and its major drawback was that it obliterated differences of status and confounded ranks to the detriment of the "native nobility" (that is, the *fonciers*), for whom Saint-Simon discreetly claimed to speak. His sometimes perceptive economic analyses were thus closely intertwined with his hierarchical obsessions. He confused an important economic distinction (between *rentier* and *foncier*) with a social distinction of a different sort (between robe and sword). The confusion is all the more misleading in that the abstract socioeconomic barrier that Saint-Simon thus created was based on a grossly oversimplified identification of *rente* with robe and land with sword. Nevertheless, Saint-Simon was right in his belief that rural "entrepreneurs" (that is, landowners) were relieved to discover that Law's system alleviated their debts, whereas *rentiers* were hurt by inflation and lower interest rates.

It is true that most *parlementaires* and "officers of the quill" belonged to the *rentier* group (one might even call it a class). To be sure, they owned land, but a considerable portion of their income derived from interest because, being wealthy but frugal, they were in a position to lend large sums of money to both the state and private individuals. Those loans were denominated in livres tournois and bore interest. Hence any devaluation that weakened the currency inevitably outraged the coupon-clipping *parlementaire* aristocracy, which felt robbed. When Law issued large numbers of banknotes, many people hitherto crushed by their burden of debt used paper to pay off loans that had been paid out in silver and gold. From the lenders' point of view this was doubly unfair: not only were they cheated of their capital, but they also suffered from the falling rate of interest. Because many loans were paid off and paper money was now plentiful, it became easy to obtain loans at low interest. While Law's system was in effect, interest rates actually fell from 4.5 to 1.25 percent.[190] In view of all this, it will come as no surprise to discover that *rentiers*, or lenders, including not only *petits robins* but especially *grands robins* and *parlementaires*, had little affection for John Law.

Conversely, the *fonciers*, or traditional landowners, whose wealth was mostly in the form of land rather than interest-bearing obligations and who often owed money themselves, had no reason to dislike the Scottish financier. On the contrary, because prices rose faster than wages, in particular the prices of agricultural products, so did the income of the landed aristocracy—both direct income (from the sale of farm products) and indirect income (from ground rents). At the same time, the debts of nobles great and small were partially wiped out by inflation. Last but not least, well-placed or highly perched aristocrats were able, through the good offices of Law's patron, the regent, to lay hands directly on bundles of banknotes from Law's bank. Although Saint-Simon has little to say on the subject, he did not deny himself any of these opportunities: indeed, he paid off 500,000 livres tournois worth of old family debt that his late father had incurred during the Fronde. Thanks to Law, Saint-Simon was able to repay not only the principal but six decades' worth of accumulated interest and still hold his head high.

It is not too much to say that, taken together, these policies constituted a system. Not only were *rentiers* deprived of their income (as interest rates fell to 2 percent by March 1720 and to 1.25 percent shortly thereafter), but many profiteers who had taken advantage of the old system were eliminated (forty-eight offices were abolished in September 1719, and the army of tax collectors was trimmed). Meanwhile, the number of loans increased as it became easier to repay borrowed money, full employment was encouraged, and agriculture "revived." The growth of the population was no longer held in check. The kingdom generally prospered.[191]

At the same time, certain *grands seigneurs* (in Saint-Simon's elevated sense) allowed themselves to speculate with precious metals obtained from opportune conversion of old notes. The Contis and Condés led by the younger Monsieur le Duc did not fail to avail themselves of the opportunity, nor did d'Antin.[192] These men were united by ties dating back to the old Monseigneur cabal of a decade earlier.

By contrast, the opponents of the system enjoyed none of the treats handed out to the *grands seigneurs*. By May or June of 1718, the cycle of inflation and devaluation that accompanied the implementation of Law's plan had begun to create enemies. In this group, *fonciers* were rare and *rentiers* far more common, magistrates of Parlement prominent among them. Indeed, among people who derived much of their income from interest, these magistrates constituted the crème de la crème, and Law's system deprived them of what they considered their due.

On 2 June 1718, Parlement therefore lodged a protest against the devaluation edict that Law had inspired and possibly even drafted.[193] "I don't give a damn about Parlement," Philippe declared a few weeks later. Tensions rose throughout the summer until August, when the High Assembly issued an ad hominem decree barring foreigners (to wit, John

Law) from playing any role in the administration of the realm's finances.[194] *In petto*, the magistrates even envisaged hanging the phenomenal financier. A horrified Saint-Simon pondered the havoc wrought years earlier by the English Parliament and the events leading to the demise of Charles I. He poured scorn on the French Parlement's claim to represent the kingdom *(le royaume)* as opposed to the monarchy *(la monarchie)*.[195]

In this controversy, Parlement enjoyed the support of the duc du Maine and part of the old court. But the regent's cabal enjoyed the advantage of being in power. By this point, its legitimacy was established, and its people had been securely in place for several years. The Orléanist faction was clearly a power to reckon with. Many higher-ranking "technocrats" were members (including d'Argenson, the younger Fagon, who served on the Council of State,[196] and of course Dubois and Law). The Orléanists also controlled the Condés and Contis, whose allegiance had been duly purchased by the regent and his Scottish financier. And they had absorbed the still impressive remains of the old Bourgogne-Beauvillier-Chevreuse group in the persons of Saint-Simon and Chaulnes junior, both of whom expressed pleasure at the measures that had been taken. After all, the new policy was supposed to humble Parlement while at the same time restoring or enhancing the status of the dukes and peers. The dukes were to be plucked from the pit into which past humiliations had plunged them. Their dignity was to be restored, and with it their morale, which under the "horrible hammer" of the late king had been obliged to survive on nothing more than wan hope and proud nostalgia.[197]

The *lit de justice* of 26 August 1718 marked the triumph of Philippe and his friends. Parlement had hoped to voice its opposition to the Law-inspired edicts and to d'Argenson's nomination as keeper of the seals. But a deployment of troops in the capital—guards, gendarmes, light cavalry, and musketeers—convinced the high Parisian tribunal that resistance was futile.[198] At the same session, the bastards were deprived of some of the privileges they had previously been granted over the dukes and peers. Responsibility for educating Louis XV was taken out of the hands of Maine (a bastard and adversary of the regent) and given to the younger Monsieur le Duc, who was adept at following orders. With one swoop, all of Saint-Simon's enemies were thus laid low. Having planned this rout, the *petit duc* was beside himself with joy.[199] Compared to the pleasures of the spirit, he remarked, the pleasures of the senses are as nothing, and still less compared to the pleasures of revenge.

The Authoritarian Regency

FALL OF 1718 TO END OF 1723

The lit de justice *of* 26 *August* 1718, *followed by the temporary* banishment of a number of high magistrates from Paris, marked the partial exclusion of Parlement from the government of France. In September of 1715, Philippe had invited the high court to join the regime in order to consolidate his own nascent power and establish the legitimacy of his regency. But even after the events of August 1718, those *bougres d'avocats,* or "damn lawyers," as Orléans called the refractory magistrates, did not suffer as they had suffered under Louis XIV. In particular, Parlement retained the right of remonstrance that Philippe had reinstated for purposes of his own in 1715, and it did not hesitate to use its restored prerogative as though it were the monarchy's supreme court. Indeed, much later, in the 1780s, it would go so far in asserting this right as to precipitate the fall of the ancien régime, which of course proved to be its own undoing. Saint-Simon had dimly foreseen the first of these two consequences— a feat of prognostication that commands a certain respect.

Concomitant with this rebirth of the power of Parlement was another innovation that Philippe introduced just after the death of the Sun King in 1715: he "brought the nobility into the government." More specifically, he granted the aristocrats of the "old court," who had previously exercised power only indirectly, an important role in the newly created system of "polysynody."[1] Among other things, he hoped thereby to disarm one potential source of opposition, namely, the previous king's old and not-so-old courtiers. In August 1718, when with the repression of Parlement the wind shifted once again, it was only logical that the councils be suppressed as well.[2] The decision to do away with polysynody was made public in September 1718.[3]

There were many reasons for this victorious offensive against polysynody. On 8 September 1718, Pope Clement XI published a pastoral letter entitled *Pastoralis officii* in which he urged all the faithful to obey the dictates set forth in *Unigenitus*.[4] All the parlements objected. Cardinal de Noailles proposed that an appeal be addressed to either the pope or some future council of the church. Although the regent studiously refrained from objecting too strenuously to this essentially pro-Jansenist proposal, he also refused to give it his blessing, whereupon Noailles immediately resigned as chair of the Council of Conscience. On 23 September, he published his appeal. On the very same day, Philippe took a step he had long been contemplating and dissolved the Council of Conscience. The next day he dissolved all the other councils except those dealing with finance, commerce, and the navy.[5]

This action was taken partly in response to pressure from the English conveyed through Stair by way of Dubois. The British were firmly convinced that in order to preserve the Dual, later Triple, and ultimately Quadruple Alliance, the French government needed to purge its pro-Spanish faction, most of whose members were associated with the old court. Foremost among the pro-Spanish officials were Huxelles and Villars, and by eliminating the councils, in particular the War Council (on which Villars sat) and the Council of Foreign Affairs (on which Huxelles sat), it was easy for Philippe to satisfy the British. This was not the first time that a foreign ambassador had exercised power in France. The Spanish ambassador had been influential in the time of the League (1590). Now it was the British ambassador's turn. Religious and financial factors also played a part in triggering the decision to abandon polysynody and "recentralize" the government. Indeed, the councils had been hanging by a thread for some time. Their contentiousness and recalcitrance had impeded the efforts of the regent and his determined aides Law and Dubois. The decision to do away with them met with widespread indifference. Even Saint-Simon had to admit that the councils had long since become the butt of ridicule.[6]

Although the suppression of the councils in some ways marked a return to the centralized monarchy of Louis XIV, substantial differences remained. To be sure, responsibilities that had been transferred from the four secretaries of state to the councils were now shifted back to the secretaries of state, the "uncrowned kings" of the ancien régime.[7] For Saint-Simon, who looked on with dismay, the change represented a revival of absolutist traditions, not least because posts in three of the four secretariats were soon filled by members of the old ministerial families. The Phélypeaux family, a powerful clan with countless branches, easily secured posts for two of their own, the young Maurepas[8] and the not-so-young La Vrillière (a fixture of the previous regime). Maurepas went to work for the Maison du Roi, while La Vrillière took up his duties in the Department of Protestant Affairs.[9] The Le Peletiers, also veterans of government service and longtime clients of the Le Tellier–Louvois clan, placed their brother-in-law Armenonville in the Secretariat of the Navy.[10] In this return of the technocrats, however, two assignments were especially worthy of note: Abbé Dubois, who had only recently been named to the Council of State, was not a product of the *robe du Conseil* from which Louis XIV had recruited his top bureaucrats. Nevertheless, he was named secretary of state for foreign affairs.[11] Henceforth, he would officially occupy the post whose duties he had already assumed. Meanwhile, Huxelles, a hanger-on from the old court and staunch supporter of Madrid, was forced out and reduced to playing "fly on the wall" while the young king made his "declaration of marriage."[12]

Another important appointment was that of Le Blanc, the former intendant of Auvergne, to the post of secretary of state for war. Le Blanc was a classic representative of the *robe du Conseil*, but he was also an active participant in the cabal that gradually formed around the regent. He was a friend of Law's and a (not very reliable) epigone of Dubois's.[13] (A few years later Dubois would unhesitatingly dismiss him from his post.) Initially Le Blanc also enjoyed the enthusiastic support of Saint-Simon.

D'Antin fell from power when the Inner Council was abolished. He saw the abolition of polysynody in September of 1718 as an attempt to deprive the high nobility of genuine power—a return to the antiaristocratic policies of Louis XIV. In this he was not entirely wrong, but it would be a serious mistake to think that the Regency simply reverted to the old pre-1715 Louis XIV model or adopted a system of government based entirely on the *robe du Conseil* and fundamentally hostile to the court nobility and nobility of the sword. A number of *grands seigneurs* such as Choiseul and princes of the church (such as Dubois, Fleury, Tencin, and Bernis) would serve as ministers under Louis XV (both young and old).[14] This would have been unthinkable in the previous reign, and in hindsight Saint-Simon discovered that he preferred Louis XIV's hostility to cardinals even though the Sun King had no more fervent opponent than himself. In any case, one needn't feel too sorry for d'Antin and others of his ilk. True, the regent, having rolled out the red carpet to win their support in 1715, now pulled it out from under them, but by way of compensation he tacitly permitted them to make millions off Law's system in dubious if not downright illegal ways. D'Antin himself proved to be one of the greediest of the lot.[15] "Let me worry about politics," Philippe seemed to say to others of his class, "and riches will be yours." Such was their reward for the loss of polysynody.

The end of polysynody signaled the transition from a "liberal" Regency backed by Parlement, the Jansenists, and the high nobility to an "authoritarian" or even (as we shall see) crypto-plebiscitary Regency. The revival of old ways of doing things was merely one aspect of the change, however, and not the most important. Day-to-day policy was Philippe's, not Louis XIV's, and to some extent it remained fundamentally liberal in its orientation.

To implement that policy the regent employed secretaries of state, but he used them in new ways inspired by those staunch Orléanists Dubois and Law, whose approaches to diplomacy and finance were new and imaginative. Soon after the return to authoritarian rule in the summer of 1718, Law's system achieved its high-water mark; the subsequent decline was rapid indeed. By November or December of 1719, following a brief war with Spain from which France easily emerged victorious, bank shares had risen to dizzying heights (as much as 10,000 livres per share).[16] Afraid that the bubble might burst, the Scottish financier tried to dampen speculation. In the following year, 1720, Law's banknotes began to depreciate. The inflated currency plummeted in value and ultimately collapsed. On 17 July a riot broke out on rue Vivienne, and one person died.[17] The duc de Tresmes, in his capacity as governor of Paris, gained notoriety on this occasion. Like Mac-Mahon after him, he is remembered for the words he addressed to the crowd in the hope of appeasing its rage: "Hey! Gentlemen, gentlemen, what's this all about? Gentlemen! Gentlemen!" History does not record whether or not this speech achieved its intended purpose.

It makes sense at this point in our story to pause long enough to assess what Law's system had accomplished thus far and what it portended for the future. Law was not so much the cause of economic recovery (which would have occurred without him) as the embodiment of it. His famous system must be seen in the context of a broader international expansion of credit (witness the South Sea Bubble in England, for example). Once the new paper had achieved its purpose, it vanished from the scene. What was that purpose? To stimulate the economy, although, again, the French economy would have recovered even without Law, owing to the general increase of economic activity throughout Europe in the second decade of the eighteenth century. Had Law never set foot on French soil, however, France's recovery might well have been less exuberant; at the very least, it would have done less to improve the lot of the vast number of people buried beneath a mountain of debt.

Speculation involving Louisiana and Mississippi was an important, perhaps even essential, ingredient of Law's system. Such speculation did not spring up overnight.[18] The French had been developing sugar plantations with slave labor in the West Indies since the end of the seventeenth century, and there had been a rapid increase in the population of French settlements (white as well as black). During Louis XIV's lifetime, France had tried hard to overtake England in this area, which was the cutting edge of capitalism at the time. Law merely promised to continue what others had begun. Unfortunately, French enterprises in Mississippi met with numerous reverses. Later the region would develop rapidly, as the growth of New Orleans attests, but this took place under the leadership of other men more prudent than John Law.

Saint-Simon several times boasted of having refused to "snatch a piece of Mississippi." He had his scruples, and he was reluctant to be seen enriching himself at other people's expense. Such integrity was rare, however, and in any case, Saint-Simon disliked wealth on paper; he preferred gold that he could touch and feel. And Law did not always have the Midas touch (although he did play Midas to Monsieur le Duc, d'Antin, and others of their ilk, but that is another story). So Saint-Simon kept his hands off the profits from Mississippi, to the amazement of the regent, who remarked that such abstention redounded to his glory. Be that as it may, the duke's ethical stance did not oblige him to forgo certain opportunities to profit indirectly from the heady economic climate of the time. As a landed aristocrat, Saint-Simon naturally eschewed the more blatant forms of speculation, but he had no compunctions about using inflated paper to pay off loans his father had made sixty years earlier, including all the interest that had accrued in the interim. He also permitted his wife to keep the stipend she received as lady-in-waiting to the duchesse de Berry, who had recently passed away. Finally, he asked for an increase of a thousand écus in his own stipend as governor of Senlis. To be sure, these were small sums compared with the colossal fortunes amassed by the speculators. Still, all things considered, Saint-Simon the *foncier* made out rather well.[19] And if he had little to say about his "small profits" in the *Memoirs*, they nevertheless disposed him to look rather favorably on Law, with whom he claims for a time to have held regular Tuesday meetings at the regent's behest.[20]

In any event, Law made a substantial contribution to France's economic recovery. Or rather, to put it more precisely, he was shrewd enough to harvest the fruits of a recovery already under way without him and make it yield enormous profits. Early in 1720, the abbé de Saint-Pierre described what the system had accomplished, or seemed to have accomplished.[21] Although his account is somewhat idealized and his enthusiasm excessive, his description is not altogether inaccurate. To begin with, the king's debts had been paid off without levying any new taxes. Troops, courtiers, and royal officials had received their normal salaries and stipends (albeit in some cases in devalued currency). Back taxes had been collected. Steps had been taken to restore the navy. State revenues had been increased (and would continue to increase as long as economic expansion continued). Citizens had been freed from their debts (which they had been able either to pay off in paper money or renegotiate at a lower rate of interest). The price of land had risen owing to the abundant supply of money, and this had enabled landowners to liquidate loans by selling off parts of their estates. Unemployment among agricultural workers and artisans had decreased. People had been given an incentive to work harder. Money and therefore goods had begun to circulate more rapidly without any decrease in prices; on the contrary, prices had risen. Trade with the East Indies had increased, and colonization of the West Indies had progressed. In France, manufacturing had expanded, and the health of the financial system had been restored.

If the Scotsman was the liberator and benefactor of the indebted, and especially the entrepreneurs and *fonciers* (to use Saint-Simon's somewhat simplistic terminology), he was also the nemesis of the *rentiers*, or creditors, who saw their position weakened and their income slashed as the money supply increased and interest rates fell. Prices of agricultural products rose, and this, too, improved the lot of farmers (whose income rose while their nominal debt remained fixed and their real debt decreased). The burden of rising prices during the brief inflationary period was alleviated by the falling interest rate, which was by no means a bad thing for the economy. Law had thus helped to "prime the pump" of the economy, which sprang to life in response to the sudden and massive influx of cash.[22]

In light of these successes, the lamentations of the minority who opposed Law's system were of little consequence. The protesters were mainly creditors who suffered when their loans were repaid in banknotes and the rate of interest declined. A curé from Angers by the name of Lehoreau prepared a detailed list of the lenders who were Law's primary victims: parish councils *(fabriques)*, ecclesiastical communities (especially nuns such as the Carmelites, Visitandines, and others), and, what was more serious, hospitals—in short, a range of charitable institutions, or institutions supposed to be charitable. All in all, the number of beneficiaries (erstwhile debtors) of the system was certainly larger than the number of victims (erstwhile creditors).[23] When the system collapsed, there were relatively few riots because, regardless of what anyone said, it left behind more good memories than bad.

Those who bemoan the "fact" that the trauma "inflicted" on France by Law made it impossible to establish a central bank in France are like those who lament the loss of India or Quebec. All three setbacks—the bank, India, Quebec—may be matters of regret for believers in France's destiny, but can they be certain that even without Law in 1720 (or the treaty of Paris in 1763) France would have been truly equipped and motivated to maintain a central bank (or colonize India or North America)? Note, for example, that on the continent of North America (in contrast to isles of the West Indies) the French colonies remained relatively small compared with the English colonies that "gradually spread" along the coasts of Virginia and New England. In Quebec, "the battle of the birth-rate" would not be won until the nineteenth or twentieth century, and even then the victory was tenuous at best. In 1750, the sparseness of the white population in Quebec stood in sharp contrast to the rapid growth of the black population on Santo Domingo.

As for the monetary problem per se, note that in 1726 the government succeeded in stabilizing the livre tournois, which then remained stable for nearly two centuries thereafter (until 1914). This would hardly have been possible without the brief period of inflation instigated by Law, which wiped out old debts and stimulated the economy. In other words, Law laid the groundwork for a sound currency, which subsequent governments were able to preserve for the next two hundred years. Before settling in for the long haul, it may well have been a good thing for France to have swallowed a dose of Law's inflationary elixir.

I t may also be worth pausing a moment to dispose of two canards often raised in this context. Some scholars compare Law's banknotes with the notes issued by the French government in 1700, others with the revolutionary *assignats* (paper currency ostensibly backed by property nationalized during the French Revolution). That Law based his system on the earlier experiment is certainly true. And many people, including perhaps some lazy historians, are apt to confound Law's notes with the later *assignats*—the better to condemn both. There are differences, however. For one thing, Law was successful, if not in a personal sense then at least in a historical one. He chose the right moment to intervene, and his intelligence, not to say genius, was buoyed by a wave of prosperity. The banknotes that Chamillart and Desmarets issued at the turn of the eighteenth century failed to produce the desired economic results, as did the *assignats* issued by the Revolution nearly a hundred years later. (Note, however, that in both cases financial expedients yielded *political* as opposed to economic benefits.) These innovations, introduced in the midst of war and economic disaster, were doomed to failure. Neither had a chance of succeeding economically. In each case, however, the real objective was not economic but military and political. In fact, both Louis XIV and the Convention got what they wanted.

W e turn now to the political history of Law's system. Which elite groups and which segments of society supported it? Once Law stumbled, of course, his support quickly evaporated. But things were different at first, and it is always wise to begin at the beginning.

Not to be counted among Law's initial supporters was Parlement. There were exceptions to this rule, as we shall see in a moment. But in general the members of Parlement were *rentiers* and thus hostile to the Scotsman. By the spring or summer of 1720, that hostility had reached the breaking point. Philippe was obliged to intervene. On 21 July 1720, almost two years after the authoritarian "coup d'état" of August 1718, Orléans exiled the Parlement of Paris to Pontoise, some twenty miles from the capital. (Saint-Simon had recommended Blois, which is even farther.)[24] Musketeers were dispatched to enforce the regent's order. Even in this extremity, however, Philippe and Law did not burn all their bridges to Parlement. In similar circumstances, Louis XIV would simply have "crushed" the insolent magistrates. By contrast, under the regent, the high court retained its right of remonstrance and suffered little in the way of material harm from its exile. Philippe's decision to involve Parlement in politics as a sort of oppositional safety valve had been carefully deliberated. His subsequent decisions to revoke some of the concessions he had made earlier had few negative consequences despite or because of Parlement's temporary exile in Pontoise. It was not until much later, in the 1750s and 1760s especially, that the battle between king and Parlement finally proved disastrous in the view of both the public and the ruling elite.

Shifting alliances were another problem. As time went by, the regent's men began to divide into two factions, one aligned with Dubois, whose star was rising, the other with Law, whose initial triumph soon turned sour. As these divisions deepened, the Scottish financier began to rely more and more on certain pro-Jansenist figures, especially Torcy and d'Aguesseau. Dubois, on the other hand, looked forward to being named a cardinal. Through d'Argenson, he therefore began to cozy up to the Jesuits. The contrast was clear during the *journées des dupes* of June 1720, when Law, whose favor had briefly plummeted, temporarily regained the upper hand. The regent dismissed the Jesuitophile d'Argenson and made the pro-Jansenist d'Aguesseau keeper of the seals (thus returning him to the post from which he had been sacked two years earlier). D'Argenson went quietly—straight to a convent in the faubourg Saint-Antoine, where he caused a scandal by making love to the abbess.[25] Now, in setting d'Aguesseau up in partnership with Law, was the regent perhaps making a discreet bid for the support of the Jansenists, which is to say, of Parlement? We will return to this theme of hostile cooperation in a moment, when we discuss the Cellamare conspiracy and the war with Spain.

Vis-à-vis the old court, Law's system was always ambivalent. Politically, the need to perpetuate the system, together with other, less important factors, led to the "coup" of August 1718 and the substitution of authoritarian for quasi-liberal rule. By laying the groundwork for the abolition of polysynody, that coup stripped whatever "cosmetic" vestiges of power remained in the hands of the titled and mitered old crocodiles left over from the era of Louis XIV—the same lizards who from 1715 to

1718 had basked in the backwaters of the soon-to-be-abolished councils. Political losses were offset by financial gains, however: whatever the high aristocracy lost in "synodal" power, it regained that much and more in notes from Law's bank—and for a time, such paper could be converted into gold. As one generation gave way to the next, elderly aristocrats such as Huxelles, Villeroy, and Villars were quietly swept out of power along with the councils on which they sat. To be sure, it became apparent during the Cellamare affair that these conspiratorial retirees had been dreaming of a comeback, but they were not men of the same fiber as Condé, Turenne, Beaufort, and Gaston d'Orléans. When the conspiracy was revealed, some of them threw themselves at the regent's feet, while others made themselves scarce.[26] Younger aristocrats, including children of these former grandees, received pecuniary favors and sacks full of banknotes. The taxpayers, as always, were fleeced and may have felt bitter about it, but nobody asked for their opinion. In truth, the gifts lavished upon the younger nobility did not cause the taxpayers undue suffering, because prosperity and rising tax revenues soon replenished coffers emptied by these advances.

Cash bonuses rained down upon the "great names" of France,[27] the successors of the old court and Parlement: Bouillon, La Feuillade, Matignon, Dangeau, Mesmes, Tresmes, Castries, Soubise, Noailles, Rouillé du Coudray (a *robin* who nevertheless worked with Noailles), Blanzac, the maréchale de Rochefort, the prince de Courtenay, and of course the Bontemps family, who as valets of the royal bedchamber represented the crème de la crème. Millions of livres were dispensed to these people in 1720.[28] Louis XIV had always made it a principle to "corrupt *les Grands* so as to rule without them, but not against them." Law and Orléans made the Sun King's watchword their own. Great aristocrats who refused to profit from the speculative frenzy touched off by the introduction of Law's system were few and far between. Among the virtuous, or rather, the virtuosos of virtue, we may include the chancellor, along with Villars and Villeroy (who were deeply enmeshed in plotting against the regent), and La Rochefoucauld (whose virtue was merely a sham, at least according to Saint-Simon, whose ill will toward the descendants of the author of the *Maxims* we have already encountered on several occasions).[29] Although what was left of the Maintenon faction had been out of favor since the death of Louis XIV, its members nevertheless received their fair share of the torrent, or rather avalanche, of bribes.

Meanwhile, Philippe and Law used similar gifts to win the allegiance of other factions that to one degree or another had failed to gain the favor of Louis XIV but were now free to flourish under the Regency. The situation of these groups had greatly improved after 1715, and to some extent they had been allowed to participate in government. In 1719 and 1720, they collected a generous tithe from the gratuities handed out by Law. The old Monseigneur, or "Meudon," cabal received any number of stipends. Among its members who battened on this largesse we may mention the princesses of Lorraine (Mlle d'Espinoy and Mlle de Melun), d'Antin, the Vendômes, Law's indefatigable friend the *grand prieur*,[30] the Condé-Contis (including the princesse de Conti, M. de Charolais, Madame la Duchesse, and of course Monsieur le Duc junior).[31] The old Fénelon-Beauvillier-Bourgogne group and its offshoots were also irrigated by the Mississippi. Here the beneficiaries included the Béthune-Sully, Lorges, Coëtquen, Saint-Simon, and Nangis families. (One of the Nangis clan, after having been the duchesse de Bourgogne's by no means platonic lover, later became a marshal of France notable only for his colorlessness.) As for the regent's faction in the strict sense, Châteautiers received substantial bonuses. Clearly the loyal lieutenants of the Palais-Royal were in no way bashful when it came to lining their pockets.[32]

Thus, the new equilibrium that established itself after the "miniputsch" of August 1718 was based on a subtle balance of power involving three main groups: the Orléanists, a coalition of two rival factions, one led by Law and the other by Dubois; Parlement, which had been sidelined but not demolished; and the old court, where innovators and reactionaries alike had been shunted aside by the regent but abundantly compensated for their loss of influence.

That the elimination of the councils did not in any simple way mark a return to the pre-1715 "ancien régime" is clear, moreover, from the Cellamare affair and the war with Spain, after which Philippe's foreign policy remained diametrically opposed to that of Louis XIV. The Cellamare conspiracy was worthy of an operetta.[33] Its goal was to increase the likelihood that Philip V, the Bourbon king of Spain, might accede to the French throne. All the maneuvering made sense, however, only if Louis XV died young, which of course he did not. Cellamare, the Spanish ambassador in Paris, participated in the plot only to the extent of conveying to Madrid plans hatched by the duchesse du Maine and two of her acolytes, Laval and Pompadour.[34] Like her Condé ancestors, the duchess hoped to play an important political role if her conspiratorial efforts succeeded.[35] Cellamare's various accomplices participated in the plot mainly by writing letters (to Philip V, to Louis XV, who was still a minor, and to Parlement).[36] Three events hastened the maturation of the plot and the final debacle. They were

1. The successful negotiation of the Quadruple Alliance (June–August 1718), which posed a direct threat to Philip V's hope of becoming king of France by guaranteeing that if Louis XV died, England would support the duc d'Orléans.[37]

2. The English defeat of the Spanish fleet at Passaro in August of 1718, which further weakened the position of the Spanish Bourbon. The regent, well aware of the significance of the event, could not conceal his joy on hearing the "great news."[38]

3. The "coups d'état" against Parlement and polysynody in August and September of 1718. Parlement was temporarily reduced to impotence, as was the old court opposition led by Maine and backed by certain members of the "non-ducal" (and in some cases provincial) nobility, who favored a convocation of the Estates General that would have complicated the regent's calculations.

A few months later, Cellamare was expelled from France, ending the conspiracy once and for all. This was a relatively mild response, even considering the fact that Cellamare was a diplomat.[39] By contrast, his French allies were arrested. The duc du Maine was seized as he left church after mass and taken to Doullens. As he was led away, he hiccuped, sighed, and muttered to himself uncontrollably, gesticulating wildly all the while.[40] The duchess proved somewhat better at maintaining her dignity as she was taken off to Dijon.[41] Their children were sent to Eu. Those lesser conspirators who had lacked the presence of mind to flee at once were locked up in the Bastille.[42] For our purposes, what is important about this rather trivial affair is that it casts a revealing light on the groups and factions involved.

Assisting the duchesse du Maine, who was far more deeply involved in the conspiracy than her prudent spouse, we find a number of individuals who had long since hitched their stars to the bastards. Among them were young Richelieu and Cardinal de Polignac.[43] The aristocratic and even intellectual opposition (Voltaire) also had ties to Cellamare, Maine, and Richelieu junior. This indecisive and loosely organized group enjoyed the often dubious support of what remained of the old court's Maintenon faction (Villeroy, Huxelles, Villars, and Aumont), as well as the even more cautious support of the Jesuits and other *constitutionnaires* (such as Père Tournemine and Bentivoglio, the papal nuncio). The fact that Cellamare was a native of Naples and that his counterpart in Madrid was also an Italian, Alberoni, lent an air of ultramontanism to what was in fact an amateurish plot.[44] The regent's men had little difficulty in crushing this "conspiracy of grammarians."[45]

Meanwhile, the ranks of the Orléanists slowly swelled. The group now included some of the regime's top "technocrats" (such as Dubois, d'Argenson, Torcy, Le Blanc, and Fagon junior) as well as the house of Condé (with the exception, of course, of the duchesse du Maine, a Condé by birth but a "Cellamarian" by political choice). And along with the Condés came, inevitably, the old Monseigneur cabal led by Monsieur le Duc and d'Antin. Finally, there was the rump of the Bourgogne cabal, most notably Saint-Simon and d'Ancenis, the son of Charost. And so the regent found himself surrounded by friends both old and new.

Among the Orléanists there were a few pro-Jesuits. D'Argenson was one, for reasons of self-interest,[46] and Dubois was on his way to becoming one in the interest of obtaining a cardinal's hat ("my kingdom for a cap," as Yves Coirault has put it). But the whole constellation of contending forces clearly indicates the degree to which Orléans was able to occupy both the center and summit of the entire apparatus. One is reminded of the words of a contemporary of ours: "Wherever I sit, that is the center." By humiliating Parlement and then sending it into exile and by destroying the Council of Conscience and Cardinal de Noailles, Philippe marked his distance from the Jansenists, traditionally associated with Parlement. In the long run, they had proven to be burdensome allies, even if their support had been indispensable for consolidating Philippe's power in the early days of his Regency. At the same time, his victory over the ultramontanist, pro-Italian, pro-Spanish, pro-Jesuit party of bigots—symbolized by the ridiculous Cellamare conspiracy, which, because it seemed to have been inspired by people who were either idiotic, disreputable, or mad, elicited nothing but contempt when it collapsed—gained him the sympathy of the same Gallican Jansenists in Parlement he had previously humiliated.[47] Score two backhanded blows for Philippe.

Law had played almost no role in exposing Cellamare and the Maines. It was in fact Dubois who had pulled the strings, under the regent's direct supervision.[48] Here we see the limits of Law's influence. Even as comptroller general of finance after 1720, the Scotsman was never more than a master technician, despite the regent's affection for him (which continued even after his downfall). The real leader of the Orléanist cabal was Dubois, whose influence became less secretive and more open as time went by. Under Orléans, Dubois, and Fleury, the post of comptroller general, resurrected for Law on 6 January 1720 and retained for his successors, never regained the vast powers it had enjoyed in the time of Colbert, Pontchartrain, Chamillart, and Desmarets.[49] When Law's ventures collapsed in 1720, interventionism in the Colbertian manner also suffered a decisive setback. To a certain extent, private capital now took over from unwieldy state-sponsored enterprises such as the one in Mississippi, which collapsed when the Scot who had encouraged it was forced out.[50] The old venture did not disappear, however. It simply reorganized and changed its name.

With the Cellamare affair out of the way, Orléans skillfully drove a wedge between the Jansenists and the Jesuits, playing each side off against the other. His maneuvering paid handsome dividends during the 1719 war with Spain, at which time Saint-Simon found himself isolated in futile opposition.[51]

The conflict was minor, but it was blown up out of proportion to its real importance. Unlike the wars of Louis XIV, this one didn't cost much, and it was easily paid for with paper issued by Law, who was then at the height of his glory. Ultimately it was financed by a nation that had once again begun to taste the fruits of economic growth. The war was actually more political than it was military. It calls to mind such recent conflicts as the British war in the Falklands and the American invasion of Grenada: expeditions launched by powerful modern nations with a minimum of resources and a maximum of publicity. In each case, one result—even if it was not necessarily the sole or initial goal—was to strengthen the hand of the ruling party, which had been in some difficulty before the event. In a way, the war with Spain was also as much a media war as a shooting war. On 8 January 1719, the French government employed the talented Fontenelle, "who was incapable of writing badly," to justify its aggressive intentions.[52] On the following day, his declaration of war, which not only announced the conflict but provided a gloss on its purposes, was posted on walls throughout Paris. In Guyenne, Berwick also published carefully argued bulletins and military notices.

The "media campaign" was a huge success. French public opinion, hesitant at first, rallied patriotically behind the regent after the exposure of the Cellamare conspiracy revealed that a foreign power was manipulating the old court opposition. The steps that Philippe and Dubois had planned in the wake of the Cellamare affair were accelerated after the fighting that broke out between France and Spain in January of 1719 created a sort of *union sacrée* atmosphere. Jansenists and *parlementaires* forgot the oppression they had suffered in August of 1718 and joined Philippe and Dubois against the party of pro-Jesuit, pro-Spanish religious bigots. With considerable skill, the regent and his advisor enlisted the support of previously rebuffed Augustinians such as Cardinal de Noailles, the maréchal d'Estrées, and the Oratorians for their temporarily anti-Spanish policy.[53]

The war, which was won as readily as it was waged, was typical of the Regency, even of the Regency in the liberal phase that seemed to have ended with the "coup" of August and September 1718. Philippe had no intention of repudiating the legacy of Louis XIV–era diplomacy. The Bourbons now occupied the throne of Spain, and for France that was a good thing, hence they should remain. That achievement had been confirmed once and for all by the Treaty of Utrecht. But Dubois's more recent accomplishments also had to be accommodated within this pre-existing framework: he had forged an alliance with England, hammered out a European union encompassing the four or five major powers, and headed off the possibility that Spain might disrupt not only the peace of the Continent but also the tranquillity of the Orléans clan and the Hanovers. All would be for naught if Philip V attempted to press his claim to the throne of France. Since Spain was unwilling to behave as a loyal ally of the house of Orléans should behave, it was up to Philippe to force her to do so. To that end, he decided to wage a small war, the goal of which would be to rid Louis XIV's legacy of one of its more outlandish— and explosive—elements, thereby protecting the rest.

Military operations in Spain were easily wrapped up by the end of 1719. In fact, the fighting ended in November. France's victory had cost her little, but for the few unfortunate soldiers who paid with their lives. After receiving this "friendly slap in the face," Spain at last decided to join the Franco-British-inspired system of collective security devised for Europe by Dubois and Stanhope. The war had been waged essentially under Dubois's leadership, with overall supervision by the regent.[54] Law's contribution was limited to coming up with the money needed to finance the army's activities. Law was thus the regent's factotum, whereas Dubois was his éminence grise (actually, as time went by, more scarlet than gray).

Once again, clear factions developed both within the Regency Council and without. The pro-Spanish faction included both overt and covert supporters of Spain: Huxelles, Villeroy, Villars, and Richelieu. They were opposed by the swelling ranks of the regent's men: top technocrats, Condéans, former Meudonians, and soldiers such as Berwick (the victor of Fontarabie) and Asfeld, who helped plan the Spanish campaign.[55] Biron and Coigny, "warriors in Spain,"[56] were only too happy to outfox old Villars, a national hero temporarily relegated to the sidelines but not yet ejected from the game. His pro-Castilian views made it impossible for him to be named commander of the army in the field, however. Indeed, Madrid would later recognize Villars's pro-Iberian sympathies by making him a grandee in 1723. Since he was a man who coveted riches and honors of any description, this award flattered him but did not altogether console him for his failure to obtain the title of imperial prince, despite assiduous efforts on his behalf at the court of Vienna.[57]

Lucky as well as clever, Orléans and Dubois were shrewd enough to exploit already powerful nationalist and Gallican sentiment in the elite and middle class in pursuing their war with Spain. When recalcitrants within the old court balked at following the government's lead, the response was twofold: on the one hand, they were paid off with Law's banknotes, while on the other, they were isolated and reduced to the role of disgruntled opposition. The dominant faction played on the country's rekindled patriotism and rising prosperity (prosperity at least by comparison with the immediately preceding period).

In view of these successes, it will come as no surprise that the Regency made quick work of the Brittany affair, an episode of resistance triggered like so many others by discontent with high taxes.[58] The days of the League and of Louis XIII were over. The Armorican nobility was no longer led by powerful court aristocrats and nobles of the sword such as Rohan and Mercoeur. Leading the high nobility of Brittany now were the magistrates of the Parlement of Rennes, where the richest and most powerful nobles in the province could be found.[59] In the early stages of the resistance (December 1715 to February 1718), when it became apparent that the spirit of rebellion had been revived on the Armorican peninsula, the region's parlement was not altogether displeased by what it saw. But the war with Spain in 1719 changed the equation. The Rennes magistrates were pro-Gallican and anti-bigot, hence anti-Spanish and perhaps discreetly pro-Jansenist, and they therefore turned against the Breton revolt that had only just gotten under way. In January 1719, they condemned the seditious manifestos that Philip V had begun to circulate in Armorica. As a result, Pontcallec and the other lesser rural nobles who formed the nucleus of the rebellion found themselves on their own, backed by at most a few isolated members of the Rennes parlement such as Sieur Lambilly. The rebels were smugglers, drunkards, and in many cases detested by their oppressed peasants. Their tragicomic uprising was doomed in advance. Yet they deluded themselves into thinking that they had the active support of the king of Spain and the duchesse du Maine (whose mythical involvement in the affair would later inspire the adventures of the duchesse de Berry in western France in 1832).[60] Although discontent with high taxes was an old Armorican tradition, it was not enough to supply the rebels with a party or an army. Their "republican," separatist hopes were destined to fail. The outcome was inevitable: Philippe, ordinarily a clement ruler, ordered the special royal court that was set up in Nantes to be especially severe with the rebels. Indeed, the regent's severity in this instance was reminiscent of Richelieu's (but to make this comparison work one has to imagine a cardinal with nothing more serious to contend with than a handful of salt smugglers). In March 1720, Pontcallec and three of his friends were executed in Nantes.[61] Sixteen of their "accomplices" had fled and were put to death only in effigy, and the remaining conspirators were granted amnesty in April. Whatever (minimal) hope of success the four executed rebels might have had at the outset was dashed once the war with Spain persuaded Jansenists in the parlements (including the Rennes parlement) that they had no choice but to back the regent's government.

Law's downfall toward the end of December 1720 gave Dubois full latitude to do as he pleased during the two and a half years he had left to live. A longtime intimate of the regent, the abbé had been shrewd enough to form an alliance against Law with the most influential representatives of the *robe du Conseil:* most notably, Le Blanc, an erstwhile provincial intendant promoted to secretary of state for war, and d'Argenson, a faithful friend of the Jesuits and former *lieutenant de police* who knew all the capital's secrets and for a time served as keeper of the seals.[62] It would be misleading, however, to speak of Le Blanc and d'Argenson as constituting a "Dubois faction." In 1723, Dubois seized on a financial scandal as a pretext for dismissing a blameless Le Blanc and replacing him as secretary of war with Breteuil, the intendant of Limoges.[63] Earlier, in June 1720, d'Argenson had to give up the seals when John Law briefly regained favor. After that he remained on the sidelines but not before lining his pockets and setting his family up in fine style.[64]

Dubois's real support came first of all from England. Stanhope and Stair consistently backed him against the "Hispanophile" old court, paradoxically incarnated by Torcy and aided by John Law in his perpetual quest for allies.[65] We say "paradoxically" in the case of Torcy because, as a member of the Colbert clan, he had already suffered in the final years of Louis XIV's reign when the group's leaders, Chevreuse and Beauvillier, were pushed off center stage.[66] The Maintenonians then turned their backs on Torcy in favor of their puppet Voysin. Yet Torcy, who had loyally carried out the old king's orders, was a Gallican and therefore not in agreement with the ultramontanist ideas of Beauvillier. Because he had remained aloof from his Colbertian cousins, it was easy for the old Maine-Maintenon-type Louis XIV "establishment" to recruit him. But he was to prove an unreliable ally. Fond of power, Torcy in the end preferred the regent's men to the old court. But was the feeling always mutual?

By contrast, the Tencins—the abbé and his sister the canoness—proved to be much more reliable allies and backers, not to say accomplices, of Dubois than Le Blanc and d'Argenson had been.[67] In financial circles, the four Pâris brothers supported Dubois against their Scottish rival, Law.[68] Born in Dauphiné, the brothers made a fortune as arms dealers, and by the end of 1718, the company they had created using the name of d'Argenson's *valet de chambre* as a front was worth a hundred million livres.[69] Sometimes known as "the anti-system," this company looked for ways to profit from the revenues of the *ferme générale*, or tax farm receipts. In 1721, when the time came to liquidate (quickly) debts backed by Law's now devalued notes, the brothers were entrusted with the official stamp.

Dubois also schemed with another powerful family, the Le Peletiers, who had supplied France with any number of ministers and mandarins. They were like soft wax, ready and willing to be molded however a government minister pleased. In the 1680s, they had served Louvois.[70] Almost four decades later, they threw their support to Dubois. Le Peletier de La Houssaye became the abbé's comptroller general in 1720, and

Armenonville, who married a Le Peletier, became keeper of the seals.[71] The Le Peletiers had always found it wise to serve a powerful minister, whether Louvois or Dubois or, later, Fleury, who would also make use of the clan's financial acumen.[72] Much the same thing can be said about the inevitable Phélypeaux clan, a perennial source of ministers for the ancien régime. The family was so ubiquitous that it seemed part of the furniture. Two of its members, the elderly La Vrillière and the young Maurepas, both became secretaries of state in 1718—or, rather, the family moved into two secretariats.[73] They, too, acted as servants of Dubois, just as they had previously served Desmarets and would subsequently serve Monsieur le Duc and, still later, Louis XVI.

Dubois himself had the ambition of becoming a cardinal. Ultimately his dream was realized, but not without difficulty. His desire to wear the red biretta of a cardinal should not be taken to mean that he totally renounced his earlier shrewd policy of discreetly favoring the Jansenists, however. One cannot overemphasize the point that Dubois did not simply throw himself into the arms of the Jesuits and the constitutional papacy. To be sure, he did try to steer French policy back toward the middle of the road. From 1719 to 1721, he was deeply enmeshed in various intrigues in Rome designed to win himself a red biretta. This brought him closer to Pope Clement XI and the Society of Jesus. After all, one of his primary agents in Italy was none other than the "Jesuit" Lafitau, the brother of the "anthropologist," who as reward for his services was given the bishopric of Sisteron.[74] Nevertheless, any number of signs suggest that in this whole business Dubois did not simply surrender body and soul to the redoubtable sirens of Rome and Saint Ignatius. To begin with, Lafitau was only a phantom Jesuit. What is more, the British diplomats Stair and Stanhope, good Anglicans both, backed the abbé's quest for a cardinal's hat to the hilt. They even approached the court of Vienna in the hope of persuading the "good daughter of the Catholic Church" to use her powerful influence with the sovereign pontiff in Dubois's behalf. The point is that Dubois's biretta, which finally landed on his head in 1721, was the product of a confluence of forces. Dubois was the embodiment of a compromise: he straddled the divide between the court of London and the court of Rome, between Anglicanism and Catholicism. In stark contrast to this figure of compromise, one thinks of a contemporary of his, a living ghost, namely, Alberoni, the disgraced former representative of narrow-minded, Jesuitical, not to say ultramontanist Spain (who was dismissed in December 1719).[75]

Dubois made his peace with the Holy See—as a cardinal, how could he have done otherwise?—but unwilling to renounce either his own plans or the regent's innovative policy, he was careful to make certain concessions to the Jansenists as well. In this period, Orléans and his teacher

Dubois were but one mind in two bodies, and both men eschewed the previous regime's brutal ways of dealing with Huguenots and Augustinians. At times the Jansenists had nothing but praise for the regent. Being totally indifferent in matters of religion and above all an enemy of extremism of any kind, Orléans had the knack of wooing those "on his left" with attractive gifts. In February and March of 1719, for example, he granted the University of Paris, Augustinian at heart, certain financial concessions intended to permit free instruction, the building of new colleges, and enhanced compensation of professors.[76] The Jesuits turned green with envy. An academic by the name of Rollin wrote an excellent *Traité des études* for the occasion. The Sorbonne and its champions organized vast pro-government processions, which one historian has rather oddly dubbed the "free-instruction festivals of 1719."[77] As for the supposed depth of the Orléans family's pro-Jansenist feelings, it is worth noting that the regent's own daughter—the charming, pistol-firing, rocket-launching abbesse de Chelles, who ran her convent with the support of a phalanx of seamstresses and flower girls—in 1718 joined several of her nuns in proposing that a general council of the church be convoked to oppose *Unigenitus*.[78] More Jansenist than that one could not be.

Dubois, though certainly less pious than the abbess, was also careful not to go out of his way to displease Jansenists alarmed by the prospect of his biretta. In June 1719, he again attempted to exert amicable influence on two friends of the Jansenists, Cardinal de Noailles and the duc d'Antin, whom the Jesuits truly hated.[79] In order to disarm the two men's hostility toward him, Dubois availed himself of the good offices of the maréchal d'Estrées and even of John Law, both of whom had on occasion shown kindness to the heirs of Port-Royal.[80] Was such kindness so surprising, after all, on the part of an erstwhile Scottish Protestant such as Law?

Dubois's cautiousness and his determination not to permit a breach with the pro-Jansenist "appellants" were evident earlier, in his reaction to the furor that erupted after the pope issued the bull *Pastoralis officii* on 8 September 1718, reaffirming *Unigenitus* in no uncertain terms. Pope Clement XI hoped that the arguments in this uncompromising text would force Cardinal de Noailles, the appellants' leader, to acknowledge the doctrinal validity of *Unigenitus*.[81] But the arguments in question were drafted in Rome and on their face unacceptable to a French "prelate" such as Dubois. If Noailles refused to acknowledge the truth of the papal text, as seemed likely, schism was but a short step away. Dubois was thus caught in a bind. Since he was looking to become a cardinal, it was difficult for him to stand in the pope's way. Yet stand he did. He thereby demonstrated that he was a staunch Gallican and in no way a puppet of the Jesuits (a charge that has often been made without foundation). In short, he refused to countenance the dangerous course advocated by Clement XI and his nephew Cardinal Albani.[82] The pope's anti-Jansenist maneuvers were thus doomed to failure.

In this affair, Dubois maintained a delicate balance between the forces to his "left" (Jansenist in coloration and perhaps even Protestant and pro-British—there were friendly contacts in the fall of 1718 between Jansenists and Anglicans)[83] and those to his "right" (ultramontane and Roman, standing watch over the old seraglio and, most important, over the path to Dubois's nomination as cardinal). To that end, the minister embarked on a cleverly orchestrated "media offensive": he sought to shape public opinion by frightening people with the specter of the Cellamare conspiracy or baiting them with the prospect of a "Gallican," possibly even pro-Jansenist, war with Spain. Under the circumstances, therefore, he could not possibly accept the crude bargain that the Roman curia was offering without dishonoring himself politically: to remove the cardinal's hat from the prestigious head of Noailles and place it on his own.

He therefore drew the line at persuading the regent to issue a royal declaration ordering Parlement, the theologians, and the faculties to begin "a new period of total silence on the subject of the Constitution" (3 June 1719).[84] This halfway measure was not enough to satisfy the pope's entourage, on whose members Dubois also lavished cash gifts at the expense of the French taxpayer.

Despite his liberal dispensation of bribes to the pope's men, however, Dubois did not hesitate to put obstacles in the way of the pro-Jesuit factions. In September 1719, he forced Rome to recall, this time for good, its nuncio Bentivoglio, who was notorious in Paris for his "criminal" intrigues on behalf of *Unigenitus.* Certain of being appointed a cardinal on his return to Italy, the diplomat was hardly inconsolable at being expelled from the French capital.[85] In Saint-Simon's eyes, he had already done "all the harm that a wolf or a rabid dog is capable of." No one missed him, except perhaps a dancer at the Opera by whom he had had a daughter. The girl later took to the stage under a name chosen in homage to her father: "La Constitution" *(Unigenitus).* The Romans had a few tricks up their sleeves themselves: late in 1719, to the outrage of the French government, the ultra-constitutionalist and anti-Gallican Mailly was named cardinal.[86] This move was a provocation to the appellants, as well as a discreet slap in the face to Dubois, whose biretta was still on hold despite the urging of the regent, England, and the Empire.

The quest for this particular cardinal's hat proved to be costly as well as corrupt. Dubois had had his heart set on becoming a cardinal for some time, and his obsession would eventually cost France eight million livres in bonuses and bribes.[87] In pursuing his goal, Dubois was by no means uncompromising in his anti-Jansenism, as we have seen. Once he had what he wanted, however, his relations with Cardinal de Noailles quickly cooled. Noailles, a man of invincible rectitude, was a staunch though moderate Augustinian. There was talk of consecrating Dubois as the new archbishop of Cambrai, but someone noticed that he was not yet ordained. This gave Noailles, shocked by the abbé's loose morals and unscrupulous ways, an opportunity for revenge.[88] Thwarted in this maneuver, Dubois then turned to less exigent churchmen who were prepared to bestow upon him whatever distinctions or orders his heart desired, from priesthood to archbishop's miter, all in one sacramental marathon. The multiple ordination procedure was completed so expeditiously that Dubois, who claimed to be following the example of Saint Ambrose, was able to grant himself dispensation from the period of retreat required of prospective archbishops. To top it all off, the ordination took place *extra tempora* (that is, outside the times prescribed by the rules of the church). With these formalities out of the way, Dubois hastened to the Louvre, where he went immediately to a meeting of the Regency Council—to the astonishment of all assembled, many of whom had been astonished by Dubois numerous times already. The duc de Mazarin summed up the reaction of council members by remarking that Dubois looked as though he had just come from his first communion. Bishop de Tressan of Nantes then asked if baptism wasn't a prerequisite for communion. But as the regent put it, the ceremony had merely been to *sacrer un sacre*, a clever but untranslatable pun, since a *sacre* is a kind of falcon, a bird of prey.[89]

Among the prelates who ordained and consecrated Dubois, we find the very same Tressan, who in addition to serving as bishop of Nantes was also *premier aumônier* to the duc d'Orléans. He belonged to an important pro-Jesuit ecclesiastical family that had long served the Palais-Royal and the late Monsieur.[90] The other two were Bezons, the archbishop of Rouen, a "crude and awkward lout" but nevertheless an accomplished courtier from an important family of soldiers and *robins*, several of whose members were longtime supporters of Philippe and his friends; and Cardinal de Rohan, a self-proclaimed pseudo-bastard of Louis XIV and "son of love and fortune," who had waited until 1715 to lend his support to Philippe and Dubois but who was for that very reason all the more zealous in serving their interests.[91] By consecrating Dubois at Val-de-Grâce, Cardinal de Rohan killed two birds with one stone: he turned the tables on Cardinal de Noailles while paying court to the regent and Dubois. Mme de Parabère, the regent's mistress at the time, was another backer of Dubois's investment in the archepiscopacy.[92] The minister shamelessly installed himself in the see of Cambrai, which had previously belonged to the late Fénelon. Grandeur and decadence! The whole episode thus revolved around the intrigues of an Orléanist subfaction that include three ecclesiastics (Tressan, Bezons, and Rohan) and a woman

(Parabère), who faithfully carried out Dubois's wishes. Anyone who passed the room in which the new archbishop was preparing to celebrate the mass that was to precede his consecration might have heard him shout, "Damn it! I'll never learn that confounded verse!"[93]

Dubois's pursuit of the biretta ended in 1721. As we have seen, it did not deter the erstwhile abbé from simultaneously pursuing the course he had long since set in foreign policy, to seek an understanding with the Protestant maritime powers while attempting to put together a "European concert" encompassing France, England, the Netherlands, the Empire, and Prussia. France isolated and attacked Spain only in order to bring her, willingly or unwillingly, into the emerging pan-Continental structure. Was Dubois playing the role of the good European? Be that as it may, he did not knuckle under to the papacy even though the pope rewarded him with a red hat. In a way, he "laid down the law" to the sovereign pontiff. For this the man with the cardinal's hat now firmly planted on his head deserves a tip of *our* hat.

It would of course be anachronistic to praise the man from Brive for his "European" vision, but the compliment would not be unwarranted. Dubois was far more than a mere opportunist. Obviously he was defending the dynastic interests of his patron Philippe, just as his English friends Stair and Stanhope were serving the dynastic interests of the Hanovers. But the abbé's pursuit of peace (even allowing for the magnification of his interest in peace in the propaganda that poured out of the French government during the war with Spain in 1719) was based on principle, and he was an inventive and creative exponent of a policy that did ultimately bear fruit. That policy marked a sharp departure from two centuries of bellicose French foreign relations that had led to war on every side and frequent diplomatic isolation under the Valois and especially the Bourbons, Louis XIV above all. Dubois elegantly raised French thinking from a national to an Anglo-Continental level. His policy drew on new ideas that the house of Orléans and the Palais-Royal may not have invented but did promote. Elderly Madame, steeped in the Protestant liberalism of the German-speaking world, which stood diametrically opposed to the Italo-Iberian culture of Louis XIV, exchanged many letters with Leibniz, whose pan-European ecumenical projects were familiar to people living on the banks of the Seine. Philippe himself was deeply influenced by Fénelon's reformist thinking. Within the Palais-Royal, Abbé de Saint-Pierre, who had served as the Princess Palatine's unorthodox chaplain since 1695, was the author of a proposal for perpetual peace in Europe that drew lessons from the very Treaty of Utrecht that its author had helped to negotiate as France's plenipotentiary.[94]

Saint-Pierre was one of the fathers of Orléanist pacifism. Dubois ably put his ideas into practice, even if he would later charge his precursor with being too audacious in his thinking and disavow his proposals. Of course, Dubois was equipped with more than ideas; he also had the resources to turn them into realities. The abbé spent 82 million livres in 1719 to finance the war in Spain and spent another 13.5 million at the Swedish court.[95] As always, he sought alliances with Protestant governments fearful of Spain's power. The strategy was Dubois's, but it was the French state that provided the sinews of war. Growth in general and John Law in particular had rescued France from poverty and even made her wealthy enough to pursue her newly conciliatory foreign policy. Finally, as so often happens, foreign and diplomatic policy became touchstones in "domestic" debates and helped differentiate the ruling factions. One sees this clearly, for instance, in February 1720, when England, suddenly adopting an aggressive posture, refused to return Gibraltar to Spain.[96] London's action outraged the regent, but his fury quickly subsided because Philippe, like his mentor Guillaume Dubois, remained steadfastly Anglophile. The British refusal also permanently raised the hackles of the Hispanophile faction of the old court, which Torcy and Law joined on this occasion for purposes of their own. The financier had become as anti-British as a Scottish exile could be, on top of which he had in the natural course of events become the rival and even adversary of Dubois within the Palais-Royal mafia, the now divided group of the regent's supporters, whose loyalty the cardinal and the financier had once shared.

We see the contending forces in a harsher light when we look at events surrounding the ultimate registration of *Unigenitus* by Parlement on 4 December 1720, in Pontoise.[97] Dubois, the regent, and their backers had made up their minds to put an end to the controversy by forcing Parlement to do their bidding. The highest court in the land was therefore ordered to condemn the Jansenists officially, but once that was done, Philippe and Dubois hoped that further offense could be avoided. On their right, however, they had to contend with Cardinal de Rohan and especially Bissy, both anti-Augustinians. Though not members of the government, they hoped to stiffen its backbone against the Jansenists. Cardinal Mailly, proud of his brand-new red skullcap, was an Ignatian fanatic and therefore a compromising ally. Forbin-Janson, the archbishop of Arles, was even more of a zealot: he compared the supporters of the Jansenists to the locusts then laying waste to Provence, lending a convenient biblical metaphor to the swirling polemics.[98] The fanaticism of the opposition briefly reunited the vast pro-Jansenist coalition (which included the Sorbonne, the parlements, the universities, and the mendicant and Benedictine orders), as did the Cellamare affair, which compromised the few pro-Spanish constitutionals, whereas it naturally left the Jansenists untarnished, briefly bucking up their courage.

It was necessary to act, however. A "centrist" reconciliation proposal known as the *Corps de doctrine* was drafted in 1720.[99] It was backed by Cardinal de Noailles and the Oratorians, many of whom were drawn to the more moderate varieties of Jansenism. For a time, this proposal seemed to garner the support of all the cardinals of France: Noailles, Rohan, Bissy, Gesvres, and Mailly. Was this papering over of cracks that had already been papered over once before capable of restoring peace within the church? Be that as it may, what did seem within reach was a third party, one that would have occupied the middle of the road between Jansenists and *zelanti*. Hotheads on both sides refused to go along, however: on the "extreme left" the pro-Augustinian Colbert of Montepellier led a group that dismissed any thought of surrender out of hand, while the "extreme right" was led by the Molinist Languet of Soissons.[100] The lukewarm *Corps de doctrine* was therefore rejected, and by June 1720 it was forgotten.

Under the circumstances, persuading a Parlement loyal to Noailles to register *Unigenitus* took a masterstroke of diplomacy, which was finally accomplished in December 1720. A shrewd compromise was disguised as an apparent surrender. Parlement, sitting in Pontoise, registered the bull even though some of its members, such as Abbé Pucelle, were still extreme partisans of Jansenius.[101] The magistrates surrounded the registration with so many ambiguous stipulations, however, "that they might as well not have registered it," for what they did "was to do nothing— it was all a game."[102] Was the reconciliation superficial? Perhaps, but the *parlementaires*, "*rentiers* first and foremost," were handsomely compensated by the departure of Law, whom they detested. By a happy coincidence, the financier left Paris on 14 December 1720.[103] He was in effect sacrificed to Parlement and for the sake of peace in the church as well as on account of his own unpopularity, which was in any case not as universal as some have claimed.

The dismissal of the erstwhile comptroller general was of course a major concession to the magistrates of Parlement, who, being *rentiers* themselves, were intransigent defenders of the value of their securities. They had felt threatened to the core by the Scot's policy of lowering interest rates and making strategic use of inflation. They had feared that their capital would be eroded and their income whittled away. So Philippe and Dubois offered them the head of Law, their bête noire, on a silver platter, in exchange for which they grudgingly agreed to register *Unigenitus*. Everybody came away with something.

The departure of Law revealed a split in the regent's cabal, of which Dubois was now the undisputed leader.[104] The revival of the economy, which had been progressing ever since Philippe came to power, had made it possible to dispense with the Scotsman's services. Law was also done in by his own tactical errors and technical problems with the "system" he had created. But the juice had been wrung from the orange, and now it was possible to throw away the rind. Law's dismissal stripped away the thin camouflage behind which certain members of the old court had been nervously hiding. Suddenly exposed, they found themselves once again in the line of fire. They would prove to be no match for Dubois's heavy artillery.

Law left Paris in December 1720. Dubois became a cardinal in July 1721. The old court remained recalcitrant, but its opposition had proved sterile.[105] Parlement, still sidelined for its earlier "infraction," was mollified by Law's departure. And not all of the millions generated by the Scotsman's system had evaporated: as has already been mentioned several times, d'Antin, the house of Condé, and more than one member of the old court were left sitting on comfortable fortunes.

The regent's faction, now the governing party, remained in the shadow of Cardinal Dubois, as we must now call him. His impressive biretta, obtained by the most dubious of means, had cost the French treasury dearly. It was by no means pure Roman crimson in color, nor had it been obtained solely by Jesuit intrigue. It also symbolized, paradoxically to be sure, further rapprochement with the Protestant powers, with England and the Germanic Empire, both of which had been glad to see Dubois get what he wanted.[106] Having produced a flood of profits, Law's system collapsed at the same time as its English counterparts (the South Seas Company went bankrupt in January 1721, one month after Law's departure).[107] Dubois's elevation to cardinal inaugurated a period in which moderate Jansenists and *parlementaires rentiers* gained, or rather regained, a certain influence within the contentious power elite. Of course Cardinal de Noailles and the *premier président* of Parlement looked upon the new cardinal with contempt. He laughed it off. Nevertheless, they were not totally excluded from his system of power, although their actual influence appears to have been of a relatively minor order.

The emerging rapprochement with Spain was similarly intertwined with issues of domestic and foreign policy. Let us cast our minds back to the year 1720, which ended, as we have seen, with Law's departure. In December of the previous year, Philip V had dismissed Alberoni following a military defeat, and this had opened up the possibility of improved relations between France and Spain.[108] In effect, Madrid had sacrificed Alberoni on the altar of reconciliation with France and England, which had made his dismissal a prerequisite to any peace negotiations. Saint-Simon, always adept at seeing things through the wrong end of the telescope, saw Alberoni's dismissal as the handiwork of Laura Pescatori, the queen's nurse. Apparently Alberoni had previously punctured the woman's pretensions, and when the time was ripe she returned the favor with interest. In other words, "Laura" was the sequel to "Nanon," yet another famous nurse who had allegedly wielded considerable influence with yet another "queen," Mme de Maintenon, and who had supposedly been able to wangle a number of nominations for her friends.[109] Nevertheless, in the summer of 1720, after Alberoni's downfall, Madrid's new ambassador to France, a Jacobite "native of Ireland" by the name of Laulès (a Gallicization of his real name, Lawless), whom Saint-Simon liked, continued to play games like those that had gotten his predecessor Cellamare, a dyed-in-the-wool Alberonian, into so much trouble.[110] Laulès made use of whatever material was at hand: he schemed with the old court, with Torcy, with Law (whose star was on the wane), and with Parlement (even though it was Jansenist in the majority and deeply hostile to Iberian-style Catholicism). He even entertained thoughts of helping the house of Bourbon defeat the regent and Dubois, whom he believed to have been tarred with Law's unpopularity.[111]

Dubois shrewdly made the first move. In order to outflank Laulès, he first made contact with Philip V's confessor, the Jesuit Daubenton, later to become a cardinal.[112] "This priest's heart remained French" despite his virulent anti-Jansenism. All Dubois had to do was to make a few friendly overtures. He permitted Daubenton to believe that rigorous measures might be instituted against the Augustinians (in the event, however, those measures were of course slow to materialize). This ecclesiastical dickering across the Pyrenees paved the way, in the period between March and July of 1721, for the successful negotiation of first a Dual Alliance between France and Spain and then a Triple Alliance of France, Spain, and England, which reinforced the Quadruple Alliance that Madrid had become a party to earlier, on 17 February 1720. Spain thus joined the European concert. Eventually she made peace with England, a Protestant power. If the goal was to sap the energy of extremist Catholicism in southern Europe, a modicum of success was achieved. In any case, the Castilian crown accepted the stipulations of the Treaty of Utrecht, which could only please the Hanoverians, the Orléans clan, and the Imperials, all of whom wished to prevent the Spanish Bourbons from acceding to the throne of France. Last but not least, Dubois rightly sought to sacrifice lesser goals for greater ones: he therefore agreed to a number of concessions to England and Spain. For instance, he allowed the English to claim a piece of the trade with Latin America, especially in the *asiento*, the slave trade with the Spanish West Indies. He also agreed to return to Spain a fortress in Pensacola, Florida, which the French had briefly occupied during the war of 1719.

Generations of historians, up to and including Leclercq, foolishly castigated Dubois for these concessions, as if they were so many acts of treason.[113] We will be more indulgent than our predecessors. Paris is well worth a mass (or even a cardinal's hat). Peace in Europe, better relations with the Protestant powers, holding on to most of Louis XIV's dynastic gains in Spain but without their dangerous implications—these were achievements for which it was well worth sacrificing the fortifications at Mardyck, the base in Pensacola, and a piece of the slave trade, which was morally repugnant in any case. With or without Mardyck and Pensacola, France was destined to retain its part of Flanders and to lose its little corner of Florida forever. As for trade in the south and central Atlantic, there would be enough growth in the eighteenth century to allow anyone who wished, English or French, a respectable portion. Leclercq to the contrary notwithstanding, the idea that France under Dubois somehow "sacrificed its commercial interests" (when in reality French foreign trade figures would soon soar) is silly.[114] A systematic anti-British policy no longer made sense, and Dubois was right to leave King George's insular subjects their "fair" share (which in this case amounted to a few shiploads of unfortunate slaves). This was the price of the first "Entente Cordiale." Finally, let us state for the record that there is no proof whatsoever that the British paid Dubois to achieve this end. His venality, in this respect at least, remains to be demonstrated.[115]

Dubois was not a man to "die for Mardyck." The subsequent course of history proved him right. A group of active diplomats saw to it that the ideas of the abbé, who in the meantime had become a cardinal, emerged triumphant.[116] They included the chevalier Destouches, the "Jesuit" Lafitau, the *robin* Chavigny, and the abbé de Mornay. Mornay's sharp wit and many talents captivated the king of Spain. In Madrid, he became the mentor of the incompetent French ambassador Maulévrier, whom the Spanish nicknamed the "hissing cat."[117] The abbé was ably assisted by Sieur Robin, who rounds out our list of diplomats. As for Maulévrier, the marquis who represented France in Madrid, he embodied all that was worst in the diplomacy of the ancien régime. When Saint-Simon was in Spain, the two got on very badly. Maulévrier made a habit of showing the Spanish the dispatches he received from Versailles. Foul-mouthed and disagreeable, he was disliked by his Iberian counterparts, who gave him no credit for the many services he rendered. But Maulévrier was undismayed by the chilly reception: he said he would rather be alone than visit with Spaniards. He criticized their customs, approved of nothing, criticized everything, and told his hosts exactly what he thought of them.[118]

In the front ranks of Dubois's group (more properly called the Orléans-Dubois group), we also find Fontenelle, a longtime servant of the house of Orléans and father of the skeptical modernist intelligentsia. It was he who prepared anti-Spanish propaganda for the abbé.[119] His manner was "deadpan humor disguised as flattery." For instance, he hailed Dubois's diplomatic success in forging the Triple Alliance with a witty jibe: "You are the minister of all the courts." Serving Dubois, who "silenced the old court by entering into an alliance with Spain without provoking a quarrel with England," Fontenelle was part of the "technocratic elite" that set and implemented France's foreign policy to the consternation of the high aristocrats and white-haired mandarins of the old court. Some of these technocrats came from *robin* backgrounds (including Fontenelle himself and Chavigny); there were also commoners (such as Robin) and clerics (such as Mornay). This shows once again that the Regency, even in its authoritarian phase, in no way represented a simple return to the narrow-minded, reactionary authoritarianism of Louis XIV; it was something altogether different.[120]

A similar remark applies to the two "Spanish marriages" that Dubois and the regent cooked up with the subsequent accord of the king of Spain (July 1721). First Mornay and later Sourdeval served as intermediaries.[121] The goal was to arrange a marriage between the prince of Asturias, Philip V's son and heir apparent, and the regent's daughter Mlle de Montpensier. The marriage ceremony proved to be something of a burlesque when the celebrant, Cardinal Borgia, displayed scandalous ignorance of Catholic ritual, to the dismay of his desperate but helpless chaplains.[122] At the same time, there was talk of a marriage between Louis XV and the Spanish infanta, Philip V's only daughter. The first of these two marriages (Asturias-Montpensier) actually took place. Plans for the second were upset after Monsieur le Duc became prime minister in 1725 and, for tactical though not doctrinal reasons, took an anti-Spanish line in foreign policy.[123]

The prospective bride and groom in this royal match were very young, to be sure, but no one was particularly shocked at the time. The children's annoyance with the whole affair showed them to be much more "human" than their parents. In Madrid, the thirteen-year-old Mlle de Montpensier once dismissed the French ambassador, none other than Saint-Simon himself, by belching three times in his face to the amazement of everyone present. The normally indomitable ambassador was struck dumb and forced to flee the room amidst raucous laughter.[124] Saint-Simon, whose genius came and went, was stupid or naïve enough (or sufficiently ironic) to have missed the obvious message in the girl's behavior: that she was tired of serving against her will as a diplomatic bargaining chip.

How did the Spanish marriages serve the foreign and domestic policy of a regency that had reverted to its semiauthoritarian ways? How, in other words, did the wedding plans fit into Dubois's strategy? For the abbé, soon to become a cardinal, arranging these marriages between French and Spanish princes and princesses was a way of preventing three other marriages whose consequences might prove devastating for France. If three daughters of the imperial family married the three sons of Philip

V, Spain would be literally wedded to the Empire, and the Quadruple Alliance would lose its significance and perhaps even fall apart. This might once again sour relations between France and the non-Catholic states of Europe. Dubois's nightmare was that if these marriages took place, all his efforts to improve France's ties to the Protestant maritime powers would be reduced to naught. Those efforts had been the centerpiece of the abbé's foreign policy, as Saint-Simon's unpublished papers make clear.[125]

Again, in the mind of the minister from Brive, the Spanish marriages did not represent a simple return to the piety-drenched, Iberophile policy of Louis XIV. Rather, their purpose was to shore up the southern and southeastern flanks of a diplomatic offensive aimed at northern Europe in concert with the rising capitalist and maritime powers of the day, England and Holland.

While attending to these international concerns, Dubois also kept one eye on the French capital. If he could bring off these Spanish marriages, he would simultaneously steal the wind from the sails of the old court, which had sought to capitalize on the differences that divided Madrid from Paris. When the Iberian weddings were announced (in September 1721), the old marshals—Villeroy, Villars, and Huxelles—were enraged to see the value of their "investment" in Spain plummet.[126] As a result of this maneuver, the "cabal opposed to the duc d'Orléans" was knocked out of the action for quite some time. It will come as no surprise to learn that Parlement joined the old court in taking a dim view of Louis XV's proposed marriage to the infanta.[127] Dubois, meanwhile, was able to consolidate his own cabal, which enjoyed the firm backing of the regent.

To that end, Dubois recruited—and subsequently bankrupted—one of the odder members of the Orléanist group, Philippe's friend Saint-Simon. At Orléans's behest, Dubois had sent the *petit duc* to Spain as head of the mission that was to submit the formal proposal for the hand of the infanta to the Catholic King and then sign the marriage contract. At the outset, Dubois was none too enthusiastic about the idea of entrusting this responsibility to Saint-Simon, but he soon realized that he had been handed an unforeseen gift: owing to the enormous costs associated with such a mission, the troublesome duke would be ruined and reduced to begging for handouts.[128] By obliging Saint-Simon and his wife to lay out enormous sums, Dubois would soon have them crawling at his feet. As proud as Saint-Simon could be in the privacy of his study, he knew how to humble himself when necessary. He did not fail to flatter Dubois, nor did he hesitate to solicit cash stipends, which Dubois disbursed with grudging contempt.[129] Saint-Simon had always been Orléans's man. Now he became Dubois's serf. It was more than he could swallow. Twenty years on, he would avenge himself on the late cardinal in his *Memoirs*, so much so that he unjustly sullied the reputation of a remarkable statesman in the eyes of posterity, which has been all too quick to take Saint-Simon's slanderous account at face value.[130] Within the privacy of his own home, Saint-Simon had been bold enough to hang a portrait of Cardinal Dubois next to his commode. To be sure, the Princess Palatine was no less kind: she habitually referred to "le Dubois" as a "dirty dog" and treated him with scorn.

The (international) Congress of Cambrai, which was convoked in 1721, limited itself to reaffirming the new European and western union— a union that symbolically bridged the English Channel. Initially, this union came about as the result of a confluence of factors, among them Dubois's diplomacy and a fortuitous harmony of interests joining the house of Hanover to the *maison* d'Orléans. Little progress was made in Cambrai, however, and little of note happened there: "The cooks were busier than their masters." This parody of diplomacy would continue until 1727.[131] Dubois's death may have had something to do with this partial failure.

L et us return to the question of the biretta, because on this as on so many other subjects Saint-Simon was by no means always wrong: disputes over precedence, even among ecclesiastics, tell us a great deal about how hierarchies were constructed. They point up the intrinsic uncertainties that the system could tolerate on occasion and indicate where power was concentrated. We already know that Dubois's biretta cost the French exchequer a good deal of money, though in the final analysis less than a war: a mere eight million livres tournois distributed to members of the pope's entourage. Dubois's hat was worth considerably more than its weight in gold. To the former abbé, now a cardinal, it was nevertheless a rare and powerful instrument, not to mention an additional source of income.

On 7 August 1721, Dubois, who had learned several days earlier that his elevation was assured, made his first move. Flattering the sensibilities of the high nobility, as was his wont, he wrote to Cardinal de Rohan: "We must look for an opportunity to restore men of the cloth to the places in government that they once occupied almost exclusively, and from which they have been driven out."[132] No sooner had he placed the red skullcap on his head than the cunning cardinal deemed it beneath him to attend meetings of the Regency Council.[133] Afraid that he might not be paid the deference due to his new rank, he sent a secretary of state (and of the council) in his stead: La Vrillière.[134] Once again the Phélypeaux clan (of whom La Vrillière was one) were pressed into service in a walk-on part. They joined Dubois as eagerly as they had once joined

Maintenon and Maine. In 1721, as so often in the past, the siren song of power filled their ears.

Dubois's second move was to drive a wedge deeper into the split that had already developed in the old court. He (elegantly) dismissed Torcy as superintendent of the Post.[135] The post office was the last bastion for this nephew of Colbert, who was locked in mortal combat with the new eminence—his only serious rival in the diplomatic realm. Torcy was nevertheless awarded a pension of 60,000 livres, to be paid out of the revenues of the Post. The superintendent's position (crucial for spying on the mail) was immediately (October 1721) absorbed into the Secretariat of Foreign Affairs—which was, of course, under the personal supervision of Dubois himself.

The third phase of Dubois's strategy involved the liquidation of Law's system. Work was proceeding deliberately under the supervision of individuals whose fortunes were linked to those of the new cardinal: Le Peletier de La Houssaye, the comptroller general of finance, and the Pâris brothers, the financiers charged with the actual mechanics of the liquidation. The process amounted to a confiscation of securities owned by some 511,000 families (or one French family in ten, which is to say, the entire elite of the kingdom). In the middle of November 1721, 400 million livres worth of shares in Law's bank were burned in an iron cage in the courtyard of the Hôtel de Nevers, to the delight of onlookers.[136]

Phase four involved Rohan, whose appearance in the scarlet robes of a cardinal earned him the epithet "Chausse-pied," or "Shoehorn." Through a series of intrigues hatched by Philippe and Dubois, Rohan was able to establish the priority of his ecclesiastical rank within the Regency Council. In any event, the privileges that he claimed had been a matter of tradition since Richelieu and Mazarin. His rank placed him ahead of the dukes and peers as well as the chancellor (although princes of the blood continued to be seated *ahead* of cardinals). If a "crimsoned" noble (that is, a cardinal) such as Rohan was entitled to such deference, could it be denied to a man of humbler origins, to be sure, but equally "crimson," namely, Guillaume Dubois? Rohan thus cleared the way for Dubois to enter the Regency Council with his head held high.[137] And a decisive entry it was.

In February 1722, the dukes and peers and marshals of France, which is to say, the old court, or "all the high nobility of the realm," in effect quit the council as a result.[138] They did not wish to concede to Dubois the superiority of rank that he was now claiming, having used his accomplice Rohan as a "cover" or stepping-stone.[139] Among those who "resigned" were Villars, d'Antin, and Noailles, symbols of the factions that had dominated the court toward the end of Louis XIV's reign. Meanwhile, d'Aguesseau, the ally of the Augustinian *parlementaires*, was once again relieved of the seals, but this time he handed them over to Armenonville, a close ally of Le Peletier and hence of Dubois himself.[140]

In the days that followed, Armenonville's son Morville replaced his father as secretary of state after the older man was promoted to keeper of the seals. The Le Peletier–Armenonville clan thus rode Dubois's coat-tails into power and adopted him as their leader. The Regency Council became a sort of private tête-à-tête: among the invited guests were the house of Condé in the person of Charolais and Monsieur le Duc, who for the time being were content to follow Dubois's lead; Toulouse, the one royal bastard with a flicker of life remaining in him; and the allies and accomplices of Philippe and Dubois, who continued to fill the leading roles (with Bouthillier, La Vrillière, Canillac, and Rohan as understud-ies). Everything ran like clockwork. With d'Aguesseau out of the way, Dubois was free to make overtures to the Jesuits. Through a subterfuge he reinstated them as confessors to the youthful king.[141] But the wily cardinal had no intention of allowing the Ignatians to clamber their way to the top. He was too crafty for that.

Dubois also seized the opportunity to purge the regent's cabal of its compromising "roués": Nocé, Brancas, and Broglie, joined before long by Canillac, were all dispatched willy-nilly to either country seats or monasteries, where they were free to enjoy life in retirement. Dubois feared that these loyal allies of the regent might overshadow him.[142] When Dubois died, they were recalled. Close friends of the regent, they had rubbed the new cardinal the wrong way, so they had been obliged to remain in exile until His Eminence was at last ready to depart this vale of tears.[143]

Before that day arrived, however, Dubois completed his purge, which was still in full swing in the summer of 1722. In June, the young king, by now almost an adolescent, returned to Versailles with the regent, the cardinal, and the "new court." It was indeed a "new" court, as the old one had vanished into gilded exile. Dubois moved into an apartment in the chateau that had once been reserved for Colbert and Louvois.[144] Like his predecessors, the cardinal-minister was virtually omnipotent. But the new prelate's almost pacifist policies had replaced the now outmoded aggressiveness of the Le Tellier–Louvois circle. By this point, the cardinal was bold enough to try anything. Having decimated the old court, he then got rid of supporters of the regent who displeased him or were of no use to him: within a few days, Noailles, Canillac, Villars, Hux-elles, Bezons, and Gramont were sent word that their presence at the chateau was no longer welcome. In August 1722, Villeroy was banished to Lyons, where he served as governor, after making the mistake of vent-ing his senile wrath on Dubois and then failing to avail himself of an offer of reconciliation. Instead of repenting for past misdeeds, "he became infatuated with the *musical* sound of his sentences" and went so far as to insult the cardinal and even threaten him. D'Artagnan then arrested the marshal, who, struck dumb by the swiftness of his fall, was hauled off to his country estate like so much merchandise.[145] Tencin, Charost (who emerged to replace Villeroy),[146] Fontenelle, and Saint-Simon (despite the considerable amount of ink he would devote to blackening Dubois's reputation after the cardinal's death) remained staunch supporters of Philippe and sometimes even of his minister and former teacher. With the house of Condé protecting the flanks, Dubois, Orléans, and their army of supporters forged ahead with their offensive.[147] Bishop Fleury, an associate of Villeroy's, hung on by the skin of his teeth after an admittedly inglorious retreat, thereby salvaging himself for the brilliant success that lay ahead.[148] He still thought of himself as very young and very green, and sure of his royal pupil's tender affection, he could afford to bide his time: after all, he was only sixty-nine.

Although Saint-Simon remained a loyal supporter of the regent, he was squeezed out of any active role in government after his return from Spain. In his *Memoirs*, he confesses that he was thereafter kept informed only of "minor and court" matters, which in any case were to his taste. He vainly opposed the exile of the duc de Noailles, whom he thought it best not to "castrate" (politically speaking).[149] Believing that he had persuaded Philippe on this point, he was surprised to learn that the regent, after being rebuked by Dubois, had "caved in" to the minister's wishes and agreed to Noailles's dismissal without mentioning Saint-Simon's opposition.[150]

On 22 August 1722, the regent took the logical next step and appointed Dubois prime minister.[151] The nomination was announced in a text drafted by Pecquet, a clerk in the Secretariat of Foreign Affairs, who had suffered no pangs of conscience in the move from serving Torcy to serving the cardinal. Although Philippe formally outranked his former teacher by one grade, he in fact acted as the kingdom's lieutenant general. The Pâris brothers, ably assisted by two *intendants de finances*, Fagon junior and d'Ormesson, continued to play an essential role in the reorganized ministry.[152] At the same time, an opposition to Dubois began to form around the regent's mediocre son, the duc de Chartres. The pattern was the same as in the past and was perhaps inevitable in a patrimonial system in which each generation becomes a potential focal point around which cabals may form. This latest cabal included the house of Condé, the naval bastard Toulouse (already on the rebound), certain members of the Estrées and Rohan families, and even two important military experts, Le Blanc and Belle-Isle.[153] The Pâris brothers, as staunchly devoted to Dubois as ever, became the target of this clandestine opposition's discreet intrigues. Indeed, when it came to intrigue, Belle-Isle, a descendant of Fouquet, had the right genes: opposition (of a relatively moderate sort) ran in his blood, biding its time until the moment was ripe.

When Louis XV attained the age of majority in February 1723, he confirmed Orléans as head of his councils, which were restored to more or less the same form as under Louis XIV.[154] Later he also confirmed Dubois as prime minister. In the interim, Dubois made himself wealthier and more powerful by annexing the revenues of a number of rich abbeys.[155] Weren't the expenses he incurred as prime minister great? He also became a member of the Académie Française. The only place from which he was still excluded was the *grand-chambre* of Parlement, the last refuge of the opposition to His Majesty.[156] On the eve of his death, Dubois, superintendent of the Post and archbishop of Cambrai as well as master of seven abbeys, was maneuvering to take control of the monasteries of Cîteaux and Prémontré. Saint-Simon estimated the cardinal-minister's annual income to be 1,534,000 livres, including the mythical stipend of 960,000 livres supposedly paid by England.[157] But even 574,000 livres was nothing to sneeze at: Dubois had enough to keep the pot boiling. If one calculates the capital represented by such an income, it is clear that his fortune was at least as large as that which Colbert had left at his death.

During the final months of Dubois's life, the various cabals crystallized in mute confrontation. The inept duc de Chartres remained the "black hole" at the center of a discreet and heterogeneous opposition that included his mother, the duchesse d'Orléans, a product of one of the Sun King's amorous escapades now disgusted by the more recent adventures of her husband, Philippe. Inevitably, Villeroy, in exile in Lyons, was also a member of the group.[158] So were various others, including some we have encountered before: Villars, d'Estrées, Noailles, d'Aguesseau, Torcy, and Toulouse, all "old court," along with Le Blanc and (in purgatory but not for long) Canillac and Nocé. This opposition was loosely organized and had no program of its own. It was merely a constellation of various groups ejected at one time or another from the *philippienne* galaxy. Elsewhere on the horizon, a pair of stars, one relatively young, the other not so young, heralded what would soon be a dazzling ascent: Monsieur le Duc, representing the collateral branch of the Bourbons, pawed the ground while awaiting his chance to become prime minister, which came after Orléans's death in 1723 and lasted until 1726. Meanwhile, Fleury, almost seventy, was preparing himself to act as the king's proxy. The young king would take his time about it, but eventually, when the moment was ripe, he did name his beloved former teacher to the post of prime minister.

For the time being, Dubois enjoyed solid support from the financial community, including the brothers Pâris. He was also backed by England, by the regent, who believed in him, and by his own family.

His brother Joseph came to Paris from Limousin and was named director of bridges and highways.[159] Dubois's nephew served as his factotum. Only his bladder seriously betrayed him: it became infected. On 10 August 1723, he died a miserable death despite the best efforts of the surgeons— or perhaps because of them. To the end, he continued to accumulate power and prebends in ever more copious quantities. On the same day that he chaired the Assembly of the Clergy, he also presided over a meeting of the stockholders of the Compagnie des Indes.[160] But death came anyway, and the wheel of fortune turned. Logically enough, Philippe d'Orléans himself replaced Dubois as prime minister.[161] But soon he too would be gone (he died on 2 December 1723).

During the few months remaining to him, the regent did nothing to alter in any fundamental way the supremely intelligent policy that his former teacher and friend had pursued under his guidance: entente cordiale with England, peace in Europe, a compromise on the religious issue between Jansenism and Jesuitry, a return to centralized administration but with de facto liberalism toward the principal forces of the elite, including Parlement, the aristocracy, and to some extent even the Jansenists (and perhaps the Huguenots). Saint-Simon, genius though he was in some respects, had—to put it charitably—understood little of all this. Louis XIV had been too far to the right for his taste, Orléans too far to the left. In each case, the *petit duc* missed the point—which does not mean that he was in the center. He thought of himself as living in an "age of monsters," and he was always either too myopic or too hyperopic to see things straight. Unbeknownst to himself, he was a rare bird— a pterodactyl surrounded by dinosaurs.

If we wish to sum up the Regency, we would do well to avoid clichés, even clichés nicely tinted to give a "period" feel. Nowadays nobody criticizes Orléans for his "debauches," even if a certain unspoken censoriousness lingers in our pejorative attitude toward the Regency. To be sure, not even the ever-vigilant moralists of the historical profession have thought to accuse Philippe of homosexuality—for good reason. In recent years, however, moralistic history has reared its head again.[162] Although it has been withering on the subject of Orléans's morals, it has oddly enough had relatively little to say about the seraglio with which Henri IV surrounded himself—Henri IV, the hero of French grade schools and of Lavissian ideology. What this demonstrates is that quite apart from all this "business about women," something else is at stake: the Jacobin tradition. Indeed, Philippe has been criticized for laxness toward Britain, Parlement, and aristocrats. The critique is only implicit, to be sure, but it would never occur to anyone to level the same charges at good King Henri, who is usually discussed in relation to the beginnings of absolutism, another ample topic.

Shennan, the author of a comprehensive biography of Philippe, similarly feels obliged to point out that the regent's qualities were offset by three serious handicaps.[163] First, he was easily bored. Second, he was an incurable hedonist. And third, he had little enthusiasm for revenge and violent aggression. The first two of these charges concern the regent's private life and are of no interest for present purposes. The third should be grounds for praise rather than blame: in order to be remembered as a great statesman, does one have to decapitate Cinq-Mars, guillotine Louis XVI, or send Bastien-Thiry before a firing squad? Although Shennan's book is excellent in many respects, he nevertheless makes the even more absurd statement that Philippe had no "vision of a permanent international order."[164] Yet Dubois, with Orléans's steadfast support and Stanhope's aid, nevertheless succeeded in putting together the first European system of collective security, in which France and England were joined by three other great powers, the Empire, Holland, and Spain. Neither Aristide Briand nor François Mitterrand, both of whom resembled Dubois in certain ways, would do any better (or any worse) in the realm of European policy.

Philippe's eight years in power were in their way a great success. Of course everything depends on one's point of view. Let us judge the prince in the light of the goals he set for himself. It was by no means his intention to rescue millions of French men and women from the poverty in which they remained mired. Lover of humanity though he was, the best he could hope for was to raise the general standard of living and improve the lot of the poorest of the poor (to put it in contemporary terms). Fortunately, a start was made toward both of these ends, thanks to the efforts of Philippe's man John Law and to the long economic recovery that began with the restoration of peace. Orléans's major concerns lay elsewhere: he hoped to transmit the royal power intact to his nephew Louis XV while ridding it of monstrous and pointlessly authoritarian outgrowths such as perpetual war, excessive taxes, and unrestrained despotism—outgrowths that had proliferated under Louis XIV. Philippe discharged this avuncular but challenging responsibility with superb skill. Even his style of government, fundamentally empirical, contributed to his success: while continuing old efforts and launching new ones, he added small touches of his own everywhere. One thing led to another, and success grew out of success in treelike fashion—in keeping with the rococo aesthetic of the age, so different from the more rigidly geometrical neoclassical style that some but not all enlightened despotic regimes would subsequently adopt, and different, too, from the *façons de faire* of a certain Louis XIV.

Sweeping changes at the top level of government were characteristic of the Regency. Law was from Scotland, Lafitau from Bordeaux. The

Tencins, brother and sister, belonged to a recently ennobled family from the Dauphiné, while the brothers Pâris were commoners from the same province. Chirac, the duc d'Orléans's physician, hailed from Rouergue. The recently deceased Fénelon was from the Périgord, and even after his death his ideas continued to inspire some of the regent's policies. Homberg, the official chemist of the Palais-Royal and darling of both Saint-Simon and Madame, was Dutch.[165] Berwick, the supreme commander of Philippe's troops during the little war with Spain, was the bastard son of a former British king and an English lady.[166] Dubois, as we have seen, was born into a middle-class family in Brive. His brother and nephew reaped the benefits of his prodigious career. In the less-than-spectacular early stages of that career, the Limousin "abbé" took an interest in English culture, that of Oxford and Cambridge as well as London. And Fleury, who was from Languedoc, would carry on after the Regency was gone, having been clever enough not to incur the regent's displeasure while he was alive. Fleury was the son of a tax collector in the diocese of Lodève—an honorable but not very exalted position, and his humble background naturally invited the scorn of certain *grand seigneurs* at court. In a sense, then, the men in whom Philippe placed his confidence were geographically and socially marginal, or at any rate peripheral.

The Regency thus drew its servants from a milieu rather different from the one in which Louis XIV's government recruited its top officials. Men like Colbert, Le Tellier, the Phélypeaux clan, La Vrillière (who would become a duke *de robe et de plume*), Voysin, Chamillart, and Villeroy were jumped-up *robins* with roots in the Paris Basin, in the region that had once been "Gothic," then became the bastion of centralized monarchy, and wound up Jacobin. Here, for a period of centuries, the basic outlines of French politics were shaped once and for all: it was always a question of unifying the nation to make war on some rival power, be it England or Holland. Dubois and Fleury took a more flexible approach: as men of the south, they were not superpatriots. Fleury was even accused of making a pact with the enemy and striking up the *Te Deum* when the duke of Savoy occupied Fréjus in 1707.[167] Although this was outright slander, Saint-Simon was quick to repeat it.[168] Such nastiness is nevertheless enlightening: talented as he was, Fleury of Languedoc was no "national royalist" in the mold of Colbert and Louvois. Clearly, with their new roster of top officials, Philippe and his royal nephew were able to adopt a policy less exclusively focused on national and dynastic glory and more conciliatory toward the forces of progress represented by the Protestant, liberal, maritime, capitalist powers to the north.

Does Philippe d'Orléans therefore deserve credit for inventing an eighteenth-century version of "Orléanism" that anticipated the nineteenth-century version? The question really transcends Philippe as an individual. Ever since the middle of the sixteenth century, when France for the first time divided into two warring ideological camps—Catholics and Protestants, followed, as time went by, by Molinists and Jansenists, traditionalists and partisans of the Enlightenment, and finally, left and right, or anticlerical and clerical, or red and white—the royal family functioned as a network (at least as long as it enjoyed power and an essential aura of sacredness). Within the family, we may distinguish certain strategic sectors (such as generations and collateral branches) around which reform tendencies influenced to one degree or another by fashionable ideologies were able to crystallize. In the 1560s, the Condés, princes of the blood, took the lead in the Huguenot revolt. During the Fronde, Condé, Beaufort, and la Grande Mademoiselle, all members of the "Holy Family," threw themselves into the antiabsolutist struggle of the parlements and the Parisians. Later, the duc de Bourgogne, Louis XIV's grandson, became the symbol of still other reform movements.[169]

Gaston d'Orléans, the younger brother of Louis XIII, led the battle against that king and his authoritarian cardinal-ministers. The singular clumsiness of that opposition effort overshadowed some of its semiliberal aspects. Philippe d'Orléans, the son of a king's brother, was obviously a man of defter touch than his great-uncle Gaston. To be sure, his pacifism and openness to innovation from whatever source, aristocratic or *parlementaire*, found expression in a regime that would in the long run retain its authoritarian essence. Nevertheless, a decisive break had been made with the rigid line of Louis XIV. What was best about the reign of Louis XV—tolerance (active or passive) of the major cultural trends and a more or less successful search for negotiated solutions (which unfortunately provoked an unparalleled degree of nationalist sentiment on the part of people quick to blame "Louis le Bien-Aimé" for giving away India, Belgium, and Quebec)—was to a great extent prefigured by the Regency.

In this sense, there was indeed a first version of Orléanism, a *philippienne* Orléanism. The regent saw himself as an innovator, though when necessary he quickly reverted to the old crypto-absolutist methods. His Regency preceded and foreshadowed the second, truly liberal form of Orléanism, which Philippe-Egalité would attempt and Louis-Philippe successfully introduce. Clearly, the traditional open-mindedness of the Orléans clan, in a way exemplified even today by the present pretender to the French throne, has an illustrious ancestry. It is by no means absurd to trace its origins all the way back to Philippe, the son of a king's homosexual, nonconformist younger brother and a German woman with Lutheran sympathies. Indeed, Juan Carlos of Spain (descended from another branch of the Bourbons) is not an unworthy heir of the seeds of liberty so tentatively sown during the Regency—seeds that would miraculously multiply in post-Franco Spain.

The Regency also invites us to take a more concrete look at a problem touched on at the beginning of this chapter: the end of autocratic rule. Or if that is putting it too strongly, how to move beyond a harsh, tightly controlled political system to something freer and more open: conservative transition or controlled adaptation? Of course, we do not mean to compare the rule of Louis XIV in any crude way with a modern twentieth-century dictatorship, totalitarian or otherwise. Nevertheless, any number of factors, including the extreme harshness of the Sun King's government after 1680 and the Revocation of the Edict of Nantes, the methods used to control the elite, the endless wars, and the heavy fiscal burden placed on the masses, made the question of transition a difficult one for anyone who hoped to preserve the system while ridding it of its more intolerable excesses. In taking up this challenge, Philippe and his aides followed four distinct courses, which for the sake of convenience we shall associate with the names of four individuals: Saint-Simon, Law, Dubois, and Cardinal de Noailles.

The name "Saint-Simon" stands for the call (in some ways farfetched) for more upper-class participation in government and some form of government by consensus.[170] Of course, in Saint-Simon's case, "upper classes" meant the aristocracy and nothing but. The *petit duc* wanted the nobility to occupy the ministries with appropriate dignity and authority, naturally at the expense of the *robe*. Indeed, Saint-Simon hoped to see the entire administration subjected to supervision by the nobility, with whatever precautions were needed to prevent abuse. Out of this idea came polysynody, which in some ways was a reactionary development (because it rescued the aristocracy from nothingness and restored it to being, as it were) but at the same time raised hopes for government by consensus and, even more, participation of the elite (in this case a very select elite, to be sure). The name "Law" stands for stimulation of the economy and therefore relief for the masses. Both the bank and the government purposely set out to improve the lot of humble folk by reducing the twin burdens of debt and taxes. "Dubois," of course, represents the reorientation of French foreign policy vis-à-vis the liberal powers of Europe—maritime, capitalist, Protestant nations that were not only liberal but also open societies. In 1715, the leading liberal powers were England and Holland.[171] Finally, "Cardinal de Noailles" stands for openness in another sense, toward nonconformism in religious matters, meaning Jansenism and *huguenoterie*.

Of course, the conservative transition thus mapped out required a certain purge of the political leadership.[172] This was carried out with a minimum of violence. At times the process had to be slowed or even reversed, and there were momentary lapses into new forms of authoritarian rule. These were necessary to prevent liberalization from moving at too rapid a pace and possibly veering out of control, thereby destroying itself. In the mind of the new prince, the goal was always to reform in order to preserve, not to destroy. At the time, the operation seemed to have been a success. It was therefore possible to complete the seamless transition by turning the reins of the humanized new regime over to a product of the system, a man who had gained experience on the job and was more of a manager than an innovator: not the duc de Bourbon, who was just a transitional figure, but old Fleury, who performed a prosaic but by no means inauspicious service during the first decades of Louis XV's majority.

The Regency can be described in metaphorical terms as a period of thaw, a description that can also be applied to other episodes in French history, such as the regency of Anne de Beaujeu, the reign of Henri IV, and the ministry of Choiseul, all analogous in certain respects to the regency of Philippe d'Orléans. In each case, the regime learned to live with its contradictors (dissidents, Protestants, Jansenists, aristocrats, *parlementaires*). It learned how to tolerate or control its opponents (as one might endure an itch) rather than crush them as the previous regime had done. Change was not valued for itself, and the goal was not so much to transform the regime as to adapt, adjust, and "regulate" it in such a way as to preserve the privileges of the elite to the maximum extent possible. Repression of opponents was mild, and honey was tried instead of vinegar. "Benign neglect" was not uncommon. In any case, recalcitrant opponents did not conduct themselves as a genuine opposition, so their threat to the future of the regime was limited. They had no authentically new political or constitutional project. In the most "extreme" cases, they behaved like dissidents whose goal was to carve out a place for themselves outside the normal institutions of society, a space in which they might be free to behave in a nonconformist manner, generally in the religious realm. Because that space was limited, it did not encroach on the traditional pastures where the silent majority grazed. Our study of the Regency thus gives rise to the more general notion of a "conservative transition" or "controlled adaptation." As noted above, examples of conservative transitions can be found in earlier regimes that resembled the Regency in some ways, as well as in later ones that, while also authoritarian, were in certain respects quite different.

When an attempt at conservative transition fails, a crisis of succession may develop. If things really get out of hand, the very legitimacy of the regime may be called into question. The historian's job is to carry out a "concrete analysis of a concrete situation" in order to "understand, or rather to recognize, similarities between events, which can then be assigned to categories for further comparative study." We are interested, then, in the comparative history of transitional processes. Such processes can occur in systems that are very different from one another chronologically, structurally, and existentially.

In conclusion, let us take another look at the question of the structure, or, rather, the genealogy, of power. From the end of the Fronde to the first decades of Louis XV's reign, five princely generations held power or prospective power in conjunction with seven associated groups. Those five generations were as follows:

1. The generation of Anne of Austria and her friend (and perhaps briefly lover) Mazarin.
2. The generation of the maturing Louis XIV, soon joined by his wife, Mme de Maintenon.
3. The generation of le Grand Dauphin, or Monseigneur, son of Louis XIV, and his exact contemporary Philippe d'Orléans, the son of Louis XIV's brother.
4. The generation of the duc de Bourgogne (the son of Monseigneur and grandson of Louis XIV) and the duc de Bourbon, also known as Monsieur le Duc (and also a grandson of Louis XIV through his mother, Madame la Duchesse). His father, also the duc de Bourbon, Monsieur le Duc senior, was a cousin of Louis XV, along with whom he belonged to the seventh generation of male descendants of Charles de Bourbon.
5. The generation of Louis XV himself, son of the duc de Bourgogne and great-grandson of Louis XIV.

These five generations (and seven groups, centered on Anne and Mazarin, Louis XIV and Maintenon, Monseigneur, Bourgogne, Orléans, Monsieur le Duc junior, and Louis XV, respectively) were the poles around which networks of power and ambition organized themselves from 1650 to 1720 (fig. 8.1).

Anne and Mazarin bequeathed their servants to Louis XIV. These included Le Tellier, Colbert, Lionne, and Fouquet (group 1). These men ruled the roost during the early years of the Sun King's personal reign, until 1680. After Fouquet was removed and Lionne faded away, the Colberts and Le Tellier–Louvois clan, fathers and sons, played a major role in governing the kingdom during Louis XIV's first quarter century on the throne.

After Louvois died in 1691, the monarch was at last able to choose his own team (group 2). He proved less adept in his choices than Mazarin had been. Indeed, the cardinal had been clever enough to enlist the support of men of genius (Colbert) and remarkable talent (Le Tellier). Although the influence of Mme de Maintenon, whom Louis secretly married in 1683, is not to be underestimated, the king nevertheless managed

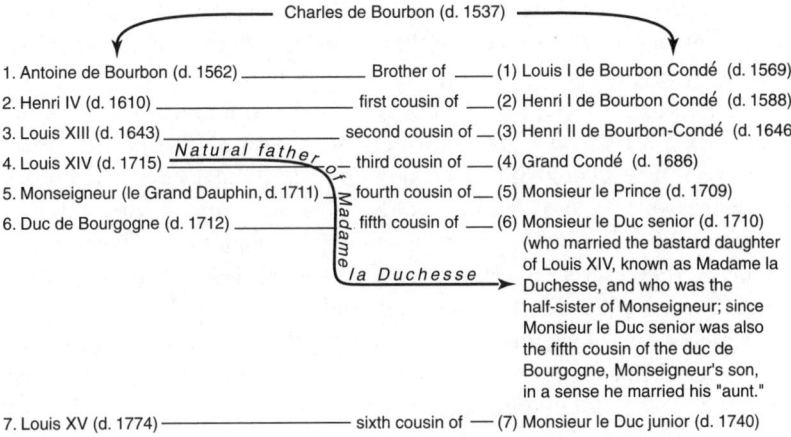

Figure 8.1. Genealogical Connections of the French Royal Family and the Bourbon-Condés

to find comptrollers general, chancellors, and secretaries of state for war who had the good fortune to please his wife, or at least not to displease her more than was tolerable. Among the various men who held these posts, let us single out the two Pontchartrains, father and son, Chamillart, Desmarets (a Colbert who hitched his star to Mme de Maintenon), and Voysin. A camarilla of *grands seigneurs*, including Villeroy, Huxelles, Harcourt, and many others, orbited around this dominant group, which under the Regency became the nucleus of what was known as the "old court"—those who looked back with nostalgia to the final years of Louis XIV's reign.

Toward the end of the seventeenth century, another cabal of ambitious men and women had grown up around the sovereign's son Monseigneur (group 3). In this group, we find important military commanders, such as Luxembourg, who soon died, and Vendôme, who was ultimately disgraced. We also find the Lorraine princesses and d'Antin, an eminent courtier, together with Madame la Duchesse, the wife of a Condé, bastard daughter of a king, and half-sister of d'Antin. Monseigneur, the leader of the group and heir apparent to Louis XIV, was not as obtuse as the memoir writers would have us believe. In 1685, he reportedly joined le Grand Condé in a (timid) protest against the Revocation of the Edict of Nantes. With some justice, he pointed out that the measure might hurt commerce, but Louis XIV swept the objection aside. Later, however, dynastic logic led le Grand Dauphin to join the party of no compromise: his son Anjou became king of Spain under the name Philip V. During the War of the Spanish Succession, therefore, Monseigneur, out of affection for his son, joined the *jusqu'au-boutistes* who insisted that French troops be kept in the Iberian Peninsula indefinitely, even though it meant prolonging a war that was costing France dearly. In the end the *jusqu'au-boutistes* were proved right—but the cost was immense.

Monseigneur's group, like Louis XIV's and Maintenon's, was opposed by the cabal of pacifists and reformers, who were the heirs of Colbert (group 4). They congregated around the representative of the fourth generation of the royal family, the duc de Bourgogne, during the first decade and a half of the eighteenth century. Disciples or relatives of the Colberts, they exercised vast influence in the ministries and behind the scenes through Chevreuse, Beauvillier, and even Torcy. They could also avail themselves of the intellectual prestige of Fénelon, who languished in an exile that was on the whole tolerable, neither too harsh nor too far from the capital. The Bourgogne-Fénelon network came to an end, however, when its principal figures passed away.

Meanwhile, the death of Louis XIV gave the Palais-Royal cabal around the duc d'Orléans (group 5) its chance. At first the group was relatively small, consisting of old and new friends of the prince: Dubois, Rémond, Bezons, Saint-Pierre, Law, and Saint-Simon. As Philippe's power grew, however it quickly drew opportunists and especially "technocrats"—civilian, military, and financial. This hastily assembled gathering of experts ensured the success of the regent's policy, which, though founded upon the principle of "openness," shrewdly sought to control the course of events. Things never got completely out of control except during the final collapse of Law's "system." Still, the consequences of that financial debacle were far less disastrous than some have maintained. The damage was quickly repaired, moreover, leaving the beneficial effects of the system in place (see fig. 8.2).

When Dubois and Orléans both passed away within a short period of time (in a manner reminiscent of the passing of another "ruling duo," Richelieu and Louis XIII), power passed to the house of Bourbon-Condé in the person of Monsieur le Duc, assisted by his mistress Mme de Prye and by the financier Pâris-Duverney (group 6). Openness was no longer in season: deflationary pressures took hold, and new repressive measures were instituted against Protestants, measures that revived the spirit of the Revocation but without its horrors, except in very small doses.

Then came the partial famine of 1725. In the following year, Louis XV, by now a teenager, was at last able to bestow power on his elderly tutor, the septuagenarian Fleury, soon to become a cardinal. In conjunction with any number of *grands robins*, including a new generation of the Phélypeaux family, the Chauvelins, the Le Peletiers, Armenonville and Morville, Orry, Le Blanc, Amelot, and d'Aguesseau (group 7), Fleury was able to stabilize the livre tournois, unify the Ferme Générale, refrain from interfering with the growth of the economy, maintain the alliance with

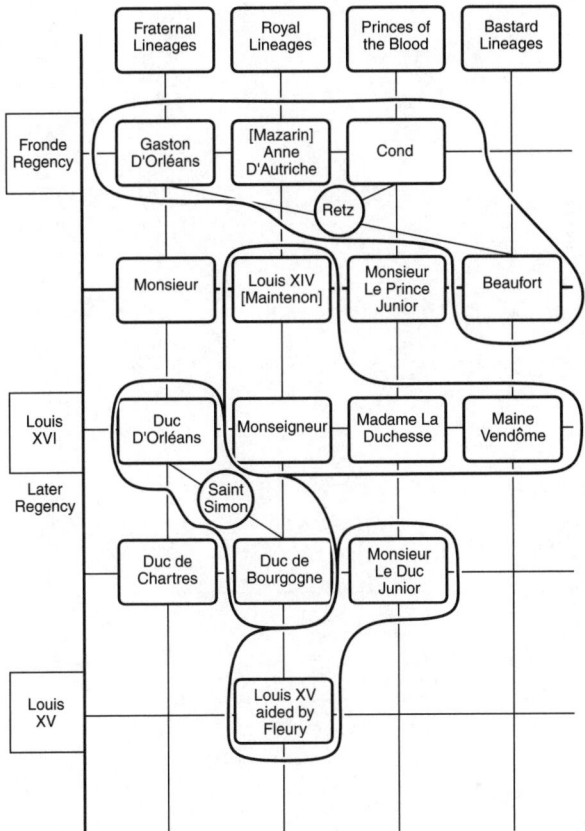

Figure 8.2. Parties, Cabals, and Factions

England, and annex Lorraine. As the heir to all of the Regency's accomplishments, Fleury, who was at once Saint-Simon's friend and his enemy,[173] was able to reap the benefit of those achievements while prudently avoiding any new initiatives. His twenty-year ministry even included the small touch of repression that one finds in most periods of consolidation: it was during Fleury's tenure that the Jansenists, persecuted once again, became the butt of ridicule when some of them, in the grip of religious fervor, began having convulsions and dancing ecstatically around the grave of Deacon Pâris.

Conclusion

I beg the reader's indulgence for quoting here a somewhat off-color remark made by my former teacher Victor-L. Tapié, whose lectures on the "very long seventeenth century" had a decisive impact on my vocation to study the history of the age of Louis XIV and beyond. "The Regency," Tapié told me in 1953, "was a mistress that Saint-Simon entered only in his dreams."

To be sure, the memoirist more or less comprehended, or at any rate tolerated, John Law's economic and financial projects, whose beneficial influence he appreciated and to some extent even enjoyed. Saint-Simon also approved of and even guided the regent's policy of reaching out to the aristocracy, moderating and liberalizing the absolutism of the previous regime, and, to a degree, replacing autocracy, at least temporarily, with a more temperate form of government. The symbol of this strategy was the introduction of "polysynody," to which both Saint-Simon and the regent fully subscribed. The strategy was not a tremendous success, to put it mildly. Furthermore, when it came to improving relations with Protestants, Saint-Simon was apt to drag his feet. He was one of the reasons why Philippe's sincere and tolerant instincts resulted in a policy toward the Huguenots of at best "benign neglect" (which wasn't always all that benign). By contrast, Saint-Simon enthusiastically applauded the decision to restrain (for a time) repressive measures against the Jansenists. This, of course, coincided with his own views. In foreign policy, however, it is fair to say that Saint-Simon understood virtually nothing of Dubois's intelligent diplomatic maneuvering to bring France closer to the major Protestant powers, England and Holland. In any case, he found it difficult if not impossible to forgive Dubois for his "filthy" petty-bourgeois origins. Saint-Simon's slander and calumny have unjustly dishonored this great statesman in the eyes of posterity. By contrast, the *petit duc* admired Philip V, in whose veins flowed "the purest blood in the universe," and he was infatuated with the idea of an alliance with Spain, a somewhat paradoxical attitude given his revulsion at the pro-Jesuit inclinations of the land of the Inquisition that he took Spain to be.

To use anachronistic political labels, then, we may situate the Regency not on the "left" of the political spectrum but in the "center left," assuming that such a thing as a political spectrum even existed between 1715 and 1723. Saint-Simon would then have to be situated on the extreme right of this center left.

Saint-Simon notwithstanding, the Regency in general took an expansive, conciliatory view of the world. Its open-mindedness (toward Anglicans, Huguenots, the Dutch, liberals, and economic expansion) was not altogether new, however: *mutatis mutandis*, we find much the same spirit in the era of Henri IV, before the great leap into absolutism under Louis XIV. One might even look farther back in time: the regency of Philippe d'Orléans bears a certain resemblance to the reign of Francis I, who also took a conciliatory approach to government (at least until the Affaire des Placards of 1534), and to the regency of Anne de Beaujeu, a woman whose name was associated with various attempts to liberalize the regime but who of course never had to deal with Huguenots (she died in 1522).

Looking forward in time, we may say that the Regency cast a long shadow over the years to come; or, to vary the metaphor, it might be better to say that it served as a bright beacon for the future of both France and the world. In some respects, it was a pioneer in what would later be dubbed, a little misleadingly perhaps, "enlightened despotism." The regent's government and others like it were not really despotic, and they did make room for a measure of liberty amid the rigidities and rigors of the old regime. Other leaders emulated Philippe d'Orléans consciously or unconsciously: Charles III of Spain, Joseph II of Austria, and the great pope of reconciliation who called himself Benedict XIV, a sort of eighteenth-century John XXIII. And if we were to take a very long view, à la Fernand Braudel and his *longue durée*, which in this context is a perfectly reasonable thing to do, we might also add Czar Alexander II, who in so many ways liberated at least a portion of his people from the bonds of serfdom and authentic autocracy. Alexander preceded the Russian revolutions of 1905 and 1917 by barely half a century, a couple of generations, while Philippe and the thaw he instigated came just sixty years before the breaking of the political and social ice-jam in France: with the pre-Revolution and then the Revolution of 1789, political and social space suddenly expanded, not to say exploded. Yet despite excesses that are all too well known and may in any case have been inevitable, no one would deny the liberating effect of those events.

On the domestic front, "Gentle" Philippe was followed by Fleury, who took up more or less where the regent had left off, and still later by Choiseul, another "liberal" minister. But in between there were phases of harsher rule, comparable in many ways with the personal reign of Louis XIV: for instance, the ministerial years of Pierre, comte d'Argenson (1743–57), and the relatively "repressive" period of Maupeou and the Triumvirate after 1770. Hawks and doves alternated, or, to use a biblical analogy, harsh Ezekiel changed places with soothing Isaiah.[1] In any case, the point is that the regime wavered between loosening the screws and tightening them.

I f there was continuity *after* Saint-Simon, there was also continuity all around him. We therefore ought to say a word about the *material* infrastructure of the château de Versailles, the cornerstone of the sacred, bastard-hating, cabal-ridden, hypergamic, and at times world-renouncing hierarchy that was the court before, during, and after the reign of Louis XIV.[2] But a great scholar from the other side of the Atlantic has been scouring the palace and national archives for details about the material aspects of life in Versailles, and we hesitate to trespass on his domain.[3] His work, when it is eventually published, will cause a stir—of that the reader may be sure.

The French Revolution would of course abruptly put an end to all this: not only the material comforts of the palace but also the ideological and sociological continuity of the court, which vanished forever in October 1791. Nevertheless, Louis-Philippe, "the king of the French" (as opposed to the "king of France"), did grasp the importance of Versailles, and he was able to make others see it as well: Versailles, an album in stone and greenery, a dazzling window onto the French past and irreplaceable compendium of the nation's history, or more precisely, the history of the monarchy. Such was the vocation of the vast Museum of the History of France that was established at the citizen-king's behest in what had been the residence of Louis XIV. Within these *salles louis-philipiennes*, today covered with layers of dust but still perfectly intact and well preserved (although closed to the public), the ghost of the *petit duc* still wanders on the eve of a new millennium (Saint-Simon was himself a student of museography).[4] Or rather, it tiptoes quietly, even though in life discretion was not Saint-Simon's style—or strong suit. Oblivious of the profanation of its mortal remains during the Revolution, the shade of Saint-Simon visits with the château's countless other phantoms—the ghosts of men who in the flesh were far more important than he politically but far less talented as writers.

France's Gaullist presidents—from the man of Colombey himself to Jacques Chirac, elected in 1995 — have naturally been champions of the national patrimony. They nevertheless missed the opportunity to restore, at little cost to the nation, this magnificent national park, which ought to be worth at least as much as has been lavished on the Astérix Park, to say nothing of the French Disneyland. It is to be hoped that with the beginning of the third millennium the public will at last be granted access to the astonishing collection of national treasures that Versailles contains—a collection housed in a very special place that bridges the gap between Saint-Simon's private testimony and the memories of the nation in general, or if not of the nation, then at least of the kingdom that preceded it.

Pierre Nora had the admirable idea of exploring the national memory of France in a series of volumes entitled *Les Lieux de mémoire*.* allowed to degenerate in the hands of epigones, some consideration ought to be given to initiatives such as the one we are proposing. The Museum of the History of France at Versailles might even resuscitate an old passion that seems to have subsided in recent years: the love of France, which lies like Sleeping Beauty in the collective unconscious. In his inimitably Gallic *mezza voce* style, Saint-Simon was one of the great interpreters of that passion, a lover of France who was not always discreet or secretive about his ardor.[5] For us, Saint-Simon himself has become an object of passion, if only because of the vast historical fresco he has left behind— a work that combines the varied talents of Rembrandt, Callot, and Rigaud with a genius for caricature in the manner of Carracci, Hogarth, Rowlandson, Toulouse-Lautrec, or his own contemporary Pier Ghezzi (1674–1755). A museum in Versailles would be a compact embodiment of the history of France under one roof. It would occupy a place of honor alongside the "museums without walls" that each of us must create within our hearts and that each culture must create in its collective memory— museums containing works not only of art but also of literature. Only then may Saint-Simon, who is unjustly neglected outside France, find his proper place alongside Goethe and Shakespeare. Europe's museums must also draw on more abstract sources, on what one German writer has called the "wellsprings of constitutional patriotism," a patriotism based not on parochialism but on reason, on a deep and considered attachment to the pacts and treaties that tie the peoples of the old continent together in an almost "religious" union. It is to be hoped, though there is reason to doubt it, that the people of France think of themselves as being in the vanguard of that union. The bonds that tie the nations of Europe together are older than one might think: they begin not with today's European Union but with the Treaty of Utrecht in 1713 and the federalist initiatives of the abbé de Saint-Pierre, vague though they might have

---

* Three volumes of the essays published in *Les Lieux de mémoire* have been translated into English by the translator of the present volume and published by Columbia University Press. Additional translations are forthcoming from the University of Chicago Press.—Trans.

been. But Saint-Pierre had to endure disgrace under the Regency, just as Saint-Simon would himself endure disgrace in 1723, as the era of the duc de Bourbon and Cardinal Fleury began.[6]

It was in that year that Saint-Simon began to judge himself, by his own standards, a total failure, or almost total failure.[7] He had failed in politics, failed at court, failed to amass a fortune, failed to secure the posterity of his line, failed in his military career, failed as a father, and failed as a duke. Within this bleak landscape, however, certain successes stand out, certain areas in which the memoirist was as successful as anyone else and perhaps even more successful: in friendship, in social life, in managing his extensive property intelligently if not profitably, in religion, in marriage, and last but not least, in literary renown, which in his case would be immense but of course purely posthumous. It hardly needs emphasizing that as an ethnographer of his times and perhaps of our own, Saint-Simon remains unrivaled. He is not only a source and prey for contemporary anthropologists but also a prophet and paragon of inequality, as well as the anti-Rousseau par excellence—though of course he lived and wrote in the period just before Jean-Jacques conceived his great egalitarian works. He was certainly a man of the eighteenth century, in the best sense of the term, but he was also a man of another era, of the classical and even baroque age. Indeed, our Louis de Saint-Simon was above all a "Ludovician": an admirer of Louis XIII, a contemporary and critic of Louis XIV, and a writer under Louis XV, whose *Memoirs* were published, recognized and admired under Louis XVI and even more under Louis XVIII and Louis-Philippe. In French culture he looms large, but as a sort of monolith displaced from its natural environment, a Pseudo-Dionysius the Areopagite somehow wandered into France— Lord knows why—in the middle of our second millennium.

Saint-Simon's thought, and more generally his worldview, remind us of what Ernst Cassirer in a book on the philosophy of the Renaissance called the *Stufenkosmos*, the social universe conceived as a series of degrees, that is, a hierarchy. Or, to cite a source from another millennium, one thinks of Maximus the Confessor and his *Scholia on Hierarchy*, which itself harks back to the Gospel of John. To this list we rather cavalierly add the learned commentaries of Dom Calmet, which are by no means anachronistic when applied to Saint-Simon: "In the house of my father there are many mansions. . . . Were that not the case, I would not have promised you a place in my kingdom" (John 14:2). In the very Saint-Simonian house of the hereditary monarch of France there were indeed many mansions.[8] His Majesty delighted in bestowing legitimacy on each, but at times he was also pleased to create barriers, degrees, and hierarchies. And when he felt the urge, he jumbled them all up again, or destroyed them, or simply transcended them.

Appendix One: On Norbert Elias

The reader will surely have noticed in the foregoing pages a dearth of references to the works of one major author, a formidable mind of international reputation. We are speaking, of course, of Norbert Elias, to whose work one will find no more than a few allusions in our text. Elias was a German sociologist, or rather a German-British sociologist. Perhaps it would be better to call him simply a European, or even a Eurafrican.[1] In this appendix, we hope to remedy any injustice we may have done by ignoring Elias, or rather, to explain our decision, which was entirely deliberate. Elias has exerted a tremendous influence on French sociology and helped to foster much of what is best in it—indeed, paradoxically, what is most authentic and original.[2] By contrast, his influence on certain topics in the historiography of the age of Louis XIV and its immediate aftermath is far more open to question. In one of his (early) works, on the court life of the ancien régime, Elias attempted to show that what he called *höfische Gesellschaft*, or "court society," was the matrix that shaped modern sociability by establishing rules of courtesy and good manners. In his view, "courtesy" as we understand it today emerged is a direct outgrowth of the courtly manners of the seventeenth century, which themselves evolved out of the "courtesies" typically associated with medieval warriors, the noble ancestors of the seventeenth century's courtiers.[3] In other words, the warriors of the Middle Ages gradually conquered their aggressive instincts and by the age of Louis XIV had transformed themselves into courtly nobles. We thus have the following progression: medieval *courtoisie* → classical "courtliness" → modern or contemporary courtesy. Such a process is obviously complex and capricious and may well appear to be filled with twists and turns.

Because the orientation of Elias's research was different from ours, we saw little reason to mention his theories up to now. In a work of his that has become a classic, Elias looked at the court in general and Saint-Simon in particular only in isolation from their immediate historical context, and only insofar as they anticipated an era that still lay far in the future: the nineteenth and twentieth centuries. In short, he took a teleological approach to history, thereby accepting the inherent risk of superficiality. Manipulated in this way, Saint-Simon was reduced to a forerunner of things to come only much later, a mere Preamble, a handmaiden of the Future, a harbinger of Tomorrow.

By contrast, our intent was to look at the memoirist as he was in himself and for himself: not a transitional coelacanth but a fish habituated to the depths, a theorist and practitioner of the inequality of rights characteristic of the ancien régime and now utterly defunct and obsolete. We wanted to look at him as the representative of a doomed species, the end of a line—and not a herald of the future, of new species and new races destined to dominate the scene until the 1930s or the 1950s. We saw ourselves as paleontologists rather than futurologists. To be sure, the *petit duc*, with his Jansenist sympathies and quiet advocacy of birth control, was not altogether a stranger to certain innovations that can be seen in retrospect to have had something to do with revolutionary stirrings. But his strongest, most consistent, most convincing trait was to have been an archaic specimen, an archeological artifact in the most fundamental sense. Saint-Simon is not the foundation or underpinning of any later edifice; he is a ruin, ripe for excavation.

What is more, Elias all too often betrayed himself or was betrayed by his German, French, and British editors. His book, which as mentioned earlier was a youthful work, is filled with errors. His few quotations from Saint-Simon were chosen arbitrarily, and not very well, on the basis of a superficial and fragmentary knowledge of the *Memoirs*. They were then translated from French into German and retranslated from German into French. (Here the fault lies with certain French publishers.) The *petit duc*'s energetic and original style was thus flattened by the steamroller of double translation. His footnotes referred to a few scattered volumes of totally outdated editions (to be fair, he was writing in the years just before World War II, not a propitious moment for such activity). Here again, the publishers come in for a substantial share of the blame: not a single publishing house, whether German, English, American, or French, took the trouble, which would not have been very great, to update Elias's footnotes, by now so out of date as to be all but unusable. These defects weaken his work and often leave his readers wondering, or would leave them wondering if they knew anything at all of the work of Saint-Simon.

Moving to a more general level of criticism, we should begin by saying that few scholars believe anymore in the heuristic value of Elias's model of court society. Few see "court society" as the remote ancestor of modern bourgeois moderation and contemporary lifestyles passed down in a continuous evolutionary process from the domesticated aristocracy of Versailles to the bourgeois elite that inhabited the wealthier sections of Paris as recently as the 1930s. Indeed, the "curial" is not necessarily the progenitor of the "convivial." Courtliness does not always lead to cordiality, no matter how carefully disciplined, controlled, and even hypocritical.

Recently, a young Dutch scholar launched the first attack on the work of the master, in terms veiled to be sure, but not sufficiently to hide the sacrilege. Dutch scholarship has long been familiar with such audacious assaults, which here and there erode and puncture the seemingly impregnable dikes that formerly held back the Zuider Zee of Knowledge. Then came the total collapse: in a part of the world where German thought inspires less awe than it does among the French, the American historian Daniel Gordon wrote a book that was clear, penetrating, and merciless.[4] Working from original texts, not only of the major authors of the period but also of the *minores*, he went to work demolishing the ingenious and in places imposing edifice that Elias had built, and when he was finished, little if anything was left standing. In particular, the idea that later developments in French sociability flowed from the court was shown to be nonsense.

What Gordon did was to show that the French elite, and to some extent the lower classes, developed their own style of sociability based on free conversation, egalitarianism, and cordial social relations. The roots of this style lay in the behavior and attitudes of broad segments of the Parisian and provincial population. The setting in which this took place was not only egalitarian but, even more significant, apolitical. It included the many salons and academies that sprang into being in the seventeenth and eighteenth centuries.[5] Elias notwithstanding, French sociability did not evolve in the court society of the great palace of the Bourbons, where conversation was inegalitarian, stiff, disciplinary, at times stifling, and pedagogically hierarchical. Gordon's orientation is of course very different from ours, for at the center of his book we find not Versailles but the Paris of the pre-Enlightenment and Enlightenment: a melting pot of elites, blue-blooded and otherwise. And we also find the provinces, which by the eighteenth century had become well acculturated to the new models of sociability, already quite remote from the court system that concerns us here.

Gordon also extends his argument to the very issue that concerned Elias, namely, the evolution of social relations in Europe between the seventeenth and the twentieth century. He suggests, indeed demonstrates in a carefully documented way, that Elias's whole outlook—based on a contrast between *völkisch* German *Kultur* and irrevocably aristocratic French *civilisation*—actually derived from the pungent writings of Thomas Mann, who for a brief period during World War I became a hypernationalist and even Francophobe (unlike Elias, who remained quite a Francophile but was nevertheless influenced by Mann's thinking). After Hitler came to power, of course, Mann's attitude fortunately changed. Gordon's account of the origins of Elias's ideas seems convincing to us, but at the end of a book concerned with questions totally different from those of Elias, we think it unwise to analyze his argument in detail. Instead, we propose to pursue elsewhere the debate that Gordon has begun. In doing so, we shall of course pay homage to Norbert Elias as a great historian of manners, but we will not hesitate to expose the weaknesses of his theory that bourgeois manners derived from the hypernoble court society of Versailles.

For the time being, then, we will simply raise several questions, the answers to which will have to be deferred. Is it not true that Elias, in holding up a mirror to court society, produced a distorted image because he was focused too much on the future and not enough on the past? Has this mirror now been smashed beyond repair by recent critiques? When we have carefully documented our criticism, we will see if the paper we hope to write is worthy of being entitled "A Tomb for Norbert Elias" and whether his ideas about court society are, to borrow a phrase from Saint-Simon, anything more "than a sad image of a vast catafalque."[6]

Appendix Two: On Pasquier Quesnel

A longtime reader of the many volumes of Quesnel's *Réflexions*, I became aware of Joseph Tans's excellent study of the great theologian's work only after writing chapter 6 of the present volume (Tans's work may be consulted in the *Dictionnaire de spiritualité*, under "Quesnel").[1] According to Tans, Quesnel was the grandson of a Scottish nobleman who was *premier peintre* to Henri III and the son of the bookseller Jacques Quesnel. The elder Quesnel's shop was located on the rue Saint-Jacques in Paris, and young Pasquier studied with the Jesuits at the Collège de Clermont before attending the Sorbonne. In November 1657, he became an Oratorian and was ordained a priest in November 1659.

In any case, Tans's article is fully consistent with the argument of chapter 6, according to which Quesnel's work was essentially anti-worldly and pro-renunciation, as Saint-Simon, a disciple of the priest (though in his own discreet and idiosyncratic way) rightly sensed. If renunciation was not always central to Quesnel's thinking, its presence was always felt. According to Tans, "Quesnel saw an abyss between the kingdom of God and the world, a place of darkness and filth. . . . The act of faith in God called for a high degree of detachment from oneself and from the world. In no case should the noise of the world be allowed to cover up the voice of God. . . . We are of the world if we partake of its cupidity." Cupidity: the thirst for glory or for the praise of one's fellow man, but also familiarity with the sacraments if linked to a pointless, idle existence. And vanity: spectacles, idle amusements, visits and conversations filled with slanderous gossip and trifles, love of fine clothing and elegant dining. Yet even such distractions are less brutish than the cupidity of the flesh, which clearly turns the world into a place of perdition. Even worse, the desires of the flesh had been refined and thereby been made even more dangerous. Like Saint Paul, Quesnel considered virginity to be one of the most precious gifts of Christ in his Church. According to Saints Jerome and Athanasius, Quesnel tells us, the Lord's seed produces a yield of thirty to one in those who seek purity in marriage, twice that much in widows who live in chastity, and a hundred to one in those who live in a state of virginal chastity. In Quesnel's ethical teachings, we hear the echoes of the Gospel according to John, for whom the "world" is summed up as concupiscence of the flesh, concupiscence of the eyes, and living pride.

"What is the world, then?" asks Quesnel, commenting on Bossuet. "The world is you who love it. You become the world by desiring to enjoy it, and one enjoys it through the pleasures of the senses, through avarice, through vain and idle curiosity of every sort, through pride and love of honor and luxury and human grandeur." Merely by seeking a career in society or in learning one becomes guilty of "diversion" in Pascal's sense. Even chess is forcefully condemned by our theologian. Of all games, chess is the one that demands the greatest concentration, takes up the most time, and is most difficult to stop playing.[2]

Tans adds, however, that Quesnel's ideas were not in themselves inimical to the social order. Participation in the life of the world was not contraindicated as long as one held fast to the spirit of prayer. Like the Puritans, moreover, Quesnel was not hostile to marriage, in which he saw "a prophetic sign of the union of Christ with His Church, a sign raised to the dignity of a sacrament by and in Christ."

Quesnel, Tans writes, "was a proponent of profound joy, of human joy, as long as it involved divine love, grace, and, in particular, *renunciation* of the self. . . . The anthropology upon which his spirituality was based remained dualist and tragic, like that of Plato. The earthly body was still a prison for the eternal soul."[3]

In my own writing on Quesnel in chapter 6, I drew primarily on Quesnel's commentaries on the Gospels of Mark, Luke, and Matthew; on the Acts of the Apostles; on Paul's Epistle to Titus, his First Epistle to the Corinthians, and his Epistle to the Romans; and on the First Epistle of John. I used volume 8 of the 1736 edition of Quesnel's works, which is one of the most complete, as well as parts of volumes 2, 3, 6, and 7. In regard to Quesnel's view of hierarchy and his argument in justification of it, I used his commentaries on the Gospel of Luke and the Acts of the Apostles (see the references under "Hierarchy" in the alphabetical index to the first volume of the 1736 edition of *Réflexions*).

To tell the truth, Quesnel writes about renunciation on nearly every page of the eight volumes of the 1736 edition. These texts are a cornerstone of his thinking. Had we tried to give complete references, we would have had to cite page after page of the great Jansenist author's work. We can do no better than to refer the reader to Quesnel's *Réflexions morales sur le Nouveau Testament*, which was first published in 1671 and which in small doses remains a pleasure to read. Many editions of the *Réflexions* exist in French, including that of 1736, for the work was a "best-seller" from the time of its first publication until well into the reign of Louis XV. Readers who wish to consult nineteenth- and twentieth-century editions, however, will be obliged to read the author in English, Italian, German, or Dutch translation. The last German edition was published, so far as I know, in 1878; the last English edition in 1900; the last Dutch edition in 1903; and the last Italian edition in 1845. It seems that Quesnel is no longer in fashion, and indeed that he went entirely out of fashion among French readers not long after the last French edition was published in Amsterdam in 1747. Chronologically and spiritually, then, Saint-Simon was very close to Quesnel. In any event the *petit duc* never made a secret of being a contemporary of the great Jansenist theologian.

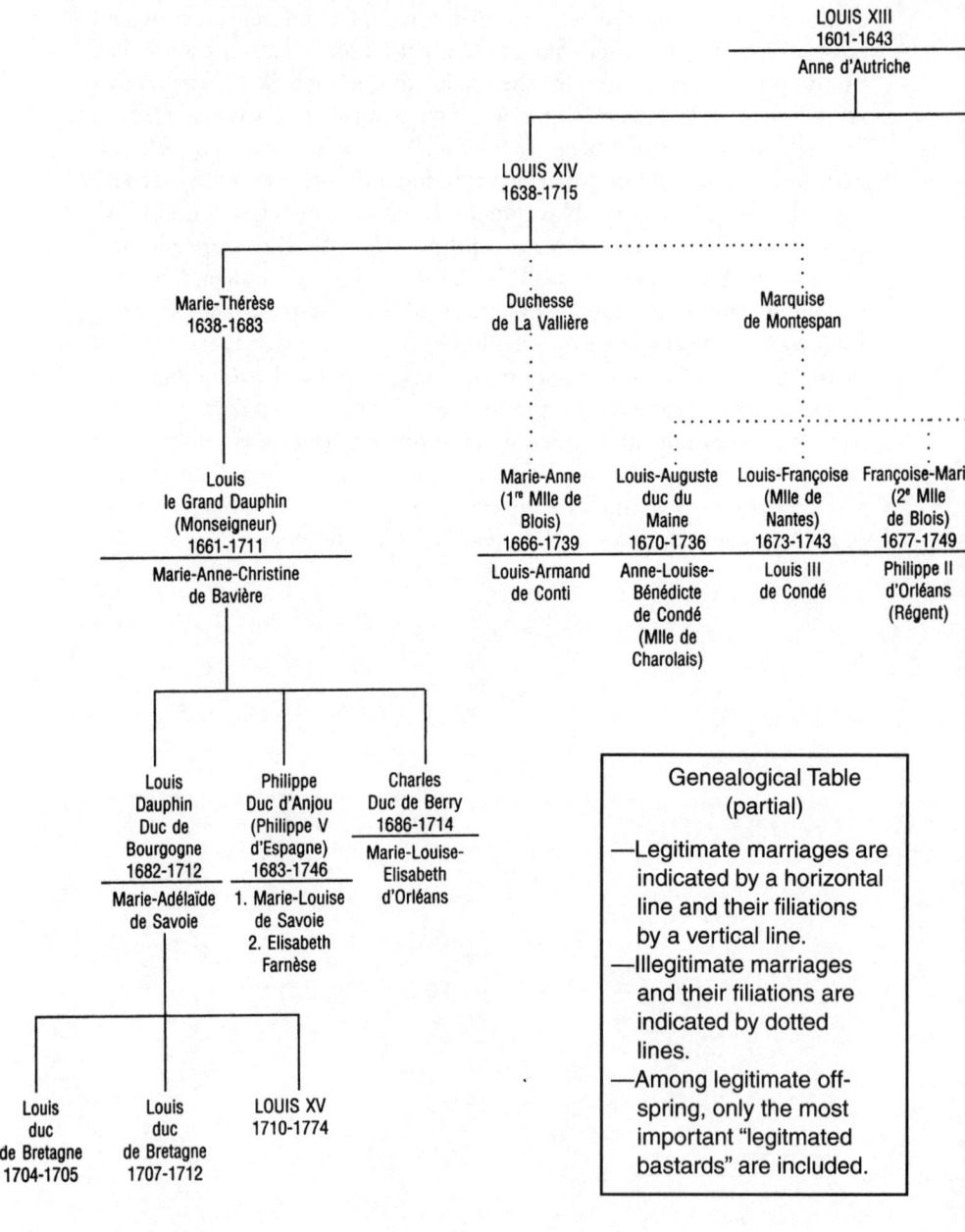

LOUIS XIII
1601-1643
Anne d'Autriche

LOUIS XIV
1638-1715

Marie-Thérèse
1638-1683

Duchesse
de La Vallière

Marquise
de Montespan

Louis
le Grand Dauphin
(Monseigneur)
1661-1711
Marie-Anne-Christine
de Bavière

Marie-Anne
(1ʳᵉ Mlle de
Blois)
1666-1739
Louis-Armand
de Conti

Louis-Auguste
duc du
Maine
1670-1736
Anne-Louise-
Bénédicte
de Condé
(Mlle de
Charolais)

Louis-Françoise
(Mlle de
Nantes)
1673-1743
Louis III
de Condé

Françoise-Marie
(2ᵉ Mlle
de Blois)
1677-1749
Philippe II
d'Orléans
(Régent)

Louis
Dauphin
Duc de
Bourgogne
1682-1712
Marie-Adélaïde
de Savoie

Philippe
Duc d'Anjou
(Philippe V
d'Espagne)
1683-1746
1. Marie-Louise
de Savoie
2. Elisabeth
Farnèse

Charles
Duc de Berry
1686-1714
Marie-Louise-
Elisabeth
d'Orléans

Louis
duc
de Bretagne
1704-1705

Louis
duc
de Bretagne
1707-1712

LOUIS XV
1710-1774

Genealogical Table
(partial)

—Legitimate marriages are
indicated by a horizontal
line and their filiations
by a vertical line.
—Illegitimate marriages
and their filiations are
indicated by dotted
lines.
—Among legitimate off-
spring, only the most
important "legitmated
bastards" are included.

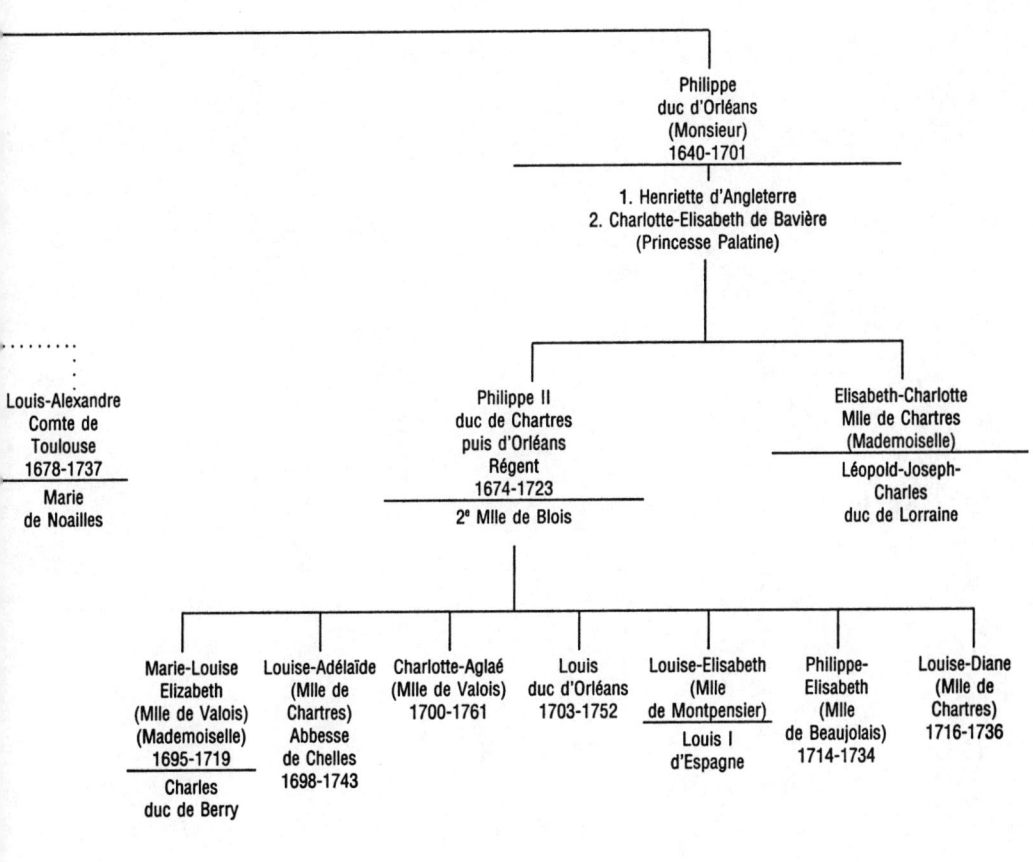

Philippe
duc d'Orléans
(Monsieur)
1640-1701

1. Henriette d'Angleterre
2. Charlotte-Elisabeth de Bavière
(Princesse Palatine)

Louis-Alexandre
Comte de
Toulouse
1678-1737

Marie
de Noailles

Philippe II
duc de Chartres
puis d'Orléans
Régent
1674-1723

2ᵉ Mlle de Blois

Elisabeth-Charlotte
Mlle de Chartres
(Mademoiselle)

Léopold-Joseph-
Charles
duc de Lorraine

Marie-Louise
Elizabeth
(Mlle de Valois)
(Mademoiselle)
1695-1719

Charles
duc de Berry

Louise-Adélaïde
(Mlle de
Chartres)
Abbesse
de Chelles
1698-1743

Charlotte-Aglaé
(Mlle de Valois)
1700-1761

Louis
duc d'Orléans
1703-1752

Louise-Elisabeth
(Mlle
de Montpensier)

Louis I
d'Espagne

Philippe-
Elisabeth
(Mlle
de Beaujolais)
1714-1734

Louise-Diane
(Mlle de
Chartres)
1716-1736

Notes

References below to the *Mémoires* of Saint-Simon indicate in some cases the Boislisle edition (B), more often the Coirault edition (C) published in the Pléiade series, or on occasion, the index in volume 18 of the Ramsay edition (R).

INTRODUCTION

1. Emmanuel Le Roy Ladurie, *L'Ancien Régime*, vol. 3 of *L'Histoire de France* (Paris: Hachette, 1991), 178.

2. See chapter 4 of this volume.

3. See part 2 of this volume.

4. Georges Poisson, *Monsieur de Saint-Simon* (Paris: Berger-Levrault, 1973), 343 passim.

5. C. 7:706 and 1491.

6. C. 7:1491.

7. The expression "thearchy," referring to the divine nature of any hierarchy worthy of the name, is taken from Pseudo-Dionysius the Areopagite, *Oeuvres complètes*, edited by Gandillac (Paris: Aubier, 1943), 70, 328, and passim.

8. Yves Coirault, *L'Optique de Saint Simon* (Paris: Armand Colin, 1965).

9. See especially the biographies by Jacques Roujon, *Le Duc de Saint-Simon, 1675–1755* (Paris: Wapler, 1958), and Georges Poisson, *Monsieur de Saint-Simon*.

10. Coirault, *L'Optique*.

11. Published in Pierre Nora, ed., *Le Lieux de mémoire* (Paris: Gallimard, 1997), vol. 3.

12. The appellation *annalistes* is not widely used in France but is common in the United States.

13. Things are beginning to change. See *Cahiers Saint-Simon* 24 (1966): 21.

1. Certain aspects of this work were treated earlier in a paper published in the *Annuaire du Collège de France*, 1981–82, 657ff. (The appellation *petit duc* refers to Saint-Simon's diminutive stature, but apparently he was not offended by it, as he was not afraid of applying it to himself.)

2. Louis Dumont, *Homo hierarchicus* (Paris: Gallimard 1966), 15, 55.

3. Louis Marin, *Le Portrait du roi* (Paris: Editions de Minuit, 1981).

4. Christian Ehalt, *Die Ausdruckformen absolutistischer Herrschaft: Der Wiener Hof im 17. und 18. Jahrhundert* (Vienna: Verlag für Geschichte und Politik, 1980).

5. B. 28:109, 110, 40:140.

6. J.-P. Labatut, *Les Ducs et pairs en France au XVIIe siècle* (Paris: Presses Universitaires de France, 1972), esp. 333–428.

7. Bosse's engravings can be found in *Le XVIIe siècle vu par Abraham Bosse* (Paris, 1967).

8. *Lettres de Madame, duchesse d'Orléans, née princesse Palatine* (Paris: Mereure de France, 1981), 27 December 1713.

9. The dauphin ranked above the other sons of France.

10. Here is the text of Madame's letter: "My son is a grandson of France. The grandsons of France are above the princes of the blood. True, they do not have as many privileges as the children of France, but they have many more than the princes of the blood. For example, my son eats at the king's table, whereas the princes of the blood do not. He has never used the title of first prince of the blood, because he is not a prince of the blood but a grandson of France. That is why he is addressed as Royal Highness. Whereas his son, who is first prince of the blood, is called Most Serene Highness and not Royal Highness. He is not with the king morning and night but only during grand ceremonies, when the entire family eats with the king. He therefore has none of the privileges that his father has, such as the sealed carriage, first equerry, first chaplain, etc. His officers cannot and must not serve him in the king's presence. He has no guards in the castle. And a hundred other things of the same sort, unlike my son. I must have made a mistake when I wrote, because my son was never a prince of the blood. The king has indeed bestowed upon the duc du Maine, his sons, and his brother the rank of princes of the blood, but after all the [other] princes and princesses of the blood. Indeed, in the duc du Maine's own home, his wife is seated above him. She always takes priority over her husband, and when a contract is signed, she signs at the rank that is hers by birth, whereas he places his name after all the [other] princes and princesses of the blood. He is therefore a long way from my son. Between them come all the princes of the blood. As for me, my position cannot change. If the king had a daughter, she would be called Madame, and I would be Madame, duchesse d'Orléans. My son's wife is called Madame *la* duchesse d'Orléans. The *la* indicates that she is not a son or daughter of France but only a granddaughter. One has to be familiar with this court to be capable of making all these distinctions. M. le Dauphin, the son of Louis XIV, committed a great injustice with respect to my son's daughter when he decided that she would come after the married princesses of the blood, when clearly she ranks first, since her brother is first prince of the blood. But Mme la Duchesse was the

first dauphin's favorite, and she could get him to do whatever she wanted, and the king did whatever M. le Dauphin asked. If he had lived, the princes of the blood would have come far behind." The duc du Maine was of course Louis XIV's illegitimate son, as was his brother the comte de Toulouse. His wife, the duchesse du Maine was born a Condé. Hence she was a princess of the blood and superior in rank to her husband, who was in principle "diminished" by his illegitimacy.

11. The hierarchy of ranks from the king to the grandsons of France and on down to the (disdained) princes of the blood was also quite apparent when Peter the Great visited Paris in 1713 (B. 31:363 to 386 and R. 18:122).

12. B. 31:194.

13. "I see that you mistake my son for a prince of the blood. But he is not. His rank is that of grandson of France. It is superior to that of princes of the blood and carries more privileges. Grandsons of France salute queens, sit in their presence, and ride in their carriages. Princes of the blood may do none of these things. Their domestics enjoy certain immunities and serve by quarter. They have a first equerry, a first chaplain, and a first majordomo. Princes of the blood have none of these things, nor do they have bodyguards, as my son does, or Swiss guards" (Madame, *Lettres*, 27 March 1707). The problem of who could be seated when pertained not only to stools and armchairs but also to carriages. In the seventeenth century, these were still seen as a relatively recent invention, which is why the question of who could ride in them was so important when it came to clarifying a hierarchy that was in part traditional.

14. B. 31:175.

15. We have all but forgotten that sitting on a chair is not a natural act but one that is culturally determined. In many civilizations chairs are not used (see Fernand Braudel, *Civilisation matérielle* [Paris, 1979], 1:247). Hence it is not surprising that questions of seating should have taken on such high symbolic importance in a ritualized society.

16. This question is dealt with in more detail below.

17. Madame, *Lettres*, 19 July 1699 and 2 August 1705.

18. B. 25:278. Here is a brief resume of the Affaire du Bonnet. In 1681 Novion, *premier président* of the Parlement of Paris, decided not to remove his distinctive judge's hat, or *bonnet*, when calling upon the peers of France to render an opinion. In this, he may or may not have been reverting to an earlier custom: that was the point in dispute. Since his purpose was to restore some of the prestige and influence that Parlement had lost under Louis XIV, the controversy was by no means pointless.

19. Jean Delumeau, ed., *Histoire de la Bretagne* (Toulouse: Privat, 1969), 346; B. 32:241.

20. B. 37:232.

21. B. 17:102 and 28:17.

22. B. 8:358.

23. B. 38:58.

24. Philippe Wolff, *Histoire de Toulouse* (Toulouse: Privat, 1986). The hierarchy in question was not an "eternal" one. Bernard Chevalier showed in *Les Bonnes Villes* (Orléans: Paradigme, 1982) how the hierarchy of urban corporations expanded with the economic revival of the second half of the fifteenth

century and later. It was therefore possible to "historicize" the hierarchical principle.

25. B. 2:203 and 11:97.

26. This comparison was inspired by the work of Louis Dumont.

27. B. 19:134, year 1710, concerning the maréchale de La Meilleraye.

28. B. 1:202; see also B. 1:386, etc.

29. Michel C. Péronnet, *Les Evêques de l'ancienne France* (Lille: Editions de l'Université de Lille III, 1977), 1:524, 1483.

30. B. 18:237 and 20:332.

31. Guy Chaussinand-Nogaret, *La Noblesse au XVIIIe siècle: De la féodalité aux Lumières* (Paris: Hachett, 1976), 54, has important things to say about the question of "merit."

32. R. 12:389 and B. 30:151.

33. B. 29:69.

34. B. 5:57.

35. B. 4:60.

36. B. 1:149.

37. Péronnet, *Les Evêques*, 1:513.

38. Claude Grimmer, *La Femme et le bâtard . . . dans l'ancienne France* (Paris: Presses de la Renaissance, 1983), 172–91.

39. B. 3:1.

40. B. 13:70.

41. B. 14:984 and 40:122.

42. Henri Brocher, *Le Rang et l'étiquette sous l'Ancien Régime* (Paris: Alcan, 1934), 17, 49.

43. R. 18:329; B. 20:32.

44. B. 10:326, 334.

45. B. 1:132 and especially R. 18:446. Emphasis added.

46. B. 1:127 and R. 18:338. Concerning what is actually known about the origins of this rank, see B. 1:129.

47. B. 1:315ff.

48. B. 17:287.

49. B. 9:62, 502.

50. B:323.

51. B. 31:206.

52. B. 23:5.

53. It is true that in B. 23:310 Saint-Simon includes the princes of the blood in "the royal house." But the essential point, leaving aside questions of vocabulary, is the distinction between the "extended royal house" (king, sons, and grandsons of France) and the even broader extended family, including royal cousins of the Bourbon, Condé, and Conti lines, that is, the princes of the blood.

54. B. 19, appendix 5.

55. B. 31:465.

56. B. 31:206. Montesquieu writes that among "the principal rules of honor" is this, "that when we have been placed in a rank, we must not do or suffer to be done anything that shows we consider ourselves inferior to that rank" (see *L'Esprit des lois*, part 1, 4:2, *in fine*).

57. B. 31:223.

58. B. 31:198 and 38:315.

59. Guy Chaussinand-Nogaret, *Le Citoyen des Lumières* (Brussels: Editions Complexe, 1994), insists in the first few chapters on the innovative character of Boulainvilliers's thought.

60. François Furet, *L'Atelier de l'histoire* (Paris: Gallimard, 1982), 175.

61. Dumont, *Homo hierarchicus*, 280.

62. B. 9:216.

63. B. 2:16.

64. B. 2:55 and 2:104.

65. B. 1:xxv.

66. B. 2:227.

67. B. 27:193 and 31:10.

68. B. 3:97.

69. R. 18:249; B. 27:162.

70. B. 2:18, 21:229.

71. B. 24:206.

72. B. 1:220.

73. B. 2:181.

74. Saint-Simon is right about there being different levels of royalty, but he is wrong about the specific terms of address: the Danish monarch addressed Louis as "Serenity," and Louis addressed him simply as "you" *(vous)*. See B. 6:247 and note 2.

75. B. 37:309 and R. 18:270.

76. R. 18:268 and B. 9:26.

77. B. 7:129 and 37:376.

78. B. 10:56 and 28:109.

79. B. 13:142, note 1.

80. B. 28:110.

81. B. 14:80.

82. B. 23:79 and 14:258, etc.

83. B. 15:343 and note 6.

84. Saint-Simon, *Ecrits inédits*, 8 vols. (Paris, 1882–92), 3:36ff.

85. B. 20:130.

86. B. 8:196 and 39:238.

87. B. 20:131.

88. B. 12:13, 14, and 15:258, 261.

89. B. 30:102.

90. Montesquieu, *L'Esprit des lois* (Paris: Editions du Seuil, 1964), 556.

91. Duc de Luynes, letter of 14 October 1754, *Mémoires*, 13:372.

92. It is true, as Hélène Himmelfarb has shown, that Saint-Simon often managed his land very intelligently in the first half of the eighteenth century, but here I am interested in his thinking about the court and not about his practice as a landowner.

93. B. 14:324 to 326.

94. B. 15:192, 20:205, and 23:79.

95. B. 18:164, 165.

96. B. 1:42.

97. B. 14:324, 326.

98. B. 17:204, 14:379.

99. B. 17:197.

100. For more information about this, see Stephen Kaplan, *Le Complot de famine* (Paris: Armand Colin, 1982).

101. B. 31:28.

102. B. 30:169; Pierre Goubert and Daniel Roche, *Les Français et l'Ancien Régime* (Paris: Armand Colin, 1984), 1:133.

103. Goubert and Roche, *Les Français et l'Ancien Régime*, 1:133; La Bruyère, *Caractères*, "De la ville," pars. 5, 7, and 8.

104. Roland Mousnier, *La Vénalité des offices* (Paris: Presses Universitaires de France, 1971), 540. See also Abbé de Choisy, *Mémoires* (Paris: Mercure de France, 1983), 24.

105. Once again, Saint-Simon's views stand in need of some correction. The truth is, rather, that the great nobles of the word were primarily landowners, and in debt, while the *parlementaires*, though primarily rentiers, also owned considerable amounts of land. Here, however, we are interested in how a mental construct came to be, not in the actual facts of wealth.

106. B. 3:34 and 20:265.

107. B. 1:194.

108. B. 32:231.

109. B. 1:239.

110. B. 29:276.

111. B. 16:123.

112. B. 11:334 (where note 6 challenges Saint-Simon's assertion about the background of Ducasse, who was certainly a commoner but not necessarily the son of a hog butcher). See also B. 23:19.

113. B. 1:63 and note.

114. B. 6:47.

115. B. 17:61. Father Tellier may not have been as lowborn as Saint-Simon claimed if he was related to the Telliers de Tournville, a family of Rouen financiers, and through them to the Harcourt-Beuvrons and therefore to the maréchal d'Harcourt (B. 17:61, note 5, and Tallemant des Réaux, *Historiettes* [Paris: Gallimard, 1932], 2:647–49 and 1422–23).

116. B. 3:4.

117. B. 37:3.

118. B. 1:33.

119. B. 31:347.

120. B. 33:97.

121. B. 29:234.

122. B. 18:110.

123. B. 15:281.

124. B. 19:413.

125. B. 20:296.

126. But not always. The duc d'Elbeuf, governor of Picardy and Artois, plundered the people he administered and "made fun of the intendants" (B. 32:221).

127. B. 23:21.

128. The story that Saint-Simon tells is accurate except for a few details, which we have corrected with the help of Boislisle's notes.

129. B. 35:288.

130. B. 35:289.

131. B. 30:315 and 19:372.

132. B. 19:35.

133. B. 36:367.

134. B. 15:381, 16:398, and 26:190.

135. B. 24:99.

136. B. 31:46ff.

137. "*Brevets de retenue* were a sort of deed to property guaranteed by the king which assured the holder of a nonvenal, nonhereditary office that if he should resign or die, no claimant would receive royal approval to hold the office without paying the former officeholder or his heirs an amount specified in the *brevet*." Thus at least the capital value of the office, if not the office itself, could be passed on (B. 1:105). If we ignore certain differences, this was tantamount to introducing venality of office into a sector where in theory it did not exist. To be sure, Montesquieu believed that venality of office was an excellent foundation for a monarchical society of orders, and therefore of ranks, since he treated office as a "family profession" and therefore a breeding ground of hereditary nobility (*L'Esprit des lois*, 1:5, 19). 138.

138. B. 38:167. 139.

139. B. 36:347. 140.

140. B. 35:283. 141.

141. B. 17:376. 142.

142. B. 41:320. 143.

143. B. 30:308 and 31:106. 144.

144. R. 18:445. 145.

145. B. 35:285. 146.

146. C. 7:640, 641; B. 1:194. 147.

147. B. 17:12. 148.

148. Yvonne Labande-Mailfert, *Charles VIII* (Paris: Fayard, 1975), 139. 149.

149. B. 11:302. 150.

150. B. 12:175. 151.

151. B. 4:150 and 10:224. 152.

152. B. 13:97. 153.

153. B. 14:76. 154.

154. B. 4:286 and 13:163. 155.

155. R. 18:225.

156. B. 13:91, 20:299, and 12:387. (The Boislisle index, which is the most complete of those available, does not always mention battlefield deaths, which makes it more difficult to establish accurate statistics.)

157. B. 2:42, 4:359, and 12:154.

158. B. 13:92.

159. B. 1:55.

160. Micheline Cuénin, *Le Duel sous l'Ancien Régime* (Paris: Presses de la Renaissance, 1982). Because the Regency temporarily dissolved the court of Versailles, where tight surveillance was in effect, there was an upsurge in dueling. Here (for once!) Norbert Elias's views on the mollification of behavior induced by the court are relevant.

161. B. 29:294 and 360.

162. In theory, the nobility monopolized the right to kill, especially in battle and in duels. Of course, mass armies (which under Louis XIV numbered 300,000

or more troops) extended this right to many commoners. The Revolution and the two centuries of modernity that followed it have further democratized this right. The right to kill takes many forms. Originally, for instance, the right to kill game was a purely noble right, but hunting rights have been democratized. In war, the number of killers and killed has multiplied many times over (as a result first of the *levée en masse* and later of compulsory military service). Where nobles once monopolized the right to kill on horseback, the automobile now kills thousands every year. And women now also claim the right to kill their own fetuses, a right that has been endlessly debated and on which we take no ideological or political position (in France in the 1990s there were some 225,000 abortions performed every year, which means that roughly one in five pregnancies ended in the death of the fetus).

163. B. 38:205.

164. B. 30:185.

165. B. 29:295 and 365.

166. B. 29:364.

167. B. 1:217.

168. B. 5:313.

169. B. 36:313.

170. B. 15:111 and 16:255.

171. Compare B. 5:422 with the somewhat different version in Tallemant, *Historiettes* (Paris: Gallimard, 1960), 1:301.

172. B. 15:111.

173. B. 25:155.

174. B. 10:310.

175. B. 7:390, 36:86, 143.

176. The maréchal de Villars was in reality an able military commander who saved Louis XIV's bacon at the end of his reign. Saint-Simon's negative judgment of this worthy captain tells us far more about Saint-Simon's obsessions than about Villars as he really was.

177. B. 20:275–76.

178. Montesquieu, *L'Esprit des lois*, part 1, 3:7: "Monarchical government implies . . . ranks. The nature of honor is such as to require preferences and distinctions. [Honor] is therefore by its very nature placed within such government." For Norbert Elias, ruse and hypocrisy, characteristic of the behavior of courtiers, were the prelude to the self-control exhibited by our contemporaries. For Montesquieu (page 538 of the 1964 Seuil edition), these behaviors were merely the logical, structural (and perhaps unfortunate) counterpart of a deferential monarchical system based on honor and rank. See also the work of Yves Castan on the importance of the point of honor among commoners in the prerevolutionary south, where a hierarchical culture related to that of Spain survived despite the barrier of the Pyrenees.

179. B. 32:329.

180. B. 19:240.

181. B. 20:73.

182. R. 18:18 and 272; B. 17:84 and 20:275.

183. B. 24:165.

184. B. 3:182 and 38:20, note 2.

185. B. 6:293. Contemporary texts cited by Boislisle in the places indicated

confirm that in regard to Dangeau and Chamillart Saint-Simon invented nothing, although the reality was obviously more complex than he makes out.

186. B. 31:177.

187. B. 6:145.

188. B. 32:239.

189. R. 18:254; B. 21:323.

190. B. 21:88.

191. B. 17:291.

192. B. 36:359 and 17:298.

193. B. 33:78.

194. B. 33:71, 81.

195. B. 18:22, 227.

196. B. 17:278.

197. B. 1:134.

198. B. 17:296.

199. B. 39:270.

200. B. 17:286.

201. B. 40:33.

202. B. 17:411, 412. Lower down the social ladder, laborers ate from earthenware, sandstone, and on occasion pewter, while wealthier peasants ate from porcelain, pewter, and in some cases crystal and silver. See D. Rosselle, "Le Béthunois sous l'Ancien Régime" (doctoral thesis, University of Lille III, 1984).

203. B. 39:5.

204. B. 7:373.

205. See Saint-Simon, *Ecrits inédits*, vol. 3, passim.

206. But Turkish ambassadors retained their turbans—a geographic exception to the rule.

207. B. 10:235.

208. B. 6:18.

209. B. 7:6.

210. B. 13:450, 452, 9:17.

211. B. 26:172, 39:78, 324, 332.

212. Saint-Simon, *Ecrits inédits*, 3:56.

213. B. 3:311 and 14:97, and more generally, the numerous references on this subject in the Boislisle index, 1:89 and 2:4.

214. We borrow this idea from Louis Dumont.

215. B. 28:235.

216. B. 7:373.

217. B. 3:63, 15:253.

218. B. 28:335.

219. B. 15:252, 253.

220. Even before carriages became commonplace, the horses ridden by nobles were stabled according to rank.

221. B. 11:186.

222. B. 9:171 and note 6.

223. Ibid., B. 2:347.

224. R. 18:63; B. 2:347.

225. B. 6:322.

226. B. 3:202.

227. B. 41:137.

228. B. 3:202. On the matter of access rights, see the index to Boislisle under *entrées*, final entry.

229. D. Dessert, *Argent: Pouvoir et société au Grand Siècle* (Paris: Fayard, 1984).

230. Chevreuse, who apparently enjoyed considerable influence at the beginning of the eighteenth century, seems to have served as emissary from a pious or *dévot* faction to the king (B. 15:402). Through him, Beauvillier, Torcy, and Desmarets, the Colbert clan remained close to the center of power.

231. B. 15:404.

232. B. 1:114.

233. B. 11:8.

234. For Montesquieu, the quintessential theorist of a monarchy based on a society of orders, nobility, and honor, civilian supremacy over the military was in no way contradictory with hierarchy as that term is used in this book: "Should civilian and military employments be conferred on the same individual? . . . In monarchy . . . they should be separate. . . . In monarchies it would nevertheless be perilous to entrust a single individual with both functions [civilian and military]. . . . In monarchies men of war have but one object, namely, glory, or at any rate honor or fortune. One should be careful not to give civilian posts to such people. On the contrary, military men should be constrained by civilian magistrates, and the men who have the confidence of the people should not at the same time have the military force to abuse it" (see Montesquieu, *L'Esprit des lois*, 5:19). Thus Louvois, who as minister of war in the fullest sense of the word was a high-ranking *robin*, was expected to "constrain" the marshals of France.

235. According to Louis Dumont.

236. B. 7:290.

237. B. 28:44.

238. B. 4:39.

239. B. 16:372 and 41:235.

240. B. 16:257.

241. B. 6:128–30.

242. B. 23:316.

243. B. 31:246.

244. B. 4:39, note 2.

245. B. 11:347.

246. Michel Antoine, *Le Conseil du Roi sous le règne de Louis XV* (Geneva: Droz, 1978), 133.

247. Ibid., 93, 190.

248. Ibid., 144.

249. B. 24:203, 399, 29:101ff.

250. Things were very different in the provinces, far from Versailles and Paris. In Brittany, for example, the *noblesse de robe* of the parlement was quite simply the nobility of that province. When necessary, it melded itself into the families of non-*robin* nobles.

CHAPTER TWO

1. B. 21:25.

2. Ibid., note 5.

3. B. 12:338 and 413.

4. Throwing money to the people was not a vulgar gesture but the survival of an old Roman tradition that lived on long after the demise of Rome, according to K. F. Werner, *Histoire de France*, vol. 1, *Les Origines* (Paris: Fayard, 1984).

5. See the chapter 1 and B. 19:88.

6. Saint-Simon wrote these texts when he was seventy-eight, in August 1753. See J.-P. Brancourt, *Le Duc de Saint-Simon et la hiérarchie* (Paris: Cujas, 1971), 242–56. See also Pseudo-Dionysus (cited in the bibliography), whose work Saint-Simon knew if not directly then through a series of intermediate authors (Coirault, *Dans la forêt san-simonienne* [Paris: Presses Universitaires de France, 1992], 183).

7. On the social hierarchy of devils in relation to the orders and *estats* of the human world, see the humorous reflections of Lesage in *Le Diable boîteux* (1707), chaps. 1ff.

8. Thomas Hobbes, *Leviathan* (Indianapolis: Bobbs-Merrill, 1958), 104, 108, 110, 127, 142.

9. Madame, *Lettres*, 3 April 1710.

10. B. 17:485.

11. B. 15:236.

12. Alexis de Tocqueville, *De la démocratie en Amérique* (Paris: Gallimard, 1951), 1:302.

13. B. 19:88. [An *aune* was a measure of length slightly under four feet— trans.]

14. B. 1:516.

15. J.-P. Babelon, *Henri IV* (Paris: Fayard, 1982), 695.

16. B. 27:278.

17. J. Jacquart, *François Ier* (Paris: Fayard, 1981), 106ff., and Lavisse, *Histoire de France*, 5, part 1: 253ff.

18. B. 9:26 and 27.

19. B. 20:75, 26:96, and 28:369.

20. B. 13:106 and 114.

21. B. 2:354, 7:149 and 151, 23:79.

22. B. 15:269.

23. B. 15:270, note 1.

24. B. 23:270.

25. Madame, *Lettres*, 17 September 1719.

26. B. 9:207.

27. B. 38:26, 9:220, 16:377, and 40:130. On all of these rites, which "half-sacralized" the royal person who physically occupied a place intermediate between clergy and nobility, see also R. 2:81 and 193, 14:39, and 17:62.

28. La Bruyère, *Caractères*, chap. 8, "De la cour."

29. R. 18:318 and B. 39:323.

30. B. 30:294.

31. B. 24:149.

32. B. 3:80.

33. La Bruyère, *Caractères*, chap. 5, "De la société et de la conversation."

34. R. Giesey, "Cérémonial et puissance souveraine (France, Xve–XVIIe siècle)," *Cahiers des Annales*, no. 41 (1987).

35. B. 21:188, 189.

36. B. 28:373.

37. According to article 25 of the original statues of 1578. See B. 16:57, note 4.

38. B. 39:338.

39. B. 39:134.

40. R. 16:3 and 17:152.

41. B. 14:282 and 26:238.

42. B. 14:114, note 6.

43. B. 26:237.

44. B. 12:194 and 26:238.

45. B. 38:310, 40:54, 23:15.

46. R. 4:403 and the Ramsay and Boislisle indexes.

47. B. 1:109, note 1.

48. B. 23:5.

49. B. 23:4, 5.

50. B. 24:74 and 39:145.

51. B. 10:204, 22:175.

52. B. 12:353.

53. B. 17:30.

54. R. 18:196.

55. R. 10:352.

56. B. 40:24, 142–46.

57. B. 24:203.

58. R. 17:138–41.

59. R. 17:138.

60. Jacques Le Goff, *Pour un autre Moyen Age* (Paris: Gallimard, 1977), 350. See B. 19:143, 144, and 164 (divine election of kings); B. 11:364 (ducal dignity emanating from king); *Ecrits inédits* of Saint-Simon, 2:121–50, cited by Brancourt, *Le Duc de Saint-Simon*, 50 (right of the nation to bestow the crown in the absence of a "Salic" prince).

61. B. 19:30, 14:411, etc.

62. B. 20:235.

63. B. 12:361, 363, and 8:282.

64. B. 4:170 and 15:277.

65. B. 16:435.

66. B. 20:238.

67. B. 23:2.

68. B. 25:185.

69. B. 41:89.

70. B. 23:2.

71. B. 38:225 and 7:20ff.

72. Boislisle index at Coëtanfao.

73. B. 22:6–8; R. 3:28.

74. B 28:224–32.

75. B. 41:43, 44.

76. B. 30:252, 253.

77. B. 30:141, 142, 144, 145.

78. B. 11:80, etc.

79. B. 4:54 and 13:304.

80. B. 10:327, 330.

81. B. 23:279.

82. B. 39:314.

83. B. 26:164.

84. B. 26:166, note 3.

85. Dumont, *Homo hierarchicus*.

86. Edmund Burke, *Reflections on the Revolution in France* (London: Penguin, 1973), 100–101.

87. R. 3:143 and B. 9:169.

88. B. 1:284, 285, and note 1.

89. B. 20:257, 375 (and "Add."), 9:169–75.

90. B. 26:296.

91. B. 6:132.

92. B. 10:198–200 and notes, esp. note 2, p. 199.

93. R. 18:328.

94. B. 5:110, note 2.

95. B. 7:78, note 5.

96. B. 7:77.

97. B. 5:268; 10:276 and 280, note 4; 33:53.

98. B. 30:167.

99. According to Théodore Godefroy, *Cérémonial français* (1649), 2:955, cited by Saint-Simon, B. 30:170 and note 1.

100. B. 40:268.

101. B. 6:418 and 25:258.

102. B. 1:57.

103. B. 2:177 and 392.

104. Ibid.

105. B. 13:458.

106. B. 4:223.

107. B. 6:222ff.

108. B. 12:559.

109. B. 36:224.

CHAPTER THREE

1. Dumont, *Homo hierarchicus*, 168–93.

2. R. 5:9.

3. R. 9:47.

4. R. 12:67.

5. R. 12:11.

6. Plate 62 of the Da Costa collection of Abraham Bosse's engravings cited in chapter 1 (*Le XVIIe siècle vu par Abraham Bosse*).

7. Piero Camporesi, paper read at a seminar at the Maison des Sciences de l'Homme, 1983.

8. Madame, *Lettres*, 145.

9. B. 37:225ff.

10. Madeleine Foisil, *L'Enfant Louis XIII* (Paris: Perrin, 1996), 57, and B. 15:43 and note 3.

11. B. 28:310.

12. At the time, the future duc d'Orléans was still only duc de Chartres.

13. Ramsay index, art. "Orléans" (18:288ff.).

14. Ramsay index, art. "Dubois" (18:132ff.).

15. Ibid. "The criminal friends—Dubois and Noailles—sniff each other out" (B. 26:367). According to Fernand Braudel, Lucien Febvre was fond of the saying, "Foxes sniff each other's tails."

16. R. 11:383 and Ramsay index, art. "Noailles" (18:280).

17. The younger Pontchartrain is another villain of the *Memoirs*. Unlike Dubois and his henchmen, such as Noailles, Pontchartrain was never mixed up in a "monstrous" marriage. His blackguardry was of another kind, including his maneuvering to prevent a decent and happy marriage, namely, that of Saint-Simon himself to Mlle de Lorges (B. 2:270). These symmetrical conjugal episodes memorably mark the beginning of the *Memoirs*.

18. See the list of relevant chapter headings in the Ramsay index under "Bastards" (18:43ff.).

19. Ibid., art. "Orléans (le chevalier d')," and B. 30:81, 36:314, 41:137.

20. R. 5:214 and 12:486; B. 35:175.

21. R. 15:58; B. 31:264, 35:257.

22. Boislisle index, art. "Bavière (Emmanuel)"; B. 9:280 and 29:296.

23. B. 31:16, 17.

24. B. 37:296.

25. B. 37:298.

26. B. 37:297.

27. B. 41:158.

28. J. Dupâquier in *Gé-Magazine*, "La Généalogie aujourd'hui," December 1985, 15ff.

29. B. 20:192.

30. B. 3:3.

31. B. 23:269.

32. Elsewhere, however, Saint-Simon asserts that it was Sala's brother who had been the archduke's coachman. See B. 23:436.

33. The "archduke" was the future emperor Charles VI.

34. B. 11:83–85.

35. B. 11:3.

36. B. 25:39.

37. B. 7:22 and note 3.

38. B. 29:50.

39. Ibid. and note 5.

40. Ibid.

41. Lev. 18:22–24, 19:19, 20:13–16.

42. B. 26:59, 60.

43. B. 22:219.

44. See reflections on *vilains* in B. 20:251.

45. Ibid., note 2, and Sévigné, letter of 12 July 1690.

46. B. 4:280.

47. B. 2:321ff.

48. B. 30:320.

49. B. 24:2.

50. B. 5:230 and 7:78.

51. B. 41:66; Ramsay index, art. "Prye" (18:334).

52. On the comte de Toulouse, see the excellent article by André Zysberg in *L'Histoire grande ouverte* (Paris: Fayard, 1997), 245.

53. R. 18:438, 439; B. 29:15 and 109, 35:57.

54. B. 38:3.

55. B. 2:253.

56. B. 14:425.

57. B. 16:293, 307, 317.

58. B. 12:60 and 17:31.

59. B. 10:99 and passim (cf. Boislisle index, art. "Maine").

60. B. 13:245.

61. B. 1:98 and passim (cf. Boislisle index, art. "Maine: Mari et femme").

62. B. 15:111.

63. B. 37:371.

64. C. 7:429.

65. B. 20:356 and 35:117.

66. B. 4:335.

67. B. 18:172, 15:8–15, 21:90 and 271.

68. B. 30:164 and Ramsay index, art. "Bâtards" (18:43).

69. B. 24:54.

70. B. 24:120.

71. B. 7:14.

72. B. 19:390.

73. B. 15:96.

74. B. 14:541.

75. Ramsay index, article "Turenne" (18:446).

76. B. 14, app. 8.

77. On La Feuillade's homosexuality, B. 29:311ff.; "muck," C. 2:320; quasi-excommunication, C. 3:325; gemstones, B. 3:117; for the rest, the indexes of Boislisle, Corault, Ramsay.

78. B. 11:41.

79. Indexes of Boislisle, Corault, and especially Ramsay.

80. B. 10:6 and Ramsay index, 18:222.

81. B. 37:144, 7:83, 14:243, and 20:50.

82. B. 7:85.

83. B. 23:122.

84. B. 30:3.

85. B. 36:292.

86. B. 37:120–27 and 398–400.

87. B. 1:209, 6:58. It is interesting to note the amusing "trifunctionalist" tone of this passage: war, court, and goods (of this world).

88. B. 17:124, 127.

89. B. 19:111.

90. B. 17:236.

91. B. 13:284, etc.

92. B. 22:27 and 335.

93. B. 20:231.

94. R. 4:145, particularly the notes; and B. 11:57.

95. B. 8:208, note 2; and C. 4:397ff. and 430; concerning the duchesse de Bourgogne, see also our chapter on the Jesuits (chap. 6).

96. Madame, *Lettres*, 14 August 1718.

97. B. 15:31 and 17:69.

98. B. 13:311.

99. B. 16:152.

100. Others took a similar view of Italy: see for example, Commynes, *Mém-oires*, ed. J. Calmette (Paris: Les Belles Lettres, 1965), 3:15: "Understand that their father [Roberto di San Severino, the father of Galeano and his half-brother Gianfrancesco] belonged to the house of Sforza because he was the son of a bastard daughter. But in Italy they make little distinction between a bastard child and a legitimate one."

101. B. 9:160.

102. B. Bennassar, *Valladolid au siècle d'or* (Paris: Mouton, 1967), 542ff.

103. B. 30:10: this text points up Saint-Simon's "Louis XIII" side: he is of course against the Habsburgs, hence against Vienna, against England (remembering Louis XIII's siege of La Rochelle), but for the Bourbon dynasty in France of course and now, in 1716, also in Spain.

104. B. 9:231 and 14:413.

105. C. 8:311.

106. B. 4:47 and C. 8:62–63. Conversely, the nuptial bed, particularly on the wedding night, had an almost public character in France. See C. 1:225 as well as the admittedly caricatural portrait in Nicolas Chorier, *L'Académie des Dames*, in *L'Enfer de la B. N.* (Paris: Fayard, 1913), 444, 459ff., etc.

107. B. 20:123 and C. 8:285.

108. In general, Saint-Simon makes fun of the Spaniards for the hyperbole in their manners and system of ranks (see C. 1:596 and 2:238ff.).

109. B. 9:235; C. 2:83.

110. B. 9:169, 179.

111. C. 2:116; B. 9:129.

112. C. 2:117.

113. C. 2:118.

114. C. 8:146 and 590.

115. C. 8:378.

116. B. 8:56 and 40:120, 121.

117. B. 39:325.

118. Louis Henry and Michel Louis Lévy, "La Démographie des ducs et pairs aux XVIIme et XVIIIme siécles," *Population: Revue de l'Institut Français d'Etudes Démographiques* (1960).

119. B. 16:138ff. and *Cahiers Saint-Simon* (1983).

120. C. 2:145 and 2:226, 324.

121. See frequent odd usage of neuter adjectives as nouns, which may be a Germanic turn of style: for example, in regard to the maréchal de Villeroy in dispute with Dubois, "il s'empêtra dans le musical de ses phrases" [he got bogged down in the musicality of his sentences] (C. 7:468ff.).

122. B. 3:189; R. 2:116 and 239.

123. "In Germany daughters do not inherit" (B. 30:222 and note 4).

124. G. Huppert, *The Idea of Perfect History* (Urbana: University of Illinois Press, 1970), chap. 4.

125. B. 25:192, note. 6.

126. Labatut, *Les Ducs et pairs de France*, 49.

127. B. 25:191ff.

128. Furet, *L'Atelier de l'histoire*, 175.

129. Boislisle index at "Boulainvilliers." See, for example, C. 8:452.

130. B. 14:127.

131. B. 39:308.

132. Ramsay index, art. "Conti," and B. 4:203ff.

133. B. 15:156–60.

134. B. 4:886.

135. Lawrence Stone, *The Family, Sex, and Marriage in England, 1500–1800* (New York: Harper and Row, 1977), 533.

136. R. 13:225, 227; B. 31:359; and in general C. 6:345.

137. Ramsay index, art. "Pérégrine," and C. 8:366, 6:345.

138. C. 6:345.

139. B. 20:270.

140. C. 4:770.

141. B. 20:261.

142. B. 5:312.

143. Stone, *Family*, 354.

144. C. 4:550.

145. C. 6:117.

146. C. 4:592ff. and 7:102.

147. Grimmer, *La Femme et le bâtard*.

CHAPTER FOUR

1. Recueil Jaeglé, 2:101–2. See B. 18:6, note 4.

2. D'O was indeed a *dévot* (C. 1:318), which corroborates the Princess Palatine on this point and therefore strengthens her credibility in regard to the system of cabals in this period. A character out of a novel, d'O began as a protégé of the comte de Toulouse. His very successful marriage led to a fine passage in the *Memoirs*, a prefiguration of the Romantic.

3. Madame, *Lettres*, 23 December 1710.

4. B. 18:5–19.

5. See Emmanuel Le Roy Ladurie, *Le Territoire de l'historien* (Paris: Gallimard, 1978), 2:275–99, concerning B. 18:5–19.

6. Madame, *Lettres*, 11 August 1686.

7. Ibid., 14 July 1718.

8. B. 11:41.

9. B. 5:123, 124.

10. B. 5:123, 124; 2:131; 11:75; 18:17, 40; 20:265.

11. B. 27:116, 206; 29:93, 131; 31:143, 225, 248; 33:22, 23; 35:3; 36:221. If there can be said to have been a group around the comte de Toulouse, the second most important of Louis XIV's bastards after Maine, its leader, after Toulouse himself, its leader was d'O.

12. On various people who were "on particularly good terms with Monseigneur," see also B. 21:277.

13. Boislisle index, "Espinoy (Elisabeth)": very complete references, in particular B. 9:43 and 15:8–10, 2:191, etc.

14. B. 6:297–99.

15. Thanks to Alain Besançon for information on this point.

16. B. 12:106 and 483, 18:183.

17. Residence of the Orléans family, the cadet branch of Louis XIII's progeny, specifically, Monsieur, brother of Louis XIV, and his son, the future regent.

18. Under France's system of government in the late twentieth century, *fonctionnaires d'autorité* are those who serve at the pleasure of "the governing authority," which substantially limits their own "authority."

19. B. 22:219.

20. Recall Helmut Kohl's statement, "Wherever I sit is the center."

21. B. 2:359.

22. B. 7:179.

23. B. 26:85 and 28:292.

24. B. 18:7, 8.

25. B. 15:403.

26. D. H. J. Van Elden, *Esprits fins et géométriques dans les portraits de Saint-Simon* (The Hague: Nijhoff, 1975).

27. In the lexicon of antiquity, a "sodality" was both a religious group and a source of influence.

28. B. 16:34.

29. B. 21:384.

30. B. 18:26.

31. B. 29:86, 122.

32. B. 17:452.

33. B. 17:61.

34. B. 17:57–61.

35. B. 24:4.

36. B. 20:98, 99.

37. B. 6:293, 294.

38. B. 2:365, 366.

39. This was the reason for the very high price of major court posts, which were reserved for the principal lords, posts such as captain of the guard. Not only were such appointments great honors, but they also made it possible to approach the king frequently and thus to obtain various favors, such as an appointment, a promotion, or a pension.

40. Think, for example, of the substantial increase in Pontchartrain's wealth as a result of financial contracts (B. 6:456). Or of the depredations of Bouchu, intendant of Dauphiné, who was simultaneously Pontchartrain's friend, maréchal de Tessé's brother-in-law, and the brother-in-law of a very well-to-do Bullion. Bouchu made a bundle from contracts for military uniforms and war taxes on Savoy (B. 12:464).

41. B. 5:295, note citing the *Mémoires* of La Rochefoucauld, 2: 68–69.

42. See the text of Madame cited above.

43. Choisy, *Mémoires*, 72.

44. Ibid.

45. Ministers became ministers because of their family background as well as their talents as individuals, as is evident from the existence of ministerial dynasties such the Colberts and the Le Tellier–Louvois clan. The fact that a minister father lived under the same roof as his secretary of state son was also useful. In 1699, for example, the elder Pontchartrain was chancellor and "lived together" with

his son, a secretary of state (B. 6:455). The same was true of Pomponne, minister of state, and his son-in-law Torcy, secretary of state (B. 3:142 to 144).

46. Choisy, *Mémoires*, 236.

47. B. 6:455.

CHAPTER FIVE

1. This assertion is based on study of the text of the *Memoirs* and of Boislisle's notes. Parts of this chapter have already appeared in print, most fully in *Résumé des cours et travaux du Collège de France*, 1989–90, 699–728. This paper represents joint work, both in research and editing, by both of us. The entire chapter was published in Emmanuel Le Roy Ladurie, *L'Historien, le chiffre, et le texte* (Paris: Fayard, 1997), 271–324.

2. For the reasons indicated above, we include only individuals born after 1620.

3. Tocqueville noted that military service on the part of young nobles was at once voluntary and compulsory: "In embarking on a military career, the noble obeyed not so much his ambition as a kind of *duty* imposed by his birth. He joined the army in search of honorable employment for the idle years of youth and in order to bring back to family and friends honorable *souvenirs* of military life. But his main goal was not to acquire property, respect, or power, because he already possessed these advantages and could enjoy them without leaving home" (see Alexis de Tocqueville, *De la démocratie en Amérique* [London: McMillan and Co., 1961], vol. 3, chap. 22).

4. A check of modal frequencies confirms these observations. The most common age of death for *robins* was 80, the same as for high-ranking officers. For dukes there were two modes, 63 and 72, that is, ten to twenty years younger. As for medians (that is, the age such that the number who died above that age equals the number who died below it), we find 71 for *robins* and 63 for dukes and princes, with military officers falling in between, again confirming our conclusions.

5. The closer to the throne a person was born, the more likely he was to be granted a high military command without experience. At the age of twenty-six the duc de Bourgogne pretended to be in charge of military operations at Oudenaarde but actually followed Vendôme's useless advice. For a more glorious example, recall that le Grand Condé's first battle experience at the age of twenty-two earned him the appellation of "new Alexander." Some young commanders demonstrated genuine military acumen (the regent was another such). A man's valor was not necessarily measured by the number of his years.

6. Tocqueville noted that "in aristocratic nations, especially those in which rank is determined by birth alone, inequality exists in the army as well as the nation. Officers are nobles, soldiers are serfs. The former are invariably called to command, the latter to obey. In aristocratic armies, the soldier's ambition is therefore strictly limited, and that of officers is not unlimited. *An aristocratic corps is not just part of a hierarchy; it always contains a hierarchy within it.* Its members are situated one above the other in an invariable fashion. *One man is naturally called by birth to command a regiment, another to command a company.* Once the limits of these hopes are fulfilled, they cease to aspire further and consider themselves satisfied with their fate" (*De la démocratie en Amérique*, vol. 3, chap. 22, emphasis added).

7. The La Rochefoucaulds' avid pursuit of pious careers was inspired by

greed, to believe Saint-Simon, who detested that family more than any other. Their strategy, moreover, was to focus exclusively on maximizing the likelihood of financial success for the eldest son in each generation: "The dukes of La Rochefoucauld had long been been in the habit of keeping under their roof only a single heir, to whom all the father's properties and fortunes were to pass, and not seeking marriages for either daughters or younger sons, whom they counted as nothing and disposed of with Malta or the church." (B. 23:227)

8. If we look not at average life expectancies but at mortality by age cohort, we arrive at the same conclusion. The pattern of death for women was substantially the same as for men, but less pronounced. Duchesses and princesses were more likely to die young (the duchesse de Bourgogne was a sad example of this). Women of the robe and nuns are underrepresented in the younger cohorts but often died between ages 40 and 49, then years earlier than their male counterparts. Nuns peaked, however, at 50–70, whereas *robines* peaked ten years later (60–89). As was the case with *robins* compared with other males, *robines* tended to die later than other women mentioned in the *Memoirs*. The differences are less pronounced in the sample of women, however, than in the sample of men for the reasons already mentioned. An examination of modal frequencies would yield similar results: for *robines* the modal age at death was 72, for duchesses and princesses, 70. Although the hierarchy persisted in the face of death, it was considerably attenuated: the modal age of death for *robines* was eight years less than for *robins*. Nuns and abbesses departed this vale of tears at a modal age of 59 (for other unmarried women the dual modes were 54 and 25). Medians were 68 for women of the robe (three years less than for *robins*), 62 for duchesses and princesses (only one year less than their male counterparts), 63 for nuns, and 54 for the luckless old maids.

9. These totals include not only subjects of the French crown but also Lorrains, Savoyards, and Walloons (see above).

10. The Boislisle index supplied us with information about a number of marriages that took place between 1723 (when the *Memoirs* were completed) and 1740. Our sample (1600–1740) is thus roughly comparable to Pierre Goubert's sample for the Beauvaisis (1600–1730). See *L'Ancien Régime*.

11. Dumont, *Homo hierarchicus*; and by the same author, *Essais sur l'individualisme* (Paris: Editions du Seuil, 1983).

12. Goubert, *L'Ancien Régime*, 1:152. Goubert insists that the nobility constituted "a race apart, which since time immemorial had been transmitting superiority by the fact of birth alone: this was how the nobility conceived of itself. Many non-nobles could not help but subscribe to this conception, which without undue anachronism can be characterized as racist" (quoted by F. Billacois, "La Crise de la noblesse européenne, 1550–1650: Une mise au point," *Revue d'Histoire Moderne et Contemporaine* 23 [1976]: 259).

13. Tocqueville, *De la démocratie en Amérique*, 246. Lémontey, for his part, refers to the "fanaticism" that sometimes distorted Saint-Simon's judgment. See P.-E. Lémontey, *Histoire de la Régence et de la minorité de Louis XV jusqu'au ministère du cardinal de Fleury* (Paris: Paulin, 1832), 1:3.

14. B. 41:238 (emphasis added).

15. We are under no illusions as to the low esteem in which Saint-Simon held the rank of "foreign prince," but we felt that it was unnecessary for our analysis to reflect every one of his prejudices, no matter how glaringly apparent.

16. Dumont, *Homo hierarchicus*, 147.

17. Norbert Elias, *La Société de cour* (Paris: Calmann-Lévy, 1974), 9. Elsewhere we have occasion to criticize some of the fundamental assumptions of this important work.

18. Labatut, *Les Ducs et pairs de France*, 187–88.

19. B. 1:142.

20. For a typical example that does not appear in Saint-Simon, see Mme de La Guette, *Mémoires* (Paris: Mercure de France, 1982).

21. B. 2:206, 207.

22. B. 4:283.

23. Emmanuel Le Roy Ladurie, *Résumé des cours et travaux du Collège de France*, 1981–82, 680. Luca Cavalli-Sforza, *Gènes peuples et langues* (Paris: Editions Odile Jacob, 1996), 204, notes that some African tribesmen married pygmy women because they cost lest to buy. Low cost or high dowry: these Africans made more or less the same calculation as the French dukes and peers in evaluating the benefits of entering into a marriage with a woman of lower status.

24. B. 16:90.

25. B. 16:93.

26. B. 26:239, 240.

27. B. 11:334–36.

28. B. 26:241.

29. Saint-Simon was not always as old-fashioned as he seems at first sight, at least in this respect. Listen to what Henri Mendras has written about marriages in contemporary French society: "(Female) hypergamy seems to provide assurance of marital bliss. . . . In general, women want their husbands to be at least as well educated as they are, whereas men do not consider this important, and some even claim to prefer women who are less well educated" (Mendras, *La Seconde Révolution, 1965–1984* [Paris: Gallimard, 1988], 227). During the French Revolution, people often said that "a *ci-devant* [former aristocrat] marries a *sans-culotte*."

30. B. 11:5.

31. B. 11:3, 4.

32. B. 11:4.

33. Dumont, *Homo hierarchicus*, 152.

34. B. 13:184.

35. B. 14:362–64.

36. On this point, see D. Dessert on the "myth of the 'lackey financier,'" *Argent, pouvoir, et société au Grand Siècle* (Paris: Fayard, 1984), 98–109.

37. Recall that Saint-Simon's wife and mother came from families that were partially *robines* and fell somewhat short of the classical "standard" for the nobility of the sword.

38. For the Princess Palatine, see D. Van der Cruysse, *Madame Palatine* (Paris: Fayard, 1988).

39. Le Roy Ladurie, *Résumé*, 681–82.

40. Ibid., 681.

41. Such thinking is not exclusive to court societies. E. M. Forster's cites an instance from Victorian England: "Mrs. Durham had of course her motives. She was looking out wives for Clive and put the Hall girls down on her list. She had a theory one ought to cross breeds a bit, and Ada, though suburban, was wealthy"

(*Maurice* [New York: Norton, 1971, 110). Golo Mann offers corroborating testimony: "Marriages between members of the nobility and young women of Jewish descent were frequent [in Weimar Germany]. It bears mentioning that the fiancée made up for her background by bringing a substantial dowry to the marriage" (see Golo Mann, *Erinnerungen und Gedanken* [Frankfurt: Fischer, 1986]). See also Jonathan Swift, *Gulliver*, part 4 ("Houyhnhnms"), chap. 6, for a very important, very Swiftian text.

42. B. 40:251.

43. B. 37:26, 27.

44. Recall once again that this distinction applied only to the court nobility. In Brittany, the wealthy parlementary nobility (of the robe) often looked town on the poor *gentilhomme*, even though he might be a *noble d'épée*.

45. B. 2:183.

46. B. 1:58–60.

47. See Dessert, *Argent, pouvoir, et société*, and Chaussinand–Nogaret, *La Noblesse au XVIIIe siècle*.

CHAPTER SIX

1. B. 5:380ff.

2. B. 30:114.

3. B. 13:263.

4. B. 16:120.

5. B. 17:119.

6. Blandine Barret-Kriegel, *L'Histoire à l'âge classique* (Paris: Presses Universitaires de France, 1988), 1:289.

7. C. 1:279.

8. C. 4:396ff. and passim.

9. Sébastien Le Prestre de Vauban, *Projet d'une dîme royale* (Paris: Imprimerie Nationale, 1992).

10. B. 4:274, note 2.

11. B. 4:258.

12. C. 4:212.

13. B. 25:69.

14. B. 11:332.

15. Louis XIV governed with a small number of ministers. In 1697 there were just four, counting Pomponne. It may be useful to recall what General de Gaulle had to say about this in 1946: "Since June of 1940, many men have come to see me. Of these I know barely three who had or acquired the head of a minister" (Claude Guy, *En écoutant de Gaulle* [Paris: Grasset, 1996], 73).

16. B. 12:114.

17. B. 3:31.

18. B. 19:386.

19. B. 15:88.

20. B. 2:93, 94.

21. B. 3:70; cf. Tallemant, *Historiettes*, 2:749.

22. B. 12:290.

23. B. 3:52, 53.

24. B. 29:343 and 41:262.

25. B. 33:100.

26. B. 16:387.

27. B. 2:180, 41:321.

28. B. 18:228, 40:132.

29. C. 1:846.

30. C. 5:155.

31. B. 31:144.

32. Saint-Simon was careful to include in his list Cardinal de Retz, who retired to Commercy after many bellicose and amorous adventures "to do penance in total solitude for his previous life" (B. 15:39).

33. B. 15:266.

34. C. 3:627.

35. C. 1:259.

36. One is reminded of the sad events that took place in 1990 in Carpentras [where a Jewish cemetery was desecrated and one of the bodies was dug up and profaned—trans.].

37. C. 5:685.

38. On hypergamy, see chap. 5 above.

39. C. 1:283ff.

40. C. 1:373.

41. C. 7:767.

42. B. 15:39.

43. C. 5:693, 6:94, 7:355.

44. C. 2:26.

45. B. 9:341.

46. C. 4:597.

47. B. 5:423; on the link between anality and money/finance, see Freud, *Gesammelte Werke* (Frankfurt: Fischer, 1972), 7:203ff. ("Charakter und Analerotik").

48. B. 12:429.

49. B. 4:311 and 24:54.

50. C. 2:469, 765.

51. One saw the same penchant for secrecy in another Bourbon king, Juan Carlos of Spain, before and shortly after the death of Franco.

52. B. 12:194, 195.

53. B. 37:332–35.

54. B. 17:347.

55. Tallemant des Réaux, *Historiettes*, 1:20–21.

56. B. 12:466.

57. B. 2:262 and B. 10:35.

58. Jacques Abbadie, *Traité de la vérité de las religion chrétienne* (Rotterdam, 1684), and numerous later editions.

59. Ibid., 3:390.

60. In the 1930s and 1940s, Simone Weil lived out similar convictions (in the minor mode, to be sure). She even contemplated the virtue of losing one's mind as the ultimate renunciation.

61. Abbadie, *De la vérité de las religion chrétienne*, 2:451.

62. Ibid., 461.

63. Ibid.

64. See chaps. 7 and 8 of this volume (on Spain).

65. Abbadie, *De la vérité de las religion chrétienne*, 2:461.

66. Texts and ideas taken from volume 2 of Abbadie, *De la vérité de las religion chrétienne*, especially the final chapters.

67. Himmelfarb, "Saint-Simon et le jansénisme des Lumières," in *Studies on Voltaire and the Eighteenth Century* 88 (1972): 768 n. 54.

68. Coirault, *Optique*, 576.

69. For example, in C. 3:629ff.

70. The duchess of Brancas was pro-Jansenist, however (B. 2:338). All of this is in Hélène Himmelfarb, "Saint-Simon et le jansénisme," 742ff.

71. Himmelfarb, "Saint-Simon et le Jansénisme," 756.

72. Malebranche, *Traité de la nature et de la grâce*, book 3, chap. 28, p. 174 of the 1628 Brussels edition. *Citations de Malebranche*, Usuels BN (BD Malebranche), 107 and passim, 298 and passim.

73. C. 4:264.

74. C. 1:453.

75. C. 1:453, 655.

76. C. 1:685.

77. C. 1:633.

78. C. 1:520.

79. C. 1:621.

80. C. 2:690.

81. C. 2:568.

82. C. 2:569.

83. C. 2:689.

84. B. 5:383–84.

85. C. 3:690.

86. C. 3:629.

87. B. 18:285.

88. C. 3:631; B. 4:273. The Molinist humanist was very unjustly attacked by Saint-Simon.

89. C. 3:622.

90. C. 3:749.

91. C. 3:521, 721.

92. C. 3:899.

93. C. 3:910.

94. C. 4:50.

95. C. 4:211.

96. C. 4:630.

97. C. 5:459.

98. C. 5:306.

99. C. 6:140.

100. C. 6:217.

101. C. 6:227 and 7:305.

102. C. 1:259.

103. C. 2:332.

104. C. 2:689.

105. B. 17:47 and C. 4:44, 45.

106. C. 5:153, 585, 688.

107. C. 7:513.

108. See appendix 2.

109. Quesnel, *Réflexions*, 8:129.

110. Ibid., 2:244.

111. Pseudo-Dionysius the Areopagite, *Oeuvres complètes*, trans. Maurice de Gandillac (Paris: Aubier, 1943), passim.

112. Quesnel, *Réflexions*, 8:419.

113. C. 1:819, 822. See also the bibliography to the present work.

114. Hélène Himelfarb (private communication) insists strongly on this point. Darricau's comments can be found in the *Dictionnaire de spiritualité* under Duguet.

115. Duguet, *Institution*, 454 and 504.

116. Ibid., 390, 423ff., 630ff., etc.

117. Ibid., 608–16.

118. Ibid., 421, 432–38.

119. Ibid., 610.

120. Ibid., 406.

121. Ibid., 390.

122. Ibid., 670.

123. Ibid., 546–48.

124. Ibid., 335–37.

125. Ibid., 669.

126. But see C. 8:1694.

127. Duguet, *Institution*, 109.

128. Saint-Simon, *Traités politiques et autres écrits*, ed. Yves Coirault (Paris: Gallimard, 1996), 590–91.

129. Ibid.

130. Ibid.

131. Saint-Simon was not always consistent. In C. 3, admittedly a somewhat unusual passage, he flatly declares himself to be on the side of Jansenius and Port-Royal against the Jesuits. For once his Augustinianism is undiluted. See also C. 2:568: "Reputed to be Jansenist, that is, regular, exact, strict in his conduct, studious, and penitent."

132. Emile Appolis, *Entre Jansénistes et zelanti: Le Tiers Parti janséniste au XVIIIe siècle* (Paris: Picard, 1960), alphabetical index of names. See also our bibliography.

133. Dumont, *Homo hierarchicus*, 235; English translation (Chicago: University of Chicago Press, 1980), 184.

134. Le Roy Ladurie, *L'Ancien Régime*, 109. One further remark is called for: in Louis Dumont's fine studies of Indian society one reads of the *sannyasi*, or male renouncer, but never of his female counterpart. Doubtless there were some, but so far from the forefront of consciousness in this somewhat male-dominated oriental culture that there was little reason to discuss them at length. By contrast, Saint-Simon goes into considerable detail about a substantial number of female renouncers. This stands to reason, since he represents a Western culture that was more accepting of certain forms of feminism—limited and moderate to be sure—than was Indian society, which ever since antiquity has been afflicted with a certain tendency to "male chauvinism" characteristic of the Indus River valley and the Deccan.

135. Dumont, *Homo hierarchicus*, 342; Emmanuel Le Roy Ladurie, *Carnaval de Romans* (Paris: Gallimard, 1979); C. 3:1043 and passim.

136. C. 3:340, 3:632, and passim.

137. Dale K. Van Kley, *The Religious Origins of the French Revolution* (New Haven: Yale University Press, 1996).

138. B. 16:62–64.

139. C. 3:346.

140. C. 3:374.

141. C. 8:10–11 and B. 8:56–57.

142. C. 4:40, 784.

143. B. 10:200.

144. C. 2:215–16.

145. C. 3:342.

146. B. 13:179.

147. B. 21:150 and C. 4:721.

148. B. 6:431ff.

149. C. 1:685.

150. B. 23:240.

151. C. 4:658.

152. C. 2:896.

153. C. 3:418.

154. C. 4:734.

155. B. 36:127.

156. B. 17:245.

157. Goethe, *Faust*, part 1, line 2039.

158. C. 3:633.

159. C. 4:646.

160. C. 1:709.

161. C. 1:864.

162. C. 3:341ff.

163. There are too many references for this paragaraph to cite them all. The basic text of Saint-Simon on the "gatekeeping" phenomenon is C. 3:628 and 633; see also C. 1:251, 2:4, 5:551 and 581: "The gateway to [ecclesiastical] benefices," etc. On the Germanic empire, see C. 7:527; on Spain, C. 1:813, 856, 864; 8:55, 183, etc. On the threat (in reality, not very serious) of a Spanish-style Inquisition in France: C. 4:915. On the Savoyard exception: C. 1:308 and 731; 2:589 and 590; 4:400, 410, and 734. On the theory of gatekeepers, see David Easton, *Analysis of Political Structure* (New York: Routledge, 1990), 84–95. On the comparison between anti-Jesuitism and anti-Semitism, see Pierre Grosclaude, *Malesherbes* (Paris), 2:642, quoting the Archives Tocqueville, file L. 135; and Léon Poliakov, *Histoire de l'antisémitisme*, vol. 3, *De Voltaire à Wagner* (Paris: Calmann-Lévy, 1968) chapter on the Enlightenment.

164. B. 22:145, 27:195, 29:396.

165. English and French horse and cattle breeders record the names and pedigrees of their prize stallions and bulls in "herd-books."

166. On the Jesuit theology of good works, true merit, and irreducible human liberty as opposed to Jansenism's quasi-fatalistic concept of predestination, see L. Lessius, *De la grâce efficace* (1610), 46, 108, 252, 254, 256–60; Dupin, *Histoire ecclésiastique de XVIIe siècle* (1714), 7, 46–47, 51–63, 84–93, 146. See also the major work of Father Luis Molina (who courageously defended Christian liberty though

forever held up to ridicule by Pascal, not to mention Saint-Simon), *Liberi aritrii gratiae donis . . . concordia* (1595), 251ff (ex. off. typ.).

167. Van Kley, *The Religious Origins of the French Revolution.*

CHAPTER SEVEN

1. B. 29:41.
2. B. 29:92.
3. B. 30:360.
4. Dom Leclercq, *Histoire de la Régence et de la minorité de Louis XV*, 3 vols. (Paris, 1921). Hereafter cited as "L."
5. B. 36:2–4.
6. B. 10:208, etc.
7. The expression "civil excommunication" is taken from Philippe Erlanger.
8. C. 5:825.
9. M. de Lescure, *Les Maîtresses du Régent* (Paris: Dentu, 1861).
10. C. 2:5.
11. C. 5:645.
12. See Hélène Carrère d'Encausse, *Le Pouvoir confisqué* (Paris: Flammarion, 1980), 27, 260, 434, 453.
13. C. 5:294–99.
14. C. 5:461.
15. On the many talents of Philippe d'Orléans himself, see, in addition to Saint-Simon's text and his quotes from the Princess Palatine, Roger Zuber, *Emerveillements de la Raison* (Paris: Klincksieck, 1997), 269, which refers to C. 5, 245ff.
16. C. 6:279.
17. J. H. Shennan, *Philippe, Duke of Orléans* (London: Thames and Hudson, 1979).
18. B. 9:288 and 30:2.
19. B. 31:165–67.
20. B. 27:176.
21. B. 25:131.
22. B. 18:74 and 19:209, especially note 4.
23. B. 21:289 and 21:384.
24. B. 27:1–10.
25. C. 1:259.
26. B. 4:298.
27. J.-P. Bardet and J. Dupâquier, eds., *Histoire des populations de l'Europe* (Paris: Fayard, 1997), 1:449 (the figures given reflect the population living within France's *present* borders, not her borders at the time).
28. C. 4:758.
29. C. 1:70, etc.
30. B. 29:2–4.
31. B. 26:266ff.
32. B. 26:280.
33. C. 8:596.
34. L. 1:327.
35. C. 5:587.
36. B. 31:146.

37. L. 1:366.

38. L. 2:28, 29.

39. L. 1:139.

40. B. 24:105.

41. L. 1:14.

42. L. 1:161.

43. C. 1:520.

44. B. 27:19–29.

45. C. 6:87; Mathieu Marais, *Journal et mémoires sous la Régence et le règne de Louis XV*, 4 vols. (Paris, Firmin-Didot, 1863–68), 1:199.

46. B. 10:8 and 9; L. 1:161.

47. L. 1:161.

48. C. 6:26.

49. C. 7:1113.

50. B. 6:264.

51. B. 6:145.

52. B. 2:249, 250; L. 2:30.

53. B. 31:159.

54. B. 17:228, 229.

55. L. 1:164.

56. B. 30:291.

57. L. 1:368.

58. B. 24:101, 102; 18:326.

59. L. 1:175.

60. B. 33:8, 9; 31:43.

61. L. 2:48.

62. L. 2:48.

63. C. 6:590.

64. B. 18:272; *Vineam* in 1705; *Unigenitus* in 1713; Port-Royal-des-Champs destroyed: B. 18:281.

65. B. 30:141–48.

66. B. 24:106.

67. B. 1:181 and note 5.

68. B. 27:108.

69. B. 25:319–39.

70. B. 27:108.

71. B. 29:15ff.

72. C. 5:336.

73. L. 1:187.

74. Shennan, *Philippe, Duke of Orléans*, 98.

75. B. 27:172, 173.

76. B. 27:10–13.

77. B. 25:248, 29:27.

78. B. 29:59–62.

79. B. 29:299.

80. B. 27:23.

81. C. 5:653.

82. B. 30:166, 167.

83. L. 2:81.

84. B. 2:106, 107.
85. L. 2:85ff.; B. 29:3.
86. L. 2:88, 89.
87. L. 2:91.
88. C. 4:803.
89. Quoted in L. 2:96.
90. B. 30:100, 191.
91. B. 30:192.
92. B. 30:194.
93. B. 27:214.
94. L. 1:xxxvii.
95. C. 5:299, 664.
96. C. 5:648.
97. B. 35:37.
98. B. 27:61.
99. L. 1:xxiii.
100. See Chaussinand-Nogaret, *Le Citoyen des Lumières*, chap. 1, on Boulain-villiers. The author sheds a good deal of light
101. C. 2:880.
102. Shennan, *Philippe, Duke of Orléans*, 24.
103. B. 35:243, 244.
104. B. 26:361, 362.
105. B. 41:300.
106. C. 5:370.
107. B. 5:46.
108. B. 1:60, 8:371ff.
109. B. 36:262.
110. B. 33:195.
111. B. 33:2.
112. B. 29:92.
113. B. 29:47, 48.
114. B. 29:234.
115. B. 28:343.
116. B. 29:125.
117. B. 5:649.
118. B. 34:7–12.
119. B. 35:57.
120. B. 24:221.
121. B. 14:73.
122. Shennan, *Philippe, Duke of Orléans*, 41.
123. C. 7:306 and L. 2:223.
124. L. 2:67.
125. B. 33:143ff., esp. 144, note 2.
126. C. 6:650.
127. B. 37:127.
128. B. 33:145.
129. B. 27:10–31.
130. Of course there was always Boulainvilliers. As for Saint-Simon, he was tied up throughout this period in an ultrapersonal and confidential sort of *samizdat*.

131. B. 30:98.
132. C. 6:317.
133. C. 6:580, 7:291.
134. C. 6:507.
135. L. 2:215.
136. C. 7:334; B. 30:86.
137. B. 30:1–7.
138. C. 7:32.
139. C. 7:320.
140. C. 5:836.
141. B. 23:285, 286.
142. B. 39:299.
143. C. 2:902.
144. B. 23:271, 385.
145. B. 1:60.
146. B. 41:117.
147. L. 1:327.
148. B. 30:16.
149. B. 26:186, 187.
150. C. 5:762.
151. B. 37:210.
152. B. 29:281.
153. L. 1:333ff.
154. *Que la fête commence*, by Bertrand Tavernier.
155. B. 26:280–82.
156. B. 34:302 and note 1.
157. B. 37:7.
158. L. 3:418.
159. C. 5:241.
160. L. 3:423.
161. B. 15:262.
162. B. 29:329, 330.
163. B. 34:266–68, 297–98.
164. Quoted in J.-L. Aujol, *Le Cardinal Dubois, ministre de la Paix* (Paris: Editions du Bateau Ivre, 1948).
165. L. 1:41–415 and Shennan, *Philippe, Duke of Orléans*, 60.
166. B. 18:50.
167. C. 6:127.
168. L. 1:388.
169. C. 7:64.
170. B. 32:245, 246.
171. B. 36:137.
172. B. 40:2, 3.
173. L. 1:381, 382; B. 19:23.
174. C. 5:835, 836.
175. B. 1:63.
176. L. 1:502.
177. B. 33:40, 41.
178. L. 1:511.

179. Brazilian gold no doubt played a role in this recovery after 1700. See C. Morrisson in Emmanuel Le Roy Ladurie, ed., *L'Histoire grande ouverte* (Paris: Fayard, 1997), 77ff.

180. B. 32:201.

181. B. 30:88–92.

182. B. 37:320.

183. Shennan, *Philippe, Duke of Orléans*, 106.

184. C. 6:504, 572.

185. B. 30:88–92.

186. B. 29:54.

187. B. 33:42.

188. G. Frèche, *Les Prix [. . .] à Toulouse* (Paris: Presses Universitaires de France, 1967), 131.

189. B. 31:281–91.

190. Le Roy Ladurie, *Les Paysans de Languedoc*, 2:1024.

191. Shennan, *Philippe, Duke of Orléans*, 118–19.

192. B. 38:91, 97.

193. L. 2:149.

194. B. 35:16.

195. B. 35:18.

196. B. 35:30.

197. B. 29:15, 16; 35:159.

198. B. 35:214ff.

199. B. 35:221ff.

CHAPTER EIGHT

1. C. 5:655.

2. C. 7:306.

3. B. 35:300.

4. L. 2:48, 205.

5. B. 35:295–300.

6. L. 2:205, 206.

7. B. 35:300.

8. B. 10:19.

9. L. II:224.

10. B. 15:382.

11. L. 2:225 and B. 1:63.

12. B. 38:271–76.

13. B. 36:142.

14. B. 34:309.

15. B. 38:90.

16. C. 7:499.

17. Marais quoted in Edgar Faure, *La Banqueroute de Law, 17 juillet 1720* (Paris: Gallimard, 1977), 484.

18. Jean Meyer, *La Vie quotidienne en France au temps de la Régence* (Paris: Hachette, 1979), 190ff.

19. L. 2:429.

20. C. 5:885.

21. L. 2:432.

22. Faure, *La Banqueroute de Law*, 55ff.

23. L. 2:472.

24. B. 37:360–62.

25. B. 37:332–35.

26. B. 36:86.

27. B. 37:21, 250, 369.

28. L. 2:429.

29. B. 37:369, 370.

30. B. 38:75.

31. C. 2:487.

32. L. 2:432.

33. B. 34:303. For the Regency period in general, readers may wish to consult Coirault, *Dans la Forêt saint-simonienne*, 88–95.

34. C. 5:279.

35. L. 2:250.

36. L. 2:254, 255.

37. B. 34:266–68.

38. B. 34:278–79.

39. B. 36:38.

40. B. 36:51–54.

41. B. 36:54–56.

42. B. 36:37.

43. B. 36:143, 36:57.

44. B. 36:14.

45. L. 1.:207, 208 (see our bibliography).

46. B. 14:379.

47. B. 36:26, note 3.

48. B. 36:27ff.

49. B. 37:128.

50. I wish to thank Guy Chaussinand-Nogaret for information he provided on this point.

51. B. 36:89–93.

52. B. 36:89.

53. L. 3:302.

54. L. 2:307.

55. B. 35:35.

56. B. 3:235.

57. B. 41:185.

58. B. 33:15.

59. B. 14:199. See also Jean Meyer, *La Noblesse bretonne au XVIIIe siècle*, 2 vols. (Paris: EHESS, 1985).

60. B. 37:232ff.

61. L. 3:60.

62. B. 41:151.

63. B. 37:333.

64. B. 30:249.

65. B. 29:262; L. 2:404.

66. B. 23:388.

67. B. 37:2–5.

68. B. 37:182ff.
69. L. 2:385.
70. B. 4:260.
71. L. 2:477; C. 7:720; B. 33:117.
72. B. 13:437.
73. B. 10:19.
74. B. 36:373.
75. L. 3:2 and B. 32:56.
76. L. 2:526ff.
77. L. 2:529.
78. L. 2:514, and in a similar spirit, B. 41:225, note 3ff.
79. L. 3:7; B. 19:206, 13:232 and 234.
80. L. 3:7.
81. L. 3:10, 11.
82. On this prelate, see also C. 4:701.
83. L. 3:12.
84. L. 3:13.
85. B. 36:354.
86. B. 37:60.
87. L. 3:1; and B. 36:1–5.
88. B. 37:191.
89. B. 37:188ff.: *sacre*, of course, refers to the ceremony of anointing with holy chrism as well as to a bird of prey, hence the pun, which literally means "to consecrate a hawk."
90. B. 37:193.
91. B. 37:192, 37:201ff.
92. B. 37:200.
93. Jean Bunat, *Journal de la Régence* (Paris: Plon, 1865).
94. C. 6:650.
95. L. 3:37.
96. L. 3:43.
97. C. 7:724; L. 3:105ff.
98. L. 3:116.
99. B. 37:82.
100. B. 31:146, 37:67.
101. L. 3:124.
102. Marais, *Journal et mémoires*, 1:484; Edmond Barbier, *Journal historique du règne de Louis XV* [or *Chronique de la Régence et du règne de Louis XV*], 1:81–88 in L. 3:125.
103. L. 3:125; Faure, *La Banqueroute de Law*, 588.
104. C. 7:729.
105. B. 38:72, 207; L. 3:204.
106. B. 38:190.
107. L. 3:143.
108. B. 37:86–92.
109. C. 1:310.
110. B. 38:303.
111. L. 3:130.
112. B. 38:356ff.

113. L. 3:150.
114. L. 3:148–65.
115. L. 3:162; C. 7:594.
116. L. 3:151.
117. B. 38:71–84.
118. B. 39:309ff.
119. L. 3:154.
120. This, nevertheless, is the hypothesis tentatively put forward by the eminent Roland Mousnier in Marcel Reinhard, ed., *Histoire de France* (Paris, 1954), 2:9.
121. L. 3:219.
122. B. 40:22.
123. B. 34:307.
124. B. 40:215, 216.
125. L. 3:208, quoting archives of foreign affairs, Spain, vol. 30, fol. 311: Dubois to Maulévrier; and E. Drumont, *Papiers inédits de Saint-Simon* (Paris, 1880), introduction, 86–87.
126. B. 38:280–82.
127. L. 3:247.
128. B. 38:285.
129. Saint-Simon, *Mémoires et lettres*, initial Pléiade edition (Paris: Gallimard, 1961), 7:444–46; L. 3:229, 242.
130. B. 26:280–82.
131. B. 38:70.
132. L. 3:261.
133. B. 38:245–74.
134. L. 3:261.
135. B. 18:314–17.
136. L. 3:263 and C. 7:680.
137. C. 8:408.
138. L. 3:264.
139. B. 40:172–78.
140. B. 40:252.
141. L. 3:271 and C. 8:457ff.
142. B. 40:253.
143. B. 41:221.
144. B. 40:263.
145. B. 40:274–93, 41:1–18.
146. B. 40:293.
147. B. 40:282.
148. B. 41:9–17.
149. B. 40:266, note 1.
150. B. 40:264–68.
151. B. 41:57–61; L. 3:285.
152. B. 26:250, 38:141.
153. L. 3:295.
154. B. 41:133, 134.
155. B. 41:193–95.
156. L. 3:407.

157. C. 8:595.
158. B. 41:17.
159. C. 7:292, 863.
160. B. 41:168.
161. B. 41:212.
162. Mousnier in Reinhard, *Histoire de France*, 2:7–8.
163. Shennan, *Philippe*, 143.
164. Ibid., 144.
165. B. 22:385.
166. C. 3:936.
167. B. 15:195.
168. B. 15, appendix 4.
169. B. 32:88.
170. B. 27:216.
171. On the union of England and Holland, B. 36:204.
172. B. 29:92, 41:4.
173. C. 7:96, 8:651.

CONCLUSION

1. Jean Bottéro et al., *La plus belle histoire du monde* (Paris: Editions du Seuil, 1997).
2. See part 1 above on renunciation. For further details about the post–Louis XIV era relevant in the present context, see the memoirs of the duc de Luynes.
3. We refer, of course, to W. Ritchey Newton's important work on Versailles, *L'Espace du roi: La Cour de France au château de Versailles, 1682–1789* (Paris: Fayard, 2000).
4. C. 7:520.
5. C. 4:264, 265; and Poisson, *Monsieur de Saint-Simon*, 136, on the notion of "patriot" in Saint-Simon; see also the fine article by Christophe Blanquie in *Cahiers Saint-Simon*, no. 24 (1996): 89.
6. B. 41:305, 15:198.
7. See the note on Philippe Alméras in our bibliography.
8. On all this, see Dom Calmet and the abbé de Vence, *Sainte Bible* (Paris, 1773), 14:638; and Gandillac, *Oeuvres complètes du Pseudo-Denys* (1943), 39 n. 89; 42 n. 100.

APPENDIX ONE

1. On the importance of the time Elias spent in Africa, see his autobiography *Norbert Elias par lui-même* (Paris: Fayard, 1991).
2. See Pierre Bourdieu, *La Noblesse d'Etat* (Paris: Les Editions de Minuit, 1989), 157 and 183; *La Distinction* (Paris: Les Editions de Minuit, 1969), 80, 251, 426, 436, 571, 575, 576; and *Méditations pascaliennes* (Paris: Editions du Seuil, 1997), 47 and passim—works in which Elias is praised and quoted in numerous places, fortunately in ways that are peripheral to the central argument of each book.
3. *Die höfische Gesellschaft*, which was originally published before World War II but republished in 1969. A French translation, *La Société de cour*, appeared in 1974. This work has often been cited by leading scholars and students of court society, such as Roger Chartier, Jacques Revel (in his excellent article for *Les*

Lieux de mémoire), Arlette Farge, and Joël Cornette in stimulating and substantial works on the archives and Louis XIV.

4. Daniel Gordon, *Citizens without Sovereignty: Equality and Sociability in French Thought, 1670–1789* (Princeton: Princeton University Press, 1994).

5. On this point, see the work of Daniel Roche on the academies of eighteenth-century France.

6. C. 5:533.

APPENDIX TWO

1. Pasquier Quesnel, *Réflexions sur l'Ancien Testament.* There are many editions of this work. We used the charming edition of 1736, which was published in eight volumes.

2. This can be found in a text written by Quesnel in 1708.

3. *Dictionnaire de spiritualité*, article "Quesnel," 2741–43.

Bibliography

The list of works below is neither exhaustive nor systematic. We include only those works that intersect in some way with our concerns in this volume. For a truly exhaustive and systematic bibliography of works relating to Saint-Simon, see the huge corpus compiled by Yves Coirault and François Formel listed below.

Abbadie, Jacques. *Traité de la vérité de la religion chrétienne.* Rotterdam, 1684. Many subsequent editions.

Alméras, Philippe. *Les Idées de Céline: Pensées politiques.* Paris: Berg International, 1992.

Saint-Simon's life was in many respects quite successful, but for a variety of reasons, people have often tried to paint him as a failure. To some extent his excellent biographer Georges Poisson does this in a rather humorous way. Here we will merely follow Philippe Alméras (260) and quote a letter from Céline to an unknown correspondent dated 20 October 1947: "Basically, a writer is someone who has failed at all the arts: poetry, music, theater, politics . . . *A bastard of all the muses!* He must be forgiven for a great deal."

Antoine, Michel. *Le Conseil du Roi sous le règne de Louis XV.* Geneva: Droz, 1978.

Appolis, Emile. *Entre Jansénistes et zelanti: Le Tiers Parti janséniste au XVIIIe siècle.* Paris: Picard, 1960.

Barbier, Edmond. *Journal historique du règne de Louis XV* [or *Chronique de la Régence et du règne de Louis XV*]. Paris, several editions, each in several volumes, published between 1847 and 1885.

Baschet, Armand. *Le Duc de Saint-Simon, son cabinet et l'historique de ses manuscrits.* Paris: Plon, 1874.

Bastide, François-Régis. *Saint-Simon par lui-même.* Paris: Editions du Seuil, 1953 and 1967.

In addition to the text by F. R. Bastide, this work contains an iconography and excerpts from the *Memoirs* of Saint-Simon.

Berliner Journal für Soziologie 7 (2): 1997, *Kapitalismus und Zivilisation: Fragen an Norbert Elias*, special issue on Norbert Elias.

On page 218, Elias's ideas about the history of civilization are still hailed as the best there are. This anthology suffers from its failure to take account of recent North American criticism of Elias, even though it appeared in 1994. This might encourage the Berlin sociologists to mute somewhat the triumphal note they strike in honoring their illustrious compatriot.

Besançon, Alain. *Présent soviétique et passé russe*. Paris: Livre de Poche, 1997.

An important work on the issue of "alternation" between open and closed phases in authoritarian regimes.

Bluche, François. *Louis XIV*. Paris: Fayard, 1986.

Boissier, Gaston. *Saint-Simon*. Paris, Hachette, 1892.

Bourdieu, Pierre. *La Distinction*. Paris: Les Editions de Minuit, 1969.

———. *Méditations pascaliennes*. Paris: Editions du Seuil, 1997.

———. *La Noblesse d'Etat*. Paris: Les Editions de Minuit, 1989.

Norbert Elias's *Court Society* has had a tremendous influence on French sociology, especially the major works of Pierre Bourdieu.

Brancourt, Jean-Pierre. *Le Duc de Saint-Simon et la monarchie*. Paris: Cujas, 1971.

Bunat, Jean. *Journal de la Régence*. Paris: Plon, 1865.

Cabanis, José. *Saint-Simon, ambassadeur, ou le Siècle des Lumières*. Paris: Gallimard, 1987.

———. *Saint-Simon l'admirable*. Paris, Gallimard, 1974.

Cahiers Internationaux de Sociologie 99 (July-December 1995), a special issue devoted to Norbert Elias.

Cahiers Saint-Simon.

This journal, obviously of fundamental importance for our subject, has been published regularly since 1973.

Cellard, Jacques. *John Law et la Régence, 1715–1729*. Paris: Plon, 1996.

Ceyssen, L. "Autour de la bulle *Unigenitus*: Le duc de Saint-Simon," *Revue Belge de Philologie et d'Histoire* 63 (3): 1985.

Chartier, Roger. *Cultural History: Between Practices and Representations*. Ithaca: Cornell University Press, 1988.

This work contains interesting and stimulating reflections on the thought of Elias, his book *Court Society*, and hierarchy, as well as on Pierre Bourdieu's book *La Distinction*. See especially the opening pages of the introduction, as well as 15 n. 3, 5, 9, 75–76. Chapter 3 is a translation of Chartier's preface to the new French edition of Elias's book, entitled *La Société de cour*, which was published by Flammarion in 1985.

———. "Distinction et divulgation: La civilité et ses livres," in *Lectures et lecteurs dans la France d'Ancien Régime*, p. 45. Paris, 1987.

———. *Lectures et Lecteurs dans la France d'Ancien Régime*. Paris: Editions du Seuil, 1987.

See 52–73, esp. 65. Chartier cleverly insists on the very "Eliasian" notion of a downward transfer of traditional signs of distinction from the court to the bourgeoisie. See also 82–84 for other references to Elias.

———. Preface to *Norbert Elias, La Société de cour*. Paris, Flammarion, 1985.

On page 24 of this preface, Chartier has important things to say about the concept of "intersocial imitation" of the court's way of life. According to Chartier, the bourgeoisie imitated courtly manners. This view has been attacked by Daniel Gordon on page 91 of his book, *Citizens without Sovereignty: Equality and Sociability in French Thought, 1670–1789.*

Chaussinand-Nogaret, Guy. *Le Citoyen des Lumières.* Brussels: Editions Complexe, 1994.
Particularly useful on Boulainvilliers, one of our de facto "Saint-Simonids," whom Chaussinand-Nogaret rightly views as a "progressive" thinker, traditional stereotypes notwithstanding (174).

———. *La Noblese au XVIIIe siècle: De la féodalité aux Lumières.* Paris: Hachette, 1976.

Chéruel, Adolphe. *Notice sur la vie et les Mémoires du duc de Saint-Simon.* Paris, 1876.

———. *Saint-Simon considéré comme historien de Louis XIV.* Paris: Hachette, 1865.
An essential book despite a number of remarks that can be characterized as hypercritical. Still, many of Chéruel's criticisms of Saint-Simon's reliability as a historian remain valid. In many cases, however, what Saint-Simon has to say is both correct and relevant and indispensable for any historical study of Louis XIV's reign and, of course, his court.

Coirault, Yves. *Dans la forêt saint-simonienne.* Paris: Universitas, 1992.
Contains a number of fundamental articles by Yves Coirault, in particular "Un Nathan invisible," "L'Orateur à la lanterne," "Un 'assez grand roi,' le Louis XIV de Saint-Simon," and "Le Duc de Saint-Simon et l'imaginaire du féodalisme," among others. This collection of essays by a master of Saint-Simon studies touches on many of the same subjects that concern us in the present volume.

———. *Grimoires de Saint-Simon: Nouveaux manuscrits inédits.* Paris: Klincksieck, Bibliothèque Française et Romane, Series C, 1975.

———. *Les Manuscrits du duc de Saint-Simon: Bilan d'une enquête aux Archives.* Paris: Presses Universitaires de France, 1970.

———. "Un lot d'inédits: Lettres du duc de Saint-Simon et documents," *Revue d'Histoire Diplomatique,* October 1967.

———. *L'Optique de Saint-Simon.* Paris: Armand Colin, 1965.
An essential book on problems of style and expression in the great writer's work.

Coirault, Yves, and François Formel. *Saint-Simon, Corpus bibliographique: Sources manuscrites et imprimées.* Preface by Jean Favier. Paris: Editions Vendôme, 1988.
Exhaustive and systematic bibliography of Saint-Simon and the Saint-Simonian "galaxy," including . . . ourselves.

Cornette, Joël. *Chronique du règne de Louis XIV.* Paris: SEDES, 1997.
Important (321).

Coutura, Johel. [*Claude de*] *Saint-Simon, favori de Louis XIII, 1626–1643.* Reignac: Editions du Glorit, 1986.
An estimable work.

Cuénin, Michèle. *Le Duel sous l'Ancien Régime.* Paris: Presses de la Renaissance, 1982.

Davis, Natalie Zemon, and Arlette Farge, eds. *Histoire des femmes en Occident.* Vol. 3, *XVIe–XVIIIe siècle.* Paris: Plon, 1991.
Our study of the court system is certainly not a contribution to the history of women per se. However, women are everywhere in Saint-Simon and therefore in our first six chapters as well, whether it be the duchesses in chapter 1, the abbesses in chapter 2,

the bastards in chapter 3, Mme de Maintenon and her "train" in chapter 4, female hypergamy in chapter 5, and female renouncers in chapter 6. Hence we think it pertinent to refer interested readers to this excellent work edited by Natalie Davis and Arlette Farge, two renowned experts on the history of women.

Debray, Régis. *Transmettre*. Paris: Odile Jacob, 1997.

See 60–71 and 200 on hierarchies à la Pseudo-Dionysius—angelic, demoniac, and terrestrial.

De Ley, Herbert. *Saint-Simon, Memorialist*. Chicago: University of Illinois Press, 1975.

"Saint-Simonism" penetrates the American Middle West with felicitous results. The phenomenon is rare and worth mentioning.

Denis, M. "Fleury, Saint-Simon . . . et Duguet." *Mémoire de l'Académie des Sciences de Caen*, 1871, 226ff.

De Waelhens, Alphonse. *Le Duc de Saint-Simon, immuable comme Dieu*. Brussels: Faculté Universitaire Saint-Louis, 1981.

A very stimulating if not always convincing attempt to interpret Saint-Simon's work and personality psychoanalytically.

Drumont, Edouard. *Papiers inédits du duc de Saint-Simon*. Paris, 1880.

Duguet, Abbé Jacques-Joseph. *L'Institution d'un prince*. Paris, 1739. 4 volumes. (Published posthumously.)

Duindam, Jeroen. "La Cour européenne au début de l'époque moderne: Problèmes et perspectives." *Cahiers Saint-Simon*, no. 24 (1996): 13–21.

Duindam's learned reflections on Norbert Elias's work on court society are often vitriolic, especially on page 21 of the text cited here.

———. *Myths of Power: Norbert Elias and the Early Modern European Court*. Translated from the Dutch. Amsterdam: Amsterdam University Press, 1994.

In this remarkable and extraordinarily well-informed text, Duindam questions Elias's assessment of the court as the central model in the civilization of manners, a model subsequently adopted, according to Elias, by the bourgeoisie (see especially 160–67). Duindam shrewdly raises a number of fundamental questions to which Daniel Gordon, in a work also published in 1994 (see below), gives detailed answers that are also highly critical of the Elias model.

Dumont, Louis. *Homo hierarchicus*. Paris: Gallimard, 1966.

Fundamental.

Easton, David. *L'analyse du système politique*. French translation. Paris: Armand Colin, 1974.

Elias, Norbert. *La Civilisation des moeurs*. French translation. Paris, Calmann-Lévy, 1973.

———. *La Dynamique de l'Occident*. French translation. Paris, Calmann-Lévy, 1975.

———. *Engagement et distanciation*. Paris, Fayard, 1993.

A striking example of the careless attitude that Elias sometimes displayed in dealing with the history of science and thought (181). Here, Elias credits Hubble with discovering the principal sequence of stellar evolution, a discovery actually made by the astronomers Hertzprung and Russell. Hubble was of course interested in the expansion of the universe and the classification of galaxies—subjects quite different from stellar taxonomy.

———. *Norbert Elias par lui-même*. French translation. Paris: Fayard, 1991.

See especially 74–80. The important subject of Elias's relation to Thomas Mann is here touched on by Elias himself (119). Specific references to *Court Society* can be found on 75–76.

————. *Qu'est-ce que la sociologie?* Paris: Pandora, 1970.
See especially 154, on the concept of configuration, and 190, on the mechanisms of social "interpenetration," which is supposed to "humanize" human relations.

————. *La Société de cour.* French translation. Paris: Calmann-Lévy, 1974.
We also used the German edition, *Die höfische Gesellschaft* (1969), which is not the original edition, as well as the English translation.

Farge, Arlette. *Des lieux pour l'histoire.* Paris: Editions du Seuil, 1997.
See especially 33 and passim, where the author has some interesting things to say about the influence of what she calls the "Elias model" on historical study. In particular, she alludes to the considerable success that *Court Society* enjoyed when it was translated into French.

Faure, Edgar. *La Banqueroute de Law, 17 juillet 1720.* Paris: Gallimard, 1977.

Febvre, Lucien. "Lettre à Fernand Braudel, 28 mai 1945." Quoted by Erato Paris in "La Genèse intellectuelle de l'oeuvre de Fernand Braudel" (doctoral diss., Ecole des Hautes Etudes en Sciences Sociales, Paris, 1997), 294.
"Never forget that this German work . . . raises difficult issues. *Culture,* they say. Of what? In any case, not of Humanity. Later, much later, of the Germans perhaps. But not those who were involved in this tragedy. . . . Much later, if we can help Germany rejoin the moral community of *civilized* nations from which she cut herself off." Febvre's letter is Thomas Mann in reverse. See below, the entry on Thomas Mann, for his relation to Elias's view of court society.

Formel, François. "Alliances et généalogie à la cour du grand roi, le souci généalogique chez Saint-Simon." Doctoral thesis, University of Paris IV–Sorbonne, 1979. 6 vols. (A more accessible edition also exists.)

————. *Alliances et généalogie.* 3 vols. Paris: Editions du Tricentenaire-Editions Vendôme, 1983–85.

————. "*Sur l'exposition Saint-Simon à la Ferté-Vidame, à l'occasion du tricentenaire de la naissane de Saint-Simon.*" La Ferté-Vidame, Comité Saint-Simon, 1975.

Gaehtgens, Thomas W. "Le Musée historique de Versailles." In *Les Lieux de mémoire,* vol. 2, ed. Pierre Nora (Paris: Gallimard, 1991).

Garrigou, Alain, and Bernard Lacroix, eds. *Norbert Elias: La politique et l'histoire.* Paris: La Découverte, 1997.
A well-informed work that contains an excellent article by André Burguière. The important connection of Elias's work with the thought of Thomas Mann by way of Jaspers is noted on page 14. Elias is portrayed as a "civilizationist," as opposed to Mann, who at that time was a "culturist." The authors seem unaware, however, that Elias's "aristocratization" of French culture was a veiled criticism, one that would eventually be turned back against Elias himself. Even worse, the book takes no account of the work of Daniel Gordon, even though it appeared in 1994. Incidentally, Garrigou and Lacroix rightly point out that François Furet and I contributed to Elias's popularity in France by publishing articles on him in 1973 and 1974 (20).

Gordon, Daniel. *Citizens without Sovereignty: Equality and Sociability in French Thought, 1670–1789.* Princeton: Princeton University Press, 1994.
An essential book, not to be missed, which levels some very severe criticism at Elias's theories, especially his ideas about the court and its aftereffects. See especially 89–92.

Grosclaude, Pierre. *Malesherbes.* 2 vols. Paris: Fischbacher, 1961.

Guilbert, Cécile. *Saint-Simon ou l'encre de la subversion*. Paris: Gallimard, 1994.

Some excellent analyses, often subtle in the best sense of the word.

Himelfarb, Hélène. "Chronologie saint-simonienne." In volume 1 of the tricentennial edition of the *Memoirs* (Paris, 1975).

A very complete chronology.

————."L'Hôtel de Saint-Simon, rue des Saints-Pères." *Cahiers Saint-Simon*, 1973.

————. "Du Nouveau sur Saint-Simon: La version des *Mémoires* soumises à Rancé." *Revue d'Histoire Littéraire de la France*, 1969.

————. "Saint-Simon et le jansénisme des Lumières." *Studies on Voltaire and the Eighteenth Century* 88 (1972): 742ff.

Fundamental.

————. "Saint-Simon et les 'nouveaux savants' de la Régence." In *La Régence* (Paris: Centre Aixois d'Etudes et Recherches sur le XVIIIe Siècle, 1970).

Interesting observations on Saint-Simon's disloyalty as a friend.

————. "Saint-Simon sans Mémoires: Soixante ans de gestion domaniale dans sa châtellenie de La Ferté-Vidame." Published in the proceedings of the colloquium "Images du peuple au XVIIIe siècle," Aix-en-Provence, 1969–1973.

Judrin, Roger. *Tableaux synoptiques de la vie et des oeuvres de Saint-Simon*. Paris: Seghers, 1970.

Kolakowski, Leszek. *Dieu ne nous doit rien*. Paris: Albin-Michel, 1997.

A rehabilitation of the Jesuits that Saint-Simon would not have found entirely to his liking.

Lachiver, Marcel. *Les Années de misère: La famine au temps du Grand Roi*. Paris: Fayard, 1991.

I have dealt with the lower classes in a number of books such as *Montaillou*, *Pierre Prion scribe*, and *Le Siècle des Platter*. Saint-Simon concerned himself with elites, indeed with the crème de la crème of the elite, court society. It is useful to have a plebeian counterpoint to his account of the upper classes. Lachiver's book provides all the necessary information about the often unfortunate situation of the "inferior" classes during Saint-Simon's lifetime, since he covers the period from 1692 to 1715 and especially the two great famines of 1693 and 1709.

La Varende, Jean de. *Monsieur le duc de Saint-Simon et sa comédie humaine*. Paris: Hachette, 1955. Reprinted in 1990 by Editions Bartillat, Etrepilly.

A pure-blooded Norman judges a mixed-breed from the Versailles stable, half Picard and half Percheron. The book is a fine collection of selected passages, some of which are accompanied by peremptory comments.

Leclercq, Dom H. *Histoire de la Régence, pendant la minorité de Louis XV*. 3 vols. Paris: Honoré Champion, 1921.

Fundamental.

Le Roy Ladurie, Emmanuel. "Auprès du roi, la cour." *Annales ESC* (1983): 21–41.

————. "Système de la cour." *L'Arc* 65 (1976): 21–35.

Lescure, M. de. *Les Maîtresses du Régent*. Paris: Dentu, 1861.

Lessius, Father Leonard, S.J. *De gratia efficaci*. Antwerp: J. Morte, 1610.

Levron, Jacques. *La Vie quotidienne à la cour de Versailles*. Paris, 1965.

In the time of Louis XV an estimated four thousand people lived in the chateau of Versailles. According to W. Ritchey Newton, this estimate is actually on the low side:

during a normal working day, there would have been some five thousand people present in the palace, but not all of them were residents.

Lougee, Carolyne. *Le Paradis des femmes*. Princeton: Princeton University Press, 1956.

Chapter 10, entitled "Le Mariage des femmes des salons" (151ff.), deals with the subject of female hypergamy, which we also consider in the present volume.

Loyseau, Charles. *Oeuvres . . . contenant les traités des ordres et simples dignités*. Paris: Editions Aubouyn, 1666.

(A hierarchical vision of ancien régime society that Saint-Simon had only to "set to music," as it were. Of course, Saint-Simon also assigned an especially privileged place in society to the dukes and peers, one that Loyseau was by no means disposed to grant them a priori.

Mandrou, Robert. *L'Europe absolutiste, 1649–1775*. Paris: Fayard, 1977.

This very useful book, which deals in particular with enlightened despotism, provides information useful for comparing the regency of Philippe d'Orléans with the power structures of other eighteenth-century European monarchies (233ff.).

Mann, Thomas. *Betrachtungen eines Unpolitischen*. Berlin: S. Fischer, 1918.

We used the French translation, *Considérations d'un apolitique* (Paris: Grasset, 1975). See especially page 52 on the supposed noble, curial, and aristocratic origins of the bourgeois spirit and French civilization and passim on the contrast between German *Kultur* and French *Civilisation*. In the English translation by Walter D. Morris, *Reflections of a Nonpolitical Man* (New York: Ungar, 1983), see 32ff. According to Daniel Gordon (see note above on *Citizens and Sovereignty*), Elias borrowed heavily from this book of Mann's in developing his ideas on the curial source of French manners and related customs continuing into the nineteenth and twentieth centuries. Elias came to know this work of Mann's as a young university student in the 1920s, when his teacher, Karl Jaspers, asked him to write a seminar paper on Mann's critique of the idea of "French civilization" (see Stephen Mennel, *Norbert Elias* [Oxford: Oxford University Press, 1989], 12, quoted in Gordon, *Citizens and Sovereignty*, 89). The central idea of Elias's *Court Society* was thus anticipated by Mann. Elias was well versed in the great German writer's work on "civilization." Germany, Mann wrote, "had no word. She was speechless, she did not love words, and she did not believe in them as did civilization [of the Roman and later French type]. . . . In the innate and eternal conviction of Roman civilization, not only humanism but humanitarianism in general, human dignity, respect for human beings, and human self-respect, are inextricably bound to literature. Not to music—or at any rate not necessarily to it. On the contrary, the relationship of music to humanitarianism is so much looser than that of literature that the musical attitude seems to the literary moral sense at the very least to be undependable, at the very least, suspicious. Nor to poetry, where the relationship is too much like that of music; in it, words and intellect play a much too indirect, cunning, irresponsible, and therefore also undependable role. Rather expressly to literature, to linguistically articulated intellect—civilization and literature are one and the same.

"The Roman West is literary: this separates it from the Germanic—or more exactly—from the German world, which, whatever else it is, is definitely not literary. Literary humanitarianism, the legacy of Rome, the classical spirit, classical reason, the generous word to which the generous gesture belongs, the beautiful, heart-stirring phrase that is worthy of a human being and that celebrates his beauty and dignity, the academic rhetoric in honor of the human race—this is what makes life worth living in the Roman West, what makes the human being human. It is the spirit that was at its height during the Revolution; it was its spirit, its 'classic form,' that spirit that in the Jacobin hardened into a scholastic-literary formula, into a murderous doctrine, a tyrannical, schoolmasterly pedantry. Its champions are the lawyer and the literary man, the spokesmen of the 'Third Estate,' and of its emancipation, the spokesmen of the Enlightenment, of reason, of progress, of 'philosophy,' against the *seigneurs*, against authority, tradition, history, 'power,' kingdom, and church—the spokesmen of the *spirit* that they consider to be the unconditional, sole, and dazzlingly true one, spirit itself, spirit in itself, while it is really just the political spirit of the middle-class revolution that they mean and understand. *It is an historical fact that cannot be denied that 'spirit' in this political-civilizing sense is a middle-class concern, even if it is not a middle-class invention (for spirit and culture in France are not originally of the middle class, but of noble-seigneurial descent; the middle class only usurped them).* Its representative is actually the eloquent citizen, the literary lawyer of the Third Estate, as I have said, the representative of its spiritual as well as, not to forget, of its material interests. The victorious advance of this spirit, its expansive process, which is the result of colossal, turbulent, explosive forces within it, can be defined as a process involving the simultaneous conquest of the world by the middle class and by literature. What we call 'civilization,' and what calls itself civilization, is nothing more than precisely this victorious advance, this propagation of the politicized and literarized middle-class spirit, its colonization of the inhabited areas of the globe. The *imperialism of civilization* is the last form of the Roman idea of unification against which Germany is 'protesting,' and she has never done so more passionately against any of its other manifestations; she has never had a more terrible battle to wage than against this one. The agreement and unity of all those communities that belong to the imperium of the middle-class spirit today is the *'entente'*—a French name, how proper—and it is truly an *entente cordiale*, a unity full of the most heartfelt, spiritual, essential agreement despite many differences in temperament and despite divergencies in power politics: directed against Germany, which is protesting the final completion and conclusive establishment of this imperium. The Battle of the Teutoburg Forest, the struggles against the Roman pope, Wittenberg, 1813, 1870 — all this was mere child's play compared to the terrible, perilous, and, in the most magnificent sense, irrational struggle against the world *entente* of civilization, a struggle that Germany has accepted with a truly Germanic obedience to her fate—or, to put it somewhat more actively, to her mission, her eternal and innate mission" (from the English translation by Walter D. Morris, 32–34).

In this bizarre text, which Mann was later somewhat ashamed of having written, we have italicized a passage that anticipates Elias on a key point, the way in which French bourgeois *Civilisation* borrowed from a preexisting noble and seigneurial entity. As Daniel Gordon rightly points out (*Citizens and Sovereignty*, 89), these lines of Mann's "fired" Elias's imagination in the 1920s. Interpreting Mann's words in his own way, Elias took the writer's "genealogical" ideas and bequeathed them to late-twentieth-century French and other Western intellectuals. As Gordon remarks (ibid., 91; we are simply paraphrasing and elaborating on his account), the ultimate irony is that so many excellent French historians have taken Elias's ideas in their most literal form. They have thus reflected the Teutonic nationalist antipathy to France of Mann at his most Gallophobic, whereas Elias himself was actually a Francophile, though at times a bit naïve and superficial and apt to misplace his admiration. Gordon further argues that these French historians have turned Mann's ideas into instruments for a kind of national self-flagellation, a Franco-French ideological self-hatred. No one would deny their competence as historians, but they see French culture as having "aristocratic" roots and an "aristocratic-bourgeois" heritage. And they believe that the aristocratic model of court society has persisted in France through a variety of different political regimes. They treat the antagonism between German *Kultur* and French *Civilisation* as if it could account for the real differences between the two countries, when in reality it is an entirely artificial construct, a purely German, purely Germano-Teutonic, invention typical of German thought during and after World War I. More specifically, it is in fact a family quarrel, a polemic initiated during the war by Thomas Mann (who at the time was an authoritarian nationalist and anti-French) against his brother Heinrich, a left-liberal Francophile (see pages 8–9 of the French edition cited above).

Marais, Mathieu. *Journal et Mémoires sous la Régence et le règne de Louis XV.* 4 vols. Paris: Firmin-Didot, 1863–68.

Meyer, Jean. *La Noblesse bretonne au XVIIIe siècle.* 2 vols. Paris: EHESS, 1985.
About a "peripheral, provincial" nobility not divided, as the court of Versailles was, by rigid boundaries between a proud nobility of the sword and a disdained nobility of the robe.

———. *La Vie quotidienne en France au temps de la Régence.* Paris: Hachette, 1979.

Molina, Father Luis, S.J. *Liberi arbitrii cum gratiae donis . . . concordia.* Ex. off. typ. Trognaesii, 1595.

Mousnier, Roland. *Les Hiérarchies sociales de 1450 à nos jours.* Paris: Presses Universitaires de France, 1969.
See especially chapter 6 on the society of orders of the seventeenth and eighteenth centuries. An extraordinarily lucid book, very Saint-Simonian in its way, and quite humorous to boot.

Muzerelle, Danielle. *Richesses de l'Arsenal.* Paris: BNF, 1997.
On page 5 one finds a caricature of the marquis de Paulmy by Pier-Leone Ghezzi, an artist and draftsman in the Saint-Simonian vein (reproduced as the frontispiece to this volume). The original is in the Bibliothèque Nationale de France *Estampes Be 12a*, Petit folio Réservé. Another sample of the work of this graphic artist and contemporary of Saint-Simon's can be found at the Art Institute of Louisville, Kentucky. Ghezzi, as we note in our conclusion, is a name to reckon with if one seeks to establish a link between Saint-Simonism and the European aesthetic of his time.

Namier, Lewis. *The Structure of British Politics at the Accession of George III.* London: Macmillan, 1961.
Factions, networks, cabals.

Newton, William R.
A fundamental work soon to be published by Fayard on the system of lodging, apartments, chambers, and other residential quarters in the palace of Versailles under Louis XIV, Louis XV, and Louis XVI.

Nora, Pierre, ed. *Les Lieux de mémoire.* Vol. 3. Paris: Gallimard, 1997.
See Jacques Revel's article "The Court" for remarks on Norbert Elias. This is a rich and substantial piece that exemplifies its author's formidable intelligence and erudition, though it may be a bit biased by its dependence on the Elias model.

Pastoureau, Mireille. *See* "Saint-Simon ou l'observateur véridique."

Petitfils, Jean-Christian. *Le Régent.* Paris: Fayard, 1986.
See also the author's very remarkable and complete *Louis XIV.*

Picot, Georges. *Les Papiers du duc de Saint-Simon aux Affaires étrangères.* Paris, 1880.

Poisson, Georges. *Album Saint-Simon.* Paris: Gallimard, 1969.

A brief, dense, and very useful work, one of the best of the Albums de la Pléiade series.

———. Anthology of reprints, 20 papers published from 1965 to 1970, Bibliothèque Nationale, 4-Z11303.

Among other things, this interesting and indispensable collection contains a fine article on Saint-Simon and the painter Rigaud, previously published in the *Bulletin de la Société de l'Art Français*, 1975, 191ff.

———. *La Ferté-Vidame, cité historique.* La Ferté-Vidame, 1975.

———. *Un Hôtel nommé de Saint-Simon.* Paris, 1988.

———. *Monsieur de Saint-Simon.* Paris: Berger-Levrault, 1973.

There are several other editions of this work, and a second updated version was published by Mazarine in 1987. This is an essential book for our subject. See in particular our introduction, which draws on it extensively.

Poliakov, Léon. *Histoire de l'antisémitisme.* Vol. 3, *De Voltaire à Wagner.* Paris: Calmann-Lévy, 1968.

Interesting comparisons of anti-Semitism and anti-Jesuitism at various times, including the eighteenth century.

Prochasson, Christophe, and Anne Rasmussen. *Au Nom de la patrie: Les intellectuels de la Première Guerre mondiale, 1910–1920.* Paris: Editions La Découverte, 1996.

A fine book that demonstrates the strength of the French nationalist enmity toward German culture in the second decade of the twentieth century. Thomas Mann's attitude was the inverted image of this, and it seems to have been the source of Norbert Elias's ideas about court society.

Projets de gouvernement du duc de Bourgogne dauphin. Text attributed to the duc de Saint-Simon, edited by Paul Mesnard. Paris: Hachette, 1860.

Pseudo-Dionysius the Areopagite. *Oeuvres complètes.* Translation, preface, and notes by Maurice de Gandillac. Paris: Aubier, 1943.

One of the more substantial publishing achievements of the occupation years. In a fine article by Yves Coirault, published in his *Dans la forêt saint-simonienne*, there is a discussion of the two dimensions of the Areopagite's thought and their relation to Saint-Simon. The theoretical aspects can serve as a kind of model for research, while the practical aspects may have influenced Saint-Simon directly. At the very least, he read works by authors who had read Dionysius, which stimulated his interest in correlations between the celestial hierarchy of angels and the terrestrial hierarchy. Those authors may have included Saint Thomas, Bérulle, and Charles Loyseau, whose *Traité des Ordres*, published in 1611, was in Saint-Simon's library, according to the inventory of 1755. For Loyseau, "celestial intelligences have their hierarchical degrees, which are immutable." This is the reason for their "excellent harmony and consonance," which human society ought to imitate, even if it cannot duplicate the perfection of the heavens (see Coirault, *Dans la forêt saint-simonienne*, 183).

Quesnel, Father Pasquier. *Le Nouveau Testament en français, avec des réflexions morales.* Paris, 1693.

There are also many later editions, including an eight-volume edition of 1736, which is the one we used. Early versions of the *Réflexions morales* date back as far as 1672, and it was in 1674 that Quesnel published the *Abrégé de la Morale de l'Evangile, ou Pensées chrétiennes sur le texte des Quatre Evangelistes pour en rendre la méditation plus facile à ceux qui souhaitent s'y appliquer*, 2d ed. (Paris: Pralard, 1674), 560 pp. Quesnel is the predecessor of Abbadie and Duguet, at least chronologically, as we argue in chapter 6 and appendix 2. They, along with Quesnel, were Saint-Simon's teachers when it came to the theology of renunciation.

Revel, Jacques. "Les Usages de la civilité." In *Histoire de la vie privée*, ed. Philippe Ariès and Georges Duby, vol. 3, *De la Renaissance aux Lumières*, ed. Roger Chartier (Paris: Editions du Seuil, 1999), 169–209.

An excellent essay, at times influenced, though without serious harm, by "Eliassomania." (See also Pierre Nora entry above.)

Rooryck, Guy. *Les Mémoires du duc de Saint-Simon, de la parole du témoin au discours du mémorialiste.* Geneva, Droz, 1972.

Roujon, Jacques. *Le Duc de Saint-Simon, 1675–1755.* Paris, Wapler, 1958.

Important.

Sabatier, Gérard. "La plus grande puissance." *Revue d'Histoire Moderne et Contemporaine,* April–June 1995, 315–19.

Interesting and substantial review of Joël Cornette, *Le Roi de guerre.* This article also draws heavily on Elias's ideas about court society, which a whole generation of historians appears to have taken as gospel. Nevertheless, Sabatier deserves credit for pointing out that alongside the *roi de guerre* ably described by Cornette there was also a *roi de cour,* and that it is difficult to separate the two.

Saint-Simon et son temps. Catalog of a show mounted in Madrid by the Institut Français en Espagne, 1956–1957.

Saint-Simon, Louis de Rouvroy, duc de. *Ecrits inédits.* 8 vols. Paris: Armand Prosper Faugère, 1882–92.

———. *Mémoires.* Paris: Editions Delroye, 1843.

This edition, today obsolete despite its beautiful nineteenth-century engravings, is "distinguished" for having been consulted, in haphazard fashion, by Norbert Elias, who makes almost no mention of any of the more recent editions, apart from a few isolated references to the Boislisle.

———. *Mémoires.* Edited by Adolphe Chéruel. 20 vols. Paris, 1856–68.

Until the great Boislisle and Corault editions were published, the Chéruel was the fundamental reference for the work of Saint-Simon, but today it has been superseded, even if it remains a valuable resource.

———. *Mémoires.* Boislisle edition. 43 vols. Published between 1879 and 1930.

A bible.

———. *Mémoires.* Pléiade edition, with an introduction by Gonzague Truc. Paris: Gallimard, 1953–61.

This first "Pléiade" edition of Saint-Simon, assembled by Gonzague Truc, is not a spectacular success. Although useful in its time, it has been supplanted by a second Pléiade edition edited by Yves Coirault, which is far preferable to its predecessor.

———. *Mémoires.* 18 vols. Paris: Editions Ramsay, 1977.

An inexpensive and unpretentious edition full of amusing typographical errors. Prefaces by a number of talented authors are included. Volume 18 is worthy of special note, for it includes several hundred pages of tables duplicating the tables that Saint-Simon himself compiled as an epilogue to his text. For that reason, we have made occasional use of volume 18 along with certain other volumes of this edition, as indicated in our endnotes.

———. *Traités politiques et autres écrits.* Edited by Yves Coirault. Paris: Gallimard, 1996.

"Saint-Simon, ou L'Observateur véridique." Paris: Bibliothèque Nationale, 1976.

Catalog of a show devoted to Saint-Simon at the Bibliothèque Nationale. Written by Mme Mireille Pastoureau.

Scheide, William H. "Thoughts on Johann Sebastian Bach, 1685–1750: History and Society." *Proceedings of the American Philosophical Society* 141 (2): 1997.

Bach was an almost exact contemporary of Saint-Simon, born a decade later and dying five years earlier than the *petit duc*. Was there more than a chronological similarity between the two men? We leave this to historical musicologists to decide.

Shennan, J. H. *Philippe, Duke of Orléans: Regent 1715–1723*. London: Thames and Hudson, 1979.

See also the work of Dom Leclercq and Jean-Christian Petitfils mentioned above.

Solnon, Jean-François. *La Cour de France*. Paris: Fayard, 1987.

Spitzer, Leo. *Approche textuelle des Mémoires de Saint-Simon*. Tübingen-Paris, 1980.

Tans, Joseph A. G. "Quesnel." In the *Dictionnaire de spiritualité* (Paris: Beauchesne, 1985), 12:2.

Van der Cruysse, Dirk. *La Mort dans les Mémoires de Saint-Simon*. Paris: Nizet, 1981.

Van der Cruysse was and is the leading Flemish-Dutch specialist on Saint-Simon.

Van Elden, D. H. J. *Esprits fins et esprits géométriques dans les portraits du duc de Saint-Simon*. The Hague: Nijhoff, 1975.

The Beauvillier-Chevreuse opposition.

Van Kley, Dale K. *The Religious Origins of the French Revolution*. New Haven: Yale University Press, 1996.

On the Jansenist factor in the period leading up to the French Revolution.

Védrine, Hubert. *Les Mondes de François Mitterrand*. Paris: Fayard, 1996.

Interesting analysis of "the court" at the Elysée Palace in the Fifth Republic—a court that was, fortunately, but a pale replica of the court of Louis XIV (66ff.).

Index

This index draws upon the index to the French edition for identifications.

Aquin, Antoine d' (1632–96); physician-in-chief to Louis XIV: 5, 87, 94

Archduke, Charles François Joseph of Austria, known as the (1685–1740): 100

Arco, Alfonso Manrique de Lara, duc del (1672–1737); gentleman of the chamber, later *grand écuyer* of Philip V: 54

Argenson, Marc René de Voyer de Paulmy, marquis d' (1652–1721); in 1697 *lieutenant de police*, in 1718 keeper of the seals: 13, 40, 134, 143, 222, 269, 294, 297, 306, 309, 310, 314

Argenson, Pierre, comte d' (1743–57): 345

Argenton, Marie Louise Madeleine Victoire Le Bel de La Boissière, demoiselle de Séry and comtesse d' (1680–1748); mistress of the Regent: 260

Armagnac, Charles de Lorraine, prince and comte d' (1684–1753); known as le Prince Charles, son of Louis: 217, 219

Armagnac, Françoise-Adélaïde de Noailles, comtesse d' (1704–76); wife of Charles: 217, 219

Armagnac, Louis de Lorraine, comte d' (1641–1718); known as Monsieur le Grand, governor of Anjou: 45, 134, 139, 196

Armenonville, Joseph Jean-Baptiste Fleuriau d' (1661–1728); in 1701 director of finance, in 1722–27 keeper of the seals: 76, 301, 315, 328, 340

Arnauld, Antoine, known as le Grand (theologian): 228, 229, 232

Arnauld d'Andilly, Robert (1589–1674); father of d'Arnauld Pomponne: 208

Arnauld-Pomponne. See Pomponne, marquis de

Arouet, François (1650–1722); notary of Claude de Saint-Simon and father of Voltaire: 2, 44

Arqien, Marie-Casimire de La Grange d' (1639–1716); wife of Jean Sobieski, king of Poland: 220

Asfeld, Claude François Bidal, chevalier later marquis and in 1734 maréchal d' (1665–1743): 76, 77, 312

Asturias, Louis Philippe de Bourbon, prince des (1707–1724); son of Philip V; in 1724 king of Spain as Louis I: 13, 325, 359

Athanasius, Saint: 356

Augustine, Saint (354–430): 81, 226, 228, 229, 245

Augustus II of Saxony (1670–1733); in 1697 king of Poland: 115

Aumale, Claude de Lorraine, duc d' (1526–73); husband of Louise de Brézé (daughter of Diane of Poitiers): 126

Aumont, Louis Marie Victor, marquis de Villequier, duc d' (1632–1704): 48, 135, 309

Aumont, Olympe de Brouilly-Piennes, marquise de Villequier, later duchesse d' (1660–1723); daughter-in-law of Louis: 183

Auvergne, Frédéric Maurice de La Tour, comte d' (1642–1707); nephew of Turenne: 189

Auvergne, Henri Oswald de La Tour, abbé, in 1737 cardinal d' (1671–1747): 108

Averne, "Mlle" d' (mistress of the Regent): 260

Balbien, Anne or Nanon, nurse of Mme de Maintenon: 322

Balladur, Edmund: 222

Baluze, Etienne (1630–1718); professor of the Royal College: 108

Barbezieux, Catherine Louise-Marie de Crussol d'Uzès, marquise de (1674–94); first wife of Louis: 183, 197

Barbezieux, Louis-François Marie Le Tellier, marquis de (1668–1701); son of Louvois: 58, 132, 141, 183, 197, 219

Barbezieux, Marie-Thérèse Eustachie d'Alègre, marquise de (1680–1706); second wife of Louis-François: 219

Barbier, Edmond Jean François (1689–1771); memoirist: 261

Bargeton, Daniel (1678–1757); lawyer in Parlement: 135

Barre, Raymond: 222

Barrillon, Henri de (1639–99); bishop of Luçon: 203

Bastien-Thiry: 333

Basville, Nicolas de Lamoignon, marquis de (1648–1724); *intendant de généralite* of Languedoc: 100, 148, 249

Bauffremont, Louis Bénigne, marquis de (1682–1755): 44

Bavaria, Louise Hollandine de, abbess of Maubuisson: 67, 210

Bâville. See Basville

Bay, Alexandre Maître, marquis de (1650–1715): 76

Beaufort, François de Vendôme, duc de (1616–69); grandson of Henri IV: 286, 307, 335, 341f

Beaujeu, Anne de France, dame de (1460 or 1461–1522); regent during the minority of Charles VIII: 337, 344

Beaujolais, Philippe Elisabeth d'Orléans, known as Mlle de (1714–34); daughter of the Regent: 178, 359

Beaumanoir, Emmanuel Charles, marquis de (1684–1703): 47

Colbert family: 6, 44, 59, 89, 124, 132, 134, 139, 141, 145, 146, 148, 154, 158, 197

Commercy, Charles François de Lorraine-Elbeuf, prince de (1661–1702): 48, 218

Concini. *See* Ancre, maréchal d'

Condé, Anne Marie Victoire de Bourbon, known as Mlle de (1675–1700): 178, 247

Condé, Henri I de Bourbon- (d. 1588): 339f

Condé, Henri II de Bourbon- (d. 1646): 339f

Condé, Louis I de Bourbon- (d. 1569): 339f

Condé, Louis II de Bourbon, prince de Condé, known as le Grand (1621–1686): 24, 156, 166, 286, 307, 335, 339f, 341f, 379n.5

Condé, Marie Anne Eléonore de (b. 1690); abbess of Saint-Antoine-des-Champs: 177

Condé (princes): 25, 53, 75, 278

Conti, François Louis de Bourbon, comte de La Marche et de La Roche-sur-Yon, in 1685 prince de (1664–1709); brother of Marie Anne de Bourbon, princesse de Conti: 49, 109

Conti, Louis-Armand II de Bourbon, comte de La Marche, later prince de (1695–1727); son of François-Louis: 24, 275–77

Conti, Louis Armand I of Bourbon, prince de (1661–1685): 137, 358

Conti, Marie-Anne de Bourbon, princesse de ("dowager princess"; 1666–1739); daughter of Louis XIV and Mlle de Vallière; wife of Louis Armand I: 96, 122–24, 136, 137–38, 153, 195, 249, 358

Conti, Marie-Thérèse de Bourbon-Condé, princesse de (1666–1732); daughter of Henri Jules, prince de Condé, and Anne of Bavaria; wife of François Louis: 308

Conti (princes of): 25, 137

Cordoba, Gonzalo Fernandez de (d. 1515): 81

Courtenay, Louis Charles, prince de (1640–1723): 307

Courtenvaux, Michel François Le Tellier, marquis de (1663–1721): 11

Courtenvaux family: 46

Crécy, Louis Verjus, comte de (1626–1709); state councilor: 250

Créquy, Anne-Charlotte Fare d'Aumont, marquise de (1665–1724): 212, 249

Créquy, François de Blanchefort de Bonne, maréchal de (1624–1687): 48

Créquy, François Joseph, marquis de (1662–1702); son of François: 48, 212

Cromwell, Oliver (1599–1658); leader in English Civil War: 65

Cronette, Joël: 57

Crozat, Antoine, marquis du Châtel (1655–1738); financier and father-in-law of the comte d'Evreux: 155, 189–90

Cusance, Béatrix de. *See* Cantcroix, princesse de

Dacier, Anne Lefèvre, dame (1654–1720): 224

Daguesseau. *See* Aguesseau d'

Dalon, Romain (d. 1738); in 1701 *premier président* of Pau, in 1703, of Bordeaux: 219

Damville. *See* Danville

Dangeau, Philippe de Courcillon, marquis de (1638–1720); state councillor, author of *Journal*: 16, 51, 72, 144, 147, 261, 307, 369n.185

Dangeau, Sophie Marie of Bavaria, comtesse de Levenstein, marquise de (1664–1736); second wife of Philippe: 212

Daniel, le P. Gabriel (1649–1728); Jesuit and historian: 103, 150, 246

Darricau, Raymond: 235

Daubenton, le P. Guillaume (1648–1723); Jesuit, confessor of Philip V: 252, 323

Dauphin. *See* Monseigneur, "le Grand Dauphin of France"; Bourgogne, duc de

Dauphine. *See* Bourgogne, duchesse de

David (Old Testament king): 81

De Gaulle, Charles (1890–1970): 17, 141, 150, 345, 382n.15

De Lancre, Pierre (d. 1630); demonologist: 91

Desmares, Christine Antoinette Charlotte (1682–1753); actress and mistress of the Regent: 45, 260

Desmarets, Nicolas (1648–1721); in 1703 director of finance, in 1708 comptroller general of finances: 2, 76, 82, 83, 131f, 145–47, 155, 172, 263, 264, 265, 281, 292–93, 294, 305, 310, 339

Desmarets family: 59

Dessert, Daniel: 129, 155

Destouches, Louis Camus, chevalier (1668–1726): 324

Dorsanne, Antoine, abbé (1664–1728); in 1715–18 secretary of the Council of Conscience, confidant of the cardinal of Noailles: 273

Dubois, Guillaume, abbé later cardinal (1656–1723)

    backers of, 76, 301, 313–15, 327, 329, 331–32

    death of, 15

    diplomatic course of, 11–12, 85, 260, 286, 289, 290, 291, 300, 312, 319, 320, 322–27, 333, 336, 343

    and elevation to cardinal, 315–319, 322, 327, 328–29

Dubois, Guillaume (*cont.*)
   and the Jansenists, 315–18
   and the Jesuits: 315–17, 329
   merits of, 265–66
   opposition to, 172, 330–32
   purge within Orléan cabal of, 327–30
   rise to power of, 13, 283, 289, 291, 297
   role of, in Regency, 108, 280, 292, 310
   Saint-Simon on, 3, 11–12, 13, 14, 97, 108,
      260, 266
   social background of, 29, 43, 288, 334
   vs. John Law: 306, 328
Dubois, Joseph (1650–1740); brother of Guillaume; doctor and director of bridges and
   highways: 290, 332
Duc, Louis Henri de Bourbon, known as Monsieur le (1692–1740); eldest son of Louis III
   de Bourbon-Condé: 78, 96, 104, 131f, 137,
   144, 195, 210, 221, 222, 263, 275–77, 278–
   79, 283, 284, 296, 297, 303, 308, 309–10,
   325, 329, 331, 338, 339, 340, 341f, 347
Duc, Louis III de Bourbon-Condé, duc de Bourbon, known as Monsieur le (1668–1710):
   123, 124, 137, 275, 338, 339f, 341f, 358t
Ducasse, Jean-Baptiste (1646–1715); lieutenant-
   general of the navy: 42–43, 185
Ducasse, Marthe. *See* Roye, marquise de
Duchamp, Marcel (1887–1968); artist: 259
Du Charmel, Louis de Ligny, comte (1646–
   1714): 201, 202, 207, 224, 234
Duchesse, Louise Françoise de Bourbon, known
   as Madame la (1673–1743); bastard of
   Louis XIV and Mme de Montespan;
   known early on as Mme de Nantes; wife of
   Louis III, duc de Bourbon-Condé: 25, 49,
   97, 106, 122, 123–24, 131f, 135–38, 142,
   149, 152, 249, 278, 308, 339f, 341f, 358
Duguet, Jacques Joseph, abbé (1649–1733); Ora-
   torian with Jansenist tendency: 15, 224,
   234–39, 241
Du Luc, Charles François de Vintimille, comte
   (1653–1740); French ambassador to Swit-
   zerland: 86
Dumas, Alexandre (1802–70); writer: 209
Dumont, Louis: 19, 93, 179, 182, 199, 241–42
Du Perchois (fortune-teller): 90
Duras, Marguerite Félice de Lévis-Ventadour,
   maréchale-duchesse de (1642?–1717): 54
Durfort, Louis de (1638–1709); comte de
   Feversham: 85

Effiat, Antoine Coiffier Ruzé, marquis d' (1638–
   1719); Regency Council advisor: 91, 131f,
   135, 280, 288

Ehalt, Christian: 23–24
Elbeuf, Charles III de Lorraine, duc d' (1620–
   92); and his family: 83, 219
Elbeuf, Françoise de Montault-Navailles,
   duchesse d' (1653–1717); third wife of
   Charles III: 83
Elbeuf, Philippe of Lorraine, prince d'
   (d. 1705): 48
Elias, Norbert: 18–19, 24, 47, 253, 349–52,
   368n.178
Elizabeth (1710–62); tsarina of Russia and
   daughter of Peter the Great: 9
Enghien, Marie Anne de Bourbon-Condé,
   demoiselle d' (1678–1718); in 1710 wife
   of the duc de Vendôme: 109
Entragues, Bernard Angélique de Crémeaux,
   abbé d' (1650–1733): 108
Entragues, Louis César de Crémeaux, marquis
   d' (1679–1747): 219
Épernon, Anne-Louise-Christine de Nogaret de
   La Valette, duchesse d' (1624–1701); Carmelite: 211
Epinoy. *See* Espinoy
Espinoy, Elisabeth de Lorraine, known as Mlle
   de Commercy, princesse d' (1664–1748);
   daughter of Anne, bastard of Charles IV of
   Lorraine, and Béatrix de Cuzance: 105,
   106, 131f, 135, 136, 138, 139, 278
Espinoy, Marie-Marguerite-Françoise de Melun,
   demoiselle d' (1671–1759): 308
Estaing, Charles-François-Marie, comte d'
   (1693–1729): 45
Estaing, François III, comte d' (1654–1732);
   lieutenant-general, governor of Douai: 45
Estaing, Henriette-Madeleine-Julie de Fontaine-
   Martel, marquise d' (1696–1733); wife of
   Charles-François-Marie: 45
Estampes. *See* Étampes
Este, Marie-Béatrice-Eléonore d' (1658–1718);
   queen of England, wife of James II: 213
Estrades, Godefroy, comte, in 1675 maréchal d'
   (1607–88); diplomat, and in 1685, guardian
   of the duc de Chartres: 87
Estrades, Jean-François, abbé d' (1642–1715);
   son of Godefroy: 206
Estrées, César, in 1671 cardinal d' (1628–1714):
   249
Estrées, Constance-Eléonore, demoiselle d'. *See*
   Ampus, comtesse de
Estrées, Jean, abbé d' (1666–1718): 212
Estrées, Victor-Marie, comte d'Estreés, in 1707
   maréchal d' (1660–1737); in 1704 grandee
   of Spain, in 1723 duc et pair: 140, 263,
   311, 316, 331

Mary (mother of Jesus): 64, 89

Massilon, Jean-Baptiste (1663–1742); Oratorian, in 1717 bishop of Clermont: 252

Matignon, Jacques III, comte de (1644–1725): 307

Matthew, Saint: 356

Maulévrier, Jean-Baptiste Louis Andrault, marquis de (1677–1754); ambassador to Spain: 75, 324

Maulévrier family: 46

Maupeou, René Nicolas Charles Augustin de (1714–1792); chancellor of France, 222, 345

Maupertuis, Louis de Melun, marquis de (1635–1721); captain of the Gray Musketeers: 3

Maurepas, Jérôme Phélypeaux, comte de. See Pontchartrain, J. de

Maximus the Confessor (580?–662); Byzantine monk: 347

Mazarin, Jules, cardinal (1602–61): 16, 42, 59, 61, 83, 156–58, 244, 287, 328, 338

Mazarin, Paul Jules de La Porte, duc de La Meilleraye, later duc (1666–1731): 318

Médard, Saint: 39

Mehemet Effendi, in 1721 Ottoman ambassador in Paris: 13

Melchizebek (Old Testament priest and king): 81

Melun, Anne Julie de Melun-Epinoy, demoiselle de (1672–1734): 308

Mercoeur, Philippe Emmanuel de Lorraine, duc de (1558–1602); governor of Bretagne: 313

Mesmes, Jean-Antoine III de (1661–1723); in 1712 *premier président* of the Parlement of Paris: 34, 102, 135, 142–43, 307

Mesmes, Jean-Jacques, bailii de (1674–1741); brother of Marie: 34

Mesmes, Judith Amasie de (b. 1672); sister of Jean, nun: 177

Mesmes, Marie-Antoinette de (1696–1767); niece of Jean and Judith. See Lorges, duchesse de

Meyer, Jean: 293

Meyrac, Albert, 260

Michelet, Jules (1798–1874): 289

Midas (mythical king of Phrygia): 303

Mignard, Catherine Marguerite (1657–1742); daughter of Pierre: 42

Mignard, Pierre (1610–95): 5, 42

Miramion, Marie Bonneau de Rubelles, dame de: 211

Mitterand, François (1916–96): 222, 333

Molière, Jean-Baptiste Poquelin, known as (1622–73): 55

Molina, le P. Luis (1535–1600); Spanish Jesuit: 230, 240, 254

Monaco, Antoine Grimaldi, princen de (1661–1724); and family of: 140

Monseigneur, Louis, "le Grand Dauphin" of France, known as (1661–1711); son of Louis XIV and Marie Thérèse, husband of Marie Anne Christine of Bavaria

cabal of, 121–23, 129–30, 131f, 133, 135–40, 149, 153, 263, 280, 339–40

cabal of, during the Regency, 263, 278, 282, 284, 308, 309

death of, 8, 34, 52, 63

within generational hierarchy, 24, 128t, 154–55, 338, 339f, 341f, 358t

and Mme Choin, 123, 195 (see also Choin)

relations with royal bastards: 106, 278

on Spain, 6, 147

title of, 53

Monsieur, Gaston Jean-Baptiste, duc d'Orléans, known as (1608–60); son of Henry IV and brother of Louis XIII: 123, 156, 307, 335, 341f

Monsieur, Philippe, duc d'Orléans, known as (1640–1701); brother of Louis XIV: 3, 6, 24, 25, 28, 34, 52, 77, 96, 107, 109, 128t, 195, 199, 280, 287, 341f, 359t

Montauban, N. de La Tour du Pin, demoiselle de (1690–1750); *fille d'honneur* of the duchesse de Maine: 135

Montausier, Charles de Sainte-Maure, duc de (1610–90); guardian of the Dauphin: 48

Montbéliard, Léopold-Eberhard, prince de (1670–1723): 98, 99

Montchevreuil, Henri de Mornay, marquis de (1622–1706): 48

Monteleone, Nicolas Pignatelli, duc de (d. 1730): 223

Montespan, Françoise Athénaïs de Rouchechou-art, marquise de (1640–1707); wife of Louis, 25, 35, 107, 116, 127, 128t, 137, 138, 142, 146, 195, 210, 211, 219, 358

Montespan, Louis Henri de Pardaillan de Grondin, marquis de (d. 1702): 135

Montesquieu, Charles de Secondat, baron de La Brède et de (1689–1755): 38, 50, 368n.178, 370n.234

Montesquiou, Pierre de Montesquiou d'Artagnan, in 1709 marèchal de (1640–1725); member of the Regency Council: 26–28, 36, 285

Montfaucon, dom Bermard de: 240

Montfort, Honoré Charles d'Albert de Luynes, duc de Chevreuse (1669–1704): 48, 147

Noailles, Louise Boyer, duchesse de (1631–97); wife of Anne: 216–17

Noailles, Marie Françoise de Bournonville, maréchale de (1656–1748): 79

Nocé, Charles de (1664–1739); in 1719 first gentleman of the chamber of the duc d'Orléans: 280, 290, 329, 331

Nora, Pierre: 346

Nostradamus, Michel de Notre-Dame, known as (1503–66): 90

O, Gabriel Claude, marquis de Villers d' (1654–1728); guardian of the comte de Toulouse: 57–58, 122, 377nn. 2, 11

Orange, William de Nassau, prince d' (1533–84); husband of Mlle de Bourbon-Montpensier: 96

Orange, house of: 227

Orléans, house of: 53, 89, 288–89

Orléans, Françoise-Marie de Bourbon, duchesse de Chartres, later d' (1666–1739); bastard of Louis XIV and Mme de Montespan and known as d'abord Mlle de Blois; in 1692 married to Philippe: 3, 28, 32–33, 36, 96, 97, 107, 125, 128, 142, 195, 280, 331, 358, 359

Orléans, Gaston d'. See Monsieur

Orléans, Jean Philippe, chevalier d' (1702–48); son of the duc d'Orléans and Mme d'Argenton, grand prior of France in the retinue of Philippe de Vendôme: 49, 97

Orléans, Louise Elisabeth d' (1709–42); known as Mlle de Montpensier, daughter of the Regent; married Louis Philippe de Bourbon, prince of Asturias: 13, 325

Orléans, Philippe, duc de Chartres, in 1701 duc d' (1674–1723); son of Monsieur; in 1715 Regent of France

and Bourgogne cabal, 124–25, 131f, 154, 155–56, 263, 272, 279

cabal of, 154, 308, 311, 321–22, 324, 329, 333–34, 340

and general orientation of cabal of, 344

in generational context, 128t, 338, 341f, 359

implementation of reforms, 259–60

and the Jansenists: 315–17, 320–21, 322

and Mainenton-Maine cabal, 131f, 271, 278–80, 284, 322, 339

marriage of, 3, 28, 96–97, 107, 113–14, 125, 195, 280

as military leader, 379n.5

and Orléanism, 302, 325, 333, 334–35

pacifism of, 335

and polysynody, 282–84, 299–300, 301–2, 308, 309, 336, 343

private life of, 260, 280, 332–33

and rank, 25, 71

and Regency as thaw, 337, 344

and Regency diplomacy, 284, 286–92, 300, 301, 308–9, 311–12, 319–20, 322, 336

and Regency fiscal policy, 287, 292–97, 301–8, 336

and Regency-noble relations, 45–46, 266, 274–78, 285, 299, 307–8, 309, 313, 322, 328

and Regency-Parlement relations, 143, 266–67, 269, 270–78, 285, 292–93, 296–97, 299, 305–8, 309, 320–21, 322

relationship with Saint-Simon, 222

and religious policies of the Regency, 248, 266–70, 285, 287, 301, 310, 317, 336, 343

royal succession of, 265

and Saint-Simon, 2, 11, 40, 50, 222, 259, 274, 343

and top officials in Regency, 333

Ormesson, Henri François-de-Paule Le Fèvre d' (1681–1756); state councilor: 330

Ormond, Jacques Butler, duc d' (1665–1747): 86

Orry, Jean (1652–1719): 223, 340

Ossone, duke of. See Osuna

Osuna, François-Marie-de-Paule Acuña Pacheco et Tellez-Giron, duc d' (1678–1716): 77, 110, 223

Osuna, Joseph Acuña Pacheco et Tellez-Giron, comte de Pinto, later duc d' (1685–1733); brother of François-Marie-de-Paule: 77

Palatin, Frederick V of Bavaria, elector of (1596–1632); father of Louise Hollandine of Bavaria: 210

Palatine, princess. See Madame

Palissot de Montenoy, Charles (1730–1814); writer: 243

Parabère, Marie Madeleine de La Vieuville, comtesse de (1693–1759); mistress of the Regent: 260, 318, 319

Pâris, François, Deacon, called the Devil (1690–1727): 217, 341

Pâris brothers: Antoine (1668–1733); Claude known as de La Montagne (1670–1745); Jean known as de Duverney (1684–1770); Jean known as de Montmartel (1690–1766): 314, 328, 330, 331, 340

Pascal, Blaise (1623–62); French philosopher and mathematician: 146, 153, 201, 230, 356

Pasquier, Etienne (1529–1615); jurist: 114

Passionei, Domenico, in 1738 cardinal (1682–1761): 240

Saxe, Frederick Augustus, electoral prince of (1696–1763); son of Augustus II of Saxony and king of Poland in 1733 under the name Augustus III: 104

Saxe, Maurice, comte and in 1744 maréchal de (1696–1750); bastard of Augustus II, king of Poland, and Maria Aurora de Königsmarck: 98, 104–5

Scotti, Annibal, marquis (1675–1752); guardian of Philip V's youngest son: 75

Ségur, Henri François, comte de (1689–1751); son of Henri Joseph; the Regent's master of the wardrobe: 45

Ségur, Henri Joseph, marquis de (d. 1737); *sénéchal* of Foix: 45, 218–19

Ségur, Philippe Angélique de Froissy, comtesse de (1700–85); bastard of the Regent and Charlotte Desmares; wife of Henri François: 45

Ségur family: 46

Seignelay, Jean-Baptiste Colbert, marquis de (1651–1690); state minister: 158

Seneca: 30

Sérignan, Guillaume de Lort de (1628–1721): 223

Servien, Augustin, abbé (d. 1716): 108, 268

Servius Tullius (578?–535? B.C.); king of Rome: 151

Séry, Marie Louise Madeleine Victoire Le Bel de La Boissière, demoiselle de. *See* Argenton, comtesse d'

Sévigné, Marie de Rabutin-Chantal, marquise de (1626–96): 5, 102, 212

Sézanne, Louis François d'Harcourt, comte de (1677–1714); brother of Henri, maréchalduc d'Harcourt: 79

Shakespeare, William (1564–1616); English playwright: 65, 288, 346

Shennan, J. H.: 261, 333

Siegfried, André: 149

Sixtus IV, pope (Francesco della Rovere; 1414–84): 43, 100

Smith, Adam (1723–1790); Scottish political economist: 65

Sobieski, Jan (1629–96); in 1674–96 elected king of Poland, 220

Sorokine, P. (1889–1968); Russian-born U.S. sociologist: 151

Soubise, Anne de Rohan-Chabot, princesse de (1648–1709); second wife of François: 103–4, 142

Soubise, Anne Julie Adélaïde de Melun-Epinoy, demoiselle de Verchin, princesse de (1697–1724); wife of Jules and governess of the children of France: 47

Soubise, Armand Gaston Maximilien, abbé de (1674–1749); son of François, in 1704 bishop of Strasbourg, cardinal in 1712: 103, 251–52, 307

Soubise, François de Rohan-Montbazon, prince de (1631–1712): 103–4, 193

Soubise, Jules François Louis de Rohan, prince de (1697–1724); nephew of Armand: 307

Soubise, house of Rohan-: 51, 103

Sourdeval, negotiator of the Regency "Spanish marriages": 325

Sourvé, Gilles, in 1615 maréchal de (1542–1626); guardian of Louis XIII: 47

Spinoza, Baruch (1632–77); Dutch philosopher and theologian: 225

Staal, Marguerite Jeanne Cordier, known as Rose de Launay, baronne de (1684–1750); lady of the chamber of the duchesse du Maine: 135

Stair, John Dalrymple, comte de (1673–1747); in 1715–1720 English ambassador to Paris: 286, 287, 288, 290, 292, 300, 314, 315, 319

Stanhope, James, in 1718 count (1673–1721); in 1709 leader of the Whig party; in 1717 first lord of the Treasury: 290, 314, 315, 319

Stuart, Marie. *See* Marie Stuart

Stuart, house of: 143, 288

Sully, Maximilien Henri de Béthune, chevalier later duc de (1669–1729): 147, 148

Sully family: 156

Tallard, Camille d'Hostun de La Baume, duc et maréchal de (1652–1728); in 1717 member of the Regency Council; in 1726 state minister: 45, 48, 131f

Tallard, Marie Isabelle Gabrielle de Rohan-Soubise, duchesse de (1699–1754) granddaughter of Camille, in 1732 governess of the children of France: 47

Tallemant des Réaux, Gédéon (1619–90); memoirist: 3, 111, 223

Tans, Joseph A. G.: 355

Tapié, Victor-L.: 343

Tellier, le P. Michel (1643–1719); Jesuit; in 1709 Louis XIV's confessor: 43, 70, 131f, 145, 148, 163, 207, 242, 246, 249, 254, 267, 268, 273, 366n.115

Tencin, Claudine Alexandrine Guérin de (1682–1749); sister of Pierre, canoness: 289, 314, 334

Tencin, Pierre Guérin, abbé, in 1739 cardinal de (1679–1758): 43, 301, 314, 330, 334

Tessé, Jacques de, *intendant* of Claude de Saint-Simon: 43

Photo Credits

Gallery follows page 246.

1. Madrid, Museo nacional del Prado / Photo © Giraudon.
2. Paris, Bibliothèque Nationale, Cabinet des Médailles / Cliché Bibliothèque nationale de France, Paris.
3. London, the Wallace Collection / Photo by permission of the Trustees of the Wallace Collection.
4. Paris, Bibliothèque Nationale, Cabinet des Médailles / Cliché Bibliothèque nationale de France, Paris.
5. Orléans, Musée des Beaux-Arts / Photo © Giraudon.
6. Paris, Musée du Louvre / Photo © R.M.N. Lagiewski.
7. Chantilly, Musée Condé / Photo Josse.
8. Arras, Musée des Beaux-Arts / Photo © G. Dagli Orti.
9. Versailles, Musée national du château / Photo © Josse.
10. Versailles, Musée national du château / Photo © Josse.
11. Versailles, Musée national du château / Photo © G. Dagli Orti.
12. Versailles, Musée national du château / Photo © G. Dagli Orti.
13. Versailles, Musée national du château / Photo © R.M.N.–G. Blot.
14. Versailles, Musée national du château / Photo © G. Dagli Orti.
15. Le Mans, Musée Tessé / Photo © G. Dagli Orti.
16. Paris, Musée du Louvre / Photo © Josse.
17. Paris, Musée Carnavalet / Photo © G. Dagli Orti.
18. Versailles, Musée national du château / Photo © G. Dagli Orti.
19. Versailles, Musée national du château / Photo © G. Dagli Orti.
20. Private collection / Photo Archives Fayard.
21. Versailles, Musée national du château / Photo © Lauros–Giraudon.
22. Paris, Musée du Louvre / Photo © Lauros–Giraudon.
23. Versailles, Musée national du château / Photo © Giraudon.
24. Versailles, Musée national du château / Photo © G. Dagli Orti.
25. Versailles, Musée national du château / Photo © Lauros–Giraudon.
26. Versailles, Musée national du château / Photo © Lauros–Giraudon.
27. Fontaine-Chaalis, Musée Jacquemart-André / Photo © G. Dagli Orti.
28. Versailles, Musée national du château / Photo © R.M.N.–G. Blot.
29. Versailles, Musée national du château / Photo © Lauros–Giraudon.
30. Versailles, Musée national du château / Photo © Lauros–Giraudon.
31. Versailles, Musée national du château / Photo © Lauros–Giraudon.
32. Versailles, Musée national du château / Photo © Josse.
33. Toulouse, Musée des Augustins / Photo © Josse.
34. Berlin, Staatliche Schlösser und Gärten, Schloßlig; Charlottenburg / Photo © AKG Paris.
35. Paris, Bibliothèque Nationale, Département des Manuscrits / Cliché Bibliothèque nationale de France, Paris.